Combined with the resources you have trusted throughout the years, we provide you with the best business resources available:

◆ In the News New current events articles are added throughout the year. Each article is summarized by our team of expert professors and fully supported by exercises, activities, and instructor materials.

◆ On-Line Study Guide Results from the automatically graded questions for every chapter provide immediate feedback for students that can be e-mailed to the instructor.

◆ Research Area Your own personal resource library includes tutorials, descriptive links to virtual libraries, and a wealth of search engines and resources.

◆ Internet Resources Provide discipline-specific sites, including preview information that allows you to review site information before you view the site, ensuring you visit the best available business resources found by our learning community.

For the Professor

◆ Teaching Resources includes resources contributed by professors throughout the world, including teaching tips, techniques, academic papers, sample syllabi, and Talk to the Team, a moderated faculty chat room.

◆ On-Line Faculty Support including downloadable supplements, additional cases, articles, links, and suggested answers to current events activities.

◆ What's New gives you one-click access to all newly posted PHLIP resources.

For the Student

◆ Talk to the Tutor Virtual office hours that allow students to post questions from any supported discipline and receive responses from the dedicated PHLIP/CW faculty team.

◆ Writing Resource Center An on-line writing center that provides links to on-line directories, thesauruses, writing tutors, style and grammar guides, and additional tools.

◆ Career Center Helps access career information, view sample résumés, even apply for jobs on-line.

◆ Study Tips An area for students to develop better study skills.

EDITION ▶ 2e

MANAGEMENT

Leading People and Organizations in the 21st Century

GARY DESSLER

Florida International University

Prentice Hall

Upper Saddle River, New Jersey 07458

Library of Congress Cataloging-in-Publication Data
Dessler, Gary
    Management: leading people and organizations in the 21st century / Gary Dessler.—
2nd ed.
      p. cm.
    ISBN 0-13-017780-6 (hardcover)
    1. Management. 2. Leadership. 3. Organization. I. Title.
HD31.D4863 2000
658.4'092—dc21

00-029345

Editor: Melissa Steffens
Editorial Assistant: Samantha Steel
Assistant Editor: Jessica Sabloff
Media Project Manager: Michele Faranda
Development Editor: Jeannine Ciliotta
Executive Marketing Manager: Michael Campbell
Managing Editor (Production): Judy Leale
Production Assistant: Keri Jean
Production Manager: Arnold Vila
Associate Director, Manufacturing: Vincent Scelta
Senior Designer: Cheryl Asherman
Design Manager: Patricia Smythe
Interior Design: Amanda Kavanaugh
Photo Researcher: Melinda Alexander
Cover Design: Cheryl Asherman
Cover Art/Photo: KnitMedia
Associate Director, Multimedia Production: Karen Goldsmith
Manager, Print Production: Christy Mahon
Composition: UG / GGS Information Services, Inc.

10 9 8 7 6 5 4 3 2 1
ISBN 0-13-017780-6

To my son Derek

BRIEF CONTENTS

CONTENTS

When he decided to drop out of college to pursue his dream, Michael Dell had a vision of a company that would sell high-quality personal computers directly to customers via catalogs and the telephone. After less than a year, with sales already bumping $80,000, he believed his idea would work. He set off on the path that would lead, in a very short time, to the mighty billion-dollar Dell Computer Corporation.

In many ways, the evolution of Dell Computer illustrates the enormous changes taking place in managing organizations today. By the mid-1990s, Michael Dell was not only selling his computers in almost every country of the world, but looking at a new channel—the Internet—as a way to reach customers directly. Within a year of organizing an Internet initiative, Dell was selling millions of dollars worth of computers and accessories over the Internet every day. Customers could not only order their equipment directly via the Net, but could also track the progress of their order as it made its way through production and finally to their front door.

Dell's transformation parallels the transformation in managing organizations. Globalization, deregulation, and technological advances mean that today's organizations have to be more competitive than ever before and be ready to respond quickly to change if they are to thrive in this intensely competitive new environment. To achieve this responsiveness and competitiveness, new management methods and philosophies have emerged, such as boundaryless organizations, team-based structures, Internet-based managing, scenario planning, and commitment building. Managing—leading people and organizations and 21st century businesses—will depend on maintaining open, communicative, and responsive organizations, in a large part by relying on human capital. Helping students understand how to manage organizations and people in this new environment is the goal at the heart of this book.

The book provides students with a practical and concrete explanation of the concepts and techniques they will need as managers in today's new organizations. It is intended for use in undergraduate or graduate courses in management or in courses that combine management and organizational behavior. The sequence of chapters follows the familiar "planning, organizing, leading, controlling" process format, and the contents and continuing themes stress the leading-edge management concepts and techniques students will need to lead today's and tomorrow's organizations.

BASIC THEMES

Within the planning, organizing, leading, and controlling framework of this book, we emphasize leading-edge management concepts and techniques by focusing on the following seven themes, which are woven into each chapter:

- **Managing today is increasingly technology- and Internet-based.** Everywhere you look, companies and their managers are relying on the Internet to manage their businesses more efficiently and responsively. Letting customers track their own products via the Net does more than make things convenient for Michael Dell's customers, it also eliminates the need to add hundreds of customer relations representatives to handle phone calls, as well as the need to house all those people and provide them with telephone support. Almost every company is using technology, and particularly the Internet, to improve its performance. That's why every chapter contains at least one concrete illustration, in a feature called "Managing @ the Speed of Thought," which shows how managers are actually using the Internet and technology to improve the performance of their organizations. For example, "Managing Groups and Teams," Chapter 13, shows how companies are using the Internet and special groupware software packages to enable geographically dispersed team members to interact in real-time. Several "Webnotes" in each chapter, illustrated with actual pages from company Web sites, show how companies are using the Internet to better manage their businesses.

- **People are part of managing.** Particularly with today's emphasis on competitiveness, team-based organizations, and responsiveness, managers can't separate their "people management" responsibilities from their strictly "managerial" ones. Thus, for example, planning requires setting and getting acceptance of goals. Similarly, re-creating the organization of a firm like Dell requires enormous leadership and motivational skills. Because human capital is so important to managing change today, this book contains one or two "The People Side of Managing" features in every chapter to show this side of management in practice. The book also contains more leadership-related chapters than competing texts.

- **Managers must manage change.** Understanding how to manage under conditions of rapid change is now a critical skill. Managing change is therefore a central theme of the book, implemented through special chapters such as "Designing Organizations to Manage Change" (Chapter 8) and examples in most chapters.

- **Entrepreneurship is driving today's economies.** Most college graduates today will go to work for smaller firms. Managing a small business is thus another major theme. Although small business examples are sprinkled throughout the text, this theme is implemented primarily with an "Entrepreneurs in Action" box in each chapter. In addition, features throughout the book related to KnitMedia (videos, video cases, "You Be the Consultant" cases, and Internet exercises) provide an in-depth look at an exciting, entrepreneurial company. (See "A Note to the Student About KnitMedia" on page xxv for more information.)

- **Teamwork is essential.** Today, work in organizations is increasingly organized not around traditional organization charts, but around teams. At the General Electric aircraft engine plant in Durham, North Carolina, for instance, there is no traditional organization chart; instead, all 180 or so employees are organized into 10- to 12-person teams, all of which report to the plant manager. A recent survey by the consulting firm Watson Wyatt concluded that about 80% of all companies in the United States today depend to some extent on teams to get their work done. Given the importance of teamwork, this book emphasizes the process of teamwork as well as team-building skills. There is one complete chapter devoted to managing teams (Chapter 13), additional material on how to organize around teams (Chapter 8), and examples of using teams in virtually every chapter.

- **Diversity must be managed.** As the workforce becomes increasingly diverse and global, it is important for managers to recognize that diversity is a positive force rather than a negative one. A portion of Chapter 3 is therefore devoted to this topic, and numerous examples in each chapter illustrate the need for techniques to manage diversity effectively.

- **Managers must change organizational culture.** Today's team-based, geographically dispersed employees are increasingly guided by a network of values and tradition—by an organizational culture. Managing that culture and establishing or changing those values are crucial management tasks. Major sections of Chapter 3, "Managing in a Cultural and Ethical Environment," and Chapter 14, "Managing Organizational and Cultural Change," are devoted to these topics and to specific issues such as culture and values, creating culture, and changing organizational culture. Other chapters and sections throughout the book address issues such as culture and communication (page 371), culture and leadership (pages 434–436), culture and ethics (pages 75–78), culture and control (pages 471–472), culture and the global environment (page 71), and the impact of values on hiring (page 475) and motivation (pages 350–351).

MANAGING GLOBALLY

Few changes in the past ten years have had more impact on managers than globalization, and this trend will no doubt continue in the current new millennium. This text covers globalization with a full chapter right up front (Chapter 2), to give students an early introduction to global issues. But because today's managers need to see all aspects of business and management from a global perspective, we also include discussions and examples of globalization in every chapter, as well as examples of how the Internet facilitates global management, for instance by providing access to instantaneous group-based communications.

Every chapter contains examples of how that chapter's material relates to the internationalization/globalization of management. To choose just a few examples: Chapter 1, "Managing in the 21st Century," discusses the impact on management of changing political systems around the world, including the explosive opening of new markets with hundreds of millions of potential customers; Chapter 2, "Managing in a Global Environment," is entirely devoted to the impact of globalization on management. For instance, it covers the reasons companies expand operations abroad and their strategies for doing so.

Chapter 6, "Strategic Management," discusses how companies, like the one that publishes the *Wall Street Journal*, achieve above-average growth rates by aggressively expanding into new geographic markets, both domestic and abroad. Chapter 12, "Interpersonal and Organizational Communication," emphasizes that cross-cultural communication is a fact of business life, and illustrates how to communicate in different cultures. Chapter 15, "Controlling and Building Commitment," points out that managing a globally dispersed workforce requires a particularly effective control system and a greater reliance on commitment-building efforts, in order to avoid the problems that can arise when employees are far away from the company's central managers.

NEW TO THIS EDITION

The previous edition of this book proved very popular with students and professors, and I've made a number of changes in this edition to make it an even more useful learning tool for management classes. I have of course thoroughly updated all the chapters and, where necessary, streamlined and revised for added clarity.

The new "Managing @ the Speed of Thought" boxes and "Webnotes" throughout the text illustrate how managers use the Internet to manage today. Material from the previous edition's chapter on managing organizational culture—topics like what is culture, creating culture, leaders and culture, and managing culture change—are now integrated into Chapters 3, 10, and 14, as well as in numerous other places throughout the text. In Part V (Controlling), the previous edition's chapter topics, managing operations and services and managing with information technology, are again fully covered, but in a slightly streamlined way. Each of these chapters appears as a module to give instructors more assignment flexibility.

PEDAGOGICAL AIDS

The pedagogical elements of this text have been carefully designed to reinforce the major themes of the text, and to make it as easy as possible for the student to learn actively and retain what he or she reads.

Each chapter contains at least one of the following three features:

- **"Managing @ the Speed of Thought."** This feature illustrates how managers are using the Internet to manage their organizations today. It includes both U.S. and international examples of managers making the Internet part of their arsenal of business management methods.

- **"The People Side of Managing."** This feature emphasizes the importance of the people or behavioral aspects of managing. For example, Chapter 4, "Decision-Making," includes a "People Side of Managing" feature illustrating the human aspects of getting employees to "buy into" the decisions managers have made.

- **"Entrepreneurs in Action."** These boxes emphasize the increasing significance of smaller companies in today's business environment and illustrate how entrepreneurs actually apply the management concepts and techniques discussed in that particular chapter.

Each chapter also contains the following aids to enhance readability and learning:

- **How it all relates—chapter introductions.** Each chapter opens with a vignette that illustrates the chapter's main point, plus an introduction that gives a bird's eye view of the material in the chapter and how it all relates to what the student has read in the previous one or two chapters.

- **Webnotes.** Each chapter contains several actual company Web pages that illustrate how managers are using the Internet to manage their organizations today.

- **Key terms.** Key terms appear in bold in the text and are defined when used; they also appear in the margin at the point of introduction. The terms are listed at the end of each chapter, and are defined again in the Glossary at the end of the book.

- **Summary and "Tying It All Together."** At the end of each chapter, the summaries do more than just summarize the material covered in that chapter. Special "Tying It All Together" overviews emphasize how that chapter's material relates to material in the previous and following chapters. They give students a continuing framework or reference point so readers always know where they stand and how that material fits in with the material in the rest of the book.

- **Cases.** Three different cases at the end of each chapter encourage students to apply that chapter's concepts to specific scenarios. A shorter case focuses on a specific question and allows for a brief in-class discussion or homework assignment on some aspect of the chapter. A longer, more comprehensive case can provide the basis for a general class discussion. "You Be the Consultant" is a continuing case that focuses on KnitMedia, a music and entertainment company. Students are asked to put themselves in the place of KnitMedia's consultants, and make decisions regarding the future direction of the company. These cases were written by the author, based on detailed information and materials provided by the officers at KnitMedia, and are therefore meaty and realistic.

- **Video cases.** "On Location at KnitMedia" is a five-part, integrated video case that focuses on KnitMedia, a music and entertainment company. The cases correspond to video clips that were custom filmed at KnitMedia's offices and edited specifically for use with this text. The video cases appear at the end of each of the five text parts.

SUPPORT MATERIALS

Instructor's Manual

Expanded to include sample syllabi for three different class structures: small, large, and distance learning, the *Instructor's Manual* is designed to guide the educator through the text. Each chapter in the manual includes a topic introduction, learning objectives, an annotated outline that includes space for instructors' own notes, answers and suggestions for all in-chapter elements, and answers to all end-of-chapter materials. A video guide section summarizes the accompanying skills video clips and the custom KnitMedia videos; it also provides suggestions for tying videos to the chapter content.

Instructor's Resource CD-ROM

This all-inclusive multimedia product is an invaluable asset for professors who prefer to work with electronic files rather than traditional print supplements. On this single CD-ROM, instructors will find the *Instructor's Manual*, the complete set of PowerPoint slides, the Test Item File, and the Prentice Hall Test Manager program.

Test Item File

The Test Item File contains over 100 questions per chapter, including multiple-choice, scenario-based, true/false, and discussion questions. Every question is section referenced to the text and is labeled easy, moderate, or challenging to satisfy all classroom needs.

Prentice Hall Test Manager

The Test Manager contains all of the questions in the printed Test Item File (TIF). Test Manager is a comprehensive suite of tools for testing and assessment. It allows educators to easily create and distribute tests for their courses, either by printing and distributing through traditional methods, or by on-line delivery via a Local Area Network (LAN) server.

PowerPoint Electronic Transparencies with Teaching Notes

PowerPoint disks allow access to over 200 figures, exhibits, and text materials.

Color Transparencies

Full-color acetates (100) based on key exhibits and concepts from the text add a visual element to your lectures.

Study Guide

Available for sale to students, this manual has been designed to reinforce key concepts of the text as well as to enhance understanding and application of concepts.

myPHLIP (Prentice Hall Learning on the Internet Partnership) Web Site

An invaluable resource for both instructors and students, myPHLIP features a wealth of up-to-date, on-line resources at the touch of a button. A research center, current events articles, interactive study guide, exercises, and additional resources all combine to give instructors and students the most advanced text-specific Web site available. Just visit www.prenhall.com/dessler.

Video Package

The video package offers two different options for enhanced learning:

- **"On Location! at KnitMedia" Video—** This customized video, shot and edited specifically for this text, focuses on a music and entertainment company called KnitMedia. The five video segments correspond to five integrative end-of-part video cases in the text, with an additional video segment that introduces students to KnitMedia.

- **Skills Videos:** Five video segments offer dramatizations that highlight various management skills. They allow students to see what it's like to conduct an interview, make management decisions, and more. The videos provide excellent starting points for classroom discussion and debate. These videos are available on VHS for classroom presentation.

WebCT On-line Course

The second edition offers a fully developed on-line course for *Management, Second Edition*.

ACKNOWLEDGMENTS

Creating a book like this is always the result of many people's efforts, and I want to take this opportunity to thank some of the people who have helped me in this endeavor. I have, first, been very lucky to have had the advantage of some of the most insightful reviewer's comments and suggestions that an author can have. In that regard, I particularly want to thank Roger Dunbar at New York University, Ron Beaulieu at Central Michigan University, and my colleagues at Florida International University, Richard M. Hodgetts and Earnest Friday. A full list of the reviewers of the first and second editions includes:

Second edition:

Roger Dunbar, New York University

Ron Beaulieu, Central Michigan University

Annette Ranft, West Virginia University

Bill Price, Howard Payne University

Mason Carpenter, University of Wisconsin-Madison

Jeff Tschetter, University of Sioux Falls

David J. Lemak, Washington State University at Tri-Cities

Peggy Brewer, Eastern Kentucky University

Richard Hodgetts, Florida International University

Earnest Friday, Florida International University

First edition:

Professor Clarence Anderson, Walla Walla College

Dr. James Bell, Southwest Texas State University

Professor Aleta Best, Texas A&M University

Professor Barbara Boyington, Brookdale Community College

Professor Monica Briedenbach, DeVry Institute of Technology

Professor James H. Browne, University of Southern Colorado

Dr. John Carmichael, Union County College

Professor Bonnie Chavez, Santa Barbara City College

Professor R. J. Dick, Missouri Western State

Professor Paul Fadil, Valdosta State University

Professor Janice Feldbauer, Austin Community College

Professor Kevin McCarthy, Baker University

Professor Mike Peng, University of Hawaii

Professor Preston Probasco, San Jose State University

Professor Rajib Sanyal, The College of New Jersey

Mr. Tim Weaver, SVP Corporate Banking

Thanks too to Dr. George Puia at Indiana State University for developing many of the end of chapter cases.

I'm also grateful for having had the opportunity to work with an extraordinarily dedicated team of Prentice Hall professionals. Natalie E. Anderson had the vision and confidence to commit to the project, and most of what is good about the book can still be attributed to her recommendations. I also benefited enormously at various stages of this project from the recommendations of a group at Prentice Hall that includes Stephanie Johnson, then Management Editor; Melissa Steffens, Management Editor; Sandy Steiner, President of the Business Publishing Division; Steve Rigolosi, then Managing Editor for Development; David Shafer, Management Editor; Jim Boyd, Vice President; and

Tamara Wederbrand, then Marketing Manager. Development editor Jeannine Ciliotta made hundreds of organizational and content recommendations for the book, and to the extent that the second edition improves on the first, she deserves much of the credit. I'm grateful to Judy Leale, Managing Editor, Production, for working tirelessly to keep this project on track. Thanks to Cheryl Asherman who, along with her design team, created a beautiful interior and cover design, and to Melinda Alexander for the fine photos. The marketing effort for the book has benefited from Marketing Manager Michael Campbell's knowledge of the market, creativity, and hard work. I am again deeply grateful to all the professionals in the Prentice Hall sales force, who have enthusiastically promoted this and the previous edition of this book, as well as my human resource management text over its eight editions. The success of this new edition of *Management: Leading People and Organizations in the 21st Century,*, now rests in their capable hands, and I thank them in advance for their efforts.

At Florida International University I appreciate the moral support I received from all of my colleagues, including Ronnie Silverblatt, Jan Luytjes, Enzo Valenzi, and of course Earnest Friday and Richard Hodgetts.

I am again grateful to Michael Dorf, CEO of KnitMedia, and to Alan Fried and the rest of the KnitMedia staff for giving us access to a fascinating business enterprise so that we could create the videos, video cases, Internet exercises, and You Be the Consultant features for this text.

Closer to home, I again want to acknowledge the support of my wife, Claudia, and her willingness to tolerate my disappearance for more evenings and weekends than I should have been gone while working on this book. However, when all the acknowledgments are said and done, if there can be a single inspiration for a book entitled *Management: Leading People and Organizations in the 21st Century*, it is again my son Derek, for whom I wrote this book in as practical and useful a way as I could, and whose unswerving support was the only motivation I needed.

Gary Dessler

You are not going to learn how to be a manager by reading this book. You know that you can't learn how to do anything—play golf, do calculus problems, or make fine furniture—just by reading about it. Instead, you have to actually apply what you read; you have to practice. As one famous commentator once replied when asked how to get to Carnegie Hall, "Practice, practice, practice."

By the time you've completed this book, we'd like you to have had an opportunity to step into a manager's shoes, and to practice what it's like to plan, organize, lead, and control (in other words, to manage) an organization. To help you do this, we've created a number of features that focus on a company called KnitMedia.

I personally find the nature of KnitMedia's business interesting, and I hope that you will, too. KnitMedia is an alternative music and entertainment company whose businesses include an independent record label, and the Knitting Factory—a live music club in New York City that specializes in alternative jazz. As you move through the book you'll see that KnitMedia is involved in other businesses, too, including radio, TV, and Internet and video-conference interactive performances.

Understanding and explaining how to manage a huge enterprise like IBM or General Motors requires quite a stretch of the imagination for most of us, and by us, I mean myself and many of the students and professors who will be using this book. On the other hand, most of us can relate more easily to and "get our hands around" the sort of small business that Michael Dorf, the founder and president, is building in KnitMedia. Here are some of the features you'll find in this book that focus on KnitMedia.

- *You Be the Consultant* (found at the end of each chapter) is a continuing case that focuses on different aspects of KnitMedia from chapter to chapter. As a result, you're going to become very familiar with just about everything about KnitMedia, its competitors, its strengths and weaknesses, its financial situation, and its managers' hopes and dreams. That way, you'll be able to make your decisions not in a vacuum but within the context of what you know about the company. For instance, you'll be able to propose a technique to help the president of the company, Michael Dorf, control his increasingly far-flung enterprise, in the context of what you know about his motives and how he likes to manage.

- *Integrative Video cases* (found at the end of each major part of the book) let you apply your knowledge of what you've learned from the preceding chapters. The cases are designed to help you think about management the way managers actually have to, in a more integrated, "it's all related" fashion.

- *KnitMedia Videos* correspond to the end-of-part integrative cases, and will let you see and hear how KnitMedia's managers and employees are actually managing their company on a day-to-day basis.

The multimedia nature of this KnitMedia component should provide you with a more realistic and concrete way to learn about making management decisions and managing companies. You'll be able to use the text, videos, and Internet to read about KnitMedia, to actually see the participants at work, to interact with some of them, and to research your answers to the exercises. And, depending upon how your professor sets up your assignments, you may even be able to interact with others in your group electronically via the Internet, to develop realistic answers to the group assignments.

I hope and believe that this integrated package will provide you with an opportunity to apply in practice what you've learned, and thus to actually see what it's like to be a manager. After all, how do you become a manager? Practice, practice, practice.

GARY DESSLER (Ph.D., business administration, Bernard Baruch School of Business) is Professor of Business at Florida International University. In addition to *Management: Leading People and Organizations in the 21st Century*, he is the author of a number of other books including, most recently, *Human Resource Management*, 8th edition (Prentice-Hall), *Essentials of Human Resource Management* (Prentice-Hall), and *Winning Commitment: How to Build and Keep a Competitive Workforce*. His books have been translated into Chinese, Russian, Indonesian, Spanish, and Portuguese, and are being used by students and managers all over the world. He has written numerous articles on employee commitment, organizational behavior, leadership, and quality improvement, and for ten years wrote the syndicated "Job Talk" column for the *Miami Herald*.

CHAPTER ▶ 1

MANAGING IN THE 21ST CENTURY

WHAT'S AHEAD?

It looked like trail's end for Apple Computer. Sales and market share were dropping fast. Expenses were soaring, the firm had just lost $1 billion, and Apple was in a "death watch," according to some employees.[1] Then Steve Jobs came back on the scene. Jobs—who had founded Apple years earlier and then been pushed out of the firm—returned as interim president. He slashed costs, refocused Apple on 4 product lines (down from 15), reduced bloated inventories, revamped distribution, spearheaded the new iMac computer, and raised morale. And now here he was, at the Flint Center in California, announcing that Apple's profits had surged to $309 million and were heading higher. The employees stood and cheered.

OBJECTIVES

AFTER STUDYING THIS CHAPTER, YOU SHOULD BE ABLE TO

- Explain, with examples, what managers do

- Describe why the people side of managing is so important

- Discuss the main trends in how modern organizations are managed

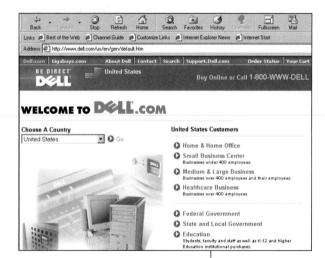

▲ WEBNOTE

Dell uses a sophisticated Internet site to communicate directly with customers and vendors.

www.dell.com

organization

a group of people with formally assigned roles who work together to achieve the stated goals of the group.

▶ **WHAT MANAGERS DO**

Managers can have the most remarkable effects on organizations. IBM floundered through much of the 1980s and early 1990s, losing market share, seeing costs rise, and watching its stock price dwindle from almost $180 per share to barely $50. Within three years, new CEO Louis Gerstner revamped the company's product line, dramatically lowered costs, changed the company's culture, and oversaw a quadrupling of IBM's stock price.[2] Dell CEO Michael Dell created a $12 billion company in just 13 years by instituting one of the world's most sophisticated direct-sales operations, eliminating resellers' markups and the need for large inventories, and keeping a vise-like grip on costs while dozens of his competitors were going down the drain.[3] And Steve Jobs (as we saw on the opening page) totally revitalized Apple Computer in barely a year.

And "manager" effects like these don't happen just at giant corporations. At this moment—as you read these words—managers at thousands of small businesses—diners, drycleaning stores, motels—are running their business well, with courteous, prompt, and first-class service, high-morale employees, and a minimum of problems like "My dinner's cold," or "You didn't press my pants." What do you think would happen if you took the competent managers out of those businesses and dropped in managers without training or skills? You know the answer because you've probably experienced the effects yourself—businesses with untrained or unprepared staff, orders not prepared on time, lost reservations, dirty rooms. About 90% of the new businesses started this year will fail within five years, and Dun & Bradstreet says the reason is generally poor management. Management is as—or more—important for the tiny start-up as it is for the giant firm.

The effect of good management is nothing short of amazing. Take an underperforming—even chaotic—organization and install a skilled manager, and he or she can soon get the enterprise humming. Take a successful enterprise that's been managed well for years—say, a neighborhood stationery store—and watch as a new, less-competent manager takes over. Shelves are suddenly in disarray, products are out of stock, bills go unpaid.

All these enterprises—IBM, Dell, the diner, the drycleaner, and the stationery store—are organizations. An **organization** consists of people with formally assigned roles who must work together to achieve stated goals. All organizations have several things in common. First, organizations needn't just be business firms; the definition applies equally well to colleges, local governments, and nonprofits like the American Red Cross. The U.S. government is an organization—certainly a not-for-profit one—and its head manager, or chief executive officer, is the president.

Organizations are, also (hopefully) "organized": Even your corner drycleaners has an organizational structure that lays out who does what (pressers press, and cleaners clean, for instance), and how the work (in this case the incoming clothes) will flow through the store and get done. An organization should also have policies that lay out how decisions will be made, such as how to reimburse a customer whose blouse has been lost, and what times and days the store will be open.

An organization that's not organized won't be much of a business (or much of a college, or local government, or what have you). To see why, think about the most disorganized person (professor?) you've ever known: lectures are unprepared and rambling, your test is always lost in some stack when you want to discuss it, and grades are never done on time and are based on unknown standards. Neither the professor nor the course are very well organized, and as a result, nothing ever goes entirely right.

Indeed, organizations, by their nature, cannot simply run themselves. Review the definition of an organization again, and you'll see why. Who would ensure that each of the people actually knew what to do? Who would see that they are trained? Who would hire them? Who would ensure that they work together, more or less harmoniously? Who would decide what the organization's goals would be, and then monitor whether each employee was doing his or her share to reach those goals?

▲ Wendy Kopp of the nonprofit "Teach for America" organization: Nonprofits are also organizations and need skilled managers.

The answer is "the manager." A manager is someone who plans, organizes, leads, and controls the people and the work of the organization in such a way that the organization achieves its goals. Management refers to two things: (1) collectively to the managers of an organization; and (2) to the study of what managers do. This is a book about management. Studying it carefully should put you well on the road to being a good manager.

The Management Process

Management writers traditionally refer to the manager's four basic functions—planning, organizing, leading, and controlling—as the management process. The rest of the book covers these in detail, but the following is a synopsis of each:

- *Planning.* Planning is setting goals and deciding on courses of action, developing rules and procedures, developing plans (both for the organization and for those who work in it), and forecasting (predicting or projecting what the future holds for the firm).
- *Organizing.* Organizing is identifying jobs to be done, hiring people to do them, establishing departments, delegating or pushing authority down to subordinates, establishing a chain of command (in other words, channels of authority and communication), and coordinating the work of subordinates.
- *Leading.* Leading means influencing other people to get the job done, maintaining morale, molding company culture, and managing conflicts and communication.
- *Controlling.* Controlling is setting standards (such as sales quotas or quality standards), comparing actual performance with these standards, and then taking corrective action as required.

You Too Are a Manager

Just as organizations needn't be business firms, managers needn't be businesspeople. In fact it's likely that you've already been (or may soon be) in the position of managing others. Let's suppose that you and some friends have decided to spend

manager
a person who plans, organizes, leads, and controls the work of others so that the organization achieves its goals.

management
the managers of an organization; or, the study of what managers do.

management process
refers to the manager's four basic functions of planning, organizing, leading, and controlling.

next summer abroad, say in France. None of you know very much about France or how to get there, so you've been elected "summer tour master" and asked to manage the trip. Where would you start? (Resist the temptation to call a travel agent and delegate the whole job to him or her, please.)

You might start by thinking through what you need to do in terms of planning, organizing, leading, and controlling. What sorts of plans will you need? Among other things, you'll need to plan the dates your group is leaving and returning, the cities and towns in France you'll visit, the airline you'll take there and back, how the group will get around in France, and where you'll stay when you're there. As you can imagine, plans like these are very important: You would not want to arrive at Orly Airport with a group of friends depending on you, and not know what you're doing next.

Developing all those plans will itself be quite a job, so you'll probably want to get some help. In other words, you'll need to divide up the work and create an organization. For example, you might delegate to Rosa—put her in charge of—checking airline schedules and prices, and Ned in charge of checking hotels, and Ruth in charge of checking the sites to see in various cities as well as the means of transportation between them. However, the job won't get done with Rosa, Ned, and Ruth simply working by themselves. Each requires guidance and coordination from you: Rosa obviously can't make any decisions on airline schedules unless she knows what city you're starting and ending with, and Ned can't really schedule any hotels unless he knows from Ruth what sites you'll be seeing and when. You'll either have to schedule weekly manager's meetings, or coordinate the work of these three people yourself.

Leadership could be a challenge, too: Ned and Ruth don't get along too well, so you'll have to make sure conflicts don't get out of hand. Rosa is a genius with numbers, but tends to get discouraged quickly, so you'll also have to make sure she stays focused and motivated.

And of course you'll have to ensure that the whole project stays "in control." If something can go wrong, it often will, and that's certainly the case when a group of people is traveling together. At a minimum, all those airline tickets, hotel reservations, and itineraries will have to be checked and checked again to make sure there are no mistakes. If you're wise, you may even ask another friend to double-check just before you leave to ensure that your group's hotel reservations are confirmed.

In other words, managing is something we all do almost every day, often without even knowing it.

Types of Managers

Most organizations contain several types of managers. In your college, for instance, there are presidents, vice presidents, deans, associate deans, and department chairs, as well as various administrators, like human resource managers. At your place of work (if you work) you might find supervisors, financial controllers, sales managers, plant managers, and a president and vice presidents. These people are managers because they all plan, organize, lead, and control the workers and the work of that particular organization in such a way that the organization achieves its goals.

There are many ways to classify managers. For example, we can distinguish managers based on their organization level, position, and functional title (see Table 1.1).

The managers at the top, of course, are the firm's top management. They are usually referred to as **executives**. Functional titles include president, chief executive officer (CEO), vice president, and chief financial officer (CFO).

Beneath this management level (and reporting to it) may be one or more levels of middle managers, positions that typically have the term *manager* or *director* in their

executives

managers at the top management level of an organization.

TABLE 1.1 Types of Managers

Organization Level	Position	Functional Title
Top managers (Have managers as subordinates)	Executives	President Vice president, production Vice president, sales Vice president, HR Chief financial officer
Middle managers (Have managers as subordinates)	Managers or directors	Production manager Sales director HR manager Finance manager
First-line managers (Have nonmanagers as subordinates)	Supervisors	Production supervisor Regional sales manager Assistant HR manager Chief bookkeeper

titles. (Particularly in larger companies like IBM, managers report to directors, who in turn report to top managers, like vice presidents.) Examples of functional titles here include production manager, sales director, HR manager, and finance manager.

First-line managers are at the lowest rung of the management ladder. These managers are often called supervisors, and might include the production supervisors who actually supervise the assembly-line employees at Toyota.

All managers have a lot in common. They all plan, organize, lead, and control the people and the work of their organizations. And all managers at all levels and with every functional title spend an enormous part of each day with people—talking, listening, influencing, motivating, and attending one-on-one conferences and committee meetings.[4] In fact, even chief executives (whom you might expect to be somewhat insulated from other people, up there in their executive suites) reportedly spend about three-fourths of their time dealing directly with other people.[5]

However, there are two big differences among the management levels. First, top and middle managers both have managers for subordinates; in other words, they are in charge of other managers. Supervisors have workers—nonmanagers—as subordinates. Managers at different levels also use their time somewhat differently. Top managers tend to spend a lot of time planning and setting goals (like "double sales in the next two years"). Middle managers then translate these goals into specific projects (like "hire two new salespeople and introduce three new products") for their subordinates to execute. First-line supervisors then concentrate on directing and controlling the employees who work on these projects.

The Manager's Changing Role

Yet the manager's job is changing so fast that some—like management guru Peter Drucker—say, "I'm not comfortable with the word *manager* anymore, because it implies subordinates."[6] What's wrong with having subordinates? Nothing, and most managers still do. But as we'll see later in this chapter, the "old style" manager who expects to give orders and be obeyed is in many situations a relic of the past. How far

first-line manager
manager at the bottom management level of an organization, also called a supervisor, who has nonsupervisors as subordinates.

do you think you'd get by barking orders at the group you'd chosen to help you manage your group's trip abroad? Probably not very far. Similarly, intense competition and rapid change mean most companies today must depend more than ever on their employees' being willing to contribute. Very often, a manager today has to be more a team leader and facilitator than a traditional command-and-control person.

MANAGING @ THE *SPEED* OF THOUGHT

■ The E-CEO

What is it like being an e-CEO, the chief executive of one of the hot new e-commerce companies? To hear the executives themselves tell it, *speed* is the word that sums up their experience best. For example, Roger Siboni, CEO of epiphany, a company which creates the software that helps e-corporations get the most from their customer data, says, "You're driving too fast—you feel the exhilaration—you must turn left and right at death-defying speed without blinking—never blink—if you go up and down with the news, you'll never make it."[7] E-CEOs must also be "brutally, brutally honest with yourself and others, because if you let a problem fester a day or two, you'll see someone in your rearview mirror coming after you."

With their markets changing so fast, e-CEOs must also constantly focus their companies' and their employees' attention on the company's mission. These companies are constantly deluged with competitive information and new ideas, so it's relatively easy for the employees to become distracted. It's the e-CEO's job to keep employees focused.

Table 1.2 summarizes why these e-CEOs are in fact a new breed. For example, they're not just younger and richer than traditional CEOs, they're also more comfortable with ambiguity and speed. They're also nearly paranoid about monitoring market trends and competitors' moves, to ensure their companies aren't blindsided by unanticipated events.

TABLE 1.2 E-CEOs Are a Brand-New Breed . . .

Operating at breakneck speed in a world with little or no margin for error, e-CEOs need a new set of qualities to thrive.

Traditional CEO	e-CEO
encouraging	evangelizing
alert	paranoid
cordial	brutally frank
infotech semiliterate (at best)	infotech literate (at least)
clearly focused	intensely focused
fast moving	faster moving
hates ambiguity	likes ambiguity
suffers from technology-confrontation anxiety	suffers from bandwidth-separation anxiety
a paragon of good judgment	a paragon of good judgment
age: 57	age: 38
rich	really rich

Source: Fortune, 24 May 1999, p. 107. © 1999 Time Inc. Reprinted by permission.

ACTION	ALL CEOs	U.S. and CANADA	EUROPE and ASIA
Setting vision and strategy	66%	67%	65%
Exploring M&As	51%	51%	51%
Reshaping corporate culture and employee behavior	47%	48%	45%
Monitoring corporate financial information	45%	47%	43%

◀ FIGURE 1.1

What Has the CEO's Attention?

Source: Adapted from "What Has The CEO's Attention?" *Management Review,* American Management Association International, September 1998, from the cover story, p.12.

The People Side of Management

Managing has always been a decidedly behavioral or people-oriented occupation, since by definition managers do their work by interacting with others. Yet the people side of managing has taken on increased importance today.

Several years ago the accounting and consulting firm PricewaterhouseCoopers interviewed 400 CEOs whose companies were in the top 2,000 in global size.[8] Their results are summarized in Figure 1.1. As you might expect, a majority of these CEOs devoted a lot of personal time to things like setting corporate strategy, exploring mergers and acquisitions, and monitoring corporate financial results. Surprisingly, about half actually spent as much or more time personally trying to shape and influence the people or behavioral side of their businesses as they did on monitoring financial results.

Why is the people side of managing so important today? Perhaps the best way to answer that is with an example.

THE **PEOPLE** SIDE OF MANAGING

▪ Allied-Signal

Honeywell Corporation and Allied-Signal merged in 1999, forming a new, much larger Honeywell Corporation. The merger was made possible by the rising fortunes of Allied-Signal, which had vastly improved under its chairman and CEO, Lawrence A. Bossidy.[9]

How did Bossidy turn Allied-Signal around? Interestingly, Bossidy's people skills had a remarkable effect on this huge industrial supplier of aerospace systems, automotive parts, and chemical products.[10] He took over a troubled company that was "hemorrhaging cash."[11] After just three years under Bossidy, Allied-Signal's net income (profits) had doubled to $708 million, profit margins had doubled, and the company's market value (the total value of its shares) had more than doubled as well, to almost $10 billion.

What did Bossidy do to bring about such a dramatic transformation in just three years? A lot of his changes were operational: Under his guidance the company merged business units, closed factories, reduced suppliers from 9,000 to 3,000, and cut 19,000 salaried jobs from the payroll, for instance.[12]

But much of what Bossidy focused on was behavioral in nature. In other words, he focused on applying his knowledge of how people, as individuals and groups, act within organizations to help bring about change. For example, in his first two months on the job, "I talked to proba-

▲ Lawrence A. Bossidy, who as Allied-Signal's CEO turned a troubled company into a roaring success in only three years.

bly 5,000 employees. I would go to Los Angeles and speak to 500 people, then to Phoenix and talk to another 500. I would stand on a loading dock and speak to people and answer their questions. We talked about what was wrong and what we should do about it."[13] His job, as he saw it, was not just to cut jobs and merge operations, since actions like these would have only short-term effects on profitability. In the longer run, Bossidy knew, he had to excite his giant firm's many employees by promoting "our employees' ability to win," by uniting the top management team "with vision and values," and in general by convincing all his employees that there was a tremendous need to change—that their "platform was burning," as Bossidy put it.[14]

Trends like technological innovation, global competition, and deregulation have created an environment that's merciless to companies and organizations whose employees aren't fully committed to doing even more than their best, every day. That's why Bossidy says that when he looks for managers, he looks for those who have a gift for working with and turning on employees. As he put it:

Today's corporation is a far cry from the old authoritarian vertical hierarchy I grew up in. The cross-functional ties among individuals and groups are increasingly important. There are channels of activity and communication. The traditional bases of managerial authority are eroding. In the past, we used to reward the lone rangers in the corner offices because their achievements were brilliant even though their behavior was destructive. That day is gone. We need people who are better at persuading than at barking orders, who know how to coach and build consensus. Today, managers add value by brokering with people, not by presiding over empires.[15]

What Else Do Managers Do?

There are, of course, many other ways to "slice and dice" what managers do. For example, some time ago, Professor Henry Mintzberg conducted a study of what managers actually do, in part by walking around and watching them as they worked. Mintzberg found that as they went from task to task, managers didn't just plan, organize, lead, and control. Instead, they wore various hats, including:

- *The* figurehead *role*. Every manager spends some time performing ceremonial duties. For example, the president of the United States might have to greet representatives of the state legislature, a supervisor might attend the wedding of a clerk, or the sales manager might take an important client to lunch.
- *The* leader *role*. Every manager must function as a leader, motivating and encouraging employees.[16]
- *The* liaison *role*. Managers spend a lot of time in contact with people outside their own departments, essentially acting as the liaison between their departments and other people within and outside the organization. The assembly-line supervisor might field a question from the sales manager about how a new order is coming. Or, the vice president of sales might meet with the vice president of finance to make sure a new customer has the credit required to place an order.
- *The* spokesperson *role*. The manager is often the spokesperson for his or her organization. The supervisor may have to keep the plant manager informed about the flow of work through the shop, or the president may make a speech to lobby

the local county commissioners for permission to build a new plant on some unused land.

- *The* negotiator *role*. Managers spend a lot of time negotiating; the head of the airline tries to negotiate a new contract with the pilots' union, or the first-line supervisor negotiates a settlement to a grievance with the union's representative.

More recently, two management experts, Sumantra Ghoshal and Christopher Bartlett, emphasized the importance of managers in creating a responsive and change-oriented company.[17] Successful managers today, say Bartlett and Ghoshal, can't afford to focus just on the mechanical aspects of managing, like designing organization charts or drawing up plans. Instead, successful managers cultivate three processes aimed at getting employees to focus their attention on creating change: *the entrepreneurial process, the competence-building process*, and the *renewal process*.

- *The* entrepreneurial *process*. Entrepreneurship, say Bartlett and Ghoshal, refers to "the externally-oriented, opportunity-seeking attitudes that motivate employees to run their operations as if they own them."[18] In their study of 20 companies in Japan, the United States, and Europe, they found that successful managers focused much of their time and energy on getting employees to think of themselves as entrepreneurs. To do this, managers emphasized giving employees the authority, support, and rewards that self-disciplined and self-directed people needed to run their operations as their own.

- *The* competence-building *process*. Bartlett and Ghoshal also found that "in a world of converging technologies, large companies have to do more than match their smaller competitors' flexibility and responsiveness. They must also exploit their big-company advantages, which lie not only in scale economies but also in the depth and breadth of employees' talents and knowledge."[19]

  Successful managers therefore also devote much effort to creating an environment that lets employees really take charge. This means: encouraging them to take on more responsibility; providing the education and training they need to build self-confidence; and allowing them to make mistakes without fear of punishment, while coaching them and supporting them to learn from their mistakes.[20]

- *The* renewal *process*. Successful managers also concentrate on fostering what Bartlett and Ghoshal call a renewal process, one "designed to challenge a company's strategies and the assumptions behind them."[21] In other words, managers have to make sure they and all their employees guard against complacency. Employees should develop the habit of questioning why things are done as they are and whether it might not be better to do things differently.

The People Side of the Management Process

To get another perspective on how managers manage, consider the behavioral or people aspects of the things managers do. Managers plan, organize, lead, and control. Obviously, leading is a very people-oriented activity, since it involves tasks like motivating employees and resolving conflicts. But, as summarized in Table 1.3, also keep in mind that the people side of managing is important to planning, organizing, and controlling, too. For instance, planning involves getting department heads to work together to craft a new plan; controlling may involve getting subordinates to correct "out of control" behavior. The people side of managing thus affects everything that managers do. We'll illustrate this in each chapter with a feature called "The People Side of Managing" that shows the people aspects of that chapter's topic.

T A B L E 1.3	Everything a Manager Does Requires Leading
Management Function	**The People or Leadership Side of the Management Function**
Planning	Getting department heads to work together to craft a new strategic plan; working with small groups of employees to encourage more creative ways of looking at the company's situation; dealing with the interdepartmental conflicts that may arise when one department's plans conflict with another's.
Organizing	Dealing with the questions of power and company politics that arise as employees in various departments jockey for positions of dominance; encouraging communication across departmental lines; understanding how personality, motivation, and skills can influence who should or should not be put in charge of various departments.
Controlling	Influencing subordinates to correct "out of control" behavior; dealing with the fact that employees may be motivated to subvert the control system to make themselves look better in the short run; and using effective interpersonal communication skills to encourage employees to change the way they do things.

Note: Leading, the management function that focuses on the people aspects of what managers do, is not just another step in the management process, but an integral part of everything managers do.

Do You Want to Be a Manager?

If you're thinking of being a manager, there's a wealth of research to help you to decide whether that's the occupation for you.

Personality and Interests   Career counseling expert John Holland says that personality (including values, motives, and needs) is an important determinant of career choice. Specifically, he says six basic "personal orientations" determine the sorts of careers to which people are drawn. Research with his Vocational Preference Test (VPT) suggests that almost all successful managers fit at least one of two personality types or orientations from that group:

- *Social orientation.* Social people are attracted to careers that involve working with others in a helpful or facilitative way (managers as well as others like clinical psychologists and social workers would exhibit this orientation). Generally speaking, socially oriented people find it easy to talk with all kinds of people, are good at helping people who are upset or troubled, are skilled at explaining things to others, and enjoy doing social things like helping others with their personal problems, teaching, and meeting new people.[22]

- *Enterprising orientation.* Enterprising people tend to like working with people in a supervisory or persuasive way in order to achieve some goal. They especially enjoy verbal activities aimed at influencing others (lawyers and public relations executives would also exhibit this orientation). Enterprising people often characterize themselves as being good public speakers, as having reputations for being able to deal with difficult people, as successfully organizing the work of others, and as being ambitious and assertive. They enjoy influencing others, selling things, serving as officers of groups, and supervising the work of others.

Competencies   Your competencies also will help determine how successful you might be at managing others. Professor Edgar Schein says career planning is a continuing process of discovery in which a person slowly develops a clearer occupational self-concept in terms of what his or her talents, abilities, motives, and values are. Schein also says that as you learn more about yourself, it becomes apparent that you have a dominant career anchor, a concern or value that you will not give up if a choice has to be made.

Based on his study of MIT graduates, Schein concluded that managers have a strong managerial competence career anchor.[23] They show a strong motivation to become managers, "and their career experience enables them to believe that they have the skills and values necessary to rise to such general management positions." A management position of high responsibility is their ultimate goal. When pressed to explain why they believed they had the skills required to gain such positions, many said they saw themselves as competent in three areas: (1) analytical competence (the ability to identify, analyze, and solve problems under conditions of incomplete information and uncertainty); (2) interpersonal competence (the ability to influence, supervise, lead, manipulate, and control people at all levels); and (3) emotional competence (the capacity to be stimulated by emotional and interpersonal crises rather than exhausted or debilitated by them, and the capacity to bear high levels of responsibility without becoming paralyzed).

Achievements   Research also suggests that you might gain some insight into your prospects by looking closely at your achievements to date. Industrial/organizational psychologists at AT&T conducted two long-term studies of managers to determine how their pre-management achievements were related to their success on the job.[24]

Some of their findings were not too surprising. Employees who had gone to college showed much greater potential when first hired for middle- and upper-management positions than did those who had not gone to college; eight years later the differences between these two groups were even more pronounced. Specifically, those who went to college rose (on average) much faster and higher in management than did those in the noncollege sample. College grades were important, too: People with higher college grades showed greater potential for promotion early in their careers, and they rose higher in management than did those with lower grades.

Also, perhaps not too surprisingly, the quality of the college attended meant a lot more early in the person's management career than it did later. Those who had attended what were considered to be better-quality colleges at first ranked higher as potential managers. But within several years college quality seemed to have little effect on who was promoted.

College major did seem to have a big effect, however, and here there were some surprises. Managers who had majored in humanities and social sciences initially scored higher as potential managers and eventually moved faster and further up the corporate ladder.[25] Business administration majors ranked second, and math, science, and engineering majors ranked third.

What accounted for the surprising performance of the humanities and social science majors? At least in this study, conducted in one company, they scored the highest in decision making, intellectual ability, written communication skills, creativity in solving business problems, and motivation for advancement. Both the humanities and social science majors and the business administration majors ranked higher in leadership ability, oral communication skills, interpersonal skills, and flexibility than did the math, science, and engineering majors.[26] Findings like these obviously don't suggest that business and science majors are lost; they may just be unique to this specific group of managers, or to AT&T. However, the findings may suggest that, whatever your major, it's important to work on improving things like decision making, creativity, and written communication skills.

career anchor
a dominant concern or value that directs an individual's career choices and that the person will not give up if a choice must be made.

managerial competence
the motivation and skills required to gain a management position, including intellectual, emotional, and interpersonal skills.

▶ WHY MANAGERS TODAY FACE INCREASED COMPETITION AND CHANGE

If there are two issues that characterize the challenges twenty-first-century managers face today, those issues can be summarized as "competition and change." A handful of forces—most notably technological advances such as the Internet, and the tendency for companies to expand their sales and manufacturing worldwide—have raised dramatically both the competition companies face and the speed with which they must cope with change. And, as a result, the way that managers manage and firms organize have both changed significantly. It is no coincidence that we've subtitled this book "Leading People and Organizations in the Twenty-First Century." We'll explain some of these forces and how they affect managers on the next few pages.

Examples of how such forces influence companies are not hard to find. For example, after more than 230 years in business, Encyclopaedia Britannica was almost put out of business in the early 1990s by Microsoft's *Encarta* CD-ROM. After selling its thirty-two-volume set of encyclopedias (and, subsequently its *Encyclopaedia Britannica* CD-ROMs) for as much as $1,200 per set, Britannica found itself on the brink of extinction, made almost obsolete by Microsoft's relatively costless *Encarta*. Today, Britannica has disbanded its door-to-door sales force and is offering its encyclopedia without charge via the Internet, and hoping that revenue from on-line ads and sponsorships will be enough to make the company grow again.

Indeed, no industry has been immune from these kinds of changes. Today, for instance, many local personnel agencies have found revenues dropping as companies search for employees via the Internet, and prospective employees list their résumés on Internet sites like hotjobs.com. And in the last few years, both Ford and General Motors announced that they are moving their entire (and enormous) purchasing operations onto the Internet, so that suppliers will be able to sell these two giant firms their supplies automatically.[27]

Similarly, in June 1999, Wall Street giant Merrill Lynch made an announcement that rocked its 14,000-member sales force and the rest of the brokerage industry: Rather than pay what often amounted to hundreds of dollars in commissions per trade, Merrill Lynch's customers would soon be able to trade on-line, for about $30 per trade. The idea was to keep Merrill Lynch's customers from jumping to low-fee on-line competitors. Said one Merrill Lynch broker, "There's a lot of very, very sore egos around here . . . we have been insulted one too many times. They basically called us dinosaurs."[28] The changes had, of course, been triggered by the rise of the Internet.

The new on-line competition spawned by the Internet thus set in motion a whole series of organizational changes at Merrill Lynch: a new on-line trading division was created, managers were reassigned, new computer systems were installed, and new plans were developed for the company, for instance. Even within the company, competition between brokers increased. The commissions Merrill Lynch brokers earned would

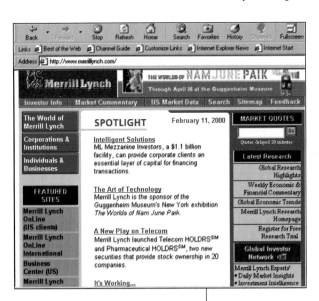

▲ W E B N O T E

Investors now do their research and buy and sell their stocks on-line, so that even traditional brokers like Merrill Lynch are becoming e-companies.

www.merrilllynch.com

Source: Copyright © 1999 Merrill Lynch & Co., Inc.

drop, and many would have to leave. Those who remained would have to work harder to provide improved services so their customers would stay loyal and pay commissions.

Such changes were not limited to Merrill Lynch. To stay competitive, other brokers would follow suit. Throughout the industry, lower fees would lead to fewer brokers, general downsizing, and more productivity and competitiveness. With giant industry mergers—such as Traveler's Group and Citibank combining to form Citigroup—added to the mix, managers today must move fast and smartly if their companies are to stay out in front.

Not all managers were able to move as quickly or smartly as those at Merrill Lynch or as Apple's Steve Jobs. In the past few years hundreds of banks, airlines, computer firms, and other businesses have failed or been gobbled up by stronger competitors. Even some of the strongest brands in the world have not been immune. After spending almost $1 billion in an unsuccessful attempt to make the company more efficient and responsive, management found that sales at Levi Strauss were heading down instead of up. Faced with smart and fast-moving global competitors like Gap and Calvin Klein, Levi's sales "fell apart" as its share in the U.S. jeans market dropped from 48% in 1990 to 25% in 1998. As this book was being written, the plans, organization, leadership, and controls of Levi's top managers were increasingly under critical scrutiny.[29]

What forces are causing such turbulence and change for companies and managers around the world today? We'll look briefly at some important ones: technological innovation, globalization, deregulation, changing political systems, category killers, the new global workforce, and new service-oriented jobs.

Technological Innovation

Technological innovations are changing the way companies are managed, and that's not just true for industry giants like Merrill Lynch. For instance, Inter-Design of Ohio sells plastic clocks, refrigerator magnets, soap dishes, and similar products. Its president explains the impact of **information technology**, which merges communications systems with computers, this way: "In the seventies we went to the post office to pick up our orders. In the early 80s, we put in an 800 number. In the late 80s, we got a fax machine. In 1991, pressured by Target [stores, a customer], we added electronic data interchange." Now, more than half of Inter-Design's orders arrive via modem, straight into company computers. Errors in order entry and shipping have all but disappeared, and both Target and Inter-Design have been able to slash finished goods inventories and therefore costs.[30]

Information technology like this has been a boon to many companies, but a near disaster for others. Wal-Mart became the industry leader in the 1990s in part because its managers used information technology to link stores with suppliers: Levi Strauss, for instance, always knew exactly how many size-10, 501-style jeans were being sold and could replenish stores' supplies almost at once. But Wal-Mart's technology advantage almost ruined K-Mart, which struggled for years without the speed and cost-effectiveness of such a system.

The Internet is having similar effects. Without physical stores and staffs, many Internet sellers like Amazon.com can offer much lower prices than local stores. And the availability of easily accessible price information means that retailers of thou-

information technology
any computerized processes, practices, or systems that facilitate the processing and transportation of data or information.

sands of products from books to boats must now drive down their own costs in order to match Internet sellers' prices. The result is continuing pressure to drive down costs and to manage firms in the most efficient and flexible manner. That's one of the reasons more conventional computer makers like Apple and Compaq have their work cut out for them in competing with the likes of Dell, which is super efficient at marketing its computers via the Internet.

Globalization

globalization

the extension of a firm's sales or manufacturing to new markets abroad.

Globalization—the extension of a firm's sales or manufacturing to new markets abroad—is also boosting competition. For instance, in the early 1980s GE, long accustomed to being the dominant lighting manufacturer in the United States, had a rude awakening. Its relatively weak competitor, Westinghouse, sold its lamp operations to Dutch electric powerhouse Philips Electronics; overnight GE's competitive picture changed. As one GE executive put it, "Suddenly we have bigger, stronger competition. They're coming into our market, but we're not in theirs. So we're on the defensive."[31]

GE did not stay there for long. It soon bought Hungary's Tungstram electronics, and is fast moving into Asia through a partnership with Hitachi.[32] In 1990 GE lighting got less than 20% of its sales from abroad; by 1993 the figure was 40%; today the estimate is more than 50%.

Production is becoming globalized too as manufacturers around the world put manufacturing facilities in the most advantageous locations. Thus, the Toyota Camry is produced in Georgetown, Kentucky, and contains almost 80% U.S.-made parts, while the Pontiac LeMans contains about two-thirds foreign-made parts.[33]

For managers, globalization is important in part because it means increased competition. In every city and town throughout the world, firms that once competed only with local firms—from airlines to car makers to banks—have discovered they must now face an onslaught of new and efficient foreign competitors. And more competition means you have to manage better and smarter to make your company succeed.

Many firms have responded successfully to this new competition, while others have failed. For instance, when Swedish furniture retailer IKEA built its first U.S. furniture superstore near Philadelphia, its unique styles and management systems grabbed market share from numerous local competitors.

But global competition is a two-way street. Ford and GM have huge market shares in Europe, for instance, while IBM, Microsoft, and Apple (thanks to those great management moves by Jobs) have major market shares around the world. As one international business expert puts it, "The bottom line is that the growing integration of the world economy into a single, huge marketplace is increasing the intensity of competition in a wide range of manufacturing and service industries."[34]

▲   Shown here is the first IKEA superstore in Elizabeth, New Jersey.

Deregulation

Competition is also keener today because the protection provided to thousands of businesses around the world by government regulation has been stripped away in many countries. In the United States hundreds of airlines, banks, and other companies have had to merge, sell out, or disappear, as deregulation exposed inefficiencies that some simply couldn't eliminate. In 1999 AT&T—formerly only a long-distance phone service provider—was poised to invade the regional Bells' local phone service turf through its purchases of various cable companies. Meanwhile, Bell Atlantic—formerly just a local service provider—was allowed to introduce long-distance service. Congress had earlier approved sweeping deregulation of local and long-distance phone service, allowing carriers to invade each other's markets. Competition in dozens of industries soared, and with it the challenge of managing the newly deregulated companies.[35]

Changing Political Systems

As nations ranging from the Philippines to Argentina, Russia, and Chile joined the ranks of democracies, central planning and communism were often replaced by capitalism. Such political changes have in turn triggered the opening of new markets, with hundreds of millions of potential customers. For business firms, the opportunities are enormous. But the burgeoning demand for goods and services also means increased global competition, as firms in more and more countries gain the wherewithal to compete in the global arena.

Category Killers

Where does a 1,000-pound gorilla sit? A 1,000-pound gorilla sits wherever it wants to, just like category killers such as Office Depot, Comp USA, and Circuit City. These mammoth stores rely on economies of scale and wide selections to drive down costs and prices and to attract huge numbers of buyers. Most small competitors— neighborhood hardware stores, stationery stores, and bookstores, for instance—can't get their costs or prices low enough to compete and haven't the product range to do so anyway. Most are squeezed out of business by the relentless competition, unless their managers and proprietors are smart enough to know how to react.

Department stores illustrate this theme too. Over the past few years many smaller retail chains like Macy's have been absorbed into giant chains like Federated Department Stores. These giant chains have powerful centralized purchasing departments that pressure clothing manufacturers to lower their prices. When the manufacturers were dealing with dozens of smaller chains, it was easier for them to negotiate. But when one giant chain accounts for half your company's sales (or more), it's much harder to resist. Manufacturers are therefore squeezed to reduce their costs, and only the most efficient and best managed survive.

The New Global Workforce

More U.S. firms are transferring their operations abroad, not just to seek cheaper labor, but also to tap what *Fortune* magazine calls "a vast new supply of skilled labor around the world."[36] Even today, for instance, most multinational firms set up manufacturing plants abroad not just to establish beachheads in promising markets, but also to utilize other countries' professionals and engineers. For example, Asea Brown Boveri (ABB; a $30 billion-per-year Swiss builder of transportation and electric generation systems) has 25,000 new employees in former Communist countries and has shifted many jobs from western to eastern Europe.

Tapping such overseas labor markets is a two-edged sword for employers. Employers gain thousands of potential new highly skilled employees, but also face the challenge of competing for and managing a geographically dispersed workforce. And for employees—especially those in the United States—it means competing for jobs with a worldwide labor force, many of whom (such as software engineers in India) may earn much lower wages than their counterparts in the U.S.

A Shift to Service and Knowledge Work

Managing today is also changing because what workers do is changing. This fact reflects several trends in the business environment. One is the growing importance of service work.[37] More than two-thirds of the U.S. workforce is now involved in producing services, not things. And of the 21 million jobs added to the U.S. economy in the 1990s, virtually all were in service industries like retailing, consulting, teaching, and law.[38] Service jobs like these put a bigger premium on worker education and knowledge than do traditional jobs, and thus they add more to a company's "human capital"—the knowledge, training, skills, and expertise of a firm's workers—at the expense of physical capital like equipment, machinery, and the physical plant.[39] As James Brian Quinn, an expert in this area, puts it, "Intellect is the core resource in producing and delivering services."[40]

▲ Knowledge-intensive, high-tech jobs proliferate: An engineer runs a space shuttle heat test simulation.

Human capital is also more important today because manufacturing jobs are changing. Particularly in the United States, jobs in the steel, auto, rubber, and textile industries are being replaced by knowledge-intensive, high-tech manufacturing in such industries as aerospace, computers, and telecommunications.[41] At Alcoa Aluminum's Davenport, Iowa, plant, for instance, computers at each workstation help employees control their machines or communicate data. As *Fortune* magazine put it, "Practically every package deliverer, bank teller, retail clerk, telephone operator, and bill collector in America works with a computer [today]."[42] Here is how Microsoft Corporation CEO Bill Gates put it:

In the new organization the worker is no longer a cog in a machine but is an intelligent part of the overall process. Welders at some steel jobs now have to know algebra and geometry to figure weld angles from computer-generated designs ... new digital photocopiers require the service personnel to have an understanding of computers and the Internet, not just skills with a screwdriver.[43]

Innovation, driven by competition, demands more highly skilled employees, too. It is not unusual for more than one-fourth of many firms' sales to come from products less than five years old. As a result, "innovating—creating new products, new services, new ways of turning out goods more cheaply—has become the most urgent concern of corporations everywhere."[44] Companies are therefore relying more on employees' creativity and skills, thus placing more stress on employees' brain power.

For managers, the challenge of human capital is that these "knowledge workers" must be managed differently than workers of previous generations. "The center of gravity in employment is shifting fast from manual and clerical workers to knowledge workers, who resist the command and control model that business took from the military 100 years ago."[45] Knowledge workers, in other words, can't just be ordered around and closely monitored. New management skills are required to turn these highly trained workers into partners in the company-building process. As a manager, you'll need to know how to lead people and organizations in the twenty-first century, in part because these people are doing jobs—designing Web sites, for instance—that workers have never done before.

▶ THE FUTURE IS NOW

The Modern Organization

Let's summarize where we are. Things are moving superfast in the world of business today; in fact, they're moving "at the speed of business," to quote a recent UPS ad. Technology, globalization, deregulation, changing political systems, the new workforce, and a shift to service and knowledge work are putting companies under tremendous pressure to respond faster and to be ever more cost-effective and competitive. What does this mean for how companies are managed? Perhaps the best way to answer that is to look at a few snapshots of how superfast businesses are being managed today. For some, being superfast means using the Internet for "Managing @ the Speed of Thought," as the following box about Dell illustrates.

MANAGING @ THE *SPEED* OF THOUGHT

■ Virtual Integration at Dell Computer

How do you build a $12 billion company in just 13 years?[46] For Dell Computer the answer meant using technology and information to "blur the traditional boundaries in the value chain among suppliers, manufacturers, and the end users."[47] What does this mean? As summarized in Figure 1.2, it basically means that there are no intermediaries like wholesalers or retailers to come between Dell and its customers and suppliers, so that Dell can be a much faster-moving company than it might otherwise be.[48] For most computer companies, the manufacturing process is like a relay race: Components come in from suppliers; these components are assembled into computers; and the computers are then handed off to be distributed through wholesalers and retailers (such as CompUSA) to the ultimate customers. Dell's system changes all that. For example, (see Figure 1.2) Dell interacts with and sells to customers directly, so it eliminates the activities of the wholesalers and retailers in the traditional distribution chain.[49]

▼ FIGURE 1.2

The Evolution of a Faster Business Model

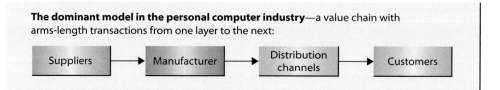

The dominant model in the personal computer industry—a value chain with arms-length transactions from one layer to the next:

Suppliers → Manufacturer → Distribution channels → Customers

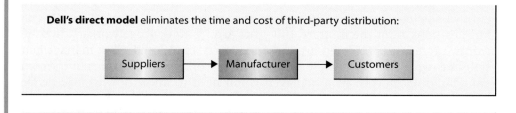

Dell's direct model eliminates the time and cost of third-party distribution:

Suppliers → Manufacturer → Customers

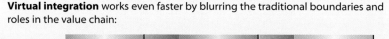

Virtual integration works even faster by blurring the traditional boundaries and roles in the value chain:

Suppliers | Manufacturer | Customers

Source: *Harvard Business Review,* March–April 1998, p. 82. Copyright © 1998 by the President and Fellows of Harvard College. All rights reserved.

"Virtual integration"—linking Dell with its suppliers and customers via the Internet—speeds things up even more. As one example, computerized information from Dell continually updates suppliers regarding the number of components to be delivered every morning, so the "outside" supplier actually starts to look and act more like an "inside" part of Dell. Similarly, instead of stocking its own monitors,

> We tell Airborne Express or UPS to come to Austin and pick up 10,000 computers a day and go over to the Sony factory in Mexico and pick up the corresponding number of monitors. And while we're all sleeping, they match up the computers and the monitors, and deliver them to the customers . . . of course, this requires sophisticated data exchange.[50]

The result of what Michael Dell calls "this virtual integration" of suppliers, manufacturing, and customers is a lean, efficient, and fast-moving operation that can turn on a dime if the products demanded by customers change:

> There are fewer things to manage, fewer things to go wrong. You don't have the drag effect of taking 50,000 people with you. . . . If we had to build our own factories for every single component of the system, growing at 57% per year just would not be possible. I would spend 500% of my time interviewing prospective vice-presidents because the company would have not 15,000 employees but 80,000. Indirectly, we employ something like that many people today. . . but only a small number of them work for us. Their contract is with other firms. . . . The vast majority [of customers] think [those people] work for us, which is just great. That's part of virtual integration.[51]

Mini-Units at ABB   Electrical equipment maker ABB (Asea Brown Boveri) makes enormously expensive machines like electric power generators and competes with giant companies like GE around the world for customers. Its business requires a unique combination of efficiency (since competitors like GE are highly efficient) and responsiveness (since each of their local customer's needs are unique and require a good deal of local technical assistance and attention. When he took over this $30 billion firm, former chairman Percy Barnevik knew dramatic steps would be needed to turn his company into an efficient and responsive competitor. He did four things to accomplish this transformation at ABB:[52]

1. First, he split its 215,000 employees into 5,000 minicompanies, each averaging only about 50 workers.[53] For example, the ABB hydropower unit in Finland is now a minicompany that serves just its own Finnish customers. Each of ABB's 50-person units is run by its own manager and three or four lieutenants. Such small units are much more manageable; it's a lot easier to monitor what everyone is doing when there are only 50 people to keep track of than when there are 1,000 or more.

2. Next, to speed decision making, the 5,000 minicompanies' employees were empowered—given the authority—to make most of their own business decisions. If a customer has a complaint about a $50,000 machine, a minicompany employee can approve a replacement on the spot, rather than having to wait for review by several levels of management. This meant faster decision-making.

3. Next, ABB "delayered"; its 215,000-employee organization now has just three management levels (a comparably sized company might have seven or eight). There is a 13-member top-management executive committee based in Zurich. Below this is a 250-member executive level that includes country managers and executives in charge of groups of businesses. A third level consists of the 5,000 minicompany managers and their management teams. By slicing out layers of management and letting lower-level employees make their own decisions, ABB employees can respond more quickly to customers' needs and competitors' moves.

4. Finally, with ABB empolyees making most of their own decisions anyway, ABB could strip away most headquarters staff. When Barnevik became CEO, he found 2,000 people working at headquarters, basically reviewing and analyzing (and slowing down) the decisions of the firm's lower-level employees. Within months, he reduced the headquarters staff to 200.

Efficiency and responsiveness are the net effect of ABB's managerial changes. Today, ABB is a lean, flat organization staffed with highly committed employees. 170,000 employees are organized into small, empowered units, each able to respond quickly to competitors' moves and local customers' needs in 100 countries, with no need to wait for headquarters approval.

Maintaining Control at Cisco Systems   As companies grow larger, it becomes more difficult for their top managers to maintain control. If you're just managing a local card shop or dry cleaning store, for instance, its fairly easy for an owner/manager to keep track of everything that's going on, at least as long as he or she is in the store. But as the company grows larger and opens subsidiaries around the world, keeping track of what is happening can become quite a challenge. Yet if top management in, say, New York City, doesn't find out until too late that expenses are out of control in the Paris office, the result could be disastrous for the company.

That's why companies like Cisco Systems are implementing special Internet-based financial control systems. For example, when you sit with Larry Carter, Cisco Systems chief financial officer (CFO), you can see the whole company laid out before you.[54] This is because Cisco, manufacturer of networking hardware and software, is in the vanguard of firms using sophisticated real-time computerized financial systems to give their top executives access to data almost instantaneously. As a relatively young company (founded in 1984), Cisco "doesn't have a bunch of incompatible, old record-keeping systems gumming things up." It could therefore start with a clean slate and computerize the entire financial control system.

Being able to continuously monitor what goes on in the company on a real-time basis has many advantages. For one thing, top management can detect changes in market conditions almost at once. Says CFO Carter, "a year ago we saw an uptick in [sales in] countries in Europe that had been flat, and we authorized accelerated hiring there long before any of our competitors did."[55]

Teamwork at Saturn Corporation You have probably seen pictures of the old-time automobile plants, where individual employees toiled night and day doing the same monotonous jobs over and over again, as the cars moved along an assembly line. As you can imagine, jobs and conditions like these didn't exactly motivate most workers to do their best or to keep quality high. Today, as we'll see in this book, one of the biggest challenges facing managers is to organize the workplace in such a way that employees become so committed to their jobs that they actually want to do those jobs as if they're the owners of the company. And that is why more and more companies are organizing their jobs around small, highly-trained and committed teams.

For example, a team-based organization is one thing that sets GM's Saturn Corporation subsidiary apart. Virtually all shop floor work is organized around work teams of 10 to 12 employees. Each team is responsible for a complete task, such as installing door units, checking electrical systems, or maintaining automated machines.

The work teams don't have traditional supervisors. Instead, the highly trained workers do their own hiring, control their own budgets, monitor the quality of their own work, and generally manage themselves. Are too many of the door parts not fitting right? Then the team must find the problem and get the parts supplier to solve it. Is a coworker always late? Then the team must discipline him or her in order to manage its own (and its team members') time.

The New Management

We've seen on the last few pages that forces like technological change, globalized competition, deregulation, political instability, and trends toward service jobs and the information age have altered the playing field on which firms must now compete. They have done this by dramatically raising the need for firms to be efficient, responsive, flexible, and capable of competing and reacting rapidly to competitive and technological changes.

Firms like ABB and Cisco are in vanguard of thousands of others that are re-creating themselves to fit these new conditions, by implementing new management methods that enable them to cope with great competition and rapid change. An overview is presented in Figure 1.3. Forces such as technological innovation, globalization, and deregulation mean that companies today must cope with much greater levels of competition, change, and unpredictability than ever before. As a result, to succeed, companies like Dell, ABB, Cisco, and Saturn have instituted new management methods (such as mini-units, Internet-based financial controls, and team-based organizations) that enable these companies to be more efficient, and also much more effective at reacting quickly to competitive and technological

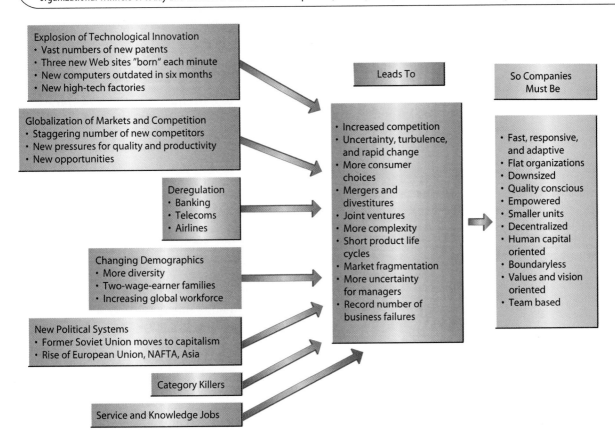

▼ FIGURE 1.3

Fundamental Changes Facing Managers A series of forces—globalized competition, technology revolution, new competitors, and changing tastes—are creating outcomes that include more uncertainty, more choices, and more complexity. The result is that the organizational winners of today and tomorrow will have to be responsive, smaller, flatter, and oriented toward adding value through people.

Explosion of Technological Innovation
- Vast numbers of new patents
- Three new Web sites "born" each minute
- New computers outdated in six months
- New high-tech factories

Globalization of Markets and Competition
- Staggering number of new competitors
- New pressures for quality and productivity
- New opportunities

Deregulation
- Banking
- Telecoms
- Airlines

Changing Demographics
- More diversity
- Two-wage-earner families
- Increasing global workforce

New Political Systems
- Former Soviet Union moves to capitalism
- Rise of European Union, NAFTA, Asia

Category Killers

Service and Knowledge Jobs

Leads To

- Increased competition
- Uncertainty, turbulence, and rapid change
- More consumer choices
- Mergers and divestitures
- Joint ventures
- More complexity
- Short product life cycles
- Market fragmentation
- More uncertainty for managers
- Record number of business failures

So Companies Must Be

- Fast, responsive, and adaptive
- Flat organizations
- Downsized
- Quality conscious
- Empowered
- Smaller units
- Decentralized
- Human capital oriented
- Boundaryless
- Values and vision oriented
- Team based

change. We'll see how managers actually do this in the rest of the book. But from their experiences, and from those of others, here is a summary of what the new management looks like.

Smaller Organizational Units First, one way or another, the actual operating units in most companies are getting smaller. For one thing, there's been an explosion of new small ventures, with thousands and thousands of "e-entrepreneurs" setting up their own new firms. And even in big firms (recall ABB), the work is increasingly organized around mini-units.

Cypress Semiconductor is another example. T. J. Rogers, president of this California firm, believes that large companies stifle innovation. So when a new product must be developed, he doesn't do it within the existing corporation. Instead, he creates a separate start-up company under the Cypress umbrella. "I would rather see our billion-dollar company of the 1990s be 10 $100 million companies, all strong, growing, healthy and aggressive as hell," Rogers says. "The alternative is an aging billion-dollar company that spends more time defending its turf than growing." True to his words, Rogers already has four successful start-ups under development.[56]

Team-Based Organizations   As at Saturn, todays' new organizations stress cross-functional teams and interdepartmental communication. There is also a corresponding de-emphasis on sticking to the chain of command to get decisions made. GE's, former Chairman Jack Welch has talked of the boundaryless organization, in which employees do not identify with separate departments, but instead interact with whomever they must to get the job done.[57]

Empowered Decision Making   Jobs today require constant learning, higher-order thinking, and much more worker commitment. This calls for more employee empowerment, and less of a 9-to-5 mentality. Experts like Karl Albrecht argue for turning the typical organization upside-down.[58] They say today's organization should put the customer—not the CEO—on top, to emphasize that every move the company makes must be aimed at satisfying customer needs. This in turn requires empowering the front-line employees—the front desk clerks at the hotel, the cabin attendants on the plane, and the assemblers at the factory—with the authority to respond quickly to these needs. The main purpose of managers in this "upside-down" organization is to serve the front-line employees, to see that they have what they need to do their jobs, and thus to serve the customers. They're not simply there to oversee what workers do and to control their actions.

Flatter Organizational Structures   Instead of the familiar pyramid-shaped organization with its seven or more layers of management, flat organizations with just three or four levels prevail. Many companies have already cut the management layers from a dozen to six or fewer, and therefore the number of managers.[59] As the remaining managers are left with more people to supervise, they are less able to meddle in the work of their subordinates, who thus have more autonomy.

New Bases of Management Power   In today's organizations, says management theorist Rosabeth Moss Kanter, leaders can no longer rely on their formal authority to get employees to follow them.[60] Instead, "success depends increasingly on tapping into sources of good ideas, on figuring out whose collaboration is needed to act on those ideas, and on working with both to produce results. In short, the new managerial work implies very different ways of obtaining and using power."[61] Peter Drucker put it this way: "You have to learn to manage in situations where you don't have command authority, where you are neither controlled nor controlling."[62] In other words, managers have to win the respect and commitment of their highly trained and empowered employees to get their jobs done today.

Knowledge-Based Organizations   Management expert Tom Peters says new organizations are knowledge based. Teams of highly trained and educated professionals apply their knowledge to clients' problems, in a setting in which the employees direct and discipline their own activities.[63]

This means managers must help their employees get their jobs done by training and coaching them, removing roadblocks, and getting them the resources they need: You can't simply "boss" teams of professionals. This highlights one big difference between the old and the new manager. Yesterday's manager thinks of himself or herself as a "manager" or "boss." The new manager thinks of himself or herself as a "sponsor," a "team leader," or an "internal consultant." The old-style manager makes most decisions alone; the new one invites others to join in the decision making. The old-style manager hoards information to build his or her personal power. The new manager shares information to help subordinates get their jobs done.[64]

An Emphasis on Vision and Values   Formulating a clear vision and values to which employees can commit themselves is more important than ever. Managers must communicate clear values regarding what is important and unimportant, and regarding what employees should and should not do. As GE's Welch said,

> Every organization needs values, but a lean organization needs them even more. When you strip away the support system of staffs and layers, people need to relearn their habits and expectations or else the stress will just overwhelm them. . . . Values [are] what enable people to guide themselves through that kind of change.[65]

Other experts agree. Drucker says today's organizations—staffed as they are by professionals and other employees who largely control their own behavior—require "clear, simple, common objectives that translate into particular actions." In other words, they need a clear vision of where the firm is heading.[66] Even without a lot of supervisors to guide them, employees can then be steered by the company's vision and values.

Managers are Change Agents   As GE's Welch puts it, "You've got to be on the cutting edge of change. You can't simply maintain the status quo, because somebody's always coming from another country with another product, or consumers' tastes change, or the cost structure does, or there's a technology breakthrough. If you are not fast and adaptable, you are vulnerable."[67]

Leadership Is Key   Empowered workers, service jobs, and the need to get workers thinking like owners puts a premium on the people side of managing. Understanding how to work with and through people and how to use behavioral science concepts and techniques at work will be more important than ever before.

More Companies Are Becoming E-based   Today virtually all companies—from tiny ".com" startups like hungryminds.com to giant companies like General Motors, Wal-Mart, and GE are reorganizing in a way that enables them to take advantage of the great potential of the Internet. Today, as we'll see in this book, managers are using the Internet in thousands of ways to help them to better plan, organize, lead, and control their organizations. In the chapters to follow we'll use "Managing @ the Speed of Thought" boxes (as we did on pages 17–18 to show how Dell has turned itself into an Internet-based company) as well as short illustrated "Webnotes" to show how managers are using the power of the Internet to help them better manage their companies today.

SUMMARY

1. An organization consists of people who have formally assigned roles and who must work together to achieve the organization's goals. Organizations needn't be just business firms.

2. Organizations cannot simply run themselves. Instead, they are run by managers. A manager is someone who plans, organizes, leads, and controls the people and the work of the organization in such a way that the organization achieves its goals.

3. Management writers traditionally refer to the manager's four basic functions of planning, organizing, leading, and controlling as the management process.

4. We can classify managers based on organizational level (top, middle, first line), position (executives, managers or directors, supervisors), and functional title (vice president of production, sales manager). All managers get their work done through people and by planning, organizing, leading, and controlling. Top managers spend more time planning and setting goals. Lower-level managers concentrate on implementing goals and getting employees to achieve them.

5. Managers play other roles too: for instance, figurehead, leader, liason. They also engage in entrepreneurial, competence-building, and renewal processes.

6. Almost everything a manager does involves interacting with and influencing people. The bottom line is that the leading, or people, side of what managers do is not just another step in the management process, but an integral part of the manager's job.

7. Managers and their organizations have to confront rapid change and intense competition today. Trends contributing to this change and unpredictability include technological innovation, globalization, deregulation, changing political systems, category killers, the new global workforce, more service-oriented jobs, and an emphasis on knowledge work.

8. Companies like ABB, Saturn, and Dell illustrate the new organization of the twenty-first century, in which responsiveness is a top priority and effective leadership is extraordinarily important.

TYING IT ALL TOGETHER

This chapter explains what managers do, and the trends (like globalization) that are forcing companies and other types of organizations to become more competitive. The fact that companies must be more competitive means that managers must organize and manage their companies to be faster and more efficient. In this book we'll see how they do that. First, in Chapter 2, "Managing in a Global Environment," we'll look more closely at one of these trends—globalization—and its effect on how managers manage.

KEY TERMS

organization 2
manager 3
management 3
management process 3

executives 4
first-line manager 5
career anchor 11

managerial competence 11
information technology 13
globalization 14

SKILLS AND STUDY MATERIALS

CRITICAL THINKING EXERCISES

1. The traditional organization is usually depicted as a pyramid-shaped hierarchy with authority and decision making flowing from the top down. As this chapter points out, the changing environment demands that new forms of organization be designed. Your assignment is to graphically depict some new organizational designs. Draw the shapes you think represent the boundaryless, team-focused, and process-oriented organizations that are evolving. Then write a brief narrative describing what you have drawn and what you think the implications behind your designs are.

2. In *The New New Thing: A Silicon Valley Story* (W. W. Norton & Co., 1999), Mike Lewis relates the contrasts that are likely to frame the next century. The story focuses on how two dif-

ferent and powerful firms are approaching their journey. Lewis argues that Jim Clark, the founder of Netscape, is the model for the future. Clark is seen as a genius "on an endless search for some unattainable solution." Clark has a talent for anarchy that well suits him at this juncture in history. In contrast, Microsoft's Bill Gates is characterized as someone who wants the future "to look exactly like the present." Lewis characterized Microsoft as a company that doesn't want to discover the new thing, but rather to tame it. Using what you have learned in Chapter 1, speculate on what management model you think will survive and why. Will it be the world of Jim Clark or the world of Bill Gates (assuming Lewis is right about both men)? Predict what the management process might involve by the year 2020.

EXPERIENTIAL EXERCISES

1. The federal government sued Microsoft for its monopolistic tendencies. In fall 1999 a judge ruled that indeed Microsoft was a monopoly. There was talk of breaking up the company into three different entities. Not so long ago, the giant Microsoft was unconcerned about the regulatory role of the federal government. Then competitors as well as the government filed a number of lawsuits against it. Some analysts felt that Microsoft believed it was so large, powerful, and dominant that it would rule without interference from anyone. Neither the government nor rivals felt the same way. Now Microsoft has hired a battery of well-known and well-connected lobbyists. However, this action may be too little, too late. Is it too powerful? Is it a monopoly, and if so, is it good for the country to have such a monopoly? What if anything does the attitude of Microsoft say about its management?

2. An excellent way to find out about entrepreneurship is to talk to an entrepreneur. By asking your professor, other professors, the Small Business Administration in your region, or another small business organization such as the Small Business Chamber of Commerce, you should be able to identify an entrepreneur or entrepreneurs who have started a business in the past five years. Contact the person and conduct an informational interview. Some questions you might want to ask are: What did it take to establish the business? Did you have a business plan? Where did you get your financing? What management challenges do you face today? How did you develop your human resource policies? Also ask any other questions that specifically fit the type of business. Then prepare a page on the major points you found about entrepreneurship and be ready to present your findings in class or in a small group.

You might want to do this project with two or three other students and divide the labor according to expertise.

Use references like *Inc.* or *Fast Company* magazines that are devoted to entrepreneurship. These resources may help you find an entrepreneur or decide what questions you want to ask an entrepreneur.

myPHLIP COMPANION WEB SITE

We invite you to visit the Dessler companion Web site at **www.prenhall.com/dessler** for this chapter's Internet resources.

Chris Sullivan and the founders of Outback Steakhouse, Inc., developed a unique vision for a restaurant concept and the management system that would make it work. Having worked for other chain restaurants in the past, Sullivan and his team wanted to do things very differently. They wanted a restaurant that exceeded customer expectations for quality and that was a fun place for employees to work. Could Sullivan's concept of a fun place to work capture the fancy of customers and employees?

Sullivan and his co-founders had originally planned to build just a few restaurants and then play a lot of golf. Life didn't work out that way. The company they created captured the imagination and appetites of the restaurant-going public. Within its first 6 years, Outback Steakhouse had become the fastest-growing restaurant chain in the casual dining segment of the restaurant industry. Outback's management team took the company public, to the delight of its shareholders. It has won numerous awards for business growth, including Entrepreneur of the Year awards from both *Inc.* magazine and the Kauffman Foundation.

Part of Outback's success has come from its unorthodox management system. First, Sullivan and his colleagues wanted restaurateurs to be able to make a career as store managers. In many restaurant chains, the best-paying positions are in a corporate office, not directly serving customers. Top store managers in those systems leave the restaurant to move to corporate in order to make a good salary.

To attract managers, Outback offered very strong financial packages (in many cases offering the manager equity in the local restaurant), assignment to a location for a minimum of five years, and a work environment serving dinner only. Outback's unique employment offers aren't just for the top employees. Recently, the company rolled out a benefits program for part-time employees. Unlike at many companies, at Outback the less you make, the less you are required to pay for health insurance.

Sullivan insists that one key for a successful restaurant is for the local team to have fun. Local Outback managers have noted that one of the first questions CEO Sullivan asks them when visiting their location is, "Are you still having fun?" Their corporate motto, "No rules, just right," is echoed in the casual style of the management team and its fiercely entrepreneurial culture.

Discussion Questions

1. What management roles does Sullivan fulfill, based on this case?

2. Why is it important in a service-oriented business like this to attract the best management talent and employees?

3. Why is the people side of management so important at Outback, and what is the company doing to maintain morale and commitment?

Has AT&T President Mike Armstrong been making the best decisions? Today investors are choosing between two competing communication technologies: cable and wireless. Armstrong has placed AT&T's bet on cable lines. In the past few years, AT&T has acquired over $100 billion in cable operations. Because of its unique technical properties, cable can carry a range of high-speed signals, including video, Internet, multimedia, data, and voice communication—potentially simultaneously.

AT&T's arch rival, MCI Worldcom, believes that wireless communications will become the technology of the future. MCI spent over $120 billion just on its acquisition of Sprint, a large wireless carrier. Sprint is also strong in data services, an area in which AT&T is considered weak. The fact that another giant company would invest its resources in an alternative technology causes investor concerns at AT&T.

The fallout from Armstrong's decisions will be profound and far-reaching. Armstrong oversees the operations of

AT&T's 126,000 workers worldwide. In addition to the challenges of people management in a company of such size, AT&T's industry—global telecommunications—is considered one of the most competitive in the world. Currently, AT&T leads the industry, with 90 million customers in 280 countries and territories. In its most recent year, AT&T generated close to $52 billion in revenue.

In addition to concerns about technology, Armstrong and his AT&T management team must consider regulation and deregulation. On the regulation side, AT&T received a major blow in summer 1999. A Florida county voted to force AT&T to open its cable networks to other local Internet providers. In essence, AT&T was forced to encourage competition.

While the U.S. market is already largely deregulated, many areas of the world that were formally strictly regulated have recently opened to market competition. Even state-owned telecommunication services have been sold to private industry. In these emerging global markets, AT&T is just one more competitor against the likes of Deutsche Telecom and Nippon Telephone and Telegraph. Competition can even come from nontelephone companies; for example, in Italy, Telcom Italia was acquired by manufacturing giant Olivetti. In 1999, about 2% of AT&T's business came from international calls, while MCI had 3.3% in international business. As global business increases, AT&T will need a strong global presence. While a giant company in its own right, there are parts of the world where AT&T is not a well-known player.

To improve its global position, AT&T completed a global joint venture agreement with British Telcom (BT). AT&T and BT announced plans in July 1998 to serve the communications needs of their multinational business customers and Internet service providers around the world. The new venture is owned equally by the two parents.

The forces of technology, deregulation, and competition have not made AT&T's executive suite an easy place to work. Since Armstrong took over as CEO, the company has lost several key senior executives. One departing executive, Robert Annunziata, left to become CEO of Global Crossing, a new company that is competing with AT&T for multinational accounts.

Finally, being CEO does not mean that Armstrong is not accountable to others. His "bosses" include the 3.5 million shareholders who are intensely interested in every decision he makes.

Discussion Questions

1. What management roles does Armstrong seem to fulfill?

2. How, specifically, have the forces of deregulation, technology, and globalization affected AT&T?

3. To what extent does AT&T's size make it susceptible to market forces? (Would a smaller company face the same forces to the same extent?) Why or why not?

4. What new management methods does AT&T seem to be adopting as a result of these market forces?

YOU BE THE CONSULTANT

KNITMEDIA IS UP AND RUNNING

When it comes to managing a business, there's nothing quite like managing a small, fast-growing enterprise like Michael Dorf's alternative music and entertainment company, KnitMedia. Managing a giant like IBM or GE requires decisions about how to organize, hire, motivate, and keep track of the activities of tens of thousands (and often hundreds of thousands) of employees and of billions of dollars. Managing a small firm like KnitMedia presents a somewhat different set of challenges: only very simple or no support systems (accountants, budget systems, control systems) in place, and only a few or no managers to call on to help get a job done. And in the highly competitive music business environment, you've got all those giants, like AOL/Time Warner and Sony, just waiting for you to make a mistake.

At the end of every chapter in this book, you'll have an opportunity to meet Michael Dorf and apply that chapter's materials to the challenges faced by his company, KnitMedia, LLC. Its businesses include several independent record labels, a festival division, a NewMedia/Internet division, and a growing chain of Knitting Factory music clubs, including two in Manhattan and Hollywood, and one soon to open in Berlin. You'll find a good deal of information about KnitMedia and its businesses in each of these end-of-chapter cases, and more information on KnitMedia's Web site, **www.knitmedia.com.**

KnitMedia began, to some extent, as a result of economic necessity. In 1985, while still a college student in Madison, Wisconsin, Dorf began managing the band Swamp Thing. He and the band started Flaming Pie

Records to record and distribute their songs. After struggling for two years to get Swamp Thing some exposure, Dorf and his partner Louis Spitzer found themselves in New York's downtown SoHo district. They rented a dilapidated office on Houston Street between the Bowery and Broadway, and the Knitting Factory was born. The initial idea (as Dorf describes it in his book *Knitting Music*) was to have an art gallery/performance space that sold coffee, tea, and a small assortment of foods. As he and Spitzer said in their first press release:

> "The Knitting Factory is primarily a showcase. Our aim is to weave strands of art mediums into a congruent whole, from the Wednesday night poetry series to the works on the walls. The Knitting Factory is also a café. It serves interesting forms of food like a fondue with fresh fruit. The Knitting Factory considers many things art and is open to suggestions. Hope to see you soon."[68]

Michael Dorf's real motivation at the time was "to earn enough money to live and to cover the rent for Flaming Pie Records." There wasn't much managing to do, since KnitMedia had few employees. Now, however, it's a different story: after nine profitable years of growth, Dorf and his company recently received an infusion of about $5 million to expand the business. And today KnitMedia, LLC, includes not only several separate businesses, but an executive management team. That team, as of 2000, is made up of Michael Dorf, president and chief executive officer; Allan Fried, chief operating officer; Glen Max, KnitMedia properties programming director; Ed Greer, senior vice president; Stephanie Oxley, vice president, KnitMedia labels; Mark Harabedian, vice president for finance; Victoria DeRose, vice president for marketing & business development; Chris Shields, director festival division; David Brenner, vice president of NewMedia; and Mitch Goldman, chief content officer.

These managers know they are in a competitive business, one that's changing very fast. They also know that as a young company they still have a way to go as far as setting up management systems is concerned. In one recent interview, for instance, Mark Harabedian, the new finance vice president, said: "My great challenge, my first great challenge when I got here was to revamp the whole finance system, so Michael and the other managers could maintain better control over the firm's fast-expanding operations."

Understanding that they face these challenges, the KnitMedia managers have asked you and your team to sign on as consultants. Many of the KnitMedia team have backgrounds in the arts and music, rather than in business, so they're looking forward to drawing on your expanding knowledge about how to plan, organize, lead, and control an organization. Since they're now in the process of planning how KnitMedia will expand in the next few years, their first questions concern the competitive challenges they can expect to face, and the broad management questions that may arise.

Team Exercises and Questions

Use what you learned in this chapter to answer the following questions from Michael Dorf and his management team:

1. Few industries are undergoing as much rapid change as music, entertainment, and Internet/NewMedia—the three industries KnitMedia is in. What are the trends (such as consolidation) taking place today for which we'll have to plan?

2. What are the key competitors in New York City for the Knitting Factory Club? (*Hint:* Use the Internet to compile a list).

3. What are the specific management tasks each of our executives can expect to have to address as part of our day-to-day duties? (*Hint:* What is the management process?)

FOUNDATIONS OF MODERN MANAGEMENT

Management existed even in antiquity. Hunters banded into tribes for protection; the Egyptians used organizations to build pyramids and control the rise and fall of the Nile; and the Romans relied on organizing to build their armies and control their empire. Management is thus a very old idea (as Figure A1.1 illustrates).

Some recurring themes become apparent when we view management over the ages. First, many of the concepts we take for granted today, such as dividing employees into departments, can be traced to the earliest human organizations, including those of the ancient Egyptians and Greeks. The close supervision and reliance on coercion and rules that management expert Peter Drucker called "command and control" is also a product of earlier times, in particular of the militaristic organizations of ancient Egypt and Rome.

Second, we will see that the forms organizations take and the ways managers manage have always been a product of the time. As futurist Alvin Toeffler says, in describing 19th-century management,

> Each age produces a form of organization appropriate to its own tempo. During the long epic of agricultural civilization, societies were marked by low transcience. Delays in communication and transportation slowed the rate at which information moved. The pace of individual life was comparatively slow. And organizations were seldom called upon to make what we would regard as high-speed decisions.[1]

So management is also an evolutionary process. Let us now look back to the beginning of modern management theory.

▼ **FIGURE A1.1**

Some All-Time Greatest Hits of Managing

2052 B.C. to 1786 B.C.	Around 59 B.C.	1906	1908	1955	1984
In the Middle Kingdom of Egypt, leaders introduce the subdivision of labor into factories (if papyrus records are to be believed).	Julius Caesar keeps people up-to-date with handwritten sheets and posters around Rome. Ever since, the greatness of leaders has been measured partly by their ability to communicate.	Sears Roebuck opens its Chicago mail-order plant. The Sears catalog makes goods available to an entirely new audience.	William Hoover sees that automobiles would kill his business, which makes leather accessories for horse-drawn carriages. So he starts the Electric Suction Sweeper Co., creating the mass-market vacuum cleaner.	Ray Kroc likes Mac and Dick McDonald's food stand in San Bernardino, California, so much that he opens his own franchised restaurant and forms McDonald's Corp.	In his dorm room at the University of Texas at Austin, Michael Dell starts selling PCs direct and building them to order.

Source: Thomas A. Stewart, "The All-Time Greatest Hits of Managing" *Fortune,* 29 March 1999, p. 192.

Management theory as we know it today is an outgrowth of the first attempts to view the management process with a new, more scientific rigor.

The Industrial Revolution

By 1750, with the advent of the Industrial Revolution, what Toeffler referred to as "the long epic of agricultural civilization" was about to end. The Industrial Revolution was a period of several decades during which machine power was increasingly substituted for human or animal labor. During these years several major trends converged. Scientific and technological discoveries, including the invention of the steam engine and the use of electricity, contributed to enormous increases in productivity and output. England, generally recognized as the epicenter of the Industrial Revolution, had a stable, constitutional government, a sensitivity to laissez-faire (hands-off) economics, and a strong spirit of self-reliance. In his book *The Wealth of Nations*, Adam Smith described the division and specialization of work—giving each worker a specialized job—as essential for efficiency and competitiveness.[2]

The Industrial Environment

For firms in the 1800s industrialization therefore meant resource accumulation and company growth. Division of work and specialization required the high volume and stability that only growth could bring. Growth led to higher profits; as sales, volume, and stability increased, efficiency went up and unit costs decreased.

But bigger operations created new problems for entrepreneurs. They needed management techniques to run their new, large-scale enterprises. Where would they learn how to manage large enterprises? These industrialists quickly adopted the structures and principles nurtured in military and religious organizations for thousands of years, such as centralized decision making, a rigid chain of command, specialized division of work, and autocratic leadership.

Frederick Winslow Taylor and Scientific Management

The race to grow and accumulate resources was particularly pronounced in the United States. The War of 1812 severed the United States from England economically and spurred the growth of domestic manufacturing operations. Technological advances included the steamboat, the cotton gin, the iron plow, the telegraph, the electric motor, and the expansion of a railroad and canal network that opened new markets for producers. In turn, these new markets provided the volume that was a basic requirement for effective division of work.

Historian Alfred Chandler pointed out that by the late 1800s many new industries were completing the resource-accumulation stage of their existence and beginning to move into what he calls a "rationalization stage."[3] The management focus shifted from growth to efficiency. As organizations became large and unwieldy, and as competition became more intense, managers needed better ways to utilize the resources they had accumulated. They sought new concepts and techniques to cut costs and boost efficiency. It was out of this environment that the classical school of management emerged.

Frederick Winslow Taylor was among the first of what historians today call the classical management writers; he developed a set of principles that became known as *scientific management*. Taylor's basic theme was that managers should study work scientifically to identify the "one best way" to get the job done. His framework for scientific management was based on four principles:

1. The "one best way." Management, through observation and "the deliberate gathering . . . of all the great mass of traditional knowledge, which in the past has been in the heads of the workmen," finds the "one best way" for performing each job.

2. Scientific selection of personnel. This principle requires "the scientific selection and then the progressive development of the workmen." Management must uncover each worker's limitation, find his or her "possibility for development," and give each worker the required training.

3. Financial incentives. Taylor knew that putting the right worker on the right job would not by itself ensure high productivity. Some plan for motivating workers to do their best and to comply with their supervisors' instructions was also required. Taylor proposed a system of financial incentives, in which each worker was paid in direct proportion to how much he or she produced, instead of according to a basic hourly wage.

4. Functional foremanship. Taylor called for a division of work between manager and worker such that managers did all planning, preparing, and inspecting, and the workers did the actual work. Specialized experts, or functional foremen, would be responsible for specific aspects of a task, such as choosing the best machine speed, determining job priorities, and inspecting the work. The worker was to take orders from each of these foremen, depending on what part of the task was concerned.[4]

Frank and Lillian Gilbreth and Motion Study

The work of the husband-and-wife team Frank and Lillian Gilbreth also exemplifies the techniques and points of view of the scientific management approach. Born in 1868, Frank Gilbreth passed up an opportunity to attend MIT, deciding instead to enter the contracting business. He began as an apprentice bricklayer and became intrigued by the idea of improving efficiency. By carefully studying workers' motions, he developed innovations—for instance, in the way bricks were stacked, in the way they were laid, and in the number of motions used—that nearly tripled the average bricklayer's efficiency.[5]

In 1904 Frank married Lillian, who had a background in psychology, and together they began to develop principles and practices to more scientifically analyze tasks. In addition to using stopwatches, these experts developed various tools, including motion-study principles, to assist in their quest for efficiency. They concluded, for example, that

1. The two hands should begin and complete their motions at the same time.

2. The two hands should not be idle at the same time except during rest periods.

3. Motions of the arms should be made at opposite and symmetrical directions and should be made simultaneously.[6]

Therbligs, another example of the tools used by the Gilbreths, were elemental motions such as searching, grabbing, holding, and transporting. (The Gilbreths created the term *therblig* by using their last name spelled backward and transposing the *th*.) *Micromotion study* was the process of taking motion pictures of a worker doing his or her job and then running the film forward and backward at different speeds so that details of the job could be examined. Used in conjunction with timing devices, micromotion study made it possible to determine precisely how long it took to complete each component activity of a task. Performance could then be improved by modifying or eliminating one or more of these components.

Henri Fayol and the Principles of Management

The work of Henri Fayol also illustrates the classical approach to management and work behavior. Fayol had been a manager with a French iron and steel firm for 30 years before writing his book *General and Industrial Management*. In it, Fayol said that managers performed five basic functions: planning, organizing, commanding, coordinating, and controlling.

He also outlined a list of management principles he had found useful during his years as a manager. Fayol's 14 principles are summarized here and include his famous principle of *unity of command*:

1. Division of work. The worker, always on the same part, and the manager, concerned always with the same matters, acquired ability, sureness, and accuracy, which increased their output.

2. Authority and responsibility. Authority is the right to give orders and the power to exact obedience. Distinction must be made between official authority, deriving from office, and personal authority, compounded of intelligence, experience, moral worth, and ability to lead.

3. Discipline. The best means of establishing and maintaining [discipline] are good superiors at all levels; agreements as clear and fair as possible; sanctions [penalties] judiciously applied.

4. Unity of command. For any action whatsoever, an employee should receive orders from one superior only.

5. Unity of direction. There should be one head and one plan for a group of activities serving the same objective.

6. Subordination of individual interests. In a business, the interests of one employee or group of employees should not prevail over those of the concern. Means of effecting it are firmness and good example on the part of superiors and agreements as far as is possible.

7. Remuneration of personnel. Remuneration should be fair and as far as possible afford satisfaction to both personnel and the firm.

8. Centralization. The question of centralization or decentralization is a simple question of proportion; it is a matter of finding the optimum degree for the particular concern. What appropriate share of initiative may be left to intermediaries depends on the personal character of the manager, on his moral worth, on the reliability of his subordinates, and also on the conditions of the business.

9. Scalar chain. The scalar chain is the chain of superiors ranging from the ultimate authority to the lowest ranks. It is an error to depart needlessly from the line of authority, but it is an even greater one to keep to it when detriment to the business ensues.

10. Order. For social order to prevail in a concern, there must be an appointed place for every employee, and every employee must be in his or her appointed place.

11. Equity. For the personnel to be encouraged to carry out its duties with all the devotion and loyalty of which it is capable, it must be treated with kindliness, and equity results from the combination of kindness and justice. Equity excludes neither forcefulness nor sternness.

12. Stability of tenure of personnel. Time is required for an employee to get used to new work and succeed in doing it well, always assuming that he possesses the requisite abilities. If, when he has gotten used to it, or before then, he is removed, he will not have had time to render worthwhile service.

13. Initiative. Thinking out a plan and ensuring its success is one of the keenest satisfactions for an intelligent person to experience. This power of thinking out and executing is what is called initiative. It represents a great source of strength for business.

14. Esprit de corps. "Union is strength." Harmony, union among the personnel of a concern, is a great strength in that concern. Effort, then, should be made to establish it.[7]

Max Weber and Bureaucratic Organization Theory

Max Weber was a contemporary of Taylor, Fayol, and the Gilbreths. His work, first published in Germany in 1921, provides further insight into the ideals of the classical management writers. But unlike most of these writers, Weber was not a practicing manager, but an intellectual. He was born in 1864 to a well-to-do family and studied law, history, economics, and philosophy at Heidelberg University.

During the 1920s Weber correctly predicted that the growth of the large-scale organization would require a more formal set of procedures for how to administer them. At the time, managers had few principles they could apply in managing organizations. He therefore created the idea of an ideal or "pure form" of organization, which he called *bureaucracy*. This term did not refer to red tape and inefficiency—bureaucracy, for Weber, was the most efficient form of organization. Weber described bureaucracy as having certain characteristics:

1. A well-defined hierarchy of authority.
2. A clear division of work.
3. A system of rules covering the rights and duties of position incumbents.
4. A system of procedures for dealing with the work situation.
5. Impersonality of interpersonal relationships.
6. Selection for employment, and promotion based on technical competence.[8]

Summary: The Classical Approach to Management

The classical approach to management generally focused on boosting efficiency. To Taylor, Fayol, Weber, and the Gilbreths, an efficiently designed job and organization were of prime importance. These writers therefore concentrated on developing analytical tools, techniques, and principles that would enable managers to create efficient organizations. Work behavior was not unimportant to the classical writers; they simply assumed its complexities away by arguing that financial incentives would ensure motivation. As a result, intentionally or not, the classicists left the impression that workers could be treated as givens in the system, as little more than appendages to their machines. "Design the most highly specialized and efficient job you can," assumed the classicist, and "plug in the worker, who will then do your bidding if the pay is right."

In the 1920s and 1930s, many changes swept the United States, and indeed the world. Increasing numbers of people moved from farms to cities and thus became more dependent on each other for goods and services. Factories became more mechanized, and the jobs became more specialized and interdependent.[9] Government became more deeply involved in economic matters, and a number of lawsuits were filed to break up industrial monopolies. Social movements worked at giving women the right to vote, electing senators by direct popular vote, establishing a minimum wage, and encouraging trade unions. Even the literature of the period became more anti-individualistic, as people questioned whether a philosophy based on hard work, individualism, and maximizing profits—the building blocks of the classical management era—might actually have some drawbacks.

The Hawthorne Studies

In 1927 the Hawthorne studies began at the Chicago Hawthorne Plant of the Western Electric Company. They eventually added an entirely new perspective to the management of people at work. Three main sets of studies took place, one of which became known as the relay assembly test studies. A group of workers was isolated and studied as a series of changes was made, such as modifying the length of the workday and altering the morning and afternoon rest breaks. Researchers noted with some surprise that these changes did not greatly affect performance, underscoring their growing belief that performance depended on factors other than physical conditions or rate of pay.

The relay assembly test studies led the researchers to conclude that the social situations of the workers, not just the working conditions, influenced behavior and performance at work. The researchers discovered, for instance, that in countless ways, their observations had inadvertently made the workers feel they were special. The observer had changed the workers' situation by "his personal interest in the girls and their problems. He had always been sympathetically aware of their hopes and fears. He had granted them more and more privileges."[10]

The Hawthorne Effect   These results have been codified as the Hawthorne effect. This is what happens when the scientist, in the course of an investigation, inadvertently influences the participants so that it is not the scientist's intended changes that affect the subject's behavior, but the way the scientist acts. In the relay assembly test, for instance, the researchers wanted to schedule rest periods when they would be most advantageous. They therefore called a meeting during which they showed the workers their output curves and pointed out the low and high points of the day. "When asked at what times they would like to have their rest, they unanimously voted in favor of ten o'clock in the morning and two o'clock in the afternoon." Accordingly, the investigators agreed to schedule the rests at these times. In retrospect, however, the researchers concluded that the subsequent rise in employee morale and performance was due to more than just the rest breaks; it was also due to the fact that the researchers had involved the workers in the decision.

Hawthorne's Consequences   The Hawthorne studies were a turning point in the study of management. As the research became more widely known, managers and management experts began to recognize that human behavior at work is a complex and powerful force. The human relations movement, inspired by this realization, emphasized that workers were not just givens in the system, but had needs and desires that the organization and task had to accommodate.

Environment, Increased Diversity, and Change

Historian Alfred Chandler said that after accumulating and then rationalizing resources, managers traditionally moved to a third stage, in which they attempted to better utilize their organizational resources by developing new products and new markets—by diversifying. In the United States, movement into this third stage was hampered in the 1930s by the Depression. However, excess production capacity ultimately stimulated research and development. Coupled with the technological and managerial advancements that emerged in the years surrounding World War II, this excess capacity finally shifted most U.S. industries into Chandler's diversification stage.[11]

To understand evolving management theory, it is important to recognize that this period was characterized by differentiated, complex, and rapidly changing environments. Even before World War II, many firms had embarked on extensive research and development to develop new products. For example, at GE and Westinghouse, research and development activities resulted in the manufacture of plastics as well as a variety of other products based on electronics. The automobile companies had begun to produce airplane engines, electrical equipment, and household appliances. After the war, companies in the rubber industry—such as United States Rubber and BF Goodrich, which had concentrated on tire manufacturing—entered into systematic research and development and began to market products such as latex, plastics, and flooring.

These changes in the business environment contributed to the development of management theory in several ways. First, the increased rate of change and novelty triggered by diversification meant that managers and management theorists could no longer view organizations as closed systems operating within predictable, unchanging environments.[12] Second, efficiency was no longer a manager's main concern. It was eclipsed by the drives to diversify and then to monitor the activities of previously unrelated companies. Third, the shift toward making organizations more responsive to their environments was characterized by a trend toward *decentralization*, which in essence meant letting lower-level employees make more of their own decisions. Decentralization required a new managerial philosophy: Allowing subordinates to do more problem solving and decision making meant that managers had to rely on their employees' self-control. This change, coming as it did just after Hawthorne's results were popularized, led to a new emphasis on participative, people-oriented leadership and a more behavioral approach to management.

Douglas McGregor: Theory X and Theory Y

The work of Douglas McGregor is a good example of this new approach. According to McGregor, the classical organization (with its highly specialized jobs, centralized decision making, and top-down communications) was not just a product of the need for more efficiency. It was a reflection of certain basic assumptions about human nature.[13] These assumptions, which McGregor somewhat arbitrarily classified as *Theory X*, held that most people dislike work and responsibility and prefer to be directed; that they are motivated not by the desire to do a good job, but simply by financial incentives; and that, therefore, most people must be closely supervised, controlled, and coerced into achieving organizational objectives.

McGregor questioned the truth of this view and asked whether traditional management practices were appropriate for the tasks faced by more modern organizations. He felt that management needed new organizations and practices to deal with diversification, decentralization, and participative decision making. These new practices had to be based on a revised set of assumptions about the nature of human beings, which McGregor called *Theory Y*. Theory Y held that people could enjoy work and that an individual would exercise substantial self-control over performance if the conditions were favorable. Implicit in Theory Y is the belief that people are motivated by the desire to do a good job and by the opportunity to affiliate with their peers, rather than just by financial rewards.

Rensis Likert and the Employee-Centered Organization

What new management procedures are called for? Researcher Rensis Likert's work is an example of trends in management theory during the postwar years. Likert concluded that effective organizations differ from ineffective ones in several ways. Less effective job-centered companies focus on specialized jobs, efficiency, and close supervision of workers. More effective organizations, on the other hand, "focus their primary attention on endeavoring to build effective work groups with high performance goals."[14] As Likert noted, in these employee-centered companies

> the leadership and other processes of the organizations must be such as to insure a maximum probability that in all interactions and all relationships with the organization, each member will, in the light of his background, values and expectations, view the experience as supportive and one which builds and maintains his sense of personal worth and importance.[15]

Chris Argyris and the Mature Individual

Chris Argyris reached similar conclusions, but approached the problem from a different perspective.[16] Argyris argued that healthy people go through a maturation process. As they approach adulthood, they move to a state of increased activity, greater independence, and stronger interests, and they pass from the subordinate position of a child to an equal or superordinate position as an adult. Gaining employees' compliance by assigning them to highly specialized jobs with no decision-making power and then closely supervising them inhibits normal maturation by encouraging workers to be dependent, passive, and subordinate. It would be better to give workers more responsibility and broader jobs.

The Behavioralist Prescriptions

Behavioral scientists such as Argyris, McGregor, and Likert soon translated their ideas into practical methodologies that became the heart of the emerging field of organizational behavior. Likert emphasized leadership style and group processes. "The low-producing managers, in keeping with the traditional practice, feel that the way to motivate and direct behavior is to exercise control through authority."[17] In contrast, "the highest-producing managers feel, generally, that this manner of functioning does not produce the best results, that the resentment created by direct exercise of authority tends to limit its effectiveness."[18] Therefore, said Likert, "widespread use of participation is one of the more important approaches employed by the high-producing managers."[19] He found that the value of participation applied to all aspects of the job and of work, "as, for example, in setting work goals and budgets, controlling costs, organizing the work, etc."[20]

McGregor had his own prescriptions. He said decentralization and pushing decision making down the company hierarchy should be the norm in order to free people from the "too-close control of conventional organization." Management should encourage job enlargement (in which the variety of tasks an employee performs is increased), so that workers' jobs are made more challenging and more interesting. Participative management (which McGregor said would give employees some voice in decisions that affect them) would similarly enhance self-control. Finally, McGregor urged using management by objectives, in which subordinates set goals with their supervisors and are measured on the accomplishment of these goals, thus avoiding the need for close day-to-day supervision.

Bridging the Eras: Chester Barnard and Herbert Simon

The work of Chester Barnard and Herbert Simon does not fit neatly into any one school of management theory. Their research actually spanned several schools and contributed to the development of an integrated theory of management.

The Zone of Indifference   Chester Barnard used his experience as an executive to develop an important new management theory. He was the president of New Jersey Bell Telephone Company and, at various times, president of the United States Organization (the USO of World War II), president of the Rockefeller Foundation, and chair of the National Science Foundation.

Barnard was the first major theorist after the Hawthorne studies to emphasize the importance and variability of the individual in the workplace. He said, for example, that "an essential element of organizations is the willingness of persons to contribute their individual efforts to the cooperative system." He added that "the individual is always the basic strategic factor in organization. Regardless of his history or obligations, he must be induced to cooperate, or there can be no cooperation."

Barnard set about developing a theory of how to get workers to cooperate. How do you get the individuals to surrender their personal preferences and to go along with the authority exercised by supervisors?[21] He believed the answer could be found in what he called the person's *zone of indifference*, a range within each individual in which he or she would willingly accept orders without consciously questioning their legitimacy.[22] Barnard saw willingness to cooperate as an expression of the net satisfactions or dissatisfactions experienced or anticipated by each person. In other words, organizations had to provide sufficient inducements to broaden each employee's zone of indifference and thus increase the likelihood that orders would be obeyed.

But Barnard, in a clear break with the classicists, said that material incentives by themselves were not enough: "The unaided power of material incentives, when the minimum necessities are satisfied, in my opinion, is exceedingly limited as to most men."[23] Several other classes of incentives, including "the opportunities for distinction, prestige, [and] personal power" are also required.

Gaining Compliance   Whereas Barnard wrote from the vantage point of an executive, Herbert Simon was a scholar who had mastered organization theory, economics, natural science, and political science, and who went on to win the Nobel Prize in economics. Like Barnard, Simon viewed getting employees to do what the organization needed them to do as a major issue facing managers. He proposed two basic ways to gain such compliance, which can be paraphrased as follows:

Decisions reached in the highest ranks of the organization hierarchy will have no effect upon the activities of operative employees unless they are communicated downward. Consideration of the process requires an examination of the ways in which the behavior of the operative employee can be influenced. These influences fall roughly into two categories:

First, the manager can establish in the employee him- or herself the attitudes, habits and state of mind that lead him or her to reach the decision that is advantageous to the organization. In other words, the manager somehow gets the worker to want to do the job. Or, second, the manager can impose upon the employee decisions reached elsewhere in the organization, for instance by closely supervising everything the person does.[24]

Therefore, according to Simon, managers can ensure that employees carry out tasks in one of two ways. They can impose control by closely monitoring subordinates and insisting that they do their jobs as they have been ordered (using the classicists command and control approach). Or managers can foster employee self-control by providing better training, encouraging participative leadership, and developing commitment and loyalty. As rapid change forced employers to depend more and more on employee initiative, developing such self-control became a major theme in management writings.

▶ THE QUANTITATIVE SCHOOL

After World War II, management theorists also began to apply quantitative techniques to a wide range of problems. This movement is usually referred to as *operations research* or *management science* and has been described as "the application of scientific methods, techniques, and tools to problems involving the operations of systems so as to provide those in control of the system with optimum solutions to the problems."[25]

The Management Science Approach

Management science has three distinguishing characteristics. First, management scientists generally deal with well-defined problems that have clear and undisputable standards of effectiveness. They want to know, for instance, whether inventory costs have been too high and should be reduced by 20% or whether a specific number of items should be produced at each of a company's plants to minimize transportation costs to customers.

Second, management scientists generally deal with problems that have well-defined alternative courses of action. A company might have four different plants from which to ship products, or various levels of Product A and Product B that can be produced to maximize sales revenues. The management scientist's task is to recommend a solution. Finally, management scientists must develop a theory or model describing how the relevant factors are related. Like any scientist, management scientists must understand the problem and relationships clearly enough to formulate a mathematical model.

Historian Daniel Wren points out that operations research/management science has "direct lineal roots in scientific management."[26] Like Taylor and the Gilbreths, today's management scientists try to find optimal solutions to problems. As Taylor and his colleagues used scientific methods to find the one best way to do a job, management scientists used the scientific method to find the best solution to industrial problems. The difference in the two approaches is twofold. First, modern-day management scientists have at their disposal much more sophisticated mathematical tools and computers. Second, management science's goal is not to try to find a science of management so much as it is to use scientific analysis and tools to solve management problems.

The Systems Approach

The management science approach is closely associated with what is called the *systems approach* to management. A *system* is an entity—a hospital, city, company, or person, for instance—that has interdependent parts and a purpose. Systems approach advocates argue that viewing an organization as a system helps managers to remember that a firm's different parts, departments, or subsystems are interrelated and that all must contribute to the organization's purpose.

According to systems approach advocates such as C. West Churchman, all systems have four basic characteristics.[27] First, they operate within an environment, which is defined as those things outside of and important to the organization but largely beyond its control. For a company these include clients, competitors, unions, and governments.

Second, all systems are composed of building blocks called elements, components, or subsystems. In an organization, these basic building blocks might be departments, like those for production, finance, and sales. The subsystems may also cut across traditional departmental lines. For example, the marketing subsystem might include sales, advertising, and transportation, because each of these elements has an impact on the task of getting the product to the customer.

Third, all systems have a central purpose against which the organization's efforts and subsystems can be evaluated. For example, the optimal inventory level for a firm that serves top-of-the-line customers would probably be higher than for a firm whose customers want the best buy in town and are willing to wait for shelves to be restocked.

Fourth, focusing on the interrelatedness among the subsystems (and between the subsystems and the firm's environment) is an essential aspect of systems thinking. Interrelatedness emphasizes the fact that a manager can't change one subsystem without affecting the rest; hiring a new production manager might have repercussions in the sales and accounting departments, for instance. Similarly, managers and management theorists need to be sensitive to the way changes taking place in their environments, since they affect the organization and management of the firm.

▶ TOWARD A SITUATIONAL MANAGEMENT THEORY AND THE FUTURE

In the early 1960s, at about the same time the systems approach was popular, organizational research studies in England and the United States began to underscore the need for a situational or contingency view of management. This was one in which the appropriateness of the organization and its management principles were contingent on the rate of change in an organization's environment and technology. In one such study, Tom Burns and G. M. Stalker analyzed a number of industrial firms in England. They concluded that whether what they called a "mechanistic" or an "organic" management system was appropriate depended on the nature of the organization's environment.

Burns and Stalker argued that a *mechanistic management system* was appropriate if the company's tasks were routine and unchanging. Thus, in a textile mill they studied, it was important to have long, stable production runs that kept surprises to a minimum and thereby prevented the necessity of shutting down huge machines. In such unchanging conditions, Burns and Stalker found that a mechanistic (or classical) management approach—characterized by an emphasis on efficiency, specialized jobs, elaborate procedures for keeping behavior in line, and an insistence that everyone play by the rules—was appropriate.

On the other hand, Burns and Stalker found that the more behavioral *organic management system* was appropriate if innovative, entrepreneurial activities were important. In high-tech electronics firms, for instance, companies and their employees are constantly under pressure to come up with new devices. Burns and Stalker found that management often ran such firms with an approach that emphasized creativity rather than efficiency. These firms placed less emphasis on specialized jobs and issued fewer rules and procedures. Instead, they delegated decisions to employees who then exercised self-control in getting their jobs done.

Also in England, Joan Woodward and researchers from the Tavistock Institute analyzed a group of firms to discover the relationship between an organization and its production technology. The organic, flexible system described by Burns and Stalker again appeared to be more appropriate where dealing with unexpected, unpredictable occurrences was of paramount concern. Thus it was used in small job shops, and in large factories that were built to run continuously and in which unexpected breakdowns were a great concern. Woodward and her team found that the mechanistic, classical approach was appropriate where predictability and efficiency were paramount, such as where mass production technologies and assembly lines were utilized.[28] These findings and others like them culminated in what came to be called a situational, or contingency, approach to management theory, the main findings of which are addressed in Chapter 8.

On to the Future   The history of management thought certainly doesn't stop with the situational theorists, as you can imagine. Writing mostly in the 1960s, what the situational theorists did was to provide a theoretical framework that allowed management writers and practitioners to focus on the relationship between the management system and the nature of the task, and in particular on how the increasingly rapid changes brought on by technological advances and globalization would have to be managed by organizations. More recently, theorists and researchers have added to our store of knowledge regarding how managers plan, organize, lead, and control their organizations under highly competitive conditions and in the face of rapid change. However, their findings are not so much a matter of history as they are a road map of things as they are today and how they will be. The following chapters are built on these modern findings.

MANAGING IN A GLOBAL ENVIRONMENT

WHAT'S AHEAD?

Customers shopping in Wal-Mart's new store in Frankfurt, Germany, were in for a big surprise. For one thing, the changes Wal-Mart had made since buying the Wertkauf chain just a year before were astonishing. In remaking the stores to fit Wal-Mart's low-price, customer-friendly image, aisles had been widened, prices reduced, and "the employees are a lot more polite than they used to be," says one shopper.[1] Wal-Mart's German competitors have gotten the message: They're already working hard to remake their own stores and management systems. Meanwhile Wal-Mart, which only began "going global" a few years ago, must grapple with the challenge of managing operations that are far removed both geographically and culturally from Benton, Arkansas.

OBJECTIVES

AFTER STUDYING THIS CHAPTER, YOU SHOULD BE ABLE TO

- Explain why companies expand operations abroad and discuss strategies for expanding abroad, such as exporting and licensing

- Give examples of the economic, legal, political, sociocultural, and technological factors that influence a manager's decision to expand abroad

- Explain how going global affects the business team in the global business

- Discuss how doing business internationally affects how managers plan, organize, lead, and control

manager

a person who plans, organizes, leads, and controls the work of others so that the organization achieves its goals.

Managers and the companies they manage don't operate in a vacuum, but instead conduct their activities within an environment that consists of things like competitors, governments, technological advances, and special-interest groups. As we saw in Chapter 1, environmental forces like these do have substantial effects on organizations and on how they are managed. For example, technological changes (such as the Internet) have both forced and given an opportunity to companies like Dell to dramatically reorganize how they deal with their customers and how they communicate with their vendors. In other words, it's difficult or impossible to understand what managers do (and how they should do it) without understanding the context in which they do it—namely, all those environmental forces such as technological change, deregulation, and globalization—that form the playing field on which companies today compete.

In this first part of the book—The Environment of Management, Chapters 1–3—we're therefore focusing mostly on the nature of these outside forces. In Chapter 1 we discuss what managers do, and itemize various forces such as technological change and deregulation that together help to explain the sorts of changes taking place in organizational management today. In the current chapter, we focus more closely on one of these forces—globalization—which is the tendency for companies to compete around the world. In the following chapter we look at the ethical environment of management, and at such issues as social responsibility and consumer affairs.

Globalization, the focus of this chapter, has had an enormous influence on businesses today. Wal-Mart's effects on its German competitors are typical: For example, they are already scrambling to merge and to install new computers and management systems. In practical terms, what globalization means is that, like Wal-Mart's German competitors, managers everywhere must be sharper and quicker than ever before, since their competitors come not just from next door, but from world-class companies. Suddenly, for instance, a self-taught grocery manager in a small town in Brazil may find herself competing with highly trained managers armed with Wal-Mart's sophisticated technology and methods.

You also should know that "globalization" doesn't apply just to big companies like GE or Royal Dutch Shell. Today, with few exceptions, there's probably not a business or organization that's not facing the need to engage in global competition, or to at least fend off a new local office of some global competitor. Indeed, several years ago, even local neighborhood drycleaners in the United States were stunned to discover that Sketchleys, a United Kingdom-based drycleaning chain, was expanding into the United States (although it subsequently sold its interests in hundreds of U.S. stores). Just about every business and manager is therefore a "global" one today. This chapter aims to give you an overview of international business and how managing in an international arena affects what managers do.

▲ Delivering Dell PCs in China: The Dell system works in China as well as it does in the U.S.

▶ DOING BUSINESS ABROAD

Why Do Companies Go Abroad?

The manager's goals determine why he or she takes the company abroad. For example, sales expansion is usually the main goal. Thus, Wal-Mart is opening stores in South America because of the high growth rate there. High growth translates into more income for South America's consumers and, Wal-Mart hopes, big sales increases for it. Similarly, when the Chicago Bulls played at Paris's Bercy Arena several years ago, the enthusiasm of the French fans underscored why the National Basketball Association has been so eager (and successful) in expanding its sales overseas: it now has more than 80 workers in 11 countries abroad.[2] And Dell Computer, knowing that China is soon to be the world's second biggest market for PCs, is now aggressively building plants and selling there.[3]

Firms go international to pursue other goals. For example, manufacturers go seeking foreign products and services to sell, and to cut their labor costs. Florida apparel manufacturers have products assembled in Central America, where the labor costs are relatively low, for instance. Sometimes high quality drives firms overseas; for example, Apple Computer recently enlisted Sony's aid in producing parts for a notebook computer.

A variety of factors—including the manager's goals, and the size and resources of his or her company—will then determine exactly how the company expands abroad. Here there are several possibilities, including exporting, licensing, franchising, foreign direct investment, joint ventures and strategic alliances, and wholly owned subsidiaries.

Exporting

Exporting is often the first choice when manufacturers decide to expand abroad, since it's relatively simple and easy. Exporting means selling abroad, either directly to target customers or indirectly by retaining foreign sales agents and distributors.[4] More than half of all such trade is actually handled by agents and distributors and other intermediaries familiar with the local market's customs and customers.

exporting

selling abroad, either directly to target customers or indirectly by retaining foreign sales agents and distributors.

Carefully selecting intermediaries, checking business reputations via local agencies of the U.S. State Department, and then carefully drafting agency and distribution agreements are essential to ensure you have the right representatives.[5] For example, Bird Corporation President Fred Schweser sought out U.S. Commerce Department trade specialist Harvey Roffman for help in generating overseas business. Roffman recommended advertising in *Commercial News USA*, a government publication designed to enlighten around 100,000 foreign agents, distributors, buyers, and government officials about U.S. products. Schweser was soon deluged with responses, and his Elkhorn, Nebraska, company now boasts customers from Japan, the United Kingdom, and many points in between. What does Bird Corporation's produce? Go-carts.[6]

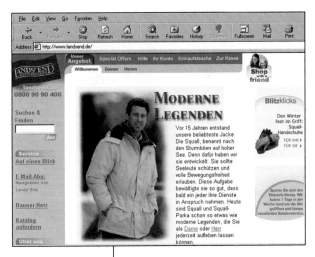

▲ **W E B N O T E**

Lands' End sells clothing and linens around the world with catalogs customized for different overseas markets.

www.landsend.de

Source: Reproduced with permission.

Whether selling directly or through agents, exporting has pros and cons. It is a relatively quick and inexpensive way of "going international," since it avoids the need to build factories in the host country.[7] Exporting is also a good way to test the waters in the host country and learn more about its customers' needs. On the other hand, transportation, tariff, or manufacturing costs can put the exporter at a disadvantage, as can poorly selected intermediaries.

One way to avoid some of these problems is by selling directly through the Internet and mail order. For example, L.L. Bean, Lands' End, and the Sharper Image all export globally via their catalogs and the Internet.[8] Since the Internet is basically borderless, almost any company can easily market its products or services directly to potential customers, often without go-betweens like salespeople or distributors.

Licensing

Licensing is another way to start-up an international operation. International **licensing** is an arrangement whereby a firm (the licensor) grants a foreign firm the right to use intangible ("intellectual") property such as patents, copyrights, manufacturing processes, or trade names for a specified period of time. The firm usually gets a percentage of the earnings, or royalties in return.[9]

Licensing arrangements also have pros and cons. For example, consider a small, underfunded U.S. inventor of a new material for reducing pollution. Working out a licensing agreement with a well-established European environmental products company could allow the U.S. firm to enter the expanding Eastern European market without any significant investment. On the downside, the U.S. firm might not be able to control the design, manufacture, or sales of its products as well as it could if it set up its own facilities in Europe. It is also possible that by licensing its knowledge and know-how to a foreign firm, the U.S. firm could eventually lose control over its patented property.

Franchising

If you've eaten at the McDonald's by Rome's Spanish Steps or on the Champs Élysées, you know that franchising is another way to start operations abroad. **Franchising** is the granting of a right by a parent company to another firm to do business in a prescribed manner.[10]

Franchising is similar to licensing, but it usually requires both parties to make a greater commitment of time and money. A franchisee must generally follow strict guidelines in running the business and make substantial investments in a physical plant (such as a fast-food restaurant). In addition, whereas licensing tends to be limited to manufacturers, franchising is more common among service firms such as restaurants, hotels, and rental services.

The advantages of franchising are similar to licensing: It's a quick and relatively low-cost way for a firm to expand into other countries. However, maintaining quality can be a problem. For example, an early McDonald's franchisee in France had to close its Paris restaurants when it failed to maintain McDonald's quality standards.

Foreign Direct Investment and the Multinational Enterprise

Exporting, licensing, and franchising can get most managers only so far. At some point they find that to take full advantage of foreign opportunities, they must make a substantial, direct investment. **Foreign direct investment** refers to operations in one country that are controlled by entities in a foreign country. A foreign firm might build new facilities in another country, as Toyota did when it built its Camry plant in Georgetown, Kentucky. Or a firm might acquire property or operations in a foreign country, as when Wal-Mart bought control of the Wertkauf stores in Germany.

Strictly speaking, foreign direct investment means acquiring control by owning more than 50% of the operation. But in practice it is possible for any firm to gain effective control by owning less than half. In any event, a foreign direct investment turns the firm into a multinational enterprise. Joint ventures and wholly owned subsidiaries are two examples of foreign direct investment.

Joint Ventures and Strategic Alliances

Some managers decide that the best way to expand abroad is through joint ventures or other strategic alliances. **Strategic alliances** are "cooperative agreements between potential or actual competitors."[11] For example, several years ago, Boeing combined with a consortium of Japanese companies to produce the 767 commercial jet. However, most experts would probably define strategic alliances as "any agreements between firms that are of strategic importance to one or both firms' competitive viability."[12] Used in that sense, even licensing or franchising agreements may come under the umbrella of strategic alliances.

A joint venture is one example of a strategic alliance.[13] A **joint venture** is "the participation of two or more companies jointly in an enterprise in which each party contributes assets, owns the entity to some degree, and shares risk."[14]

Companies use such relationships every day. For example, America Online, Philips Electronics, and Direct TV recently formed a joint venture to develop and offer an interactive service that lets customers access the Internet via their TV sets. The joint venture aims to develop a set-top box to allow Internet access while watching TV.[15] Some Ace hardware stores are joint ventures. For example, Ace Hardware Corporation, the umbrella company for the Ace cooperative, formed a joint venture with Sunshine Ace, which currently operates 3 Ace stores, to open 10 new stores in southwest Florida over the next few years. Sunshine Ace will supply the initial capital investment, and Ace Hardware Corporation will help the new venture stock the store.[16] Airline alliances, such as the American Airlines–British Airways One World Alliance, are also examples of strategic alliances. The airlines here don't share investments, but share seating on some flights, and let passengers use the alliance members' airport lounges.[17]

Alliances like these have many advantages. The overriding aim is usually to quickly gain some complementary strengths that would otherwise take too long to develop: The flights on American and British Airways tend to complement each other, so that both Americans and BA's customers gain by being able to use the other airline's flights and lounges. Furthermore, as one consultant points out, "in a complex, uncertain world filled with dangerous opponents, it is best not to go it alone."[18] A joint venture lets a firm gain useful experience in a foreign country, using the expertise and resources of a locally knowledgeable firm. Joint ventures also help both companies share what may be the substantial cost of starting a new operation. But, as in licensing, the joint venture partners also risk giving away proprietary secrets, and joint ventures also almost always mean sharing control. Each partner runs the risk that the venture may not be managed the way it would have chosen.

strategic alliance
an agreement between potential or actual competitors to achieve common objectives.

joint venture
the participation of two or more companies in an enterprise such that each party contributes assets, owns the entity to some degree, and shares risk.

▲ **W E B N O T E**

Airlines use the Internet to support their global alliances; for instance by making it easier to book flights on partner airlines.

www.aa.com

Source: Copyright 1999 American Airlines, Inc. All rights reserved.

Joint ventures can be a necessity. In China, for instance, foreign companies that want to enter regulated industries like telecommunications must enter into joint ventures with well-connected Chinese partners. The partnership of Britain's Alcatel and Shanghai Bell to make telephone switching equipment is an example.[19]

Wholly Owned Subsidiaries

Sometimes, the company has the knowledge and resources to go it alone. As the name implies, a wholly owned subsidiary is owned 100% by the foreign firm. Thus, in the United States today, Toyota Motor Manufacturing, Inc., and its Camry facility in Georgetown, Kentucky, is a wholly owned subsidiary of Toyota Motor Corporation, which is based in Japan. In Japan, Toys "R" Us, Inc., was the first large U.S.-owned discount store, and the company is expanding its wholly owned subsidiary there.[20]

Wholly owned subsidiaries have pros and cons. They let the company do things exactly as it wants, since there are no partners to worry about. Similarly, the firm needn't share its proprietary knowledge. However, this is a more costly way to expand abroad, since the company must make the entire investment itself (rather than with a partner).

The Language of International Business

Once the manager decides to do business abroad, he or she must become familiar with the basic vocabulary of international business. An international business is any firm that engages in international trade or investment.[21] International business also refers to those activities, such as exporting goods or transferring employees, that require the movement of resources, goods, services, and skills across national boundaries.[22] International trade refers to the export or import of goods or services to consumers in another country. International management is the performance of the management functions of planning, organizing, leading, and controlling across national borders. As Wal-Mart managers expand abroad, for instance, they necessarily engage in international management.

The multinational corporation is one type of international business. A multinational corporation (MNC) is an international business that is controlled by a parent corporation and owned and managed essentially by the nationals of the firm's home country. An MNC operates manufacturing and marketing facilities in two or more countries; these operations are coordinated by a parent firm, whose owners are mostly based in the firm's home country. Firms like GE and GM have long been multinational corporations. However, thousands of small firms, like KnitMedia, are now MNCs, too.

Some experts say that the MNC is slowly being displaced by a special multinational enterprise called the global (or transnational) corporation. The MNC operates in a number of countries and adjusts its products and practices to each. The global corporation, on the other hand, operates as if the entire world (or major regions of it) were a single entity. Global corporations sell essentially the same things in the same way everywhere. Thus a global corporation such as Sony sells a standardized Walkman around the world, with components made in or designed in different countries.[23] Ikea's furniture is much the same the world over. Coke tastes the same everywhere, and Chanel and Lanvin sell the same products around the globe. However, global companies may still reflect their national roots.[24] For example, when the German firm DeutscheBank took over a British bank, the traditionally high incentive pay of the British managers created considerable tension between them and their new, lower-paid German bosses (tension that took some time to resolve).

▶ THE MANAGER IN AN INTERNATIONAL ENVIRONMENT

Going international or, certainly global, presents the manager with new and often perplexing problems. He or she must be adept at dealing with a wide range of economic, legal, political, sociocultural, and technological factors, since the manager's plans, organization, and incentives and controls will be molded by them.

The Economic Environment

For example, managers doing business abroad need to be familiar with the economic systems of the countries in question, the level of each country's economic development, and exchange rates and economic integration.

The Economic System   For one thing, countries still vary in the extent to which they adhere to a capitalistic economic system like America's. For example, consider the dilemma facing business managers in Hong Kong. In 1997 the People's Republic of China resumed governing Hong Kong. How did this affect Hong Kong's existing economic structure, and how did foreign firms react?

Hong Kong is an example of a market economy. In a pure market economy, the quantities and nature of the goods and services produced are not planned by anyone. Instead, the interaction of supply and demand in the market for goods and services determines what is produced, in what quantities, and at what prices.

At the other extreme, the People's Republic of China until recently was a pure command economy. In a command economy, central planning agencies try to determine how much is produced by which sectors of the economy, and by which plants and for whom it is produced. Countries like these usually base their yearly targets on five-year plans. They then establish specific production goals and prices for each sector of the economy (for each product or group of products) and for each manufacturing plant.

By agreement, China is to let Hong Kong keep its capitalist system for 50 years, and so far that generally seems to be going fairly smoothly. A shipping magnate, Tung Chee-hwa, was elected Hong Kong's first post-handover chief executive. However, Hong Kong's political administration is governed closely by Beijing, and Hong Kong's new legislature recently imposed limits on opposition activities and on the number of people eligible to vote. If the politicians start to pass laws that limit private ownership and free trade in any way, Hong Kong's capitalist system may be in for some rough sailing. Therefore, developing long-run management plans under such circumstances can be quite a challenge.

In a **mixed economy**, some sectors of an economy are left to private ownership and free market mechanisms, while others are largely owned by and managed by the government.[25] "Mixed" is, of course, a matter of degree. For example, France is basically a capitalist country, but is mixed to the extent that the government still owns shares of industries like telecommunications (France Telecom) and air travel (Air France).

Shifting economic systems can lead to social instability, as occurred in the newly capitalized Russia. Free-market economies require things like commercial

mixed economy
an economy in which some sectors are left to private ownership and free market mechanisms, while others are largely owned and managed by the government

laws, banking regulations, and an effective independent judiciary and law enforcement, without which business transactions are difficult. Without such a political and legal infrastructure in Russia, the first years of transition to a market economy there were especially turbulent for business managers: They had to cope not just with competitors, but with criminals, lax law enforcement, and the virtual control of several industries by friends of powerful politicians. Some experts warn of the possibility of similar turbulence in other developing economies including South Korea, Malaysia, and Vietnam.[26] Managers taking their firms into such areas therefore must be concerned, not just with the economic system, but with the turbulence caused as the country moves from a command economy to a capitalist one.

Economic Development Countries also differ dramatically in levels and rates of economic development. For example, some countries—the United States, Japan, Germany, France, Italy, and Canada, for instance—have large, mature, well-established economies with extensive industrial infrastructures (industry, telecommunications, transportation, and regulatory and judicial systems, for instance). Their **gross domestic product** (the market value of all goods and services that have been bought for final use during a period of time, and therefore the basic measure of a nation's economic activity) ranges from about $700 billion for Canada, to $1.0 trillion for France, $1.5 trillion for Germany, almost $3 trillion for Japan, and $7.5 trillion for the United States.[27]

However, some countries are growing much faster than others. For example, the growth rate of mature economies like those above generally averages around 4% per year. On the other hand, China, India, and Taiwan are generally growing at just over 7.5%, 5.0%, and 5.2%, respectively. Many multinationals are therefore boosting their investments in these high-growth (and thus high-potential) countries.[28]

Exchange Rates Managers engaged in international business must also juggle exchange rates. The **exchange rate** for one country's currency is the rate at which it can be exchanged for another country's currency. As the foreign exchange chart in Figure 2.1 shows, in July 1999, one Brazilian real was worth about $0.56 in U.S. currency. Similarly, a French franc was worth about $0.16. Exchange rates can have a big impact on a company's performance. A dramatic drop in the value of the dollar relative to the pound could have a devastating effect on a small U.S. company that suddenly found it needed 30% more dollars to build a factory in Scotland than it had planned.

Economic Integration and Free Trade The existence of "free trade" agreements among some countries is a big part of the economic environment facing managers. **Free trade** means that all trade barriers among participating countries are removed.[29] Free trade occurs when two or more countries sign an agreement to allow free flow of goods and services, unimpeded by trade barriers such as **tariffs** (special governmental taxes on imports which boost the costs of international trade). **Economic integration** occurs when two or more nations obtain the advantages of free trade by minimizing trade restrictions between them.

Economic integration occurs on several levels. In a **free trade area**, all barriers to trade among member countries are removed, so that goods and services are freely traded among member countries. A **customs union** is the next higher level of economic integration. Here members dismantle trade barriers among

gross domestic product
the market value of all goods and services that have been bought for final use during a period of time, and therefore the basic measure of a nation's economic activity.

exchange rate
the rate at which one country's currency can be exchanged for another country's currency.

free trade
the unrestricted exchange of goods among participating countries.

tariff
government tax on imports.

economic integration
the result of two or more nations minimizing trade restrictions to obtain the advantages of free trade.

free trade area
a type of economic integration in which all barriers to trade among members are removed.

customs union
a situation in which trade barriers among members are removed and a common trade policy exists with respect to nonmembers.

TRADES OF OVER $1 MILLION

Foreign Exchange, New York prices.	Fri.	Thur.
Argent (Peso)	1.0010	1.0005
Australia (Dollar)	.6500	.6461
Austria (Schilling)	.0777	.0780
Belgium (Franc)	.0265	.0266
Brazil (Real)	.5557	.5574
Britain (Pound)	1.6221	1.6189
Canada (Dollar)	.6646	.6640
Chile (Peso)	.001945	.001945
China (Yuan)	.1208	.1208
Colombia (Peso)	.000549	.000547
Czech Rep (Koruna)	.0291	.0289
Denmark (Krone)	.1437	.1435
Dominican Rep (Peso)	.0627	.0627
Ecudr (Sucre)	.000085	.000087
Egypt (Pound)	.2930	.2930
Euro (Euro)	1.07050	1.07300
Finland (Mark)	.1799	.1805
France (Franc)	.1632	.1636
Germany (Mark)	.5473	.5486
Greece (Drachma)	.003294	.003303
Hong Kong (Dollar)	.1288	.1288
Hungary (Forint)	.0042	.0042
India (Rupee)	.0231	.0231
Indnsia (Ruplah)	.000146	.000147
Ireland (Punt)	1.3581	1.3626
Israel (Shekel)	.2410	.2424
Italy (Lira)	.000553	.000554
Japan (Yen)	.008735	.008666

Foreign Exchange, New York prices.	Fri.	Thur.
Jordan (Dinar)	1.4104	1.4104
Lebanon (Pound)	.000663	.000663
Malaysia (Ringgit)	.2632	.2632
Mexico (Peso)	.106326	.106101
Nethrinds (Guilder)	.4854	.4870
N. Zealand (Dollar)	.5315	.5289
Norway (Krone)	.1284	.1280
Pakistan (Rupee)	.0195	.0194
Peru (New Sol)	.3000	.3000
Philpins (Peso)	.0260	.0261
Poland (Zloty)	.2604	.2611
Portugal (Escudo)	.005335	.005353
Russia (Ruble)	.0413	.0413
SDR (SDR)	1.36420	.36210
Saudi Arab (Riyal)	.2667	.2667
Singapore (Dollar)	.5945	.5926
Slovak Rep (Koruna)	.0240	.0238
So. Africa (Rand)	.1621	.1623
So. Korea (Won)	.000831	.000831
Spain (Peseta)	.006428	.006449
Sweden (Krona)	.1221	.1221
Switzerland (Franc)	.6708	.6716
Taiwan (Dollar)	.0311	.0310
Thailand (Baht)	.02698	.02703
Turkey (Lira)	.000002	.000002
U.A.E. (Dirham)	.2723	.2723
Uruguay (New Peso)	.0869	.0869
Venzuel (Bolivar)	.0016	.0016

◄ F I G U R E   2 . 1

Foreign Exchange

International travelers should be familiar with exchange rates between various countries. For example, on July 31, 1999 one Brazilian real was worth about $0.56.

Source: The *Miami Herald*, 31 July 1999, p. 9C.

themselves while establishing a common trade policy with respect to nonmembers. In a **common market**, no barriers to trade exist among members, and a common external trade policy is in force; in addition, factors of production, such as labor, capital, and technology, move freely between member countries, as in Figure 2.2

Economic integration is taking place around the world. In 1957 the European Economic Community (now called the European Union, or EU) was established by founding members France, West Germany, Italy, Belgium, the Netherlands, and Luxembourg (Figure 2.3). Their agreement, the Treaty of Rome, called for the formation of a free trade area, the gradual elimination of tariffs and other barriers to trade, and the formation of a customs union and (eventually) a common market. By 1987 the renamed European Community had added six other countries (Great Britain, Ireland, Denmark, Greece, Spain, and Portugal) and signed the Single Europe Act. This act "envisages a true common market where goods, people, and money move among the twelve EC countries with the same ease that they move between Wisconsin and Illinois."[30] Austria, Finland, and Sweden joined in 1995, and several more countries are preparing to join in the years ahead.

In Asia, the Association of Southeast Asian Nations (ASEAN) was organized in 1967 (Figure 2.4). It includes Brunei, Indonesia, Malaysia, the Philippines, Singapore, Thailand, and Vietnam. These countries are cooperating in reducing tariffs and in attempting to liberalize trade, although the results at this point have been limited.[31] Asia also formed the Asia Pacific Economic Cooperation (APEC)

common market

a system in which no barriers to trade exist among member countries, and a common external trade policy is in force that governs trade with nonmembers; factors of production, such as labor, capital, and technology, more freely among members.

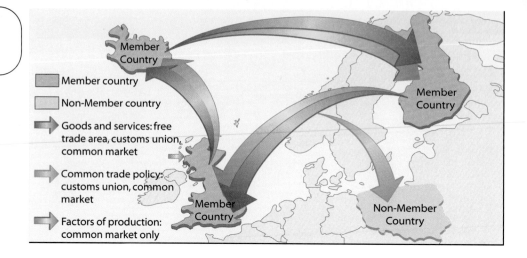

forum, which is a loose association of 18 Pacific Rim states that aims to facilitate freer trade in its region. Members include Australia, Chile, China, Japan, Malaysia, Mexico, Singapore, and the United States.[32]

Canada, the United States, and Mexico have together reestablished a North American Free Trade Agreement (NAFTA; see Figure 2.5). NAFTA creates the world's largest free trade market, with a total output of about $6 trillion.

Economic integration has a big effect on company managers. For one thing, it vastly increases the level of competition. In Europe today, for instance, airlines and telecommunication firms that once had little or no outside competition face new

► FIGURE 2.3

EU Member Countries

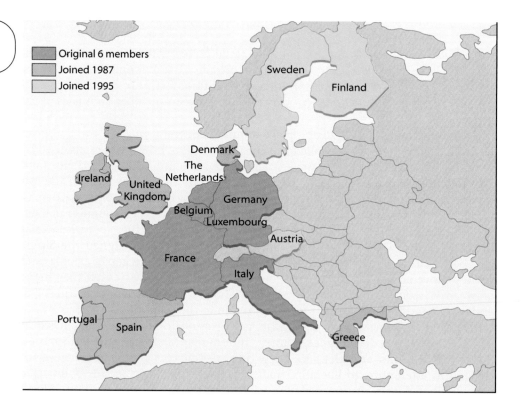

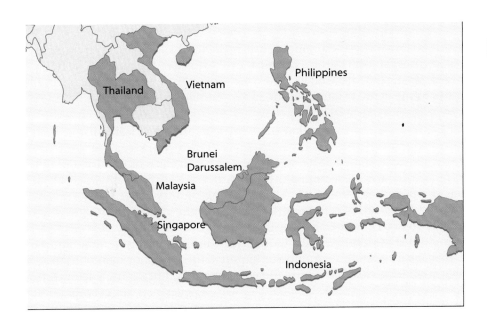

FIGURE 2.4
ASEAN Member Countries

competitors from similar firms within their trading blocs. However, it can also, of course, let more effective companies expand into new markets. Some fear that the EU's existence will lead to a "fortress Europe to which non-EU firms will find it increasingly difficult to export goods."[33] Many U.S. managers are therefore entering joint ventures with European partners, to establish local beachheads from which to sell throughout the EU.

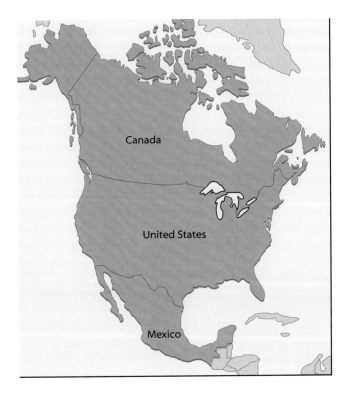

◄ FIGURE 2.5
NAFTA Member Countries

The Political and Legal Environment

International managers also must consider the legal and political environments of the countries in which they do business. Consider the uneven playing field between Japan and the United States, for example. A Chrysler LeBaron sells for $18,176 in the United States, but for $33,077 in Japan.[34] How could this be?

Trade Barriers   The answer is that trade barriers can dramatically distort the prices companies must charge for their products. Trade barriers are governmental influences usually aimed at reducing the competitiveness of imported products or services. Tariffs, the most common trade barrier, are governmental taxes levied on goods shipped internationally.[35] The exporting country collects export tariffs, the importing country collects import tariffs, and the country through which the goods are passed collects transit tariffs.

A multitude of nontariff trade barriers exist too. For example, in addition to the fact that Japan sets high automobile import tariffs, cars not made in Japan must meet a complex set of regulations and equipment modifications. Side mirrors must snap off easily if they come into contact with a pedestrian, for example. And any manufacturer selling 1,000 or fewer cars of a particular model annually must test each car individually for gas mileage and emission standards.

Some countries make direct payments to domestic producers. These are called subsidies, and they can make an otherwise inefficient producer more cost competitive. Other countries impose quotas—legal restrictions on the import of particular goods—as further barriers to trade.[36]

trade barrier
a governmental influence that is usually aimed at reducing the competitiveness of imported products or services.

subsidiary
a direct payment a country makes to a domestic producer.

quota
a legal restriction on the import of particular goods.

Political Risks   The international manager must be concerned not just with governmental influences on trade, but with political risks as well. For example, companies doing business in Peru must be vigilant against terrorist attacks. In 1999 ethnic violence in the former Yugoslavia brought economic activities for many companies exporting to that area to a standstill.[37] Similarly, racial strife in South Africa, civil unrest in Ireland, and religious attacks in Egypt and Israel make doing business in these areas more difficult than it would otherwise be, and obviously influence how managers run their businesses.

Legal Systems   There are also important differences in legal systems. Many countries adhere to a system known as common law, which is based on tradition and depends more on precedent and custom than on written statutes. England and the United States are examples of countries that use common law.

Other countries have a code law system, or a comprehensive set of written statutes. Some countries use a combination of common law and code law. For example, the United States adheres to a system of common law in many areas, but to a written Uniform Commercial Code for governing business activities.

International laws and agreements can also affect a manager's strategy, as the "Entrepreneurs in Action" box shows. International law is not so much an enforceable body of law as it is agreements embodied in treaties and other types of agreements. For example, international law governs intellectual property rights (such as whether KnitMedia's music can be reproduced in Japan without its permission).

▲   The city of Pristina, capital of Kosovo, after a bombardment in July 1999.

▶ When he paid Hewlett-Packard $80,000 for the remains of a canceled engineering project back in 1982, Charlie Trimble never thought the business he was starting would be involved in an international incident. What he bought—shelves of research notes, and a circuit board that could pick up a signal from the first of what would soon be a ring of 24 military satellites orbiting the globe—were the rights to commercialize what would become the global positioning system.

As most people know by now, when a global positioning system (GPS) receiver picks up satellite signals, it calculates its position based on its distance from 8 satellites. With one of these handheld systems, someone can now almost instantaneously determine his or her location to within 20 or 30 feet, anywhere on the globe. GPS receivers are now used worldwide not only by sea captains and hikers keeping track of their locations, but by naturalists tracking wild goats in the Galapagos Islands and scientists measuring movements atop Mount Everest.

There was a time, though, when it looked like GPS would never be a worldwide system (although it would have been ironic to have something called a global positioning system that couldn't be used in vast areas of the globe). The technology was developed by the United States Department of Defense, which in fact still maintains and controls the satellites. The problem was that many foreign users, both governmental and private, didn't want to be at the mercy of the U.S. government when it came to critical positioning and navigating information. The problem almost torpedoed the use of the GPS system abroad when 47 member countries of the International Telecommunications Union (including Britain, Germany, France, Italy, Japan, Korea, and Mexico), voted to take a big part of the radio spectrum used by the GPS satellites and use it for mobile phones instead. Only the direct intervention of NATO's commander at the time, General Wesley Clark, convinced the ITU that it should back off, and let the GPS system be used worldwide.

Today, it's still not all clear sailing for Charlie Trimble. The market for the GPS devices never took off the way he thought it would, and he was recently removed as CEO of the company he founded by his own Board of Directors because of disappointing sales. However, like a true entrepreneur, Trimble is still dedicated to the eventual success of GPS, especially since, having overcome cultural and political resistance from abroad, the system can now be used worldwide.

Source: Claire Tristram, "Has GPS Lost Its Way?" *Technology Review*, July–August 1999, pp. 78–75.

Among other things, legal issues influence the strategy a manager uses to expand abroad.[38] For example, joint venture laws vary. In India, for instance, a foreign investor may own only up to 40% of an Indian industrial company, while in Japan up to 100% of foreign ownership is allowed.[39] Some managers go global by appointing sales agents or representatives in other countries. But in some countries that's not legally an option. In Algeria, for instance, agents are not permitted to represent foreign sellers, and in other countries agents are viewed as employees subject to those countries' employment laws.[40]

The Sociocultural Environment

Managers who travel to other countries quickly learn they must also adapt to cultural differences. In Latin America, for instance, *machismo* ("maleness") is defined as virility, zest for action, daring, competitiveness, and the will to conquer. This is translated into business life by demonstrating forcefulness, self-confidence, courage, and leadership.[41] In Japan, saving face and achieving harmony are very important. Indirect and vague communication is therefore preferred, with sentences frequently left unfinished so the other person may draw his or her own conclusions. The people of Saudi Arabia, it is said, love the spoken word and tend not to get to the point quickly. This can frustrate U.S. managers, who must be careful not to show impatience or annoyance. In France, a firm and pumping handshake may be considered uncultured; instead, a quick shake with some pressure on the grip is more appropriate.

Cross-Cultural Challenges: An Example Cultural differences can have very practical consequences, such as affecting how disagreements are resolved. Consider the challenge of negotiating with people abroad. A researcher at Georgetown University found that Japanese, German, and U.S. managers tended to use very different approaches when resolving workplace conflict.[42] The Japanese prefer the power approach, tending to defer to the party with the most power. Germans tend to emphasize a more legalistic, "sticking to the rules" approach. U.S. managers tend to try to take all parties' interests into account and to work out a solution that maximizes the benefits for everyone.

Such "cross-cultural differences may complicate life for expatriate managers who find themselves trying to manage conflict in a foreign cultural system."[43] For example, American managers may be shocked to learn that those from other countries aren't so interested in finding solutions that benefit everyone. They may also become upset at endlessly discussing bureaucratic regulations and practices (which Germans did significantly more than U.S. managers).

values

basic beliefs about what is important and unimportant, and what one should and should not do.

Values Research by Geert Hofstede shows that a society's values are among the most influential of cultural differences. Values are basic beliefs we hold about what is good or bad, important or unimportant. Values (such as West Point's famous "duty, honor, country") are important because they shape the way we behave. Hofstede says that different societies reflect four basic values as follows:

- *Power distance.*[44] *Power distance* is the extent to which the less powerful members of institutions accept and expect that power will be distributed unequally.[45] Hofstede concluded that the institutionalization of such an inequality was higher in some countries (such as Mexico) than it was in others (such as Sweden).

- *Individualism versus collectivism.* The degree to which ties between individuals are normally loose or close is measured as individualism or collectivism. In more individualistic countries, "all members are expected to look after themselves and their immediate families."[46] Individualistic counties include Australia and the United States. In collectivist countries, people are expected to care for each other more; Indonesia and Pakistan are examples.

- *Masculinity versus femininity.* According to Hofstede, societies differ also in the extent to which they value assertiveness (which he called "masculinity") or caring ("femininity"). Japan and Austria ranked high in masculinity; Denmark, Costa Rica, and Chile ranked low.

- *Uncertainty avoidance.* Uncertainty avoidance refers to whether people in the society are uncomfortable with unstructured situations in which unknown, surprising, novel incidents occur. In other words, how comfortable are people in a society when it comes to dealing with surprises? People in some countries (such as Sweden, Israel, and Great Britain), according to Hofstede, are relatively comfortable dealing with uncertainty and surprises. People living in other countries (including Greece and Portugal) tend to be uncertainty avoiders.[47]

Differences in values manifest themselves in very real ways. In Russia, for instance, changing occupations, being unemployed, or looking for work is rare (or at least it was, until quite recently). Workers therefore try exceptionally hard to avoid being out of work: "Even an indefinite paid leave is accepted by employees hoping to return later."[48] Differences in values also manifest themselves in different working conditions. While child labor and even work produced by prisoners is much less common today, long hours and low pay are still widespread in many Asian factories. One recent report referred to "sweatshop Barbie" in describing conditions at one Asian plant of a Mattel subcontractor.[49]

Language and Customs   The international manager must also deal with differences in language. For example, one airline's "Fly in Leather" slogan was embarrassingly translated as "Fly Naked" for the company's Latin American campaign.[50] A country's traditional manners and customs can also be important. Campbell's, for instance, learned that Japanese drink soup mainly for breakfast. A country's predominant religions, cultural orientations (such as styles of music and art), and educational processes can all influence the manner in which business should be conducted in that country. In the United States or Japan, inviting a businessperson out for an alcoholic drink is sometimes done, for instance, whereas in Saudi Arabia such an invitation might be shocking.

The Technological Environment

A country's technological environment—such as the relative ease with which technology can be transferred from one country to another—can determine a product's success abroad. **Technology transfer** is the "transfer of systematic knowledge for the manufacture of a product, for the application of a process, or for the rendering of a service, and does not extend to the mere sale or lease of goods."[51]

Successful technology transfer depends on several things. First, there must be a suitable technology to be transferred—for instance, pollution filter devices. Second, social and economic conditions must favor the transfer. Pollution-reducing technology might be economically useless in a country where pollution reduction is not a priority. Finally, technology transfer depends on the willingness and ability of the receiving party to use and adapt the technology.[52] If using the pollution control filters requires chemical engineers to whom the receiving country has no access, the technology transfer might be impossible. Similarly, opening a new plant, or franchising a process, requires an acceptable level of technical expertise on the receiving country's end. If this is absent, the expansion into this country may well fail.

> **technology transfer**
> the transfer, often to another country, of systematic knowledge for the manufacturing of a product, for the application of a process, or for the rendering of a service; it does not extend to the mere sales or lease of goods.

▶ THE MANAGEMENT TEAM IN A GLOBAL BUSINESS

In most companies today, most managers are attached to specific functional departments or teams, such as production, marketing, finance, or human resources. Managing in a global business creates some special challenges in that regard. Managers in each function must analyze how best to manage their functions abroad, while working together with the other teams to make sure they achieve overall company goals. We'll look next at some examples.

Global Marketing

Marketing abroad is often a necessity today. As one expert says, "Even the biggest companies in the biggest countries cannot survive on their domestic markets if they are in global industries. They must be in all major markets."[53]

Wal-Mart is a good example. Between 1998 and 1999 its total company sales rose by 16%, but its international sales jumped by 26%. In just the first quarter of

1999, it opened nine international units, including three in Mexico. As of April 30, 1999, Wal-Mart's international units included stores in Argentina (13 stores), Brazil (14), Canada (154), Germany (95), Mexico (423), and Puerto Rico (15), as well as units in China and Korea.[54] About 10%—or 135,000—of Wal-Mart's employees are outside the United States. Its Web site (www.wal-mart.com) is a good example of how giants like Wal-Mart (or tiny companies, for that matter), can market their products or services globally, often without ever leaving their home countries.

Expanding sales abroad confronts the marketing manager with several challenges. For example, plans for the move must take local tastes into consideration. While it's true that for many products the tastes and preferences of consumers in different nations are beginning to converge on some global norm, the fact is that even global companies like McDonald's and the Gap (both of which tend to emphasize standardized products) need to fine-tune those products when they go abroad.[55] You won't find beef in McDonald's restaurants in India. And, you'll find several unusual products including sparkling water on sale at the McDonald's on the Champs Elysees.

Therefore, whether it's a giant firm like McDonald's or a smaller one like KnitMedia, considerable market research and analysis is required before the marketing plans for expanding overseas can be finalized. Similarly, incentive plans that work for salespeople in the United States may not work for the marketing manager's sales force in Argentina. She will also have to decide how to organize the sales effort abroad, particularly since she—while still in charge of overall company sales—will be many miles away.

Globalization of Production

Globalizing production means placing parts of a firm's production process in various locations around the globe. Thus the productions manager might place plants in France and Peru, and distribution warehouses in Germany and Brazil. One aim is to provide manufacturing and supply support for local markets abroad. Another is to take advantage of national differences in the cost and quality of production—it might be cheaper to produce certain items in Peru, for instance.

For many production managers, the overall aim today is to integrate their global operations into a unified and efficient system of manufacturing facilities around the world.[56] This can present a considerable challenge when it comes to managing the coordination of such an effort. Xerox Corporation's worldwide manufacturing system is an example. In the early 1980s, each Xerox company in each country had its own suppliers, assembly plants, and distribution channels. Each country's plant managers gave little thought to how their plans fit into Xerox's global needs. This approach became unworkable as international competition in the copier market grew more intense. Canon, Minolta, and Ricoh penetrated Xerox's U.S. and European markets with low-cost copiers.[57]

The competitive threat prompted Xerox's senior managers to coordinate their global production processes. They organized a new central purchasing group to consolidate raw materials purchases, and thereby cut worldwide manufacturing costs. They instituted a "leadership through quality" program to improve product quality, streamline and standardize manufacturing processes, and cut costs. Xerox managers also eliminated over $1 billion of inventory costs by installing a computer system that linked customer orders from one region more closely with production capabilities in other regions.

With the proper training and guidance, the production manager can develop and expand the role of his or her foreign facilities. Consider the story of the Hewlett-Packard factory in Singapore. When originally built, its purpose was to produce simple labor-intensive components at low cost. Within several years it was upgraded to produce a complete, low-cost calculator. As the Singapore plant managers became more experienced at manufacturing complete products, they improved their ability to redesign products as well. By redesigning one calculator— the HP 41C—they cut production costs by 50%. By building on their new design capabilities, plant managers and engineers were gradually entrusted by Hewlett-Packard's U.S. headquarters with increasingly sophisticated assignments. Today, Singapore is Hewlett-Packard's global center for the design, development, and manufacture of portable printers for markets worldwide.[58]

MANAGING @ THE *SPEED* OF THOUGHT

Using the Internet as a Global Management Tool

Managing a global production operation is always a challenge: The distances involved are usually enormous, and it's easy for home-office managers to lose track of what's going on in the field, especially when the field is 8,000 miles away. If that happens, the benefits of efficiency sought by firms like Xerox and Hewlett-Packard in the examples above will not materialize.

Production managers today are therefore using the Internet to keep tabs on their global operations. Schlumberger Ltd. is a good example. Schlumberger, which manufactures oil-drilling equipment and electronics, has headquarters in New York and Paris. The company operates in 85 countries, and in most of them employees are in remote locations.[59] How do the company's managers maintain control over so many far-flung locations? Here's how experts describe the company's system:

> To install their own network for so few people at each remote location would have been prohibitively expensive. Using the Internet, Schlumberger engineers in Dubai (on the Persian Gulf) can check e-mail and effectively stay in close contact with management at a very low cost. In addition, the field staff is able to follow research projects as easily as can personnel within the United States. Schlumberger has found that since it converted to the Internet from its own network, its overall communications costs are down 2% despite a major increase in network and information technology infrastructure spending. The main reason for the savings is the dramatic drop in voice traffic and in overnight delivery service charges (they attach complete documents to their e-mail messages).[60] At Schlumberger, the Internet plays a central role in creating an efficient world-wide production system.

Global Staffing

Companies around the world are also tapping a vast new supply of skilled labor.[61] Thus, 3M makes tapes, chemicals, and electrical parts in Bangalore, India, and Hewlett-Packard assembles computers and designs memory boards in Guadalajara, Mexico. In Jamaica, 3,500 office workers make airline reservations, process tickets, and handle calls to toll-free numbers via satellite dishes for U.S. companies. Back in Bangalore, an educated workforce has drawn Texas Instruments and 30 more firms, including Motorola and IBM, to set up software programming offices in the area.[62] Firms like these aren't just chasing cheap labor: They are moving plants and jobs overseas to tap the growing pool of highly skilled employees in Latin America and Asia.

Any decision to do business abroad usually triggers global staffing issues. Setting up factories abroad requires first analyzing employment laws in the host country and establishing a recruiting office. Even a more modest expansion abroad requires a global staffing outlook. For example, sending the company's sales manager abroad for several months to close a deal means deciding how to compensate her for her expenses abroad, what to do with her house here, and how to make sure she is trained to handle the cultural demands of her foreign assignment. Developing effective staffing policies and plans and then coordinating these with production, marketing, and other functions can thus be a challenging aspect of going abroad.

THE PEOPLE SIDE OF MANAGING

■ Managing in Mexico

Managers must carefully consider the people side of managing when staffing production facilities abroad.[63] For example, consider some of the following issues in setting up a factory in Mexico.

Workplace Harmony. The Mexican workplace has a low tolerance for adversarial relations. While getting along with others is important in U.S. factories, too, Mexican employers put much more emphasis on hiring employees who have a record of working cooperatively with authority. Mexican employers, according to one expert, "tend to seek workers who are agreeable, respectful, and obedient rather than innovative and independent."[64] This can lead to counterproductive behavior, even on the part of supervisors. For example, in attempting to preserve the appearance of harmony, supervisors may hide defective work rather than confront the problem or report it to a manager.

Role and Status. Mexican employees often put a relatively high emphasis on social order and on respecting one's status. In one factory in Chihuahua, Mexico, for instance, a U.S. manager wore jeans and insisted that everyone call him Jim. He assumed those around him would prefer that he reduce the visible status gap between himself and the workers. He was then amazed to learn that the local employees considered him "uncultured and boorish."[65]

Exercising Authority. Mexican employees tend to have a more rigid view of authority than do their U.S. counterparts. Therefore, attempts by U.S. managers to encourage input and feedback from employees may cause confusion. As one expert puts it:

> [Mexican] supervisors see their role as strictly following orders to the best of their ability, never questioning nor taking matters into their own hands, and this is exactly how they view the proper role of their subordinates. The Mexican supervisor's style is to supervise closely, and look for willing obedience. Opinions expressed by employees are often regarded as backtalk.[66]

Globalization of markets, production, and labor is coinciding with the rise of the global manager. To managers like Wal-Mart's CEO David Glass, the bonds between company and country are thinning. A global manager is one who views markets and production globally and who seeks higher profits for his or her firm on a global basis.[67] He or she is also able to deal effectively with cultural differences like those in the Mexico factory example above.

Being a global manager is easier said than done. It's one thing to say that you view your markets and production globally and intend to integrate operations so as to maximize profits around the world. It's quite another thing to be sitting in your office in Kansas and to actually be willing to give your customers and employees in France or India the same attention that you give to customers and employees who are in the next town. Not everyone has what it takes to be so global in outlook.

Cosmopolitan Managers

For one thing, global managers tend to be cosmopolitan in the way they view people and the world. What do we mean by "cosmopolitan?" Webster's dictionary defines cosmopolitan as "belonging to the world; not limited to just one part of the political, social, commercial or intellectual spheres; free from local, provincial, or national ideas, prejudices or attachments."[68] Global managers must be comfortable anywhere in the world, and being cosmopolitan helps them to be so.

How can you tell if you're cosmopolitan? Cosmopolitan people have a clear identity that also values others' views, a sensitivity to what is expected of them in any context in which they find themselves, and the flexibility to deal intelligently and in an unbiased way with people and situations in other cultures. International travel can certainly contribute to one's cosmopolitanism (by exposing you to people and cultures around the world). However, travel is certainly neither a prerequisite nor a guarantee that the traveler will be cosmopolitan. Yet travel is often one thing that sets such managers apart. Take the travel schedule of Ellen Knapp, chief knowledge and information officer for the accounting and consulting firm PricewaterhouseCoopers.[69] In an average month, Knapp is lucky to spend two days in the office; the rest of the time she's on the road, mostly outside the United States. One week recently, for instance, she took three red-eye (overnight) flights in six days. She uses office space wherever she may be, sticks to airlines and hotels she knows well. "My place of work is simply where I am," is how she puts it.[70]

To a great extent, cosmopolitanism reflects a person's values—the basic beliefs he or she has regarding what people should or should not do. As a result, the philosophy of the company's top managers tends to both reflect and affect how cosmopolitan its managers are, and influences its managers' willingness to take that company global. For example, an ethnocentric (home-base-oriented) management philosophy may manifest itself in an **ethnocentric** or home-market-oriented firm. A **polycentric** philosophy may translate into a company that is limited to several individual foreign markets. A **regiocentric** (or geocentric) philosophy may lead managers to create more of an integrated global production and marketing presence.

Do You Have a Global Brain?

In addition to being cosmopolitan, global managers also have what some experts call a *global brain*, which means, for instance, that they accept the fact that, at times, their home-grown ways of doing business are not always best. For example,

ethnocentric
a management philosophy that leads to the creating of home-market-oriented firms.

polycentric
a management philosophy oriented toward pursuing a limited number of individual foreign markets.

regiocentric
a management philosophy oriented toward larger areas, including the global marketplace.

when Volkswagen formed a partnership with Skoda, a Czech Republic car maker, it focused on training Skoda's managers in Western management techniques; however, it was wise enough to follow Skoda's suggestions about how business was conducted in its country.[71] This sort of willingness to understand that going global means choosing the best solutions from different systems and then applying them to the problems at hand is what management writers mean by having a global brain.

Again, though, being global does not mean acting like a chameleon. As one expert put it, "A company's goal shouldn't be to operate like a French company in France and a Brazilian company in Brazil. Instead, a company—whether it is multinational or local—should bring a multinational approach to each business issue."[72] Ernst and Young, a consulting firm, takes exactly that approach. It is therefore developing a global database of "best practices" that can be accessed by its consultants. As one of Ernst and Young's officers put it, "a solution that works in India may have a component that works in the UK. . . . Sharing best practices helps each office respond more rapidly"[73] (and also helps make the firm truly global).

How do managers with global brains behave? For one thing, "global thinkers have a real interest in other cultures."[74] They also tend to be more sensitive to the possibility of important contributions by other societies, and so give ideas from other nations as much credence as those from their own or other Western nations.[75] You needn't have lived or traveled extensively abroad or be multilingual to have a global brain, although such experiences can help. The important thing is that you be deeply interested in the greater world around you, make efforts to learn about other people's perspectives, and take those perspectives into consideration when you make your own decisions.[76] For a manager, the result might be, for example "applying a successful Brazilian marketing solution to a similar situation in Malaysia, or honoring the local communications hierarchy while keeping the appropriate people in your company in the loop."[77]

Would Your Company Choose You to Be an International Executive?

Of course, there's more involved in getting picked to be a global manager than liking to travel or having a global brain. What do companies look for in trying to identify international executives?

A recent study by behavioral scientists at the University of Southern California provides some answers. The researchers studied 838 lower-, middle- and senior-level managers from 6 international firms in 21 countries, focusing particularly on personal characteristics. Specifically, they studied the extent to which personal characteristics such as "sensitivity to cultural differences" could be used to distinguish between managers who had high potential as international executives and those whose potential was not so high.

Fourteen personal characteristics successfully distinguished those identified by their companies as having high potential from those identified as lower performing in 72% of the cases. To get an initial, tentative impression of how you would rate, see Table 2.1, which lists the 14 characteristics (along with sample items). For each, indicate (by placing a number in the space provided) whether you strongly agree (number 7), strongly disagree (number 1), or fall somewhere in between.

Generally speaking, the higher you score on each of these fourteen characteristics, the more likely it is you would have been identified as a high-potential international executive in this study.[78]

Characteristics of More Successful International Managers

TABLE 2.1

Scale	Score	Sample Item
Sensitive to cultural differences		When working with people from other cultures, works hard to understand their perspectives.
Business knowledge		Has a solid understanding of our products and services.
Courage to take a stand		Is willing to take a stand on issues.
Brings out the best in people		Has a special talent for dealing with people.
Acts with integrity		Can be depended on to tell the truth, regardless of circumstances.
Is insightful		Is good at identifying the most important part of a complex problem or issue.
Is committed to success		Clearly demonstrates commitment to seeing the organization succeed.
Takes risks		Takes personal as well as business risks.
Uses feedback		Has changed as a result of feedback.
Is culturally adventurous		Enjoys the challenge of working in countries other than his or her own.
Seeks opportunities to learn		Takes advantage of opportunities to do new things.
Is open to criticism		Appears brittle—as if criticism might cause him or her to break.*
Seeks feedback		Pursues feedback even when others are reluctant to give it.
Is flexible		Doesn't get so invested in things that he or she cannot change when something doesn't work.

*Reverse scored.

▶ THE PROCESS OF INTERNATIONAL MANAGEMENT

Today, almost every manager is an international manager because almost every business is involved in some way in international trade (and if that trade spans the globe, *global manager* would of course be the better term).

International management means carrying out the management functions of planning, organizing, leading, and controlling on an international scale. Doing business internationally obviously affects the way each of these functions is carried out. We will present several examples here, and then continue our discussion of international management in each chapter.

Planning Issues

Planning involves setting goals and identifying the courses of action for achieving those goals. It therefore also requires identifying opportunities and threats, and balancing these with the strengths and weaknesses of the enterprise. Planning in

planning
the process of setting goals and courses of action, developing rules and procedures, and forecasting future outcomes.

an international arena uses this same basic approach. However, global planning also means dealing with some unique issues.

For one thing, as we've seen, international planners must consider special political, legal, and technological issues. In Germany, for instance, Wal-Mart discovered it was illegal to advertise that it would refund to customers the difference in price if they found the same items elsewhere for less. International planners must also consider the possibility of political instability, since many countries have frequent changes of government.[79] Similarly, currency instability, competition from state-owned enterprises, and pressures from national governments (including changing trade barriers) can all throw even the best-laid plans into disarray.

Instabilities like these are not just a characteristic of developing countries. Between 1993 and 1995, Italy embarked on a sweeping privatization of its nationalized businesses. During that time, Italy sold banks and companies worth about $60 billion, including some of the country's largest telecommunications, oil and gas, and insurance companies.[80] At the same time, sweeping criminal investigations created havoc among the country's political and managerial elite. The resulting upheaval brought enormous opportunities for foreign firms doing business in Italy. But it also increased the risks by boosting both the competitiveness of the newly privatized Italian firms and the uncertainties of dealing with the country's political institutions.

Other complications arise in international planning.[81] A domestic U.S. planner faces a relatively homogeneous home market, while the international planner faces a relatively fragmented and diverse set of foreign customers and needs. For U.S. planners, data are usually available and relatively accurate and easy to collect. Internationally, collecting information—about demographics, production levels, and so on—can be a formidable task, and the actual data are often of questionable accuracy.

Organizing Issues

How do you organize an international business?[82] Figure 2.6 shows the typical options, including the traditional domestic organization, the export-oriented organization, the international organization, and the multinational organization.

These organizational structures differ in how they maintain authority over the foreign operations. In a domestic organization, each division handles its own foreign sales, which may come largely from unsolicited overseas orders. In response to increasing orders from abroad, the firm may move to an export-oriented structure. Here, one department (often called an import-export department) coordinates all international activities such as licensing, contracting, and managing foreign sales. In an international organization, the company is divided into separate domestic and international divisions. The international division focuses on production and sales overseas, while the domestic division focuses on domestic markets. Reynolds Metals, for instance, is organized into six worldwide businesses, with a U.S.-focused group and a separate international group.[83]

Finally, the firm may move to a multinational organization, in which each country where the firm does business will have its own subsidiary. The oil firm Royal Dutch Shell is organized this way. It has separate subsidiaries for Shell Switzerland and Shell U.S.A. (as well as many other countries), for instance.[84]

Globalization also complicates a firm's human resource decisions. New policies will have to include how to select, train, and compensate the managers who will be sent to foreign posts and how to deal with intercountry differences in labor laws.

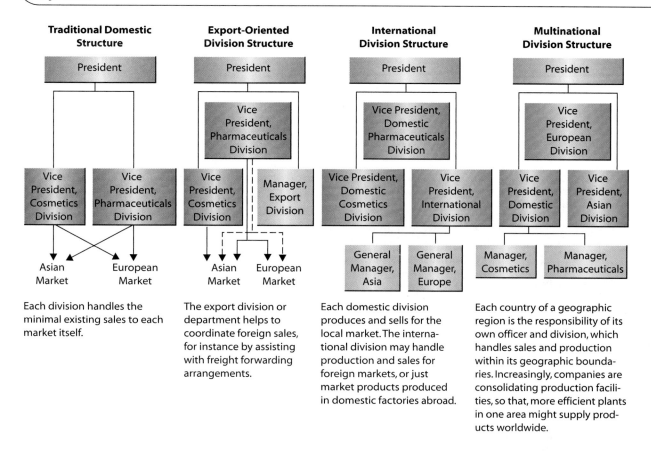

▼ **F I G U R E 2 . 6** **International Organizations**

As firms evolve from domestic to multinational enterprises, their increasing international operations necessitate a more globally oriented organization.

Traditional Domestic Structure

President

Vice President, Cosmetics Division

Vice President, Pharmaceuticals Division

Asian Market

European Market

Each division handles the minimal existing sales to each market itself.

Export-Oriented Division Structure

President

Vice President, Pharmaceuticals Division

Vice President, Cosmetics Division

Manager, Export Division

Asian Market

European Market

The export division or department helps to coordinate foreign sales, for instance by assisting with freight forwarding arrangements.

International Division Structure

President

Vice President, Domestic Pharmaceuticals Division

Vice President, Domestic Cosmetics Division

Vice President, International Division

General Manager, Asia

General Manager, Europe

Each domestic division produces and sells for the local market. The international division may handle production and sales for foreign markets, or just market products produced in domestic factories abroad.

Multinational Division Structure

President

Vice President, European Division

Vice President, Domestic Division

Vice President, Asian Division

Manager, Cosmetics

Manager, Pharmaceuticals

Each country of a geographic region is the responsibility of its own officer and division, which handles sales and production within its geographic boundaries. Increasingly, companies are consolidating production facilities, so that, more efficient plants in one area might supply products worldwide.

Global staffing policies like these can be very important. For example, when international managers fail, they generally fail either because they can't adapt to the customs of the new country or because their families can't deal with the emotional stress that relocation entails.[85] Global companies must therefore provide training that focuses on cultural differences, on raising trainees' awareness of the impact of these cultural differences on business decisions, and on other matters like building language and adaptation skills. Explaining intercountry differences in labor laws (such as the fact that what is sexual harassment in one country might not be in another) is another example.[86] Yet few firms actually provide such "going abroad" training to employees.[87]

Issues in Leading the International Enterprise

Globalizing also influences the people side of managing. In Latin America, for instance, bosses are expected to be more autocratic, so participative management (in which employees are encouraged to make work-related decisions) can cause problems. At the other extreme, Japanese managers value consensus and rarely welcome the kind of take-charge leader who wants to make all the decisions personally.

In their book *Working for the Japanese*, Joseph and Suzy Fucini describe the cultural problems between the Japanese and U.S. workers that eventually caused Denny Pawley, the highest-ranking American at the Mazda Michigan plant, to leave for a new job with United Technologies Corporation:

> Pawley did not quit for the money. He left Mazda because he had become frustrated with the constraints that the company's Japanese management had placed on him. After two years and one month with Mazda, it had become obvious . . . that because he was an American he would never be given real authority at Flatrock. As he would later observe, "it started looking more and more to me [like] the real decision-making would always come out of Hiroshima, and [this] just didn't offer me the opportunity to use my broad-based management experience."[88]

Controlling Issues

For managers, maintaining control means monitoring actual performance to ensure it's consistent with the standards that were set. However, doing so can be easier said than done, especially when the thing you're trying to keep tabs on is 5,000 miles and an ocean away. In June 1999, for instance, Coca-Cola was hit by a rude surprise as country after country in Europe required Coke to take its beverages off store shelves. While Coke has perhaps the industry's highest standards for product quality and integrity, keeping an eye on what's happening at every plant can be a challenge. It turned out that chemicals had seeped into the beverages at one of Coke's European plants, and many consumers had apparently become sick as a result.

Going global also usually means the company must install effective computerized information systems so that managers can monitor and maintain control over worldwide operations. For example, for many years Kelly Services, Inc., the Troy, Michigan-headquartered staffing service, let its offices in each country operate with their own individual billing and accounts receivable systems. However, according to Tommi White, Kelly's executive vice president and chief technology officer, with the international division now representing about 25% of the company's total revenue, "we are consolidating our operations in all countries and subsidiaries under a standard [information system]. . . All our customers expect us to deliver consistent practices, metrics, and measurement. Establishing global standards is an important part of meeting and exceeding that expectation."[89]

SUMMARY

1. Companies can pursue several strategies when it comes to extending operations to foreign markets. Exporting is the route often chosen by manufacturers, and licensing and franchising are two popular alternatives. At some point, a firm may decide to invest funds in another country. Joint ventures and wholly owned subsidiaries are two examples of foreign direct investment.

2. An international business is any firm that engages in international trade or investment. Firms are globalizing for many reasons, the three most common being to expand sales, to acquire resources, and to diversify sources of sales and supplies. Other reasons for pursuing international business include reducing costs or improving quality by seeking products and services produced in foreign countries and smoothing out sales and profit swings.

3. Free trade means that all barriers to trade among countries participating in an agreement are removed. Its potential benefits have prompted many nations to enter into various levels of economic integration, ranging from a free-trade area to a common market.

4. Globalizing production means placing parts of a firm's production process in various locations around the globe. The aim is to take advantage of national differences in the cost and quality of production and then integrate these operations in a unified system of manufacturing facilities around the world. Companies also are tapping new supplies of skilled labor in various countries. The globalization of markets, production, and labor coincides with the rise of a new type of global manager, who can function effectively anywhere in the world.

5. International managers must be adept at assessing a wide array of environmental factors. For example, managers must be familiar with the economic systems, exchange rates, and level of economic development of the countries in which they do business. They must be aware of import restrictions, political risks, and legal differences and restraints. Important cultural differences also affect the way people in various countries act and expect to be treated. Values, languages, and customs are examples of elements that distinguish people of one culture from those of another. Finally, the relative ease with which technology can be transferred from one country to another is an important consideration in conducting international business.

TYING IT ALL TOGETHER

Chapter 1 explained how trends like globalization are boosting the level of competition companies face, and therefore the challenges managers face in managing their companies successfully. In the present chapter we turned our spotlight on managing in a global environment—what globalizing means, and specifically how going global affects what managers do and the skills they need. We saw that globalizing confronts the manager with many international management issues and challenges. The effectiveness with which he or she deals with these new issues—whether they involve planning, organizing, leading, managing human resources, controlling, or managing the people side of a firm—determines whether the decision to internationalize turns out to be a good one.

One of the main things discussed in this chapter is that managers must take into account a society's values and culture when dealing with people from other cultures. However, cross-cultural issues don't necessarily involve just dealing with people abroad. Particularly with today's diverse workforce, differences in values and cultures may be as pronounced in one's own office as they are when dealing with people overseas. That's one reason why, in the following chapter, we'll look more closely at the issue of values and ethics and how they influence what people do.

KEY TERMS

manager 42	multinational corporation (MNC) 46	common market 49
exporting 43		trade barrier 52
licensing 44	global corporation 46	subsidiary 52
franchising 44	mixed economy 47	quota 52
foreign direct investment 44	gross domestic product 48	values 54
strategic alliance 45	exchange rate 48	technology transfer 55
joint venture 45	free trade 48	ethnocentric 59
wholly owned subsidiary 46	tariff 48	polycentric 59
international business 46	economic integration 48	regiocentric 59
international trade 46	free trade area 48	planning 61
international management 46	customs union 48	

CRITICAL THINKING EXERCISES

1. At the end of the 20th century, an admiral of the U.S. Navy predicted that as the Mediterranean had been the sea of the past and the Atlantic the sea of the present, so the Pacific would be the sea of the future. What do you think he meant? Is the Pacific Rim the leading market for goods and services in the twenty-first century? Write your own version of the admiral's prediction, looking ahead to the year 3000.

2. As we look around the globe, there seems to be war or conflict on most continents. Africa continues to have tribal warfare. Poverty is rampant. Technology is somewhat rare. Disease is everywhere. In the former USSR, Russia continues to fight with its former satellite countries, while the country itself seems to be falling apart. There is famine in the military, an inadequate food supply for regular citizens, a growing black market, and dissatisfaction from the many unemployed Russians. The European Union (EU) seems to be working on the surface, but not without conflict. The United Kingdom and France are boycotting each other's meat and other products. Not all nations have decided to join the EU; for example, Sweden has yet to join. The conflict in Bosnia involved the United States and other European nations. In Asia, Pakistan and India are at odds on a regular basis. Indonesia has been at odds with itself and the people of East Timor. Taiwan and China are at odds. The United States is not without its problems, ranging from the need for better schools to crime. In terms of business, the United States seems to be thriving. How does the above picture affect future global investment and business opportunities? How would you prepare for these problems if expanding your business abroad?

EXPERIENTIAL EXERCISES

1. You have just taken an assignment to move to Russia. Your company is heavily invested in biotechnical farming techniques. The company is located in David, California, a community known for a heavy sense of social responsibility, progressive agricultural techniques, and a liberal political atmosphere. You have a week to prepare to go to St. Petersburg and then to Moscow. How would you begin to prepare? Would you look at political turmoil in Russia and its relationships with the former members of the USSR? Would you study the social customs? Would you take a crash course in the language? How would you prepare yourself to enter this new world of Russia? Would you interview recent immigrants from Russia? What might reading history tell you about how to conduct business meetings in Russia?

2. It is projected that by the middle of the next century, if not before, India will surpass China in population. What do you know about either of these countries? They are home to approximately two-fifths of the world population. Some of the richest and poorest people live in these two nations. Wealth is not distributed as it is in the United States. China is still a communist country, developing an entrepreneurial and capitalistic economy. India is a democratic country, ruled by religion and other ancient values. How does religion (mainly Confucianism in China and Hinduism in India) affect managerial thinking? How do you think these countries' ancient history and religions affect their respective approaches to business and the global marketplace? What types of governmental structures do they have, and how do these structures affect business? What political issues in these regions would make them potential risks for U.S. investment? With a team of four or five people, research each country's history and current situation. Look at the political, social, economic, technological, and environmental issues, concerns, and attitudes. Then write up this information in the form of a recommendation to companies that might wish to invest in either country. Be sure to note ethical and moral issues in the recommendation.

myPHLIP COMPANION WEB SITE

We invite you to visit the Dessler companion Web site at **www.prenhall.com/dessler** for this chapter's Internet resources.

U.S. BOOKSELLER FINDS A STRONG PARTNER IN GERMAN MEDIA GIANT

When Barnes & Noble was exploring ways to become more competitive in its battle with Amazon.com, there were hundreds of U.S. companies to which it could turn. Research clearly demonstrated that the cultural differences which characterize cross-border ventures made them far more complicated than domestic ones. Yet, Barnes & Noble surprised competitors when it chose to form its Internet joint venture with the German media giant Bertelsmann. Was Barnes & Noble mistaken to look abroad for a partner?

Bertelsmann is best known among college students for its record label and music club, BMG (now both owned by Universal). At the time, BMG entertainment was second in the market with $1.9 billion in sales. The BMG music club is well known to US college students with its buy 1 get 10 free CD offers posted on campus bulletin boards nationwide. With $3.9 billion in sales and nearly 65,000 employees, Bertelsmann is much more than a CD club. Its holdings include Random House, the world's largest English-language book publisher, and Offset Paperback, a firm that manufactures nearly 40% of all the paperback books sold in the U.S. Bertelsmann had also actively pursued e-commerce on its own. By the end of the twentieth century, Bertelsmann had quietly staked out a position as the world's third largest Internet business.

To fund barnesandnoble.com, the two created a separate company and conducted an initial public offering (IPO) to raise capital. The offering raised $421 million for the new venture, after commissions and expenses, making it the largest e-commerce offering in history. Since launching its on-line business in May 1997, barnesandnoble.com has quickly become one of the world's largest e-commerce retailers. The company has successfully capitalized on the recognized brand value of the Barnes & Noble name to become the second largest on-line retailer of books.

Discussion Questions

1. What may have motivated Barnes & Noble to partner with the German firm Bertelsmann?

2. In general terms, what advantages would Barnes & Noble gain by having an international partner?

3. With all its experience in e-commerce, why wouldn't BMG just set up its own competitor to Amazon.com?

4. What are a few of the planning, organizing, leading, and controlling issues Barnes & Noble's managers faced in joining forces with Bertelsmann?

SHOULD FORD OUTSOURCE THE FINAL ASSEMBLY OF AUTOS?

As CEO of one of the world's largest auto manufacturers, Jacques Nassar has spearheaded a number of major initiatives aimed at making Ford more competitive globally. (Within the past year, for instance, Ford announced the acquisition of the Volvo car business from AB Volvo for $6.45 billion.) Ford was also in the process of considering a subtle but profound change in its strategy: the company was beginning to articulate a vision that did not include final assembly of its vehicles as a core competence. Chairman William Clay Ford, Jr., described Ford's 21st century vision as becoming "the world's leading consumer company that provides automotive products and services." Nassar was

thinking of taking that vision a step further. He was considering outsourcing the final assembly of Ford cars—in other words, letting other companies actually assemble their cars.

At the same time, Ford had radically internationalized its operations. In addition to its acquisition of Volvo, Ford had acquired Aston-Martin and Jaguar. The Ford brand was already immensely popular in Europe. Fifty-five leading motoring journalists in Europe had selected Ford's new Focus as the 1999 European car of the year. However, in its manufacturing operations worldwide, Ford had continued its practice of performing the final assembly on all its autos and light trucks.

Ford had a long and proud history of manufacturing. In the early 1970s the Michigan Rouge Plant was Ford Motor Company's testament to large-scale manufacturing. Starting with iron ore and sand, the company manufactured its own steel and glass. Completed autos rolled off the assembly line, comprised almost entirely of Ford-made parts. But over the decades, the business environment in which Ford competed changed dramatically. Competition in the industry became progressively more global; auto companies actively sought parts sources and assembly operations around the globe. In the tumultuous 1980s, Ford became the best-selling car in Europe, while Nissan, Honda, and Toyota captured the U.S. market.

Throughout the 1990s, Ford continued to assemble its own cars with parts from worldwide sources. In late 1999, however, Nassar signaled a potential major change in Ford's manufacturing practices. Beginning with its plant in Northeast Brazil, Ford was considering having its equipment manufacturers and parts suppliers perform vital parts of the final assembly of its cars. Under the plan, Ford would pay only for the units produced. If the Bahia Brazil plant was suc-cessful, Ford would begin outsourcing final assembly world-wide. In essence, Ford would signal that auto assembly was not one of its core activities.

Ford would not be the first auto maker to move in this direction. DaimlerChrysler and Volkswagen have already introduced similar plans. Under Nassar's plan, a division of the Italian firm Fiat would provide management and main-tenance services, as well as body assembly.

Discussion Questions

1. What motivated Ford to become a more global manu-facturing operation?

2. If Ford no longer considers assembling cars as part of its core business, on what activities should management focus its attention?

3. Why would this "outsource assembly" decision likely be made only at the highest levels of the Ford organiza-tion?

4. What specific global management problems would you see Ford encountering if it decides to let other firms assemble its cars around the world?

KNITMEDIA

KNITMEDIA GOES GLOBAL

When it comes to the music industry, "abroad" is one place a music company has to be. About one-third of the $50 billion or so in global recorded music sales comes from outside the United States, and all the major music firms, including Sony, Warner/EMI, and Universal, are expanding into foreign mar-kets. They are setting up joint ventures and company-owned offices. They are doing so not just to sell American performers like Madonna overseas, but also to identify and to develop local talent, since it's local talent that music lovers abroad often want to hear. That helps explain, for example, why Eiffel 65's "Blue"—the number one hit in Italy and in Europe in 1999—was quickly signed by Universal. It hit the U.S. charts at number 6 in January 2000. In Europe, as in the United States, recording companies are continually searching for new talent. You'll find their representatives sift-ing through the CDs at a music store in London's Camden Town, for example, trying to find the next new break-out band from a small independent label.

"The Knitting Factory is at the center of the international music movement," the *Wall Street Journal* recently noted, and increasingly that's the case. Almost from the beginning KnitMedia has had international aspirations, but today "going global" is a major part of the company's plans.

In some respects, going global is easier for companies like KnitMedia, but in other respects it's getting a lot more difficult. Technologies like the Internet and videoconferenc-ing make it easier to track what's happening abroad and to communicate across borders and oceans quickly and easily. On the other hand, the industry is also consolidating, mak-ing it a lot more difficult for independents like KnitMedia to break in. Today, for instance, the majors are down from six companies to three: Warner Music and EMI, which merged in 2000; Universal and B.M.G., which merged in 1999; and Sony. Independent record labels ("Indies") have about 22% of the market, while Universal has about 32%, Warner has about 27%, and Sony has about 17%. More and more, inde-pendents are doing battle with companies that have enor-mous marketing clout.

Michael Dorf and KnitMedia have been doing business overseas since 1990. Going overseas began with a 24-city European tour with bands like Sonny Sharrock, the Jazz Passengers, and Miracle Room. It was a good start, but not everything went smoothly. For one thing, a first-time agent booked the tour into a stop in Helsingbourd, Sweden, that held only 30 people—barely enough for Knit's three bands, let alone customers. A date scheduled in East Berlin just before the Wall fell ended up losing money when German Chancellor Helmut Kohl decided to start the reunification by offering three East German marks for one Deutsche mark, instead of the six or seven East German mark exchange rate that existed at that time. However, the tour was successful in introducing Europeans to the KnitMedia name and artists, and the company's next tours were much more profitable.

KnitMedia has long had an office in Holland to coordinate its European tours and other operations and currently plans to move that office to Berlin. The company also devoted considerable time and resources to developing a strategic alliance with the South Bank Center in London, with the aim of opening a Knitting Factory club along the Thames in 1997. However, a variety of factors caused KnitMedia to change its plans: now it will open its first club abroad in Berlin. (KnitMedia is currently in the midst of opening its first U.S. club outside of New York, in Hollywood, California.) As more clubs are added, they'll be linked into a digital KnitMedia community that should provide a global outlet for the company's artists and products.

KnitMedia is also involved in other international operations. Like other independents, says Dorf, "we're trying to sell American acts abroad and find acts abroad to bring to America. We're working with Tower Records in the United States on a possible strategic alliance that would have Tower opening special KnitMedia kiosks in the jazz sections of more than 100 Tower stores, an idea that can possibly be exported to Europe. And that's not all. Other European tours and festivals are planned, and we're working with telecom-munications and Internet firms to develop global Internet music broadcasting. Alliances with companies like Sony Music should help KnitMedia expand to South America, Asia, Africa, and the South Pacific." Given all these possibilities, the Knit Media executive team would like some advice on how to further its aspirations to expand abroad.

Team Exercises and Questions

Use what you learned in this chapter to answer the following questions from Michael Dorf and his management team:

1. What international strategies have we used thus far to go global? What specific strategies would you suggest KnitMedia use for the next few years, and why?

2. How have the economic, sociocultural, and technological components of the international environment affected KnitMedia up to now? Based on what you know about the international environment in Europe today (or based on what you can find out), what do you think are the main economic, sociocultural, and technological challenges KnitMedia will face over the next year or two?

3. What "international management" challenges do we at KnitMedia seem to have faced to date in planning, organizing, leading, and controlling the company's expansion abroad, and what challenges do you anticipate as we open the new Knitting Factory in Berlin? What specific steps would you suggest we take to meet those challenges?

4. What competition do you see us facing in Europe as KnitMedia expands abroad? How do you suggest we address that competition?

3

MANAGING IN A CULTURAL AND ETHICAL ENVIRONMENT

OBJECTIVES

AFTER STUDYING THIS CHAPTER, YOU SHOULD BE ABLE TO

- Explain the nature of ethical decisions, including what makes a decision a moral one

- Discuss the factors that influence whether specific people in specific organizations make ethical or unethical decisions

- Explain how to create a company's culture

- Explain the main approaches to corporate social responsibility

- Discuss techniques managers can use to manage workforce diversity

WHAT'S AHEAD?

It was a public relations disaster of global proportions. It seems that some people were so anxious to make Salt Lake City home to the 2002 Winter Olympics that they apparently bribed several members of the Olympics selection committee to get their way. And, after further investigation, it turned out that Salt Lake City was probably not the first to boost its chances with some well-placed bribes: A number of other cities had used much the same tactics. The Olympics—often viewed as a shining example of amateur sports and international harmony—came out of this with its reputation tarnished and with some of its committee members openly accused of questionable ethics and forced to resign. For many years, people would wonder about the culture and values that the Olympics leadership had allowed to take root.

Chapter 2 explained the challenges of managing in a global environment, and emphasized the problems that can arise from cross-cultural differences in values and points of view. In this chapter we'll turn to other environmental challenges, and focus on the subjects of culture, ethics, social responsibility, and diversity, and on why they are important.

Environmental challenges like these are interrelated. For example, globalizing forces companies to deal more effectively with diversity and particularly with a more diverse workforce. Similarly, globalizing and ethics are inseparable. Consider the international corruption index shown in Figure 3.1. The figure highlights a truism that many managers deal with every day: Bribes and unethical behavior are the price of doing business in many countries around the world. In Albania, for instance, it's been estimated that businesses pay out bribes equal to about 8% of their sales (about one-third of their potential profits) as a cost of doing business.[1] Similarly, it's been estimated that U.S. businesses in one recent year lost $15 billion in orders abroad to firms from countries that allow bribes (which are prohibited in the United States by the Foreign Corrupt Practices Act). Businesspeople hope a number of steps, among them an "antibribery" treaty recently signed by 34 trading

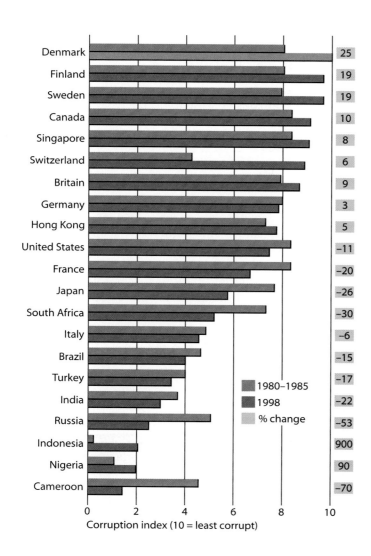

◄ F I G U R E 3 . 1

The International Corruption Index

Source: © 1999 The Economist Newspaper Group, Inc. Reprinted with permission. Further reproduction is prohibited. www.economist.com

nations, including those responsible for most of world trade, will reduce the incidence of corruption.

The problems facing the Olympics Committee are just one example of how an organization's value set—what we'll call in this chapter it's *culture*—can create a powerful environment that affects everything its employees and other stakeholders do. There are therefore few more important things a manager can do than to infuse his or her company with the right values. We'll discuss how to do that, and several related matters, in this chapter.

▶ WHAT DETERMINES ETHICAL BEHAVIOR AT WORK?

We all face ethical choices every day. Consider this dilemma: Your best friend sits next to you in a large college class, and can't afford to miss any more sessions since attendance counts so much in the final grade. She's just called to ask that you sign the class roll for her tomorrow, and you know that she does in fact have a serious family matter to attend to. There are 190 students in the hall, so your chances of getting caught are virtually zero. Should you help your best friend? Or would it be unethical to do so? How can you decide? What factors will influence whether you say yes or no? These are some of the questions we address here. Let's look first at the meaning of ethics.

The Meaning of Ethics

ethics

the study of standards of conduct and moral judgment; also, the standards of right conduct.

Ethics refers to "the principles of conduct governing an individual or a group,"[2] and specifically to the standards you use to decide what your conduct should be. Ethical decisions always involve normative judgments.[3] A **normative judgment** implies that "something is good or bad, right or wrong, better or worse."[4] "You are wearing a skirt and blouse" is a non-normative statement; "That's a great outfit!" is a normative one.

normative judgment

a comparative evaluation stating or implying that something is good or bad, right or wrong, or better or worse.

Ethical decisions also always involve **morality**, in other words, society's accepted ways of behavior. Moral standards differ from other types of standards in several ways.[5] They address matters of serious consequence to society's well-being, such as murder, lying, and slander. They cannot be established or changed by decisions of authoritative bodies like legislatures,[6] and they should override self-interest. Moral judgments are never situational: Something that is morally right (or wrong) in one situation is right (or wrong) in another. Moral judgments tend to trigger strong emotions. Violating moral standards may make you feel ashamed or remorseful. If you see someone else acting immorally, you may feel indignant or resentful.[7]

morality

a society's accepted norms of behavior.

It would simplify things if it was always crystal clear which decisions were ethical and which were not. Unfortunately, this is not always true. Ethics—principles of conduct—are rooted in morality, so in many cases it's true that what is ethical is pretty clear. (For example, if the decision makes the person feel ashamed or remorseful, or involves a matter of serious consequence such as murder, then chances are it's pretty clear that it is probably unethical.) Yet there are many borderline situations you must consider. In Albania, for instance, it may be that bribing is so widely ingrained and viewed as a necessary evil that most people there would not view it as "wrong." The fact that "everyone is doing it" is certainly no excuse. However, the fact that a society as a whole doesn't view bribery as wrong may suggest that a local businessperson making a bribe may not be doing something that we should consider wrong, at least in terms of his or her own frame of reference.

Ethics and the Law

So there you are, trying to decide whether or not to sign your friend's name on the class roll. What will you do? Several factors influence whether specific people in specific situations make ethical or unethical decisions. The law is one. Is there a law against signing your friend's name? Well, perhaps there's just a college rule, so chances are other factors will influence your decision. Let's look at them.

First, something may be legal but not right. You can make a decision that involves ethics (such as firing an employee) based on what is legal. However, that doesn't mean the decision will be ethical, since a legal decision can be unethical (and an ethical one illegal). Firing a 38-year-old employee just before she has earned the right to her pension may be unethical, but generally it is not illegal. Charging a naïve customer an exorbitant price may be legal but unethical.

Some retailers survey their customers' buying habits by using electronic and infrared surveillance equipment.[8] Videocart, Inc., of Chicago, used infrared sensors in store ceilings to track shopping carts, and video screens on shopping carts as well. Other firms compile information from credit card purchases. These activities are not illegal at the present time. But many believe that such encroachment into a person's privacy is unethical.

▲ This Videocart is equipped with a video screen activated by radio transmitters located in each aisle to show information relevant to that aisle. Other information is also presented, such as a store map, news from *USA Today*, coupons, and store specials.

Individual Standards

People bring to their jobs their own ideas of what is morally right and wrong, so the individual must shoulder most of the credit (or blame) for the ethical decisions he or she makes. Every decision we make and every action we take reflects, for better or worse, the application of our moral standards to the question at hand.

Here's an example. A national survey of CEOs of manufacturing firms was conducted to explain the CEOs' intentions to engage (or to not engage) in two questionable business practices: soliciting a competitor's technological secrets and making payments to foreign government officials to secure business. The researchers concluded that the CEOs' ethical intentions were more strongly affected by their personal predispositions than by environmental pressures or organizational characteristics.[9]

It's hard to generalize about the characteristics of ethical or unethical people, although older people—perhaps because they're more experienced—do tend to make more ethical decisions.

In one study, 421 employees were surveyed to measure the degree to which age, gender, marital status, education, dependent children, region of the country, and years in business influenced responses to ethical decisions. (Decisions included "doing personal business on company time," "not reporting others' violations of company rules and policies," and "calling in sick to take a day off for personal use.") With the exception of age, none of the variables were good predictors of whether a person would make the "right" decision. Older workers in general had stricter interpretations of ethical standards and made more ethical decisions than younger employees.

This generation gap in business ethics has also been found by other researchers.[10] One Baylor University study surveyed 2,156 individuals who were grouped by age; those ages 21–40 represented the younger group, and those age 51–70 represented the older group. As in the previous study, respondents were asked to rate the acceptability of a number of ethics-related vignettes.[11] The following are several of the 16 vignettes used in the study:

1. A company president found that a competitor had made an important scientific discovery that would sharply reduce the profits of his own company. He then hired a key employee of the competitor in an attempt to learn the details of the discovery.

2. In order to increase profits, a general manager used a production process that exceeded legal limits for environmental pollution.

3. Because of pressure from his brokerage firm, a stockbroker recommended a type of bond that he did not consider to be a good investment.

4. A small business received one-fourth of its gross revenue in the form of cash. The owner reported only one-half of the cash receipts for income-tax purposes.

5. A company paid a $350,000 "consulting" fee to an official of a foreign country. In return, the official promised assistance in obtaining a contract that should produce a $10 million profit for the contracting company.

In virtually every case, the older group viewed the ethically questionable decision as more unacceptable than did the younger group. Of course, such findings don't suggest that all older employees are ethical, or that all younger ones are unethical. But they do raise the question of whether the younger employees' relative lack of experience leaves them more open to making "wrong" decisions. One danger is that most people view themselves as being more ethical than others. In other words, most people tend to have a distorted view of how ethical they really are.[12]

The Organization Shapes Ethical Practices

Although ethical crises are sometimes caused by unscrupulous employees, most often that isn't the case. One employee's character flaws rarely cause corporate misconduct. More typically, says one ethics expert,

> Unethical business practice involves the tacit, if not explicit, cooperation of others and reflects the values, attitudes, beliefs, language, and behavioral patterns that define an organization's operating culture. Ethics, then, is as much an organizational as a personal issue.[13]

Sears, Roebuck and Company provides a good example.[14] In 1992 consumers and attorneys general in more than 40 states accused Sears of misleading customers. The specific complaint was that Sears service writers had sold customers unnecessary parts and services, from brake jobs to front-end alignments. Could so many Sears employees have had ethical lapses?

Research by Sears management and by outside experts suggests that a number of organizational factors contributed to the problem. Faced with declining revenues, Sears management tried to boost the financial results of its auto centers by introducing new quotas and incentives for center employees. Advisers later reported that those failing to meet quotas would not only lose commissions, but might be transferred to other jobs or have their work hours reduced.

While building pressure for sales, Sears management apparently didn't do enough to establish a company culture that would encourage ethical decisions. As the then-CEO of Sears Edward Brennan acknowledged, management was responsible for a compensation and goal-setting system that "created an environment in which mistakes did occur."[15] Indeed, the program was probably an honest attempt to boost sales. This is perhaps the scariest lesson of all: Honest people with good intentions can create conditions in which unethical decisions can flourish. Once the allegations became public, Sears' top management took steps to prevent further occurrences. Unfortunately for Sears and its stockholders, the total cost of settling the various lawsuits and providing customer refunds was an estimated $60 million.[16]

Is Sears an isolated case? Psychologist Saul Gellerman would say No. He describes how more than 40 years ago, information began to reach Johns Manville Corporation's medical department—and through it the firm's top executives—indicating that asbestos inhalation was a cause of asbestosis (a debilitating lung disease) among its employees. Subsequent testimony in a California court revealed that Manville had hidden the asbestos danger from its employees rather than looking into safer ways to handle it.[17] A New Jersey court was blunt. It "found that Manville had made a conscious, cold-blooded business decision to take no protective or remedial action, in flagrant disregard of the rights of others."[18] After reviewing all the evidence, Gellerman concluded it is inconceivable that for 40 years all Manville managers could have been immoral. Instead:

> The people involved were probably ordinary men and women for the most part, not very different from you and me. They found themselves in a dilemma, and they solved it in a way that seemed to be the least troublesome. The consequences of what they chose to do—both to thousands of innocent people, and, ultimately, to the corporation—probably never occurred to them.[19]

Does paying a hefty fine and having the stock price plummet make companies act more ethically the next time around? Apparently not. Sears had to pay that $60 million, but in 1999 the firm was accused of much the same behavior all over again. Even stockholders don't seem to care. One study focused on what happened after a giant retail food chain had to pay millions of dollars for back wages and civil fines after being accused of child labor violations. The researchers found that the managers "may dismiss fines and slight declines in stock price as inconsequential", and that "investors may also be insufficiently grasping the implications of a conviction."[20] Something more than the threat of getting caught and paying a fine is obviously required to head off unethical behavior.

The Influence of Top Management

The behavior of superiors is an important factor influencing ethical decisions.[21] In fact, many managers seem to feel that unethical actions are acceptable if their superior knows about them and says nothing. One writer gives these examples of how supervisors knowingly (or unknowingly) lead subordinates astray ethically:

- Tell staffers to do whatever is necessary to achieve results.
- Overload top performers to ensure that work gets done.
- Look the other way when wrongdoing occurs.
- Take credit for others' work or shift blame.
- Play favorites.[22]

Ethics Policies and Codes

The leader's actions may be "the single most important factor in fostering corporate behavior of a high ethical standard," but surveys rank an ethics policy as very important, too.[23] A policy signals that top management is serious about ethics and wants to foster a culture that takes ethics seriously.

Many firms have ethics codes. One study surveyed corporate accountants. The researchers found that 56% of the respondents' firms (but only about 25% of small firms) had corporate codes of conduct. Here are some other conclusions from this survey:[24]

Top manager's role. Top management must make it clear that it is serious about code enforcement.[25] Top management also must ensure that customers, suppliers, and employees are all aware of the firm's stress on ethics.

Approval of Code. The researchers concluded that "it is important for the code to be endorsed by executives at or near the top of the organization chart and by employees throughout the organization.[26] In 95% of the firms with codes, the code had been approved by the CEO, the board of directors, or both.

Communication of Code. To influence employee behavior, the ethics code must be communicated. The researchers found that the first step was generally to have top management assign responsibility for implementation of the code to a high-ranking manager, who in turn communicates the code to employees. Although this is an important step, only about 57% of the firms actually sent a copy of their conduct codes to all employees.

Increased workforce diversity may make ethics codes even more important in the future. One expert contends that, with the flow of immigrants across national borders, it may become harder to rely on a shared organizational culture to control ethical behavior. In other words, because it is more difficult to infuse common values and beliefs in a diverse workforce, it may become more necessary to emphasize explicit rules, expectations, and ethics codes.[27]

Recent changes in U.S. federal sentencing guidelines also make it more important than in the past to have an ethics code. Under the new guidelines, the more effort management can show it made to ensure ethical behavior, the lower the fine the company can expect to pay if it is sued for unethical practices and loses. For example, if a company had a published ethics code and program, discovered and reported a violation of law, and then cooperated with authorities and accepted responsibility for the unlawful conduct, the firm might be fined only 5% of the loss suffered by customers. If it had no program and no reporting, offered no cooperation, and took no responsibility, the fine might be 200% of the loss suffered by customers.[28]

Ethics Programs in Practice: Johnson & Johnson

The recurring problems at Sears, as well as those associated with the 2002 Olympics, show that heading off ethical problems is easier said than done. A recent study by the American Society of Chartered Life Underwriters and Chartered Financial Consultants found that 56% of all workers felt some pressure to act unethically or illegally, and that the problem seems to be getting worse. For example, 60% of the workers said they felt more pressure to act unethically than they did five years before, and 40% felt greater pressure than they did just a year before the study was made.[29]

How are well-known companies tackling this problem? We can get a better perspective on how to encourage ethical behavior by looking at an actual corporate ethics program: Johnson & Johnson's. Ethical decision making at Johnson & Johnson has long been symbolized by what the company calls "Our Credo." The credo, presented in Figure 3.2, provides the ethical pillars on which the firm is built and on which it continues to produce its pharmaceutical and health care products. It begins with the statement "We believe our first responsibility is to the doctors, nurses and patients, to mothers and all others who use our products and services."[30] Other elements include "in meeting their needs, everything we do must be of high quality," and "our suppliers and distributors must have an opportunity to make a fair profit."

Stories abound about how the credo's moral standards guide the firm. One describes how Johnson & Johnson reacted when a few poisoned Tylenol capsules

Our Credo

We believe our first responsibility is to the doctors, nurses and patients,
to mothers and fathers and all others who use our products and services.
In meeting their needs everything we do must be of high quality.
We must constantly strive to reduce our costs
in order to maintain reasonable prices.
Customers' orders must be serviced promptly and accurately.
Our suppliers and distributors must have an opportunity
to make a fair profit.

We are responsible to our employees,
the men and women who work with us throughout the world.
Everyone must be considered as an individual.
We must respect their dignity and recognize their merit.
They must have a sense of security in their jobs.
Compensation must be fair and adequate,
and working conditions clean, orderly and safe.
We must be mindful of ways to help our employees fulfill
their family responsibilities.
Employees must feel free to make suggestions and complaints.
There must be equal opportunity for employment, development
and advancement for those qualified.
We must provide competent management,
and their actions must be just and ethical.

We are responsible to the communities in which we live and work
and to the world community as well.
We must be good citizens — support good works and charities
and bear our fair share of taxes.
We must encourage civic improvements and better health and education.
We must maintain in good order
the property we are privileged to use,
protecting the environment and natural resources.

Our final responsibility is to our stockholders.
Business must make a sound profit.
We must experiment with new ideas.
Research must be carried on, innovative programs developed
and mistakes paid for.
New equipment must be purchased, new facilities provided
and new products launched.
Reserves must be created to provide for adverse times.
When we operate according to these principles,
the stockholders should realize a fair return.

Johnson & Johnson

◄ FIGURE 3.2

**Johnson & Johnson's
Corporate Credo**

Source: Courtesy of Johnson & Johnson.

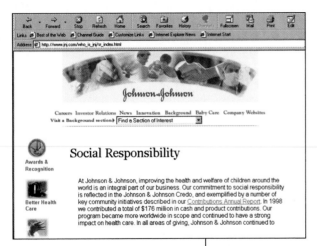

Social Responsibility

At Johnson & Johnson, improving the health and welfare of children around the world is an integral part of our business. Our commitment to social responsibility is reflected in the Johnson & Johnson Credo, and exemplified by a number of key community initiatives described in our Contributions Annual Report. In 1998 we contributed a total of $176 million in cash and product contributions. Our program became more worldwide in scope and continued to have a strong impact on health care. In all areas of giving, Johnson & Johnson continued to

▲ **WEBNOTE**

Johnson & Johnson uses the Web to communicate its credo to its employees, investors, and others.
www.johnsonandjohnson.com
Source: Used with permission.

were discovered some years ago. Because "our first responsibility is to the doctors, nurses and patients," Johnson & Johnson recalled all outstanding capsules. The decision cost the firm hundreds of millions of dollars in lost sales. But in five months, J&J had produced a new tamper-resistant Tylenol product and regained 70% of its market share. Within several years, its market share was fully restored.

The credo has also been described as the glue that helps hold the firm together and the heart of its ethics culture.[31] Johnson & Johnson is a widely diversified international company with over 160 businesses in 50 countries. Its products range from baby powder to toothbrushes to contact lenses.[32] It is also very decentralized, with the presidents of its subsidiaries "usually left very much on their own in terms of the way in which they will manage their particular company."[33] By evaluating, promoting, and continually reminding all employees of the credo's importance, the company has used it to give its far-flung managers a common focus and set of standards. Whether the managers are working in Asia, South America, France, or the United States, the firm's home office can be assured that company values will be adhered to by employees around the world.

How to Foster Ethics at Work

After a review of the ethics programs at eleven major firms, one study concluded that fostering ethics at work involved five main steps:

1. *Emphasize top management's commitment.* "To achieve results, the chief executive officer and those around the CEO need to be openly and strongly committed to ethical conduct, and give constant leadership in tending and renewing the values of the organization."[34]

2. *Publish a "code."* Firms with effective ethics programs set forth principles of conduct for the whole organization in the form of written documents.[35]

3. *Establish compliance mechanisms.* For example, pay attention to values and ethics in recruiting and hiring; emphasize corporate ethics in training; institute communications programs to inform and motivate employees; and audit to ensure compliance.[36]

4. *Involve personnel at all levels.* For example, use roundtable discussions among small groups of employees regarding corporate ethics and surveys of employee attitudes regarding the state of ethics in the firm.[37]

5. *Measure results.* All eleven firms used surveys or audits to monitor compliance with ethical standards.[38] The results of audits should then be discussed among board members and employees.[39]

► CREATING THE RIGHT CULTURE

You know from your own experience that it's not just what you say that's important; it's what you do. A father can talk about being ethical till he's blue in the face, but if his children see him always cutting ethical corners—bringing home "free" office supplies from where he works, or bragging about buying stocks based on "inside" information, for instance—his children may learn that "being unethical is really ok."

The same is true in organizations. Whether it's in regard to ethics or some other matter, the manager—and especially the top manager—creates a culture by what he or she says and does, and the employees then take their signals from that behavior and from that culture.

What Is Organizational Culture?

Organizational culture can be defined as the characteristic traditions and values employees share. Values (such as "be honest," "be thrifty," and "don't be bureaucratic") are basic beliefs about what you should or shouldn't do and what is or is not important. Values guide and channel behavior; leading and influencing people and molding their ethical behavior therefore depends in part on influencing the values they use as behavioral guides.

Let's take a closer look at what organizational culture means. To do that, think for a moment about what comes to mind when you hear the word *culture* applied to a country. In France, China, or the United States, you'd probably think of at least three things. Culture means, first, the *physical aspects* of the society, things like art, music, and theater. Culture also means the *values* citizens share—for instance, the emphasis on "equality" and fraternity in France, or on democracy and hard work in the United States, and the assumptions—such as "people can govern themselves"—that the values stem from. By culture you'd also probably mean the characteristic way the people of that country *behave*—the patience of the people in England, or the emphasis on fine food and art among the people of France.

▲ Autodesk, Inc., a software company in San Rafael, California, welcomes employees' dogs in the workplace.

We can use this country culture analogy to get a better understanding of the components of organizational culture. **Cultural artifacts** are the obvious signs and symbols of corporate culture, such as written rules, office layouts, organizational structure, and dress codes.[40] Organizational culture also includes the company's **patterns of behavior**, such as ceremonial events, written and spoken comments, and actual employee behaviors. For example, the firm's managers and employees may engage in behaviors such as hiding information, politicking, or expressing honest concern when a colleague requires assistance.

In turn, these cultural signs and behaviors are a product of **values and beliefs**, such as "the customer is always right" or "don't be bureaucratic." These guiding standards—these values and beliefs—lay out what ought to be, as distinct from what is.[41] If management's *stated* values and beliefs differ from what the managers actually value and believe, this will show up in their behavior. For example, Fred Smith, founder and chairman of FedEx, says that many firms *say* they believe in respecting their employees and putting their people first.[42] But in a lot of these firms it's not what the managers say, but the way they behave—insisting on time clocks, routinely downsizing, and so on—that makes it clear what their values really are.

Organizational culture is important to ethics because a firm's culture reflects its shared values, and these in turn help guide and channel employees' behavior. At Sears, for instance, the service advisers and mechanics apparently had little to go by in making decisions other than the "boost sales"–oriented incentive plan and quotas top management had put in place. There was not a strong set of shared values

organizational culture
the characteristic set of values and ways of behaving that employees in an organization share.

cultural artifacts
the obvious signs and symbols of corporate culture, such as organizational structure, policies, and dress codes.

patterns of behavior
in organizational behavior, the ceremonial events, written and spoken comments, and actual behaviors of an organization's members that contribute to creating the organizational culture.

values and beliefs
the guiding standards of an organization, such as "the customer is always right" or "don't be bureaucratic," that affirm what should be practiced, as distinct from what is practiced.

throughout the company that said, for instance, "potentially unethical sales practices will not be tolerated," and "the most important thing is to provide our customers with top-quality services that they really need."

The Managers' Influence

Managers play a major role in creating and sustaining a firm's culture, through the actions they take and the comments they make. Following are some specific ways in which managers can shape their organization's culture.

Clarify Expectations   First, make it clear what your expectations are with respect to the values you want subordinates to follow. For example, investment banking firm Goldman Sachs has long been guided by a set of written principles, such as "our client's interests always come first," and "we take great pride in the professional quality of our work."

Publishing a formal core values statement is thus a logical first step in creating a culture. For example, Figure 3.2 summarizes the core values credo of Johnson & Johnson: "We believe our first responsibility is to the doctors, nurses and patients, to mothers and fathers and all others who use our products and services. In meeting their needs everything we do must be of high quality.[43]

A firm's values should then guide the company's behavior. When Johnson & Johnson faced the poisoned Tylenol capsules crisis several years ago, the management knew from the credo what it had to do: Be responsible to patients, mothers, and so on, emphasize high quality, and be good citizens.[44]

Use Signs and Symbols   Remember that it's not just what the manager says but what he or she does that subordinates will pick up on. At Sears, for instance, it was important that top managers not just pay lip service to the importance of top-quality ethical service. After problems arose, they also tried to engage in practices that symbolized those values. For example, they eliminated the service quotas and the commission incentive plan for service advisers. And they instituted unannounced shopping audits. Yet, given the problem's apparent reoccurrence in 1999, the steps they took may have been insufficient.

Many believe that the symbolism—what the manager says and does and the signals he or she sends—ultimately does the most to create and sustain the company's culture. At Saturn Corporation—known for its culture of quality, teamwork, and respect for the individual—one of the firm's top managers said this about company culture:

> Creating a value system that encourages the kind of behavior you want is not enough. The challenge is then to engage in those practices that symbolize those values [and] tell people what is really O.K. to do and what not [to do]. Actions, in other words, speak much more loudly than words.[45]

Signs and symbols, stories, and rites and ceremonies are concrete examples of such actions.

signs and symbols
practices and actions that create and sustain a company's culture.

Signs and symbols are used throughout strong-culture firms to create and sustain the company's culture. At Ben & Jerry's, the "joy gang" is a concrete symbol of the firm's values (charity, fun, and goodwill toward fellow workers). The joy gang is a voluntary group that meets once or twice a week to create new ways to inject fun into what the Ben & Jerry's people do, often by giving out "joy grants," which are "five hundred quick, easy, no-strings attached dollars for long-term improvements to your work area."[46] Sam Walton's hula dance on Wall Street (after Wal-Mart met its goals) is another example of a culture-building symbol.

Stories illustrating important company values are also widely used to reinforce the firm's culture. Thus, at Procter & Gamble there are many stories about relatively trivial decisions going all the way to the top of the company.[47] IBM has similar stories, such as how IBM salespeople took dramatic steps (like driving all night through storms) to get parts to customers.

Rites and ceremonies can also symbolize the firm's values and help convert employees to them. At JC Penney (where loyalty and tradition are values), new management employees are inducted at ritualistic conferences into the "Penney Partnership." Here they commit to the firm's ideology as embodied in its statement of core values. Each inductee solemnly swears allegiance to these values and then receives his or her "H.C.S.C. lapel pin." These letters symbolize JC Penney's core values of honor, confidence, service, and cooperation.

The following "People Side of Managing" box provides an example of culture in action.

THE **PEOPLE** SIDE OF MANAGING

▥ Corporate Culture at Procter & Gamble

Procter & Gamble's culture reflects what one management theorist has called the firm's legendary emphasis on "thoroughness, market-testing, and ethical behavior," values that are transmitted to new employees through selection, socialization, and training processes.[48]

The basic elements of Procter & Gamble's strong corporate culture go back to the founders, William Procter and James Gamble. They started P&G in Cincinnati in 1837 to produce relatively inexpensive household products that were technically superior to those of the competition, quickly consumed, and an integral part of their customers' lifestyle.[49] Their intention was to "foster growth in an orderly manner, to reflect the standards set by the founders, and to plan and prepare for the future."[50]

This philosophy was translated into several core P&G values. The emphasis on orderly growth manifests itself in "tremendous conformity."[51] A new recruit soon learns to say *we* instead of *I*.[52] This conformity bolsters thoroughness and a methodical approach. Its result, according to one past chair, is a "consistency of principles and policy that gives us direction, thoroughness, and self-discipline."[53]

Procter & Gamble's culture manifests itself in and is sustained by various management practices. College graduates are recruited and placed in highly competitive situations. Those who can't learn the system are quickly weeded out; the remainder enjoy the benefits of promotion from within. As a result, no one reaches middle management without 5 to 10 years of close scrutiny and training. This in turn creates what one researcher called "a homogeneous leadership group with an enormous amount of common experience and strong set of shared assumptions."[54]

New recruits may assume major responsibility for projects almost immediately, but the authority for most big decisions is made far up the chain of command, usually by committees of managers. Nearly everything must be approved through a written memo process. Stories abound that reinforce this process; one describes the decision about the color of the Folger's coffee lid, supposedly made by the CEO after four years of extensive market testing.[55]

Internal competition is fostered by the brand management system: Brands compete for internal resources, have their own advertising and marketing, and act as independent cost centers. The extensive use of memos, the continual rechecking of each other's work, and the rigid timeline for promotions also contribute to (and reflect) P&G's strong culture and emphasis on thoroughness.

Corporate social responsibility refers to the extent to which companies should and do channel resources toward improving one or more segments of society other than the firm's own stockholders. Socially responsible behavior might include creating jobs for minorities, controlling pollution, or supporting educational facilities or cultural events.

As you know from reading and watching the news, social responsibility issues comprise a major part of the environmental forces with which managers must cope. Hardly a day goes by without news reports about companies grappling with problems like oil spills, pollution control, or manufacturing products in sweatshops. As you can see from these examples, social responsibility is also largely an ethical issue, since it involves questions of what is morally right or wrong with regard to the firm's responsibilities. As you will see, though, there is less unanimity regarding what is right or wrong in this area than there is with respect to traditional ethical issues such as bribery, stealing, and corporate dishonesty. Many perfectly ethical people strongly believe that a company's only social responsibility is to its shareholders.

Being Socially Responsible Today

The Asia Monitor Resource Center   Hidden on a small street in Hong Kong's Kowloon area is the tiny headquarters of the Asia Monitor Resource Center, whose job is to monitor working conditions in mainland China. Its reports often shock huge U.S. firms like Disney, and help to illustrate what socially responsible behavior means today. Its aim is to uncover and publicize unacceptable working conditions in plants producing products for global firms. It hopes to thereby improve working conditions for manufacturing workers in mainland China.

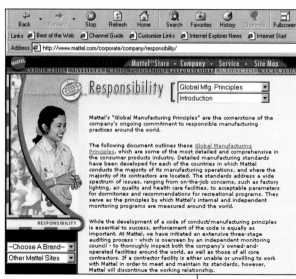

What sorts of unethical practices does the center report? Its Disney report alleges that some mainland Chinese employed by Disney contractors were working up to 16 hours a day, seven days a week, and paid little or no overtime. Another report, on China's toy industry, describes what some have called "sweatshop Barbie" assembly lines, because of abuses including long work hours and heavy fines for workers.

Companies with brands especially vulnerable to such criticism have been among the first to react in a socially responsible way. In fact, the plants of contractors for firms like Disney and Mattel are now reportedly among some the most progressive in mainland China.[56] Both Disney and Mattel have codes of conduct, and Disney has carried out tens of thousands of inspections of its contractors' plants to make sure they comply. Disney even cut off one of its noncomplying factories. Mattel emphasizes that it has received the certificate of workplace standards that Asia Monitor itself calls for.

▲   **W E B N O T E**

Mattel was one of the first companies to react in a socially responsible way to charges that workplace conditions in its mainland China plants were poor: Mattel has a code of conduct called Global Manufacturing Principles, and its plants are now reportedly some of the most progressive in China.

www.mattel.com

Source: © 1999 Mattel, Inc. All rights reserved.

Ben & Jerry's   Managers must make up their own minds regarding where on the social responsibility scale their firm should lie. For Ben &

Jerry's ice cream company, the decision was never in doubt. Founders Ben Cohen and Jerry Greenfield started a company that had, as part of its mission,

> To operate the company in a way that actively recognizes the central role that business plays in the structure of a society by initiating innovative ways to improve the quality of life of a broad community: local, national and international.[57]

How does Ben & Jerry's put its socially responsible mission into practice? The firm has "green teams" responsible for assessing environmental impact and for developing and implementing programs to reduce any negative impact. The firm donates (at its board's discretion) 7.5% of its pretax earnings to the Ben & Jerry's Foundation, a nonprofit institution established by personal contributions from founders Cohen and Greenfield. And, in explaining Ben & Jerry's choice of suppliers, Ben Cohen says:

> Wild Maine Blueberry is another step in how we are defining what caring capitalism is all about. Our goal is to integrate a concern for the community in every business decision we make. We are trying to develop a system that improves the quality of life through socially conscious purchasing of our ingredients. For example, the brownies in Chocolate Fudge Brownie benefit the employment of underskilled persons.[58]

To Whom Should the Corporation Be Responsible?

Mattel's run-in with the Asia Monitor Resource Center helps to crystallize the dilemma that lies at the heart of social responsibility: To whom should a company be socially responsible? Improving workers' living standards in China is certainly a laudable and socially responsible goal. But would it not be more socially responsible, others ask, for the company to concentrate on boosting its profits, so that its stockholder-owners and their families would gain?

Managerial Capitalism   The classic view of social responsibility is that a corporation's primary purpose is to maximize profits for its stockholders. Today, this view is most notably associated with economist and Nobel laureate Milton Friedman, who said,

> The view has been gaining widespread acceptance that corporate officials and labor leaders have a "social responsibility" that goes beyond the interest of their stockholders or their members. This view shows a fundamental misconception of the character and nature of the free economy. In such an economy, there is one and only one social responsibility of business—to use its resources and engage in activities designed to increase its profits so long as it stays within the rules of the game, which is to say, engages in open and free competition, without deception and fraud. . . . Few trends could so thoroughly undermine the very foundation of our free society as the acceptance by corporate officials of a social responsibility other than to make as much money for their stockholders as possible.[59]

Friedman's position is built on two main arguments.[60] First, stockholders are owners of the corporation and so the corporate profits belong to them and to them alone. Second, stockholders deserve their profits because these profits derive from a voluntary contract among the various corporate stakeholders—the community receives tax money, suppliers are paid, employees earn wages, and so on. Everyone gets their due, and additional social responsibility is not needed.

► FIGURE 3.3

A Corporation's Major Stakeholders

One view of social responsibility is that a firm must consider and serve all the stakeholders that may be affected by its business decisions.

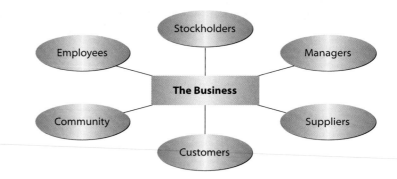

Stakeholder Theory An opposing view is that business has a social responsibility to serve all the corporate stakeholders affected by its business decisions. A **corporate stakeholder** is "any group which is vital to the survival and success of the corporation."[61] As in Figure 3.3, six stakeholder groups are traditionally identified: stockholders (owners), employees, customers, suppliers, managers, and the local community (although conceivably others could be identified as well).[62] To stakeholder advocates, being socially responsible means more than just maximizing profits; being up front with employees (unlike the manager in the cartoon) is important too.

Whereas Friedman's corporation focuses on maximizing profits, stakeholder theory holds that[63]

> the corporation should be managed for the benefit of [all] its stakeholders: its customers, suppliers, owners, employees, and local communities. The rights of these groups must be ensured, and, further, the groups must participate, in some sense, in decisions that substantially affect their welfare.[64]

corporate stakeholder

any person or group that is important to the survival and success of the corporation.

"Some things, Morris, are more easily expressed through puppets."

The Moral Minimum Between the extremes of Friedman's capitalism and stakeholder theory is an intermediate position known as the **moral minimum**. Advocates agree that the purpose of the corporation is to maximize profits, but subject to the requirement that it must do so in conformity with the moral minimum,[65] meaning that the firm should be free to strive for profits so long as it commits no harm. By this view, a business would certainly have a social responsibility not to produce exploding cigarette lighters or operate chemical plants that poison the environment. However, it is unlikely that the social responsibilities of the business would extend to donating profits to charity or educating the poor, for instance.

moral minimum
the idea that corporations should be free to strive for profits so long as they commit no harm.

It would be a mistake to assume that this brief discussion of managerial capitalism, stakeholder theory, and the moral minimum adequately summarizes the complicated field of corporate responsibility. For example, "the moral minimum" is certainly not the only intermediate position between managerial capitalism and stakeholder theory. Indeed, many find the idea that maximizing profits is acceptable, as long as the company adheres to the moral minimum of committing no harm, is itself unacceptable. Similarly, while many definitely do view managerial capitalism as a worthy goal, many others would tell managers that in reality ignoring the interests of non-owner stakeholders—ignoring the needs of the community in which the corporation has facilities, for instance—is bound to be counterproductive. The bottom line is that when it comes to being socially responsible there are a range of options a manager can pursue. How he or she decides to deal with these issues should reflect an intelligent and informed decision, one built around a strong sense of what is right and wrong.

How to Improve Social Responsiveness

The question of how to improve a company's social responsiveness isn't easy to answer because, as we've seen, there's no agreement on what being socially responsible means. Some companies take a proactive approach: They make being socially responsible the core of almost all their decisions. Other companies seem to pay as little attention to being socially responsible as they can. Others (such as Disney and Mattel) fall somewhere in the middle: They pursue socially responsible aims after being gently reminded to do so. Being proactively socially responsible is not the only option pursued by companies today.

Corporate Social Monitoring: The Social Audit Given a commitment to being socially responsible, how can firms ensure that they are in fact responsive? Some firms monitor how well they measure up to their aims by using a rating system called a **corporate social audit**.[66]

corporate social audit
a rating system used to evaluate a corporation's performance with regard to meeting its social obligations.

The Sullivan Principles for Corporate Labor and Community Relations in South Africa was one of the first such rating systems.[67] The Reverend Leon Sullivan was an African-American minister and GM board of directors member. For several years during the 1970s he had tried to pressure the firm to withdraw from South Africa, whose multiracial population was divided by government-sanctioned racist policies, known as *apartheid*.

As part of that effort, Sullivan formulated the code that came to be named for him, the purpose of which was "to guide U.S. business in its social and moral agenda in South Africa."[68] The code provided for measurable standards by which U.S. companies operating in South Africa could be audited, including nonsegregation of the races in all eating, comfort, and work facilities, and "equal pay for all employees doing equal or comparable work for the same period of time."[69] In the 1990s he pro-

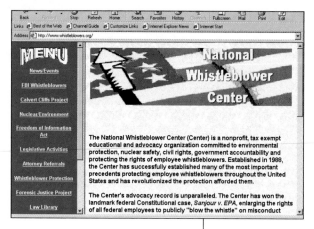

▲ **WEBNOTE**

Employees today can more easily "blow the whistle" on employers' misdeeds thanks to Web-based information and applications like those in this site.

www.whistleblowers.org

Source: Used with permission of National Whistleblowers Center, Washington, DC.

whistle-blowing

the activities of employees who try to report organizational wrongdoing.

posed a new code for companies returning to South Africa after *apartheid* had ended stressing the protection of equal rights and the promotion of education and job training.

Whistle-Blowing Many firms have a reputation for actively discouraging whistle-blowing, the activities of employees who try to report organizational wrongdoing. Yet many arguments can be made for actually *encouraging* whistle-blowers. In a firm that adheres to the moral minimum view, for instance, whistle-blowers can help the company avoid doing harm. As one writer put it, whistle-blowers "represent one of the least expensive and most efficient sources of feedback about mistakes the firm may be making."[70] Other firms find the "benefit of muffling whistle-blowers is illusory."[71] Once the damage has been done—whether it is asbestos hurting workers or a chemical plant making hundreds of people ill—the cost of making the damage right can be enormous.[72]

▶ MANAGING DIVERSITY

The workforces of countries around the world are becoming increasingly diverse. Almost half the net addition to the U.S. workforce in the 1990s was nonwhite and almost two-thirds female.[73] Similarly, it's been estimated that minorities comprise 8%–10% of the population in France, 5% in the Netherlands, and a growing proportion in Italy, Germany, and much of Europe.[74] Even Japan, historically a homogeneous society, will have to find ways to accommodate at least many more women in its workforce.[75]

Diversity is thus a central part of most managers' environments and will confront managers with ethical and other challenges of epic proportions. For example, as we've seen in this and the preceding chapter, people from different cultures often have values, traditions, and ways of looking at things that are unique to their culture: that's why it's important for managers to have global brains.

Diversity is both a blessing and a curse. Bringing together people with different values and views can, for instance, ensure that problems are attacked in a richer, more multifaceted way. On the other hand, research findings show that diversity makes it harder to create a smoothly functioning team: "These findings are consistent with the idea that the more similar people are in background [traits] such as socio-economic status or attitudes, the more attractive they are likely to be to each other, at least initially."[76] Creating a close-knit and efficient multicultural team can therefore be quite a challenge.

▲ Workplace diversity: the night crew at a Home Depot store in California.

But diversity also creates enormous opportunities. There is, for instance, the opportunity to attract and retain the best possible human talent, and to boost creativity and innovation by bringing different points of view to bear on problems. In any case, diversity is increasingly a necessity. For example, most industrialized countries are becoming more diverse, so from a practical point of view, diversity at work can't be avoided. And in a business environment that's increasingly global, virtually every company's workforce will have to be multi-national and multi-ethnic. **Managing diversity** means "planning and implementing organizational systems and practices to manage people so that the potential advantages of diversity are maximized while its potential disadvantages are minimized."[77]

Bases for Diversity

A workforce is **diverse** when it is composed of two or more groups, each of whose members are identifiable and distinguishable based on demographic or other characteristics. The bases on which groups can be distinguished are numerous. However, when managers talk of diversity, they usually do so based on at least the following groups:[78]

- *Racial and ethnic groups.* African Americans, Pacific Islanders, Asian Americans, Native Americans, and other people of color now comprise about 25% of the U.S. population.
- *Women* will represent about 48% of the U.S. workforce by 2005.
- *Older workers.* By 2005, the average age of the U.S. workforce will be 40, up from an average of 36 years and reflecting the gradual aging of the workforce and the larger number of older people remaining at work.
- *People with disabilities.* The Americans with Disabilities Act makes it illegal to discriminate against people with disabilities who are otherwise qualified to do the job, and this act has thrown a spotlight on the large number of people with disabilities in the U.S. workforce.
- *Sexual/affectional orientation.* It has been estimated that about 10% of the population is gay, which may make gays a larger percentage of the workforce than some racial and ethnic minorities.[79]

Barriers in Dealing with Diversity

Any attempt at managing diversity has to begin with an understanding of the barriers that may prevent a company from taking full advantage of the potential in its diverse workforce. These barriers include the following.

Stereotyping and Prejudice   Stereotyping and prejudice are two sides of the same coin. **Stereotyping** is a process in which specific behavioral traits are ascribed to individuals on the basis of their apparent membership in a group.[80] **Prejudice** is a bias that results from prejudging someone on the basis of some trait.

Most people form stereotyped lists of behavioral traits that they identify with certain groups. Unfortunately, many of these stereotypes, in addition to being inaccurate, carry negative connotations. For example, stereotypical "male" traits might include strong, cruel, aggressive, and loud; "female" traits might include weak, softhearted, meek, and gentle.[81] When someone allows stereotypical traits like these to bias them for or against someone, then we say the person is prejudiced.

managing diversity
planning and implementing organizational systems and practices to manage people in a way that maximizes the potential advantages of diversity while minimizing its potential disadvantages.

diverse
describes a workforce comprised of two or more groups, each of which can be identified by demographic or other characteristics.

stereotyping
attributing specific behavioral traits to individuals on the basis of their apparent membership in a group.

prejudice
a bias that results from prejudging someone on the basis of the latter's particular trait or traits.

ethnocentrism

a tendency to view members of one's own group as the center of the universe and to view other social groups less favorably than one's own.

Ethnocentrism Ethnocentrism is prejudice on a grand scale. It can be defined as a tendency "for viewing members of one's own group as the center of the universe and for viewing other social groups (out-groups) less favorably than one's own." Ethnocentrism can be a very significant barrier to managing diversity. For example, white managers have been found to attribute the performance of blacks less to their ability and effort and more to help they received from others; conversely, white managers attributed the performance of whites to their own abilities and efforts.[82]

Discrimination Whereas prejudice means a bias toward prejudging someone based on that person's traits, discrimination refers to taking specific actions toward or against the person based on the person's group.[83] Of course, in many countries, including the United States, many forms of discrimination are against the law. In the United States it is generally illegal to discriminate against someone solely based on that person's age, race, gender, disability, or country of national origin.

discrimination

a behavioral bias toward or against a person based on the group to which the person belongs.

Discrimination continues to be a barrier to diversity management. For example, many argue that there is an invisible "glass ceiling," enforced by an "old boys' network" and friendships built in places like exclusive clubs, that effectively prevents women from breaking into the top ranks of management.

Tokenism Tokenism occurs when a company appoints a small group of women or minority-group members to high-profile positions, rather than more aggressively seeking full representation for that group. Tokenism is a diversity barrier when it slows the process of hiring or promoting more members of the minority group.

tokenism

symbolically appointing a small number of minority-group members to high-profile positions instead of more aggressively achieving full representation for that group.

Token employees often also fare poorly. Research suggests, for instance, that token employees face obstacles to full participation, success, and acceptance in the company. There is also a tendency for their performance, good or bad, to be magnified because of the extra attention their distinctiveness creates.[84]

gender-role stereotype

usually, the association of women with certain behaviors and possibly (often lower-level) jobs.

Gender Roles In addition to problems like glass ceilings, working women confront gender-role stereotypes, in other words, the tendency to associate women with certain (frequently nonmanagerial) jobs. In one study, attractiveness was advantageous for female interviewees only when the job was nonmanagerial. When the position was managerial, there was a tendency for a woman's attractiveness to reduce her chances of being hired and getting a good starting salary.[85]

Boosting Performance by Managing Diversity

As mentioned above, managing diversity means maximizing diversity's potential advantages while minimizing its potential barriers. In practice, doing so includes both legally mandated and voluntary management actions.

There are, of course, many legally mandated actions employers must take to minimize workplace discrimination. For example, employers should avoid discriminatory employment advertising (such as "young man wanted for sales position"), and prohibit sexual harassment. Yet, while actions like these can reduce the more blatant barriers, blending a diverse workforce into a close-knit community also requires other steps, as Figure 3.4 shows. Based on his research, one diversity expert

▲ **W E B N O T E**

Companies like JCPenney use the Web to promote their commitment to diversity.
www.jcpenny.net
Source: Courtesy of JCPenny.

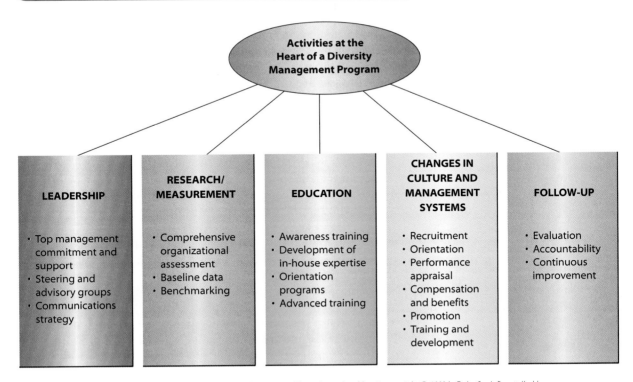

concludes that five sets of activities are at the heart of a managing diversity program, as follows:

Provide Strong Leadership Companies with exemplary reputations are typically led by chief executives who champion diversity's cause. Leadership in this case means taking a strong personal stand on the need for change; becoming a role model for the behaviors required for the change; and providing the mental energy and financial and other support needed to implement actual changes, for instance in hiring practices. It can also mean writing a statement that defines what you mean by diversity and how diversity is linked to your business.[86]

Research: Assess Your Situation The company must assess its current situation with respect to diversity management. This might include using surveys to measure current employee attitudes and perceptions toward different cultural groups in the company and about relationships between the groups.

Provide Diversity Training and Education One expert says "the most commonly utilized starting point for . . . managing diversity is some type of employee education program."[87] Employers typically use several types of programs, most often a one- to three-day workshop aimed at increasing awareness and sensitivity to diversity issues.

What might such a seminar cover? Suggestions include involve a diverse group of employees in the process, and ask them: What does diversity mean to you? Why do you have those perceptions of diversity? What does it mean to our organization? How can we develop an inclusive and positive definition of diversity that will be understood and accepted by everyone?[88] Since disagreements may arise, it's usually best that meetings like this be managed by professional facilitators.

Change Culture and Management Systems Education programs should be combined with other steps aimed at changing the organization's culture and management systems. For example, the performance appraisal procedure might be changed so that supervisors are appraised based partly on their success in minimizing intergroup conflicts. Many companies also institute mentoring programs. Mentoring is defined as "a relationship between a younger adult and an older, more experienced adult in which the mentor provides support, guidance, and counseling to enhance the protégé's success at work and in other arenas of life."[89]

Mentoring can contribute to diversity management efforts: After all, why attract a diverse workforce and then simply leave the new people to sink or swim? A good mentor provides the advice and counsel required to deal with challenges at work, particularly for those who may be new to the workforce.[90]

Evaluate the Diversity Program The evaluation stage is aimed at measuring the diversity management program's results. For example, do the surveys now indicate an improvement in employee attitudes toward diversity? How many employees have entered into mentoring relationships, and do these relationships appear to be successful?

What effects do diversity programs have on employee attitudes and points of view? Do they actually boost mutual understanding? Many peoples' first experience with formal diversity programs is in college, so schools' experiences with such programs can be informative. A study conducted by the former presidents of Harvard and Princeton was recently reported in the *Harvard Business Review*: Some results are presented in Figure 3.5.[91]

The findings suggest that diversity has generally had a positive impact on university education and on student attitudes. For example, the study found "a strong and growing belief in the value of enrolling a diverse student body," and "[a] belief among graduates that college had contributed much to their ability to work well and get along with members of other races."[92] At least in college, in other words, programs aimed at encouraging and managing diversity seem to be having the desired effects.

▶ **FIGURE 3.5**

The Impact of Diversity on Education

Source: Reprinted by permission of *Harvard Business Review.* An exhibit from "A Report Card on Diversity," January–February 1999, Copyright © 1999 by the President and Fellows of Harvard College. All rights reserved.

What College Diversity Management Survey Data Show

- A strong and growing belief among graduates in the value of enrolling a diverse student body;

- the affirmation by 79% of white graduates that race-sensitive admissions policies at their alma mater should either be retained or strengthened;

- almost exactly the same level of support for diversity by white matriculants who had been turned down by their first-choice school (and who might therefore be expected to resent race-sensitive admissions policies);

- a significant degree of social interaction between the races during college;

- the belief among graduates that college had contributed much to their ability to work well and get along with members of other races.

1. Managers face ethical choices every day. Ethics refers to the principles of conduct governing an individual or a group. Ethical decisions always include both normative and moral judgments.

2. Being legal and being ethical are not necessarily the same thing. A decision can be legal but still unethical, or ethical but still illegal.

3. Several factors influence whether specific people in specific organizations make ethical or unethical decisions. The individual making the decision must ultimately shoulder most of the credit (or blame) for any ethical decision he or she makes. However, the organization itself—including its leadership, culture, and incentive/compensation plan—also shapes an individual employee's behavior.

4. Ethics policies and codes are important. They send a strong signal that top management is serious about ethics and are a sign that it wants to foster a culture that takes ethics seriously.

5. Managers take several steps to foster ethics at work: emphasizing top management's commitment, publishing a code, establishing compliance mechanisms, involving personnel at all levels, and measuring results.

6. Organizational culture may be defined as the characteristic traditions, norms, and values that employees share. Values are basic beliefs about what you should or shouldn't do and what is and is not important.

7. Several things contribute to creating and sustaining the corporate culture. One is a formal core values statement. Leaders also play a role in creating and sustaining culture. One of a leader's most important functions is to influence the culture and shared values of his or her organization. Managers also use signs and symbols, stories, and rites and ceremonies to create and sustain their companies' cultures.

8. Social responsibility is largely an ethical issue, since it involves questions of what is morally right or wrong with regard to the firm's responsibilities. People differ in answering the question, To whom should the corporation be responsible? Some say solely to stockholders, and some say to all stakeholders. Some take an intermediate position: They agree that the purpose of the corporation is to maximize profits, but subject to the requirement that it must do so in conformity with the moral minimum.

9. As the workforce becomes more diverse, it becomes more important to manage diversity so that the benefits of diversity outweigh any potential drawbacks. Potential barriers to managing diversity include stereotyping, prejudice, and tokenism. Managing diversity involves taking steps such as providing strong leadership, assessing the situation, providing training and education, changing the culture and systems, and evaluating the program.

Organizations and their employees get things done within an environment that is continually shifting. Outside forces such as globalization, deregulation, and technological change create a competitive environment, within which managers must do their jobs. Within the company too there's an "environment," consisting of its values, ethics, and culture. Chapters 1 through 3 focused on these outside and inside environments and on how they affect what managers and employees do.

Now, having looked at the things that surround and influence what managers do, we can turn to a detailed discussion of what managers do and how they do it—in others words, to the management process topics of planning, organizing, leading, and controlling. Since making good decisions underlies just about everything else managers do, we turn first to making decisions in Chapter 4.

KEY TERMS

ethics 72
normative judgment 72
morality 72
organizational culture 79
cultural artifacts 79
patterns of behavior 79
values and beliefs 79
signs and symbols 80

stories 81
rites and ceremonies 81
social responsibility 82
corporate stakeholder 84
moral minimum 85
corporate social audit 85
whistle-blowing 86
managing diversity 87

diverse 87
stereotyping 87
prejudice 87
ethnocentrism 88
discrimination 88
tokenism 88
gender-role stereotype 88
mentoring 90

SKILLS AND STUDY MATERIALS

CRITICAL THINKING EXERCISES

1. You work for a medical genetics research firm as a marketing person. You love the job. The location is great, the hours are good, and work is challenging and flexible. You receive a much higher salary than you ever anticipated. You hear via the rumor mill that the company's elite medical team has cloned the first human, the CEO. It was such a total success that you have heard that they may clone every employee so that they can use the clones to harvest body parts as the original people age or become ill. You are not sure you believe in cloning. You joined the firm for reasons of its moral and ethical reputation. You feel that the image presented to you was one of research and development of life-saving drugs and innovative medical procedures. The thought of cloning was never on your mind, but now it must be. What would you do? What are the ethical and cultural issues involved? Do you think that managers in Japan, Sweden, Chile, or France would manage the discovery differently? Why? Do you think cloning will become even a more controversial ethical and moral issue in the future as cloning becomes part of the medical decision making model?

2. A key to ethical perception is realizing that all people bring different views, experiences, and other relevant influences to decisions. This is particularly true in U.S. society. Read the following narratives about perception, and relate them to ethical decision making examples in the workplace.

First narrative, by Taoist writer Lieh-tse: A man noticed that his axe was missing. Then he saw the neighbor's son pass by. The boy looked like a thief, walked like a thief, behaved like a thief. Later that day, the man found his axe where he had left it the day before. The next time he saw the neighbor's son, the boy looked, walked and behaved like an honest, ordinary boy.[93]

Second narrative, by Taoist writer Chuang-tse: An archer competing for a clay vessel shoots effortlessly, his skill and concentration unimpeded. If the prize is changed to a brass ornament, his hands begin to shake. If it is changed to gold, he squints as if he were going blind. His abilities do not deteriorate, but his belief in them does, as he allows the supposed value of an external reward to cloud his vision.[94]

1. In teams of four or five class members, research and then write about the ethical philosophies and attitudes toward business in the following nations: Russia, India, Egypt, Israel, the Congo, Norway, Saudi Arabia, and Australia. Compare and contrast their respective approaches to ethics and corporate social responsibility. Explain why there are differences.

2. You were taking a month's holiday in Europe. In your first week there, you became very ill with a recurring ailment for which you have been treated with limited success in the United States. In fact, it is a chronic condition that is inhibiting your ability to advance your career. The doctors who treated you in Europe have given you some medication that is legal there but has not been approved by the U.S. Food and Drug Administration. You feel better than you have in years. Because the European drug restrictions allow this drug to be purchased across the counter without a prescription, you are able to buy a year's supply. However, you know that it is listed as an illegal drug in the United States and you must pass through customs. What would you do? What are the ethical and moral dilemmas facing you? Is there any action you can take as an individual to change the situation? If your decision is to smuggle the drug in and you are successful, what will you do in a year?

We invite you to visit the Dessler companion Web site at **www.prenhall.com/dessler** for this chapter's Internet resources.

ALLSTATE PLANS TO RESTRUCTURE—CUTTING 4,000 JOBS

C A S E   1

Like many companies, Allstate faces pressure to be both cost competitive and provide new services to its customers. It also faces pressure for continuous improvement in its financial performance from its shareholders. Assuming that for Allstate to survive and prosper it needs to respond to both customers and shareholders, what responsibilities does it have toward another important group of stakeholders, its employees?

Here is the situation. In November 1999 the Allstate Corporation announced a series of strategic initiatives to expand its selling and service capabilities, buy back company shares to raise its stock price, and cut expenses by reducing the workforce. As part of its restructuring, Allstate would transfer its existing captive agency program to a single exclusive agency independent contractor program, thus markedly reducing the need for agency support staff. In its press release on this initiative, Allstate management also announced it would eliminate 4,000 current non-agent positions by the end of 2000, or approximately 10 percent of the company's non-agent workforce.

Said Allstate CEO Edward Liddy, "Now, many of our customers and potential customers are telling us they want our products to be easier to buy, easier to service and more competitively priced. We will combine the power of our agency distribution system with the growth potential of direct selling and electronic commerce. . . . This unique combination is without parallel in the industry and will make Allstate the most customer-focused company in the marketplace."

Proponents of this type of restructuring might argue that Allstate is simply taking the steps needed to be competitive. They might even say that if Allstate did not cut jobs to create the cash flow needed to fund new competitive initiatives, it might ultimately fail as a business, putting all 54,000 of its employees at risk.

Yet Allstate's program raises concerns. One analyst noted that by encouraging customers to purchase insurance products directly from the Internet, Allstate could threaten the commissions of its more than 15,000 agents. The announcement of cost cutting came one day after Allstate announced it would meet its regular quarterly dividend of $0.15 per share. The company has raised its dividend annually since 1993.

Discussion Questions:

1. Is reducing the number of employees in a company in and of itself unethical? Why or why not?

2. If you decided it was generally ethical, what would the company have to do to make the employee dismissals unethical?

3. What responsibilities does a company like Allstate have toward its employees?

4. Is there a moral dimension to the question of marketing Allstate insurance via the Internet?

MITSUBISHI AND ENVIRONMENTALISTS BATTLE OVER BAJA SALT FACTORY

CASE 2

Mitsubishi's proposal must have seemed like a dream to the Mexican government. Mexico has long been known for its *maquilladoras,* factories along the U.S.–Mexican border that produce products in Mexico for export to the rest of North America. While these factories had been a great help to the economy, the Mexican government wanted to see a greater diversity in Mexican manufacturing. It also needed still greater foreign direct investment.

As part of its campaign to secure more foreign investment, the Mexican government proposed a joint venture with the Japanese manufacturing giant, Mitsubishi, to develop the world's largest salt factory, to be located on Mexico's Pacific coast in Baja California. The plant would be adjacent to the breeding habitat of the Pacific gray whale. Several environmental groups opposed the plant location, saying the operation would ruin over 100 square miles of coastal breeding grounds. The area is also host to abalone fishing and is a breeding ground for more than 70 animal species. Mitsubishi earned the wrath of local environmentalists when another plant it operated in Mexico proved to be responsible for the death of 94 endangered turtles.

The International Fund for Animal Welfare (IFAW) announced a campaign in California to boycott Mitsubishi, claiming that the salt project poses a threat to the gray whale. One month later, the money managers of 13 U.S. mutual funds announced they would no longer buy stock in Mitsubishi and urged other funds to do the same. These funds have combined investments of nearly $14 billion.

Mitsubishi had yet to file its environmental impact study. It noted in a public response to IFAW that whale populations have risen to record levels near an existing salt facility. "These latest antics demonstrate a complete abandonment of truthfulness on the part of IFAW," stated James E. Brumm, an executive vice president with Mitsubishi. "They know

better, but they're using the whales as an icon anyway. That doesn't serve anyone's interests—not their donors, [not] the activist community as a whole, and most certainly not the whales. Think of the resources they've wasted on fundraising mailers and celebrity events that could have gone toward legitimate research, education or conservation."

Mitsubishi's corporate code of ethics includes an active position on environmental issues: "Environmental responsibility is an integral part of Mitsubishi Corporation's corporate philosophy. To set forth a clearly defined framework, the company drafted its internal Environmental Guidelines for Business Activities in 1992. After four years of addressing environmental issues, the company formulated an Environmental Charter in 1996 in line with the basic concepts of the ISO 14001, the international standard for environmental management systems. This charter provides a strong base for the company to strive for further progress as a sound global enterprise."

Environmental activists noted that Laguna San Ignacio, the proposed factory site, is the last pristine Pacific gray whale nursery in the world, and is part of a UNESCO World Heritage Site and the Vizcaíno Biosphere Reserve. As part of their campaign against the facility, thirty-four scientists, including nine Nobel Prize winners, have expressed opposition to the project.

Two separate scientific reports were expected to be presented concerning the salt factory. An independent, international team of scientists from the International Union for the Conservation of Nature (IUCN) was to issue a report to the World Heritage Committee Bureau. Following the IUCN publication, a two-year multidisciplinary study by some 40 scientists from prestigious Mexican universities and from the Scripps Institution of Oceanography commissioned by the salt factory would be completed. Unlike the IUCN project, this study will examine every aspect of the potential impact of a new facility—both the environmental impacts and the socioeconomic impacts. Mexico, however, responded to the pressure by cancelling the project.

Discussion Questions:

1. What should Mitsubishi's corporate position be in regard to the environment?

2. How might the initial positions taken by the different stakeholders in this case have affected their evaluation of the scientific reports?

3. What would you have done differently if you were Mitsubishi's CEO? Why?

YOU BE THE CONSULTANT

KNITMEDIA

ETHICS AND CON EDISON

One of the many differences between managing a small business like KnitMedia and a giant like GE is this: You rarely have your local electric utility coming in and shutting off the power when you're the president of GE.

The Knitting Factory faced a dilemma as Con Edison, New York City's electric utility, came close to putting the club out of business, at least for one long weekend. With bills of about $2,000 a month, the Knitting Factory was occasionally late with its payments. Con Edison reacted by demanding an $800 deposit, and even Michael Dorf's letters, formal complaint, and visit to the local Con Ed office weren't enough to get Con Ed to change its mind. Now it's 5:45 PM Friday—the start of the Knitting Factory's heavy weekend schedule. Four refrigerators are filled with chilled products. A Con Edison employee has just come into the bar, saying he's there to read meters. He proceeds to turn off the Knitting Factory's electric service.

Michael Dorf has what you might say is an ethical and managerial dilemma. On the one hand, it's too late to pay Con Ed, and a company KnitMedia's size simply can't afford to just walk away from a full weekend of performances. There is one choice: There is a living area above the club and the electricity is still turned on in that space. Dorf and his managers could quickly rig up extension cords from the apartment and keep the Knitting Factory running all weekend. Doing so would raise some questions, however. For instance, is that the ethical thing to do? And what would be the ethical and moral implications if the electric lines overheated and something went wrong? Michael Dorf asks you what to do.

Team Exercises and Questions

Use what you learned in this chapter to answer the following questions from Michael and his management team:

1. Assume the Knitting Factory will incur a substantial loss without electric power for the weekend, and that Con Ed was aware of that. Do you believe Con Ed's decision to cut the power was an ethical one? Regardless of the decision to cut off the power, do you think the manner in which Con Ed did the power cut was ethical?

2. Given the fact that Con Ed could not be contacted until the following Monday, should KnitMedia go ahead and run the extension lines down from the apartment to keep the club open? Why or why not? What are the ethical and moral pros and cons?

Managing in a Global Environment

The Knitting Factory, an alternative downtown jazz club in New York City, is also the heart of what *Inc.* magazine (*Inc. 500, 1999*) calls "a wildly growing business" under the leadership of its cofounder and CEO, Michael Dorf. KnitMedia, the holding company, includes a Web site, Webcast operation, recording studio, four record labels, touring and festival promotion operations, videoconferenced educational programs for high school and college, and new Knitting Factory clubs in Los Angeles and abroad. Plans for the future include additional European clubs, a nonprofit foundation to provide (among other things) health insurance for Knitting Factory performers, retail KnitMedia merchandise, and a stronger Internet presence via jazzE.com and a broadband media project that will provide both audio and video. Dorf envisions the Knitting Factor as the preeminent jazz "brand"—a name that jazz lovers everywhere will associate with a downtown culture that he calls "more than a zip code—it's a philosophy."

KnitMedia took its first steps into the international marketplace with an office in Amsterdam, opened several years ago to develop relationships with European musicians, agents, promoters, and retailers. Plans for opening the first Knitting Factory club in London recently fell through due to difficulties with the site, but Michael Dorf says his business plan has not changed at all. A new club is set to open in Berlin, and to streamline the European operation, the Amsterdam office will soon close to be reopened in Berlin. London is still a likely home for a future club, and Paris may be as well, although Michael is aware of French concerns over U.S. "cultural imperialism," the tendency for U.S. cultural values and icons to swamp respected national traditions when they are exported abroad. Like the Knitting Factory club in Los Angeles, each European club will have its own local general manager, and its own contacts with local musicians and music and retail communities. Each will report back to the central New York operation.

One of the consequences of KnitMedia's rapid growth over the last several years is the increased complexity of the management tasks and issues at every level of the business. The organization has changed, by necessity, from a loose and informal structure with Michael Dorf at its center, to a layered, hierarchical structure with Michael at the top. Its members now do many of the tasks Michael once did himself as he finds it increasingly necessary to delegate. The number of employees has nearly doubled, and the size of the management staff has tripled. Communication has become more formal, with increasing use of the written

word, particularly in the form of e-mail. Budgets are constructed and plans are made. Formal goals are set, and an employee evaluation system is underway.

All these internal changes are taking place at a time when close links between the Internet and the music industry are offering KnitMedia ever more ways to reach a worldwide audience. As excited as the organization's managers are about using technology, however, they agree that nothing can substitute for the thrill of a live performance. Knitting Factory clubs will continue to be at the forefront of KnitMedia's international expansion efforts.

Listen as Michael describes the difficulties of operating abroad now that KnitMedia's success has put it "in the spotlight." You will also hear from Mary Noelle Dana, Festival Programming Director and Jazzchool Coordinator and a native of France, as she contrasts the United States and France in terms of their cultural differences and approaches to financial support for the arts. Consider how some of these factors will affect KnitMedia's global expansion and prospects for success in Europe. Other managers address the organization's internal culture and the dedication to music that draws people to work there, sometimes by unlikely paths. Think about how expansion abroad will affect, and be affected by, KnitMedia's changing culture.

Questions

Based on the case, the video, the text chapters you've read so far, and your knowledge from other sources, answer the following.

1. What are some of the issues KnitMedia's managers must face in deciding to open a new club (a wholly owned subsidiary) in a European city? (*Hint:* What questions do you think Michael Dorf and his team should ask themselves as they consider opening a new club abroad?) Since they want to avoid the problems they ran into with the planned London club, what is your advice to Michael for planning his expansion abroad?

2. What specific cultural differences do you think would challenge KnitMedia's European expansion? How would you suggest Michael and his management team overcome these?

3. How would you describe the corporate culture of KnitMedia? What do you think is motivating for the people who work there? Is it a place where you would like to work?

CHAPTER ▶ 4

MAKING DECISIONS

WHAT'S AHEAD?

Seated in his cramped office–conference room in Barnes & Noble's old building in lower Manhattan, CEO Len Riggio had some decisions to make. While Barnes & Noble sells almost 30% of all books sold in U.S. bookstores, the bookselling battle-ground is shifting, and shifting fast. More and more people are buying their books on the Web, and that means booming sales for Amazon.com. In fact, according to a recent *Fortune* magazine report,[1] several large investors, including Fidelity Funds, unloaded millions of shares of Barnes & Noble stock after hearing Amazon's Jeff Bezos outline his strategy for capturing more of the book market.

Anticipating all this, Riggio had created BarnesandNoble.com way back in 1997, but it still lagged far behind Amazon in total customers. To make matters worse, it was becoming increasingly obvious that much of Amazon's on-line sales were com-ing at the expense of Barnes & Noble's bricks-and-mortar stores. Riggio had to decide what to do about expanding B & N's presence on the Internet.

OBJECTIVES

AFTER STUDYING THIS CHAPTER, YOU SHOULD BE ABLE TO

- Summarize the decision-making process

- Compare rational decision making with decision making in practice

- Identify the barriers to effective decision making

- Use at least three techniques for making better decisions

- Use groups more effectively in the decision-making process

decision

a choice made between available alternatives.

decision making

the process of developing and analyzing alternatives and choosing from among them.

problem

a discrepancy between a desirable and an actual situation.

Everyone is continually faced with the need to choose—the route to school, the job to accept, or the computer to buy. A decision is a choice from among the available alternatives. Decision making is the process of developing and analyzing alternatives and making a choice.

Most decisions, like Len Riggio's, are prompted by problems. A problem is a discrepancy between a desirable and an actual situation. If you need $50 for a show but can afford to spend only $10, you have a problem.

Decisions don't always involve problems. On the other hand, problem solving always involves making decisions, so we'll use the terms *decision making* and *problem solving* interchangeably. *Judgment* refers to the cognitive, or "thinking," aspects of the decision-making process.[2] We'll see in this chapter that the decision-making process is often subject to distortions and biases, precisely because it is usually a judgmental, not a mechanical, process.

Managers make decisions every day, and these often decide the success or failure of their firms. Barnes & Noble must decide whether to pour more money into its Web site or to build more stores. FedEx recently decided to enter the domestic heavy freight market, a substantial expansion over its traditional business of delivering packages.[3] In 1999, faced with increased competition from on-line traders, the New York Stock Exchange decided to postpone its decision on late-hours trading for a year or two, until the competitive landscape becomes clearer.[4]

In chapters 1 through 3 we focus on the things that surround what managers do, specifically on environmental forces such as globalization, deregulation, and values, culture, and ethics. Within this managerial environment, the manager's first task is to develop plans for his or her enterprise. This chapter starts Part 2 of the book, which deals with planning. Since good decisions obviously underlie planning and just about everything we do, in this chapter we focus on *making decisions*.

Decisions and the Management Process

Indeed, decisions are a big part of everything managers do. Planning, organizing, leading, and controlling are the basic management functions. However, as illustrated in Table 4.1, each of these calls for decisions—which plan to implement, what goals to choose, which people to hire.

Every manager on the company's business team therefore makes decisions. This is illustrated in Table 4.2. For example, the accounting manager decides what outside auditing firm to use and how many days a customer can be allowed to wait before it pays its bills. The sales manager decides which sales representatives to use in each region and which advertising agency to hire. The production manager decides between alternative suppliers and whether or not to recommend building a new plant. Nearly everything a manager does involves making decisions.

Programmed and Nonprogrammed Decisions

However, not all decisions are alike. For one thing, many management experts distinguish between programmed decisions and nonprogrammed decisions. As we'll see, programmed decisions tend to be repetitive and can be solved through mechanical procedures that usually can be laid out in advance.[5] In contrast, nonprogrammed decisions (like the one facing Len Riggio) tend to be unpredictable and to require lots more intuition and creativity.

TABLE 4.1	Everything Managers Do Involves Decisions

Management Function	Typical Decisions
Planning	What are the organization's long-term objectives? What strategies will best achieve these objectives? What should the organization's short-term objectives be? How difficult should individual goals be?
Organizing	How many subordinates should report directly to me? How much centralization should there be in the organization? How should jobs be designed? When should the organization implement a different structure?
Leading	How do I handle employees who appear to be low in motivation? What is the most effective leadership style in a given situation? How will a specific change affect worker productivity? When is the right time to stimulate conflict?
Controlling	What activities in the organization need to be controlled? How should these activities be controlled? When is a performance deviation significant? What type of management information system should the organization have?

Source: Stephen P. Robbins and Mary Coulter, *Management*, 5th ed. (Upper Saddle River, NJ. Prentice Hall, 1996), p. 193.

TABLE 4.2	Decisions Business Team Managers Make

Manager	Decisions
Accounting Manager	What accounting firm should we use? Who should process our payroll? Should we give this customer credit?
Finance Manager	What bank should we use? Should we sell bonds or stocks? Should we buy back some of our company's stock?
Human Resource Manager	Where should we recruit for employees? Should we set up a testing program? Should I advise settling the equal employment complaint?
Production Manager	Which supplier should we use? Should we build the new plant? Should we buy the new machine?
Sales Manager	Which sales rep should we use in this district? Should we start this advertising campaign? Should we lower prices in response to our competitor's doing so?

There are two main reasons why it's useful for managers (or future managers) to understand the differences between these two types of decisions. For one thing, the manager's time is precious. The more decisions he or she can program or make routine, the less time he or she needs to devote to them, since subordinates or systems can make these decisions more or less automatically. (This is related to what classical management experts call the "principle of exception," which basically says that only exceptions to the way things are supposed to be need to be brought to the manager's attention.) The second reason for distinguishing between the two stems from the first: Each type of decision is solved in a different way, using different methods, and so it's important to know what resources are available for solving each type. Let's look at this.

Programmed Decisions   Luckily for managers, not every decision must be handled as a brand-new situation. Instead, many decisions can be classified as programmed decisions, so standard rules or methods can be used to make them more or less automatically. **Programmed decisions** are repetitive and routine and can be solved through mechanical procedures such as by applying rules, and through mathematical procedures like those in the appendix. For example, to expedite its refund process, a department store may use this rule: "If the customer returns a jacket, you may give that person a refund if the tag is not removed, if the jacket is not damaged, and if the purchase was made within the past two weeks."

Some writers estimate that up to 90% of management decisions are programmed.[6] In many universities, for example, the question of which students to admit is made by mathematically weighting each candidate's test scores and grades. In most companies, the calculation of overtime pay and weekly payroll benefits is made by computer software. In fact, the advent of computers has dramatically boosted the number of decisions that can now be programmed. When your credit card is swiped at a point of purchase, the decision to accept it is generally computerized. The decision is referred to a credit manager only if there is a problem.

It makes sense to try to determine whether particular decisions can be programmed. If they can, the decisions can be left to subordinates, or to computers.

Nonprogrammed Decisions   In contrast, **nonprogrammed decisions** are unique and novel. Crisis decisions—like managing the rescue work for a plane crash—are one example.

Nonprogrammed decisions are generally "the kinds of [major] decisions which managers are paid to address."[7] Len Riggio's decision about how to respond to the Amazon.com threat was a nonprogrammed decision. Deciding what career to pursue, which job to take, and whether to move across the country are personal nonprogrammed decisions we all make.

Generally speaking, nonprogrammed decisions rely heavily on judgment and focus on the firm's strategic development and survival. With the big and unexpected changes of the past few years—deregulation, global competition, and the Internet, for instance—nonprogrammed decisions are increasingly common. Table 4.3 compares programmed and nonprogrammed decision making.

Top-level managers tend to face more nonprogrammed decisions, while lower-level managers face more programmed ones. This is illustrated in Figure 4.1. Lower-level managers tend to spend more time addressing programmed decisions, such as "How many employees should I put on the assembly line today, given our production quota?" Top managers face more decisions like "How should we respond to our competitor's moves?"

programmed decision
a decision that is repetitive and routine and can be made by using a definite, systematic procedure.

nonprogrammed decision
a decision that is unique and novel.

TABLE 4.3	Comparing Programmed and Nonprogrammed Decisions	
	Programmed	**Nonprogrammed**
Type of Decision	Programmable; routine; generic; computational	Nonprogrammable; unique; innovative
Nature of Decision	Procedural; predictable; well-defined information and decision criteria	Novel; unstructured; incomplete channels of information; unknown criteria
Decision-Making Strategy	Reliance on rules and computation	Reliance on principles; judgment; creative problem-solving processes
Decision-Making Technique	Management science; capital budgeting; computerized solutions; rules	Judgment; intuition, creativity

The "Rational" Decision-Making Process

Suppose you are the owner of a big retail store and must decide which of several cars to buy for deliveries. What process would you use to select among the many alternatives? The answer depends on how rational a decision-making process you want to use. The idea that managers are entirely rational in their approach has a long and honorable tradition in economic and management theory. Early economists needed a simplified way to explain economic phenomena, like how supply and demand were related. Their solution was to accept a number of simplifying assumptions about how managers made decisions. Specifically, they assumed that the rational manager (the manager who approached decision-making rationally):

1. Had complete or "perfect" information about the situation, including the full range of goods and services available on the market and the exact price of each good or service;

2. Could perfectly define the problem and not get confused by symptoms or other obstacles;

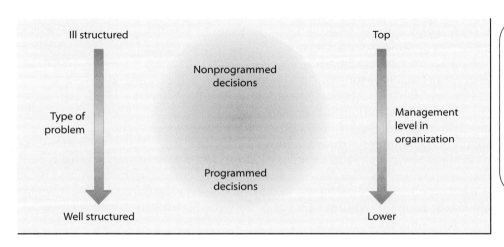

◄ FIGURE 4.1

Different Levels, Different Decisions

Top managers tend to confront more ambiguous situations; and lower managers tend to confront more structured decisions.

Source: Management 5th Ed. by Robbins and Coulter © 1996. Reprinted by permission of Prentice Hall, Inc.

3. Could identify all criteria and accurately weigh all the criteria according to his or her preferences;

4. Knew all possible alternatives and could accurately assess each against each criterion; and

5. Could accurately calculate and choose the alternative with the highest perceived value.[8]

The rational manager's approach to making a decision would thus include the steps described in the following sections.

Define the Problem[9]　Managerial decision making is usually sparked by the identification of a problem. Perhaps you need to expand your retail chain, or you are faced with increased advertising by competitors.

Identifying, defining, or "framing" the problem correctly is not always easy. Common mistakes include emphasizing the obvious and being misled by symptoms.[10] Here is a classic example. Office workers in a large office building were upset because they had to wait so long for an elevator to pick them up, and many tenants were threatening to move out. The owners called in a consulting team and told them the problem was that the elevators were running too slowly.

If you assume, as did the owners, that the problem could be defined as "slow-moving elevators," the solutions are both limited and expensive. The elevators were running about as fast as they could, so speeding them up was not an option. One solution might be to ask the tenants to stagger their work hours, but that could cause more animosity than the slow-moving elevators. Another alternative might be to add one or two more elevators, but this would be tremendously expensive.

The point of this example is that the alternatives you develop and the decision you make are both linked to the way you define or frame the problem. What the consultants actually did in this case was to define the problem as "the tenants are upset because they have to wait for an elevator." The solution they chose was to have full-length mirrors installed by each bank of elevators so the tenants could admire themselves while waiting! The solution was both inexpensive and satisfactory, and the complaints virtually disappeared.

This case shows that managers must be careful how they define problems. Don't take the accuracy of how the problem is stated to you for granted! The Entrepreneurs in Action box provides another example of how defining or "framing" the problem right can make a big difference.

Identify and Weight the Criteria　In most decisions you'll want to achieve several objectives or satisfy several criteria. This is illustrated in Figure 4.2 on page 104. In buying a computer, for instance, you may want to maximize reliability, minimize cost, obtain adequate support, and so on.

Having criteria is important because they largely determine which alternatives you should choose. Consider Len Riggio, trying to decide whether to redeploy assets from bookstores to the Internet. What are his objectives? In other words, what criteria should he apply when the time comes to evaluate his options? Let us assume, for the sake of argument, that his decision must satisfy three criteria: increase revenues by 20% per year; don't lose market share to Amazon; and be the world's dominant seller of books. In making his choice with our rational manager approach, Riggio should therefore ask, "To what extent will this alternative help us to satisfy our three criteria?"

▶ Some software entrepreneurs, seeing the success of superstores for products like building supplies and office equipment, might have asked themselves, "How big a retail store can we build to sell software, and thereby knock off our smaller competitors?" But that's not how David Prais and Tim Burton defined the problem. They believed that "the software-retail system breeds big inefficiencies," and "no one is looking five years out." They therefore created chumbo.com, which became the first company to sell Windows 98 and Microsoft Office 2000 over the Web, and the first to let customers preorder software. This Web site was soon offering about 15,000 titles from almost 500 publishers, and its sales were approaching $20 million per year.

Here's how they did it. In deciding how to proceed, Prais and Burton were guided by the needs of the hardware (not software) manufacturers themselves. When a company like IBM sells an Aptiva computer, for instance, many of its customers go to IBM's site to find out about buying new software. Dave and Tim decided to build their new Web site in part around servicing those hardware companies' Web sites. So now when you click on Aptiva's site, you're first guided to IBM's on-line easychoice.com, which then has chumbo.com supply the software. This was a good decision for two entrepreneurs who decided not to define their problem as "how to sell software through bigger stores."[11]

Some criteria may be more important to you than others. (For example, minimizing cost may be more important than having service support.) Rational decision makers may therefore give more weight to some criteria than to others.

Develop Alternatives   Whether selecting among alternative plans, job candidates, cars, or computers, the existence of some choice is a prerequisite to effective decision making. When a manager has no choice, there really isn't any decision to make—except perhaps to "take it or leave it." Developing good alternatives is not easy; it takes a great deal of creativity and judgment, as we'll see later in this chapter.

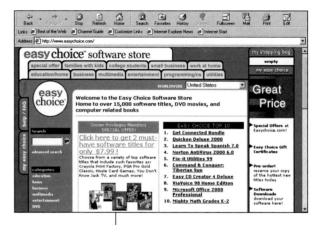

▲   **W E B N O T E**

David Prais and Tim Burton (see the "Entrepreneurs in Action" box) decided to build their new Web business by linking it to hardware suppliers' sites, such as IBM's easychoice.com.

www.easychoice.com

Analyze the Alternatives   The next step is to analyze the alternatives. Should the factory buy Machine A or Machine B? How does each alternative stack up, given the criteria on which the decision is to be based?

One expert says, "This is often the most difficult part of the decision-making process, because this is the stage that typically requires forecasting future events."[12] Under the most perfectly rational conditions, a decision maker would be able to assess the potential consequences of choosing each alternative. However, such perfect conditions rarely exist. Some quantitative tools for analyzing alternatives are explained in the appendix to this chapter.

Make a Choice, and Then Implement and Evaluate the Decision   All your analyses are useless unless you finally make a choice. Under perfect conditions, making the choice should be a straightforward matter of computing the pros and cons of each alternative and choosing the one that maximizes your benefits. But in practice, as you know, making a decision—even a relatively straightforward matter like choosing a computer—usually can't be done so accurately or rationally. To see why, let's move on to decision making in practice.

The Rational Decision-Making Process

Source: *Management* 5th Ed. by Robbins/Coulter © 1996. Reprinted by permission of Prentice Hall, Inc.

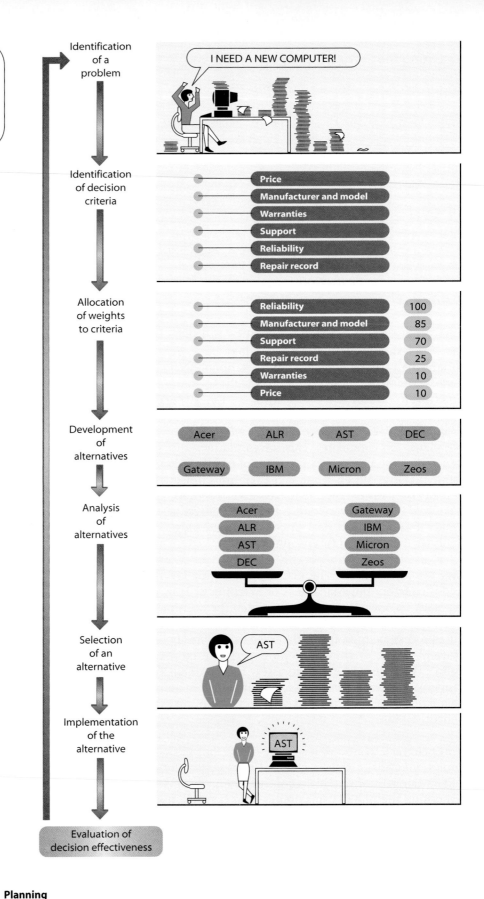

Identification of a problem

Identification of decision criteria

Allocation of weights to criteria

Development of alternatives

Analysis of alternatives

Selection of an alternative

Implementation of the alternative

Evaluation of decision effectiveness

"It was precisely this kind of indecisiveness that got us into trouble in the first place!"

▶ HOW MANAGERS MAKE DECISIONS

Many factors limit how rational a decision maker can be. That does not mean the rational model is useless: Far from it. Most managers probably do try to make rational analyses. But in practice we know the following barriers to rationality can trip up the decision maker.

Individual Differences

The ability to absorb, analyze, and generally process information varies from person to person, and is also quite limited. In one series of lab studies, participants were required to make decisions based on the amount of information transmitted on a screen.[13] Most people quickly reached a point of "information overload," and they then began adjusting in several ways. Some people omitted or ignored some of the information transmitted on the screen; others began making errors by incorrectly identifying some of the information; others gave only approximate responses (such as "about 25" instead of "24.6"). (Of course, today computers can vastly increase the number of options most of us mortals can review and consider).

Perception   The way someone perceives a situation is a good example of how individual differences influence the way decisions are made. **Perception** is the selection and interpretation of information we receive through our senses and the meaning we give to the information. Many things, including our individual needs, influence how we perceive stimuli. (For example, a thirsty person in the desert may perceive faraway heat waves as a mirage, whereas his healthy rescuer sees nothing but sand.) In organizations, a person's prior experiences and position in the company can have a big effect on how the person perceives a problem and reacts to it.

perception

the unique way each person defines stimuli, depending on the influence of past experiences and the person's present needs and personality.

In the classic study of this phenomenon, 23 executives, all employed by a large manufacturing firm, were asked to read a business case.[14] The researchers found that a manager's position influenced how he or she defined the "most important problem" facing the company. For example, of six sales executives, five thought the most important problem was a sales problem. "Organization problems" were mentioned by four out of five production executives, but by only one sales executive and no accounting executives.

Findings like these illustrate the importance of the people side of managing. In this study a person's experiences and functional role molded and influenced how he or she saw the problem. The managers looked at the same data, but interpreted or saw it differently, and each would probably have taken action based on his or her own view of the problem. You know from your experience that things like this happen every day: You might be a lot less happy with a B in a course after finding out that your friend got an A with more or less the same test grades.[15]

Systematic Versus Intuitive Decision Styles   Individuals also differ in how they approach decision making. *Systematic decision makers* tend to take a more logical, structured, step-by-step approach to solving a problem.[16] At the other extreme, *intuitive decision makers* use a more trial-and-error approach. They disregard much of the information available and rapidly bounce from one alternative to another to get a feel for which seems to work best.

One study compared systematics (who took a systematic approach to searching for information, and to slowly and thoroughly evaluating all alternatives) with intuitives (who sought information nonsystematically or selectively, and quickly reviewed the data on just a few alternatives). The study clearly showed that for most situations the intuitive approach was best.[17] The lesson seems to be that plodding through all the options may be fine if time permits, but in the real world there's a lot to be said for not letting yourself get overly involved in the process: Follow your instincts and "just do it," as the Nike ads say.[18]

Decision-Making Shortcuts

heuristic
a rule of thumb or an approximation applied as a shortcut to decision making.

Decision-making shortcuts also distort how decisions are made. People take shortcuts when solving problems by applying rules of thumb, or heuristics. For example, a banker might follow the heuristic "people should spend only 30% of their disposable income for mortgage and interest expenses."[19] Applying this rule of thumb may expedite decision making, but it may also mean that an otherwise qualified applicant is rejected.

Managers apply heuristics in many ways. A manager might predict someone's performance based on that person's similarity to other individuals with the same ethnic background that the manager has known in the past. Or a manager might base a decision on what is most readily available in memory. A common problem in appraising someone's performance is to evaluate the person based on recent performance only—the past few weeks rather than the whole year—because those experiences are more available in memory.

Using shortcuts (heuristics) has its pros and cons. On the one hand, to the extent that doing so limits the number of alternatives or information that the decision maker reviews, the ultimate decision may be less than perfect. On the other hand, it's obvious that heuristics do enable managers to make faster decisions than they might otherwise. And from a practical point of view, it's useful to keep in mind that this is generally how most people actually do make decisions.

How the Problem Is Framed

Misdefining the problem may be the biggest barrier to making good decisions. Remember how much money the building owners would have wasted if their elevator consultants had accepted at face value the owners' claim that the problem was slow-moving elevators? Here's how three decision-making experts put it:

> The greatest danger in formulating a decision problem is laziness. It's easy to state the problem in the most obvious way, or in the way that first pops into your mind, or in the way it's always been stated in the past. But the easy way isn't necessarily the best way.[20]

In other words, managers need to work hard to understand what the problem really is.

Care to test your framing skills? Since you should be an expert at solving "mirror" problems by now, here's another one for you. You just bought a new but small apartment, and you'd like to make it look roomier. On your right as you enter is an eight-foot-wide closet with a set of two bifold doors. Mirrors make a room look bigger, so your significant other has suggested you have mirrors mounted on the door panels. Unfortunately, the estimates you've gotten so far are much too high. So you are about to give up. But first you ask, "Did I frame the problem correctly?"

Well, probably not. What did you do wrong? For one thing, you've defined the problem as "How do we mount mirrors on the door panels?" Even if we assume that mirroring the closet is the best way to make your place look roomier, why limit yourself to accomplishing that by *mounting* mirrors on the closet doors? You don't really care if you *mount* mirrors there, do you? The problem really is this: "What's the best way to put mirrors where we now have closet doors?" A quick trip to your local building supply store and you discover a set of inexpensive sliding-door mirror panels that can replace your bulky doors; and which slide back and forth on a track you install yourself. Total cost: one-half the previous estimates.

Anchoring

Errors in framing are sometimes caused by **anchoring**, which means unconsciously giving disproportionate weight to the first information you hear.

Anchors pop up in the most unexpected ways. Let's say you're selling your car, which you know is worth about $10,000. Joe has responded to your classified ad; when he arrives, he offhandedly remarks that the car is only worth about $5,000. What would you do? On the one hand, you know that Joe is probably just positioning himself to get a better deal, and you know that $5,000 is absolutely ridiculous. On the other hand, Joe is the only game in town at the moment (one other person called, but never showed up) and you don't really feel like killing more weekends placing ads and waiting around for buyers who don't show up. So you start bargaining with Joe: He says $5,000, you say $10,000, and before you know it you've arrived at a price of $8,000, which Joe graciously points out is "better than splitting the difference" from your point of view.

What happened here? You just got anchored (to put it mildly). Without realizing it, you gave disproportionate weight to his offhand comment, and your decision making (and bargaining) from that point on revolved around his price, not yours. (What should you have done? One response might have been "$5,000? Are you *kidding*? That's not even in the *ballpark*!" It might not have worked, but at least you'd have loosened that subliminal anchor, so the bargaining could be on your terms, not his.)

anchoring
unconsciously giving disproportionate weight to the first information you hear.

Psychological Set

psychological set

the tendency to rely on a rigid strategy or approach when solving a problem.

The tendency to focus on a rigid strategy or point of view is called **psychological set**.[21] This mental trait can severely limit a manager's ability to think of alternative solutions. A classic example is presented in Figure 4.3. Your assignment is to connect all nine dots with no more than four lines running through them, and to do so without lifting your pen from the paper. Hint: Don't fall into the trap of taking a rigid point of view. The answer is provided on page 110.

Organizational Barriers

Too often the company itself—how it's organized, or its policies and procedures, for instance—undermines employees' ability to make good decisions. You've probably experienced that yourself. For example, you ask a salesperson at a department store to make a simple change, and you're told, "You'll have to get that approved first by customer service." Microsoft went through a major reorganization in 1999, in part to ensure that lower-level managers could make more decisions themselves, without referring decisions up to Bill Gates.

In a recent study nearly two-thirds (62%) of the 773 hourly workers surveyed said their organizations were operating with half or less than half the employee brain power available to them. This observation was shared by 63% of the 641 managers responding to the survey. The numbers in the figure help to explain why this is so. About 40% of all employees gave "organizational politics" as one of the three big barriers to effective thinking in their firms. Time pressure and a lack of involvement in decision making were the other two big barriers. Less important barriers included lack of rewards, lack of skills, procedures/work rules/systems, lack of training, and unclear job expectations.[22] Obviously managers can undermine decision making in many ways if they aren't careful.

Decision Making: How It Should Be Versus How It Is

bounded rationality

the boundaries on rational decision making imposed by one's values, abilities, and limited capacity for processing information.

satisfice

to stop the decision-making process when satisfactory alternatives are found, rather than reviewing solutions until an optimal alternative is discovered.

The existence of these barriers means that the ideal rational model of what management decision making *should be* must be taken with a grain of salt. Herbert Simon and his associates say that, in practice, "bounded rationality" more accurately represents how managers actually make decisions. **Bounded rationality** means that a manager's decision making is only as rational as his or her unique values, capabilities, and limited capacity for processing information permit him or her to be. Decision making in practice is limited by the sorts of barriers—information overload, selective perception, and anchoring, for instance—discussed in this section.[23]

One particularly important difference between the rational and the bounded rational decision maker is: the rational manager continues to review solutions until he or she finds the optimal choice. In contrast, managers in practice often **satisfice**. Managers tend to be concerned with just discovering and selecting *satisfactory* alternatives, and only in exceptional cases with finding *optimal* alternatives.[24]

■ **So Many Decisions, So Little Time**

Perhaps the best way to illustrate "decision making: how it should be vs. how it is" is with an example. This one is from Dominic Orr, president and CEO of Alteon WebSystems Inc. Ask him what his main management problem is, and he responds that "like a lot of young companies in new industries, we have to make choices every day about competitive strategy and product development.[25] So how can we make decisions that we trust without wasting valuable time?" As he puts it, "fast execution and fast delivery—that's easy. Fast decision making is harder. Young industries and startups are constantly changing—which means that even day-to-day decisions take on huge strategic importance . . . [Therefore] making high stakes decisions as a team is important. But we don't have time for endless debate or for office politics."[26]

So how do they actually make decisions at Alteon? "We focus on collecting as many facts as quickly as we can, and then we decide on the best—but not necessarily the perfect—solution." In Alteon's decision making process, the people element is particularly important: for example, they aim to encourage lively debate while avoiding dysfunctional, personal comments. As Orr says, "there's no silent disagreement, and no getting personal, and definitely no "let's take it off-line" mentality. Our goal is to make each major decision in a single meeting. People arrive with a proposal or a solution—and with the facts to support it. After an idea is presented, we open the floor to objective, and often withering, critiques. And if the idea collapses under scrutiny, we move onto another: no hard feelings. We're judging the idea, not the person. As the same time, we don't really try to regulate emotions. Passionate conflict means that we're getting somewhere, not that the discussion is out of control. But one person does act as referee—by asking basic questions like "is this good for the customer?" Or "does it keep our time to market advantage impact?" By focusing relentlessly on the facts, we're able to see the strains and weaknesses of an idea clearly and quickly."[27]

The bottom line is that in reality, the people side of making decisions is extremely important. Decisions like those at Alteon usually need to be made quickly and under constantly changing conditions. As a result, it often happens that not all the facts can be brought to bear. Furthermore, as at Alteon, managers need to be vigilant as the decision is being discussed, since politicking, unregulated emotions, personal comments and other characteristically human actions can undermine the decision-making process.

This is not to say that managers don't try to be rational; it is simply recognizing the fact that, in practice, their attempts to be rational are limited, or bounded. Luckily, several decision-making tools are available to help minimize the adverse effects of these barriers and thus improve managers' decisions.

▶ HOW TO MAKE BETTER DECISIONS

Some people assume that good judgment is like great singing—either you can do it or you can't. But overcoming the many decision-making barriers we've identified can lead almost anyone to making better decisions. Some techniques that can help you avoid problems at every step of the process follow.

Be Creative

Creativity—the process of developing original, novel responses to a problem—plays a big role in making good decisions. It is essential for decision-making activities like framing the problem and developing new alternatives. Remember the consultant's creative redefinition of the "slow-moving elevators" problem. Creativity *can* be cultivated. Here are some suggestions.

Check Your Assumptions   Decision-making barriers like anchoring and psychological set can be avoided in part by forcing yourself to check your assumptions. Let's look again at the problem of the nine dots, which is shown in Figure 4.4. Remember that your instructions were to connect all nine dots with no more than four lines running through them, and to do so without lifting your pen from the paper.

Psychological set, the tendency to take a rigid view of a problem, may be the decision-making barrier at work here. Most people tend to view the nine dots as a square, but this of course limits your solutions. In fact, there is no way to connect all the dots with just four lines as long as you make this assumption.

Figure 4.5 shows one creative solution. The key to this solution was breaking through your assumptions about how the problem needed to be solved. In fact, one managerial decision-making expert refers to creativity as, in essence, "an assumption-breaking process."[28] Now try to solve the problem in Figure 4.6. Remember: Always check your assumptions.

Think Through the Process   Forcing yourself to think through the decision and each of its consequences, as if you were actually there experiencing them, can also help you be more creative. Consider this problem: An extraordinarily frugal person named Joe can make one whole cigar from every five cigar butts he finds. How many cigars can he make if he finds twenty-five cigar butts? Before you answer "five," think through Joe's cigar-making process, step by step. There he sits on his park bench, making (and smoking!) each of his five cigars. As he smokes each cigar, he ends up with one new cigar butt. Thus, in smoking his five hand-made cigars, Joe ends up with five new butts, which of course he combines into his sixth, and in this case final, whole new cigar.[29]

This problem illustrates how process analysis can boost creativity and insight. Process analysis means solving a problem by thinking through the process involved from beginning to end, imagining, at each step, what actually would happen.[30] In this case, process analysis meant envisioning Joe sitting on his park bench

process analysis

solving problems by thinking through the process involved from beginning to end, imagining, at each step, what actually would happen.

► F I G U R E   4 . 4

Looking at the Problem in Just One Way

Source: Lester A. Lefton and Laura Valvatine, *Mastering Psychology*, 4th ed. Copyright © 1992 by Allyn & Bacon. Reprinted by permission.

► F I G U R E   4 . 5

The Advantage of Not Just Looking at the Problem in One Way

Source: Max H. Bazerman. *Judgment in Managerial Decision Making.* Copyright © 1994 Wiley, p. 93. Reprinted by permission of Wiley.

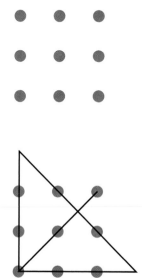

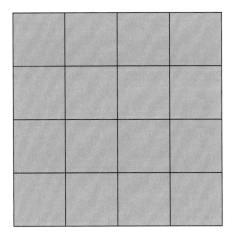

◀ FIGURE 4.6

Using Creativity to Find a Solution

How many squares are in the box? Now, count again. Only sixteen? Take away your preconception of how many squares there are. Now, how many do you find? **You should find thirty!**

Source: Applied Human Relations, 4th ed., by Benton/Halloran © 1991. Reprinted by permission of Prentice Hall, Upper Saddle River, NJ.

and thinking through each of the steps he would take as if we were there. By using process analysis to look over Joe's shoulder in this way, we boosted our creativity and discovered that he made a sixth cigar.

Increase Your Knowledge

"Knowledge is power" someone once said, and that's particularly true when it comes to making decisions. Even the simplest decisions—mapping your route to work in the morning, or deciding which cereal to buy, for instance—become problems if you lack basic information, such as the distances involved or the costs of each of the various products. And making major, more complex life decisions of course depends even more on what you know about the situation. For example, Ed (not his real name), a highly intelligent medical doctor practicing for many years in a major Southeast town, accepted a job with a group of young doctors in another state, only to find that what he was expected to do and the hours he had to work were much more than he had anticipated. After less than a year of being run ragged, he had to leave, albeit as a wiser man: Knowledge is power, and the more you know about the elements of the decision before you make that decision, the better the decision will be.

That's easy to say, of course, but how do you go about getting the knowledge you require? There are several things you can do. First, ask, ask, ask. In formulating your questions, always keep the six main question words in mind: who, what, where, when, why, and how. Then, even for a smaller decision, like buying a used car, make sure to do your research. Who is selling the car, and who has owned it? What do similar cars sell for? What if anything is wrong with this car? Where has it been serviced? Why does the owner want to sell it? How well has the car been maintained? And how much does the owner want to sell it for? Think of how much trouble Dr. Ed could have saved himself if he had just sat down and asked his prospective partners a few incisive questions about the job!

Second, get experience. For many endeavors, there's simply no substitute for getting some experience. That's certainly true on a personal level: Many students find that interning in a job similar to the occupation they plan to pursue can help enormously in clarifying whether that's the right occupation for them. And it's certainly true when it comes to managing organizations. In Chapter 2 we saw that some companies expand abroad by opening their own facilities, while others enter into joint ventures. What do you think determines which route a company's managers choose? It turns out that experience has a lot to do with it. Multinational corporations that

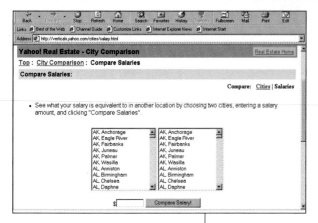

already have a great deal of experience in doing business in a particular country generally opt for full ownership of foreign affiliates. Less experienced companies tend to establish joint ventures in foreign markets, in part so they can get the necessary expertise.[31]

Third, do your research. Whether the decision involves a new job, a new car, expanding abroad, or the sorts of issues now facing Barnes & Noble (such as whether to expand the Web site and if so, how), there is a wealth of information out there that managers can tap. For example, thinking of moving from New York to Los Angeles? How do salaries in Los Angeles compare with those in New York? That question is easily answered on an Internet Web site such as Yahoo.com/cities/salary. Want to know what your used car is worth? Then tap into edmunds.com.

Fourth, use consultants. In fact, that's basically what business consultants are for. The consultants' experience in some areas (such as personnel testing or strategic planning) can be used to supplement the managers' lack of experience in those areas. And the consultants needn't be management consultants, of course. If our Dr. Ed had had the foresight to meet with an employment lawyer to draw up an employment contract before taking his new job, the lawyer probably would have asked a lot of the questions Ed neglected to ask. Sometimes just talking the problem over with other people can help, particularly if they've had experience solving similar problems.

Fifth, force yourself to recognize the facts when you see them. "Well of course I'll recognize the facts when I see them," you might say, but in fact doing so is easier said than done. It's always easy to overlook some facts when you really want to do something. (For example, it's always easy to make the financials involved in a vacation look better when you really want to take that vacation.) In other words, endeavor to maintain your objectivity, so that your decision is based on an intelligent review of the facts as they really are.

MANAGING @ THE SPEED OF THOUGHT

■ Knowledge Management

In today's highly competitive business environment, it's often the company with the best information that's the most successful. As one expert recently put it, "it is a competitive advantage if your company is learning faster than the competition."[32] As a result, many managers today are emphasizing what they call "knowledge management." Knowledge management refers to any efforts aimed at enabling the company's managers and employees to better utilize the information available anywhere in their companies.

Part of the problem in effectively managing knowledge is that, as one expert puts it "only two percent of information gets written down—the rest is in people's heads."[33] For any company, and especially a large one, capturing such information and transforming it into knowledge that others can use can be quite a challenge.

Xerox provides a useful example of how one company dealt with this challenge. As an example of the magnitude of the knowledge management problems Xerox faced, the company has 23,000 repair technicians around the world fixing copiers at clients' sites. In many cases, the repair solutions exist "only in the heads of experienced technicians, who can solve complex problems faster and more efficiently than less experienced ones."[34] The challenge for Xerox was to find a way to access all that brain-based knowledge and translate it into a form that could be used by the company's entire 23,000-person worldwide repair force.

Xerox's solution was to create an Intranet-based communications system named Eureka, which was linked with a corporate database. Repair technicians around the world are encouraged to share repair tips by inputting them into the database via Eureka, a task facilitated by having the technicians use laptop computers. At the current time, more than 5,000 tips have been entered. This experienced-based knowledge is then easily accessible by other service reps around the world.

Use Your Intuition

Overemphasizing rationality and logic can actually backfire by blocking you from using your intuition. *Intuition* can be defined as a cognitive process whereby a person unconsciously makes a decision based on his or her accumulated knowledge and experience. Here is what the psychiatrist Sigmund Freud had to say about making important decisions:

> When making a decision of minor importance I have always found it advantageous to consider all the pros and cons. In vital matters, however, such as the choice of a mate or a profession, the decision should come from the unconscious, from somewhere within ourselves. In the important decisions of our personal life, we should be governed, I think, by the deep inner needs of our nature.[35]

WHAT IS MY ORIENTATION?

You can get a rough idea of your relative preferences for the rational and intuitive ways of dealing with situations by rating yourself on four items. For each statement, rank yourself on a six-point scale— 1 (never), 2 (once in a while), 3 (sometimes), 4 (quite often), 5 (frequently but not always), 6 (always)—and place your response in the box to the right of the item:

1. When I have a special job to do, I like to organize it carefully from the start. ☐

2. I feel that a prescribed, step-by-step method is best for solving problems. ☐

3. I prefer people who are imaginative to those who are not. ☐

4. I look at a problem as a whole, approaching it from all sides. ☐

Now add the values for the first two items for one total, and for the last two items for another total. Subtract the second total from the first. If your total has a positive value, your preference is *Rational* by that amount, and if your total has a negative value, your preference is *Intuitive* by that amount. Ten represents the maximum possible rational or intuitive score from the equally preferred midpoint (0). Mark your position on the range of possible scores:

Intuitive −10 −9 −8 −7 −6 −5 −4 −3 −2 −1 0 1 2 3 4 5 6 7 8 9 10 Rational

These items are taken from a 30-item Personal Style Inventory (PSI) assessment of preferences for Rational and Intuitive behavior created by William Taggert.

◄ **FIGURE 4.7**

Are You More Rational or More Intuitive?

Source: Adapted and reproduced by permission of the Publisher, Psychological Assessment Resources. Inc., Odessa FL 33556, from the Personal Style Inventory by William Taggart, Ph.D., and Barbara Hausladen. Copyright 1991, 1993 by PAR, Inc.

▲ Price wars are a form of escalation of commitment, in which step-by-step decision making leads each party to become more and more entrenched in a position.

Another expert says you can usually tell when a decision fits with your inner nature, for it brings an enormous sense of relief. Good decisions, he says, are the best tranquilizers ever invented; bad ones often increase your anxiety. So always consult your inner feelings: Never disregard your intuition.[36] Intuitiveness can be measured. The short test in Figure 4.7 provides an approximate reading on whether you are more rational or intuitive in your decision making.[37]

Don't Overstress the Finality of Your Decision[38]

Very few decisions are forever; there is more "give" in most decisions than we realize. While many major strategic decisions are certainly hard to reverse, most poor decisions won't mean the end of the world for you, so don't become frozen in the finality of your decision.

In fact, it's the manager's job to see that a decision needs changing, and to drive through the change. For example, when Len Riggio saw that Barnes & Noble's strategy of emphasizing bricks and mortar bookstores was no longer adequate, he made the decision to create Barnes & Noble on-line. When Steve Jobs took over Apple Computer several years ago, he decided that the company's previous strategy of offering a wide number of products was misguided. He pared the number of products being produced and sold, and focused instead on the company's iMac computer.

Indeed, knowing when to quit is sometimes the smartest thing a manager can do. The London City government recently lost millions as its efforts to automate the London Stock Exchange collapsed due to technical difficulties. Experts studying the problem subsequently said the venture might have been a victim of what psychologists call "escalation." *Escalation* is the act of making a wrong decision and losing even more because of continued adherence to the decision.[39] So don't let fear that the decision is forever scare you into not making the decision. And once the decision is made, stick with it if you believe you're on the right track, but know when to fold if the decision turns out to be a poor one.

Make Sure the Timing Is Right

You've probably noticed that, as with most people, your decisions are affected by your mood. For example, deliberately cut off by another driver while speeding down the highway, even a usually conservative driver might unwisely decide to engage in some retaliation. At work, a small business owner we'll call Tom is famous (or maybe infamous) among his workers for his passing moods. After a bad night on the home front or after losing a big sale, the mercurial Tom is usually ready to lash out at anyone and anything around, so his managers learned long ago to steer clear of asking him for a decision when he's in one of his dark moods. Researchers know that when people feel "down," their actions tend to be aggressive and destructive. When they feel good, their behavior swings toward balance and tolerance. Similarly, people tend to be lenient when they're in good spirits and tough when they are grouchy. How would you like to have your class presentation evaluated by a professor who is in a particularly bad mood?

Decision makers in general (and managers in particular) can derive a lesson from this: It's important to take into account your emotions when making important decisions. Whether it's appraising an employee, hiring a supervisor, or buying a new machine, do a quick reality check to make sure you're not in the midst of an unwelcome mood swing. Good managers usually have stable, mature personalities. And the successful ones know enough to take their moods into consideration before making a decision.

▶ USING GROUPS TO MAKE BETTER DECISIONS

Whether they are called workgroups, teams, or committees, groups accomplish much of the work in organizations. Since we've focused on individual decision making until now, it's important that we turn our attention to using the power of groups to make better decisions.

Although we'll discuss groups in more detail in Chapter 13, some working definitions are in order now. A **group** is defined as two or more persons interacting for some purpose and who influence one another in the process. The board of directors of Microsoft is a group, as is the Lexington, Kentucky, work team that installs the dashboards on Toyota's Camry line.

Groups are important at work in part because of the effect they have on their members. For example, pressure by other group members can cause a member to raise or lower his or her output. In turn, the extent to which a group can influence its members depends on several things, including the **cohesiveness** of the group—the attraction of the group for its members—and on the group's **norms**—the informal rules that groups adopt to regulate and regularize members' behavior.[40]

Pros and Cons of Group Decision Making

You have probably found from your own experience that groups to which you belong can and do influence how you behave and the decisions you make. It is therefore not surprising that having groups make decisions has pros and cons. These pros and cons are summarized in Figure 4.8.

The old saying that "two heads are better than one" can be true when you bring several people together to arrive at a decision. Pooling the experiences and points of view of several people can lead to more points of view regarding how to define the problem, more possible solutions, and more creative decisions in general. Groups that analyze a problem and come up with their own decisions also tend to "buy in to" those decisions; this acceptance boosts the possibility that the group will work harder to implement the decision once it's put into effect.[41]

While advocates say "two heads are better than one," detractors say "a camel is a horse put together by a committee." Using a group can sometimes actually short-circuit the decision process.

Several things can go wrong when groups make decisions. The desire to be accepted tends to silence disagreement and to favor consensus, a fact that can actu-

group
two or more persons interacting in such a manner that each person influences and is influenced by each other person, and who may or may not have unanimity of purpose.

cohesiveness
the attraction of the group for its individual members.

norms
the informal rules that groups adopt to regulate and regularize the behavior of group members.

PROS	CONS
• "Two heads are better than one" • More points of view • Fosters acceptance • Group may work harder to implement decisions	• Pressure for consensus • Dominance by one individual • Escalation of commitment: pressure to "win your point" • More time-consuming • Groupthink

◀ FIGURE 4.8

Pros and Cons of Using Groups to Make Decisions

ally reduce creative decisions instead of enhancing them.[42] In many groups, a dominant individual emerges who effectively cuts off debate and channels the rest of the group to his or her point of view. Escalation of commitment can be a problem, too: When groups are confronted by a problem, there is often a tendency for individual members to become committed to their own solutions; the goal then becomes winning the argument rather than solving the problem. Groups also take longer to make decisions than do individuals. The process can therefore be inherently more expensive than having an individual make the decision.

Groupthink

Groupthink is another potential problem. **Groupthink** has been defined as "a mode of thinking that people engage in when they are deeply involved in a cohesive group, when the members' desire for unanimity overrides their personal motivation to realistically appraise alternative courses of action."[43]

The classic, often cited, groupthink example involved the Kennedy Administration's disastrous decision to invade Cuba at the Bay of Pigs in 1961. Midway through the National Security Council's discussions of the pros and cons of the invasion, then-Attorney General Robert Kennedy reportedly told one detractor: "You may be right and you may be wrong, but President Kennedy has made his decision, so keep your opinions to yourself." The desire for unanimity overrode the potential advantage of including more varying points of view and contributed to what turned out to be a bad decision. The warning signs of groupthink, such as pressuring, are presented in Figure 4.9.

Improving Group Decision Making

The manager's job is to use groups in such a way that the advantages of group decision making outweigh the disadvantages. For this there are several decision-making tools the manager can use.[44]

Brainstorming **Brainstorming** is one way to amplify the creative energies of a group. It has been defined as a group problem-solving technique whereby group members introduce all possible solutions before evaluating any of them.[45] The

▶ **FIGURE 4.9**

Signs That Groupthink May Be a Problem

Source: Adapted from information provided in Irving James, *Group Think: Psychological Studies of Policy Decisions and Fiascos,* 2nd ed. Boston: Houghton Mifflin, 1982.

"Don't ask, don't question."	Group members censor themselves, refuse to ask probing questions, and withhold disagreement.
"You must conform."	Someone, probably a group member, pressures others to withhold dissent and to go along with the group decisions.
"We all agree."	Group members press on with making their decisions, under the erroneous impression that all group members agree—possibly due to dissenters' silence.
"We're on a mission."	Group members frame their arguments in terms of what's right for the group's mission—electing the U.S. president, attacking a country, or beating a competitor, for instance—and assume therefore that what they're doing is right and ethical.
"Masters of the world."	Group members come to believe that the group is totally in command of the mission and can therefore do anything, regardless of the risks—they come to feel invulnerable.

technique is aimed at encouraging everyone to introduce solutions, without fear of criticism. The process typically has four main rules:

1. Avoid criticizing others' ideas until all suggestions have been made;
2. Share even wild suggestions;
3. Offer as many suggestions and supportive comments as possible; and
4. Build on others' suggestions to create your own.[46]

Brainstorming can produce creative solutions even if group members feel too inhibited to make wild suggestions.[47]

A recent and effective innovation is to use electronic brainstorming, by letting group members interact via groupware (a type of software) and PCs, instead of face-to-face. Doing so results in a relatively large increase in the number of high-quality ideas generated by the group, compared with face-to-face groups.[48]

Devil's-Advocate Approach   One way to guard against the tendency for one group member's efforts to dominate the discussion and stifle debate is to formalize the process of criticism. The devil's-advocate approach is one way to do this. An advocate defends the proposed solution, and a second, "devil's," advocate is appointed to prepare a detailed counterargument listing what is wrong with the solution and why it should not be adopted.

The Delphi Technique   The Delphi Technique aims to maximize the advantages of group decision making and minimize its disadvantages. Basically, you obtain the opinions of experts who work independently, with the experts' written opinions from one stage providing the basis for other experts' analyses of each succeeding stage. Delphi analysis steps are as follows:

1. A problem is identified;
2. Expert opinions are solicited anonymously and individually through questionnaires (for example, on a problem such as "What do you think are the five biggest breakthrough products our computer company will have to confront in the next five years?");
3. The expert opinions are then analyzed, distilled, and resubmitted to other experts for a second round of opinions;
4. This process is continued for several more rounds, until a consensus is reached.

This can obviously be a time-consuming process; on the other hand (as in electronic brainstorming), problems like groupthink can be reduced by eliminating face-to-face meetings.

The Nominal Group Technique   The nominal group technique is a group decision-making process in which participants do not attempt to agree as a group on any solution, but rather meet and vote secretly on all the solutions proposed after privately ranking the proposals in order of preference.[49] It is called the "nominal" group technique because the "group" is a group in name only: Members vote on solutions not as a group, but individually.

The process is this:

1. Each group member writes down his or her ideas for solving the problem at hand;

2. Each member then presents his or her ideas orally, and the ideas are written on a board for other participants to see;

3. After all ideas have been presented, the entire group discusses all ideas simultaneously;

4. Group members individually and secretly vote on each proposed solution; and

5. The solution with the most individual votes wins.

The Stepladder Technique   The stepladder technique also aims to reduce the potentially inhibiting effects of face-to-face meetings. Group members are added one-by-one at each stage of the process so that their input is untainted by the previous discussants' points of view. The process involves these steps:

1. Individuals A and B are given a problem to solve, and each produces an independent solution;

2. A and B then meet, develop a joint decision, and meet with C, who had independently analyzed the problem and arrived at a decision;

3. A, B, and C jointly discuss the problem and arrive at a consensus decision, and they are joined by person D who has individually analyzed the problem and arrived at his or her own decision;

4. A, B, C, and D meet and arrive at a final group decision.[50]

How to Lead a Group Decision-Making Discussion

The person leading the discussion can have a big effect on whether the group's decision is useful. If a chairperson monopolizes the meeting and continually shoots down others' ideas while pushing his or her own, it's likely that other points of view will go unexpressed.

According to a series of group decision-making studies, an effective discussion leader therefore has a responsibility to do the following:

1. See that all group members participate. As discussion leader, it is your responsibility to ensure that all group members participate and have an opportunity to express their opinions. Doing so can help ensure that different points of view emerge and that everyone takes ownership of the final decision.

2. Distinguish between idea getting and idea evaluation. These studies conclude that evaluating and criticizing proposed solutions and ideas actually inhibit the process of getting or generating new ideas. Yet in most group discussions, one person presents an alternative, and others begin immediately discussing its pros and cons. As a result, group members quickly become apprehensive about suggesting new ideas. Distinguishing between the idea getting and idea evaluation stages—in particular, forbidding criticism of an idea until all ideas have been presented—can be useful here.

3. Not respond to each participant or dominate the discussion. Remember that the discussion leader's main responsibility is to elicit ideas from the group, not to supply them. As a discussion leader, you should therefore work hard to facilitate free expression of ideas and avoid dominating the discussion.

4. See that the effort is directed toward overcoming surmountable obstacles. In other words, focus on solving the problem rather than on discussing historical events that cannot be changed. Some groups make the mistake of becoming embroiled in discussions about who is to blame for the problem or what should

have been done to avoid the problem. Such discussions can't lead to solutions because the past can't be changed. As a discussion leader, your job is to ensure that the group focuses on obstacles that can be overcome and on solutions that can be implemented.[51]

SUMMARY

1. A decision is a choice from among available alternatives. Decision making is the process of developing and analyzing alternatives and making a choice.

2. Decisions can be either programmed (repetitive and routine) or nonprogrammed (unique and novel). Nonprogrammed decisions require more intuition and judgment of decision makers.

3. Rational decision making assumes ideal conditions such as accurate definition of the problem and complete knowledge about all relevant alternatives and their values.

4. In contrast, decision making in reality is bounded by differences in managers' ability to process information, reliance on heuristics or shortcuts, framing, anchoring, escalation, psychological set, and factors in the organization itself.

5. "Bounded rationality" describes decision making in reality and often implies satisficing, or accepting satisfactory (as opposed to optimal) alternatives.

6. Guidelines for making better decisions include increase your knowledge, use creativity, use intuition, don't overstress finality, and make sure the timing is right.

7. A group consists of two or more persons who interact for some purpose and who influence each other in the process. Group decision making can result in the pooling of resources and strengthened commitment to the decision, but it can also be flawed by groupthink, an overwhelming desire for unanimity.

8. Tools for better group decisions include brainstorming, the devil's-advocate approach, the Delphi and nominal group techniques, and the stepladder technique.

9. Knowing how to lead a group decision-making discussion is important. Some hints include see that all group members participate; distinguish between idea getting and idea evaluation; don't respond to each participant or dominate the discussion; and see that the effort is directed toward overcoming surmountable obstacles.

TYING IT ALL TOGETHER

In this chapter we moved from the environment of the manager's job to a more detailed discussion of what managers actually do. Because all the management functions (planning, organizing, leading, and controlling) require making decisions, we began this part of the book with information on making decisions—the process, the barriers, and the techniques you can use to make better decisions.

Decisions underlie everything managers do. Riggio must decide how to respond to the challenge of Amazon.com. Tom, a small business owner, must decide what computers to buy and what people to hire or fire (hopefully, once he's back in a good mood). Everything revolves around decisions. It's not coincidental that we placed the decision-making chapter at the start of Part II, which focuses on planning. After all, the decisions we make when planning are among the biggest decisions we will ever make, whether the plans concern a choice of career or which new products to introduce. What plan should Barnes & Noble craft to compete with Amazon.com over the next few years? How should Gates and Microsoft respond to the increasing threat of the Internet to their Windows system? Questions like these point to the close relationship between decisions and planning.

KEY TERMS

decision 98
decision making 98
problem 98
programmed decision 100
nonprogrammed decision 100
perception 105
heuristics 106
anchoring 107
psychological set 108
bounded rationality 108

satisfice 108
process analysis 110
group 115
cohesiveness 115
norms 115
groupthink 116
brainstorming 116
breakeven analysis 125
linear programming 126

waiting-line/queuing techniques 127
statistical decision theory techniques 127
certainty 127
uncertainty 128
risk 128
decision tree 128
expected value 128

SKILLS AND STUDY MATERIALS

CRITICAL THINKING EXERCISES

1. To paraphrase philosopher Bertrand Russell, there are two kinds of workers: those that roll the rock up the hill and those that tell them to do so. Since you are probably in college as you read this text, it can perhaps be assumed that you wish to be the one giving the directions (the brainwork), rather than rolling the rock (the brawn work). The brain-based economy reinforces the necessity of education if you neither wish to roll the rock up the hill nor have it roll down on you, if you are the manager. Times are continuously changing. With those changes there are new things you need to know as a manager to make good decisions. How do you think managerial decision making is different in a brain-based economy than in an industrial, or a brawn-based, one? What are the most important factors or variables that go into making managerial decisions in the new millenium? What do you think decision making will be like in the year 2100? Will the rational model prevail, or will some form of computerized process displace the time-honored tradition of Western thought and Descartes' dictum: "I think, therefore I am"? Be prepared to discuss these questions in class.

2. In his provocative book, *Managing as a Performing Art*, Peter Vaill argues that there are seven myths in managing organizations. Three are as follows:

   ■ The myth of a single person, called "the manager" or "the leader." Vaill contends that all kinds of people without the title or power have opportunities for management and leadership in modern organizations.

   ■ The myth that what the leader leads and the manager manages is a single, freestanding organization. Vaill states that thinking of organizations as singular things allows us to ignore the fact that organizations are a part of their environment and must therefore be aware of their impact on that environment.

   ■ The myth of rational analysis as being the primary means of understanding and directing organizations. Intuition is important; change is so constant and discontinuous that we must be creative constantly, and there is much mystery in our decisions today.

   Analyze and discuss the points made by Vaill in light of what you now know about decision making and organizations from this chapter. Do you agree with him?

1. As a team, analyze the following story about Taoist thinker Chuang-tse: While sitting on the banks of the P'u River, Chuang-tse was approached by two representatives of the Prince of Ch'u, who offered him a position at court. Chuang-tse watched the water flowing by as if he had not heard. Finally, he remarked, "I am told that the Prince has a sacred tortoise, over two thousand years old, which is kept in a box, wrapped in silk and brocade." "That is true," the officials replied. "If the tortoise has been given a choice," Chuang-tse continued, "which do you think he would have liked better—to have been alive in the mud, or dead within the palace?" "To have been alive in the mud, of course," the men answered. "I too prefer the mud," said Chuang-tse. "Goodbye." (From Benjamin Hoff's *The Tao of Pooh*, 1982, p. 42.) In our rapidly changing world, we must all make a number of decisions as to how we wish to live our lives. As a team, do research on decision-making methods and information sources that are available for making decisions about career choices today.

2. People from other countries are often puzzled and intrigued by the complexity and enigmas of U.S. culture. Here are some examples from Nancy J. Adler's, *International Dimensions of Organizational Behavior:*

   - India: "Americans seem to be in a perpetual hurry. Just watch them walk down the street. They never allow themselves the leisure to enjoy life; there are too many things to do."

   - Kenya: "Americans appear to us rather distant. They are not really close to other people—even fellow Americans— as Americans overseas tend to portray. It's almost as if an American says, 'I won't let you get too close to me.' It's like building a wall."

   - Turkey: "Once we were out in a rural area in the middle of nowhere and saw an American at a stop sign. Though he could see in both directions for miles and no traffic was coming, he still stopped."

   - Colombia: "The tendency of the United States to think that life is only work hits you in the face. Work seems to be the one type of motivation."

   - Indonesia: "In the United States everything has to be talked about and analyzed. Even the littlest thing has to be 'Why, Why, Why?' I get a headache from such persistent questions."

   - Ethiopia: "The American is very explicit; he wants a 'yes' or 'no.' If someone tries to speak figuratively, the American is confused."

   - Iran: "The first time . . . my (American) professor told me, 'I don't know the answer, I will have to look it up,' I was shocked. I asked myself, 'Why is he teaching me?' In my country, a professor would give the wrong answer rather than admit ignorance."[50]

   There are two parts to this exercise. Part one is to discuss and analyze how decision making is made more complex when representatives of different cultures are attempting to make decisions and do business together.

   Part two is to discuss how you would manage the group decision-making process if all these parties were represented around a table and needed to make a decision that would affect your organization as well as theirs.

With a booming market on Wall Street, brokerage firm Charles Schwab & Co. has been growing at more than 20% per year. By 1998 the company had grown to 6,500 employees. But by the end of the year, Schwab was at least considering downsizing. In an interview in *Executive Excellence* Schwab CEO David Pottruck put forth his ideas on downsizing and Schwab's plan to prevent it.

Schwab had become one of the nation's largest financial services firms, serving 6.1 million active investor accounts, with $564 billion in customer assets through 302 branches, four regional customer telephone service centers, and automated telephonic and online channels. It received the most attention recently for its outstanding on-line services. Gomez Advisors, a leading on-line provider of objective e-commerce research and analysis, ranked Schwab first in a number of key categories, including customer confidence.

But while Schwab was adding staff, other firms were engaged in "cutting the fat." Technology could help firms replace repetitive jobs, reducing the need for some employees. Other firms found they could cut fat by reducing the number of employees whose jobs had become less valuable over time.

While these decisions made economic sense, there were high human costs. Research had indicated that only 35% of laid-off workers ended with jobs that paid as well as their old ones.

Pottruck said his company might be able to avoid downsizing if it adhered to five commitments:

1. Long-term growth
2. Industry leadership
3. Business expansion
4. Commitment to technology
5. Commitment to change

If Schwab could maintain these commitments, then management felt they would grow without adding the fat that growing organizations often add. As a result, they would not need to downsize in the future.

Discussion Questions

1. Schwab is basing its decision on five commitments. Are those five commitments the most important criteria of the downsizing/outsourcing decision?
2. Will fulfilling these commitments guarantee that Schwab will not need to downsize?
3. What factors would you consider in making your decision if you were Pottruck?

Shareholders of British Petroleum (BP) were faced with a challenging decision. BP CEO Sir John Browne had recommended that the venerable British company purchase long-time American competitor Amoco for $57 billion.

Browne had just led BP in the purchase of Atlantic Richfield just six months earlier for $27 billion. If the shareholders approved the deal, BP-Amoco would become the second largest oil producer in the world—not bad for a company that had been in serious financial trouble just seven years prior.

In a presentation to press and industry analysts, Sir Browne presented his view of the merger. Browne's presentation to shareholders was straightforward. The merger would make BP a "super-major" oil company, holding the third largest volume of oil and gas reserves. Browne portrayed the new company as having distinctive assets, global reach, and strongly competitive returns.

The company would be lightly restructured. The resulting synergies gained by the new firm would result in a net $2 billion pretax savings. The merger would also geographically diversify BP, improving the balance in its revenues between the United States, Europe, and the rest of the world.

BP's earnings in 1997 were $4.6 billion and Amoco's totaled $2.7 billion. Combined revenues of the two giants would total $108 billion. The current combined market capitalization (the total value of its shares) of some $110 billion would create Britain's largest company.

Critics of the proposal suggested it was not so simple. Among other issues, Sir Browne needed to develop a strategy for BP's natural gas assets. The merger was scheduled to make BP the world's third largest producer of natural gas (only smaller than the Russian giant Gazprom and the U.S. Company Exxon). Analysts had predicted that demand for natural gas would grow twice as fast as that for oil, yet there were questions about BP's knowledge and skills in this area. Former Amoco executives said the company did not understand the global nature of the gas business.

There was also concern that Browne might not be able to grow the new business. Browne had shown great skill in cutting costs and gaining efficiencies, but analysts were still concerned. It takes a different set of skills to cut a company than to grow it. For all his success, Browne had not clearly demonstrated to everyone's satisfaction that he could move a company to sustained growth.

Still, the numbers presented by Browne and his management team were impressive. They were careful to document the sources of their estimated $2 billion in cost savings, providing assurances that these moves were well planned. Further, the management team suggested its numbers were conservative as they did not reflect any synergies that

might occur in revenue generation—only those that came from cost cutting. As a result, the $2 billion improvement in profit might be conservative. Further, the management team at BP had linked its own management compensation to meeting the strategic cost targets.

In describing the merger to BP shareholders, Browne described the BP-Amoco link-up in glowing terms, as "a superb alliance of equals with complementary strategic and geographical strengths which effectively creates a new super-major that can better serve our millions of customers worldwide."

There was a great deal of information to consider when making the decision. The Securities and Exchange Commission (SEC) filings alone concerning the acquisition were more than 100 pages. There were strong opinions for and against the acquisition.

Discussion Questions

1. What criteria do you think BP used in making its decision? Why do you think BP chose those criteria? Would you consider their decision process rational?

2. What criteria might you use as an investor that would be different from BP's?

3. What decision do you think the shareholders should make, and why?

YOU BE THE CONSULTANT

WHERE TO OPEN NEXT?

Some of the biggest decisions Michael Dorf and his executive team have to make concern the locations of their new Knitting Factory music clubs. Indeed, much of the millions of dollars they recently raised from private investors is earmarked to go into building new clubs, so the decisions KnitMedia makes regarding these clubs will have a big effect on the company's success.

When you talk to Dorf, it's apparent how complicated making one of these club location decisions can be. For example, for many years KnitMedia worked on opening its first club abroad in London, but it never happened. Why? According to Dorf, "The real estate deal fell through. It was a joint venture with the South Bank, which is a publicly supported arts institution that gets its funding from the British Arts Council, which receives its funding from the lottery, and due to all kinds of political reasons beyond our control, the

lottery did not grant to the Arts Council, which in turn didn't grant to the South Bank, the funding for them to do their whole complex and renovation of which we were to be part."

It therefore looks like KnitMedia's first club abroad will open in Berlin, Germany. But as Dorf explains it, opening a club anywhere—and particularly abroad—is "not as easy as building a Web site. You know, there are local laws and local politics and numerous elements that go into a large facility like a Knitting Factory." Just building the balcony for the new club in Hollywood involved over 200 tons of steel, for instance, plus dealing with building codes, union regulations, and inspections. And construction problems are just part of the overall decision-making process when it comes to deciding where to open a new club.

Michael Dorf is a very, very smart person whose business has thrived so far in large part because of his decision-making ability. However, he wants to make sure that he's using all the decision-making tools he can when it comes to deciding where to open his next club abroad. He wants your advice.

Team Exercises and Questions

Use what you learned in this chapter to answer the following questions from Michael Dorf and his management team:

1. We want to make sure we don't make any unnecessary errors. What are the main stumbling blocks to good decision-making that we ought to be on the lookout for?

2. In our opinion, the problem we want to address here is, "Where should we open our next Knitting Factory abroad?" Do you agree that we've defined the problem accurately? If not, what do you think the problem statement should be?

3. You've told us that information is very important in making decisions. What specific kinds of information do you think we need to make our new club abroad decision? Where specifically do you think we ought to get that information?

4. We obviously ran into unanticipated consequences in opening the London Knitting Factory (actually, in *not* opening the London Knitting Factory, as it turned out). What do you think we did wrong in London? Did we choose the wrong location? Did we not manage the process properly? How can we avoid making the same mistakes again?

QUANTITATIVE DECISION-MAKING AIDS

Many decisions (particularly programmed ones) lend themselves to solution through quantitative analysis. Here are several of the more popular quantitative decision-making techniques.

▶ BREAKEVEN ANALYSIS

In financial analysis, the breakeven point is that volume of sales at which revenues just equal expenses, and you have neither a profit nor a loss. **Breakeven analysis** is a decision-making aid that enables a manager to determine whether a particular volume of sales will result in losses or profits.[1]

breakeven analysis
a financial analysis decision-making aid that enables a manager to determine whether a particular volume of sales will result in losses or profits.

Breakeven Charts

Breakeven analysis makes use of four basic concepts: fixed costs, variable costs, revenues, and profits. *Fixed costs* (such as for the plant and machinery) are costs that basically do not change with changes in volume. In other words, you might use the same machine to produce 10 units, 50 units, or 200 units of a product. *Variable costs* (such as for raw material) rise in proportion to volume. *Revenue* is the total income received from sales of the product. For example, if you sell 50 dolls at $8 each, then

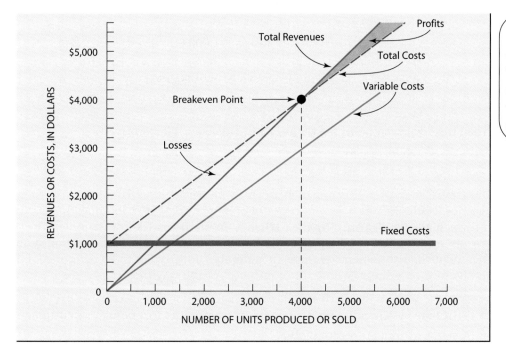

◀ **F I G U R E   A 4 . 1**

A Breakeven Chart

The breakeven point is that number of units sold at which total revenues just equal total costs.

your revenue is 8×50, or $400. *Profit* is the money you have left after subtracting fixed and variable costs from revenues.

A *breakeven chart*, as in Figure A4.1, is a graph that shows whether a particular volume of sales will result in profits or losses. The fixed costs line is horizontal, since fixed costs remain the same, regardless of level of output. Variable costs, however, increase in proportion to output and are shown as an upward sloping line. The total costs line is then equal to variable costs plus fixed costs at each level of output. The *breakeven point* is the point where the total revenue line crosses the total costs line. Beyond this point (note the shaded area in Figure A4.1), total revenue exceeds total costs. In this example, an output of about 4,000 units is the breakeven point. Above this, the company can expect to earn a profit. But if sales are fewer than 4,000 units, the company can expect a loss.

Breakeven Formula

The breakeven chart provides a picture of the relationship between sales volume and profits. However, a chart is not required for determining breakeven points. Instead, you can use a formula:

$$P(X) = F + V(X)$$

where

$$F = \text{fixed costs}$$

$$V = \text{variable costs per unit}$$

$$X = \text{volume of output (in units)}$$

$$P = \text{price per unit}$$

Rearranging this formula, the breakeven point is $X = F(P - V)$. In other words, the breakeven point is the volume of sales where total costs just equal total revenues. If, for example, you have a product in which

$$F = \text{fixed costs} = \$1,000.00$$

$$V = \text{variable costs per unit} = \$.75$$

$$P- = \text{price per unit} = \$1.00 \text{ per unit}$$

then the breakeven point is $1,000/($1.00 - $.75) = 4,000$ units.

▶ LINEAR PROGRAMMING

linear programming
a mathematical method used to solve resource allocation problems.

Breakeven analysis is only one of many quantitative decision techniques. Decision-science techniques are a second category of programmed decision-making aids, all of which are distinguished by their reliance on mathematics. For example, **linear programming** is a mathematical method used to solve resource allocation problems, which arise "whenever there are a number of activities to be performed, but limitations on either the amount of resources or the way they can be spent."[2] For example, it can be used to determine the best way to

- Distribute merchandise from a number of warehouses to a number of customers;
- Assign personnel to various jobs;

- Design shipping schedules;
- Select the product mix in a factory to make the best use of machine and labor hours available while maximizing the firm's profit;
- Route production to optimize the use of machinery.

In order for managers to apply linear programming successfully, the problem must meet certain basic requirements: There must be a stated, quantifiable goal, such as "minimize total shipping costs"; the resources to be utilized must be known (a firm could produce 200 of one item and 300 of another, for instance, or 400 of one or 100 of another); all the necessary relationships must be expressed in the form of mathematical equations or inequalities; and all these relationships must be linear in nature. An example can help illustrate:

> Shader Electronics has five manufacturing plants and twelve warehouses scattered across the country. Each plant is manufacturing the same product and operating at full capacity. Since plant capacity and location do not permit the closest plant to fully support each warehouse, Shader would like to identify the factory that should supply each warehouse in order to minimize total shipping costs. Applying linear programming techniques to this problem will provide an optimum shipping schedule.

▶ WAITING-LINE/QUEUING TECHNIQUES

Waiting-line/queuing techniques are mathematical decision-making techniques for solving waiting-line problems. For example, bank managers need to know how many tellers they should have. If they have too many, they are wasting money on salaries; if they have too few, they may end up with many disgruntled customers. Similar problems arise when selecting the optimal number of airline reservations clerks, warehouse loading docks, highway toll booths, supermarket checkout counters, and so forth.

waiting-line/queuing techniques
mathematical techniques used to solve waiting-line problems such that the optimal balance of employees available to waiting customers is attained.

▶ STATISTICAL DECISION THEORY TECHNIQUES

Statistical decision theory techniques are used to solve problems for which information is incomplete or uncertain. Suppose a shopkeeper can stock either Brand A or Brand B, but not both. She knows how much it will cost to stock her shelves with each brand, and she also knows how much money she would earn (or lose) if each brand turned out to be a success (or failure) with her customers. However, she can only estimate how much of each brand she might sell, so her information is incomplete. Using statistical decision theory, the shopkeeper would assign probabilities (estimates of the likelihood that the brand will sell or not) to each alternative. Then she could determine which alternative—stocking Brand A or Brand B—would most likely result in the greatest profits.

statistical decision theory techniques
techniques used to solve problems for which information is incomplete or uncertain.

Three Degrees of Uncertainty

Statistical decision theory is based on the idea that a manager may face three degrees of uncertainty in making a decision. Some decisions are made under conditions of **certainty**. Here, the manager knows in advance the outcome of the decision. From a practical point of view, for example, you know that if you buy a $50 U.S. savings bond, the interest you will earn to maturity on the bond is, say, 6%. Managers rarely make decisions under conditions of certainty.

certainty
the condition of knowing in advance the outcome of a decision.

At the opposite extreme, some decisions are made under conditions of **uncertainty**. Here, the manager cannot even assign probabilities to the likelihood of the various outcomes. For example, a shopkeeper may have several new products that could be stocked, but no idea of the likelihood that one brand will be successful or that another will fail. Conditions of complete uncertainty are also relatively infrequent. Most management decisions are made under conditions of **risk**. Under conditions of risk, the manager can at least assign probabilities to each outcome. In other words, the manager knows (either from past experience or by making an educated guess) the chance that each possible outcome (such as Product A being successful or Product B being successful) will occur.

Decision Tree

A **decision tree** is one technique for making a decision under conditions of risk. With a decision tree like the one in Figure A4.2, an expected value can be calculated for each alternative. **Expected value** equals (1) the probability of the outcome multiplied by (2) the benefit or cost of that outcome.

For example, in the figure, it pays our shopkeeper to stock Brand B rather than Brand A. Stocking Brand A allows a 70% chance of success for an $800 profit, so the shopkeeper has to balance this possible expected $560 profit against the possibility of the $90 loss (.30 × possible loss of −$300). The expected value of stocking Brand A is thus $470. By stocking Brand B, though, the expected value is a relatively high $588.

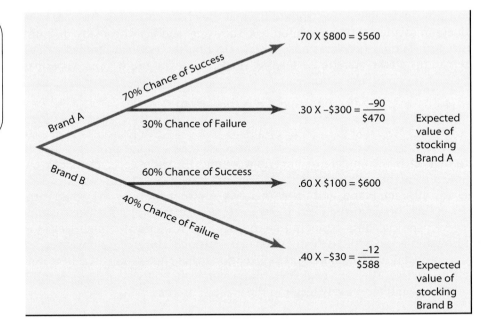

► **FIGURE A4.2**

Example of a Decision Tree

The expected value of each alternative is equal to (1) the chance of success or failure times (2) the expected profit or loss.

PLANNING AND SETTING OBJECTIVES

WHAT'S AHEAD?

While most people assume Wal-Mart's people-friendly stores and great selection account for the firm's success, some planning experts believe it's actually the firm's data warehouse. What's a data warehouse? It's a computerized repository of information. Wal-Mart's data warehouse collects information on things like sales, inventory, products in transit, and product returns from Wal-Mart's 3,000 stores. Wal-Mart managers can monitor this information to see what's actually "occurring on the ground", analyze trends, understand customers, and more effectively manage inventory. For example (as we'll see later in this chapter), the data warehouse enables Wal-Mart managers to make uncannily accurate forecasts about how much of what products will be sold (based on past experience). It therefore helps the company, and vendors like Warner-Lambert, develop amazingly accurate and realistic manufacturing plans, and is a good example of how leading-edge managers plan today.[1]

OBJECTIVES

AFTER STUDYING THIS CHAPTER, YOU SHOULD BE ABLE TO

- Define planning
- List the five steps in the planning process
- Formulate effective objectives
- Create a hierarchy of objectives
- Write an executive action plan

"We've finished your tower."

Planning, the subject of this chapter, is often called the "first among equals" of the four management functions (planning, organizing, leading, and controlling), since it establishes the goals that are (or should be) the basis of all these functions. The people you hire, the incentives you use, and the controls you institute all relate to what you want to achieve and to the plans and goals you set. (Conversely, the way your plans are implemented—the final results—will be no better than the people you have doing the work and how they do it.) In this chapter we'll focus on planning and on the techniques for setting goals and objectives. Then, in Chapter 6, we'll turn to the crucial subject of strategic planning, in other words to setting the long-term, companywide plans for your enterprise.

▶ **THE NATURE AND PURPOSE OF PLANNING**

Why Plan?

Plans, as Wal-Mart knows well, are methods formulated for achieving a desired result. All plans specify goals (such as "boost sales by 10%") and courses of action (such as "hire a new salesperson and boost advertising expenditures by 20%"). Plans should specify, at a minimum, what you will do, how you will do it, and by when you'll get it done.[2] **Planning**, therefore, is "the process of establishing objectives and courses of action, prior to taking action."[3] **Goals**, or **objectives**, are specific results you want to achieve. Wal-Mart's data warehouse helps its managers forecast what its customers will buy, and therefore to plan to have that merchandise in their stores when it is needed. In this section we'll look at the nature of planning, and then turn to the methods managers use to forecast the future.

plan
a method for doing or making something and consisting of a goal and a course of action.

planning
the process of setting goals and courses of action, developing rules and procedures, and forecasting future outcomes.

goal
a specific result to be achieved; the end result of a plan.

objectives
specific results toward which effort is directed.

As you can see from these descriptions, planning and decision making (the subject of Chapter 4) are closely intertwined. Planning means choosing your objectives and the courses of action that will get you there. In other words, when you make a plan, you're really deciding ahead of time what you or your company are going to do in the future. A plan is thus a group of premade decisions that will allow you to achieve a future goal.

So if you're planning a trip to Paris, your plan might include the following decisions: the date you leave; how you get to the airport; your airline and flight; the airport of arrival; how you'll get into Paris; your hotel; and (of course) a fairly detailed itinerary (or plan) for each day you're in Paris. You could just wing it, and many people do. If you don't decide ahead of time how you're getting to or from the airport, or what you'll be doing on each of your days in Paris, what will happen? Perhaps nothing. More likely, though, you'll find yourself having to make a lot of last-minute decisions under stressful conditions. Instead of arranging ahead of time to have a friend take you to the airport, you may be scrambling at the last minute to find a cab. Instead of researching and pricing your options ahead of time, you may find yourself at Orly Airport, tired, and faced with a bewildering variety of buses and cabs, including some high-priced "gypsy" cabs. And instead of deciding ahead of time in the comfort of your home (and with all your guidebooks) what you'll do each day, you may kill two hours or more each day deciding what to do and finding out what is open, or drifting aimlessly through the Paris streets (which is not necessarily all bad, of course). Done right, planning also forces you to get in touch with what's actually happening "on the ground"—for instance, to check to see if the Louvre is closed the day you arrive because it's a national holiday. Your Paris plans thus will be quite useful, and your trip a lot more pleasant than it might be without a plan.

The point, again, is that planning gives you the luxury of deciding ahead of time what you're going to do. You don't have to plan, but if you don't, you're going to find yourself scrambling, probably under less-than-hospitable conditions, to make those decisions on the run. And this can lead to lots of errors.

Here's another example. If you are like most readers of this book, you're probably reading it as part of a management course. And why are you taking this course? Chances are the course is part of your program of studies. This program (it is hoped) is planned. It identifies your goal (say, getting a degree in business in two years), and it identifies how you will get that degree, by specifying the courses you'll need to graduate. Your plans may not end with earning the degree (although for many students, just doing so while working may be hassle enough for now). You may also have a broader goal, a vision of where you're headed in life. If you do, then your degree may be just one step in a longer-term plan. For example, suppose you dream of running your own management consulting firm by the time you are 35. Now (you ask yourself), "What do I have to do to achieve this goal?" The answer may be to work for a nationally known consulting firm, thus building up your experience and your reputation in the field. So here is your plan: Take this course to get the degree, get the degree to get the consulting job, and then work hard as a consultant to achieve your dream.

What Planning Accomplishes

In discussing the trip to Paris, we mentioned one big benefit of planning: You get to make your decisions ahead of time, in the comfort of your home (or office), and with the luxury of having the time to do research and weigh your options. There are a few other benefits of planning.

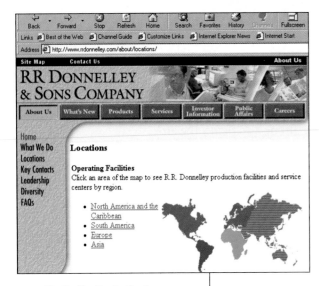

Planning provides direction and a sense of purpose. "If you don't know where you're going, any path will get you there," Alice is told as she stumbles into Wonderland. The same is true for all your endeavors: In the career example above, knowing ahead of time your goal is to have your own consulting firm provides a sense of direction and purpose for all the career decisions you have to make, such as what to major in and what experience you'll need along the way. This helps you avoid piecemeal decision making: It's a lot easier to decide what to major in and what courses to take when you've got a clear career objective.

The same is true in management: A plan provides a unifying framework against which decisions can be measured. For example, R. R. Donnelley & Sons Company is in the business of printing documents and other materials for a broad range of clients including investment bankers. Indeed, the company today is a leading content manager and printer of books, magazines, and catalogs, and is one of the world's largest manager, storer, and distributor of books in electronic form.[4] Donnelley's planning led its managers to anticipate a demand caused by the globalization of its customers. The company therefore invested heavily in advanced technology and a worldwide network. Now, with the help of satellites, R. R. Donnelley can print a securities prospectus simultaneously in locations around the globe.[5]

It would have been wasteful for R. R. Donnelley to spend its investment dollars building ever-bigger printing factories in the United States. The globalization of its customers demanded—and technological advances made possible—that it be capable of transmitting and creating documents via satellite around the globe. Its plan for doing so helped ensure that the firm channeled all its resources toward those desired results, thus avoiding activities—such as building unneeded domestic printing plants—that were inconsistent with the firm's overall direction.

Management theorist Peter Drucker says that planning can also help identify potential opportunities and threats and at least reduce long-term risks.[6] For example, R. R. Donnelley's planning process helped identify the opportunity for satellite-based global printing.

Planning facilitates control. Control means ensuring that activities conform to plans; it is a three-step process in which standards are set, performance is measured against these standards, and deviations are identified and corrected. Planning is the first step in this cycle—specifying what is to be achieved. Thus, a company's plan may specify that its profits will double within five years. This goal can then be a standard against which the manager's performance is measured, compared, and controlled.

descriptive plan

a plan that state's what is to be achieved and how.

budget

a financial plan, showing financial expectations for a specific period.

graphic plan

a plan that shows graphically or in charts what is to be achieved and how.

Types of Plans

While all plans specify goals and the courses of action chosen for reaching them, the plans themselves can come in all shapes and sizes, and each makes sense under different circumstances. For example, plans differ in format, or the way they are expressed. **Descriptive plans**, like the career plan above, state in words what is to be achieved and how. Plans stated in financial terms are called **budgets**. **Graphic plans** show what is to be achieved and how in charts.

Plans also differ in the spans of time they cover. Top management usually engages in long-term (5- to 10-year) strategic planning. A **strategic plan**—such as Wal-Mart's plan to expand abroad and apply its leading-edge planning methods globally—specifies the business or businesses the firm will be in and the major steps it must take to get there. Middle managers typically focus on developing shorter-term tactical plans (of up to five years' duration). **Tactical plans** (also sometimes called **functional plans**) show how top management's plans are to be carried out at the departmental level. First-line managers focus on shorter-term **operational plans**, or detailed day-to-day planning. These might show, for instance, exactly which workers are to be assigned to which machines or exactly how many units will be produced on a given day.

Andrew Carnegie, an early-20th-century multimillionaire, supposedly once happily paid $10,000 (a royal sum at the time) for a remarkably simple day-to-day operational planning system, one that millions of people use to this day. "I will show you a way to plan your day," a planning expert supposedly told Carnegie, "and if you like my idea, you'll pay me $10,000 for it." The idea—which may seem obvious today—was to write a daily to-do list. "Each night before you go to bed," the advisor told Carnegie, "list in priority order the things you need to get done the following day. Then, when tomorrow comes, methodically cross off each task as you do it." Carnegie was reportedly so impressed with how it boosted his efficiency that he paid the adviser the very next day.

Some plans are made to be used once, and others over and over. For example, some plans are **programs** established to lay out in an orderly fashion all the steps in a major one-time project. In contrast, **standing plans** are made to be used repeatedly, as the need arises.[7] Policies, procedures, and rules are examples of standing plans. **Policies** usually set broad guidelines. For example, it might be the policy at Saks Fifth Avenue that "we sell only high-fashion apparel and top-of-the-line jewelry." **Procedures** specify what to do if a specific situation arises. For example, "Before refunding the customer's purchase price, the salesperson should carefully inspect the garment and then obtain approval for the refund from the floor manager." Finally, a **rule** is a highly specific guide to action. For example, "Under no condition will the purchase price be refunded after 30 days." Standing plans like procedures or rules are usually written so that the standing plan's purpose is clear.

▶ THE MANAGEMENT PLANNING PROCESS

There is nothing mysterious about the planning process, since, as we said, planning is something we all do every day, often without even knowing it. For example, what planning process would you follow to choose a career? Here are the basic steps you would probably take: (1) set a tentative career goal, such as "to work as a management consultant"; (2) analyze the situation to assess your skills and to determine the future prospects for management consulting; (3) determine what your alternative courses of action are for getting there—in other words the paths you'll follow (college major, summer experiences, etc.) to reach your goal of management consultant; (4) evaluate them; and finally (5) choose your plan, and write it down (including a budget to show the money you'll need and where it will come from). This process is summarized in Figure 5.1.

You may notice that the planning process parallels the decision-making process; this makes sense, since developing plans involves deciding today what you'll do tomorrow. Both involve establishing objectives on criteria, developing and analyzing alternatives based on information you obtain, evaluating the alternatives, and then making a choice.

---

strategic plan

a plan that outlines the course of action a firm plans to pursue in becoming the sort of enterprise it wants to be, given the firm's external opportunities and threats and its internal strengths and weaknesses.

tactical plan

a plan that shows how top management's plans are to be carried out at the departmental, short-term level.

functional plan

a tactical short-term plan showing how each department of a business will contribute to top management's plans.

operational plan

planning a short-term plan that shows the detailed daily steps of business operations.

program

a plan that lays out all the steps in proper sequence to a single-use, often one-time business project.

standing plan

a plan established to be used repeatedly, as the need arises.

policy

a standing plan that sets broad guidelines for the enterprise.

procedure

a plan that specifies how to proceed in specific situations that routinely arise.

rule

a highly specific guide to action.

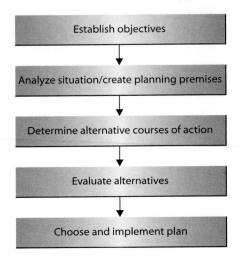

The planning process is basically the same when managers plan for their companies, but there are two added complications. First, there's usually a *hierarchical aspect* to management planning: Top management approves a long-term plan first; then each department creates its own budgets and other plans to show how it will contribute to the company's long-term plan.

Second—and especially in big companies—the planning process may be quite formal and involve much interaction and give-and-take between departments and a group we might call "corporate central." In other words, in many firms plans are bounced back and forth between the departments and a centralized planning staff, whose main purpose is to review and help define the plans of each department.

The Planning Hierarchy

In some respects, step 5 in Figure 5.1 (choose and implement the plan) is not the final step in the process. It is actually just the beginning because top management's goals then become the targets for which subsidiary units must formulate derivative plans. One result of the planning process is, therefore, a **hierarchy of plans**. The hierarchy includes (1) the enterprisewide plan and objectives and (2) subsidiary units' derivative plans and objectives, each of which contributes to achieving the enterprisewide plan and objectives.

hierarchy of plans

a set of plans that includes the enterprisewide plan and the derivative plans of subsidiary units required to help achieve the enterprisewide plan.

Example: Sunbeam In practice, a hierarchy of plans evolves. Several years ago the Sunbeam Corporation, which makes kitchen appliances, decided to drive down costs by at least 20%, by dramatically reducing the size of the firm (downsizing, in other words.) What evolved was a top-management plan to reduce the number of employees by half, roll out 30 new products per year, and shrink the number of factories and warehouses from more than 40 to just 13.

With that framework as a guide, lower-level plans then had to be crafted. For the coming year, for instance, managers for each product group had to formulate and have approved plans for the new products they would add, and those they would drop. The production head had to craft plans showing which plants were to close to meet the goal of closing almost 30 facilities.

Once these second-level plans were in place, third-level operational plans were needed. For example, once the HR manager knew which plants were to be closed, she would need specific plans for handling the dismissals. And each plant manager would need specific monthly production plans, once he or she knew the targets top management had set for the facility. There would thus evolve a hierarchy of plans of increasing specificity (and increasingly more short-term oriented the lower in the hierarchy the plan was) from the top of the firm to the bottom.

Example: Executive Assignment Action Plan Table 5.1 shows an executive assignment action plan for linking management's goals at one level to the derivative plans at the next level down.[8] (It actually specifies, as you can see, each executive's assignment for carrying out the overall plan.)

TABLE 5.1 Executive Assignment Action Plan for Achieving a Long-Term Objective

LONG-TERM OBJECTIVE: HAVE A MINIMUM OF 55% OF SALES REVENUE FROM CUSTOMIZED PRODUCTS BY 2003

Executive Assignments/ Derivative Objectives	Accountability		Schedule		Resources Required			Feedback Mechanisms
	Primary	Supporting	Start	Complete	Capital	Operating	Human	
1. Complete market study on sales potential for customized products	VP Marketing	VP Sales	Year 1	**Year 1**		$10,000	500 hrs.	Written progress reports
2. Revise sales forecasts for Years 1, 2, and 3 to reflect changes	VP Sales	VP Marketing		**Year 1**			50 hrs.	Revised forecasts
3. Convert Building C to customized manufacturing operation by 2003	VP Mfg.	VP Engineering VP Administration	Year 1	**Year 2**	$500,000	$80,000	1,100 hrs.	Written progress reports
4. Change compensation structure to incentivize customized sales	VP HR	VP Sales	Year 1	**Year 1**		$50,000	100 hrs.	Revised structure report
5. Train sales staff in new technology	Director of Training	VP Sales	Year 2	**Year 2**		$50,000	1,000 hrs.	Training plan reports
6. Expand production of customized products —to 25% —to 30% —to 40% —to 50% to 55%	VP Mfg.	VP Engineering	Year 1	**Year 2** **Year 2** **Year 3** **Year 3**		Budgeted	Budgeted	Production reports
7. Increase sales of customized products —to 25% —to 30% —to 40% —to 55%	VP Sales	VP Marketing	Year 1	**Year 2** **Year 2** **Year 3** **Year 3**				Sales reports
8. Revise sales forecasts	VP Sales	VP Marketing		**Year 3**				Revised forecasts

Note: This executive assignment action plan shows the specific executive assignments required to achieve top management's long-term objective, "Have a minimum of 55% of sales revenue from customized products by 2003."

In this case, one of top management's long-term goals is to "have a minimum of 55% of sales revenue from customized products by 2003." The action plan summarizes the derivative targets to be achieved by each department if that long-term objective is to be met. Thus, the vice president of marketing is to "complete market study on sales potential for customized products" within one year. The vice president of manufacturing is to "convert Building C to customized manufacturing operation" within a year.

Each vice president's assigned goals then become the target for which they must develop their own plans. This is illustrated in Table 5.2. Here the manufacturing vice president's goal of converting Building C to customized manufacturing is the target for which derivative plans must be formulated. For instance, converting Building C will entail completing a feasibility study, and purchasing and installing new equipment. The action plan helps ensure coordinated effort by the management team.

TABLE 5.2 **Action Plan for a Specific Executive Assignment**

EXECUTIVE ASSIGNMENT: CONVERT BUILDING C TO CUSTOMIZED MANUFACTURING OPERATION BY 2003*

Assignments/ Derivative Objectives	Accountability		Schedule		Resources Required			Feedback Mechanisms
	Primary	Supporting	Start	Complete	Capital	Operating	Human	
1. Complete feasibility study on conversion requirements	Director Engineering	VP Manufacturing	Year 1	**Year 1**		$10,000	100 hrs.	Written progress reports
2. Complete converted production line design and equipment specifications	Director Engineering	VP Manufacturing		**Year 1**		$50,000	500 hrs.	Design review meetings
3. Purchase and install new equipment	Purchasing	VP Manufacturing	Year 1	**Year 1**	$400,000		100 hrs.	Written progress reports
4. Modify existing equipment	VP Mfg.	VP Engineering	Year 1	**Year 1**	$100,000	$10,000	100 hrs.	Written progress reports
5. Train production staff	Director of Training	VP Manufacturing	Year 1	**Year 1**		$10,000	300 hrs.	Training plan reports
6. Initiate customized production line	VP Mfg.	VP Engineering				Budgeted	Budgeted	Production reports
7. Increase production of customized products —to 25% —to 30% —to 40% —to 50% to 55%	VP Mfg.	VP Engineering	Year 1	**Year 2** **Year 2** **Year 3** **Year 3**		Budgeted	Budgeted	Production reports
8. Reassess future production capacity	VP Mfg.	VP Engineering		**Year 3**				Production forecast

Source: Reprinted with permission from George Morrisey: *A Guide to Long-Range Planning.* Copyright © 1996 Jossey-Bass, Inc. All rights reserved.
*Note: This action plan shows the subsidiary assignments required to achieve the specific executive assignment, "Convert Building C to customized manufacturing operations by 2003."

■ The Importance of Top-Management Teamwork

As illustrated in the action plan, no single person can formulate and implement a strategy for a complex organization alone.[9] Therefore, creating a cohesive top-management team including the CEO and his or her subordinate officers is a precondition if a firm is to implement its plans and achieve its goals. Planning experts list several reasons why top-management teamwork is crucial for success[10]:

- The CEO has a complex coordination task and cannot be effective without working closely with the people who are in charge of the company's major activities (such as functions, products, or regions).

- The CEO's subordinate officers usually possess greater expertise about the operating components of the organization and their own fields of expertise than does the CEO.

- The team members can be more understanding of and supportive of the CEO's strategic decisions if they have a voice in shaping those decisions.

- Teamwork among the members of the top-management team enhances communication and coordination among them.

- Technical and administrative innovations will be more likely when team members have more opportunity for cross-functional communication.

Most CEOs therefore spend considerable time molding their subordinates into a cohesive team. Former Chairperson and CEO Stephen Wolf of United Airlines' reportedly worked closely on a daily basis with the executives in charge of areas like finance, marketing, and employee relations. His success in turning that company around is partially attributed to his ability to assemble a talented top-management team.[11]

The Goals Hierarchy

As you can see, the planning process produces not just a hierarchy of plans, but also a hierarchy of goals from the top to the lowest-level managers.[12] This is illustrated in Figure 5.2. At the top, the president and his or her staff set strategic goals (such as to have a minimum of 55% of sales revenue from customized products by 2003), to which each vice president's goal (such as to convert Building C to customized manufacturing operation) is then tied. A hierarchy of supporting departmental goals down to tactical and functional goals and finally short-term operational goals is then formulated.

The method needn't be complicated. When Gregg Foster purchased the troubled metal-converting Elyria Foundry, he knew the key to long-term prosperity was setting goals and then getting employees—from the shop floor to the top—committed to achieving them. "Goals are specific, but they also create a picture of how we want to be."[13]

Foster used a hierarchical approach. First, he set a few strategic goals to point out a broad direction for the firm. He next turned to his department managers, who each submitted five to ten supporting goals. Next, input from lower-level employees yielded goals ranging from retirement plan participation to qualifying for ISO 9000 (international quality management) certification.

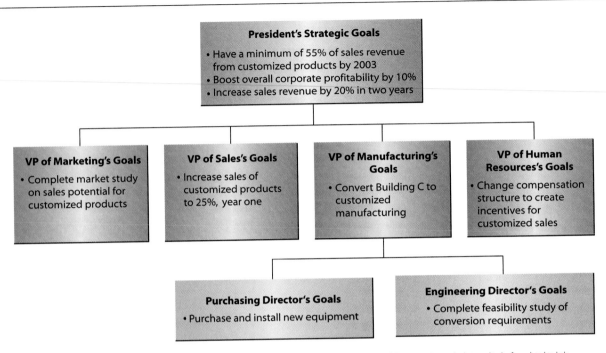

President's Strategic Goals
- Have a minimum of 55% of sales revenue from customized products by 2003
- Boost overall corporate profitability by 10%
- Increase sales revenue by 20% in two years

VP of Marketing's Goals
- Complete market study on sales potential for customized products

VP of Sales's Goals
- Increase sales of customized products to 25%, year one

VP of Manufacturing's Goals
- Convert Building C to customized manufacturing

VP of Human Resources's Goals
- Change compensation structure to create incentives for customized sales

Purchasing Director's Goals
- Purchase and install new equipment

Engineering Director's Goals
- Complete feasibility study of conversion requirements

Note: A hierarchy of goals like this is one important byproduct of the planning process. This figure shows some (not all) of the supporting goals that need to be formulated to help achieve the company's overall goal of having a minimum of 55% of its sales revenue from customized products by 2003.

The resulting goals hierarchy showed how each level's efforts contributed to attaining the goals at the next higher level and for the foundry as a whole. It also helped identify the dozens of things employees and managers felt needed to be fixed if the firm were to achieve Foster's overall goals. And the plan was realistic, since it was based on input from managers who were actually at ground level doing the job on a day-to-day basis.

► HOW TO SET OBJECTIVES

There is one thing on which every manager can expect to be appraised: the extent to which he or she achieves his or her unit's goals or objectives. Whether it's a work team or a giant enterprise, the manager in charge is expected to move the unit ahead, and this means visualizing where the unit must go and helping get there. Organizations exist to achieve some purpose, and if they fail to move forward and achieve their aims, to that extent they have failed. As Peter Drucker put it, "There has to be something to point to and say, we have not worked in vain."[14]

Effectively setting goals is important for other reasons. Objectives (or goals—we'll use the terms interchangeably) are the targets toward which plans are aimed, and the anchor around which the

▲ CEO Gregg Foster of Elyria Foundry cured a sick company by setting goals.

hierarchy of goals is constructed. Goals can also aid motivation. Employees—individually and in teams—focus their efforts on achieving concrete goals with which they agree, and usually perform better with goals than without them. In fact, when performance is inadequate, it is often not because the person or team is loafing, but because the individual or team doesn't know what the goals are.

All managers today require a good working knowledge of how to set goals or objectives. We'll look first at the various types of objectives, and then at how to set and express them.

Types of Objectives

The range of activities for which goals or objectives may be set is virtually limitless. In a classic analysis, Peter Drucker listed eight areas in which objectives should be set:

1. Market standing
2. Innovation
3. Productivity
4. Physical and financial resources
5. Profitability
6. Managerial performance and development
7. Worker performance and attitude
8. Public responsibility[15]

One planning expert listed more than a dozen other areas in which objectives may be set, including the following:

1. Market penetration
2. Future human competencies
3. Revenue/sales
4. Employee development
5. New product/service department
6. New/expanded market development
7. Program/project management
8. Technology
9. Research and development
10. Customer relations/satisfaction
11. Cost control/management
12. Quality control/assurance
13. Productivity
14. Process improvement
15. Production capability/capacity
16. Cross-functional integration
17. Supplier development/relations
18. Unit structure (reorganization)[16]

It is clear from these lists that profit maximization alone is not a good enough guide. It is true that in economic theory and in practice managers aim to maximize profits (although other goals, including social responsibility, are crucial too). However, managers also need specific objectives in areas like market penetration and customer service if they are to have any hope of boosting profits. (At the same time, top management must also take care that the goals are complete. People put their efforts where they know they count, so if you measure only market penetration or revenue, profits may be ignored.)

How to Set Motivational Goals

goal-setting studies
organizational behavior research that provides useful insights into how to set effective goals.

Goals are useful only to the extent that employees are motivated to achieve them. Managers can do several things to ensure that the goals they set do motivate employees. Research known as **goal-setting studies** provides useful insights into setting effective goals. They suggest the following:

Assign Specific Goals   Employees who are given specific goals usually perform better than those who are not. One study that illustrates this was conducted in an Oklahoma logging operation.[17] The subjects were truck drivers who had to load logs and drive them to the mill. An analysis of the truckers' performances showed that they often did not fill their trucks to the maximum legal net weight. The researchers believed this happened largely because the workers were urged to "do their best" when it came to loading the truck.

The researchers arranged for a specific goal ("94% of a truck's net weight") to be communicated to each driver. Performance (in terms of weight loaded on each truck) jumped markedly as soon as the truckers were assigned specific goals, and it generally remained at this much higher level. This and other evidence shows that setting specific goals with subordinates, rather than setting no goals or telling them to "do their best," can improve performance in a wide range of settings.[18]

Assign Measurable Goals[19]   Goals should be stated in quantitative terms and include target dates or deadlines. Goals set in absolute terms (such as "an average daily output of 300 units") are less confusing than goals set in relative terms (such as "improve production by 20%"). If measurable results will not be available, then "satisfactory completion"—such as "satisfactorily attended workshop" or "satisfactorily completed his or her degree"—is the next best thing. In any case, target dates or deadlines should always be set.

Assign Challenging but Doable Goals   Goals should be challenging, but not so difficult that they appear impossible or unrealistic.[20] Particularly in areas such as sales management, where immediate and concrete performance is obvious and highly valued, goals consistent with past sales levels—realistic yet high enough to be challenging—are widely used.[21]

When is a goal too difficult or too hard? As Yukl says:

A goal is probably too easy if it calls for little or no improvement in performance when conditions are becoming more favorable, or if the targeted level of performance is well below that of most other employees in comparable positions. A goal is probably too difficult if it calls for a large improvement in performance when conditions are worsening, or if the targeted level of performance is well above that of people in comparable positions.[22]

Encourage Participation Should managers assign their subordinates goals, or should they permit their subordinates to participate in developing their own goals? Research evidence on this point has been mixed, but we can reach five conclusions concerning the relative superiority of participatively set versus assigned goals:

First, employees who participate in setting their goals in fact tend to perceive themselves as having had more impact on setting those goals than do employees who are simply assigned goals.[23] *Second*, participatively set goals tend to be higher than the goals the supervisor would normally have assigned.[24] *Third*, even when goals set participatively are more difficult than the assigned ones, they are not perceived as such by the subordinates.[25] *Fourth*, participatively set goals do not consistently result in higher performance than assigned goals, nor do assigned goals consistently result in higher performance than participatively set ones. However, when the participatively set goals are higher and more difficult than the assigned goals, as is usually the case, the participatively set goals usually lead to higher performance. (The fact that the goal is more difficult, not the fact that it was participatively set, seems to account for the higher performance.)[26] *Finally*, goals unilaterally assigned by managers can trigger employee resistance, regardless of their reasonableness. Insofar as participation creates a sense of ownership in the goals, it can reduce resistance.[27]

▲ Like this interior design team, employee teams at Saturn's Spring Hill, Tennessee, plant, often participate in setting goals.

How to Express the Goal

Knowing how to express the goal is important, too. As Table 5.3 illustrates, it's important to distinguish between an *area to be measured* (such as sales), a *yardstick* (such as sales revenue), and a *goal* (such as $85,000 per month). There are usually several possible yardsticks for any measurable area. The area of "sales" could be measured in terms of sales revenue or market share. Remember to state any goal in measurable terms.

TABLE 5.3 **Examples of Yardsticks and Goals**

Area to Be Measured	Yardstick	Goal
Sales	Sales revenue	$85,000 per month
Production	Productivity	Produce at least five units per labor hour
Customer reactions	Satisfaction	Zero complaints
Quality	Number of rejects	No more than three rejects per 100 items produced
Employee behavior	Absenteeism Accidents Turnover	No more than 3% absences/week No serious accidents permitted 10% turnover maximum
Finances	Profitability Turnover	20% profit margins Sales − inventory = 8%
Expenses	Phone bill Raw materials Supplies	$300 per month maximum 20% of sales 5% of sales

TABLE 5.4	Examples of Well-Stated Objectives

MORRISEY'S FOUR-POINT MODEL	
To (1) (*action/verb*)	(2) (single measurable *result*)
by (3) (*target* date/time span)	(4) *at* (*cost* in time and/or energy)

EXAMPLES OR OBJECTIVES THAT FOLLOW THE MODEL

- To (1,2) complete the Acme project by (3) December 31 at a (4) cost not to exceed $50,000 and five hundred work-hours.
- To (1) decrease the (2) average cost of sales by a minimum of 5 percent, effective (3) June 1, at an (4) implementation cost not to exceed forty work-hours.
- To release (1, 2) product A to manufacturing by (3) September 30 at a cost not to (4) exceed $50,000 and five thousand engineering hours.
- To (1) reduce (2) average turnaround time on service requests from eight to six hours by (3) July 31 at an implementation cost (4) of forty work-hours.

Source: Reprinted with permission from George Morrisey, *A Guide to Tactical Planning.* Copyright © 1996 Jossey-Bass, Inc. All rights reserved.

Planning expert George Morrisey presents a four-point model for use in formulating objectives:

To (1) (action/verb)

(2) the (single measurable *result*)

by (3) (*target date/time span*)

(4) at (*cost in time and/or energy*)

Table 5.4 presents several examples.

Using Management by Objectives

management by objectives (MBO)

a technique in which supervisor and subordinate jointly set goals for the latter and periodically assess progress toward those goals.

Management by objectives (MBO) is a technique used by many firms to assist in the process of setting organizationwide objectives as well as goals for subsidiary units and their employees. Supervisor and subordinate jointly set goals for the latter and periodically assess progress toward those goals. A manager may engage in a modest MBO program by setting goals with his or her subordinates and periodically providing feedback. However, the term *MBO* almost always refers to a comprehensive organizationwide program for setting goals, one usually reserved for managerial and professional employees. One advantage of this technique (in terms of the goal-setting studies just reviewed) is that, implemented properly, it can lead to specific, measurable, and participatively set objectives.

The MBO process generally consists of five steps:

1. *Set organization goals.* Top management sets strategic goals for the company.

2. *Set department goals.* Department heads and their superiors jointly set supporting goals for their departments.

3. *Discuss department goals.* Department heads present department goals and ask all subordinates to develop their own individual goals.

4. *Set individual goals.* Goals are set for each subordinate, and a timetable is assigned for accomplishing those goals.

5. *Give feedback*. The supervisor and subordinate meet periodically to review the subordinate's performance and to monitor and analyze progress toward his or her goals.[28]

Managers can do several things to make an MBO program successful. They can state goals in measurable terms, be specific, and make sure each person's goals are challenging but attainable. Goals should also be reviewed and updated periodically, and be flexible enough to be changed if conditions warrant.[29]

Again, however, an effective MBO program requires more than just setting goals. The main purpose is integrating the goals of the individual, of the unit in which the individual works, and of the company as a whole. In fact, to Drucker, the creator of MBO, the method was always more a philosophy than a rigid sequence of steps. As he said, "the goals of each manager's job must be defined by the contribution he or she has to make to the success of the larger unit of which they are part." MBO therefore basically gives managers a road map for how to link the goals at each level and across the firm's departments, and to thereby create the company's hierarchy of goals.

▶ DEVELOPING PLANNING PREMISES

Good plans—whether for a career, a trip to Paris, or an expansion by Wal-Mart into Europe—are built on premises, assumptions we make about the future. Managers use several techniques to produce the premises on which they build their plans. These include forecasting, marketing research, and competitive intelligence.

Sales Forecasting Techniques

IBM's strategy in the new century—for instance to make all its products more Internet-compatible—reflects the assumptions it made regarding demand for its traditional products like mainframe computers. Forecast means to estimate or calculate in advance or to predict.[30] In business, forecasting often starts with predicting the direction and magnitude of the company's sales.

There are two broad classes of sales forecasting methods: quantitative and qualitative. Quantitative forecasting methods use statistical methods to examine data and find underlying patterns and relationships. Qualitative forecasting methods emphasize human judgment.

Quantitative Methods Quantitative methods like time-series methods and causal models forecast by assuming that past relationships will continue into the future. A time series is a set of observations taken at specific times, usually at equal intervals. Examples of time series are the yearly or monthly gross domestic product of the United States over several years, a department store's total monthly sales receipts, and the daily closing prices of a share of stock.[31]

If you plot time-series data on a graph for several periods, you may note various patterns. For example, if you were to plot monthly sales of Rheem air conditioning units, you would find seasonal increases in late spring and summer, and reduced sales in the winter months. For some types of time series, there may also be an irregular pattern, such as a sudden blip in the graph that reflects unexplained variations in the data.

premise
an assumption made about the future.

forecast
to estimate or calculate in advance or to predict.

quantitative forecasting
a type of forecasting in which statistical methods are used to examine data and find underlying patterns and relationships; includes time-series methods and causal models.

qualitative forecasting
predictive techniques that emphasize logical, unbiased human judgment and may include both technological and judgmental methods.

time series
a set of observations taken at specific times, usually at equal intervals, to identify fundamental patterns.

The basic purpose of all time-series forecasting methods is to remove irregular and seasonal patterns so that management can identify fundamental trends.

Managers often need to understand the causal relationship between two variables, such as their company's sales and an indicator of economic activity, like disposable income. **Causal methods** develop a projection based on the mathematical relationship between a company factor and those variables that management believes influence or explain the company factor.[32] The basic premise of causal models is that a particular factor—such as company sales of television sets—is directly influenced by some other, more predictable, factor or factors—such as the number of people unemployed in a state or the level of disposable income in the United States.[33] **Causal forecasting** thus estimates the company factor (such as sales) based on other factors (such as advertising expenditures or level of unemployment). Statistical techniques such as correlation analysis (which shows how closely the variables are related) are generally used to develop the necessary relationships.

Companies like Wal-Mart use sophisticated technology to forecast sales; the "Managing @ the Speed of Thought" box provides an example.

causal methods

forecasting techniques that develop projections based on the mathematical relationship between a certain factor and the variables believed to influence or explain that factor.

causal forecasting

estimating a company factor (such as sales) based on other influencing factors (such as advertising expenditures or unemployment levels).

MANAGING @ THE *SPEED* OF THOUGHT

■ Demand Forecasting at Wal-Mart

When it comes to retailing, Wal-Mart is larger than its three closest competitors combined, and that's not just because it buys its merchandise inexpensively. Wal-Mart has what is probably the most sophisticated information technology system in all of retailing, and it uses that system's power to give its customers what they want, while squeezing every bit of extraneous cost from its products.

Wal-Mart's data warehouse (introduced in the chapter opener) is a good example of how Wal-Mart does this. Recall that the data warehouse collects information on things like sales, inventory, products in transit, and product returns from Wal-Mart's 3,000 stores. These data are then analyzed to help Wal-Mart's managers analyze trends, understand customers, and more effectively manage inventory. How is this information used? As one example, Wal-Mart is implementing a new demand-forecasting system. Its data warehousing tracks the sale by store of 100,000 Wal-Mart products. This powerful system lets Wal-Mart managers examine the sales of individual items for individual stores, and also creates seasonal profiles for each item. Armed with this information, managers can more accurately plan what items will be needed for each store and when.

Wal-Mart is also teaming with vendors like Warner-Lambert to create an Internet-based collaborative forecasting and replenishment (CFAR) system. Wal-Mart collects data (on things like sales by product and by store, and seasonal trends) for its sales of Warner-Lambert products. Managers at Wal-Mart and Warner-Lambert then collaborate to develop forecasts for sales by store for Warner-Lambert products, such as Listerine. Once Warner-Lambert and Wal-Mart planners decide on mutually acceptable figures, a purchase plan is finalized and sent to Warner-Lambert's manufacturing planning system. So far, CFAR has helped cut the supply cycle time for Listerine from 12 weeks to 6, and that means less inventory, lower costs, and better buys for Wal-Mart customers.[34]

Qualitative Forecasting Methods   Time series and causal forecasting have three big limitations: They are virtually useless when data are scarce, such as for a new product with no sales history; they assume that historical trends will continue into the future.[35] They also tend to disregard unforeseeable, unexpected occurrences. Yet it is exactly these unexpected occurrences that often have the most profound effects on companies.

Qualitative forecasting techniques emphasize and are based on human judgment. They gather, in as logical, unbiased, and systematic a way as possible, all the information and human judgment that can be brought to bear on the factors being forecast.[36] Don't underestimate the value of qualitative forecasting methods. It's true that in developing adequate plans hard data and numbers are usually very important. However, it's also true that if you want plans to be realistic, there's usually no substitute for an intelligent human analysis of the situation and its possible consequences for the company.

The **jury of executive opinion** is one such qualitative forecasting technique. It involves asking a jury of key executives to forecast sales for, say, the next year. Generally, each executive is given data on forecasted economic levels and anticipated changes. Each jury member then makes an independent forecast. Differences are reconciled by the president or during a meeting of the executives. In an enhancement of this approach, experts from various departments gather to make the forecast.

The **sales force estimation** method is similar to the jury of executive opinion technique, but it gathers the opinions of the sales force regarding what they think sales will be in the forthcoming period. Each salesperson estimates his or her next year's sales, usually by product and customer. Sales managers then review each estimate, compare it with the previous year's data, and discuss changes with each salesperson. The separate estimates are then combined into a single sales forecast for the firm.

Marketing Research

Tools like causal models and sales force estimation can help managers explore the future to develop more accurate planning premises. However, there are times when, to formulate plans, managers want to know not just what may happen in the future, but what customers are thinking right now. **Marketing research** refers to the procedures used to develop and analyze customer-related information that helps managers make decisions.[37]

Marketing researchers depend on two main types of information. One source is **secondary data**, or information that has been collected or published already. Good sources of secondary data include the Internet, libraries, trade associations, company files and sales reports, and commercial data, for instance from companies such as A. C. Nielsen. **Primary data** refer to information specifically collected to solve a current problem. Primary data sources include mail and personal surveys, in-depth and focus-group interviews, and personal observation (watching the reactions of customers who walk into a store).[38]

jury of executive opinion
a qualitative forecasting technique in which a panel of executives are given pertinent data and asked to make independent sales forecasts, which are then reconciled in an executive meeting or by the company president.

sales force estimation
a forecasting technique that gathers and combines the opinions of the sales people on what it predicts sales will be in the forthcoming period.

marketing research
the procedures used to develop and analyze current customer-related information to help managers make decisions.

secondary data
information for analyzing a situation that has already been collected or published.

primary data
information specifically collected to address a current problem.

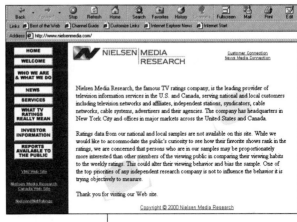

▲ **W E B N O T E**

Nielsen uses the Web to communicate with its customers (such as advertising firms) who in turn use the Nielsen data for planning purposes.

www.nielsenmedia.com

Copyright © 1999 Nielsen Media Research, Inc.

▲ A focus group is an example of a primary data source. Here we see the videotaping of a focus group through a two-way mirror at an ad agency.

competitive intelligence
systematic techniques used to obtain and analyze public information about competitors.

Competitive Intelligence

Developing useful plans often requires knowing as much as possible about what competitors are doing or are planning to do. **Competitive intelligence** (CI) is a systematic way to obtain and analyze public information about competitors. Although this sounds (and is) a lot like legalized spying, it's become much more popular over the past few years. According to one report, the number of large companies with CI groups has tripled since 1988, to about 1000.[39]

Competitive intelligence (CI) practitioners use a variety of techniques to find out what clients' competitors are doing. These include keeping track of existing and new competitors by having specialists visit their facilities, and hiring their workers and questioning their suppliers and customers. CI firms also do sophisticated Internet searches to dig up all available information about competitors, as well as more mundane searches like reading stock analysts' reports on the competitors' prospects. Several private CI consulting firms, including Kroll Associates, have built successful businesses using prosecutors, business analysts, and former FBI and Drug Enforcement Agency employees to ferret out the sorts of information one might want before entering into an alliance with another company or before deciding to get into a given business.

As Table 5.5 illustrates, CI consultants provide a range of information. For example, a firm can help client companies learn more about competitors' strengths and vulnerabilities, product strategies, investment strategies, financial capabilities, and current or prior behavior. Other CI services include evaluating the capabilities, weaknesses, and reputation of potential or existing joint-venture partners; identifying the major players in a new market or industry the firm is thinking of entering; and helping planners boost sales opportunities, for instance by identifying the decision makers who actually do the purchasing and the critical factors they look for in vendors.

Managers using CI must beware of slipping into activities that are ethically or legally wrong. Reading brokers' reports on a competitor or finding information about it on the Internet would be viewed as legitimate by almost everyone. However, when CI practitioners dig through the target's trash on public property to search for memos or hire former employees to pick their brains, ethical alarms should start ringing.

Some CI investigators may cross the line. For example, in a recent court case involving a large American chemical firm, former news reporters allegedly worked as investigators on behalf of one of the parties, posing as journalists to try to unearth confidential information about the firm. Another former reporter was allegedly offered a $25,000 bonus to get any national newspaper to publish a negative article about the company.[40]

	Competitive Intelligence: Kroll's Business Intelligence and
TABLE 5.5	**Analysis Services and Capabilities**

CI Can Address Four Critical Management Concerns	By Providing Intelligence Like This on Companies, Industries, and Countries
COMPETITION: Learning enough about competitors to devise proactive and reactive strategies, including competitors' strengths and vulnerabilities, product strategies, investment strategies, financial capabilities, operational issues, and anti-competitive behavior.	**Operations:** Nature of business, sales, locations, headcount. **Financial:** Ownership, assets, financing, profitability.
BUSINESS RELATIONSHIPS AND TRANSACTIONS: Evaluating the capabilities, weaknesses, and reputation of potential or existing joint venture partners, strategic alliances, acquisitions, distributors, licensees/licensors, critical suppliers/vendors, and project finance participants.	**Management:** Organization structure, decision makers, integrity/reputation, management style, history as partner, political connections. **Marketing/Customers:** Market position, major accounts, pricing, distribution, sales force, advertising.
ENTRY INTO NEW MARKETS: Developing entry strategies into new geographic and/or product markets, including identifying players in an industry, analyzing industry structure and trends, assessing local business practices, and ascertaining entry barriers, government regulation, and political risk.	**Manufacturing:** Plant and equipment, capacity, utilization, sourcing materials/components, shifts, labor costs, unions. **Technology:** New products and processes, research and development practices, technological assessment.
SALES OPPORTUNITIES: Maximizing opportunities to win contracts, develop major new customers, or maintain existing ones, including identifying purchasing decision makers and critical factors, determining current suppliers, understanding the competition, and assessing the status of bids.	**Strategic Directions:** Business priorities, diversification, geographic strategy, horizontal/vertical integration, strategic relationships. **Legal:** Lawsuits, judgments, potential liabilities, environmental exposure.

► **PLANNERS IN ACTION**

So far in this chapter we've explained the planning process and some techniques for setting goals and predicting the future. In this final section we turn to a discussion of how planners actually plan, in other words to illustrations of planners and planning departments in action.

Who Does the Planning?

Who does the planning depends a lot on the size of the firm. The basic process—set goals, develop background information such as forecasts, develop and evaluate alternatives, and finalize the plan—is pretty standard. However, in a small business the entrepreneur (such as Gary Steele in the following "Enterpreneurs in Action" box) will likely do most of the planning himself or herself, perhaps informally bouncing around ideas with a few employees or using business planning software. In larger firms there's usually a central corporate planning group (some call it corporate central) whose role it is to work with top management and each division to continually challenge and refine the company's plans.

Over the past few years, most large companies have made dramatic changes in the way they do their planning. For example, most large companies like General Electric have moved from centralized to decentralized planning.[41]

▶When Gary Steele joined Internet startup Netiva, the company looked like a sure bet. It had big-name venture-capital backers, and a product, the Netiva Internet application system, which let larger companies build databases, using the Java programming language.

Steele soon discovered, though, that most of the company's plans were based on some erroneous assumptions. Its software was designed for the customer to run and maintain, but that meant Netiva's technical people had to get deeply involved up front in selling the software, and the deals were taking too long to complete. The original business plan also assumed that customers would develop multiple applications based on Netiva's software (and thereby have to pay multiple license fees); that wasn't happening, so Netiva was doing a lot of work for just the one-time license fee of $25,000.

Steele quickly concluded that the company was doomed unless drastic measures were taken. Forty percent of the employees were laid off the next week. Working mostly on his own, Steele produced an eight-point plan of action, laying out what the company had to do in the following six weeks. Several weeks later he and four members of his executive team held 75 fact-finding meetings with executives at medium- and large-sized firms to get the information they required about what customers wanted and thus what Netiva's plans should be. ServicePort was one new product to come out of these meetings; it is basically a Web portal for consulting firms to enable their employees (who are often out of town) to conveniently plug in to their companies' databases and share things like client reports.

Now called Portera, the company has 70 employees, and Steele has raised more money, thanks in large part to his ability to almost single-handedly develop his company's new plan.[42]

Today, in other words, the people doing the actual planning in big firms like GE are generally not specialists housed in large, centralized headquarters departments. Instead, the actual planning is carried out by product and divisional managers, often aided by small headquarters advisory groups. Pushing planning down from centralized departments to product managers reflects the fact that the latter are usually in the best position to sense changes in customer, competitive, and technological trends and react to them.

In practice, many entrepreneurs and managers turn to packaged planning software when it comes to developing and creating their business plans. Used in this context, the phrase "business plan" means a comprehensive plan—often prepared for prospective funding sources—for all aspects of the business for the next two to three years. Such a plan traditionally begins with a brief overview called an executive summary and then covers topics such as company summary, products or services, market analysis, strategy and implementation, and financial plan.

The basic idea of such a plan is usually to give the bank or other funding source a clear picture of your business, the industry and the competition, what you intend to accomplish, and how you will use your new funds. The following "Entrepreneurs in Action" box presents one planning package.

Using Computerized Business Planning Software

▶There are several good business planning software packages available, and we can use one—Business Plan Pro from PaloAltoSoftware, to illustrate what they do and how they're used. Business Plan Pro basically contains all the information and planning aids someone would need to create a business plan from beginning to end. In addition to 30 actual sample plans, its files contain detailed sample plan outlines, complete, step-by-step instructions (with examples) for creating each part of a plan (executive summary, market analysis, and so on), financial planning spreadsheets, easy-to-use tables (for instance for making sales forecasts), and automatic programs for creating color 3 D charts for showing things like monthly sales and yearly profits.

An important aspect of Business Plan Pro is that its Planning Wizard "takes you by the hand" and helps you develop your plan on a step-by-step basis. The result is a totally integrated plan complete with charts, tables, and professional formatting. For example, click "start a plan," and the Planning Wizard presents a series of questions, including Does your company sell products, services or both? Would you like a detailed or basic business plan? Does your company sell on credit? Is your company classified as a home office? Then, as you go to each succeeding part of the plan—such as the executive summary—the Planning Wizard shows you instructions with examples, so that typing in your own executive summary becomes relatively easy. Then, as you move into the quantitative part of your plan, such as making sales and financial forecasts, the numbers you give the planning wizard can be easily translated into tables and charts. One section from a sample plan is shown in Figure 5.3.

▼ **FIGURE 5.3** **Acme Consulting**

Executive Summary

Acme Consulting will be formed as a consulting company specializing in marketing of high-technology products in international markets. Its founders are former marketers of consulting services, personal computers, and market research, all in international markets. They are founding Acme to formalize the consulting services they offer.

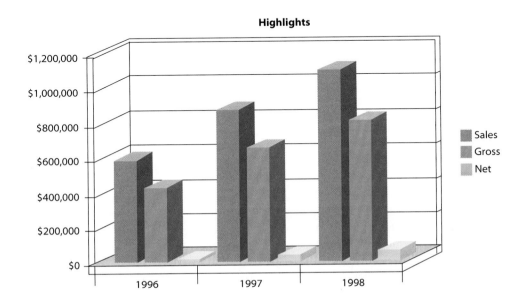

What Planners Do

Most large companies still have small central planning departments, and these planners still play a crucial role. For example, the corporate-central planning departments of multinational firms like GE engage in several basic planning activities:[43]

- *Act as "information central."* They compile and monitor all planning-related data such as data on divisions' progress toward meeting planned financial targets, and competitor intelligence.
- *Conduct competitor and market research.* They help the divisions analyze global competition, for instance, by identifying major global competitors.
- *Develop forecasts.* They develop forecasts that are applicable companywide.
- *Provide consulting services.* They help divisions conduct industry analyses and provide divisional planners with training in the techniques they could or should be using.
- *Create a common language.* They devise corporationwide planning reports and forms so that the divisions' plans are comparable in the information they provide.
- *Communicate companywide objectives.* They communicate companywide objectives to divisional managers, who then formulate plans for achieving their assigned objectives.

Planning in Action

The idea that planning is done by lower-level managers rather than a planning department is in fact somewhat misleading, since the actual process in larger firms involves much give and take. Based on input from product and divisional managers and other sources, top management sets an overall strategic direction for the firm. The resulting objectives then become the targets for which the product and divisional managers formulate specific tactical and operational plans. Strategic planning and direction setting are still mostly done by top managers, usually with their planning unit's assistance. However, more of the premising, alternatives-generating, and product-planning input goes up the hierarchy than in previous years.

GE's recent planning activities provide a "big company" example. In 1998–1999, three themes guided organizationwide planning at GE: globalization, product–services, and "six-sigma quality" (what GE calls its quality improvement–cost minimization process.) These basic themes, or "growth initiatives," provided the guidelines for the top managers of various divisions (such as Aerospace, GE Capital, and NBC). For example, with Asia in economic crisis in 1998, several of GE's divisions moved fast to take advantage of extraordinary global opportunities in Japan. GE's Edison Life quickly became a force in the Japanese insurance industry, acquiring over $6 billion of Japanese insurance assets.

Companywide, GE also wants to move to providing more high-value, information technology–based productivity services. Several GE divisions have therefore invested hundreds of millions of dollars to allow them to provide services to upgrade the competitiveness and profitability of customers as wide-ranging as utilities, hospitals, railroads, and airlines. Finally, the first of GE's six-sigma–guided products are now coming to market from various GE divisions. One, the LightSpeed scanner, dramatically reduces (from 3 minutes to 17 seconds) the time a trauma patient must spend being scanned to diagnose an illness such as a pulmonary embolism.[44]

Planning in action, in other words, is really an interplay between headquarters and divisions, particularly in large, multi-business firms. In a typical company, top management and the board might formulate a few guiding themes at the start of the year. The divisions might then complete reviews of their businesses in April, and forward these to corporate planning. In June the board might adopt a set of planning assumptions and guidelines prepared by the corporate planning department. At the same time, central planning might be preparing various financial forecasts, again based in part on projections from the divisions.

In July the board reviews and sets the firm's financial objectives, and in early August these goals are sent to each business unit. The units then use these financial targets (as well as other guidelines, like GE's three growth initiatives) to prepare their own plans. These are submitted for approval in January. Once adopted, the plans are monitored by central planning, perhaps via quarterly reports from the operating units. After the broad divisional plans are approved, the divisions and their departments develop their shorter-term tactical plans.

▲ If a planning team is separated by distance, videoconferencing can offer an effective way to communicate and build cohesiveness, as it does for this group of Chase Manhattan bank executives.

There's No One Best Way

Planning can sometimes be more trouble than it's worth. Even on something as simple as a trip to Paris, for instance, blind devotion to the plan could cause you to miss a great opportunity that pops up at the last minute. In a company, such inflexibility can be even more dangerous. For example, department stores like JC Penney would be foolish to ignore the possibility of Internet catalog sales just because the word *Internet* didn't appear in their long-term plans two or three years ago.

A recent *Harvard Business Review* article explains some other ways misguided planning can destroy a company's value. An extensive and time-consuming planning process can be a waste of time and money unless top management and its planning group can coax divisional managers to do things differently than they would have done on their own. Yet, "at many companies, business unit plans get through the process largely unscathed." The result is that a lot of time and money has been spent for very little gain.

The opposite is also true: If they're not careful, top managers and central planning may insist on counterproductive changes in the division managers' plans. Top managers, after all, can spend only a fraction of their time understanding the details of each of the many separate businesses of the company, so "the potential for misguided advice is high, especially in diversified companies."[45]

Problems like these don't have to happen. One way to avoid them, says one expert, is to remember that a planning process that works for one company won't necessarily work for another. A good planning process, he contends:

is not a generic process but one in which both analytic techniques and organizational processes are carefully tailored to the needs of the businesses as well as to skills, insight, and experiences of senior corporate managers. A mature electrical-products business, for example, has different planning needs than a fast growing entertainment business or a highly cyclical chemicals business.[46]

What this means is that each company must develop a planning process that's right for it, starting with what it wants its planning process to achieve. The planning process at Granada, a British conglomerate that has businesses in television programming and broadcasting, hotels, catering, and appliances, emphasizes *not* relying on comparing or benchmarking its financial results to those of the industry. When you do that, "you lock yourself into low ambitions" the CEO says.[47] Granada's planning process is therefore built around challenging business managers to find ways to achieve huge leaps in their divisions' sales and profitability. "Planning is about raising ambitions and helping businesses get more creative in their search for ways to increase profits."[48]

On the other hand, Dow Chemical Corporation's planning process is aimed at finding small, incremental improvements in processing costs—such as a 2% savings in maintenance costs—because in the slow-growing chemicals industry costs are very important. The whole planning process at Dow is therefore very formal, analytical, comparative, and numbers oriented. The point, says one planning expert, is that managers must define what they want to achieve from their planning before establishing a planning process.

SUMMARY

1. Plans are methods formulated for achieving desired results. Planning is the process of establishing objectives and courses of actions prior to taking action. Plans differ in format, timetable, and frequency.

2. The management-planning process consists of a logical sequence of five steps: establish objectives; conduct situation analysis; determine alternative courses of action; evaluate alternatives; and choose and implement the plan. In practice, this produces a planning hierarchy because top management's goals become the targets for which subsidiary units must formulate derivative plans.

3. Every manager can expect to be appraised on the extent to which he or she achieves assigned objectives, which makes setting objectives an essential management skill. The areas for which objectives can be set are virtually limitless, ranging from market standing to innovation and profitability.

4. The goal-setting studies suggest these guidelines for goal setting: Assign specific goals; assign measurable goals; assign challenging but doable goals; and encourage participation where feasible.

5. In setting goals, remember also to distinguish between an area to be measured, a yardstick, and an objective, and to specify what is to be done, when, and at what cost or in what time period. Management by objectives can be used to create an integrated hierarchy of goals throughout the organization.

6. Among the techniques for developing planning premises are forecasting, marketing research, and competitive intelligence. Forecasting techniques include quantitative methods such as time-series analysis and causal methods. Qualitative forecasting methods such as sales-force estimation and jury of executive opinion emphasize human judgment.

7. Most companies have moved from centralized to decentralized planning in the past few years, in part to place the planning responsibility with the product and divisional managers who are probably in the best position to understand their customers' needs and competitors' activities. However, central planning units in larger companies, though dramatically downsized, still carry out important planning-related activities such as competitor and market research, communicating companywide objectives, and providing planning-related consulting services to the divisions.

TYING IT ALL TOGETHER

As we've seen, planning and decision making are closely intertwined. Planning means choosing, ahead of time, your objectives and the courses of action that will get you there. So your plan is actually a set of prior decisions.

This chapter focuses on the overall planning process and goals, and on the hierarchical nature of corporate planning. We saw that all of a company's plans tend to revolve around and service top management's longer-term strategic plan. Setting strategy—deciding what businesses the company will be in and how it will compete—is a primary management function, and is discussed in more detail in Chapter 6.

KEY TERMS

plan 130
planning 130
goal 130
objectives 130
descriptive plan 132
budget 132
graphic plan 132
strategic plan 133
tactical plan 133
functional plan 133
operational plan 133

program 133
standing plan 133
policy 133
procedure 133
rule 133
hierarchy of plans 134
goal-setting studies 140
management by objectives
  (MBO) 142
premise 143
forecast 143

quantitative forecasting 143
qualitative forecasting 143
time series 143
causal methods 144
causal forecasting 144
jury of executive opinion 145
sales force estimation 145
marketing research 145
secondary data 145
primary data 145
competitive intelligence 146

SKILLS AND STUDY MATERIALS

CRITICAL THINKING EXERCISES

1. Consider an ancient country with a long tradition of religious philosophy, an ethic of hard work, and strong warrior instincts. Imagine this country emerging into the world marketplace almost overnight, a country with over 1.2 billion consumers. Many of its citizens have a per capita income of only $500, but economists estimate that as many as 200 million middle-class consumers have dispos-able income to spend on a variety of products. There are believed to be at least one million millionaires in this socialistic-capitalistic country.

This country has had most-favored-nation trade status since 1980. However, because it does not allow freedom of emigration as called for by a 1974 U.S. amendment, it must have its trade privileges reauthorized by the president every year. Many U.S. citizens are concerned with the civil and intellectual rights of the people of this country, which has imposed government sanctions on demonstrators and has a history of human-rights violations. Bilateral trade between the United States and this country recently reached $57 billion. U.S. investment rose from $358 million in 1990 to $25 billion in 1996.

The country, of course, is the world's largest: China. There is great potential and opportunity for business here. However, there are also threats. Using the concepts presented in this chapter, explain how you would go about developing a plan for doing business in China for the next five years.

2. The Internet is increasingly a part of our lives. We can bank with it; shop for groceries, cars, and homes; go to college; be our own travel agents; research topics; talk with others in chat rooms; and use it for a host of other uses. The long-term implications of the Internet are amazing. The Internet can provide a much more flexible and convenient lifestyle for many. But there are potential downsides. What happens to all the jobs that are displaced by technology? For example, many of us have not been into a bank for years because we use ATMs. Now we can bank over the Internet from home. We can pay bills. We can shop and have goods delivered. Critical questions arise in terms of the planning and setting of objectives for companies, individuals, and society. What will happen to displaced workers? Will there be enough jobs for everyone? What about those who are not technologically literate or do not own a computer? What about the cost of the Internet for those who cannot afford to use the service? Explain how you would use the concepts and techniques in this chapter to write an essay titled "The Impact on Society of the Internet".

EXPERIENTIAL EXERCISES

1. One of the chronic complaints of employers about prospective employees, especially those just out of universities who have limited work experience, is that they don't have well-honed presentation skills. A recent issue of *Fast Company* outlined an eight-point program for presentations guaranteed to keep your listeners on the edge of their seats.[49] The eight points are as follows.

   ▪ Incite, don't inform. Effective presentations don't end with nodding heads and polite applause, they end with *action*.

   ▪ Don't talk to strangers. Know your audience by doing research prior to the presentation.

   ▪ First (and last) impressions are everything. The two most important parts of your presentation are the first 30 and the last 15 seconds.

   ▪ Simpler is better. Make your presentations short and candid.

   ▪ Perform, don't present. The impact of a typical presentation is 55% visual (how you look), 38% vocal (how you talk), and only 7% verbal (what you say). In other words, you don't deliver presentations, you *perform* them.

   ▪ The show must go on. Concentrate on the performance factor.

   ▪ There's one in every crowd. That is, there is always a hostile member you must handle. The first rule is to disagree without being disagreeable, and don't pick a fight.

   ▪ Practice, practice, practice.

   Select a topic from this chapter on planning and prepare a 5-minute presentation, following the rules outlined here. Be ready to give your presentation to your class.[50]

2. You are the chancellor of the California State University system, which has 23 campuses. California has a population of about 37 million people who represent a microcosm of the world's population. You know that with an increasing birthrate and continuing immigration into the state, your college system could be swamped by the year 2010. Many of the campuses are already filled to capacity. There have been limited funds allocated for introducing technology into every classroom. Some faculties are not as computer literate as their students. This situation may worsen as the years go by. The freshmen of 2010 are likely to be more sophisticated than the current freshmen. The world of technology seems to grow geometrically in terms of knowledge you need to understand and effectively use computers. You have quite a planning challenge. Outline how you would use the information provided in the chapter about planning and setting objectives to formulate a plan for the California State University system. Assume that there is increased funding, along with increased pressures to educate a larger percentage of the population as 2010 approaches.

We invite you to visit the Dessler companion Web site at **www.prenhall.com/dessler** for this chapter's Internet resources.

ONCE A COMPANY MEETS ITS OBJECTIVES, CAN IT REST?

CASE 1

In the early 1990s the Chubb Corporation, one of the nation's premiere insurance companies, set very challenging objectives for itself. For example, the property and casualty insurer had set a target of selling 25% of its policies outside the United States by 2000. It reached 24% in 1995. Rather than slow down, Chubb management felt the only response was to increase the difficulty of its objectives.

Chubb had correctly forecasted an increasing trend toward internationalization: Companies were already looking across borders for new markets and new suppliers, so they were also likely to look overseas for their insurance. Chubb wanted to be there when international companies came looking.

Part of Chubb's strategy to achieve international business success was to position itself as the insurance firm that best understood global business. To meet that challenge, Chubb developed a policy to help exporters manage the broad array of unique risks they face when doing business abroad. Called the *Exporters Package Portfolio*, the insurance policy includes insurance for such unique international risk challenges as kidnap/ransom and extortion, open-ocean cargo, political risk, and products-withdrawal expense.

By 1997 Chubb was again achieving its globalization goals ahead of schedule. Chubb had more then 100 offices operating in the world's top insurance markets. Chubb's aggressive strategy of opening its own offices rather than using joint ventures or cooperative marketing agreements clearly differentiated the company from other global insurers like AIG and CIGNA. At the same time Chubb was having great success abroad, it was winning service awards in the United States. *Worth Magazine*'s readers' choice survey named Chubb the top pick for homeowners' insurance.

Given Chubb's track record for success, it would seem that setting more difficult objectives would be in order. Yet Chubb's management might wonder, could Chubb continue to meet all its challenging goals, or at some point would it falter? Was now a time for Chubb to slow down, or should it push on?

Discussion Questions

1. In what way does Chubb's behavior reveal a well-thought out planning process?

2. What risks might Chubb face if it continues to push for more difficult objectives?

3. Should Chubb push for higher levels of international revenue in its next round of objective setting? Use what you just learned about planning to answer, why or why not?

KMART'S HIGH HOPES

CASE 2

Kmart president and CEO Floyd Hall believes his company will ultimately be identified as one of the top five retailers in the country—in any area. Could Hall's vision for Kmart be translated into meaningful objectives, or is it too ambitious for the merchandising firm? Hall feels there is sufficient room for growth in the discount retailing industry for the next five years. Given the strength of Kmart's brands, its savvy store managers, and competitive pricing, Hall envisions customers coming back to Kmart.

As part of Kmart's objective to be one of the top five retailers, the company is expanding its physical presence in the market. In October 1999 Kmart Corporation announced that it expects to expand or open 400 new stores over the next five years, half of them supercenters. In 2000, Kmart opened more than 70 new stores in key metropolitan markets across the country. All this expansion comes from a company that can already boast that 80% of the U.S. population is within a 15-minute drive of one of its 2,153 Kmart, Big Kmart, or Super Kmart stores.

One of Kmart's successful tactics for meeting its sales objectives involves merchandising. Kmart promotes heavily to get customers into its stores, and then merchandizes to them when they are there. Kmart uses a wide range of tactics to get customers into the stores. For example, Kmart has nearly 1,560 pharmacies, making it the third largest pharmacy chain in the United States. While customers are waiting for their prescriptions, they are likely to browse one of the artfully crafted display areas. Kmart is also the world's largest photo processor. More than 25 million rolls of film per year are brought to Kmart stores to be developed. The end result is that specialty traffic means increased sales for Kmart's branded lines. Kmart's Jaclyn Smith clothing line, for example, is the fourth most popular sportswear line in America, with sales of more than 30 million pieces.

Hall feels that Kmart must develop an identity to which the customer can relate. Hall has Kmart pursuing a differentiation strategy by further developing the company's own labels, especially the Martha Stewart line. Kmart also offers the Penske auto products line, Sesame Street, Thom McAn, and others. In this way it hopes to differentiate itself from competitors like Wal-Mart, and to underscore that Kmart has items and brands that others do not.

In addition to its in-store merchandising, the company is also pursuing more innovative promotional channels. Kmart has developed sophisticated database marketing capabilities. With this information technology, Kmart can track 2 billion transactions annually from more than 85 million households. One use of this data is to reach customers through targeted direct mail. The database may also help Kmart in a move to Internet marketing.

In addition to its Super Kmart offering, the company plans to renovate more than 160 smaller stores to its new small-store prototype. Kmart has successfully positioned itself as the largest discount retailer in urban markets, which is one of the ways that Kmart differentiates itself from rival Wal-Mart.

Outside analysts feel that one of Kmart's greatest strengths is its current management team. Most feel this team can carry Kmart to a bright future. Kmart's target, however, is constantly moving. While Kmart may be meeting its current sales objectives, its competitors are also developing new products and promotional strategies.

Some feel that continued growth at Super Kmart may be tied to an alliance with a food retailer, which could provide Kmart with some important benefits. For example, such an alliance would allow Kmart to focus on its traditional general merchandise, an area where Kmart has more expertise and more profit than in groceries.

Discussion Questions

1. What evidence can you see that Kmart's growth is the result of management's plans rather than just chance?

2. How do you think Kmart's departmental plans link together to help it achieve its objectives?

3. Can Kmart become one of the top five retailers, as Hall envisions? Why or why not?

YOU BE THE CONSULTANT

TO PLAN OR NOT TO PLAN, THAT IS THE QUESTION

You don't raise $5 million and run a successful, growing business for more than 10 years unless you know where you're going. But when it comes to making detailed business plans, KnitMedia and its managers still have some doubts. For example, when asked if the company does much planning, Michael Dorf replies: "Sure, we actually are, you know, starting to use, well, budgets—I can't even say it because it's so hard for me to adhere to them, but, you know, we are using budgets to some extent. [In fact] every so often, I put together the business plan and I talk with every team member and try and consolidate all our ideas and our plans. [However] it's difficult to be very fast-moving, especially at Internet speeds, if everything has to be constricted to a pure schedule and plan."

In fact, Dorf's dilemma is often the dilemma that all startups (and especially technology-oriented startups) face every day. As he says, KnitMedia's managers have to adapt very quickly to stay ahead of the competition, and it's not easy to do that if every step was decided several months or years ago.

Alan Fried, KnitMedia's chief operating officer, makes much the same point. As he says: "I mean, we are very much a media company and as some of the clichés around go, Internet years happen much quicker than calendar years. And if you have to move so fast, you have to move fast because if you're thinking of it, somebody else's thinking of it and first player advantage means a lot. So, sometimes we don't have the good fortune to just sort of sit down and plan everything. [What we do, though] is have an idea, and we have some meetings about it and we just move where I think we have to." That way, the company is always moving in the new direction even though it doesn't have a rigid, pre-determined plan.

The problem is, Dorf and his team are not entirely convinced that this more or less seat-of-the-pants approach to planning is necessarily the best, although it's certainly worked so far. Furthermore, as more people invest money in the business, it's become increasingly important to develop formal plans so others will know where you're planning on going. The management team has approached you to help it formalize KnitMedia's planning process.

Team Exercises and Questions

Use what you learned in this chapter to answer the following questions from Michael Dorf and his management team:

1. At a bare minimum, what sorts of plans do you think we should develop and use at KnitMedia? Why?

2. Our immediate task is opening the Berlin club. Can you provide us with an outline of an executive assignment action plan that we can use to guide us in opening that location?

3. You already know something about how we are organized here at KnitMedia: for instance, you know Michael Dorf is CEO, and that we have basically four divisions—Knitting Factory clubs, music labels, the festivals, and Internet KnitMedia. What specific types of objectives do you think Michael should be assigning to each of his top managers?

4. Is it possible for us to assign specific goals even though we don't have a formal planning process? If so, how can we do that? Would it be a good idea for us to set goals without a formal planning process? Why or why not?

STRATEGIC MANAGEMENT

W H A T ' S   A H E A D ?

To Microsoft Corporation, the phrase "The network is the computer" is anything but benign. Every company needs to know who it will compete with and where and how it will compete—in other words, to have a strategy. For years Microsoft's strategy was to produce operating systems for desktop computers. But the growing success of Sun Microsystems's new strategy may well change all that. Under CEO Scott McNealy, Sun is focusing on using its Java Internet-based software to enable anyone anywhere to tap into an almost limitless range of computer applications via the Internet, even if their computers are fairly primitive. Already, through alliances with companies like AOL and Netscape, Sun is making its new strategy a reality. But if the network is the computer, who's going to need all those expensive Microsoft operating systems? Microsoft must therefore move fast to reorient how it defines its core business and how it intends to compete with the likes of Sun, while dealing with many lawsuits accusing it of anti-competitive practices.

O B J E C T I V E S

AFTER STUDYING THIS CHAPTER, YOU SHOULD BE ABLE TO

- List the steps in the strategic management process

- Compare and contrast the three main types of strategies

- Develop a strategy

- Use three strategy-development tools

Planning, as we saw in Chapter 5, means setting objectives and deciding on the courses of action for achieving them. We also saw that plans are usually hierarchical, since the firm's long-term strategic plan provides the framework within which its other plans must fit. So defining your occupational business (or strategy) as "management consultant" will lead you to make short-term plans—regarding which college to attend and which courses to take, for instance—which are vastly different than they would be if you had decided to be a dentist. In business management too, says management guru Peter Drucker, top management's primary task is thinking through the mission of the business—that is, asking the question "What is our business and what should it be?" This leads to the setting of objectives, the development of strategies and plans, and the making of today's decisions for tomorrow's results.[1]

In this chapter, we therefore turn to strategic planning and management. Planning and strategic planning have much in common: Both involve assessing your situation today and predicting the future; both involve setting objectives; and both involve crafting courses of action to get you from where you are today to where you want to be tomorrow.

But we'll see in this chapter that strategic planning is also in a class of its own. Tom Peters, another management guru, reportedly once offered $100 to the first manager who could demonstrate that he or she had created a successful strategy from a planning process.[2] His point is that a highly-structured planning process may actually produce worse—not better—strategic plans.

Why? Because, unlike shorter-term plans (What courses should I take this term?), strategic planning (What occupation is best for me after I graduate?) requires looking far ahead and using insight and creativity to make sense of a great many imponderables. (For your personal strategic plan, these might include Will I be a good consultant? Will I enjoy that career? and Will there be enough jobs to make being a consultant worth my while?). As two experts put it, "Planning processes are not designed to accommodate the messy process of generating insights and molding them into a winning strategy."[3] So, do not be misled into believing that strategic planning is (or could ever be) entirely mechanical: Insight and creativity always play a very big role.

▶ THE STRATEGIC MANAGEMENT PROCESS

How do firms like Sun Microsystems know what strategy they should pursue to stay competitive? **Strategic management** is the process of identifying and pursuing the organization's mission by aligning the organization's internal capabilities with the external demands of its environment.[4] As Figure 6.1 shows, the strategic man-

strategic management
the process of identifying and pursuing the organization's strategic plan by aligning internal capabilities with the external demands of its environment, and then ensuring that the plan is being executed properly.

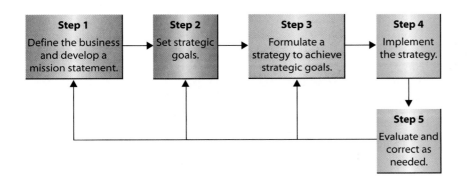

◀ F I G U R E   6 . 1

The Five Strategic Management Steps

agement process consists of five tasks: defining the business and developing a vision and mission; translating the mission into specific goals; crafting a strategy to achieve the goals; implementing and executing the strategy; and evaluating performance, reviewing the situation, and making adjustments.

Let's look at each step in turn.

Step 1: Define the Business and Its Mission[5]

Strategic management starts with answering the question What business should we be in? This is tricky because two companies can be in the same industry but answer that question in very different ways. For example, Ferrari and Toyota both make cars. However, Ferrari specializes in high-performance cars, and its competitive advantage is built on craftsmanship and high-speed performance. Toyota produces a range of automobiles, and many of its own supplies and parts; its competitive advantage is built on cost-efficient production and a strong dealer network.

Wal-Mart and Kmart are also in the same industry. Wal-Mart, however, distinguished itself from Kmart by at first concentrating its stores in small southern towns, and by building a state-of-the-art satellite-based distribution system. Kmart opened stores throughout the country (where it had to compete with a great many other discounters, often for expensive, big-city properties). Kmart also based its competitive advantage on its size, which it (erroneously) assumed would provide it with the economies of scale necessary to keep costs below those of competitors.

Answering the question, What business should we be in? may require both a vision statement and a mission statement (although the two are often the same). The company's **vision** is a "general statement of its intended direction that evokes emotional feelings in organization members."[6] As Warren Bennis and Bert Manus say:

> To choose a direction, a leader must first have developed a mental image of a possible and desirable future state for the organization. This image, which we call a vision, may be as vague as a dream or as precise as a goal or mission statement. The critical point is that a vision articulates a view of a realistic, credible, attractive future for the organization, a condition that is better in some important ways than what now exists.[7]

vision

a general statement of an organization's intended direction that evokes emotional feelings in its members.

"Never choose a mission statement on a dark, rainy day."

APEX ELEVATOR
To provide a high reliability, error-free method for moving people and products up, down, and sideways within a building.

UNITED TELEPHONE CORPORATION OF DADE
To provide information services in local-exchange and exchange-access markets within its franchised area, as well as cellular phone and paging services.

JOSEPHSON DRUG COMPANY, INC.
To provide people with longer lives and higher-quality lives by applying research efforts to develop new or improved drugs and health-care products.

GRAY COMPUTER, INC.
To transform how educators work by providing innovative and easy-to-use multimedia-based computer systems.

For example, Rupert Murdock (chairman of News Corporation, which owns the Fox network and many newspapers and satellite TV operations) has a vision of an integrated global news-gathering, entertainment, and multimedia firm. Bill Gates had a vision of a software company serving the needs of the microcomputer industry.

Thanks to the Internet, even young entrepreneurs with the right vision and the skills to implement it can be enormously successful, almost overnight. Take Jeffrey Arnold, the CEO of WebMD. Jeff had a crystal-clear vision of a Web site supplying everything a consumer might want to know about medical-related issues, and today the startup he founded in late 1999 is valued at over $3.5 billion. That kind of success took more than luck and a clear vision, of course. He was also able to put in place all the elements of his strategy, for instance by getting Microsoft to invest over $250 million in WebMD, and getting CNN to make it a partner on its own Web site.[8]

The firm's **mission statement** operationalizes the top manager's vision. A mission statement "broadly outlines the organization's future course and serves to communicate 'who we are, what we do, and where we're headed.'"[9] Some examples are presented in Figure 6.2.

mission statement
a statement that broadly outlines the enterprise's purpose and serves to communicate "who the organization is, what it does, and where it's headed."

Step 2: Translate the Mission into Strategic Goals

The next strategic management task (remember the hierarchy of goals, from Chapter 5?) is to translate top management's vision and mission into operational strategic goals. For example, strategic goals for Citicorp include building shareholder value through sustained growth in earnings per share; continuing its commitment to building customer-oriented business worldwide; maintaining superior rates of return; building a strong balance sheet; and balancing the business by customer, product, and geography.[10]

Step 3: Formulate a Strategy to Achieve the Strategic Goals

A **strategy** is a course of action that explains how the enterprise will move from the business it is in now to the business it wants to be in (as stated in its mission), given its opportunities and threats and its internal strengths and weaknesses. For example, Wal-Mart decided to pursue the strategic goal of moving from being a relatively small, southern-based chain of retail discount stores to becoming the national leader in low-cost merchandise. One of Wal-Mart's strategies was to reduce distribution costs and minimize inventory and delivery times through a satellite-based distribution system.

strategy
a course of action that explains how an enterprise will move from the business it is in now to the business it wants to be in.

Step 4: Implement the Strategy

Strategy implementation means translating the strategy into actions and results. Doing so requires drawing on all management functions: planning, organizing, leading, and controlling. For instance, employees need to be hired and motivated, and budgets need to be formulated so progress toward strategic goals can be measured. (That's one reason it's called the strategic *management* process.)

Step 5: Evaluate Performance

strategic control

the process of assessing the firm's progress toward its strategic objectives and taking corrective action as needed to ensure optimal implementation.

Finally, strategic control—the process of assessing progress toward strategic goals and taking corrective action as needed—keeps the company's strategy up to date. Strategic control should also ensure that all parts and members of the company are contributing in a useful way toward the strategy's implementation.

Managing strategy is thus an ongoing process. Competitors introduce new products, technological innovations make production processes obsolete, and societal trends reduce demand for some products or services while boosting demand for others. Managers must therefore be alert to opportunities and threats that might require modifying or totally redoing their strategies.

Strategic Planning

strategic planning

identifying the current business of a firm and the business it wants for the future, and the course of action or strategy it will pursue.

Strategic planning is the process of identifying the business of the firm today and the business it wants for the future, and then identifying the course of action it will pursue, given its opportunities, threats, strengths, and weaknesses. It specifies who the firm will compete with and how it will compete with them.

Strategic planning is part of the overall strategic management process. As illustrated in Figure 6.1, it represents the first three of the strategic management tasks: defining the business and developing a mission, translating the mission into strategic goals, and crafting a strategy or course of action to move the organization from where it is today to where it wants to be.

We'll look more closely at how to develop and implement strategic plans later in this chapter. First, we'll look at the types of strategies a firm might pursue.

▶ TYPES OF STRATEGIES

corporate-level strategy

a plan that identifies the portfolio of businesses that comprise a corporation and how they relate to each other.

There are three main types of strategies, as summarized in Figure 6.3. Many companies consist of a portfolio of several businesses. For instance, Disney includes movies, theme parks, and the ABC TV network. These companies need a **corporate-level**

▶ **FIGURE 6.3**

Relationships Among Strategies in Multiple-Business Firms

Companies typically formulate three types of strategies: Corporate strategies, business-level/competitive strategies, and functional strategies.

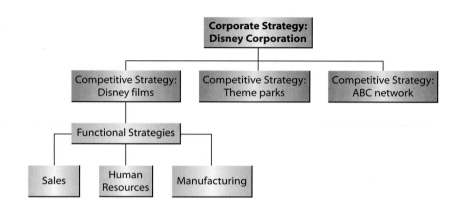

strategy, which identifies the portfolio of businesses that comprise the corporation and the ways in which these businesses fit together.

Each of these businesses then has its own business-level or **competitive strategy**. This strategy identifies how to build and strengthen the company's long-term competitive position in the marketplace.[11] It identifies, for instance, how Microsoft will compete with AOL/Netscape.

Each business is in turn composed of departments, such as manufacturing, marketing, and HR. **Functional strategies** identify the basic courses of action each functional department will pursue to contribute to attaining the business's competitive goals. We'll look at each type of strategy in turn.

Corporate-Level Strategies

Every company must choose the number of businesses in which it will compete and the relationships that will exist among those businesses. These decisions are driven by the firm's corporate-level strategy, which identifies the portfolio of businesses that will comprise the company. Companies can pursue one or more of the following corporate strategies when deciding what businesses to be in and how these businesses should relate to each other.

Concentration   A concentration/single business strategy means the company focuses on one product or product line, usually in one market. Organizations that have successfully pursued single business strategies include McDonald's, KFC, and WD-40 Company. The main advantage of a concentration strategy is that the company can focus on the one business it knows well, allowing it to do that one thing better than competitors (Thus Gerber stresses that "baby foods are our only business"). The main disadvantage is the risk inherent in putting all one's eggs into one basket. Concentrators must always be on the lookout for signs of decline. McDonald's, after years of concentrating in the hamburger franchise business, tried unsuccessfully to diversify into franchising children's play areas in covered shopping malls. Harley Davidson, on the other hand, successfully diversified into clothing, restaurants, and finance from motorcycles.

Concentrating in a single line of business need not mean the firm won't try to grow. Indeed, some traditional concentrators like the Coca-Cola Company have achieved very high growth rates through concentration.

Four strategies can contribute to growth.[12] Single-business companies can grow through **market penetration**. This means taking steps to boost sales of present products by more aggressively selling and marketing into the firm's current markets. **Geographic expansion** is another alternative. The *Wall Street Journal* has achieved above-average growth rates while concentrating on its traditional business by aggressively expanding into new geographic markets, domestic and overseas. Growth can also be achieved through **product development**, which means developing improved products for

competitive strategy
a strategy that identifies how to build and strengthen the business's long-term competitive position in the marketplace.

functional strategy
the overall course or courses of action and basic policies that each department is to follow in helping the business accomplish its strategic goals.

market penetration
a growth strategy to boost sales of present products by more aggressively permeating the organization's current markets.

geographic expansion
a strategic growth alternative of aggressively expanding into new domestic and/or overseas markets.

product development
the strategy of improving products for current markets to maintain or boost growth.

▲ **W E B N O T E**

Harley-Davidson is diversifying: The planned Harley-Davidson motorcycling experience complex will include, in addition to exhibits, a restaurant, a retail store, and an outdoor special events area.
www.harley-davidson.com
Used with permission.

horizontal integration

acquiring ownership or control of competitors who are competing in the same or similar markets with the same or similar products.

current markets. **Horizontal integration**, acquiring ownership or control of competitors in the same or similar markets with the same or similar products, is another option. For example, the Humana hospital chain has grown rapidly while remaining a concentrator by acquiring hundreds of hospitals.

Vertical Integration Instead of staying in one business, a firm can expand into other businesses through a vertical integration strategy. **Vertical integration** means owning or controlling the inputs to the firm's processes and/or the channels through which products or services are distributed. (The former is backward integration, and the latter is forward integration.) Thus, Ford owns Libby-Owens glass, which supplies it with windshields; major oil companies like Shell not only drill and produce their own oil, but also sell it through company-controlled outlets.

vertical integration

a growth strategy in which a company owns or controls its own suppliers and/or distribution channels.

Diversification **Diversification** means a strategy of expanding into related or unrelated products or market segments.[13] Diversifying helps to move the organization into other businesses or industries, or perhaps just into new product lines. In any case, it helps the firm avoid the problem of having all its eggs in one basket by spreading risk among several products or markets. However, diversification adds a new risk: It forces the company and its managers to split their attention and resources among several products or markets instead of one. To that extent, diversification may undermine the firm's ability to compete successfully in its chosen markets.

diversification

a corporate strategy whereby managers try to better utilize their organizational resources by developing new products and new markets.

Several forms of diversification are widely used. **Related diversification** means diversifying into other industries in such a way that a firm's lines of business still possess some kind of fit.[14] When women's-wear maker Donna Karan expanded into men's clothing, that was related diversification. Campbell's Soup purchased Pepperidge Farm Cookies because it felt that Pepperidge Farm's customer base and channels of distribution were a good fit.

related diversification

a strategy of expanding into other industries or markets related to a company's current business lines.

Conglomerate diversification, in contrast, means diversifying into products or markets that are *not* related to the firm's present businesses or to one another. For example, Getty Oil diversified into pay television, and several years ago Mobil Oil Company purchased (and then sold) the Montgomery Ward retail chain.

conglomerate diversification

diversifying into other products or markets that are not related to a firm's present businesses.

Status Quo Strategies Unlike other growth-oriented strategies, a stability or status-quo strategy says "the organization is satisfied with its rate of growth and product scope." Operationally, this means it will retain its present strategy and, at the corporate level, continue focusing on its present products and markets, at least for now. Status quo is one corporate strategy pursued by the lubricant company that makes WD-40, which rarely advertises or aggressively pursues increased market share.

Investment Reduction Strategies Investment reduction and defensive strategies are generally corrective actions required due to overexpansion, ill-conceived diversification, or some other financial emergency. They are taken to reduce the company's investments in one or more of its lines of business. For example, Levi Strauss, suffering a dramatic loss of market share, recently closed many of its U.S. clothing plants.

There are several ways to reduce investment. **Retrenchment** means the reduction of activity or operations. IBM engaged in a massive retrenchment effort, dramatically reducing (downsizing) the number of its employees and closing many facilities. **Divestment** means selling or liquidating individual businesses. (Divestment usually denotes the sale of a viable business, while liquidation denotes the sale or abandonment of a nonviable one.)

retrenchment

the reduction of activities or operations to reduce investment.

divestment

selling or liquidating the individual businesses of a larger company.

Strategic Alliances and Joint Ventures   Sometimes the firm's corporate strategy involves forming a partnership with another company, rather than growing internally. In such cases, strategic alliances and joint ventures are corporate strategic options.

As we noted in Chapter 1, both terms generally refer to a formal agreement between two or more separate companies, the purpose of which is to enable the organizations to benefit from complementary strengths. For example, a small, cash-poor Florida-based company with a patented industrial pollution control filter might form a joint venture with a subsidiary of a major European oil firm. In this case, the joint venture might be a separate corporation based in Europe to which each partner contributes funds and other resources. The oil firm gets access to a product that could revolutionize its distilling facilities; the filter company gets access to the oil firm's vast European marketing network.[15]

The Virtual Corporation   For many firms encountering rapid change, the ultimate strategic alliance is the **virtual corporation**, "a temporary network of independent companies—suppliers, customers, even erstwhile rivals—linked by information technology to share skills, costs, and access to one another's markets."[16] Virtual corporations don't have headquarters staffs, organization charts, or the organizational trappings that we associate with traditional corporations. In fact, virtual corporations are not corporations at all, in the traditional sense of common ownership or a chain of command. Instead, they are networks of companies, each of which lends the virtual corporation/network its special expertise. Information technology (computer information systems, fax machines, electronic mail, and so on) then helps the virtual corporation's often far-flung company constituents stay in touch and quickly carry out their contributions.[17] When a virtual corporation is managed correctly, the individual contributors aren't just impersonal suppliers or marketers. Instead, successful virtual corporation relationships are built on trust and on a sense of "co-destiny." This means that the fate of each partner and of the virtual corporation's whole enterprise is dependent on each partner doing its share.[18]

Virtual corporations abound today. For example, AT&T called on Japan's Marubeni Trading Company to help it link up with Matsushita Electronic Industrial Company when it wanted to speed production of its Safari notebook computer (which was designed by Henry Dreyfuss Associates).[19] And when start-up company TelePad came up with an idea for a handheld, pen-based computer, a virtual corporation was its answer for breathing life into the idea: An industrial design firm in Palo Alto, California, designed the product; Intel brought in engineers to help with some engineering details; several firms helped develop software for the product; and a battery maker collaborated with TelePad to produce the power supply.[20] (Unfortunately, the idea didn't click, and TelePad went out of business).

The Internet, not surprisingly, is spawning a multitude of virtual operations. For example, the Web site eLance (www.elance.com) lets freelance consultants, graphic designers, and anyone else who wants to sell business services to businesses compete for work with one another by posting information on their skills and fees.[21] Denver-based graphic designer Serena Rodriguez now gets about 10% of her business through that site, and works, virtually—long distance, and without seeing them or being a formal part of their company—with firms like pharmaceuticals manufacturer Merck. Getting a big project often means recruiting other free agents to join your virtual team. For example, says Web designer Andrew Keeler, "I work with lots of people here in San Francisco whom I've never even met . . . It happens so fast, and it's all done by e-mail."[22]

virtual corporation
a temporary network of independent companies linked by information technology.

Competitive Strategies

Whether a company decides to concentrate on a single business or to diversify into several different ones, it should develop a competitive strategy for each business. Strategic planning expert Michael Porter defines competitive strategy as a plan to establish a profitable and sustainable competitive position against the forces that determine industry competition.[23] The competitive strategy specifies how the company will compete; for instance, based on low cost or high quality. Porter says three basic or generic competitive strategic options are possible: cost leadership, differentiation, and focus.

Cost Leadership Just about every company tries to hold down costs. In this way, a company can price its products and services competitively. Cost leadership as a competitive strategy goes beyond this. A business that pursues this strategy is aiming to become *the* low-cost leader in an industry. The unique characteristic is the emphasis on obtaining absolute cost advantages from any and all possible sources. Wal-Mart is a typical industry cost leader. Its distribution costs are minimized through a satellite-based warehousing system, the stores themselves are plain, and Wal-Mart negotiates the lowest prices from suppliers.

Pursuing a cost leadership strategy requires a tricky balance between pursuing lower costs and maintaining acceptable quality. Southwest Airlines, for instance, keeps its cost per passenger mile below those of most other major airlines while still providing service as good as or better than that of its competitors.

cost leadership
a competitive strategy by which a company aims to be the low-cost leader in its industry.

Differentiation In a differentiation strategy, a firm seeks to be unique in its industry along some dimensions that are valued by buyers.[24] In other words, it picks one or more attributes of the product or service that its buyers perceive as important, and then positions itself to meet those needs.

In practice, the dimensions along which you can differentiate range from the "product image" offered by cosmetics firms, to concrete differences such as the product durability emphasized by Caterpillar. Volvo stresses safety, Apple Computer stresses usability, and Mercedes-Benz emphasizes quality. Firms can usually charge a premium price if they successfully stake out their claim to being different in some important way.

differentiation strategy
a competitive strategy aimed at distinguishing a company from its competitors by focusing on the attributes of its products or services that consumers perceive as important.

Focus Differentiators like Volvo and low-cost leaders like Wal-Mart generally aim their business at all or most potential buyers. A business pursuing a focus strategy selects a market segment and builds its competitive strategy on serving the customers in its market niche better or more cheaply than its competitors.

The basic question in choosing whether to pursue a focus competitive strategy is this: By focusing on a narrow market, can we provide our target customers with a product or service better or more cheaply than our generalist competitors?

Examples of focusers abound. Pea in the Pod, a chain of maternity stores, focuses on selling stylish clothes to pregnant working women. By specializing in "working woman maternity clothes," the company is able to provide a much wider range of such clothes to its target customers than can generalist competitors like Macy's or JCPenney.

focus strategy
a strategy in which a business selects a narrow market segment and builds its strategy on serving those in its target market better or more cheaply than its generalist competitors.

The Five Forces Model To formulate a competitive strategy, the manager should understand the competitive forces that together determine how intense the industry's rivalries are and how to best compete. Based on that analysis, the company must

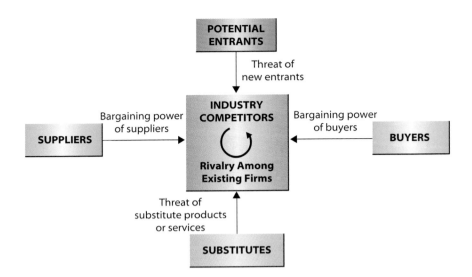

▶ F I G U R E   6 . 4

Forces Driving Industry Competition

Source: Reprinted with the permission of The Free Press, a division of Simon & Schuster from *Competitive Strategy: Techniques for Analyzing Industries and Competitors* by Michael E. Porter. Copyright © 1980 by The Free Press.

find a sustainable **competitive advantage**, that is, a basis on which to identify a relative superiority over competitors. Strategy expert Michael Porter argues that how a company competes—its competitive strategy—depends on the intensity of the competition in its industry. Years ago when competition was not so keen in the auto industry, GM was not so concerned with competing on cost and quality.

Competitive intensity, says Porter, reflects five competitive forces, as shown in Figure 6.4. The task is to analyze them so that management can decide how best to compete in that industry.[25] We'll look at each of the five forces in turn.

competitive advantage
the basis for superiority over competitors and thus for hoping to claim certain customers.

Threat of Entry   Intensity of industry competition depends first on the threat of new entrants. For instance, the competitive landscape for Encyclopaedia Britannica changed when Microsoft introduced Encarta.

In general, the more easily new competitors can enter the business, the more intense the competition. However, several things can make it harder for new competitors to enter an industry. For example, it's not easy to enter the auto industry because of the high investment required for plant and equipment. Making it more expensive for customers to switch to a competitor is another entry barrier: For instance, after a travel agent signs up for the American Airlines computerized reservation system, it's expensive for that agent to switch to the Delta system.

▲ W E B N O T E

With its Internet-based Encarta Encyclopedia and related learning materials, Microsoft simultaneously undermined conventional competitors and built its own strategy of becoming everyone's main link with the Internet.

www.encarta.msn.com

Microsoft and Encarta are registered trademarks, and trademarks of Microsoft Corp. in the United States and other countries.

Rivalry Among Existing Competitors   Rivalry among existing competitors manifests itself in tactics like price competition, advertising battles, and increased customer service.[26]

The rivalry in some industries is more intense and warlike than in others. For example, for many years the rivalry among law firms and CPA firms could be characterized as cordial. Recently, it has turned quite cutthroat. This in turn has motivated many law firms to emphasize efficiency, to offer special pricing plans to clients, and to merge.

Pressure from Substitute Products   Intensity of competition also depends on substitute products. For example, frozen yogurt is a substitute for ice cream, and synthetics are a substitute for cotton.

Substitute products perform the same or similar functions. The more substitute products, then, in effect, the more competitive the industry. To the extent that few substitutes are available (as would be the case with certain patented drugs), rivalry is reduced and the industry is more attractive and less cutthroat.

Bargaining Power of Buyers   The buyers' power is another competitive factor. For example, a buyer group is powerful if it purchases large volumes relative to the seller's sales; Toyota has a lot of clout with its suppliers, for instance. Similarly, when the products purchased are standard or undifferentiated (such as apparel elastic), and when buyers face few switching costs or earn low profits, then buyers' bargaining power over suppliers tends to be enhanced.

Bargaining Power of Suppliers   Suppliers can also influence an industry's competitive intensity and attractiveness, for instance by threatening to raise prices or reduce quality.

Suppliers tend to have greater bargaining power when they are dominated by a few firms and are more concentrated. When few substitute products are available, when the buying industry is not an important customer of the supplier group, and when the supplier's product is an important input to the buyer's business, the supplier's power rises. In its lawsuit, for example, the U.S. government claimed that Microsoft exerted tremendous power as the only Windows supplier.

Analyzing an industry using the five forces model helps a company choose competitive strategy options. For example, where rivalry among existing competitors is very intense or there is a threat of new entrants, boosting product differentiation is a sensible option. That's one reason law firms now try to stress their differences and why image-oriented advertising is important to cosmetics firms. Boosting switching costs (as American Airlines did when it convinced thousands of travel agents to use its SABRE computerized reservation system) can also reduce rivals' (or new entrants') ability to compete, even when the product or service itself is fairly undifferentiated. Building competitive barriers is illustrated in the "Entrepreneurs in Action" box.

Functional Strategies

At some point, each business's competitive strategy (low-cost leader, differentiator, or focuser) is translated into supporting functional strategies that each of its departments must pursue. Note that in some very large firms like GE, similar businesses are first grouped into strategic business units for control purposes. A **strategic business unit** (SBU) is an organizational entity that contains several related businesses. A firm's forest products SBU, for instance, might include separate fine papers, newsprint, and pulp businesses.

A functional strategy is the basic course or courses of action each department will follow in enabling the business to accomplish its strategic goals. Wal-Mart competes as the industry's low-cost leader. To implement this competitive strategy, it formulated departmental functional strategies that made sense for moving Wal-Mart toward its desired position. For example, the distribution department pursued a strategy (satellite-based warehousing) that ultimately drove down distribution costs to a minimum; the company's land development department found locations that fit the firm's customer profile and kept construction costs to a minimum; and the merchandise buyers found sources capable of providing good-quality merchandise

strategic business unit
an organizational entity that contains several related businesses.

►The success of Russ Leatherman and his colleagues at MovieFone illustrates how a smart entrepreneurial company put these competitive strategy ideas into practice. In 1989 Leatherman dreamed up the idea for an interactive telephone movie guide he called MovieFone. Callers in many cities get complete up-to-the-minute listings of theater offerings and show times in their area and can even purchase tickets over the phone. Leatherman's task, once his firm was launched, was to build barriers to keep potential competitors like Ticketmaster at bay.

To build these competitive barriers, MovieFone managers sought the following:

1. *Exclusivity.* MovieFone acquired highly desirable phone numbers in each of its area codes, such as 777-FILM, and registered these as trademarks. The numbers are easy for callers to remember, differentiating MovieFone and keeping competitors out.

2. *Focus.* By focusing on movie listings instead of branching out into other markets such as theaters or sporting events, MovieFone has become the industry expert when it comes to supplying listings and tickets. It knows its customers' profiles and has mastered the hardware, software, and logistics required to obtain, compile, and deliver listings and tickets better than anyone else.

3. *Expert systems.* MovieFone has developed what it calls *expert systems*, comprising special hardware, software, and electronic "will-call windows" in which customers can automatically pick up tickets. These systems further differentiate MovieFone and create substantial barriers to any new competitors that might be considering entering the market.

4. *Strategic alliances.* Many of the electronic will-call windows are placed in movie theaters, with which MovieFone has formed strategic alliances for this purpose. The alliances provide an additional source of income for the theaters and strengthen MovieFone's relationship with them.[27]

Today, MovieFone is growing fast. Moviegoers can reach it not just by phone, but on the Internet, too.

---

at the lowest possible prices. Functional strategies can't be formulated intelligently unless the business has a clear direction in terms of the competitive strategy it wants to pursue. Then its functional strategies must fit its competitive strategy.

► CREATING STRATEGIC PLANS

Strategic plans like that of Sun's Scott McNealy (the network is the computer) usually don't just appear overnight. Instead, considerable thought goes into creating good plans, since a mistake—in terms of choosing the wrong way to compete—can be deadly. In this section we'll look more closely at how to create a strategic plan.

The Strategic Planning Process

"Define the business's mission," "set strategic goals," and "formulate a strategy to achieve those goals" are basic steps in strategic planning (see Figure 6.1). But strategic planning in practice is more complicated: Most managers don't formulate strategic missions or goals without first scanning the firms environment to see what competitors are doing. And once the strategy is in place, subsidiary plans to support the goals must be crafted.

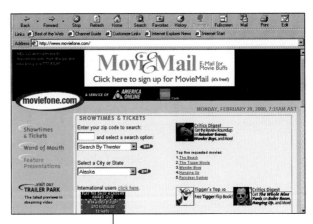

▲ WEBNOTE

Moviefone has grown quickly by using four strategies to keep competitors at bay: exclusivity, focus, expert systems, and strategic alliances. And it's not just a telephone system any more—now it's on the Internet as well.

www.moviefone.com

Used with permission.

▲ A Home Depot megastore in Paramus, New Jersey.

Strategic planning therefore usually starts with identifying the driving forces in a firm's environment. These include the economic, demographic, technological, and competitive forces that shape a company's strategy.

There are several tools you can use to identify and assess these forces, but remember that it's important to avoid being too mechanical in your approach: you don't want to miss important forces. Encouraging insight and creativity is therefore necessary. Brainstorming (discussed in Chapter 4) can be a useful tool at this first stage. One strategy expert suggests having the top management team spend several hours brainstorming all the possible forces that might influence the firm. They must be sure to avoid criticizing or disposing of any until its potential usefulness and impact have been thoroughly aired.[28] Only then can the managers move on to actually formulating a strategy. Here again, brainstorming is useful for generating strategic options.

It's hard to overestimate the importance of this strategy formulation stage. A recent *Fortune* article emphasizes how the 17 companies that topped the *Fortune* 1000 in shareholder return did so in large part based on brilliant strategies. For example: "While many of its competitors in the biotech industry let the disease lead them to the science, Amgen stays ahead by taking the opposite approach. It develops its drugs by identifying areas of promising research that may lead to breakthrough products."[29] "Worldcom saw there was more than one way to be a telephone company. By offering customers not only long distance but also local and Internet services, it broke out of the pack and became a powerhouse in the U.S. telecommunications industry."[30] Here's another example: "Seeing opportunity and a market made up of mom-and-pop hardware stores, Home Depot launched a national chain of mega stores. Economies of scale let the giant retailer offer better prices, selection, and service to the home-improvement crowd."[31] For a view of the Internet's effect on strategy, see the accompanying "Managing @ the Speed of Thought" box.

MANAGING @ THE *SPEED* OF THOUGHT

■ **Strategy for the Internet**

Strategies can't be crafted today without considering how information technology (IT) and the Internet could and should affect the company's strategy.

This is nothing new. For example, Wal-Mart has grown fast thanks to its satellite-based warehouse and distribution system. UPS, the world's largest air and ground package distribution company, has maintained its competitive edge in large part due to the $1 billion invested on an annual basis in information technology. UPS drivers use hand-held computers to capture customers' signatures, along with pickup, delivery, and time card information, and automatically transmit this information to headquarters via a cellular telephone network. For companies like these and thousands more, IT lies at the heart of their strategies.

But it's likely that the Internet's effect on companies' strategies will be even more profound. On-line companies like Amazon.com are perhaps the most obvious examples here. Consider how the strategies of traditional booksellers like Barnes & Noble and countless smaller ones have had to change in reaction to Amazon.com. Barnes & Noble has had to create its own on-line bookstore. Many smaller booksellers have had to reconsider whether they even want to or can remain in business, given the new competitive landscape. And in January 2000, AOL and Time Warner announced that they would combine. Their new strategy would involve using Time Warner's cable access and content along with AOL's system to reach hundreds of millions of customers.

And it's not just information businesses that must adapt to the Internet.[32] Two experts argue that even businesses not widely considered information businesses are or will be highly dependent on the Net. For example, GE's divisions used to purchase their supplies from suppliers with which they had long and established relationships. Today, GE has created special on-line purchasing Web sites, and any supplier can bid on the GE orders. That drives down GE's purchasing costs and gives it a new competitive advantage; meanwhile, its former suppliers must adapt their strategies to make themselves a lot more Web friendly.[33] GE's divisions have also been told to create Internet businesses that would replace their traditional brick and mortar businesses.

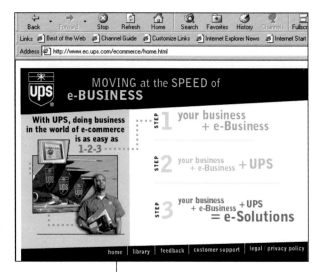

▲ **W E B   N O T E**

UPS customers use a Web site to find solutions to their shipping needs.
www.ec.ups.com
Used with permission.

Finally, once the firm's mission and strategy are in place, the manager must of course create subsidiary plans for actually implementing the strategy. This brings the strategic planner back to the hierarchical planning process discussed in Chapter 5. Specific strategy-related goals are formulated and assigned to the company's managers, who in turn are responsible for crafting plans to ensure that those goals are achieved.

Choosing the Right Strategic Planning Tools

Strategic planning always involves predicting the future, but some futures are more predictable than others. For example, the president of Delta Airlines needs a strategy for dealing with low-cost airlines such as Southwest entering Delta's markets. While such planning involves some uncertainty, this situation and the range of Delta's strategic options is fairly clear. However Delta would face a much more uncertain situation if, for instance, it were considering entering emerging markets like India or Russia. Here the possible outcomes aren't neatly circumscribed by relatively homogeneous U.S. laws, demographics, and political stability. The number of imponderables would be enormous, from potential political instability to criminal activities to economic collapse. How do you plan for a threatened nuclear attack by Pakistan?

Recognizing and accepting that some future situations are more predictable than others is important to strategic planners since it determines the strategic planning tools they use. This is summarized in Figure 6.5. Sometimes the future is clear

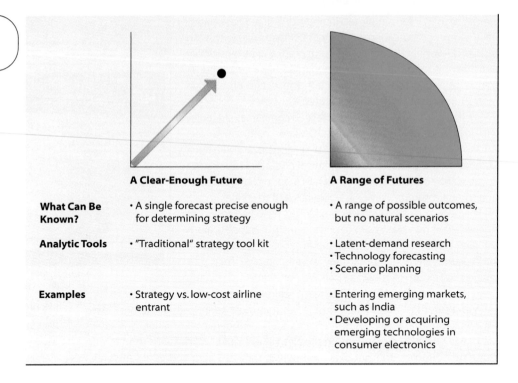

	A Clear-Enough Future	A Range of Futures
What Can Be Known?	• A single forecast precise enough for determining strategy	• A range of possible outcomes, but no natural scenarios
Analytic Tools	• "Traditional" strategy tool kit	• Latent-demand research • Technology forecasting • Scenario planning
Examples	• Strategy vs. low-cost airline entrant	• Entering emerging markets, such as India • Developing or acquiring emerging technologies in consumer electronics

enough, and here tools like the SWOT analysis discussed below are used. Sometimes the strategic planner faces a more uncertain range of futures. Here a more flexible approach (like scenario planning, also discussed below) is required. Let's look at the tools for these two situations.

When the Future Is More Predictable

You are the president of Delta Airlines and need a strategy to deal with the possible entrance of a low-cost, no-frills airline into one of your major markets. What strategies might you pursue? Options include introducing a low-cost Delta service, surrendering the low-cost niche to the new entrant, or competing more aggressively on price and service to drive the entrant out of the market.[34]

The question is, What kind of information would you need to make your decision? Generally, you need the sorts of information provided by traditional planning tools. For example, you'll need market research on the size of the different markets, on the likely responses of customers in each market segment to different combinations of pricing and service, and information about the new entrant's competitive objectives. There are also traditional strategic planning tools you might use, including SWOT analysis, environmental scanning, benchmarking, and portfolio analysis.

SWOT analysis

a strategic planning tool for analyzing a company's strengths, weaknesses, opportunities, and threats.

SWOT Analysis   SWOT analysis is used to list and consolidate information regarding a firm's internal strengths and weaknesses and external opportunities and threats. As illustrated in Figure 6.6, potential strengths might include adequate financial resources, economies of scale, and proprietary technology. Potential internal weaknesses include lack of strategic direction, obsolete facilities, and lack of managerial depth and talent.

POTENTIAL STRENGTHS	POTENTIAL WEAKNESSES
• Market leadership	• Large inventories
• Strong research and development	• Excess capacity for market
• High-quality products	• Management turnover
• Cost advantages	• Weak market image
• Patents	• Lack of management depth

POTENTIAL OPPORTUNITIES	POTENTIAL THREATS
• New overseas markets	• Market saturation
• Falling trade barriers	• Threat of takeover
• Competitors failing	• Low-cost foreign competition
• Diversification	• Slower market growth
• Economy rebounding	• Growing government regulation

Formulating strategic plans is partly a process of identifying strategic actions that will balance these strengths and weaknesses with the company's external opportunities and threats. Opportunities might include the possibility of serving additional customers (market penetration), the chance to enter new markets or segments (market development), or falling trade barriers in attractive foreign markets. Threats might include the likely entry of new lower-cost foreign competitors, rising sales of substitute products, and slowing market growth. Delta's managers would consider all these facts, summarize them on the four quadrants of a SWOT chart, and use this information to help develop a corporate strategy, and then a competitive strategy.

Environmental Scanning We saw in Chapters 1–3 that all companies operate in an external environment. The **external environment** of an organization is the set of forces with which that organization interacts.[35] These forces include all the things—like economic trends, regulatory policies and laws, and competitors' actions—that influence the company. **Environmental scanning** means obtaining and compiling information about the environmental forces that might be relevant to the company's strategic planners.

Six key areas of the company's environment are usually scanned to identify opportunities or threats. A form like that in Figure 6.7 can be used for this:

external environment
the set of forces with which an organization interacts.

environmental scanning
a strategic control method aimed at identifying previously unidentified or undetected critical events that could influence the company's strategy.

1. *Economic trends*. These are factors related to the level of economic activity and to the flow of money, goods and services. For example, there has been a trend for people living in Asia to hoard more of their money in gold and gold items. What opportunities and threats would such a trend imply for bankers or for companies in the business of selling gold items?

2. *Competition trends*. These are the factors that involve actions taken or possibly taken by current and potential competitors. For example, Microsoft's move into Internet browsers helped push Netscape into the waiting arms of AOL, which acquired it.

3. *Political trends*. These are factors related to dealings with local, national, and foreign governments. For example, cigarette manufacturers like R. J. Reynolds must monitor trends in the regulation of cigarette smoking around the globe.

4. *Technological trends*. These factors relate to the development of new or existing technology, including electronics, machines, tools, and processes. Several years ago, Microsoft's Bill Gates noticed that the Internet's explosive growth provided both opportunities and threats to his company. The threat lay in the possibility that computer users might come to rely on the Internet itself for

computer processing and thus need less sophisticated personal computers and Microsoft programs (the Sun Microsystems "the network is the computer" threat). The opportunity lay in the possibility of linking more and more Microsoft programs directly to the Internet, thus making Microsoft the gateway to the Internet. (Microsoft chose to include browsers in its Windows operating systems, triggering a federal antitrust charge against the firm.)

▶ FIGURE 6.7

Worksheet for Environmental Scanning

Economic Trends
(such as recession, inflation, employment, monetary policies)

_____
_____
_____
_____

Competitive Trends
(such as competitors' strategic changes, market/customer trends, entry/exit of competitors, new products from competitors)

_____
_____
_____
_____

Political Trends
(such as national/local election results, special interest groups, legislation, regulation/deregulation)

_____
_____
_____
_____

Technological Trends
(such as introduction of new production/distribution technologies, rate of product obsolescence, trends in availability of supplies and raw materials)

_____
_____
_____
_____

Social Trends
(such as demographic trends, mobility, education, evolving values)

_____
_____
_____
_____

Geographic Trends
(such as opening/closing of new markets, factors effecting current plant/office facilities location decisions)

_____
_____
_____
_____

5. *Social trends.* These are factors that affect and reflect the way people live, including what they value. In the United States, for instance, the proportion of Hispanic people is rising quickly. What impact might this have on major advertising companies?

6. *Geographic trends.* This includes factors related to climate, natural resources, and so forth. In Florida, for instance, an apparent long-term cooling trend has reduced the growing area for oranges, so that "Florida oranges" now increasingly come from South America.

Scanning can be done in several ways. For example, employees can be assigned to watch particular areas (economic, social), perhaps by scouring publications like the *New York Times* and the *Wall Street Journal*, as well as the Internet, consultants' reports, information services, and industry newsletters. Other firms use consultants called *environmental scanners*, who read and abstract a wide variety of publications to search for environmental changes that could affect the firm. You can also set up Internet news services to continuously and automatically screen thousands of news stories and provide precisely the types of stories in which you're interested.

Benchmarking Sometimes a company must develop its strengths to become a better competitor. **Benchmarking** is the process through which a company learns how to become the best in some area by carefully analyzing the practices of other companies that already excel in that area (best-practices companies). The basic benchmarking process typically follows several guidelines:[36]

1. Focus on a specific problem and define it carefully. Such a problem might be, What order-fulfillment processes do best-practices companies use in the mail-order business? L.L. Bean is often analysed by other firms, since it's viewed as a best-practice company for the way it expeditiously handles customers' questions and fulfills orders.

2. Use the employees who will actually implement those changes to identify the best-practices companies and to conduct on-site studies. Having the employees who will actually implement the best practices do the study helps ensure their commitment to the required changes.

3. Studying best practices is a two-way street, so be willing to share information with others.

4. Avoid sensitive issues such as pricing, and don't look for new product information.

5. Keep information you receive confidential.

Portfolio Analysis In developing their corporate strategies, most firms (like Pepsi) end up with several businesses in their "portfolio" (such as Colas and Frito-Lay in Pepsi's case). How do you decide which businesses to keep in (or drop from) a portfolio? Several portfolio analysis tools are used to help managers decide.

The BCG Matrix, developed by the Boston Consulting Group (BCG), helps to identify the relative attractiveness of each of a firm's businesses. As shown in Figure 6.8, it does this by comparing growth rate and relative competitive position (market share) for each of the company's businesses. Each business is usually placed in a matrix as in Figure 6.8. Once all businesses have been placed on the matrix, it's easier to decide which to keep or drop. **Stars** are businesses in high-growth industries

benchmarking
a process through which a company learns how to become the best in one or more areas by analyzing and comparing the practices of other companies that excel in those areas.

star in strategic planning
a business in a high-growth industry that also enjoys a high relative market share.

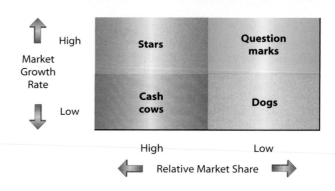

question mark

in strategic planning, a business in a high-growth industry, but with low relative market share.

cash cow

a business with a high relative market share in a low-growth industry such that minimal investments can and need be made to continue to withdraw relatively high quantities of cash.

dogs

a business in a low-growth, unattractive industry that also has low relative market shares and thus should usually be divested.

in which the company has a high relative market share. For example, Intel's microprocessor business (microprocessors are the heart of computers such as IBM's Pentium-driven PCs) has a high growth rate and Intel has a relatively high market share. Star businesses usually require large infusions of cash to sustain growth. However, they generally have such a strong market position that much of the needed cash can be generated from sales and profits.

Question marks are businesses in high-growth industries, but with low market shares. These business units face a dilemma: They are in attractive high-growth industries, but they have such low market shares that they lack the clout to fend off larger competitors. A company must either divert cash from its other businesses to boost the question mark's market share or get out of the business.

Cash cows are businesses in low-growth industries that enjoy high relative market shares. Their being in a low-growth, unattractive industry argues against making large cash infusions into these businesses. However, their high market share generally allows them to generate high sales and profits for years, even without much new investment. Cash cows can thus be good cash generators for the company's question mark businesses.

Finally, **dogs** are low-market-share businesses in low-growth, unattractive industries. Having a low market share puts the business in jeopardy relative to its larger competitors. As a result, dogs can quickly become "cash traps," absorbing cash to support a hopeless and unattractive situation. They are usually sold to raise cash for stars and question marks.

The GE Business Screen, shown in Figure 6.9, is another, somewhat more elaborate portfolio analysis aid. This is a nine-cell matrix originally used by GE to analyze its own business portfolio. Each company is plotted into the appropriate cell according to its industry attractiveness and business unit position. Industry attractiveness, as illustrated, reflects things like industry size, market growth, and industry profitability. Business unit position reflects relative size, market share, and profitability. Like the BCG matrix, the GE Business Screen helps a manager decide whether the firm should boost or reduce its investment in each business. As in the upper left of Figure 6.9, businesses in attractive industries that are relatively strong competitors justify further investment and a growth strategy like market development. Businesses in the lower right of the matrix no longer deserve investment: They either become cash cows or are divested. Those falling in the three blue (diagonal) cells need to be monitored for any changes in industry attractiveness or business strengths, since this might signal the need for increased or decreased investment.

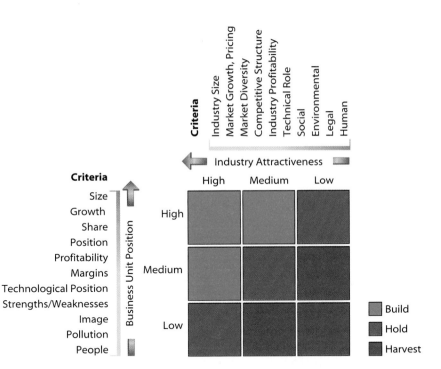

► FIGURE 6.9

Company Position/Industry Attractiveness (GE) Screen

Source: Michael Porter, *Competitive Strategy: Techniques for Analyzing Industries and Competitors* (New York: The Free Press, 1980), p. 365.

When There Is a Range of Futures

Sometimes managers face more uncertainty and a range of possible futures; in this case several scenarios might be applicable, and it's difficult or even impossible to decide ahead of time what will happen. For example, in the United States in the mid-1990s Congress was formulating legislation aimed at deregulating the telecommunications market. Phone companies such as Bell Atlantic, AT&T, and MCI had to develop strategies based on what this legislation might require (regarding, for instance, letting regional Bell companies enter the long-distance market). In situations like these there's great uncertainty and a whole range of possible futures. But how do you predict the future when it's so difficult to foresee? Environmental scanning is not enough. Scenario planning is one tool managers use to identify and plan for the relevant driving forces when the future is unusually unpredictable.

Scenarios have been defined as

hypothetical sequences of events constructed for the purpose of focusing attention on causal processes and decision points. They answer two kinds of questions: (1) precisely how might some hypothetical situation come about, step by step, and (2) what alternatives exist, for each situation at each step, for preventing, diverting, or facilitating the process?[37]

For example, Shell Oil uses scenario planning. As one of its officers said, "The Shell approach to strategic planning is, instead of forecasting, to use scenarios, which are 'stories' about alternative possible futures. These stories promote a discussion of possibilities other than the 'most likely' one, and encourage the consideration of 'what-if' questions."[38]

As in most instances of scenario planning, Shell's planners were asked to write what amounted to stories about their worst possible nightmares, given the forces of change they deemed most crucial to their company.[39] Shell was reportedly the only oil company prepared when a number of years ago oil producers took control away

scenario

a hypothetical sequence of events constructed for the purpose of focusing attention on causal processes and decision points.

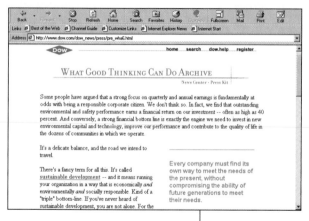

▲ **W E B N O T E**

Companies like Dow use scenario planning to try to "see the future" and to anticipate how they might adapt their strategy to that future.

www.dow.com

Used with permission.

from the oil companies and caused major price increases. It was Shell's scenario planning that helped it anticipate such a scenario, and to act quickly when it actually occurred.

Scenario planning doesn't have to produce just nightmare scenarios (although these are often the ones that companies are most interested in anticipating and planning for). Some scenarios just call for the planning team members to develop narratives of a fundamentally different but better world. For example, the Dairy Council of California (which supplies most of California's classroom nutrition education instruction) could see that education was moving out of the classroom via technology.[40] However, while the council knew that was happening, "it wasn't until the group went through a scenario planning process, that participants, for the first time, clearly pictured the technology trends' ramifications on their world and the need for action."[41] As their scenario developed, a vision emerged of a so-called net generation, a new segment of learners from toddlers to college students who would require dramatically new nutrition education instruction and delivery. This in turn led the council to develop a strategy aimed at creating a new education program using cutting-edge technology to be delivered on-line.

Many companies use scenario planning, and use it successfully.[42] For example, scenario planning helped Pacific Gas & Electric Company prepare for the California earthquake; and an Austrian insurance company was able to anticipate changes in eastern and central Europe and to enter new markets there. Electrolux uses scenario planning to spot new consumer markets, and Krone, a wiring and cable supplier in Berlin, used scenario planning to develop 200 new product ideas.

Scenario planning forces planners to think creatively, to examine possible "what if" scenarios. For instance: What if Internet-based video education replaces most conventional classroom learning? What if most people start using the Internet for all their long-distance calls? What if the market for consumer goods doubles in China? Businesses and other organizations such as universities can then better anticipate changes that may affect how they do business, and plan for them.

▶ STRATEGIC PLANNING IN PRACTICE

Because strategic planners are almost always dealing with the uncertainties of the future, it would be wrong to assume that strategic planning could ever be a purely mechanical process. Indeed, methods like scenario planning are specifically aimed at forcing managers to think creatively about what their company's strategic plans should be. Let's look at some other aspects of strategic planning in practice.

Achieving Strategic Fit

Strategic planning expert Michael Porter says that in practice, managers can't just formulate a competitive strategy and expect it to be effective. Instead, all the firm's activities must be tailored to or fit that strategy, by ensuring that the firm's functional strategies support it's corporate and competitive strategies. As Porter says: "It's this 'fit' that breathes life into the firm's strategy."[43]

Let's look at an example.[44] Southwest Airlines "tailors all its activities to deliver low-cost convenient service on its particular type of short-haul route."[45] By getting fast, 15-minute turnarounds at the gate, Southwest can keep its planes flying longer hours than rivals and have more departures, with fewer aircraft. Southwest also shuns frills like meals, assigned seats, and premium classes of service on which other full-service airlines build their competitive strategies.

Figure 6.10 illustrates the idea that Southwest's successful low-cost competitive strategy is the result of activities that all "fit both each other and Southwest's low-cost competitive strategy." The activities at the heart of Southwest's low-cost activity system are represented by the darker circles: limited passenger services; frequent, reliable departures; lean, highly productive ground and gate crews; high aircraft utilization; very low ticket prices; and short-haul, point-to-point routes. Each of these activities is, in turn, supported by various sub-activities and decisions. For example, limited passenger service means things like no meals, no seat assignments, no baggage transfers, and limited use of travel agents. Lean, highly productive ground and gate crews require high compensation of employees, flexible union

▶ **FIGURE 6.10** **The Southwest Airlines' Activity System**

Companies like Southwest tailor all their activities so that they fit and contribute to making their strategies a reality.

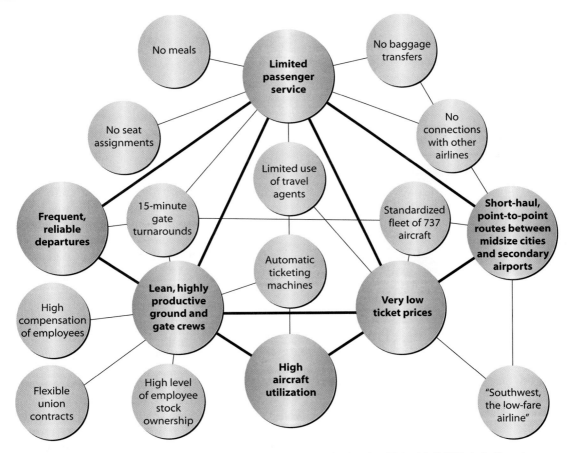

contracts, and a high level of employee stock ownership. Together, these activities combine to create a successful low-cost strategy. If these activities don't each fit the low-cost strategy, then that strategy will probably fail.

In practice, the relationship between strategy and the firm's activities should be reciprocal. In formulating the strategy, for instance, you'll want to build on the company's unique core competencies or strengths and weaknesses, such as a highly trained workforce. On the other hand, implementing the strategy will require ensuring that (as at Southwest) every activity contributes to and fits the strategy.[46]

Strategy As Stretch and Leverage

leverage

to gain a competitive edge by concentrating a company's resources on key strategic goals or competencies.

core competencies

the collective learning in an organization, especially the knowledge of how to coordinate diverse design and production skills and integrate multiple streams of technologies.

Strategic fit is important, but strategy experts Gary Hamel and C. K. Prahalad caution that managers shouldn't become preoccupied with it.[47] They agree that every company "must ultimately effect a fit between its resources and the opportunities it pursues."[48] However, they argue that being preoccupied with fit can limit growth. That's why they say that the concept of "stretch" should supplement fit. Specifically, Hamel and Prahalad argue that leveraging resources—supplementing what you have and doing more with what you have—can be more important than just fitting the strategic plan to current resources.

For example, "If modest resources were an insurmountable deterrent to future leadership, GM, Phillips, and IBM would not have found themselves on the defensive with Honda, Sony, and Compaq."[49] Similarly, Kmart would not have found itself overtaken by Wal-Mart. Companies, they say, can **leverage** their resources by concentrating them more effectively on key strategic goals. For example, Wal-Mart focused its relatively limited resources on building a satellite-based distribution system and gained a competitive advantage that helped it overtake Kmart.

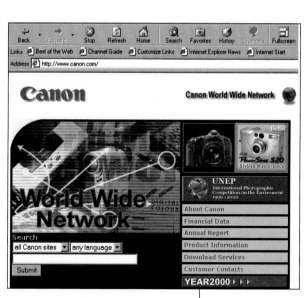

The Strategic Role of Core Competencies

According to Hamel and Prahalad, it's a company's core competencies that should be leveraged. They define **core competencies** as "the collective learning in the organization, especially [knowing] how to coordinate diverse production skills and integrate multiple streams of technologies."[50]

Canon Corporation provides one example. Over the years it has developed three core competencies: precision mechanics, fine optics, and microelectronics. These competencies reflect collective learning and skills that cut across traditional departmental lines. They result from hiring and training in such a way as to create accumulated knowledge and experience in these three areas.

Canon starts by drawing on its core competencies to produce core component products like miniature electronic controls and fine lenses. Then, businesses—its camera business, computer business, and fax business, for instance—are built around these core products. In other words, the businesses use the core products to create end products such as digital cameras, laser printers, and fax machines.

Growing its businesses and end products out of a handful of core competencies this way makes it easier for Canon's managers to quickly change its product mix. Regardless of how the demand for products shifts—for instance, from one type of fax machine to another—Canon's "eggs" aren't all in its products but in its core competencies of precision mechanics, fine optics, and microelectronics. If Canon's managers sense changes in customer demand, they can reach across departmental lines to marshal these core competencies. Suppose managers sense the need for a tiny new consumer electronic product like a compact camera to take PC-based video Internet pictures. Its managers can "harmonize know-how in miniaturization, microprocessor design, material science, and ultra thin precision casting—the same skills it applies in its miniature card calculators, pocket TVs, and digital watches—to design and produce the new camera."[51]

THE PEOPLE SIDE OF MANAGING

▓ It's the People That Make the Strategy Work

While strategic tools like scenario planning are important in strategic planning, as a practical matter the people side of managing is crucial, too. One nationwide survey of 9,144 employees illustrates this. The results showed that the vast majority (83%) of surveyed employees understood their employers' goals and their own job responsibilities (87%), both important factors in getting employees to cooperate in carrying out the firm's strategies. Yet fewer than half of the employees (43%) said they were given the skills and training and information they needed to achieve their goals.[52] The problem, of course, is that having a strategy that's widely known and accepted is of little use if the employees don't have the ability to implement it.

Smart companies know that, and are doing something about it. In companies like Motorola, Saturn, and 3M, employees average between 40 and 80 hours per year of training. And many, including The Lane Group, practice "open-book management," which means keeping all employees continuously informed about the company's financial and other situations so that the employees are, in a real sense, treated like partners.

In other words, the CEOs of most successful companies today understand that even creating a brilliant strategy is a job that's only half done. As Herb Kelleher, CEO of Southwest Airlines once put it, his company's ability to keep costs down (for instance, by turning aircraft around in half the time it takes competitors) is not the result of special equipment or methods. Instead, it's the work of a group of highly motivated managers and employees who believe in Southwest's low-cost strategy, and who have the skills and wherewithal to implement it.

How Entrepreneurs Actually Craft Strategies

Entrepreneurs often take a short cut when it comes to actually creating a strategy for their firms. Interviews with the founders of 100 of the fastest-growing private companies in the United States and research on 100 other thriving ventures showed that entrepreneurs use three general guidelines in formulating strategies:[53]

1. *Screen out losers quickly.* Successful entrepreneurs know how to quickly discard ideas for new products and services that have a low potential. Their decision-making tends to emphasize judgment and intuition, rather than lots of data.

2. *Minimize the resources devoted to researching ideas.* With limited resources, entrepreneurs can obviously do only as much planning and analysis as are absolutely necessary. They then make subjective judgment calls, sometimes based on very limited data. Indeed, about 20% of entrepreneurs got the ideas for their businesses by replicating or modifying an idea encountered in their previous employment. Apparel designer Ralph Lauren reportedly got the kernel of his idea for classic men's and women's wear when he began his career as a salesperson with Brooks Brothers. About 20% got their ideas serendipitously—building a temporary job into a business, developing a family member's idea, or "thought up during honeymoon in Italy," for instance.

3. *Don't wait for all the answers, and be ready to change course.* Large companies often use a fairly ponderous planning process. Plans are carefully drawn up; a hierarchy of goals is assigned; and duties are allocated to actually get the work done. Entrepreneurs often "don't know all the answers before they act." In fact, many entrepreneurs change the traditional motto "Ready, aim, fire" to "Ready, fire, aim." They try a product or service based on the most preliminary market data and then quickly drop or modify the product if it doesn't click with customers.

SUMMARY

1. A primary task of top management is to think through the mission of the business and ask, What is our business, and what should it be? Strategic management is the process of identifying and pursuing the organization's mission by aligning internal capacity with the external demands of the environment.

2. There are five steps in the strategy management process: define the business and develop a mission; translate the mission into strategic objectives; formulate a strategy to achieve the strategic objectives; implement the strategy; and evaluate performance and initiate corrective adjustments as required. Strategic planning includes the first three steps of this process.

3. There are three main types of strategies. The corporate-level strategy identifies the portfolio of businesses that in total will comprise the corporation and the ways in which these businesses will relate; the competitive strategy identifies how to build and strengthen the business's long-term competitive position in the marketplace; and functional strategies identify the basic courses of action that each department will pursue to contribute to the attainment of its goals.

4. Each type of strategy contains specific standard or generic strategies. Generic corporate strategies include concentration, market penetration, geographic expansion, product development, horizontal integration, vertical integration, and diversification, as well as status quo and retrenchment strategies.

5. Generic competitive strategies include being a low-cost leader, differentiator, or focuser. Formulating a specific competitive strategy then requires understanding the competitive forces that determine how intense the competitive rivalries are and how best to compete. The five forces model helps managers understand the five big forces of competitive pressure in an industry: threat of entry, intensity of rivalry among existing competitors, pressure from substitute products, bargaining power of buyers, and bargaining power of suppliers.

6. Creating strategic plans involves: identifying environmental forces, formulating a plan, and creating implementation plans. Useful techniques include SWOT analysis, environmental scanning, benchmarking, portfolio analysis, and scenario planning.

7. Implementing the organization's strategy involves several activities, among them achieving strategic fit, leveraging the company's core competencies, and effectively leading the change process.

TYING IT ALL TOGETHER

Creating a plan is just the first step in the strategic planning process; like any plan, it must then be carried out. In practice, for instance, implementation requires achieving strategic fit—in other words, crafting functional plans so that all the firm's activities, from maintenance to sales to finance, contribute in a coordinated way to what the company wants to achieve. In practice, implementation also requires that work assignments be made; authority delegated to carry them out; employees hired, trained, and motivated; and final results compared to the plan and adjusted if required (in other words, controlled). Therefore, implementing the company's plans ultimately depends on how good a job the manager does with the remaining management functions of organizing, leading, and controlling. In the next Chapter, 7, we'll turn to organizing (which is the first of the remaining management functions) and specifically to the fundamentals of organizing.

KEY TERMS

strategic management 159
vision 160
mission statement 161
strategy 161
strategic control 162
strategic planning 162
corporate-level strategy 162
competitive strategy 163
functional strategy 163
market penetration 163
geographic expansion 163
product development 163
horizontal integration 164

vertical integration 164
diversification 164
related diversification 164
conglomerate diversification 164
retrenchment 164
divestment 164
virtual corporation 165
cost leadership 166
differentiation strategy 166
focus strategy 166
competitive advantage 167

strategic business unit 168
SWOT analysis 172
external environment 173
environmental scanning 173
benchmarking 175
star in strategic planning 175
question mark 176
cash cow 176
dogs 176
scenario 177
leverage 180
core competencies 180

SKILLS AND STUDY MATERIALS

CRITICAL THINKING EXERCISES

1. You have just been appointed to a strategic planning committee for Apple Computer. You know that in the late 1990s the company had been having a difficult time with its strategies. Do some research on the history of Apple. (Both *Fortune* and *Business Week* have many articles on Apple.) Using this information, apply the ideas, concepts, and approaches discussed in this chapter to develop a strategic plan for Apple.

2. You are a strategic planner for GM. In the late 1990s you saw the merger of DaimlerChrysler. By fall 1999 the Germans had taken greater control of the company and put some Chrysler people off the board of directors, and you saw the somewhat early departure of the Chrysler CEO. Rumor has it that the cultures of the two companies did not completely "merge." Now there is a rumor that Ford and Toyota are thinking of merging. What would you recommend that GM do? Using the concepts presented in the chapter, analyze the situation and make recommendations to the GM board.

EXPERIENTIAL EXERCISES

1. With three to four other students in the class, form a strategic management group for your college or university. In a 2-hour time period, identify what "business" your college or university is in, where it is in terms of implementing a strategy, and where it needs to be strategically headed. Prior to meeting to develop your plan, look at what your college or university has developed in the way of a strategic plan by interviewing some administrators, faculty members, and students about their knowledge of the strategic plan. From the information gathered, prepare some strategic alternatives for the other students to discuss in a class brainstorming session.

2. You are the newest member of the design team for a major toy manufacturer. You just saw a show on the A&E channel that identified the most popular toys of the last century. The top five were, in ascending order, Playdoh, Lionel trains, Barbie, the Crayon, and the Yo-Yo. Your job is to design a new toy that could be the top toy of the twenty-first century. In a team of four to five students, do a strategic analysis for the purpose of developing such a toy, and propose a toy.

myPHLIP COMPANION WEB SITE

We invite you to visit the Dessler companion Web site at **www.prenhall.com/dessler** for this chapter's Internet resources.

HOW MANY BRAND NAMES CAN A COMPANY SUCCESSFULLY MANAGE?

C A S E 1

The merger of the German giant Daimler, maker of the Mercedes-Benz, with U.S. giant Chrysler, seemed to be a good match. Mercedes has long been respected for its quality engineering and high reliability, and often been criticized for the rather boxy design of its autos. And while successful in selling its expensive Mercedes autos in the United States, Mercedes has been losing share to Lexus and BMW (even James Bond has switched from his British Aston-Martin to a BMW). Also, Daimler has not had a successful strategy for penetrating the lucrative lower-cost general U.S. auto market. Chrysler Corporation, on the other hand, although the number three U.S. maker, behind Ford and GM, has long been recognized for innovative designs. Chrysler was the first company to produce a minivan, and its Jeep brand was the first sports utility vehicle. While it has been successful in these areas, Chrysler has been less successful in establishing a global presence. The marriage of Daimler and Chrysler therefore seemed a good fit. The question, however, was Would the new DaimlerChrysler be able to exploit the synergies created by the merger?

The new company was faced with an unusual situation. It had several successful brand names, including Mercedes,

Chrysler, Plymouth, and Jeep: What should it do with them? Brand names are powerful assets. A well-known brand, when placed on a new product, tells the customer that the new product can be trusted. Many consumers develop brand loyalty. When faced with a new purchase decision, they buy the familiar brand they know and can trust. Brand management, however, is not free. Maintaining a brand requires constant advertising and promotion.

U.S. consumers have known for some time that Chrysler and Plymouth have many overlapping designs. The problem is, there are many Plymouth owners who are loyal to Plymouth, whose recent product lineup included Neon, Breeze, Voyager, Grand Voyager, and Prowler. In an attempt to establish a more consistent global image, DaimlerChrysler has now decided to drop the Plymouth brand name. This will allow the company to focus more of its marketing resources on the Chrysler brand. Daimler wants to establish a strong brand image for small and midsize cars worldwide and does not feel it can accomplish that for more than one brand. It has selected Chrysler as its global car for the future: "Our goal is to increase our automotive presence around the world, and to do that, we need to focus our resources and our efforts on our growth opportunities," said company President James P. Holden. "The Chrysler brand has tremendous worldwide growth potential for cars." The question is, has DaimlerChrysler made the right decision in dropping the Plymouth brand?

Discussion Questions

1. Perform a SWOT analysis for DaimlerChrysler. What are its greatest strengths and weaknesses? Opportunities and threats?

2. What corporate strategy does DaimlerChrysler appear to be pursuing?

3. In what ways might the decision to drop Plymouth strengthen DaimlerChrysler strategically? What risks does this decision pose?

IT'S A "GOOD THING" TO HAVE A WELL-KNOWN BRAND NAME

CASE 2

Very few new companies begin the initial public offering (IPO) stage of their history with the brand identity of Martha Stewart Omnimedia (MSO). On the day of her company's IPO, Martha Stewart came to Wall Street to serve croissants, muffins, and scrambled egg brioches to startled traders on the floor of the stock exchange. By the end of the day, Stewart's small company (only 385 employees) had raised $2.3 billion in working capital. The question is, with its new-found capital, does MSO have the strategy required to gain and sustain competitive success?

Stewart describes her firm as a leading creator of how-to content and related products and services for homemakers and other consumers. The firm's prospectus makes clear that MSO intends to leverage the well-known Martha Stewart brand name to gain access to key promotional and distribution channels.

Stewart's business is built around seven core content areas: home, cooking and entertaining, gardening, crafts, holidays, keeping, and weddings. For each of these areas, the MSO team puts together a library of articles, books, television programs, newspaper columns, radio segments, and products. The firm has two strategic objectives: Provide original how-to content and information to as many consumers as possible, and turn consumers into doers by offering them the information and products they need for do-it-yourself ingenuity, the "Martha Stewart way."

MSO distributes its content through a broad media platform that includes two magazines, an Emmy Award–winning television program, a weekly TV segment on *CBS This Morning*, a daily cable TV program, a weekly syndicated newspaper column, a radio program, periodic primetime television broadcasts, and to date 27 how-to books. Stewart's two magazines alone, *Martha Stewart Living* and *Martha Stewart Weddings*, have an estimated readership of 9.9 million per month. MSO also has a Web site that now boasts close to 1 million registered users.

In addition to its impressive communication outlets, the company also has created what it calls its "omnimerchandising" platform. The platform consists of products with the Martha Stewart name. At the time of the IPO, the company had more than 2,800 distinct variations of products, including bed and bath products, interior paints, craft kits, outdoor furniture, and garden tools, as well as a line of branded products sold at Kmart. Products are also marketed through national department stores, the upscale catalog *Martha by Mail*, and the on-line store.

While Stewart's brand name has given her firm a great start, to sustain advantage MSO plans to position itself as "a leading authority across key categories of domestic arts." To accomplish this goal, the firm plans to capitalize on what it sees as a number of key strengths besides its brand name: a highly experienced team of creative and business personnel; strong relationships with key distribution, fulfillment, and marketing channels; an extensive research and development process; and an extensive library of high-quality products and designs.

The firm is not comfortable resting on its existing reputation, but has very specific strategies to build revenue over the next few years. These strategies include plans to expand the company's merchandising along its core content lines, amortize the cost of developing high-quality content by sharing it across media and merchandising platforms, exploit the revenue potential of the Internet, and cross-sell and promote its brands.

One of MSO's strategies is somewhat controversial. The firm has publicly stated that it plans to "evolve our brands through team-based content and reduce dependence on our founder." Some analysts feel it is dangerous to remind the market of Stewart's mortality since so much of the promotional strategy depends on her many media appearances. The company has taken out a $67 million life insurance policy to reduce its exposure to risk in the event that it loses Stewart for any reason. This move has also made some investors edgy. At age 58, Stewart is only 7 years away from the time the average person retires. To signal her commitment to the firm, Stewart has signed a five-year contract.

Currently, Martha Stewart owns 70% of the outstanding shares of MSO.

Consumer companies generally face tremendous pressure. First, consumer preferences can be unpredictable. Fads like Furbys and Pokémon are nearly impossible to predict. There has also been significant consolidation in retail distribution channels. The risk here is that in losing one key distributor, MSO could lose several chains of stores. Further, MSO's competitors will not sit still, each will work to find ways to throw MSO off track.

Stewart's new publicly traded firm is off to a great start. She clearly has a well-known brand name, and her slogan, "It's a good thing," is memorable. Now, MSO will have to move past image and slogans to the difficult task of effectively implementing strategy.

Discussion Questions

1. Which of the generic corporate strategies seems best to describe MSO? What competitive strategy does it seem to be pursuing for most of its lines?

2. Based on what you know about MSO or can find out, to what extent do the firm's activities seem to reflect a well-thought-out policy of strategic fit?

3. Perform a brief SWOT analysis for MSO.

4. Based on your results from question 2, have Stewart and her team positioned MSO so that it can gain and sustain a competitive advantage? Why or why not?

YOU BE THE CONSULTANT

KNITMEDIA'S STRATEGIES FOR GROWTH AND EXPANSION

Up to now, you might say that KnitMedia's remarkable growth has been vision-rather than strategy-based. Looking back, it seems apparent that Michael Dorf had a vision of a vertically integrated music company, one in which a new artist could be discovered, showcased in the Knitting Factory clubs, recorded by KnitMedia's record labels, publicized by KnitMedia's festivals division, and marketed by KnitMedia's marketing arms. Therefore, as chief operating officer Allan Fried puts it, leveraging KnitMedia's name and its artists is at the heart of everything the company does. The Knitting Factory is not just a club: "It's an entertainment destination that was leveraged over the Internet, and that was leveraged in what became the Knitting

Factory festivals. So, it's leveraging or expanding the [KnitMedia] brand that we're looking to do." That's why KnitMedia launched the new Web site jazze.com, which started with alternative jazz and now is moving into what Fried calls "more commercial, more smooth jazz."

Basically, therefore, KnitMedia hopes that the synergies created by the integration of the company's various divisions will enable it to compete better in the marketplace and to provide a single source of management, promotion, and distribution for its products and services. In fact, some of KnitMedia's literature presents the company's strategy in terms of a pyramid: In a triangle at the top of the pyramid are the Knitting Factory clubs and the studios whose live recordings and artists, filmmakers, shows, and stories generate the content for everything the company does. Just below this content source are the "brick and mortar" distribution divisions, including record labels and music festivals. These distribute the content generated by the top of the pyramid. At the base are KnitMedia's many online operations, including jazze.com, knittingfactory.com, jazzschool.com, knitfilms.com, and knitradio.com. Along with Internet partners like AOL and Bell Atlantic, KnitMedia's managers plan to use these online properties to deliver KnitMedia's content directly to consumers.

As Dorf and his team explain it, the company's basic strategies for growth and expansion include: offering a broad integrated family of products and services; leveraging existing products, artists, and expertise; expanding international businesses; expanding and strengthening merchandising businesses; expanding and strengthening product licensing; and continuing to target consumers, especially those aged 25 to 49.

However, several recent events have been a little unnerving for the KnitMedia management team. For one thing, in 1999 and 2000 most of the large record companies around the world merged, so that today there are basically only three major record companies left: Warner Music/EMI, Universal/BMG, and Sony Music. Independent record labels still account for about one-fourth of all record companies' market share, but competing with the marketing and distribution resources of these giants is becoming increasingly demanding. Perhaps even more disconcerting was the merger, announced in early 2000, of AOL and Time Warner, a merger that gives that company and its library of hits automatic access to AOL's tens of millions of customers.

So, part of the strategic question facing Michael Dorf and his team is whether a company the size of KnitMedia is really up to competing with giants like Universal and Warner, and if so what strategy it should pursue. On the one hand, these giant businesses are, as Dorf has said, relatively slow and ponderous when it comes to finding new talent and making decisions. It's also true that the Internet is certainly making it easier for independent record labels like KnitMedia to distribute content directly to consumers. On the other hand, the giants do have the financial and human resources to buy the top talent and then market and distribute it effectively.

In a nutshell, Dorf and his team want to make sure they don't end up getting steamrollered while KnitMedia is busy spreading itself across so many businesses. They need your strategic advice.

Team Exercises and Questions

Use what you learned in this chapter to answer the following questions from Michael Dorf and his management team:

1. Of the generic corporate strategies that strategic planning experts use, which is or are the ones that KnitMedia is currently pursuing? Do you think pursuing this (these) strategy(ies) is a good idea? Why or why not?

2. Do you think KnitMedia will be able to achieve the sorts of vertical integration synergies it desires (for instance, by having its clubs spotlight talent that can then be put under contract, recorded, and sent out on music tours)? Why or why not? What do you see as the pros and cons of KnitMedia pursuing this integration strategy?

3. Based on what you know about the company, about strategic planning, and about the music business and the Internet, what corporate strategy would you recommend KnitMedia pursue, and why? What competitive strategy do you think KnitMedia should pursue for each of its separate businesses? Why?

Planning and Setting Objectives

Planning—the process of setting goals, forecasting, and developing courses of action—is in a state of evolution at KnitMedia. From its small and loosely structured beginnings, the organization has nearly doubled in size and grown in complexity. Its goals have broadened considerably, to take advantage of a fruitful overseas market for U.S. jazz music and explosive growth in the power of the Internet. Its managers are still finding new ways of planning, organizing, leading, and controlling efficiently. At the same time that they are creating new positions, shaping an organizational hierarchy, and adding to staff, KnitMedia's managers also face an ever-increasing pace of change. This phenomenon, experienced by every business firm today, is particularly evident at the vibrant crossroads of music and technology that KnitMedia occupies.

All these factors combine to raise planning at KnitMedia to a new level of importance. Planning for the long term receives perhaps the most attention. Long-term goals include opening Knitting Factory clubs in new markets, as we saw in the video for Part One, and leveraging the Knitting Factory brand into new ventures and new media, such as electronic commerce and interactive Webcasts. As Chief Operating Officer Allan Fried points out, KnitMedia's vision changes as the Internet changes and grows, and as its capabilities for reaching and interacting with audiences become clearer. At the same time, it's important for KnitMedia's managers to keep in touch with their market, and with the rate at which the new communication technologies they are exploring are being adopted by consumers.

Some planning still takes place on an ad-hoc basis. Good ideas may just pop up at night or on a weekend, for example. However, most of KnitMedia's managers expect they will be doing more formal planning in the future, not less. Dave Brenner, Vice President for New Media, follows a coherent plan for creating new Web sites with his designers that includes setting goals with them and checking periodically to see whether the work is on schedule and the goals still realistic. Everyone has noticed that there are more meetings than in the past.

Dave also recognizes that flexibility is a key characteristic of good planning, particularly when looking several years ahead. If audiences don't have the hardware necessary to receive super-fast media streams on the Internet, for instance, he foresees scaling back the technology part of the Webcasting goal and refocusing that plan on the audience as it exists at the time, wherever that audience may be in terms of technological capability. The overall goal, however, is likely to remain the same as in CEO Michael Dorf's original vision—to make the Internet a conduit between the artist and the consumer. As Michael sees it, only the tools are changing.

The speed of business also dictates flexibility in planning, according to Ed Greer, Senior Vice President of Club Operations. KnitMedia is working hard to create more proactive plans and do less reacting, or catching up, to events and opportunities that arise without warning. While no one can accurately predict every new trend or spot every new talent, the organization still wants to be in a position to develop plans that help it respond in time to rapid changes in its environment. Ed believes KnitMedia has strengthened its planning function in this respect over the last five years.

More KnitMedia managers are preparing and using budgets, essentially financial plans. Michael Dorf believes that KnitMedia must and will remain "fast and nimble" in order to stay ahead of the curve. He recognizes, however, that for him, tighter planning will only help the process of delegation that the organization's growth has made necessary. Now he regularly prepares and revises his business plan and coordinates the plans of each of his managers. In this way he ensures that the team is achieving the proper balance between formalized planning and "gut" innovation that makes KnitMedia a dynamic and successful operation.

Questions

Based on the case, the video, the text chapters you've read so far, and your knowledge from other sources, answer the following:

1. Dave Brenner, KnitMedia's Vice President for New Media, says the planning process in his department is not as formal as he would like it to be. How do you think he might begin to introduce more formality into the planning process? What particular difficulties do you think he will have to overcome?

2. What are some of the goals articulated at KnitMedia? What other organizational goals can you infer for this firm? What types of goals do you think they should have?

3. Describe the decision-making process at KnitMedia. In what ways do you think it might differ from decision making at larger, more established organizations? In what ways do you think it is the same? Given that KnitMedia is still a small entrepreneurial company, how would you suggest it might improve the decision-making process?

CHAPTER ▶ 7

THE FUNDAMENTALS OF ORGANIZING

WHAT'S AHEAD?

Howard Schultz, head of Starbucks Corporation[1] knows that with more than 2,200 Starbucks stores in the U.S., organizing the company is no easy task. There must be training departments to turn college students into café managers (who know, for example, that every espresso must be pulled within 23 seconds or be thrown away); departments to sell coffee to United Airlines and supermarkets; and a way to manage stores as remote as the Philippines and Beijing. How to organize is, therefore, not an academic issue to Howard Schultz.

OBJECTIVES

AFTER STUDYING THIS CHAPTER, YOU SHOULD BE ABLE TO

▪ Define organizing

▪ Describe and give examples of the basic alternatives for organizing departments

▪ List the types of authority in organizations and provide examples of how authority can be delegated

▪ Illustrate what is meant by decentralization by providing two real-life examples

▲ Howard Schultz cuts the ribbon to open Starbucks' Tokyo store—the first Starbucks outside North America.

Starbuck's Howard Schultz is discovering that planning (Chapters 4–6) and organizing (covered in this and the next two chapters) are inseparable. When his firm was small, its strategy focused on offering high-quality coffee drinks through small, specialized neighborhood coffee houses. This strategy in turn suggested the main jobs for which Schultz had to hire lieutenants—for example store management, purchasing, and finance and accounting. Departments then grew up around these jobs.

As Schultz's strategy evolved to include geographic expansion across the United States and abroad, his organization also had to evolve. Regional store management divisions were established to oversee the stores in each region. Today, with Starbucks coffee also sold to airlines, bookstores, and supermarkets, the company's structure is evolving again, with new departments organized to sell to and service the needs of these new markets. What Schultz is discovering, in other words, is that the organization is determined by the plan: strategy determines structure.

We All Have Things to Organize

The planning–organizing link applies, whether it's General Motors, or Starbucks, or a small start-up business. Let's go back to the management task we first addressed in Chapter 1—your assignment as summer tour master. What's your organization's strategic mission? To plan, organize, and execute a successful trip to France. What job assignments will that require? One way to organize (and the one we chose in Chapter 1) is to break the job into the main functions that must be performed. So we put Rosa in charge of airline scheduling, Ned in charge of hotels, and Ruth in charge of city sites.

How might your organization change if your strategic mission were different? Suppose next year your friends promote you (you lucky thing): You are now in charge of simultaneously planning several trips—to England, to Sweden, and to the south of France. Your organization's strategic mission has therefore changed, too; it is now to plan, organize, and execute three successful trips, and to do so more or less simultaneously. How would you organize now? Perhaps by putting each of last year's trusted lieutenants in charge of a country (say, Rosa—England, Ned—Sweden, and Ruth—South of France). You'd then have a sort of "regional" organization, and each lieutenant might in turn hire trusted friends to arrange for airline tickets, hotels, and sites to see. Again, the tasks to be done, and thus how you organize, have flowed logically out of your plan.

What Is Organizing?

Organizing means arranging the activities in such a way that they systematically contribute to enterprise goals. An organization consists of people whose specialized tasks are coordinated to contribute to the organization's goals.

The usual way of depicting an organization is with an **organization chart**, as shown in Figure 7.1. It shows the structure of the organization; specifically, the title of each manager's position and, by means of connecting lines, who is accountable to whom and who is in charge of what area. The organization chart also shows the **chain of command** (sometimes called the *scalar chain* or the *line of authority*)

organizing

arranging the activities of the enterprise in such a way that they systematically contribute to the enterprise's goals.

organization chart

a chart that illustrates the organization-wide division of work by charting who is accountable to whom and who is in charge of what department.

chain of command

the path a directive and/or answer or request should take through each level of an organization; also called a scalar chain or the line of authority.

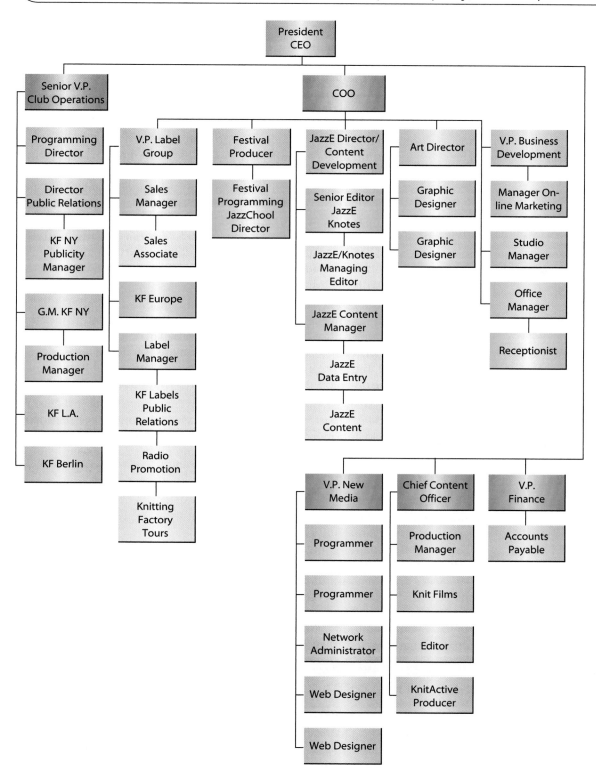

between the top of the organization and the lowest positions in the chart. The chain of command represents the path a directive should take in traveling from the president to employees at the bottom of the organization chart or from employees at the bottom to the top of the organization chart.

In a corporation, the stockholders generally elect a board of directors to represent their interests, so the board, strictly speaking, is at the top of the chain of command. The board's main functions are to choose the top executives, to approve strategies and long-term plans, and to monitor performance to make sure that the stockholders' interests are protected. The board then delegates (we discuss delegation in more detail below) to the CEO the authority to actually run the company—to develop plans, to hire subordinate managers, and to enter into agreements. This is how an organization chart and chain of command evolve.

informal organization
the informal contacts, communications, and habitual ways of doing things that employees develop.

One thing the organization chart does not show is the **informal organization**—the informal, habitual contacts, communications, and ways of doing things that employees develop. Thus, a salesperson might develop the habit of calling a plant production supervisor to check on the status of an order. The salesperson might find this quicker than adhering to the chain of command, which would entail having the sales manager check with the plant manager, who in turn would check with the supervisor.

In fact, there's more informality in most organization charts than most managers would probably like to admit. An executive, hoping to amuse his audience, opened his speech with the following story:

> A young and enthusiastic lion, straight out of lion school, was hired by a circus. After his first day on the job, the lion, by now famished, was surprised to be served not a huge plate of meat, but a bunch of bananas. The lion stormed over to the ringmaster and said "I'm the lion, what are you doing feeding me bananas?" "Well, the problem is," the ringmaster said, "our senior lion is still around, so you're down on the organization chart as a monkey."

The moral of the story is, an organization chart is not always what it seems. For example, the president's assistant may be "only" a secretary, but as the president's gatekeeper may wield enormous authority. The computer systems manager may be so crucial to the company that even the president and other senior executives routinely defer to her decisions. And sometimes a young lion gets hired thinking he is going to be the president, only to find out that the president remains as chairman of the board and effectively second-guesses and undercuts almost everything the president does. You have to learn to exercise some healthy skepticism when reviewing a company's organization chart.

The rest of this chapter is organized around four main topics. The first two focus on what you might call the "horizontal" aspects of organizing—namely, creating departments and then coordination among departments. The final two sections focus on the "vertical" aspects of organizing—namely, delegating or pushing authority down from the top to the bottom of the chain of command, and comparing companies with many levels (and therefore a tall chain of command) with companies that have fewer levels (and therefore a flatter chain of command).

▶ CREATING DEPARTMENTS

Every enterprise—including your summer tour organization—must carry out various activities to accomplish its goals. In a company, these activities might include manufacturing, selling, and accounting. In a city, they might include fire, police, and health protection. In a hospital, they might include nursing, medical services, and radiology. **Departmentalization** is the process through which an enterprise's activities are grouped together and assigned to managers; it is the organizationwide division of work. Departments—logical groupings of activities—are often called divisions, units, or sections.

departmentalization

the process through which an organization's activities are grouped together and assigned to managers; the organizationwide division of work.

The basic question is, Around what activities should you organize departments? Should you organize people around functions such as airline scheduling and hotels, or around places such as England and the south of France? In a company, should departments be organized for sales and manufacturing? Or should there be separate departments for industrial and retail customers, each of which then has its own sales and manufacturing units? As we'll see, many options are available.

Creating Departments Around Functions

Functional departmentalization means grouping activities around basic functions like manufacturing, sales, and finance. Figure 7.2 shows the organizational structures for STM (your summer tour organization) and for the ABC car company. At ABC each department is organized around a different business function—sales, finance, and production. Here the production director reports to the president and manages ABC's production plants. The directors carry out the sales, finance, and production functions.

functional departmentalization

a form of organization that groups a company's activities around essential functions such as manufacturing, sales, or finance.

Service businesses like STM can be built around business functions too—scheduling, reservations, and sightseeing destinations. And the basic business functions around which banks are often departmentalized include operations, control, and loans. In a university, the business functions might include academic affairs, business affairs, and student affairs.

There are other types of functions, too. For example, organizing around managerial functions means putting supervisors in charge of departments like planning, control, and administration. Departmentalization based on technological functions means grouping activities such as plating, welding, or assembling. The basic idea of any functional departmentalization is to group activities around the core functions the enterprise must carry out.

FUNCTIONAL ORGANIZATIONS

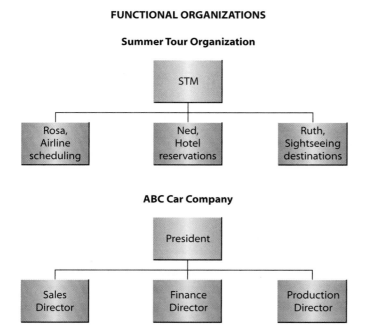

Summer Tour Organization

```
                    STM
     ┌───────────────┼───────────────┐
  Rosa,            Ned,            Ruth,
  Airline          Hotel         Sightseeing
  scheduling     reservations    destinations
```

ABC Car Company

```
                 President
     ┌───────────────┼───────────────┐
  Sales            Finance        Production
  Director         Director        Director
```

◀ F I G U R E   7 . 2

Functional Departmentalization

This chart shows *functional* organizations, with departments for basic functions like finance, sales, and production.

Advantages   Organizing departments around functions has several advantages (see Table 7.1):

1. It is simple, straightforward, and logical; it makes sense to build departments around the basic functions in which the enterprise must engage.

2. Functional organizations usually have single departments for areas like sales, production, and finance that serve all the company's products, rather than duplicate facilities for each product. Because the volume in these departments is relatively high, the firm typically gets increased returns to scale—in other words, employees become more proficient from doing the same job over and over again, and the company can afford larger plants and more efficient equipment. Functional organizations are therefore often associated with efficiency.

3. The managers' duties in each of the functional departments tend to be more specialized (a manager may specialize in finance or production, for instance); the enterprise therefore needs fewer general managers—those with the breadth of experience to administer several functions at once. This can simplify both recruiting and training.

4. Functional department managers also tend to receive information on only part of the big picture of the company—on that which concerns their own specialized functions. This can make it easier for top management to exercise control over the department managers' activities.

Disadvantages   Functional organizations also have disadvantages (see Table 7.1):

1. Responsibility for the enterprise's overall performance rests on the shoulders of one person, usually the president. He or she may be the only one in a position to coordinate the work of the functional departments, each of which is only one element in producing and supplying the company's product or service. This may not be a serious problem when the firm is small or does not work with a lot of products. But as size and diversity of products increase, the job of coordinating, say, production, sales, and finance for many different products may prove too great for one person; the enterprise could lose its responsiveness.

T A B L E 7 . 1	Advantages and Disadvantages of Functional Departmentalization
Advantages	**Disadvantages**
1. Managers are functionally specialized and therefore more efficient	1. Responsibility for overall performance with chief executive only
2. Less duplication of effort	2. Can overburden chief executive and lead to slower decision making and less responsiveness
3. Increased returns to scale	3. Reduces the attention paid to specific products, customers, markets, or areas
4. Simplified training	4. Results in functionally specialized managers rather than general managers
5. Simple and proven over time	
6. Tight control by chief executive	

2. Also, the tendency for functional departments to result in specialized managers (finance experts, production experts, and so forth) makes it more difficult to develop managers with the breadth of experience required for general management jobs like president.

Creating Departments Around Products

With product departmentalization, departments are organized for each of the company's products or services, or for each family of products. Department heads in this type of organization are responsible for both creating and marketing a product, a family of products, or a service. Figure 7.3 shows the organization charts for the Summer Tour Organization and for a product-related company, Bright Star Pharmaceuticals. In Bright Star, a president heads North Atlantic operations. Three product divisions report to this person: one for drugs and pharmaceuticals, one for personal care products, and one for stationery products. Each of these three product divisions then has its own staff for activities such as production and sales.

Arranging departments around products in this way is sometimes called **divisionalization**. Divisionalization exists *when the firm's major departments are organized so that each can manage all the activities needed to develop, manufacture, and sell*

divisionalization
a form of organization in which the firm's major departments are organized so that each can manage all or most of the activities needed to develop, manufacture, and sell a particular product or product line.

▼ **FIGURE 7.3** **Product Departmentalization**

In product departmentalizations like these, separate departments or divisions are set up for services—tour management—or products—drugs, pharmaceuticals, personal care, and stationery.

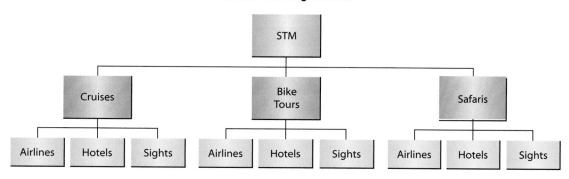

Summer Tour Organization

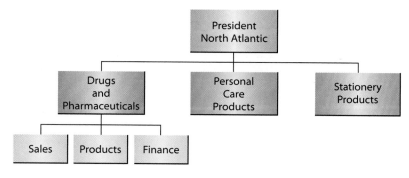

Bright Star Pharmaceuticals

▶Between May 5, 1994 (when it started corporate life as Mosaic Communications), and March 1999 (when it was bought by America Online), Netscape went from nothing to a company valued at over $10 billion. How it built its organization in such a short time provides some interesting insights into how start-up companies organize to grow rapidly under conditions of hyper-change.[2]

Like most startups, Netscape began with a simple functional organization, with separate departments for activities like marketing, development, legal, and finance. However, even at this early date, one of the company's big challenges was maintaining the intensity of a startup, so the development group was divided into small teams of around six engineers each, with each group enjoying considerable autonomy.

The company even used the Internet to create a virtual development organization. In 1994, for example, Netscape had only 115 employees and so didn't really have the resources to test and debug its new browser. It therefore posted a beta version of Navigator on the Internet, thus allowing users to serve as a sort of virtual quality assurance team. Within a month, more than 1.5 million users had given Navigator a trial run, and provided the design engineers with invaluable information about what had to be changed.

As the company grew, its functional organization was replaced by a structure built around product divisions. As one researcher pointed out, Netscape executives did this in part because "they believed that combining the functional groups needed to build a product under a single general manager will enable the product groups to be closer to customers, to focus more effectively on specific markets and competitors, and to act more autonomously."[3]

As the size of the product divisions increased, Netscape's top managers needed a more formal way to coordinate the activities of its different groups. In early 1998 various organizational changes were made to add more formality; for example, a new position was created for "quality and customer satisfaction." And the company began to emphasize a more systematic, longer-term way of looking at things by building activities around 36-month plans.

a particular product, product line, or service. The head of such a division usually has functional departments—say, for production, sales, and personnel—reporting to him or her. As a result, each of these product divisions is *self-contained.* In other words, each controls all or most of the resources required to create, produce, and supply its product or products.

Netscape is a good example of how a company went from a functional to a product organization, as discussed in the "Entrepreneurs in Action" box.

Advantages   Divisionalization can be advantageous in several ways.

1. A single manager is charged with overseeing all the functions required to produce and market each product. Each product division can therefore focus its resources on being more sensitive and responsive to the needs of its particular product or product line. (The manager in charge of the North American personal care group in Figure 7.3, for example, has his or her own research, manufacturing, and sales departments. As a result, the division can usually respond quickly when a competitor brings out a new and innovative product.) The manager need not rely on research, manufacturing, or sales managers who are not within his or her own division. Divisionalization is thus appropriate where quick decisions and flexibility (rather than efficiency) are paramount.

2. Performance is more easily judged. If a division is doing well (or not doing well), it is clear who is responsible because one person is managing the whole division.

3. Being put in charge of "the whole ball game" can help motivate the manager to perform better.

4. Self-contained divisions can also be good training grounds for an enterprise's executives because they are exposed to a wider range of problems, from production and sales to personnel and finance.

5. Finally, divisionalization helps shift some of the management burden from top management to division executives. Imagine if the North American president had to coordinate the tasks of designing, producing, and marketing each of the company's many products. The diversity of problems he or she would face would be enormous. Therefore, virtually all very large companies, as well as many small ones with diverse products and customers, have divisionalized.[4]

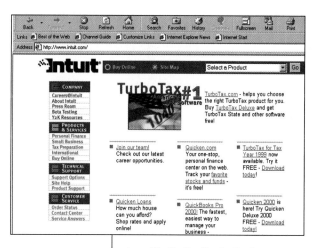

That helps explain why Bill Harris, then executive vice president of software company Intuit, praised the company's divisional structure:

> Two years ago, it was becoming clear that the bigger we got, the more being organized by functions was a liability. . . . The executive team had become a real bottleneck. We needed a new structure [and decided] to bust the organization apart. [Our new CEO] created eight business units, each with its own general manager and customer mission. The basic goal was to flatten the organization and fragment the decision-making process. Each business unit would be the size that Intuit had been a few years ago, and each would focus on one core product or market.

The effects of the reorganization have been dramatic. The new organization forces Intuit's top managers to give more decision-making authority to the individual business units. The executive team used to make or approve most product-related decisions. Now these decisions are left to the business units, and within these units they are usually left to the individual product teams. Intuit has become more responsive and effective at managing change.[5]

Disadvantages   Organizing around divisions can also produce disadvantages, such as the following:

1. Divisions breed an expensive duplication of effort. The fact that each product-oriented unit is self-contained implies that there are several production plants instead of one, several sales forces instead of one, and so on. Related to this, the company's customers may become annoyed at being visited by many salespeople representing different divisions.

2. Divisionalization may also diminish top management's control. As at Intuit, the division heads often have great autonomy because they are in charge of all phases of producing and marketing their products. Top management therefore tends to have less control over day-to-day activities. A division might run up excessive expenses before top management discovers there is a problem. In fact, striking a balance between providing each division head with enough autonomy to run the division and maintaining top management control is crucial.

3. Divisionalization also requires more managers with general management abilities. Each product division is, in a sense, a miniature company, with its own production

TABLE 7.2 **Advantages and Disadvantages of Product Departmentalization**

Advantages	Disadvantages
1. One unit is responsible for giving continuous, undivided attention to the product, so the unit is more sensitive and responsive to the unique needs of the product.	1. Duplication of effort, perhaps reduced efficiency. In some situations, customers may be bothered by representatives of more than one division.
2. Part of the burden is lifted from the shoulders of the top manager.	2. Finding and training people to head each division is a more difficult job.
3. Performance is more easily identified and judged; this in turn may motivate good performance.	3. Since division heads now do their own coordinating without checking with the top manager, the latter could begin to lose control. He or she no longer coordinates and oversees the day-to-day *activities* by which managers do their jobs, just the *ends*—whether or not the division makes a profit at the end of the year.
4. It provides a good training ground for future top executives.	

plant, sales force, personnel department, and so forth. Divisional managers therefore cannot just be sales, production, or personnel specialists. Companies with divisional structures and strong executive development programs tend to be prime hunting grounds for executive recruiters. GE is often listed as the place where recruiters look first when trying to find CEOs for other companies.

The advantages and disadvantages of product (divisional) departmentalization are summarized in Table 7.2.

Creating Departments Around Customers

customer departmentalization

similar to divisional organization except that generally self-contained departments are organized to serve the needs of specific groups of customers.

Customer departmentalization is similar to product departmentalization, except that here departments are organized to serve the needs of specific customers. Figure 7.4, for instance, shows the organization chart for the Grayson Steel Company. Notice how the company's main divisions are organized to serve the needs of particular customers, such as metals and chemicals customers, packaging systems customers, aerospace and industrial customers, and the international group.

Advantages and Disadvantages Organizing around customers has several advantages. As in product departmentalization, a manager is charged with giving continuous, undivided attention to a customer or group of customers. This can result in faster, more satisfactory service to each of the company's customers, particularly when their needs are substantially different.

As in product departmentalization, the main disadvantage is duplication of effort. The company may have several production plants instead of one, and several sales managers, each serving the needs of his or her own customers, instead of one. This can reduce overall corporate efficiency.

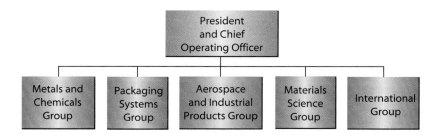

◄ **F I G U R E   7 . 4**

Customer Departmentalization, Grayson Steel Company

With customer departmentalization, separate departments are organized around customers such as aerospace and metals and chemicals customers.

Creating Departments Around Marketing Channels

With **marketing-channel departmentalization**, top-level departments are organized around each of the firm's marketing channels (instead of products, services, or customers). A **marketing channel** is the conduit (wholesaler, drugstore, grocery, or the like) through which a manufacturer distributes its products to its ultimate customers.

Marketing-channel departmentalization is illustrated in Figure 7.5. As you can see, it is similar to customer departmentalization, but there are several differences. In customer departmentalization, each customer-oriented department is usually responsible for both manufacturing and selling its own product to its own customers. In marketing-channel departmentalization, the same product (such as Ivory soap) is typically marketed through two or more channels. Usually one department is chosen to manufacture the product for all the other marketing-channel departments.

Organizing around marketing channels assumes that each marketing channel's unique needs must be catered to. For example, Revlon may sell through both department stores and discount drugstores. Yet the demands of these two channels are quite different: The department store may want Revlon to supply specially trained salespeople to run concessions in its stores. The discount druggist may just want quick delivery and minimal inventory. Putting a manager and department in charge of each channel can help ensure these diverse needs are met quickly and sat-

marketing-channel departmentalization

an arrangement in which departments of an organization focus on particular marketing channels, such as drugstores or grocery stores.

marketing channel

the means through which a manufacturer distributes its products to its ultimate customers.

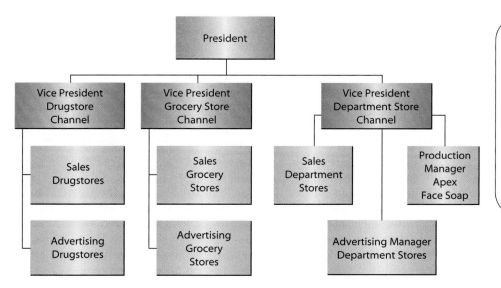

◄ **F I G U R E   7 . 5**

Marketing Channel Departmentalization

With marketing channels, the main departments are organized to focus on particular marketing channels such as drugstores and grocery stores.

Note: Only the department-store channel produces the soap, and each channel may sell to the same ultimate consumers.

isfactorily. As in product and customer departmentalization, the resulting duplication—in this case, of sales forces—is the main disadvantage.

Creating Departments Around Geographic Areas

Finally, as when you put Rosa in charge of England, Ned in charge of Sweden, and Ruth in charge of the south of France, you can organize departments around geographic regions. With geographic, or territorial, departmentalization, separate departments are organized for each of the territories in which the enterprise does business. Territorial geographic departments are usually examples of divisional departmentalization: Each area tends to be self-contained, perhaps with its own production, sales, and personnel activities.

Advantages and Disadvantages   The main advantage of territorial departmentalization is that one self-contained department focuses on the needs of its particular buyers—in this case, those in its geographic area. This can lead to speedier, more responsive, and better service. A department store chain like JCPenney might organize territorially to cater to the tastes and needs of customers in each area. Like product, customer, and marketing-channel departmentalization, territorial departmentalization is advantageous insofar as it ensures quick, responsive reaction to the needs of the company's clients.

Also like the other types of departmentalization, however, territorial departmentalization may create duplication of effort. And again, with these types of divisions, the company needs to hire and train managers capable of managing several functions (like production, sales, and personnel).

An Example: Heinz   To some extent, organizing geographically was a product of a time when it was difficult to communicate across borders, particularly international borders. Taking the pulse of consumer needs and monitoring operations in a far-flung global operation is no easy task. As a result, many companies departmentalized globally, so that local managers could run their regional or country businesses as more or less autonomous companies. Two trends are making the geographic organization less practical today.

First, global competition is becoming much more intense, so it's increasingly important for a company to be able to apply product improvements it obtains in one locale to another. If H. J. Heinz in Japan, for instance, discovers a new way to formulate one of its soups, it will want to make sure that the improvement is implemented in all the company's markets, including Europe and the United States. A geographic organization—with its relatively compartmentalized country divisions—may hamper such cross-fertilization.

Second, information technology is reducing the impediments to cross-border communication. Video conferencing, e-mail, fax, and computerized monitoring of operations means that an executive in one region—say, the United States—can now easily keep his or her fingers on the pulse of operations around the world.

Many companies are therefore switching from a geographic to a product organization. For example, Heinz's new CEO, William Johnson, said he will end the company's system of managing by country or region.[6] Instead, the company will manage by products or categories, so that managers in the United States can work with managers in Europe, Asia, and other regions to implement the best ideas from one region in other regions as well.

Procter & Gamble recently said it was taking the same approach. Its new organization eliminates its old four business units based on regions of the world, and puts profit responsibility in the hands of seven executives who will report directly to new CEO, Durk Jager. Each executive will globally manage product units such as baby care, beauty, and fabric and home care. The company said the reorganization will speed decision making and send products to market faster.[7]

▓ Using the Internet for Global Communications

Companies like Heinz can use the Internet in many ways to improve global communications. Videoconferencing is one of them. For the cost of a local telephone call, companies now have global, face-to-face communications that help eliminate the barriers distance formerly placed in the way of such face-to-face talk.[8]

CU-SeeMe is one of the systems companies use to hold multiparty video-conference meetings over the Internet. This system uses a "reflector" program, which sends simultaneous transmissions to every participant. While the system is used primarily for "talking head" meetings (each participant appears on the screen in a 4-inch box), it provides an inexpensive and effective way to hold long-distance meetings.

The World Bank, which is headquartered in Washington, DC, is an example of how one organization uses CU-SeeMe. With offices or partners in 180 countries, the World Bank has an urgent need to communicate quickly and efficiently across borders. It uses CU-SeeMe to conduct small meetings and virtual seminars. While the images may be small and the video may not always be very smooth, the system's low cost and ease of use makes it easy for the World Bank and other organizations and companies to communicate instantly and face to face around the globe. It therefore reduces the need to depend so heavily on a global organization structure.

▲ A participant using the CU-SeeMe video-conferencing system. The camera is on top of the computer monitor.

Creating Matrix Organizations

A **matrix organization**, also known as matrix management, is an organization in which one form of departmentalization is superimposed on another.[9] In one example, illustrated in Figure 7.6, product departments are superimposed on a functional departmentalization. This company's automotive products division is functionally organized, with departments for functions like production, engineering, and personnel. Superimposed over this functional departmentalization are three product groups—for the Ford project, the Chrysler project, and the GM project. Each of these product groups has its own product manager, or project leader. One or more employees from each functional department (like production and engineering) is temporarily assigned to each project.

Combining customer and geographic organizations is another common matrix approach.[10] For example, a bank may be organized geographically, with separate officers in charge of operations in each of several countries. At the same time, the bank has a customer structure superimposed over this geographic organization. Project heads for major bank customers such as IBM lead teams comprised of bank employees from each country who concentrate on the local and worldwide financial interests of IBM. Bank employees in each country may report to both their country man-

matrix organization
an organization in which one or more forms of departmentalization are superimposed on an existing one.

▼ FIGURE 7.6 **Matrix Organization Departmentalization**

With a matrix organization, a project structure is often superimposed over a functional organization.

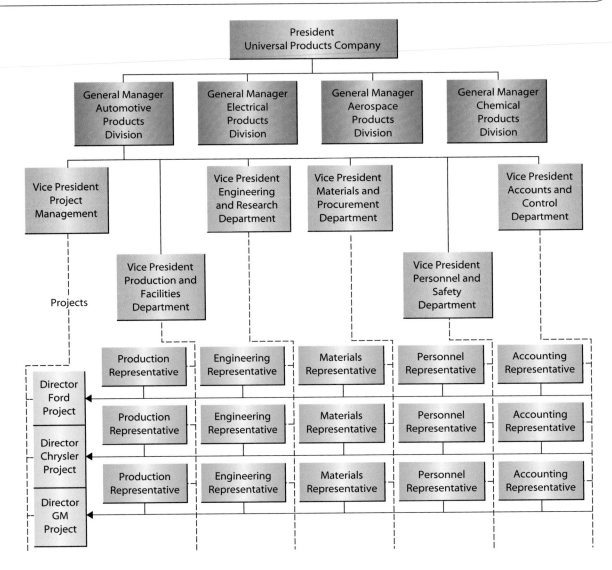

agers and their project managers. Some matrix organizations are more formal than others. Sometimes temporary project managers are assigned to provide coordination across functional departments for some project or customer. Other firms sometimes add a semipermanent administrative structure (including, for instance, project employee appraisal forms) to help build the project teams' authority.[11]

Matrix organizations have proved successful in a wide range of companies, including Citicorp, TRW Systems, NASA and many of its subcontractors, UNICEF, and various accounting, law, and security firms.[12]

Advantages and Disadvantages Matrix departmentalization can help give bigger companies some of the advantages of smaller ones. For example, a self-contained project group can devote undivided attention to the needs of its own project, product, or customer, yet the entire organization need not be permanently organized around what may turn out to be temporary projects. Another advantage is that management avoids having to establish duplicate functional departments for each project.

However, matrix organizations can also trigger problems that, although avoidable, are potentially serious.

- *Power struggles and conflicts.* Since authority tends to be more ambiguous and up for grabs in matrix organizations, struggles between managers who head the functional and project groups may be more common than in traditional organizations.

- *Lost time.* Matrix organizations tend to result in more intragroup meetings, which can make people feel decision making takes too long.

- *Excessive overhead.* Matrix organizations may tend to raise costs because hiring more managers and secretaries raises overhead.

- *Confusion.* Dual reporting lines can cause confusion, and are appropriate only "for complex tasks and uncertain environments" where ambiguity is a reasonable price to pay for dealing with rapid change.[13]

THE **PEOPLE** SIDE OF MANAGING

■ Implementing Matrix Management at Texas Instruments

As you may imagine, the people side of managing holds the key to effectively implementing a matrix organization. This is illustrated by a recent reorganization in the Materials & Controls division (M&C) of Texas Instruments Corp.[14]

Texas Instruments M&C is headquartered in the Netherlands, and specializes in the design of low-cost, high-quality, customer-specific sensors, controls, and materials. As the industry's product life cycle—the time required to design, introduce, and then redesign or replace a product—became shorter, the company decided it needed to develop new products faster. At the time, M&C had a functional organization, with separate departments for design, engineering, manufacturing, purchasing, and quality engineering. After participating in a training course on project management, the division's management and staff became enthusiastic about organizing around projects, but decided doing so would require instituting a matrix management structure.

In the division's "balanced matrix" organization, "the project managers and functional managers share roughly equal authority and responsibility for the project."[15] Project managers were appointed and project teams installed, so that team members reported to both a project manager and their existing functional managers. This new structure "required the teams and their managers not only formally but also actively to commit themselves to a project."[16]

Yet getting that kind of commitment in the face of the ambiguities created by dual reporting lines is often easier said than done, and relies heavily on the people side of managing. For example, some project managers who were initially appointed reportedly lacked the skills, time, or commitment to perform the job and had to be replaced. M&C's managers soon discovered that having project teams which didn't have a strong team culture was undermining the effectiveness of the teams. Implementing the matrix structures there-

▲ **W E B N O T E**

Texas Instruments' Materials & Controls division's Web homepage emphasizes the project team orientation that is the basis for its matrix structure.

www.ti.com

Used with permission.

fore led management to introduce activities aimed at team building, such as pre-project motivation exercises.

Even this wasn't enough. The teams seemed to divide into two factions, one focusing on manufacturing employees, and one on design engineers. Meetings were organized to promote interaction, but, as the researcher notes, promoting interaction is one thing, and collaboration is another. Ultimately, Texas Instruments M&C got its matrix structure to work right, but doing so required enormous attention to the people side of managing.

▼ FIGURE 7.7 A Hybrid Organization

Particularly in large organizations, several types of departmentalization are typically combined, in this case functional, product, and geographic.

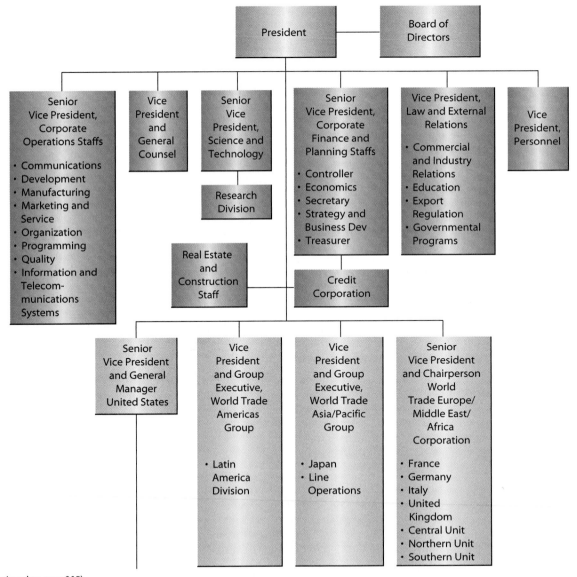

(continued on page 205)

Departmentalization in Practice: A Hybrid

Most enterprises use several forms of departmentalization: They are hybrids. For example, top management might decide to establish functional departments for production, sales, and finance. They then break the sales department into geographic areas, with separate sales managers for the north, east, south, and west.

An example of this type of hybrid is presented in Figure 7.7, which shows a large multinational organization. Within the United States, this is basically a divisional

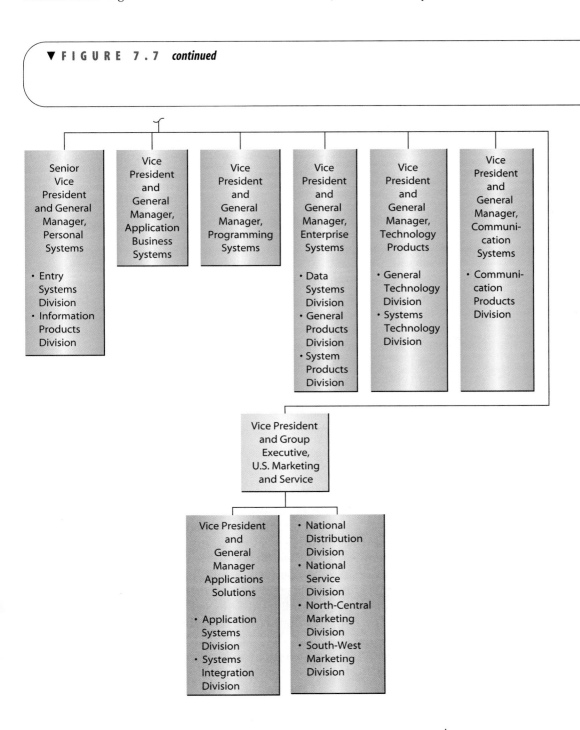

▼ FIGURE 7.7 *continued*

Senior Vice President and General Manager, Personal Systems
- Entry Systems Division
- Information Products Division

Vice President and General Manager, Application Business Systems

Vice President and General Manager, Programming Systems

Vice President and General Manager, Enterprise Systems
- Data Systems Division
- General Products Division
- System Products Division

Vice President and General Manager, Technology Products
- General Technology Division
- Systems Technology Division

Vice President and General Manager, Communication Systems
- Communication Products Division

Vice President and Group Executive, U.S. Marketing and Service

Vice President and General Manager Applications Solutions
- Application Systems Division
- Systems Integration Division

- National Distribution Division
- National Service Division
- North-Central Marketing Division
- South-West Marketing Division

structure, with separate departments organized around business systems, programming systems, and so forth. However, this firm also uses territorial departmentalization, with separate officers in charge of Asia, the United States, and the Middle East. As is often the case with divisional structures, the headquarters itself is organized around managerial functions (general counsel, finance and planning, and law, for instance).

Hybrid Organization: An Example Rosenbluth International is a fast-growing 1,000-office global travel agency, but the way it is organized is based on what CEO Hal Rosenbluth learned on a cattle farm.

Standing on a field in rural North Dakota several years ago, Rosenbluth made a discovery: "The family farm is the most efficient type of unit I've ever run across, because everybody on the farm has to be fully functional and multifaceted." He decided to look for an organizational design that would embody that approach to getting everyone fully involved in helping to run the company. He knew doing so would help his managers.

▲ Hal F. Rosenbluth, Chairman and CEO of Rosenbluth International, illustrates quality service by serving tea to new associates (employees) attending orientation at the company's world headquarters in Philadelphia. All new associates come to headquarters to learn about all facets of the company and to understand how all the business units interact with the central service centers at the Philadelphia headquarters.

His company is a good example of how smart managers blend several organizational styles to build fast-moving, successful firms. Rosenbluth broke his company into more than 100 geographic units, each functioning like a farm, serving specific regions and clients. Corporate headquarters became more like what Rosenbluth calls "farm towns," where "stores" like human resources and accounting are centralized so all the farms can use them. Its computerized Global Distribution Network links each of its travel agents to the company's minicomputers in Philadelphia. There, centralized data on clients help ensure that the work of all the offices is coordinated to serve the needs of Rosenbluth clients.[17]

▶ ACHIEVING COORDINATION

What Coordination Is and Why It's Important

coordination

the process of achieving unity of action among interdependent activities.

Congratulations: You have split or divided the tour work to be done into several departments. Now—as with your assignments to Rosa, Ned, and Ruth—that work must be coordinated. **Coordination** is the process of achieving unity of action among interdependent activities. Coordination is required whenever two or more interdependent individuals, groups, or departments must work together to achieve a common goal. For example, what good would it do for your trip to France if Rosa got airline tickets that weren't coordinated with Ned's hotel reservations or Ruth's sightseeing plans? The only way your efforts (and the trip) will work is if Rosa's, Ned's, and Ruth's activities are coordinated, so that all the dates in the schedule make sense and your group arrives for its hotel reservations when it's supposed to. In companies, organizing usually creates specialized and differentiated jobs, such as managers for production and for sales, or for product A and product B. Somewhere along the line the work of these people must be coordinated. We'll see in this section that managers use various methods to achieve such coordination.

Departmentalization always creates the need for coordination, but some types of departmentalization create the need for more coordination than others. Functional departmentalization tends to create departments that are highly interdependent and that rely heavily on someone to make sure the work is coordinated. This is the case with your group's trip to France, for instance: You had better coordinate the work of your three lieutenants, or you might find your group arrives in Paris on Tuesday but the hotel reservations don't begin until Friday. Similarly, for the ABC Car Company Organization in Figure 7.2, the president must coordinate the work of the sales director, finance director, and production director. If the president is not careful, for instance, he or she might find that the production director plans to produce 10,000 cars one month, but the finance director hasn't arranged to finance that many cars, or the sales director is unprepared to sell that many.

On the other hand, coordination tends to be simpler with divisional types of departments. In the case of your three-country trip, for instance, putting each lieutenant in charge of a country would mean that, at least within each country, you could be fairly sure that all the plans will be coordinated without much input from you. Rosa will make sure that all the airline, hotel, and sightseeing plans within England make sense. As another example, consider the separate customer divisions established by the Grayson Steel Company (Figure 7.4). The separate divisions are pretty much-self-contained. Each division—such as those for metals and chemicals, and aerospace—has its own research, production, and sales units. In such an organization, each division can be managed more or less as an autonomous business. The job of achieving coordination between the more-or-less separate divisions would be relatively simple, because it is not essential for the divisions to work in unison on most day-to-day matters.

Methods for Achieving Coordination

What methods do managers use to achieve coordination? There are several:[18,19] mutual adjustment, rules or procedures, direct supervision, divisionalization, staff assistants, liaisons, teams and committees, independent integrators, standardization.

Use Mutual Adjustment Mutual adjustment means achieving coordination by relying on face-to-face interpersonal interaction. It is used in both the simplest and most complex situations. In a simple situation (such as two people moving a heavy log) coordination could be achieved by having one person count "one, two, three, lift," at which time both people lift the log in unison. Or, you could have Rosa, Ned, and Ruth meet before making any final decisions on the trip to Europe.

Mutual adjustment is also used in more complex situations. A platoon of marines planning its attack, for instance, may follow formal procedures and stick to the chain of command. But when the marines hit the beach, most coordination will likely take place through an ongoing process of mutual adjustment, with the marines continually interacting with and responding to one another as they meet with unanticipated problems.

Rules or Procedures If the work can be planned in advance, you can specify ahead of time what actions your subordinates should take. Rules and procedures are useful for coordinating routine, recurring activities. They specify what course of action each subordinate should take if a particular situation should arise. Thus, a restaurant manager could have a rule that bussers will clear tables as soon as customers

mutual adjustment
achieving coordination through personal interactions and communicated responses to a situation.

finish eating. This ensures that the table is ready for the next course and that the work of the waiters and bussers is coordinated.

Direct Supervision   Direct supervision achieves coordination by having one person coordinate the work of others, issuing instructions and monitoring results.[20] When problems arise that are not covered by rules or procedures, subordinates are trained to bring the problem to the manager. In addition to using rules and mutual adjustment, all managers use the chain of command in this way to achieve coordination.

Divisionalization   Functional departmentalization creates additional demands for managerial coordination, since the work of the functional departments is both specialized and interdependent. Divisional types of departments tend to reduce such interdependence, and take the coordinative burden off the president. For example, in a divisional organization, the president does not have to work as hard coordinating the efforts of his or her product divisions, because they are relatively independent of each other.

Staff Assistants   Some managers hire staff assistants to ease the job of coordinating subordinates. When subordinates bring a problem to the manager, the assistant can compile information about the problem, research it, and offer advice on available alternatives. This effectively boosts the manager's ability to handle problems and coordinate the work of his or her subordinates.

Liaisons   When the volume of contacts between two departments grows, some firms use special liaisons to facilitate coordination. For example, the sales department manager might appoint a salesperson to be his or her liaison with the production department. This liaison is based in the sales department but travels frequently to the factory to learn as much as possible about the plant's production schedule. When an order comes in to the sales department, the sales manager can then quickly determine what the production schedules are and knows whether a new order can be accepted.

Teams and Committees   Many firms achieve coordination by appointing interdepartmental committees, task forces, or teams. These are usually composed of representatives of the interdependent departments. They meet periodically to discuss common problems and ensure interdepartmental coordination.

independent integrator
an individual or a group that coordinates the activities of several interdependent departments, but is independent of them.

Independent Integrators   An **independent integrator** is an individual or a group that coordinates the activities of several interdependent departments.[21] Integrators differ from liaisons in that integrators are independent of the departments they coordinate. They report to the manager who oversees those departments.

Using independent integrators has proved useful in high-tech firms where several interdependent departments must be coordinated under rapidly changing conditions. In the plastics industry, for instance, developing new products requires close coordination between the research, engineering, sales, and production departments in a situation where competitors are always introducing new and innovative products. Some firms have established new-product development departments whose role is to coordinate (or integrate) the research, marketing analysis, sales, and production activities needed for developing and introducing a new product.

Standardization of Targets, Skills, and Shared Values   Firms also achieve coordination by standardizing their employees' efforts. First, you can standardize the *goals*, or *targets*, employees are to reach. For example, as long as the sales, finance, and production managers reach their assigned goals, the president can be reasonably sure that their work will be coordinated because adequate financing and production will be provided to meet the sales target.

Standardizing *skills* also facilitates coordination. That's one reason firms like Saturn spend millions of dollars training workers. Whether a work team is installing door panels or solving a problem, training ensures that each team member knows how his or her efforts fit with the others and how to proceed. Standardized skills reduce the need for outside coordination.[22]

Creating *shared values* is another approach. For example, every year Unilever brings 300 to 400 of its managers to its executive development center and also gives 100 to 150 of its most promising overseas managers temporary assignments at corporate headquarters.[23]

This gives the visiting managers a strong sense of Unilever's strategic vision and values. Such knowledge helps to ensure that, wherever they are around the world, Unilever managers will contribute in a coordinated way to that vision, while adhering to the values of the firm. As one of its managers put it: "The experience initiates you into the Unilever club and the clear norms, values, and behaviors that distinguish our people—so much so that we really believe we can spot another Unilever manager anywhere in the world."[24]

These coordination methods differ in several ways. For instance, relying on rules or procedures is more impersonal than relying on liasons. Another difference is that some methods are more useful when the situation is predictable than when it is not. In other words, in deciding how coordination will be achieved, managers have to ask (among other things) to what extent they can predict the sort of situation employees are going to face.

Giving a manager a book of rules and procedures to follow works well as long as those rules and procedures cover situations that can be anticipated in advance, such as what to do when a customer comes into a store and requests a refund. However, forcing a commando landing team to follow predetermined rules to coordinate their efforts would probably be pretty silly (not to mention dangerous). Here the Marine commander would probably rely more on interpersonal, face-to-face mutual adjustment, so the soldiers could adapt quickly to a changing situation.

MANAGING @ THE SPEED OF THOUGHT

■ Construction Central

Coordination is a real and obvious challenge in the construction industry. Particularly where huge projects are involved—Boston's 15-year, $10 billion "big dig," New York City's planned Second Avenue subway, or the San Francisco Giants new stadium, for instance—coordinating the work of hundreds or thousands of suppliers and contractors can be an overwhelming job.

That's why several companies including Blueline Online, a Palo Alto CA-based startup, are providing Web-based software that some are referring to as "construction junction." This software helps construction companies managing jobs coordinate all the hundreds or thousands of parties involved. As Blueline CEO James Dhillon puts it, "We link companies together and streamline information from design to completion." Our application enables the effective flow of information."[25]

► FIGURE 7.8

Construction Central

Web sites today can be used to replace phone, fax, and overnight mail to coordinate the updating of progress of a construction job.

Source: Adopted from Delia Craven, "Click and Mortar," *Red Herring*, November 1999, p. 208.

Figure 7.8 illustrates how coordination software works. By using the Internet and a PC, everyone involved in the project from owners to architects, to contractors and subcontractors receives instantaneous updates regarding design changes and construction status. That way, instead of having to send time-consuming reports back and forth or to coordinate personally or by phone and fax, any of the parties in the project need only to click on their PC to see the project status to know when their activity is scheduled to start and end.

► DELEGATING AUTHORITY IN ORGANIZATIONS

So far in this chapter we have focused mostly on the horizontal aspect of organizing, and specifically on creating departments and achieving coordination among these departments. Now, in the final two sections, we'll turn to the vertical aspect of organizing, and specifically to delegating or pushing authority down the chain of command, and to comparing companies with many levels with ones that have fewer levels.

Sources of Authority

authority

the right to take action, to make decisions, and to direct the work of others.

Authority is the right to take action, to make decisions, and to direct the work of others. It is an essential part of organizing because managers and employees must be authorized to carry out the jobs assigned to them. What use would it be to put Rosa in charge of airline scheduling, if you don't also authorize her to check with the airlines and to make the reservations?

Authority derives from several sources, one of which is the person's position. For example, the president of software manufacturer Intuit, has more authority based on rank than does one of his senior vice presidents. In a corporation, the stockholders/owners choose a board of directors and authorize the directors to choose corporate officers. The board in turn chooses officers and authorizes them to run the company. But authority can stem from other sources, too. Some people have authority because of personal traits, such as intelligence or charisma. Others are acknowledged experts in an area or have some knowledge that requires others to depend on them. (Even the president of Intuit might have to defer on some highly technical matters to the head of R&D.)

Some management writers argue that authority must come from the bottom up and be based on subordinates' acceptance of supervisors' orders. Theorist Chester Barnard was an early proponent of this view. Barnard argued that for orders to be carried out, they must lie within a subordinate's "zone of acceptance"—in other words, they must be viewed as acceptable.

From a practical point of view, there is a great element of truth in this. A president might have considerable authority based on rank but be unable to get anyone to follow orders. Experts such as Rosabeth Moss Kanter and Tom Peters argue that getting employees' acceptance is increasingly important today, given the growing emphasis on empowered workers and team-based organizations.

Line and Staff Authority

In organizations, managers distinguish between line and staff authority. **Line managers**, like the president, production manager, and sales manager, are always in charge of essential activities, such as sales. They are also authorized to issue orders to subordinates. **Staff managers**, on the other hand, generally cannot issue orders down the chain of command (except in their own departments); they can only assist and advise line managers. For example, an HR manager—even a senior vice president—can advise a production supervisor regarding the types of selection tests to use. However, it would be unusual for the HR manager to order the supervisor to hire a particular employee. On the other hand, the production supervisor's boss—the production manager—usually could issue such orders.

There is an exception to this rule: A staff manager (such as an HR manager) may have functional authority. **Functional authority** means that the manager can issue orders down the chain of command within the very narrow limits of his or her authority. For example, the president might order that no screening tests be administered without first getting the HR manager's approval. That manager then has functional authority over the use of personnel tests.

Line and Staff Organizations

Some small organizations use only line managers, but most larger ones have departments headed by staff managers too. Figure 7.6 illustrates a line and staff organization for a large multinational corporation. The division heads have line authority; these are therefore all line divisions. The project managers also have line authority and head up the project teams. However, staff departments have also been established, for accounts and controls, and personnel and safety.

Line–staff conflict refers to disagreements between a line manager and the staff manager who is giving him or her advice. For example, a production manager may want to use a particular personnel test, but the HR manager may insist that the test not be used. Conflict usually results when line managers feel that staff managers are encroaching on their duties and prerogatives, or when staff managers feel that line managers are resisting good advice. One way to reduce such conflict is to make clear who is responsible for what.

The Delegation Process

Organizing departments would be useless without **delegation**, which we can define as the pushing down of authority from supervisor to subordinate. The assignment of responsibility for some department or job traditionally goes hand in hand with the delegation of authority to get the job done. It would be inappropriate, for example, to assign a subordinate the responsibility for designing a new product and then deny him or her the authority to hire designers to create the best design.

But while *authority* can be delegated, *responsibility* cannot. A manager can assign responsibility to a subordinate. However, the manager is still ultimately responsible for ensuring that the job gets done properly. Because the supervisor retains the ulti-

line manager
a manager authorized to issue orders to subordinates down the chain of command.

staff manager
a manager without the authority to give orders down the chain of command (except in his or her own department); generally can only assist and advise line managers in specialized areas such as human resources management.

functional authority
narrowly limited power to issue orders down the chain of command in a specific functional area such as personnel testing.

line–staff conflict
disagreements between a line manager and the staff manager who is giving him or her advice.

delegation
the act of passing down authority from supervisor to subordinate.

mate responsibility, delegation of authority always entails the creation of accountability. Subordinates become accountable—or answerable—to the supervisor for the performance of the tasks assigned to them, particularly if things go wrong.

Today, the terms *delegation* and *empowerment* are intertwined; however, empowerment is the broader term. Specifically, **empowerment** means authorizing *and enabling* workers to do their jobs. Assembly workers at Toyota do not just have the authority to solve problems on the line. They are also given the training, tools, and management support to enable them to solve most production problems. In this way, Toyota workers are empowered to continuously improve production quality.

Decentralized Organizations

A **decentralized organization** is one in which authority for most decisions is delegated to the department heads (usually the heads of product, customer, or geographic divisions). Control over essential companywide matters is maintained at the headquarters office. *Decentralized* and *divisionalized* usually go together.

Companies organized around product divisions are usually referred to as *decentralized*. Managers of product divisions are often in charge of what amounts to their own miniature companies. Decisions that have anything to do with their products are delegated to them and can be made with little or no communication with other divisions or the firm's CEO.

Decentralization is increasingly popular today. Implemented properly, it can stimulate responsiveness, with the managers and employees who are actually "at ground level" the ones who are making the split-second decisions.[26] As we've seen, this kind of responsiveness is especially important given the kinds of challenges currently facing business organizations. For example, globalization of competition is forcing more companies to rely on strategic partnerships and alliances and to push decision-making down. Luckily, information technology (including the Internet) is making it more practical to keep track of what's going on in even far-flung decentralized units.[27]

Decentralization at successful decentralized companies always represents a shrewd balance between delegated authority and centralized control over essential functions. On the one hand, division managers have considerable autonomy and the means for quickly servicing local customers. On the other hand, headquarters maintains control by centralizing major decisions regarding activities such as making capital appropriations, managing incoming cash receipts, and setting profitability goals.

The possibility of losing control in a decentralized organization is a particular problem today. As one expert recently put it: "Despite its popularity and even urgency, downward shifting provokes serious questions. Is it possible to reduce a manager's operational control too much?"[28] Until recently, decisions were mostly decentralized to subordinate managers. In today's world of strategic alliances and partnerships, however, it's common to outsource numerous business activities to temporary firms or to "virtual" manufacturing partners. Increasingly, even the firm's own employees are not in the office, but are telecommuting most days of the week.

What this all adds up to is the need to be particularly diligent about monitoring performance and maintaining control as companies become increasingly decentralized. Pressures like these put particular emphasis on the manager's ability to maintain control, since in many cases the company being managed is basically a virtual one. Often, with no clear organization chart, high decentralization, and a flexible, ever-changing set of responsibilities, CEOs in companies like these "must

empowerment
the act of giving employees the authority, tools, and information they need to do their jobs with greater autonomy and confidence.

decentralized organization
an organization in which department heads have authority for most decisions in their divisions, while the company's headquarters office focuses on controlling essential companywide matters.

be a unifying force" both in their respective organizations and in the umbrella organization that is managing the overall project.[29]

In any case, the degree of decentralization has both a communication aspect and a delegation aspect.[30] The communication aspect refers to the extent to which employees must channel all their communications directly through the head or hub of the organization.[31] For example, must the finance, production, and sales managers communicate with each other *only* through the president, or are they permitted to communicate directly when arriving at a joint decision? The more communications must be channeled through the president, the more centralized the firm. The more managers can communicate directly with one another, the more decentralized the firm.

The delegation aspect of decentralization can be summed up as follows: The more decisions and the more areas in which authority is delegated from the president to subordinates, the more decentralized the organization.

For example, Cirque du Soleil, producer of an internationally celebrated traveling circus, is headquartered in Montreal, with 2,100 employees worldwide and offices in Amsterdam, Las Vegas, and Singapore. How do you manage such an enterprise? The answer for this firm is combining decentralization with a small-company atmosphere.

▲ Guy Laliberte, founding director of Cirque du Soleil, and co-owner Daniel Gauthier.

Most of the 2,100 employees are attached to local, geographic division tours, with two-thirds of the workforce located outside Montreal. Employees are from 40 different countries and speak more than 15 languages. Decision making for such areas as human resources is decentralized to the tour managers because employment law, for example, can vary drastically from country to country. The company maintains cohesion through its strong culture of shared values and beliefs. Jobs are posted on the Internet, employees write the company newspaper, and, for example, members of the Las Vegas finance department can videotape themselves on the job and swap tapes with the casting crew in Montreal to keep the community feeling.

Strategy and Organizational Structure

The strategy–structure link mentioned earlier helps explain why companies like General Electric decentralize.[32] The classic, and still the most influential, study in this area was conducted by economic historian Alfred Chandler a number of years ago.[33]

Chandler analyzed the histories of about 100 of the largest U.S. industrial enterprises. Information was obtained from annual reports, articles, and government publications, as well as interviews with senior executives. Chandler wanted to discover why companies like GE had adopted decentralized, divisionalized organizational structures, while others, such as steel industry firms, had remained functionally departmentalized.

Based on his analysis, Chandler concluded that "structure follows strategy," or that a company's organizational structure has to fit its strategy. He concluded, for instance, that

> The prospect of a new market or the threatened loss of a current one stimulated [strategies of] geographical expansion, vertical integration, and product diversification.... [In turn] expansion of volume ... growth through geographical dispersion ... [and finally] the developing of new lines of products ... brought the formation of the divisional structure.[34]

Thus, the new-product development and technological change with which the company's strategy required its managers to cope apparently explained the strategy–structure link. In the steel industry, for instance, the strategy was to concentrate on just one product, and the main strategic objective was to boost efficiency. Here the sorts of duplication inherent in setting up separate product divisions was unnecessarily inefficient, so these companies generally kept functional departmentalization.

At the other extreme, Chandler found that companies in the electronics and chemical industries emphasized research and development, product development, and a strategy of expansion through product diversification. This meant that those companies had to market an increasingly diverse range of products to an increasingly diverse range of customers. Having to deal with so many products and customers made the original functional structures obsolete. As one early Westinghouse executive pointed out to Chandler:

> All of the activities of the company were [originally] divided into production, engineering, and sales, each of which was the responsibility of a vice president. The domain of each vice president covered the whole diversified and far-flung operations of the corporation. Such an organization of the corporation's management lacks responsiveness. There was too much delay in the recognition of problems and in the solution of problems after they were recognized.[35]

▶ TALL AND FLAT ORGANIZATIONS AND THE SPAN OF CONTROL

Flat Versus Tall Organizations

When he became CEO of GE in the late 1980s, Jack Welch knew he had to make some dramatic organizational changes—and fast. Welch had climbed the ranks and seen how GE's chain of command was draining the firm of creativity and responsiveness. Business heads had to get approval from the headquarters staff for almost every big decision they made: In one case, the light bulb business managers spent $30,000 producing a film to demonstrate the need for some production equipment they wanted to buy. The old GE, Welch knew, was wasting hundreds of millions of dollars and missing countless opportunities because managers at so many levels were busily checking and rechecking each others' work.

Therefore, the first thing he did as CEO was strip away unneeded organizational levels. Before he took over, "GE's business heads reported to a group head, who reported to a sector head, who reported to the CEO. Each level had its own staff in finance, marketing, and planning, checking and double checking each business."[36] Welch disbanded the group and sector levels, thus dramatically flattening the organizational chain of command. No one stands between the business heads and the CEO's office now. In disbanding those two levels, Welch got rid of the organizational bottlenecks they caused and the salaries of the almost 700 corporate staff that composed them. Now that it is flatter and leaner, GE is a much more responsive company and its results reflect its new effectiveness.

▲ Jack Welch, who restructured GE into a leaner, flatter, more responsive organization.

The restructuring at GE has been repeated many times at many companies. Everywhere you look, from GM to IBM to Levi Strauss to Pratt and Whitney, CEOs are hammering down their chains of command and pushing authority down to lower levels.[37] In flat companies, there are few levels, and each manager has a relatively large number of subordinates reporting to him or her. The result is an organization in which employees tend to have high autonomy and the ability to respond quickly to customers' needs. Perhaps because of this, morale tends to be higher too.[38]

The Span of Control

The **span of control** is the number of subordinates reporting directly to a supervisor. In the country-based geographic organization shown in Figure 7.9, the span of control of the country general manager is 13: There are 6 business managers, 5 directors, 1 innovation manager, and 1 manufacturing manager.

span of control
the number of subordinates reporting directly to a supervisor.

The average number of people reporting to a manager is related to the number of management levels in an organization. For example, if an organization with 64 workers to be supervised has an average span of control of 8, there will be 8 supervisors directing the workers and 1 manager directing the 8 supervisors (a flat organization). If, on the other hand, the span of control were 4, the same number of workers would require 16 supervisors. The latter would in turn be directed by 4 managers. These 4 managers would in turn be directed by 1 manager (a tall organization). There would be an extra management level.

Classic management theorists such as Henri Fayol believed that tall organizational structures (with narrow spans of control) improved performance by guaranteeing close supervision.[39] However, as recent experience (like GE's) has shown, taller organizations and narrow spans can backfire by slowing decisions. Therefore, as the rate of technological change and new-product introductions has increased, many more firms have opted for flatter structures and wider spans.[40] We will pursue this point in Chapter 8.

▶ **FIGURE 7.9** **Spans of Control in Country-Based Organization**

In this chart, the span of control of the general manager is 13—6 business managers, 5 directors, 1 innovation manager, and 1 manufacturing manager.

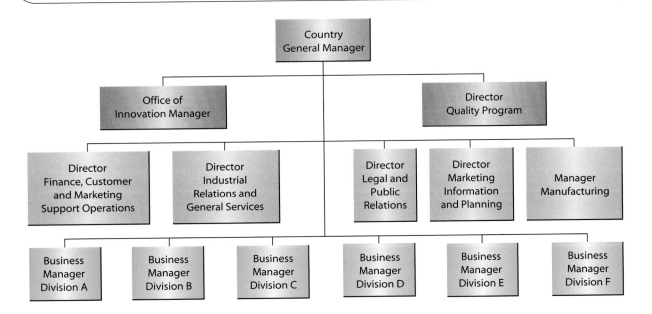

SUMMARY

1. Organizing is the arranging of an enterprise's activities in such a way that they systematically contribute to the enterprise's goals. An organization consists of people whose specialized tasks are coordinated to contribute to the organization's goals.

2. Departmentalization is the process through which an enterprise's activities are grouped together and assigned to managers. Departments can be grouped around functions, products, customer groups, marketing channels, or geographic areas.

3. A matrix organization, or matrix management, is defined as an organization in which one or more forms of departmentalization are superimposed on an existing one. In practice, most enterprises are hybrids and use several forms of departmentalization.

4. Coordination is the process of achieving unity of action among interdependent activities. It is required when two or more interdependent entities must work together to achieve a common goal. Techniques for achieving coordination include mutual adjustment; the use of rules or procedures; direct supervision; departmentalization; the use of a staff assistant, a liaison, a committee, independent integrators; and the standardization of targets, skills, or shared values.

5. Authority is the right to take action, to make decisions, and to direct the work of others. Managers usually distinguish between line and staff authority. Departments could not be organized without delegation, which is defined as the pushing down of authority from superior to subordinate. In a decentralized organization, authority for most decisions is delegated to the department heads.

6. Many companies are adopting flatter structures in an effort to eliminate duplication of effort, inspire creativity, and increase responsiveness. The span of control in a company is the number of subordinates reporting directly to a supervisor.

TYING IT ALL TOGETHER

Planning (covered in Chapters 4–6) helps to determine what tasks must be done, and therefore the activities around which you should organize. For example, a plan to expand to Europe may mean organizing new departments for European sales and manufacturing. In this chapter we covered the fundamentals of organizing, in particular setting up departments, providing coordination, and delegating authority down the chain of command. In today's fast-changing world, new ways of organizing are required if a firm is to be able to respond quickly enough to competitive and technological changes. We turn to organizing to manage change in Chapter 8.

KEY TERMS

organizing 190
organization chart 190
chain of command 190
informal organization 192
departmentalization 193
functional departmentalization 193
divisionalization 195

customer departmentalization 198
marketing-channel departmentalization 199
marketing channel 199
matrix organization 201
coordination 206
mutual adjustment 207
independent integrator 208

authority 210
line manager 211
staff manager 211
functional authority 211
line–staff conflict 211
delegation 211
empowerment 212
decentralized organization 212

1. Organizations and how managers structure them to accommodate a changing set of circumstances is increasingly important to company survival. New organizational models are required. In less turbulent times, the bureaucracy with its top-down control and hierarchically arranged roles and authority was relatively efficient and effective. With the advent of the global economy, constantly changing technology, and immense competitive pressures, most managers are looking for a way to more efficiently and effectively structure the flow of work in their organizations. One of the most frequently touted means is the use of groups or teams. Warren Bennis's and Patricia Ward Biederman's *Organizing Genius: The Secrets of Creative Collaboration* (Addison-Wesley, 1997), explores the workings of famous collaborations from what they call "Troupe Disney" to The Manhattan Project. Their thesis is "None of us is as smart as all of us." They come to a number of interesting conclusions, including the following:

Greatness starts with superb people; great groups and great leaders create each other; every great group has a strong leader; leaders of great groups love talent and know where to find it; and great groups see themselves as winning underdogs and always have an enemy. To survive in the next millennium, we can speculate that all our brainpower and creativity will be needed. Given the structures discussed in the chapter and the information about needing teams-based organizations in *Organizing Genius*, design a new structure for a company in the following industries: retail sales, the aerospace industry, hospitals, auto manufacturing, and construction.

2. Think about the university or college you are attending. How is it organized? Could it be organized more efficiently, using the concepts discussed in this chapter? How would you reorganize the university to be more effective and efficient for all stakeholders?

1. Imagine that you are attending a college that is about to transform its structure. The environment around the university is changing. The senior faculty decides that a new structure is required to accommodate the changing demands of students and society. They vote to decentralize their power as the sole decision makers on issues of personnel and curriculum matters, as well as other organizational policies. The new structure is fluid, and amoebae-like. There is no all-powerful head. There is still a dean and administrators, but they are only advisory to some committees and have only a partial vote on some important matters. The dean and administrators still take care of the overall running of the college, but they must include input from all members of the college.

The college holds meetings four times a year to gather, debate, and decide important matters. Anyone connected or once connected to the college, such as alumni, is welcome to attend the meetings and has one vote on policy matters. Each current college student, faculty member, and staff member has one vote on matters of importance. Matters discussed may include merging with another part of the university or changing the name of the college or the college's mission.

At the first meeting, three committees are elected. One is the Policy Committee, which deals with major policy issues. Anyone may be elected to this committee, such as students or faculty members. The second committee is the Personnel Committee, whose members are elected by representative groups (e.g., the students elect their representatives). This committee makes tenure decisions and other decisions of importance to the college. The third committee is the Academic Affairs Committee, which is voluntary and usually consists of faculty and students. This committee deals with curricular matters and course offerings.

With this approach to structure in mind, redesign your college's organization chart around these structural principles. Be sure to consider the environment the college is in, the type of student body that usually attends the university, and the mission of the university or college or school or department. Also think about the problems that might arise, why change might be difficult, and where resistance might come from.

2. By the time the office opens at 8:45 A.M., the line of people waiting to do business at the Registry of Motor Vehicles (RMV) in Watertown, Massachusetts, will be 25 deep. By mid-day, especially if it is near the end of the month, the line may extend around the building. Inside, motorists wait in slow-moving rows before poorly marked windows to get a driver's license or to register an automobile. When someone gets to the head of the line, he or she is often told by the clerk that it is the wrong line. The customers grumble impatiently. The clerks act harried and sometimes speak rudely.

Not far away, people also wait in line at a McDonald's fast-food restaurant. There are several lines; each is short and moves quickly. The menu is clearly displayed on attractive signs. The workers behind the counter are invariably polite. If someone's order cannot be filled immediately, he or she is asked to step aside for a moment while the food is prepared, and then is brought back to the head of the line to receive the order. The atmosphere is friendly and good natured. The room is immaculately clean.

What might the RMV learn from McDonald's? What are some of the issues and problems in redesigning the RMV to be more like McDonald's? What concepts discussed in the chapter might help the RMV and maybe even improve McDonald's?

Source: James Q. Wilson, *Bureaucracy* (New York: Basic Books. 1989), p. 112.

myPHLIP COMPANION WEB SITE

We invite you to visit the Dessler companion Web site at **www.prenhall.com/dessler** for this chapter's Internet resources.

ORGANIZING AT GREENLEY COMMUNICATIONS

CASE 1

Louis Greenley had been presented with a difficult decision. His company, Greenley Communications, was a diversified communications company that operated primarily in the western United States. The firm owned and operated newspapers and radio and television stations. For years there had been an invisible wall between the print operations and television.

The existing structure was organized by industry. There was a newspaper division, a radio division, and a television production division. Each division had its own bookkeeping, sales, marketing, operations, and service divisions. Accounting and financial management were handled at the corporate level.

In the newspaper division, there was a clear distinction between the news and the financial sides of the business. Coming from a family of journalists, Greenley was always concerned that the sale of advertising to local clients would influence the paper's coverage of the news—editors might ignore potential stories that might reflect negatively on an advertiser.

The vice president of broadcast operations, Greenley's television arm, proposed a major structural change. The proposal called for the organization to be restructured geographically. This would allow regional managers to have a single sales force that could sell advertising in any form: print, radio, or TV. The approach had some appeal. There was significant geographic overlap at Greenley—the company tended to own multiple properties in the same region. Certainly there would be savings in personnel, as the company would need a far smaller sales staff.

Discussion Questions

1. What factors should influence Greenley's decision to restructure?

2. What risks does the proposed restructuring create?

3. If you were Greenley, what choice would you make? Why?

How should a company based in Zurich that employs approximately 170,000 people in more than 100 countries organize itself to compete globally? That was the problem faced by Asea Brown Boveri (ABB) leaders Percy Barnevik, chairman, and Göran Lindahl, CEO. Indeed, ABB's complexity goes far beyond its geographic scope. Much of the company's revenue comes from custom projects that may not necessarily generate repeat business.

ABB is not a household name in the United States, but it should be. For example, Lindahl was recently named *Industry Week*'s CEO of the year. Lindahl is the first non-U.S. CEO to win this honor. Previous recipients were IBM's Lou Gerstner, Dell Computer's Michael Dell, GE's Jack Welch, and Microsoft's Bill Gates. The *Industry Week* award is the top honor bestowed by this premier industry publication.

In its report to shareholders, ABB described its approach to business as helping customers be more successful by providing them with the resources of a fully globalized company. These global resources are delivered locally by ABB employees who understand the unique technical and cultural needs of the local customer.

ABB had originally organized its company using a regional structure. The task of the regional managers was to establish a market presence and brand reputation for ABB worldwide. Each regional manager had a geographic territory for which he or she was accountable. This system worked so well that ABB decided it had in fact accomplished its mission—it had become a truly global company.

But as a global company, ABB became concerned that it was becoming less responsive. The firm wanted to serve customers better, and to do that it needed to move faster and organize its resources to exploit a unique combination of speed and flexibility. As a result, ABB decided to eliminate the regional management level. ABB now prides itself on having a decentralized management culture. Managers at the local level are encouraged to make tough and important decisions. The illustration shows ABB's current organizational structure.

Discussion Questions

1. How would you characterize ABB's current structure?

2. Do you think ABB's decision to remove its regional managers was prudent? (Defend your answer.)

3. What are the strengths and weaknesses of the current structure?

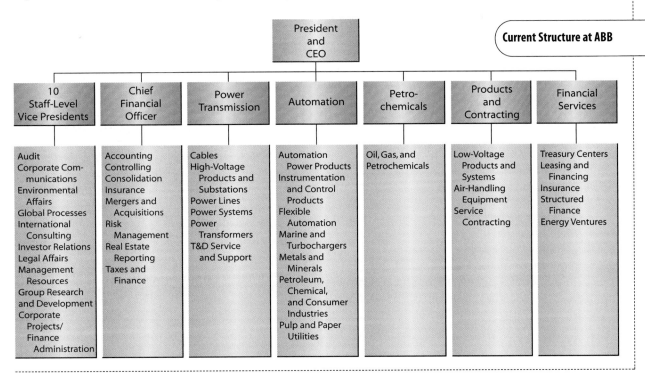

Current Structure at ABB

KNITMEDIA GETS ORGANIZED

In terms of the numbers, KnitMedia's growth has been phe-nomenal. For example, revenues shot from $269,000 in 1994 to over $7 million in 1999, and the number of staff members shot up from 11 to almost 100. Organizationally, KnitMedia has therefore gone from a traditional "mom and pop" type organization, in which the owner-founder (in this case, Michael Dorf) could stand in the middle of all the action and make all the decisions himself, to a larger company with the type of organization chart presented earlier in this chap-ter, in Figure 7.1. In the organization chart, as you can see, Michael Dorf is president and CEO, and has reporting to him Ed Greer as senior vice president for club operations, Allan Fried as chief operating officer, Dave Brenner as vice presi-dent for NewMedia, Mitch Goldman as chief content officer, and Mark Harabedian as vice president for finance.

While the chart is a fairly accurate representation of how things really are at KnitMedia, two important things must be taken into consideration. First, since a lot of the plans and vision are still in Michael Dorf's head, a company like this has to be careful that not a lot happens that Michael Dorf doesn't know about. Here's how Dorf puts it:

> Having a chief operating officer in place has certainly freed me up to do more, for instance to work in the finance side of the business, and maybe more of what I like to do, which is in strategic deal making, and less on the operational side of managing the club, the record label, even some of the festival day-to-day [activities]. So in some respects, when it comes to these things I feel a little clueless although at the same time, you know, I like to drill down to really look at what is actually happening and selling so we can make an analysis of whether we're doing the job correctly.

In other words, the new organization has freed Michael Dorf to help the company grow, but it also, in some respects, took him away from the day-to-day operations.

The second important thing to remember about this organization chart is that with a company growing this fast, everyone has to pitch in to do things that may not, strictly speaking, be their job on the organizational chart. For exam-ple, Ed Greer is senior vice president of club operations, but he might also be pulled into working with Mark on some

financial systems problem. Greer is also responsible for jug-gling the operations of the lucrative New York Knitting Factory club, as well as those of the KnitMedia's Knitting Factory clubs in Los Angeles, Berlin, and the other sites under development.

To hear Michael Dorf tell it, opening the clubs outside of New York actually helped KnitMedia breathe life into its organization chart. "[Opening the Hollywood/LA site has been a great exercise, one] I'd recommend to anybody try-ing to learn how to manage a company. Leaving for three months [while Dorf was in Hollywood opening the new club] helped us all understand what [our] roles were and force the proper delegation. When I'm in that office, how easy it was for someone to go around Allan and talk to me. [With me in Hollywood for three months] there wasn't any opportunity for that, so it was a great exercise."

Great exercise or not, Michael and his team want to make sure that creating the organization chart in Figure 7.1 was the right way to proceed, and also that the new structure won't stifle the company's responsiveness. They'd like your advice.

Team Exercises and Questions

Use what you learned in this chapter to answer the following questions from Michael Dorf and his management team:

1. What are the benefits and potential drawbacks to KnitMedia of our having organized in the manner depicted in the organization chart in Figure 7.1?

2. How would you suggest we avoid the potential draw-backs you mentioned in your answer to question 1 above?

3. The Knitting Factories are basically the "cash cows" that produce the revenues we use to build KnitMedia's other operations. Given that fact, and the fact that more of these clubs are going to be opened abroad, should we reorganize KnitMedia in such a way as to include a sep-arate executive for handling international operations? What would be the pros and cons of doing so?

4. Let's suppose we decide to throw away our organization chart and come up with a new one. What kind of new organization chart would you suggest for KnitMedia?

CHAPTER 8

DESIGNING ORGANIZATIONS TO MANAGE CHANGE

WHAT'S AHEAD?

Technical and Computer Graphics Company (TCG) is at the forefront of information technology. It makes high-tech communication devices, such as handheld data terminals (like those used by UPS) and electronic data interchange systems. You probably could not find a company whose competitive and technological terrain is changing as fast or unexpectedly as TCG's. To succeed in such a fast-changing environment, TCG has to make sure it's organized for speed. In TCG's case, this means what the company calls a cellular organization. TCG is actually composed of 13 small, more-or-less autonomous and self-reliant firms (or cells), each interacting with the others and with partners and customers outside the company.

OBJECTIVES

AFTER STUDYING THIS CHAPTER, YOU SHOULD BE ABLE TO

- Give examples of traditional ways managers redesign organizations to make them more responsive

- Explain how to organize and lead team-based organizations

- Give examples of network-based and boundaryless organizations

- Describe the horizontal corporation

- List the factors affecting how organizations are designed and structured

Companies from giants like IBM to relatively small ones like TCG, are creating new means of organizing their operations: They hope these will help them better respond to today's fast-moving competition, and thus to manage change. Chapter 7 covered the fundamentals of organizing, such as basic ways to departmentalize and how to provide coordination and delegate authority. However, those are just the basic elements and language of how to organize. Now we turn to organizing to manage change, and specifically to the new ways companies are organizing to better respond to competitive, technological, and political pressures.

▶ MOVING BEYOND ORGANIC ORGANIZATIONS

Early, "classical" management theorists were not oblivious to the fact that organizations sometimes had to move fast. Most of these experts (such as Henri Fayol, Frederick Taylor, and Luther Gulick) were managers or consultants. They were therefore savvy enough to know that there are times when sticking to the chain of command results in slow decisions and slow responses. Henri Fayol, for instance, said that orders and inquiries should generally follow the chain of command. But, in very special circumstances, a "bridge" communication could take place, say between a salesperson and a production supervisor, if a decision was required at once.

Prescriptions like these worked fairly well in the less intense environment of the time. Competition was local, not global, new-product introductions were relatively slow, and consumers tended to be much less demanding. Giving every employee a specialized job and achieving coordination by making most people stick to the chain of command was an effective way to do things. But as the number of unexpected problems and issues—new competitors, new product or technological innovations, customers suddenly going out of business, and so on— becomes unmanageable, a classical-type organization gets overloaded and errors start to mount.

That's why today, says management expert Tom Peters, success in a fast-changing global environment "is directly proportional to the knowledge that an organization can bring to bear, how fast it can bring that knowledge to bear, and the rate at which it accumulates knowledge."[1] In other words, companies must be organized to respond to rapid change.

Fitting the Organization to the Task

The idea that fast-moving business environments demand fast-moving organizational designs makes sense. For example, suppose your family owns a small chain of supermarkets in the northeastern United States. The stores have been in your family for many years, and for many years your traditional structure (a fairly large central staff of produce and food buyers, a layer of regional managers, a layer below that of store managers, each with two or three layers of department managers), worked fairly well, since things weren't changing very quickly.

You've had basically the same competitors for the past 30 years, you and your competitors all sold more or less the same line of products, and everyone used more or less the same technology—namely, telephones and fax machines and an occasional personal computer—to run their operations. No one was a lot more efficient than anyone else, no one was introducing new technologies, and everyone was selling at about the same prices, since they all had about the same costs. Your whole operation was kept quite busy, but you didn't really have to make a lot of split-second decisions, nor did you face a lot of unpredictable events.

Luckily, though, you went to business school, so you could clearly see that things were changing. Two of your competitors just merged into a much larger chain, and are building superstores complete with pharmacies. That means they can also consolidate backroom operations (functions like accounting, and purchasing, for instance) and you know that that's going to drive down costs and prices. As if that weren't enough, you just read in your local paper that Wal-Mart is building a huge superstore right outside of town, as is Costco. You know that with their super-efficient satellite-based distribution systems, costs and prices are going to fall even more. You can see that, in other words, the decision-making tempo is picking up, and picking up fast.

All of a sudden, every day, managers are coming to you with emergencies, with complaints, and with decisions that have to be made. You know you're going to have to make your whole organization structure a lot smarter and faster-moving than it's ever been before. For one thing, you can't afford to have so many people passing requests for decisions up and down the chain of command like some kind of relay race. For another, you have to find a way to get the answers you need a lot faster than you can now. You've got to streamline your organizational structure and reorganize. The idea that fast-moving environments need fast-moving organizations is actually an idea that was stumbled upon a number of years ago.

Much of this earlier research occurred in the United Kingdom. For example, in one study researchers Tom Burns and G. M. Stalker found that a stable, unchanging environment demands a different type of organization than does a rapidly changing one.[2] A stable environment, they said, can be characterized as having characteristics like these: (1) Demand for the organization's product or service is stable and predictable; (2) there is an unchanging set of competitors; and (3) technological innovation and new product developments are evolutionary rather than revolutionary; necessary product changes can be predicted well in advance and the required modifications made at a leisurely pace.

A textile manufacturer they studied operated in just such a stable environment. To be successful, this firm had to keep costs down and be as efficient as possible. Its existence therefore depended on keeping unexpected occurrences to a minimum, so as to maintain steady, high-volume production runs.

At the other extreme, some companies, they found, had to compete in fast-changing "innovative" environments. Here, (1) Demand for the organization's product or service can change drastically, sometimes overnight, as competitors introduce radically improved products; (2) sudden, unexpected changes occur in the nature of the organization's competitors;[3] and (3) an extremely rapid rate of technological innovation and new product development is common. Several of the electronics firms Burns and Stalker studied were competing in such an innovative environment. Their existence depended on being able to continually introduce innovative electronic components. They also had to be constantly on the alert for innovations by competitors, so responsiveness and creativity (rather than efficiency) were paramount.

Findings like these led Burns and Stalker to distinguish between two types of organizations, which they called mechanistic and organic. The textile firm was typical of mechanistic, classic organizations; the electronics firms were typical of the organic ones. **Mechanistic organizations**, they said, are characterized by: Close adherence to the chain of command; a functional division of work; highly specialized jobs; use of the formal hierarchy for coordination; and detailed job descriptions that provide a precise definition of rights, obligations, and technical methods

mechanistic organization
an organizational structure characterized by close adherence to the established chain of command, highly specialized jobs, and vertical communications.

▲ (1) Mechanistic organization: Toyota truck assembly line. (2) Organic organization: Microelectronic Research Center—making chips.

organic organization

an organizational structure characterized by flexible lines of authority, less specialized jobs, and decentralized decisions.

for performing each job. **Organic organizations** on the other hand are characterized by: Little preoccupation with the chain of command; a more self-contained, divisionalized structure of work; job responsibility not viewed by employees as a limited field of rights and obligations (employees don't respond to requests by saying, "That's not my job."); and lateral rather than vertical communication and an emphasis on consultation rather than command.

Burns and Stalker concluded that different organizational structures are appropriate for, or contingent on, different tasks.[4] At one extreme are organizations dealing with predictable, routine tasks like running a textile firm,[5] where efficiency is emphasized, and successful organizations tend to be mechanistic. They stress adherence to rules and to the chain of command, are highly centralized, and have a more specialized, functional departmentalization.

At the other extreme, some organizations—and, increasingly, the ones you'll have to deal with—have more unpredictable tasks and are constantly faced with the need to invent new products and respond quickly to emergencies. Here creativity and entrepreneurial activities are emphasized, and to encourage these activities such organizations tend to be organic. Like many of today's boundaryless and team-based organizations, they do not urge employees to "play by the book" or to stick to the chain of command. Decision making is decentralized, and jobs and departments are less specialized.[6] They use the sorts of organizational devices we'll discuss in the rest of this chapter. The differences are summarized in Table 8.1.

As globalization and technological change created an increasingly unpredictable and competitive environment in the last few years, managers initially reacted to the more rapid change in several ways. Many downsized. **Downsizing** means dramatically reducing the size of a company's workforce.[7] At the same time, they and others often took their existing structures and (1) reduced the levels of management (flattening the structures); (2) reorganized around mini-units; and (3) reassigned support staff from headquarters to the divisions, thus decentralizing decisions: Let's look at these.

downsizing

dramatically reducing the size of a company's workforce.

	Type of Organization	
Characteristics	**Mechanistic**	**Organic**
Type of Environment	Stable	Innovative
Comparable to	Classical organization	Behavioral organization emphasis on self-control
Adherence to Chain of Command	Close	Flexible—chain of command often bypassed
Type of Departmentalization	Functional	Divisional
How Specialized Are Jobs?	Specialized	Unspecialized—jobs change daily, with situation
Degree of Decentralization	Decision making centralized	Decision making decentralized
Span of Control	Narrow	Wide
Type of Coordination	Hierarchy and rules	Committees, liaisons, and special integrators

TABLE 8.1 Contingency Approach to Organizing

Reducing Management Layers

Reducing management layers—first mentioned in Chapter 7—is one popular structural way to help a company manage change. Eliminating layers can reduce costs and boost productivity by cutting salaries. It may also speed decision making by reducing the number of people whose approvals and reviews are required, and by letting people "on the ground" actually make the decisions. For example, when he took over the troubled Union Pacific Railroad (UPRR), former CEO Mike Walsh inherited a bureaucratic and slow-moving organization. As Walsh said:

> Suppose a customer was having difficulty [finding] a railroad car—it was either not the right one, or wasn't where the customer needed it for loading or unloading. The customer would go to his UPRR sales representative—who "went up" to the district traffic manager, who in turn "went up" to the regional traffic manager. The regional boss passed the problem from his sales and marketing organization, across a chasm psychologically wider than the Grand Canyon, to the operations department's general manager. The general manager then "went down" to the superintendent, who "went down" to the train master to find out what had gone wrong.[8]

Then, of course, the whole process was repeated in reverse. The information went up the operations chain and then down the sales and marketing chain, until the annoyed customer finally got his or her answer—often several days later. Multiplied hundreds or thousands of times a week, that sort of unresponsiveness, Walsh knew, helped explain why UPRR was losing customers, revenues, and profits.

The first thing he did therefore was flatten the firms 30,000-person operations department, by squeezing out five middle management layers (see Figure 8.1). When Walsh arrived, there were nine layers of managers between the executive vice president of operations and the railroaders themselves. After reorganizing, only four levels remained. In about three months, five layers and 800 middle managers were stripped from the chain of command.[9]

► FIGURE 8.1

Union Pacific Railroad Hierarchy: Before and After

Source: From *Liberation Management* by Tom Peters. Copyright © 1992 by Excel, a California Limited Partnership. Reprinted by permission of Alfred A. Knopf, Inc.

FIGURE A	FIGURE B
BEFORE REORGANIZATION	**AFTER REORGANIZATION**
Executive VP Operations	Executive VP Operations
VP Operations	VP Field Operations
General Manager	Superintendent Transportation Services
Assistant General Manager	Manager Train Operations
Regional Transportation Superintendent	Yardmaster
Division Superintendent	*Railroaders*
Division Superintendent Transportation	
Trainmaster/Terminal Superintendent	
Assistant Trainmaster/ Terminal Trainmaster	
Yardmaster	
Railroaders	

Yet, delayering can also backfire. For example, several years ago a trader named Nicholas Leeson brought down Barings Bank by losing over $1.4 billion with a series of fraudulent trades. As one observer recently put it, "Numerous organizations have been removing layers of management—layers sometimes depicted as performing no useful function ... but as [Leeson's book] *Rogue Trader* underlines, management may also provide experience and judgment, curbing actions on the part of enthusiastic, novice employees that may otherwise have disastrous consequences."[10] Even UPRR hasn't been immune. For example annual losses after Walsh left were approaching $1.3 billion, due to severe traffic delays, a lack of rail cars, congestion problems, and accidents. The losses were caused in part by UPRR's merger with another railroad, and in part, one might assume, by the elimination of all those experienced midlevel managers.[11]

Establishing Mini-Units

When it comes to being responsive, many companies have concluded that "smaller is better." Many managers therefore advocate splitting companies into minicompanies. The resulting smaller units tend to be more entrepreneurial: Everyone (including the top executive) knows everyone else, layers of management aren't required for an approval, and interactions and communications are more frequent, given the employees' close proximity to one another.

Many companies take this route. At ABB the former CEO "deorganized" his 215,000 employees into 5,000 smaller profit centers averaging about 50 people each. At Intuit the new CEO broke the company

▲ Nicholas Leeson arriving in London after serving three and a half years in jail for fraudulent trading that helped bring down Barings Bank.

into eight separate businesses, each with its own general manager and mission.[12] Hal Rosenbluth of Rosenbluth International broke his company into more than 100 business units, each focused on special regions and clients.[13]

Reassigning Support Staff to the Divisions

Some companies still have large central headquarters' support staffs composed of managerial groups engaged in analytical duties like industrial engineering and market research. The original thinking was that these centralized groups could help the firm's top managers better monitor and control what was going on in their far-flung enterprises. Today, more and more managers believe that the benefits of control are outweighed by the fact that these big central staffs actually slow decisions by inserting a whole new approval level between the divisions and top management. They thus reduce the firm's ability to respond to competitive pressures. It's therefore better, the thinking now goes, to eliminate many of these central-staff managers, or to redeploy them to the divisions, where they can give their advice to local executives while being closer to the division's customers and competitors.

Reassigning support staff has therefore been a popular way to streamline organizations in order to make companies more responsive. For example, candy maker Mars, Inc., is a $7 billion company with a 30-person headquarters staff. Mars does have staff employees. But as is true in more and more firms, these staff employees are assigned directly to the individual business units. Here they can help their business unit be successful in the marketplace rather than act as gatekeepers who check and recheck divisional managers' plans. Similarly, when Percy Barnevik took over as CEO of Sweden's ABB, it had a central staff of 2,000 which he quickly reduced to 200. When his firm then acquired Finland's Stromberg company, its headquarters staff of 880 was reduced within a few years to 25.[14]

Reassigning support staff is not without its downside. The employees who are reassigned may have to relocate, enter their new positions at the bottom of the promotion system, and need extensive training; this can lead to morale problems. And, while reassigning staff may help the company retain experienced employees, it also limits its ability to hire new ones (such as recent college graduates). The dynamism new people bring to the firm is thereby lacking.[15]

▶ BUILDING TEAM-BASED STRUCTURES

Increasingly, steps like delayering, reassigning support staff, and establishing mini-units are not enough. Managers have sought additional ways to streamline how decisions are made. New structural approaches are therefore being tried. Specifically, managers are using teams, networks, and "boundaryless" structures to redesign their organizations so as to better manage change. We'll look at these in this and the next few sections.

The Building Blocks of Team-Based Organizations[16]

Many firms today, for example, organize activities around self-contained and self-managing work teams. A **team** is a group of people who work together and share a common work objective.[17]

For example, at the GE jet engine plant in Durham, North Carolina, over 170 employees work with only one manager—the plant manager—and are organized into small, self-managing teams.[18] At Johnsonville Foods in Wisconsin, the CEO organized most of the firm's activities around self-managing, 12-person work

team
a group of people committed to a common purpose, set of performance goals, and approach for which they hold themselves mutually accountable.

teams. At Johnsonville, work teams are responsible for running and maintaining the firm's packaging equipment. But unlike in traditional management structures, such teams are empowered to manage themselves and make fast, on-the-spot decisions. For example, the duties of a typical Johnsonville work team include:

- Recruit, hire, evaluate, and fire (if necessary)
- Handle quality control, inspections, subsequent troubleshooting, and problem solving
- Develop and monitor quantitative standards for productivity and quality
- Suggest and develop prototypes of possible new products and packaging[19]

At Chesebrough-Ponds USA, a functional organization was replaced with a structure built around self-directed teams that now run the plant's four production areas. Hourly employees make employee assignments, schedule overtime, establish production times and changeovers, and even handle cost control, requisitions, and work orders. They are also solely responsible for quality control under the plant's Continuous Quality Improvement Challenge, a program in which employees can post suggestions or challenges to improve quality. Team member Sherry Emerson summed up employee sentiments: "The empowerment is exciting. If we see something that will affect the quality to customers, we have the freedom to stop a process. They [management] trust us." And the results have been extraordinary. Quality acceptance is 99.25%. Annual manufacturing costs are down $10.6 million; work-in-process inventory has been reduced 86%; and total inventory is down 65%.[20]

As these examples suggest, team-based organizations are different from the traditional departmentalized and hierarchical organizations described in Chapter 7. Companies were traditionally organized with individuals, functions, or departments as the basic work units or elements. This is evident in the typical organization chart, which might show separate boxes for each functional department, and perhaps even separate tasks for individual workers at the bottom of the chart.

In team-based organizations, the team is the basic work unit or element. Employees work together as a team, and do much of the planning, decision making, and implementing required to get their assigned jobs done, while being responsible for things like receiving materials, installing parts, and dealing with vendors who ship defective parts. Or, instead of simply organizing around traditional publishing functions like production, editorial, and sales, some publishers create more of a team-based organization; they create, for each book in process, a multidisciplined and self-managing team whose members work together to develop, produce, and market the book.

If you've ever worked on a team (say, to present a project at school), you know that such an approach can have many advantages. Everyone's attention tends to be focused on the team's goal; everyone tends to the more committed to achieving that goal; and everyone generally tends to be more willing to pitch in and get the job done. And since these teams tend to be small and don't have the traditional departmental barriers separating its members, communication and interaction tends to be open and free-flowing. At least, that's the theory. In practice, smoothly functioning team-based organizations don't arise spontaneously; instead, they depend on the presence of several supporting mechanisms, to which we now turn.

Designing Organizations to Support Teams[21]

Managers can't create team-based organizations without providing the supporting mechanisms that will allow the teams to flourish. At least five support mechanisms are required to enable work teams to do their jobs: The firm must have the right philosophy, structure, systems, policies, and employee skills (Figure 8.2).

- *Organizational philosophy.* The philosophy underlying a team-based organization is obviously different in several ways from the philosophy in companies that are organized traditionally. In facilities like GE/Durham and Johnsonville, the workers are basically responsible for supervising themselves and for making sure that their work is getting done and getting done properly. There's no supervisor looking over their shoulders.

    To establish a team-based organization, management therefore can't just pay lip service to the idea that employees should be involved and trusted. For example, organizing around self-managing teams and then showing employees you don't trust them by having supervisors second-guessing everything they do is counterproductive.

    Committing to the right organizational philosophy is thus the first step managers have to take before setting out to create a team-based organization. What people believe and value tends to guide what they do, and if top management doesn't really buy into the philosophy of employee involvement and trust, it's liable to institute practices that end up undermining the entire team effort. Successful team-based organizations are run by managers committed to a philosophy and core values emphasizing high employee involvement and trust.

▼ **FIGURE 8.2** **Designing Organizations to Manage Teams**

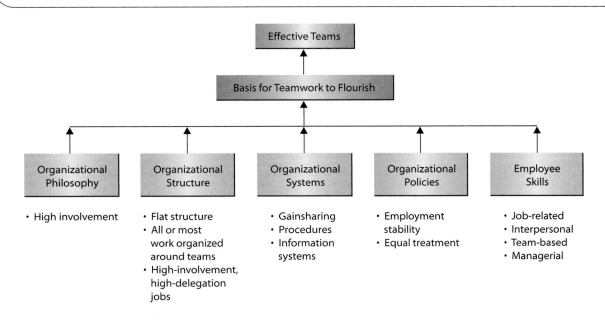

Source: Adapted from James H. Shonk, *Team-Based Organizations* (Homewood, IL: Irwin, 1997), p. 36.

- *Organizational structure.* In team-based organizations, teams are the basic work units. Firms are characterized by flat structures with few supervisors, and delegation of much decision-making authority to the work teams. In turn, the work teams in firms like GE/Durham carry out supervisory tasks ranging from scheduling overtime to actually doing the work.

- *Organizational systems.* Every company depends in part on standard operating systems to make sure that everything goes smoothly. These systems range from performance appraisal and financial rewards to the systems used to gather marketing data and to keep track of sales and production levels.

  Instituting team-friendly support systems is another building block of team-based structures. For example, team-based companies often use a performance appraisal system called "360-degree appraisals," since systems like these are based on feedback from all the worker's teammates, not just the facility's managers. Similarly, financial incentives tend to be paid to the team as a whole rather than to individual employees.

- *Organizational policies.* We've also seen that every company uses organizational policies (such as "the customer is always right" and "we only use fresh ingredients") as standard guidelines regarding how the work of the organization is to be accomplished. Policies like these can play an important role in supporting the company's team effort. For example, organizing around self-managing teams means building close-knit, stable teams of highly trained employees, and it hardly pays to do so if employees are fired every time revenue dips.

  Team-based organizations therefore tend to emphasize employment stability. At Toyota's Camry facility in Lexington, Kentucky, for instance, slack demand might mean that more employees spend time being trained to develop new skills rather than being laid off. Similarly, rigid policies such as "any employee coming to work more than 12 minutes late will not be allowed on the premises" would be counterproductive in a team-based organization, since here the teams themselves usually have the responsibility to supervise their own team member-employees.

- *Employee skills.* Work teams typically have wide-ranging responsibilities (such as scheduling their own time, hiring team members, and managing their own quality). It's therefore essential that all team members have a wide range of skills, including (1) the skills to actually do the job (such as welding); (2) the interpersonal skills to work in a healthy manner with and in the team (listening, communicating, and so on); (3) team skills (such as problem solving and running decision-making meetings); and (4) management skills (including planning, leading, and controlling).

▶ BUILDING NETWORK-BASED ORGANIZATIONS

organizational network
a system of interconnected or cooperating individuals.

Many firms today superimpose "organizational networks" over their existing structures. An **organizational network** is a system of interconnected or cooperating individuals.[22] We'll look at three: formal organizational networks, informal organizational networks, and electronic networks.

Whether formal, informal, or electronic, the network enhances the likelihood that the work of even far-flung units can be accomplished promptly and in a coordinated manner, especially if quick decisions must be made. All organizational networks share the same core idea: They link managers from various departments, levels, and geographic areas into a multidisciplinary team whose members communicate across normal organizational boundaries.

Formal Networks

A **formal organizational network** has been defined as

> A recognized group of managers assembled by the CEO and the senior executive team. . . . The members are drawn from across the company's functions, business units, and geography, and from different levels of the hierarchy. The number of managers involved almost never exceeds 100 and can be fewer than 25—even in global companies with tens of thousands of employees.[23] The cross-functional nature of formal networks is illustrated in Figure 8.3. Note the number of organizational levels and departments represented by the blue boxes.

Formal networks differ from teams or cross-functional task forces in three ways.[24] First, unlike most task forces, networks are *not temporary*. In fact, each manger's continuing experience in the network helps build the shared understanding among members and explains the network's effectiveness. Second, unlike most teams and task forces, networks *take the initiative* in finding and solving problems. In other words, they do not just solve the specific problems they are given. Third, the existence of the formal network changes—or should change—the nature of top management's job. With the networks in place, CEOs "no longer define their jobs as making all substantive operating decisions on their own.[25] Instead, although CEOs still make many decisions, the network can handle more of the interunit coordination the CEO might otherwise have to do, leaving him or her more time for strategic planning.

A formal network is used at the railroad firm Conrail. Here, 19 middle managers from various departments and levels constitute the firm's operating committee, which is actually a formal network, and thereby influence most of the firm's key operating decisions. They meet for several hours on Monday mornings to review and decide on tactical issues (delivery schedules and prices, for instance) and work on longer-term issues such as five-year business plans.[26] But, as a formal network, they are also expected to communicate continuously during the week to monitor operations activities across their departments.

formal organizational network
a formally assigned, permanent group of managers or other employees drawn from across a company's functions, geographic areas, and hierarchical levels to take the initiative in finding and solving problems.

◄ **FIGURE 8.3**

How Networks Reshape Organizations

The members of a formal network may be selected from various departments and organizational levels.
Source: Reprinted by permission of *Harvard Business Review*. From "How Networks Reshape Organizations—For Results," by Ram Charan, September–October 1991. Copyright © 1991 by the President and Fellows of Harvard College; all rights reserved.

The vacuum cleaner company Electrolux provides another example. When Leif Johansson took over an Electrolux division that stretched from Norway to Italy, he inherited a daunting task. Electrolux's line included 20 products, numerous acquired companies, and more than 200 plants in many countries. Each presented unique market positions, capabilities, plant capacity, and competitive situations. Johansson saw that his strategy had to be to create strengths across functional and geographic borders if he was to derive maximum economies of scale from the multiproduct, multiplant, multinational operation.

Local managers convinced him that abandoning local brands would jeopardize existing distribution channels and customer loyalty. How could he derive the benefits of Electrolux's multicountry scale while maintaining local brand autonomy? His solution was to create a formal network composed of managers from various countries. The network structure helped keep operations flexible and responsive. Local managers still had wide authority to design and market local brands. But the formal network helps provide the overall multinational and multiproduct coordination in areas like production and inventory management that helped Electrolux obtain economies of scale.[27]

While our focus here is mostly on internal formal organizational networks, such formal networks are also increasingly important in international trade. For example, in telecommunications, the Global One joint venture, led by Sprint, Deutsche Telecom, and France Telecom, is managed by a formal network serving 65 countries and functioning as one company to serve the global telecommunications needs of corporations.[28] In fact, it's been estimated that by the year 2000, more than 20,000 such strategic alliances were in place and operating around the world. Other examples include the major strategic alliances in the airline business, such as the Star Alliance, which includes United, Lufthansa, SAS, Varig, and others. As with internal formal organizational networks, strategic alliances are also managed by formal networks: a recognized group of managers—in this case, in each of the various alliance member companies—is appointed to achieve the day-to-day and strategic coordination required to make the strategic alliance a success.

Informal Networks

Networks needn't be formal, and indeed many firms, particularly multinationals, encourage the growth of informal networks. "Here," as one expert put it, "Creating confidence in the work of colleagues around the world and building up personal relationships are the key factors."[29] **Informal organizational networks** consist of cooperating individuals who are connected only informally. They share information and help solve each other's problems based on personal knowledge of each other's expertise.

There are several ways to nurture the personal relationships on which informal networks are built. Multinationals like Philips and Shell build personal relationships through international executive development programs. They bring managers from around the world to work together in training centers in New York and London. Other firms, like GE, have international management development centers near their home cities.

Moving managers from facility to facility around the world is another way to build these informal networks. Some firms, such as Shell, transfer employees around the world in great numbers. In one case, for instance: "[International mobility] has created what one might call a 'nervous system' that facilitates both corporate strategic control and the flow of information throughout the firm. Widespread transfers

informal organizational network

cooperating individuals who are interconnected only informally to share information and help solve each other's problems.

have created an informal information network, a superior degree of communication, and mutual understanding between headquarters and subsidiaries and between subsidiaries themselves, as well as a stronger identification with the corporate culture, without compromising the local subsidiary cultures."[30]

Management development programs like these help build informal networks in several ways. The socializing that takes place builds personal relationships among managers. Such personal relationships then facilitate global networking and communications. So if a new Shell Latin America sales manager needs to get in to see a new client, she might call a Shell Zurich manager she knows who has a contact at the client firm.

Electronic Networks

The rise of the Internet and of collaborative computing networking software lets companies make better use of existing formal and informal networks and, indeed, encourages all employees throughout the firm to network. Collaborative computing software includes packages such as Lotus Notes that help employees "get together" and make decisions, even at great distances.

Electronic networking—networking through e-mail and the use of collaborative computing software like Lotus Notes—helps manage businesses today. PricewaterhouseCooper's 18,000 accountants stay in touch thanks to **electronic bulletin boards**. Thus a Dublin employee with a question about dairy plant accounting might have her question answered by a networked colleague half a world away.[31] Group decision support systems allow employees—even those in different countries—to brainstorm ideas and work together on projects.[32]

Indeed, collaborative packages like Lotus Notes are changing how companies are managed and organized.[33] For example, a product called IP Team 3.0 includes new decision-building tools that automate and document the making of engineering decisions. One of its key features is that it integrates suppliers and contractors into the product development cycle. It thus lets a geographically dispersed group from the company and its suppliers work together to develop a product, and then automates the bidding procedure.[34] Another collaborative groupware product called OneSpace allows several design teams "to collaborate over the Internet and across fire walls in real-time by working directly on the 3 D solid model. . . ."[35] When it comes to using the Internet for networking business processes, the UK-based British Telecommunications PLC (BT) provides a good illustration of "managing@the speed of thought." BT has developed an Intranet—an internal network based on Internet technologies—which is used by over 60,000 employees, customers, and suppliers. For example, the Intranet is used for BT's project proposal submission process and helps everyone involved to instantaneously submit, review, and track the status of each project.[36] The system uses a simple security/authentication system to ensure that only involved parties have access to the project data. But by linking everyone together via the Internet, all those involved in a project (both within and outside BT) are able to monitor and manage their project, thanks to Internet-based networking.

Products like these do more than expedite the company's design process or automate its purchasing. By linking employees, customers, suppliers, and partners electronically (often over the Internet), they enable companies to create what amount to electronic networked organizations. Here communications and relationships ignore traditional departmental boundaries, and even the traditional boundaries separating the company from its customers and suppliers largely cease to exist. In fact, companies today use the Internet, intranets, and similar links between them-

electronic networking
Networking through the use of collaborative computing software like Lotus Notes.

electronic bulletin board
an example of e-mail-based communications that allow one or more group members to file messages on various topics to be picked up by other group members via telecommunications links.

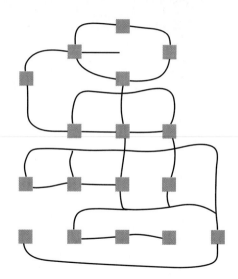

hyperarchies

companies today use the internet, intranet, and similar links between themselves and customers and suppliers to communicate.

selves and customers and suppliers to communicate in what two experts call **hyperarchies**. Figure 8.4 illustrates the effect of such networking. In a hyperarchy, the network is so complete that basically everyone can communicate with anyone else, and is encouraged to do so. As these experts put it: "Hyperarchy challenges all hierarchies, whether of logic or of power, with the possibility (or the threat) of random access and information symmetry."[37] Everyone, in other words, from first-line employees on up can communicate digitally with everyone else. The result is an organization where communications aren't restricted by the organization chart or the chain of command—a sort of digital boundaryless organization, as we'll see in a moment.

MANAGING @ THE *SPEED* OF THOUGHT

▓ Knowledge Management

To Microsoft's Bill Gates, making sure that employees can communicate is a good example of knowledge management. Here's how he puts it:

> Knowledge management is nothing more than managing information flow, getting the right information to the people who need it so they can act on it quickly. . . .And, knowledge management is a means, not an end. The end is to increase institutional intelligence, or corporate IQ. In today's dynamic markets a company needs a high corporate IQ to succeed. By corporate IQ I don't mean simply having a lot of smart people at your company—although it helps to start with smart people. Corporate IQ is a measure of how easily your company can share information broadly and of how well people within the organization can build on each other's ideas. . . . The workers in a company with a high corporate IQ collaborate effectively so that all of the key people on a project are well-informed and energized. The ultimate goal is to have a team develop the best ideas from throughout an organization and then act with the same unity of purpose and focus that a single, well-motivated person would bring to bear on the situation.[38]

"Old-style" organizations have boundaries. Vertically, the chain of command implies clearly defined authority boundaries: The president gives orders to the vice president, who gives orders to the managers, and so on down the line. There are also clearly delineated horizontal or departmental boundaries. Most companies are separated into what some call "smokestacks." The production department has its own responsibilities, the sales department has its own, and so on. If the company happens to be divisionalized, the work of each division is self-contained and each division often proceeds on the assumption that it can (and should) do its job with little or no interaction with other divisions.[39]

We've seen that such boundary-filled organizations once served a useful purpose. Jobs were specialized, lines of communication were well defined, and the slow-arriving problems could be solved in a relatively mechanical, step-by-step manner by an organization in which all knew exactly where they stood. For most firms, things are different today. Rapid change demands a more responsive organization: First-line employees may need quick responses from managers two levels up, or someone in the U.S. division may need a quick response from someone in Europe. As a result, yesterday's neat organizational boundaries need to be pierced, as they are with teams and formal and informal networks. As two experts summarized it: "Companies are replacing vertical hierarchies with horizontal networks; linking together traditional functions through interfunctional teams; and forming strategic alliances with suppliers, customers, and even competitors."[40] In so doing, they are creating boundaryless organizations.

A **boundaryless organization** is one in which the widespread use of teams, networks, and similar structural mechanisms means that the "walls" which typically separate organizational functions and hierarchical levels are reduced and made more permeable.[41] Taken to the extreme, the boundaryless company is one in which not only internal organizational boundaries are stripped away, but also those between the company and its suppliers and customers.

boundaryless organization
an organization in which the widespread use of teams, networks, and similar structural mechanisms means that the boundaries separating organizational functions and hierarchical levels are reduced and more permeable.

authority boundary
the boundary represented by differences in organizational level or status across which communications may be distorted or constrained due to the status difference.

Piercing Organizational Boundaries

In practice, four specific boundaries must be pierced if the company is to take full advantage of teams and networks: the authority boundary, the task boundary, the political boundary, and the identity boundary.[42] A summary of these four boundaries and the managerial tensions and feelings that must be addressed in order to pierce them is shown in Figure 8.5.

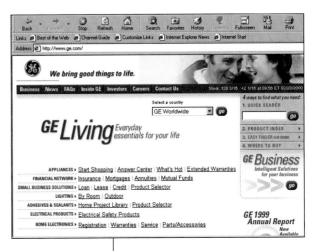

▲ W E B N O T E

Through Web sites like this, GE enables customers and suppliers to link with it and to make GE more boundaryless as an organization.
www.ge.com
Used with permission.

The Authority Boundary   In every company, superiors and subordinates—even those in self-managing teams or formal networks—always meet at an **authority boundary**. Therein lies the problem: To achieve the responsiveness required of a team-based or network structure, just issuing and following orders "is no longer good enough."[43] For example, a manager in a formal network who happened to be a vice president would inhibit the network's effectiveness if she demanded the right to give orders based solely on the fact that she was the highest-ranking

	KEY QUESTIONS	TENSIONS DEVELOPING DUE TO THIS BOUNDARY
Authority Boundary	"Who is in charge of what?" →	How to lead but remain open to criticism. How to follow but still challenge superiors.
Task Boundary	"Who does what?" →	How to depend on others you don't control. How to specialize yet understand other people's jobs.
Political Boundary	"What's in it for us?" →	How to defend one's interests without undermining the organization. How to differentiate between win–win and win–lose situations.
Identity Boundary	"Who is—and isn't—'us'?" →	How to feel pride without devaluing others. How to remain loyal without undermining outsiders.

person in the network. Doing so would undermine the collaboration and the reliance on experts that are two advantages of teams and networks.

Piercing the authority boundary thus requires three things. Bosses must learn how to lead while remaining open to criticism. They must be willing to accept "orders" from lower-ranking employees who happen to be experts on the problems at hand. And "subordinates" must be trained and encouraged to follow but still challenge superiors if necessary.

The Task Boundary Creating a boundaryless organization also requires managing the **task boundary**. This means changing the way employees feel about who does what when employees from different departments work on a task. Managing the task boundary means training and encouraging employees to rid themselves of the "It's not my job" attitude that typically compartmentalizes one employee's area from another's:

> Indeed, their own performance may depend on what their colleagues do. So, while focusing primarily on their own task, they must also take a lively interest in the challenges and problems facing others who contribute in different ways to the final product or service.[44]

The Political Boundary Differences in political agendas often separate employees as well. For example, manufacturing typically has a strong interest in smoothing out the demand for its products and in making the firm's products as easy to produce as possible. Sales, on the other hand, has an equally legitimate interest in maximizing sales (even if it means taking in a lot of custom or last-minute rush orders). The result of such opposing agendas in a traditional organization can be a conflict at the departments' **political boundary**.

task boundary

the perceived limited actions of a specific organizational position.

political boundary

the special interests or agendas within an organization that may oppose each other.

Members of each special-interest group in a boundaryless firm may still ask "What's in it for us?" when a decision must be made. But they have to be encouraged to take a more collegial, consensus-oriented approach, to defend their interests without undermining the best interests of the team, network, or organization.

The Identity Boundary Everyone identifies with several groups. For example, a General Motors accountant might identify with her colleagues in the accounting profession, with her co-workers in the GM accounting department, and perhaps with GM itself, to name a few. The **identity boundary** means that we tend to identify with groups with which we have shared experiences and with which we believe we share fundamental values.

identity boundary
the boundary caused by identifying with those groups with which one has shared experiences and with which one believes one shares fundamental values.

Unfortunately, such identification tends to foster an "us" versus "them" mentality. The problem at the identity boundary arises because people tend to trust those with whom they identify but distrust others. Attitudes like these can undermine the free-flowing cooperation that responsive networked or team-based organizations require.

There are several ways to pierce the identity boundary. One is to train and socialize all the firm's employees so they come to identify first with the company and its goals and ways of doing things: "The company comes first" becomes their motto. Another is to emphasize that while team spirit may be laudable, employees must avoid "devaluing the potential contribution of other groups."[45]

IBM's research facilities provide an illustration of how the boundaryless process works in practice.[46] IBM has eight labs worldwide, employing about 3,000 researchers. While the labs' results are obviously brilliant—they generated $1.3 billion in licensing revenues in one recent year—it's not just the discoveries but how they're developed and implemented that makes IBM's R&D effort truly unique.

As in many organizations, the usual way of doing things tends to be much different in the research group than on the development side. As IBM's senior vice president for research puts it: "The development side is highly disciplined, with a lot of checkpoints, tests, and milestones." On the other hand, "The research side is the exact opposite; it's much more freewheeling." A big reason for IBM's success in commercializing its discoveries has been it's ability to eliminate barriers between the research and development groups. While they're separate departments, their efforts are more like that of a joint venture group. In other words, by reducing the barriers created by the authority, task, political, and identity boundaries, IBM has been able to blend the work of two very different departments into a concerted team-like effort.

Horizontal Corporations

In many firms today, boundarylessness translates into what management experts call a horizontal corporation. As illustrated in Figure 8.6, the **horizontal corporation** is a structure organized around customer-oriented processes such as new-product development, sales and fulfillment, and customer support. Employees work together in multidisciplinary teams; each team performs one or more of the processes.

horizontal corporation
a structure that is organized around customer-oriented processes performed by multidisciplinary cross-functional teams rather than formal functional departments.

In its purest form, a horizontal structure eliminates functional departments, instead sprinkling functional specialists throughout the key process teams. They then work together on those teams with other functional specialists to accomplish the process-oriented team's mission, be it product development, sales and fulfillment, customer support, or some other goal. The horizontal structure usually has a small team of senior executives to give strategic direction and to provide essential staff support functions like human resource management.[47]

▼ FIGURE 8.6 The Horizontal Corporation

In the horizontal corporation the work is organized around cross-functional processes with multifunction teams carrying out the tasks needed to service the customer.

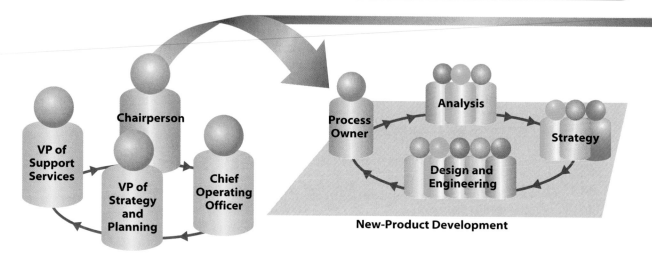

Source: John A. Byrne, "The Horizontal Corporation." *Business Week*, December 20, 1993, p. 80.

Companies organize horizontally for several reasons. Many (including AT&T and DuPont) found that downsizing did not change the fundamental way departments accomplished work. The work—from getting the sales order to processing an invoice—was still handed from department to department like a baton in a relay race. At truck rental firm Ryder Systems, for instance, purchasing a vehicle for subsequent leasing required as many as 17 handoffs, as the relevant documents made their way from one department to another. Since such handoffs occurred both horizontally and vertically, the amount of time and energy wasted was enormous. Ryder remedied the situation by "reengineering" the job so that all vehicle purchasing tasks were handled by a single multispecialist horizontal vehicle purchase group.

► FIGURE 8.7 How to Create a Horizontal Corporation

Creating a horizontal organization involves several steps, starting with determining the firm's strategic objectives, and including such steps as flattening the hierarchy and using teams to accomplish the work.

Identify strategic objectives.

Analyze key competitive advantages to fulfill objectives.

Define core processes, focusing on what's essential to accomplish your goals.

Organize around processes, not functions. Each process should link related tasks to yield a product or service to a customer.

Eliminate all activities that fail to add value or contribute to the key objectives.

Source: Reprinted from the December 20, 1993, issue of *Business Week* by special permission. Copyright © 1993 by the McGraw-Hill Companies, Inc.

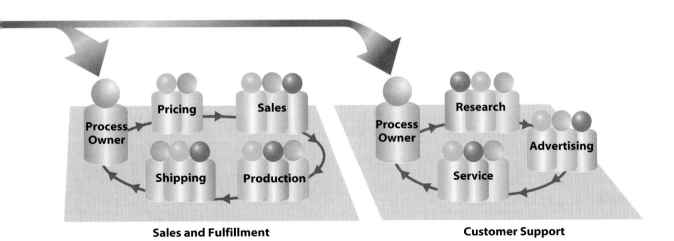

Sales and Fulfillment

Customer Support

Horizontal structures also help to obliterate organizational boundaries. Even in divisionalized firms, functional areas tend to grow into fiefdoms in which protecting one's own turf can take priority over satisfying customer needs. Such territorial thinking is less likely to occur when the "departments" are essentially multifunctional teams organized to provide basic customer-oriented processes. Thus the horizontal new-product-development process team might replace the new-product-development sequence, in which each department (such as engineering, production, and sales) did its part and then passed the responsibility to the next department.

Several companies are moving toward the horizontal model. For example, AT&T's Network Services division, with 16,000 employees, identified 13 core processes around which to reorganize. GE's lighting business similarly organized around multidisciplinary teams, each carrying out more than 100 processes, from new-product design to improving manufacturing machinery efficiency. As Figure 8.7 shows, the essence of creating a horizontal corporation is defining the firm's core processes and then organizing teams around these, while linking each process team's performance to specific customer-related objectives. Once the horizontal heart of the organization is in place, the firm eliminates the functions, levels, and staff departments that do not directly contribute to the work of the process-oriented teams.

Cut function and staff departments to a minimum, preserving key expertise.

Appoint a manager or team as the "owner" of each core process.

Create multidisciplinary teams to run each process.

Set specific performance objectives for each process.

Empower employees with authority and information to achieve goals.

Revamp training, appraisal, pay, and budgetary systems to support the new structure and link it to customer satisfaction.

■ Organizing Horizontally

Many companies organize around complete, horizontal processes to speed decision making and get orders out faster to the customers, but doing so requires more than just reorganizing.[48,49] In successful reorganizations, management fosters what researchers in one study called a "collective sense of responsibility." In other words, employees took an active interest in their colleagues and in improving the outcome of their mutual efforts. They were willing to offer colleagues a helping hand and to work hard so the team would succeed.

How do you cultivate that kind of collective responsibility in a horizontal organization? These researchers found four ways:[50]

■ *Make responsibilities overlap.* Design individual jobs as broadly as possible and keep the number of job titles to a minimum. That way, responsibility boundaries blur, and employees are more inclined to pitch in and help each other.

■ *Base rewards on unit performance.* In this study the most successfully reorganized companies based employees' rewards (for example, salaries, incentives, recognition) on the performance of the units to which they belonged. That helped to emphasize the importance of everyone working together.

■ *Change the physical layout.* In other words, don't just reorganize. Change the physical layout so it promotes collective responsibility, such as by letting people see each other's work.

■ *Redesign work procedures.* Work procedures should encourage collective responsibility. Provide computer terminals so employees can communicate more readily; use the e-mail network to keep employees informed of how they're doing as a team; and make sure managers are available if the team or any member has an issue to discuss.

Two experts say some managers underestimate the difficulty of breaking the functional mindset. They spend all their time fine-tuning new (process-oriented) tasks, instead of concentrating on the people side of the problem:

> Such managers overlook the importance of changing their organizations' culture. They fail to see that collective responsibility is an attitude, a value, a concern. It means taking an interest in one's colleagues and in improving the outcome of mutual (as opposed to individual) efforts. People who feel collectively responsible are willing to work especially hard to not let the team down. They will take the initiative in offering a colleague a helping hand with a work problem, even though doing so might make it more difficult for them to meet their own deadlines.[51]

The managing and the people sides of organizations are really inseparable. Designing organizations for managing change—for instance, by creating a horizontal corporation—is crucial today and can be done successfully. However, managers must take into consideration the human element.

▶ FEDERAL-TYPE ORGANIZATIONS

federal organization

an organization in which power is distributed between a central unit and a number of constituents, but the central unit's authority is internationally limited.

For some companies, managing change means moving to federal organizations. In **federal organizations** (as in federal governments), power is distributed between a central authority and a number of constituent units, but the central unit's authority is intentionally limited.[52] Organizing and disbursing power in this way enables a company to marshal resources and bring them to bear quickly, while giving remote units the authority and flexibility they need to respond quickly to local challenges.

ABB, mentioned above, is an early example. Recall that the CEO broke the company into 5,000 profit centers, each containing about 50 employees. Each unit had wide authority to act more or less like a mini-company in its dealings with customers and suppliers. However, the parent firm retained control over matters like companywide strategy and financing major projects. Let's look at two more recent federal-type organizations: virtual organizations and cellular organizations.

Virtual Organizations

If often happens that a company has to organize considerable resources to accomplish some significant project, but can't afford the time or expense of acquiring and owning those resources itself. The question then is, "How can we accomplish that?" For many firms, the answer (as we first saw in Chapter 6) is a virtual corporation, "a temporary network of independent companies—suppliers, customers, perhaps even rivals—linked by information technology to share skills, costs, and access to one another's markets."[53] Virtual corporations are usually not corporations at all in the traditional sense, but rather networks of companies, each of which brings to the virtual corporation its special expertise. For example, AT&T worked with Matsushita Electronics Industrial Co. to speed production of its Safari notebook computer, which was designed by Henry Dreyfuss Associates.

Organizationally, virtual organizations have two main features. First, "the central feature of virtual organizations is their dependence on a federation of alliances and partnerships with other organizations."[54] "A virtual organization operates as a federated collection of enterprises tied together through contractual and other means, such as partial ownership arrangements. Specific arrangements include joint ventures, strategic alliances, minority investments, consortia, coalitions, outsourcing, and franchises."[55]

The virtual organization's second feature stems from this first characteristic: Corporate self-interest (rather than authority) generally plays a major role in maintaining organizational integrity. In traditional organizations, authority is dispersed down the chain of command, and employees who actually do the work are generally expected to follow legitimate orders. In virtual organizations, on the other hand, its not a company's employees who are doing the work, but the principals and employees of its virtual partners, so that "giving orders" and relying solely on a chain of command is usually not a constuctive way to get things done. Instead, assignments are made, partners are chosen for competence and reliability, and arrangements are made to provide for equitable incentives.[56]

Cellular Organizations

Do you remember biology? If you do, it will be easier to understand what some experts have called **cellular organizations**. In biology cells are the microscopic structural building blocks of the body, just as bricks are the building blocks of a house. But there the similarity ends. Cells are not just brick-like building blocks, but are also independent functional units, each able to live, to grow, to repair itself, and often to learn and thus adapt on its own. All cells have certain things in common (such as nuclei and cell membranes), yet cells also differ markedly in the jobs they have to do. Humans are composed of billions and billions of specialized cells (skin, hair, and eye cells, for instance), each alive and making its own unique contribution to the organism.

cellular organization
an organization composed of small, individual, more or less autonomous and self-reliant firms.

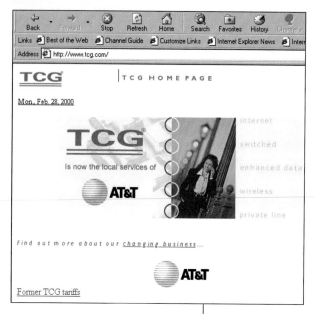

Cellular organizations are much the same. Cells—usually small independent companies but sometimes, also self-managing teams—are the basic building blocks of cellular organizations. As in biology, each cell is organized to be self-sufficient, to live on its own and adapt, and to perform a specialized function. And (also as in biology), each individual cell contributes to the overall functioning of the company, while simultaneously deriving needed resources from the parent firm.

Team-based organizations and mini-unit structures (like ABB's) have cellular features, but *cellular organization* usually denotes something more. For example, consider the cellular organization at TCG, discussed in the chapter opener.[57] TCG, which develops a wide variety of products such as portable and handheld data terminals, is organized around 13 individual small firms: "Like a cell in a large organism, each firm has its own purpose and ability to function independently, but shares features and purposes with all of its sister firms."[58]

Figure 8.8 summarizes how TCG's cellular structure works. At TCG, each individual firm continually searches for new product and service opportunities. Then, when a particular venture—say, for developing and selling a new product—shows concrete progress, the initiating firm acts as project leader for what the company calls its *triangulation process*. Triangulation means that the initiating firm creates and leads a three-way partnership consisting of (1) one or more TCG firms, (2) an external joint venture partner, and (3) a principal customer for the product or service.[59] The triangulation process and mutual support among the 13 firms help

▶ **FIGURE 8.8**

TGC's Cellular Organization

Source: Reprinted with permission of the *Academy of Management Executive*, from "Organizing in the Knowledge Age: Anticipating the Cellular Form," Raymond Miles, vol. 11, no. 4, © 1997; permission conveyed through Copyright Clearance Center, Inc.

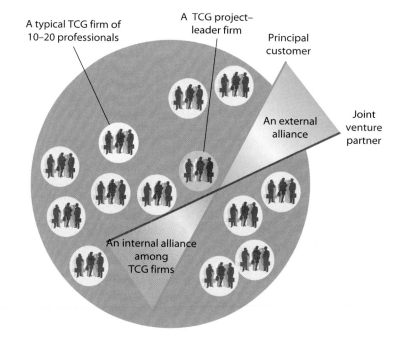

make TCG more than just the sum of its parts. For example, the firms learn from one another, have access to one another's customers, and help to capitalize and fund one another's projects.

TCG's cellular approach is based on three underlying principles: (1) Each individual firm must accept its entrepreneurial responsibilities, for instance with respect to identifying new project opportunities and pursuing customers; (2) each individual firm is self-organized, meaning it is a self-contained and functioning firm with "both the ability and freedom to reach a dip deeply into its own knowhow to create responses to a continuously evolving set of customer and partner needs"; and (3) each firm has the responsibility to be profitable and the opportunity to invest in—and even own stock in—the other TCG firms.

SUMMARY

1. Managers can make a number of basic structural changes to make their organizations operate more responsively. Simplifying or reducing structure by reducing layers of management, creating mini-units, reassigning support staff, and widening spans of control are examples we discussed.

2. Research suggests that different organizational structures are appropriate for, or contingent on, different tasks. Routine, efficiency-oriented tasks seem best matched with mechanistic organizational structures. At the other extreme, rapid change and technological innovation seem more suited to organic structures.

3. Some managers find that to manage change, responsive organizational structures are advisable. Team-based organizations built around self-managing teams are an example. Here the team is the basic work unit, and teams do much of the planning, decision making, and implementing required to get their assigned jobs done.

4. Many firms superimpose organizational networks over existing structures. A network is a system of interconnected or cooperating individuals. It can be formal or informal, and it can be electronically based. The basic idea is to link managers from various departments, levels, and geographic areas so they form a multidisciplinary team whose members communicate across normal organizational boundaries.

5. Taken to its logical conclusion, a networked organization results in a boundaryless organization in which managers have taken the steps required to pierce the organizational boundaries that often inhibit networked communications and decision making. These are the authority boundary, the task boundary, the identity boundary, and the political boundary.

6. The horizontal corporation is a structure organized around basic processes such as new-product development, sales fulfillment, and customer support. Everyone works together in multidisciplinary teams, with each team assigned to perform one or more of the processes.

7. Federal organizations are organizations in which power is distributed between a central unit and a number of a constituent units, but the central unit's authority is intentionally limited; virtual organizations and cellular organizations are two examples. A virtual organization is a collection of independent enterprises tied together by contracts and other means, such as partial ownership arrangements. In a cellular organization, small independent companies are the basic building blocks, and while each is self-sufficient, they all contribute to each other's and to the parent firm's success.

After plans are made, managers have to organize the work to be done. In Chapter 7 we focused on the fundamentals of organizing, including departmentalization (by function or product, for instance), coordination, and delegation. In this chapter we turned to designing organizations to manage change, and to structures such as boundaryless and cellular organizations.

However, designing the organization and organization chart is only part of the overall job of creating an organization: Having a box that says "Finance Department" doesn't really tell you very much about what the employees in that department actually do on a day-to-day basis. Nor is an organization chart of much use without employees to fill its positions. In Chapter 9 we therefore turn to staffing, and to the methods managers use to find and select employees to do the organization's jobs.

KEY TERMS

mechanistic organization 223
organic organization 224
downsizing 224
team 227
organizational network 230
formal organizational network 231

informal organizational network 232
electronic networking 233
electronic bulletin board 233
hyperarchy 234
boundaryless organization 235

authority boundary 235
task boundary 236
political boundary 236
identity boundary 237
horizontal corporation 237
federal organization 240
cellular organization 241

SKILLS AND STUDY MATERIALS

CRITICAL THINKING EXERCISES

1. New organizational structures are all around us. Teams largely manage some companies, such as Whole Food Markets. At Whole Foods Markets, the financial books are open to all, teams hire and fire team members, and they measure every aspect of performance. At Southwest Airlines, a team spirit that involves cross-training and employee input is deeply valued by the management. UPS management took its company public in November 1999, making its employees—most of whom own stock in the company—wealthier. Some organizations are virtual. Some are primarily made up of telecommuters who never come to the office. Many businesses are merging into giant corporations: Think of DaimlerChrysler. With such trends in mind, describe what you think will be the typical organization of the twenty-first century.

2. Max Weber, the German sociologist, is considered by most to be the father of the mechanistic or bureaucratic organization. Writing in the late 1800s and the early 1900s, Weber was analyzing the ushering in of what 1990s management expert Charles Handy has called "The Century of Organizations." For Weber it was a time when the new large-scale organizations would emphasize the importance of authority in the system: "In the past the man has been first, in the future the system must be first." What do you think he meant by that statement? How would he see today's team-based and boundaryless organizations? How might today's new structures change the relationship between the system and the human beings?

1. In *The Horizontal Organization* (Oxford University Press, 1999), Frank Ostroff argues that the vertical organizational design with its chain of command is of the past and the flat, horizontal organizational design is for now and the future. The vertical organization has inherent shortcomings in our competitive, technological, and workforce-focused environment, he says. Among the shortcomings are its internal focus on functional goals rather than an outward-looking concentration on delivering value and winning customers; the loss of important information as knowledge travels up and down multiple levels and across the functional departments; the fragmentation of performance objectives brought about by a multitude of distinct and fragmented functional goals; the added expense involved in coordinating overly fragmented work and departments; and the stifling of creativity and initiative of the workers at lower levels.

   Among the reasons Ostroff gives for saying the horizontal corporation is the structure of today and the future are that horizontal organizations organize around core processes, not tasks or functions; they install process owners or managers who will take responsibility for the core process in its entirety; teams, not individuals, are the cornerstone of the organizational design and performance; and they empower people by giving them the tools, skills, motivation, and authority to make decisions essential to the team's performance.

   Would you rather work in a vertical or horizontal organization and why? Which structure do you think will survive better in the future and why?

2. There is a new system of organizing that gets every employee thinking like a businessperson, that is, like an owner. Called "open-book management,"[60] it is getting remarkable results for companies such as Springfield Remanufacturing Corp., Case Company, and Cin-Made. In a nutshell, open-book management is a way of running a company that gets everyone to focus on helping the business make money.

   There are three essential differences between this approach and conventional approaches to management: (1) every employee sees—and learns to understand—the company's financial records, along with all the other numbers that are critical to tracking the business's performance; (2) employees learn that, whatever else they do, part of their job is to move those numbers in the right direction; and (3) employees have a direct stake in the company's success: If the company makes a profit, they get a share, and if it doesn't, they don't.

   You work for an old-line industrial firm with a mechanistic organizational structure that has been managed by basically the same team for the past 30 years. The company has developed a paternalistic culture: employees are expected to do their jobs, but not question their orders. Financial data, including salaries and compensation packages, are kept secret. In fact, if you share information about your pay with others, you may be fired. Your competitors seem to have a very motivated workforce and aggressive sales and marketing people, as well as technologically sophisticated products. As the newest member of the management team, you are very interested in introducing new ideas about organizational design, including open-book management.

   Your assignment is to write a brief report on *how* you would introduce these new concepts into this organization. The report should be only two pages and basically outline the issues and your recommendations based on concepts from the chapter. You should be ready to present your report either to a group in class or to the whole class.

m y P H L I P   C O M P A N I O N   W E B   S I T E

We invite you to visit the Dessler companion Web site at **www.prenhall.com/dessler** for this chapter's Internet resources.

How can a smaller entertainment company compete with U.S. giants like Warner Brothers and Disney? Canadian-owned Lions Gate Entertainment Corp. has two organizational strategies for taking its competitors to the mat: Imitate the best of the competitor organizations' existing structures, and use external networks of resources to make up for your smaller size.

Like its U.S. competitors, Lions Gate Entertainment employs an integrated media model. That is, it has separate operating divisions that can deliver stand-alone products, or serve as support services for each of its other divisions. The four main operating divisions at Lions Gate are motion pictures, television, animation, and studio facilities.

Recent projects demonstrate how a smaller firm like Lions Gate can use networked resources to strengthen its market position. To produce and distribute Class A feature films (large-budget films with international distribution), Lions Gate developed a joint venture, Mandalay Pictures, with a major U.S. film producer. The venture's first film, *Sleepy Hollow*, opened as the Number 2 film in the U.S., with a first-weekend take of more than $30 million.

In a similar move for the television market, Lions Gate formed a partnership with Paramount International Television and signed a contract with the Fox Family Network for a TV series before the first episode of a new series was filmed. The series, *Higher Ground*, began its life with a full-season 22-episode agreement from the Fox Family Channel.

Lions Gate, like most major film companies, uses a network of banks and financial institutions to finance its projects. Single banks are often uncomfortable financing projects as risky as major films. By arranging a consortium of lenders, film companies like Lion's Gate can receive financing without a single bank having to bear all the risk associated with a project. Lions Gate also uses its network for film distribution. (Since Lions Gate has no distribution system of its own, it relies on its network partners for the theatrical release of its films.)

Discussion Questions

1. In terms of what we discussed in this chapter, what modern organization structures does Lions Gate use?

2. In what ways does Lions Gate benefit from having a network structure?

3. What limitations would Lions Gate face without its networking capabilities?

4. Could a small firm like Lions Gate be competitive by using just its own resources?

Would you offer someone a high-salary position without knowing what job they would have? W. L. Gore & Associates does. It is one of the many unusual practices that have helped Gore, makers of the waterproof fabric GORE-TEX®, to be repeatedly named to the *Fortune* list of 100 Best Companies to Work for in America, most recently ranking as the 11th best firm. While only 40 years old, Gore has amassed revenues in excess of $1 billion and operates in 45 countries, while employing only 6,100 people.

Gore operates a high-tech company in a market (textiles) that is traditionally low-tech. As a high-tech company, Gore must be prepared to change rapidly when the market changes. To do this, Gore's structure and processes are distinguished by three unique characteristics: sponsors rather than bosses, a "lattice" organization, and the "waterline principle."

Gore sees the way it organizes and works as one of the things that sets it apart from its competitors. Gore militates against bureaucracy: it sees hierarchies as the enemies of innovation. Gore hires "associates" (not *employees*) into general work areas. When hired, these employees don't have specific job titles or positions. With the help of their Gore *sponsors* (*bosses*), associates select and commit to projects that seem to match their skills and interests. One of the sponsors' jobs is to help associates find a place in Gore that will offer personal fulfillment and maximize their contribution to the enterprise. Gore does not assign managers. In the company's view, leaders are people who have followers. If the organization is left on its own, leaders will emerge naturally, by demonstrating the character, knowledge, and skills that attract followers. To become a leader at Gore, you need to perform in a way that attracts followers.

This self-selecting process leads to what Gore calls the *lattice organization*. In the lattice, there are no chains of command; decision making is delegated to the point where the decision must be made. It is assumed that employees are sufficiently concerned about the good of the organization to make good decisions on behalf of the organization. Gore's lattice has no preestablished channels of communication. New associates are coached by their sponsors to communicate directly with each other. Associates work in multidisciplinary teams and are accountable to each other. The goal of this innovative structure is to unleash the creative potential of all of the associates, thus allowing Gore to become a truly innovative company.

The last commitment, the *waterline principle*, is cited by many as a key to Gore's successful ability to adapt. The company is viewed as a ship. Holes above the waterline are unattractive and even uncomfortable, but not deadly. Holes below the waterline would sink the ship. If you are a Gore associate and you see an action or event that could hit Gore below the waterline, then it is your individual responsibility to do something, even if the event or action happens outside your department or area. Failing to act on a waterline issue would earn you a severe reprimand from your peers, the other associates. After all, it is the role of every employee to protect the ship. With these principles firmly in place, Gore has been able to be remarkably flexible, to change constantly to meet the needs of current and future clients.

The results of Gore's structure and processes have been impressive. Its world-renowned fluoropolymer technology has allowed it to extend the product line far beyond the well-known GORE-TEX® brand. The same technology has allowed the company to produce Glide®, a nonstick dental floss, and Elixir®, a corrosion-resistant guitar string. Lesser known but equally impressive products, including next-generation materials for printed circuit boards and fiber optics, and new methods to detect and control environmental pollution, are marketed in the industrial sector. Gore has also been recognized for its work in advancing the science of regenerating tissue destroyed by injuries.

The Company's founder, Bill Gore, originally articulated the Company's unique structure and culture. To Gore, the company would be successful only if it could create an environment that was naturally conducive to the highest levels of innovation and productivity. Gore envisioned associates making a commitment to four basic principles: fairness to each other and everyone they came in contact with; freedom to encourage, help, and allow other associates to grow in knowledge, skill, and scope of responsibility; the ability to make one's own commitments and keep them; and consultation with other associates before undertaking actions that could affect the reputation of the company by hitting it "below the waterline."

Discussion Questions

1. In what ways is Gore's lattice structure similar to the structures discussed in this chapter?

2. In what ways does Gore's lattice structure make it better suited to change?

3. Gore asserts that its structure makes it more innovative. Could a traditionally structured company be as innovative as W. L. Gore & Associates? How?

4. What difficulties might you encounter if you tried to apply Gore's structural principles to an existing company?

YOU BE THE CONSULTANT

HOW CAN WE ORGANIZE WITHOUT LOSING IT?

KnitMedia is at the epicenter of several industries that are undergoing very rapid change. Record distribution and music publishing are two related industries that are rapidly consolidating, with giants like Warner, Sony, and Universal now responsible for over three-fourths of the total industry revenues. New Media, including music Web sites and music cybercasts, is undergoing similar explosive growth. Not only are substantial players like KnitMedia increasingly active in this industry, but so are tiny "one person bands" with their own Web sites and—at the other extreme—the Web sites and networks of giants like Viacom, Sony, and Apple Computer.

KnitMedia therefore finds itself competing in a marketplace dominated by both multinational corporations and tiny independent operations. The large corporations have enormous resources, but their great size may also be a potential weakness. As KnitMedia's management has said: "Due to the multinationals' international structures, they are restricted in their ability to react quickly to market demands. This has historically caused late entry for major record labels in many new markets. Because the size of the large organizations also precludes them from a certain familiarity with a consumer, this has created an inability to see shifts in a marketplace."[61]

On the other hand, particularly with all those tiny independent bands and labels using the Internet to distribute their music, KnitMedia also has to guard against having the same sort of institutional isolation set in as it grows larger. In other words, it has to make sure its organization is such that Michael Dorf and his management team don't become isolated from the consumer so that they are no longer able to see shifts in the marketplace and react quickly and appropriately.

Dorf and his management team certainly recognize this potential problem and have tried to make sure it doesn't occur. For one thing, KnitMedia tries to take a team approach to most of the things it does. For example, in describing the job of Ed Greer, chief operating officer Allan Fried put it this way: "Ed Greer's been around, I think, for about 13 years. So to say Ed, you should just be involved with the clubs and we don't want your opinion on anything else, would just be to waste his talent, his intelligence, his energy, and because . . . people are passionate about what goes on here, they all have good ideas and we like to think

that the best idea wins, not just my idea because it's my idea. I think we're all fighting for a common cause [and I think, overall] that we're very much of a team."

Of course the problem is that saying you're operating like a team is one thing, and doing it in practice is another, particularly when you start with the fairly conventional KnitMedia organization chart depicted in Figure 7.1. Michael Dorf and his team certainly want to take advantage of the latest thinking when it comes to designing organizations to manage change; the question is how to do that. They've come to you for advice.

Team Exercises and Questions

Use what you learned in this chapter to answer the following questions from Michael Dorf and his management team:

1. Do you think KnitMedia's current organization chart provides our company with the ability to manage rapid change? Why or why not?

2. We want to be more team oriented in the way we organize and in the way we deal with problems; what exactly can we do to inject more of a team orientation into the way we organize?

3. Would it be helpful for us to also apply the latest thinking with regard to network-based organizations, boundaryless organizations, and/or horizontal organizations at KnitMedia? Why or why not? And if so, how would you suggest we do it?

STAFFING THE ORGANIZATION

WHAT'S AHEAD?

When it comes to leading-edge, fast-changing companies, it's hard to think of one more on the edge than Cisco Systems. Cisco is the worldwide leader in Internet networking, and it supplies the network solutions that let people transfer information over the Internet. With offices in more than 115 countries worldwide and growing at hyper-speed, Cisco has a constant need to hire the best of the best employees. To keep growing fast in this high-tech field, Cisco needs a constant supply of new top candidates, and outstanding training and HR programs to assimilate and motivate them.

Cisco has some of the most sophisticated HR programs anywhere. And as you'd expect from the world's Internet networking leader, much of its recruiting and initial screening takes place via the Internet.[1]

OBJECTIVES

AFTER STUDYING THIS CHAPTER, YOU SHOULD BE ABLE TO

- Explain why human resource management is crucial today

- Use five methods to recruit a pool of good candidates

- Use testing in selecting new employees

- List and briefly discuss the main steps in conducting an employment interview

- Describe three other important employee selection techniques

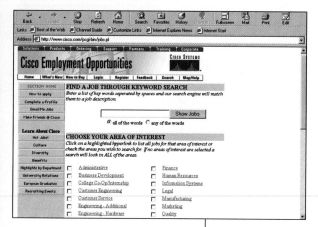

Having a box in an organization chart that says "Finance Department" as we noted in Chapter 8, doesn't really tell you much about what the employees in that department actually have to do, or what kinds of people should be hired for these positions. In the last two chapters we focused on organizing, including organizational fundamentals (like how to departmentalize and achieve coordination). Now we turn to staffing, and in particular to developing job descriptions and to the methods managers use to recruit and select the employees who will actually fill job slots.

Staffing, personnel, or (as it is generally known today) **Human Resource Management** (HRM) is the management function devoted to acquiring and training the organization's employees, and then appraising and paying them. This chapter emphasizes those staffing functions that relate most directly to organizing (such as recruiting and selecting employees). Toward the end of the chapter we'll briefly cover appraisal and compensation (which we talk about more in the motivation chapter, Chapter 11). Once a company is organized and staffed, its employees are ready to be motivated and led. These are the topics we'll turn to in the next part of the book.

All managers are, in a sense, personnel managers, because they all get involved in activities like recruiting, interviewing, selecting, and training. But most large firms also have Human Resource (HR) departments with their own human resource managers

human resources (HR) management

the management function devoted to acquiring, training, appraising, and compensating employees.

▶ HUMAN RESOURCE MANAGEMENT AS A STRATEGIC PARTNER

Intense global competition means that companies today need competent and committed employees more than they ever have before. To be more competitive, companies must now rely on things like self-managing work teams and empowering employees. In turn, organizing like this boosts the need for motivated and self-directed employees: You can't very well have self-managing work teams if the employees don't have the skills or attitudes to manage themselves.

Many experts describe this situation by saying that employees have become for most companies, their main competitive advantage or "competitive edge." For example, the reason Southwest Airlines can be so efficient is that its employees are all driven to make their company succeed. But if employees are a competitive advantage, then selecting, training, and managing them should be an important part of the company's strategic planning process. This in turn has led to the emergence of strategic human resource management.

strategic (HR) management

the linking of the human resource function with the company's strategies to accomplish that strategy.

Strategic human resource management has been defined as "the linking of HRM with strategic goals and objectives in order to improve business performance and develop organizational cultures that foster innovation and flexibility."[2] Strategic HR means accepting the fact that human resource management plays an important role in *formulating* company strategies, as well as in *executing* those strategies through its activities like recruiting, selecting, and training personnel.

HR's Role in Formulating Strategy

HR management can play a crucial role in helping companies formulate their strategies. For example, HR management is in a good position to supply competitive intelligence that the firm's top managers need to know. Details regarding incentive plans being used by competitors, opinion surveys from employees that elicit information about customer complaints, and information about pending legislation like labor laws or mandatory health insurance are examples.

HR also supplies information regarding the company's internal strengths and weaknesses. IBM's decision to buy Lotus was prompted in part by IBM's conclusion that its own human resources were inadequate to enable the firm to reposition itself as an industry leader in networking systems, or at least to do so quickly enough.

HR's Role in Executing Strategy

HR also can play a big role in executing the company's strategy. For example, FedEx's competitive strategy is to differentiate itself from its competitors by offering superior customer service and guaranteed on-time delivery. Since basically the same technologies are available to UPS, DHL, and FedEx's other competitors, it is FedEx's workforce that gives it a crucial competitive advantage. The firm's HR processes and its ability to create a highly committed, competent, and customer-oriented workforce are crucial to FedEx's ability to execute its strategy. FedEx has therefore implemented many leading-edge HR practices, including extensive incentive plans and a grievance process that goes all the way to the FedEx president.

▲ FedEx's human resources—its committed, competent, customer-oriented employees—give the firm its competitive advantage.

▶ PERSONNEL PLANNING AND RECRUITING

Once the firm's organization is in place, its positions must be filled. For most companies, the heart of the human resource management system (as illustrated in Figure 9.1) is a sequence of steps in which employees are recruited, screened, and finally trained to do their jobs. This is also referred to as the manager's **staffing** function, the function that involves actually filling the firm's open organizational positions. In most companies, this process begins by looking at the organization chart and then deciding specifically what each job entails and who (both in and out of the company) might be available to fill it. It begins, in other words, with analyzing the company's personnel requirements and then recruiting applicants to fill them.

Job Analysis and Personnel Planning

Developing an organization chart (see Chapters 7 and 8) creates jobs to be filled. **Job analysis** is the procedure used to determine the duties of the jobs and the kinds of people (in terms of skills and experience) who should be hired for them.[3] These data are then used to develop a **job description,** or a list of duties showing

staffing

actually filling a firm's open positions; also, the personnel process that includes six steps: job analysis, personnel planning; recruiting, interviewing, testing and selection, and training and development.

job analysis

the procedure used to determine the duties of particular jobs and the kinds of people (in terms of skills and experience) who should be hired for them.

job description

a document that identifies a particular job, provides a brief job summary, and lists specific responsibilities and duties of the job.

The recruitment and selection process is a series of hurdles aimed at selecting the best candidate for the job.

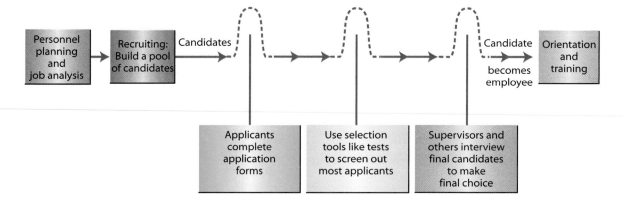

job specification

the human qualifications in terms of traits, skills, and experiences required to accomplish a job.

job analysis questionnaire

a form used by managers to determine the duties and functions of a job through a series of questions that employees answer.

what the job entails, and **job specifications,** a list of the skills and aptitudes sought in people hired for the job. A job description like the one in Figure 9.2 identifies the job, provides a brief job summary, and then lists specific responsibilities and duties.

Managers often use a **job analysis questionnaire** (see Figure A9.1, page 286) to determine a job's duties and responsibilities. This generally requires employees to provide detailed information on what they do, such as briefly stating their main duties in their own words, describing the conditions under which they work, and listing any permits or licenses required to perform duties assigned to their positions. Supervisors and/or specialists from the company's HR department may then review this information, question the employees, and decide exactly what each job does—or should—entail.

MANAGING @ THE *SPEED* OF THOUGHT

■ JobDescription.com

There was a time, not too long ago, when producing job descriptions meant spending hours going through job description manuals. Today, it's possible to produce the job description you need almost instantaneously by using an Internet-based job description service.

JobDescription.com is one example. When the manager clicks on the site, he or she begins (for a fee) by choosing a job title from the 3,700 jobs listed in the JobDescription.com library. Then the manager follows the prompts to provide the requested information and/or customize the samples provided by JobDescription.com for each of the job description's sections (such as summary, duties and responsibilities, job information, and supervisory responsibilities).

The description in Figure 9.2—in this case for a marketing manager—provides an example. As you can see, the description is quite complete and includes such essential elements as summary, duties, and the human qualifications for the job.

OLEC CORP.
Job Description

Job Title:	Marketing Manager
Department:	Marketing
Reports To:	President
FLSA Status:	Non Exempt
Prepared By:	Micheal George
Prepared Date:	April 1, 2000
Approved By:	Ian Alexander
Approved Date:	April 15, 2000

SUMMARY

Plans, directs, and coordinates the marketing of the organization's products and/or services by performing the following duties personally or through subordinate supervisors.

ESSENTIAL DUTIES AND RESPONSIBILITIES include the following. Other duties may be assigned.

Establishes marketing goals to ensure share of market and profitability of products and/or services.

Develops and executes marketing plans and programs, both short and long range, to ensure the profit growth and expansion of company products and/or services.

Researches, analyzes, and monitors financial, technological, and demographic factors so that market opportunities may be capitalized on and the effects of competitive activity may be minimized.

Plans and oversees the organization's advertising and promotion activities including print, electronic, and direct mail outlets.

Communicates with outside advertising agencies on ongoing campaigns.

Works with writers and artists and oversees copywriting, design, layout, pasteup, and production of promotional materials.

Develops and recommends pricing strategy for the organization which will result in the greatest share of the market over the long run.

Achieves satisfactory profit/loss ratio and share of market performance in relation to pre-set standards and to general and specific trends within the industry and the economy.

Ensures effective control of marketing results and that corrective action takes place to be certain that the achievement of marketing objectives are within designated budgets.

Evaluates market reactions to advertising programs, merchandising policy, and product packaging and formulation to ensure the timely adjustment of marketing strategy and plans to meet changing market and competitive conditions.

Recommends changes in basic structure and organization of marketing group to ensure the effective fulfillment of objectives assigned to it and provide the flexibility to move swiftly in relation to marketing problems and opportunities.

Conducts marketing surveys on current and new product concepts.

Prepares marketing activity reports.

SUPERVISORY RESPONSIBILITIES

Manages three subordinate supervisors who supervise a total of five employees in the Marketing Department. Is responsible for the overall direction, coordination, and evaluation of this unit. Also directly supervises two non-supervisory employees. Carries out supervisory responsibilities in accordance with the organization's policies and applicable laws. Responsibilities include interviewing, hiring, and training employees; planning, assigning, and directing work; appraising performance; rewarding and disciplining employees; addressing complaints and resolving problems.

QUALIFICATIONS

To perform this job successfully, an individual must be able to perform each essential duty satisfactorily. The requirements listed below are representative of the knowledge, skill, and/or ability required. Reasonable accommodations may be made to enable individuals with disabilities to perform the essential functions.

EDUCATION and/or EXPERIENCE

Master's degree (M.A.) or equivalent; or four to ten years related experience and/or training; or equivalent combination of education and experience.

LANGUAGE SKILLS

Ability to read, analyze, and interpret common scientific and technical journals, financial reports, and legal documents. Ability to respond to common inquiries or complaints from customers, regulatory agencies, or members of the business community. Ability to write speeches and articles for publication that conform to prescribed style and format. Ability to effectively present information to top management, public groups, and/or boards of directors.

MATHEMATICAL SKILLS

Ability to apply advanced mathematical concepts such as exponents, logarithms, quadratic equations, and permutations. Ability to apply mathematical operations to such tasks as frequency distribution, determination of test reliability and validity, analysis of variance, correlation techniques, sampling theory, and factor analysis.

REASONING ABILITY

Ability to define problems, collect data, establish facts, and draw valid conclusions. Ability to interpret an extensive variety of technical instructions in mathematical or diagram form.

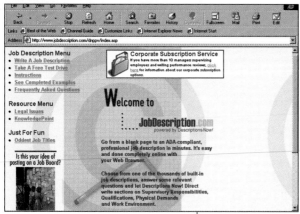

personnel planning

the process of determining the organization's future personnel needs, as well as the methods to be used to fill those needs.

personnel replacement chart

company records showing present performance and promotability of inside candidates for the most important positions.

position replacement card

a card prepared for each position in a company to show possible replacement candidates and their qualifications.

recruiting

attracting a pool of viable job applicants.

Job analysis is part of personnel planning. **Personnel planning** is the process of determining the organization's personnel needs, as well as the methods to be used to fill those needs. If Sears decides to create a new department to handle Internet retail sales, it will need to do personnel planning. This will involve developing job descriptions and specifications to determine what sorts of people it will need to staff the new department. And its personnel plans should lay out where those new employees will come from (from within or from outside the current Sears employee pool), and how they should be trained and developed to function effectively.

Thanks to computers, personnel planning is becoming increasingly sophisticated. Many firms maintain data banks containing information on hundreds of traits (like special skills, product knowledge, work experience, training courses, relocation limitations, and career interests) for each of their employees. Such systems can make it much easier to identify promotable current employees and their training needs.[4]

The availability of so much employee data can obviously make it easier to plan for and fill positions in big companies. However, it also intensifies the need to protect the privacy of the data that are stored in the firm's computers.

Personnel planning needn't always involve sophisticated computer systems, especially in smaller firms. For example, many employers use **personnel replacement charts** (Figure 9.3) to keep track of inside candidates for their most important positions. These show the present performance and promotability for each potential replacement for important positions. As an alternative, you can use a **position replacement card**. You make up a card for each position, showing possible replacements as well as present performance, promotion potential, and training required by each possible candidate.

Employee Recruiting

Once you know what jobs must be filled, **recruiting**—attracting a pool of viable job applicants—becomes very important. If you have only two candidates for two openings, you may have little choice but to hire them. But if many applicants appear, you can use techniques like interviews and tests to hire the best.

Effective recruiting is especially important today, for several reasons. First, the U.S. unemployment rate has been declining for several years, which has led some experts to refer to the current recruiting situation as one of "evaporated employee sources."[5] Many also believe that today's Generation X employees (those born between 1963 and 1977) are less inclined to build long-term employment relationships than were their predecessors.[6] High average turnover rates for some occupations is another problem; the average annual turnover rate for high-tech employees is 14.5%, according to one recent study.[7]

Current Employees   While *recruiting* often brings to mind employment agencies and classified ads, current employees are often the largest source of recruits. Filling open positions with inside candidates has both pros and cons. On the plus side, employees see that competence is rewarded and morale and performance may thus

▼ **FIGURE 9.3** **Management Personnel Replacement Chart**

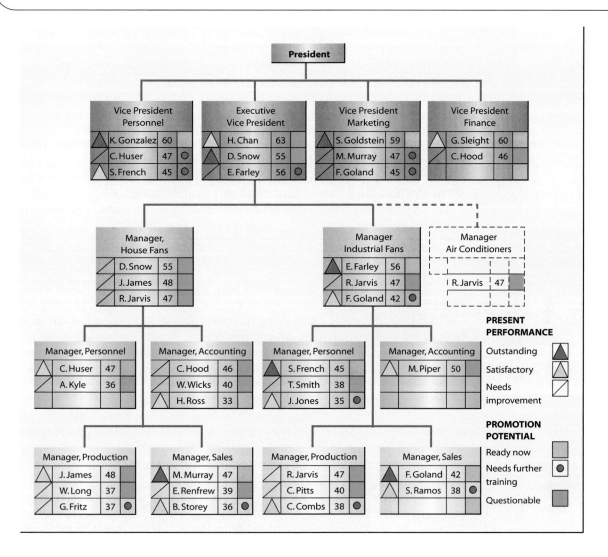

be enhanced. Inside candidates are also known quantities in terms of performance and skills, and may already be committed to the company and its goals.

On the other hand, current employees who apply for jobs and don't get them may become demoralized. Inbreeding is another drawback: When an entire management team has been brought up through the ranks, there may be a tendency to maintain the status quo when innovation and a new direction are needed. Some companies (like Delta Airlines) have thus recently gone outside to hire their CEOs.

Promotion from within generally requires job posting.[8] **Job posting** means publicizing the open job to employees (often by literally posting it on bulletin boards and Intranets) and listing the job's attributes, like qualifications, supervisor, working schedule, and pay rate (see Figure A9.2 on page 287). Some union contracts require job posting to ensure that union members get first choice of new and better positions. Job posting can be a good practice, even in nonunion firms, if it facilitates the transfer and promotion of qualified inside candidates.[9]

job posting

publicizing an open job to employees (often by literally posting it on bulletin boards) and listing its attributes, like qualifications, supervisor, working schedule, and pay rate.

Advertising   As you know from the many help-wanted ads that appear in your local newspaper, advertising is a major way to attract applicants. The main issue here is selecting the best advertising medium, be it the local paper, the *Wall Street Journal*, or a technical journal.

The medium chosen depends on the type of job and on how wide a net the company believes it has to use. The local newspaper is usually best for blue-collar help, clerical employees, and lower-level management employees. For specialists, employers often advertise in trade and professional journals like *American Psychologist, Sales Management*, and *Chemical Engineering*. Executive jobs are often advertised in the *Wall Street Journal*.

Employment Agencies   An employment agency is an intermediary whose business is to match applicants with positions. There are three types of agencies: (1) those operated by federal, state, or local governments; (2) those associated with not-for-profit organizations; and (3) those that are privately owned.

Public employment agencies exist in every state and are often referred to as *job service* or *unemployment service agencies*. Agencies like these are a major free source of hourly blue-collar and clerical workers and are increasingly establishing themselves as agents for professional and managerial-level applicants as well.

Other employment agencies are associated with not-for-profit organizations. For example, most professional and technical societies have units to help members find jobs.

Private agencies charge a fee for each applicant they place. These fees are usually set by state law and are posted in the agencies' offices. Whether the employer or the candidate pays the fee is mostly determined by market conditions. The trend in the past few years has been toward "fee paid" jobs, in which the employer pays the fees. These agencies are important sources of clerical, white-collar, and managerial personnel.

Temporary Help Agencies   Many employers today supplement their permanent employee base by hiring **contingent** (or **temporary**) **workers**, often through special agencies. The contingent workforce is big and growing, recently accounting for about 20% of all new jobs created in the United States. It is broadly defined as workers who don't have permanent jobs.[10]

Contingent staffing owes its growing popularity to several things. First, corporate downsizing seems to be driving up the number of temp workers firms employ. For example, while DuPont cut its workforce by 47,000 in recent years, it also estimates that about 14,000 workers returned in some temporary capacity, or as vendors or contractors.[11] Employers have always used temps to fill in for the days or weeks that permanent employees were out sick or on vacation. Today's desire for ever-higher productivity also contributes to temp workers' growing popularity. In general, as one expert puts it, "Productivity is measured in terms of output per hour paid for." "If employees are paid only when they're working, as contingent workers are, overall productivity increases."[12]

Executive Recruiters   **Executive recruiters** (also ominously called *headhunters*) are agencies retained by employers to look for top management talent, usually in the $70,000 and up category.

These firms have many business contacts, and are adept at contacting qualified candidates who are employed and not actively looking to change jobs. They can also keep a client firm's name confidential until late in the search process. The recruiter saves management time by doing the work of advertising for the position

contingent worker
a temporary worker hired by an employer to fill short-term needs; not a permanent full-time, or part-time employee.

executive recruiter
an agency retained by employers to seek out top management talent.

and screening what could turn out to be hundreds of applicants. The process usually starts with the recruiter meeting with the client to formulate a description of the position to be filled and the sort of person required to fill it. The recruiter then uses various methods to identify candidates, interview these people, and present a short list to the client for final screening.

Top firms used to take up to seven months to complete a search, with much of that time spent shuffling between head-hunters and researchers who dig up the initial long list of candidates.[13] This often takes too long in today's fast-moving environment. Most search firms are therefore creating Internet-linked computerized databases, the aim of which, according to one senior recruiter, is "to create a long list [of candidates] by pushing a button."[14] Recruiter Korn/Ferry launched a new Internet service called Futurestep to draw more managerial applicants into its files; in turn, it has teamed up with the *Wall Street Journal*, which runs a career Web site of its own.[15] The "Entrepreneurs in Action" box shows how Melba Duncan built a search firm from scratch—and how she chooses great candidates.

▲ Melba Duncan of Duncan Group, Inc.: Duncan's screening techniques enable her to successfully place top-ranked executive/administrative assistants.

Referrals and Walk-ins Particularly for hourly workers, walk-ins—people who apply directly at the office—are a major source of applicants. Encouraging walk-in applicants may be as simple as posting a handwritten help-wanted sign in a window. Some organizations encourage walk-in applicants by mounting employee referral campaigns. Announcements of openings and requests for referrals are made in the company's newsletter or posted on bulletin boards and Intranets.

Employee referral programs are increasingly popular. Of the firms responding to one survey, 40% said they use an employee referral system and hire about 15% of their employees through such referrals. A cash award for referring hired candidates is the most common incentive. The cost per hire, however, was uniformly low; average per-hire expenses were only $388, far below the cost of an employment service.[16] Recruiting high-tech employees is especially amenable to such programs. In fact, some experts contend that the most effective recruiting method is to encourage existing employees to refer qualified friends and colleagues.[17]

College Recruiting College recruiting—sending employers' representatives to college campuses to pre-screen applicants and create an applicant pool from that college's graduating class—is an important source of management trainees, promotable candidates, and professional and technical employees. One study of 251 staffing professionals concluded, for instance, that about 38% of all externally filled jobs requiring a college degree were filled by new college graduates.[18] What do recruiters look for in new college grads? The report presented in Figure 9.4 is typical. Traits assessed include motivation, communication skills, education, appearance, and attitude.[19]

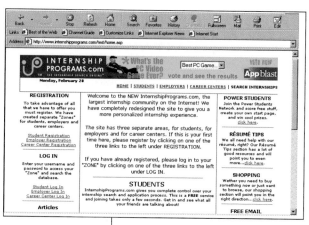

▲ **W E B N O T E**

Many companies today use the Internet to search for applicants to fill their internship programs.

www.internshipprograms.com

Source: Copyright © 1998–1999, InternshipPrograms.com, Inc.

"One day," as Melba J. Duncan recalls, "I woke up, and I knew: This is a business!"[20] After years as an administrative assistant to CEOs at companies like Wall Street's Lehman Brothers, Duncan decided to strike out on her own. She correctly believed that top-ranked administrative/executive assistants were an overlooked region of the retained-search industry. Today her company successfully places administrative assistants who command salaries ranging from $55,000 to $130,000 per year, not counting bonuses and benefits, with clients including IBM, Home Depot, Bankers Trust, and the Boston Consulting group.

With years as a top assistant herself, Duncan combines a complete understanding of what the job calls for with a comprehensive system for selecting great candidates. For Duncan, it all starts with recruiting: She knows that to send three great finalists to a client, she'll need to start with a pool of 100. Her recruiters therefore work the phones "like air-traffic controllers," and review their files and their network of contacts. An initial screening cuts the original candidate pool to about 50; these complete a 15-page questionnaire, after which the pool is further cut to about 15.[21]

The screening doesn't stop there. Those 15 then go through a four-hour testing and profiling process that helps highlight their written and oral communication and clerical skills, and their management aptitude and personality. A clinical psychologist spends two days per week in Duncan's office, interviewing candidates and compiling profiles. Clients usually get their first three solid prospects within five days of the official opening of the search, along with a complete file on each candidate's background and work history. Duncan's favorite questions for applicants are summarized below.[22]

Duncan's Five Fave Questions for Applicants

At the Duncan Group candidates are asked to complete a 15-page questionnaire. It's jammed with mind-benders such as "What does service mean to you?" and "What places, people, ideas, or things arouse your curiosity?" The questionnaire doesn't change, but the questions Duncan is inspired to ask during face-to-face interviews always do. Here are her current favorites, culled from the questionnaire and the interviews:

1. Describe your worst boss and best boss. ("I'm partly thinking about discretion," says Duncan. "How much are you telling me that I shouldn't know?")

2. What would a previous employer have to say about you? ("For perspective on flexibility, judgment, and maturity.")

3. What are some of the qualities that enable you to perform successfully in a support role? ("People are more important than technology in this job; of course you need both, but does the answer reveal a technician?")

4. Given the opportunity, what new activities would you try? ("Are you curious, outgoing, strong, confident? Whiners aren't good.")

5. Please write a brief paragraph on the subject of your own choosing. You may want to focus on your life, your family, your aspirations, your goals, or your achievements. ("There's nothing as important as having people's best interests at heart; I want to guide them into the right position and this answer will help me do that. I want to know they have a sense of direction. I want to know what they care about. Also, attention to detail: please, no typos!")

Source: Reprinted with permission of Inc. Magazine, from "First Aide," by Nancy Austin, September 1999, copyright © 1999; permission conveyed through Copyright Clearance Center, Inc.

CAMPUS INTERVIEW REPORT

Name_____ Anticipated Graduation Date_____

Current Address_____
If different than placement form

Position Applied For_____
_____

If Applicable (Use Comment Section if necessary)

      Driver's License   Yes _____ No _____

      Any special considerations affecting your availability for relocation?
_____
_____

      Are you willing to travel? _____ If so, what % of time? _____

EVALUATION	Outstanding	Above Average	Average	Below Average
Education: Courses relevant to job? Does performance in class indicate good potential for work?	_____	_____	_____	_____
Appearance: Was applicant neat and dressed appropriately?	_____	_____	_____	_____
Communication Skills: Was applicant mentally alert? Did he or she express ideas clearly?	_____	_____	_____	_____
Motivation: Does applicant have high energy level? Are his or her interests compatible with job?	_____	_____	_____	_____
Attitude: Did applicant appear to be pleasant, people-oriented?	_____	_____	_____	_____

COMMENTS: (Use back of sheet if necessary)
_____
_____
_____

Given Application   Yes_____ No_____ Received Transcript Release Authorization _____

Recommendations Invite _____ Reject _____

Interviewed by: _____ Date: _____

Campus _____

Source: Adapted from Joseph J. Famularo, *Handbook of Personnel Forms, Records, and Reports* (New York: McGraw-Hill, 1982), p. 70.

Many college students get their jobs through college internships; it's estimated that today almost three-quarters of all college students take part in an internship before they graduate, compared to 1 in 36 in 1980, for instance.[23]

Internships can be win–win situations for both students and employers. For students, it may mean being able to hone business skills, check out potential employers, and learn more about their likes (and dislikes) when it comes to choosing careers. And employers, of course, can use interns to make useful contributions while they're being evaluated as possible full-time employees.

MANAGING @ THE SPEED OF THOUGHT

■ Recruiting on the Internet

A growing number of employers recruit via the Internet. In one survey, 32% of the 203 respondents said they were using the Internet as a primary recruitment source.[24]

Many Internet job-placement and recruiting sources are available today (Figures 9.5 and 9.6). For example, the personnel journal *Workforce* has a Web site (www.workforceonline.com/postajob/) with links to various sites, including "best Internet recruiter," general recruitment Web sites, college recruitment Web sites, and specific industry recruitment Web sites. It also lets you place your own help-wanted ad on-line at the *Workforce* Web site. Yahoo (employment.yahoo.com/) is another site where you can place and access employment classified ads.

▼ **FIGURE 9.5**

Employment Services on a Company's Web Site

Progressive Corp. is just one of many firms that posts a recruiting page on its Web site. Such pages often include a means for job applicants to e-mail their resumes and research what it would be like to work at the firm.

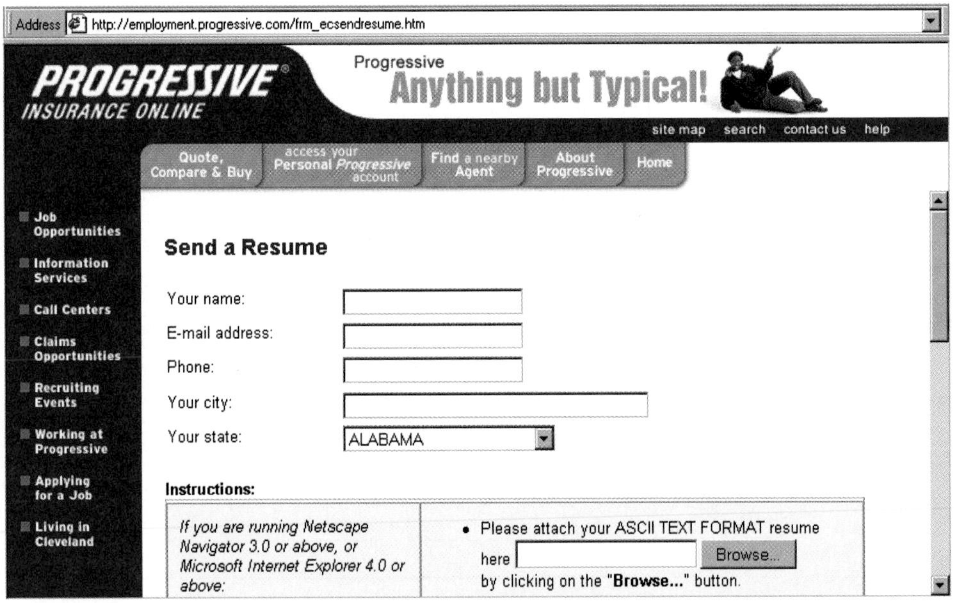

Many Web site services permit employers to post their open positions, in this case for a fee.

| Address | C:\TEMP\hrcc52.htm |

JOBS Direct Placement

Welcome to JOBS Direct Placement. As an employer, you can use this online service to post your job openings in a database which currently receives **over 450,000 queries every day.**

If you are a new advertiser interested in posting your employment opportunities on CareerMosaic's JOBS Database, please register on the new advertiser form. Once we receive your form, a representative from JOBS Direct Placement will contact you, via email, to give you an ID number, verify your submission, and arrange for payment. If you have previously posted jobs directly through this section of CareerMosaic and have been assigned an ID number, go directly to the registered advertiser form. A representative from JOBS Direct Placement will contact you, via email, to confirm your job posting.

You may also request additional information regarding advertising on CareerMosaic.
Questions? Call us at our toll free number: 1-888-339-8989.

Here are some guidelines to help get your job into immediate circulation:

- Each job record is **$160.**
- Each job record should contain **one job title** and **one job description**.
- Job records run in our database for 30 days. They expire automatically.
- Make sure to complete **all** fields.
- You may include information about your company in the job description field.
- Make sure the job description is comprehensive. The more information you provide for the job seeker, the better the chance it will be found by the right people. You have plenty of room -- up to 16,000 characters...or about 40 paragraphs.
- The description should also include **clear response instructions**.
- Please indicate your preferred payment method (**credit card** or **invoice**) for each job.

Employers are using Internet recruiting in various ways. One Boston-based recruiting firm posts job descriptions on its Web page.[25] NEC Electronics, Inc., Unisys Corp., and LSI Logicorp have all used Internet-based "cyber fairs" to recruit applicants.[26] A Minneapolis-based computer firm uses the Internet to search for temporary workers with extensive knowledge of Microsoft Excel.[27] And Cisco Systems, Inc., (as noted earlier) has a Web site with an employment opportunities page. It offers links to such things as hot jobs (job descriptions for hard-to-fill positions), Cisco culture (a look at Cisco work life), Cisco College (internships and mentoring program information), and jobs (job listings).[28]

Getting résumés and listings via the Web is only part of the Web's possibilities. At Peoplesoft Company, for instance, applications sent via the Web or fax are automatically deposited into a database (those submitted on paper are first scanned into a computer). When a hiring manager selects an applicant for interview, the system automatically phones the applicant and asks him or her to select an interview time by punching buttons on a touch-tone phone. After the call, the database system notifies the interviewers of the appointment, and sends a reminder on the day of the interview—all without human interaction.[29] Now that's managing @ the speed of thought!

Recruiting a More Diverse Workforce   Recruiting a diverse workforce is not just socially responsible; it's a necessity, given the rapid growth in the number of minority and female candidates. This means taking special steps to recruit older workers, minorities, and women.

There are many things an employer can do to assist it in these efforts. Because some minority applicants may not meet the educational or experience standards for a job, many firms offer remedial training in basic arithmetic and writing.[30] Diversity data banks or nonspecialized minority-focused recruiting publications are another option. For example, Hispan Data provides recruiters at companies like

▲ Recruiting a diverse workforce: many companies are actively recruiting older workers, minorities, and women.

McDonald's access to a computerized data bank; it costs a candidate $5 to be included.[31] Checking with your own minority employees can also be useful: About 32% of job seekers of Hispanic origin cited "check with friends or relatives" as a strategy when looking for jobs.[32]

Employers are also implementing various "welfare-to-work" programs for attracting and assimilating former welfare recipients. In 1996 President Clinton signed the Personal Responsibility and Welfare Reconciliation Act of 1996. The act required 25% of people receiving welfare assistance to be either working or involved in a work-training program by September 30, 1997, with the percentage rising each year to 50% by September 30, 2002.[33]

The key to a welfare-to-work program's success seems to be the employer's "pretraining" assimilation and socialization program, during which participants receive counseling and basic skills training.[34] Marriott International has hired 600 welfare recipients under its Pathways to Independence program. The heart of the program is a six-week preemployment training program teaching work and "life skills designed to rebuild workers' self-esteem and instill positive attitudes about work."[35]

▶ SELECTING EMPLOYEES

With a pool of applicants to fill open slots, the employer can turn to screening and selecting. These processes use one or more techniques, including application blanks, interviews, tests, and reference checks, to assess and investigate an applicant's aptitudes, interests, and background. The company then chooses the best candidate, given the job's requirements.

In terms of strategic human resource management, how you select employees and who you select also ties in to the company's overall strategic plan. For example, Microsoft has always been a very intense and competitive company, and its human resource strategy therefore includes a rigorous selection process aimed at hiring the best and most intelligent employees it can find. As another example, Toyota Motor Manufacturing builds its manufacturing strategy in large part around letting highly motivated and well-trained self-managing teams do most of the work. Its HR strategy therefore emphasizes selecting employees who have the decision-making and interpersonal skills to thrive in such an environment.

Employee selection is important for several specific reasons. As a manager, your job performance always hinges on subordinates' performance. A poor performer drags a manager down, and a good one enhances the manager's performance. The best time to screen out undesirables is before they have their foot in the door—not after.

Screening applicants is also expensive, so it is best to do it right the first time. Hiring a manager who earns $60,000 a year may cost as much as $40,000 or $50,000, including search fees, interviewing time, and travel and moving expenses. The cost of hiring even nonexecutive employees can be $3,000 to $5,000 or more.

Application Forms

Once you have a pool of applicants, the selection process can begin. For most employers, the **application form** is the first step. (Some firms first require a brief prescreening interview.) The application form is a good way to quickly collect verifiable and therefore fairly accurate historical data from the candidate. It usually includes information about such areas as education, prior work history, and hobbies.

In practice, most organizations need several application forms. For technical and managerial personnel, for example, the form may require detailed answers to questions concerning education and experience. The form for hourly factory workers might focus on the tools and equipment the applicant has used.

application form

a form that requests information such as education, work history, and hobbies from a job candidate as a means of quickly collecting verifiable historical data.

Testing for Employee Selection

A *test* is basically a sample of a person's behavior. It is used in personnel management for predicting success on the job. Tests are widely used today. For example, about 45% of 1,085 companies surveyed by the American Management Association in 1998 tested applicants for basic skills (defined as the ability to read instructions, write reports, and do arithmetic at a level adequate to perform common workplace tasks).[36] Another survey by the American Management Association recently concluded that 38.6% of the companies it surveyed said they performed psychological testing on job applicants, ranging from tests of the applicants' cognitive abilities to "honesty testing."[37] If you want to see what such tests are like, try the short test in Figure 9.7 to see how prone you might be to on-the-job accidents.

CHECK YES OR NO	YES	NO
1. You like a lot of excitement in your life.		
2. An employee who takes it easy at work is cheating on the employer.		
3. You are a cautious person.		
4. In the past three years you have found yourself in a shouting match at school or work.		
5. You like to drive fast just for fun.		

Analysis: According to John Kamp, an industrial psychologist, applicants who answered no, yes, yes, no, no to questions 1, 2, 3, 4, and 5 are statistically likely to be absent less often, to have fewer on-the-job injuries, and, if the job involves driving, to have fewer on-the-job driving accidents. Actual scores on the test are based on answers to 130 questions.

◀ **FIGURE 9.7**

Sample Test

Source: Courtesy of NYT Permissions.

© 1997 Randy Glasbergen.

GLASBERGEN

"Rusty, you've been my dog for three years now and I'm afraid you're getting stale. I'd like you to be my parakeet for the next six months."

Many types of tests are available. Intelligence (IQ) tests like the Stanford-Binet or the Wechsler or Wonderlic tests are designed to measure general intellectual abilities. For some jobs, managers are also interested in testing other abilities. The Bennett Test of Mechanical Comprehension (illustrated in Figure 9.8) helps to assess an applicant's understanding of basic mechanical principles and might be

▶ **FIGURE 9.8**

Bennett Test of Mechanical Comprehension, Example

Human resource managers often use personnel tests, like this one, to measure a candidate's skills and aptitudes.

Source: Bennett Mechanical Comprehension Test. Copyright 1942, 1967–1970, 1980 by The Psychological Corporation, a Harcourt Assessment Company. Reproduced by permission. All rights reserved. "Bennett Mechanical Comprehension Test" and "BMCT" are registered trademarks of The Psychological Corporation.

Look at Sample X on this page. It shows two men carrying a weighted object on a plank, and it asks, Which man carries more weight? Because the object is closer to man B than to man A, man B is shouldering more weight; so blacken the circle under B on your answer sheet. Now look at Sample Y and answer it yourself. Fill in the circle under the correct answer on your answer sheet.

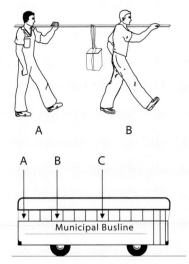

X
Which man carries more weight? (If equal, mark C.)

Examples

A B C
X ○ ● ○

A B C
Y ○ ○ ○

Y

Which letter shows the seat where a passenger will get the smoothest ride?

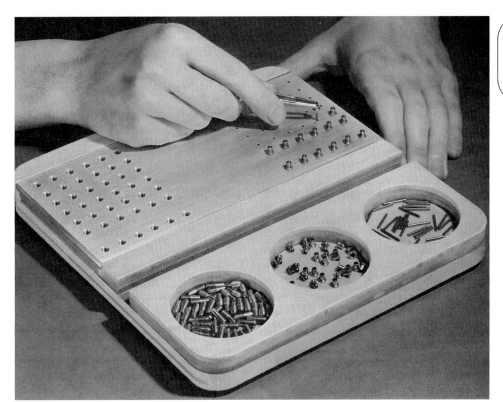

useful for predicting success on a job such as machinist or engineer. A test like the Crawford Small Parts Dexterity Test (see Figure 9.9) is used to measure the applicant's speed of finger, hand, and arm movements. This would be useful if the job in question involves manipulating small items (for instance, assembling computer circuit boards).

It is also sometimes useful to measure personality and interests. For example, you probably wouldn't hire someone for an entry-level job as an accounting clerk if he or she had no measurable interest in working with numbers![38] As another example, service management expert Karl Albrecht says that service jobs require high levels of emotional labor. *Emotional labor* is any work in which the employee's feelings are the tools of his or her trade (for instance, an airline reservation clerk is expected to deal courteously with each caller). Most of us have had some experience dealing with service people who are obviously not psychologically suited for such jobs. A personality test might have screened them out.

A **management assessment center** is another selection technique. In such centers, about a dozen candidates spend two or three days performing realistic management tasks (like making presentations) while being observed by expert appraisers. Each candidate's potential is assessed.[39] The center's activities might include individual presentations, objective tests, interviews, and participation in management games. Participants engage in realistic problem solving, usually as members of two or three simulated companies that are competing in a mock marketplace.

management assessment center

a development and/or selection device wherein management candidates spend two or three days performing realistic management tasks under the observation of appraisers.

■ Hiring Happy Employees

With all the aptitudes, skills, and traits for which managers can test applicants, there is still one thing that's usually not tested for but that perhaps should be—at least if some recent research findings are valid. Particularly in companies being rocked by downsizings and competitive pressures, there's something to be said about hiring people who are inclined to remain happy even in the face of unhappy events. A recent line of research suggests that it might be possible to do so.

Basically, this line of research suggests that happiness seems to be largely determined by the person's genetic makeup—that, in other words, some people are simply born to be somewhat happier than others.[40] The theory, in a nutshell, says that people have a sort of "set point" for happiness, a genetically determined happiness level to which the person quickly tends to gravitate, no matter what failures or successes he or she experiences. So confront a high-happiness-set-point person with the prospect of a demotion or an unattractive lateral transfer, and he or she will soon return to being relatively happy once the short blip of disappointment has dissipated. On the other hand, send an inherently low-set-point, unhappy person off on a two-week vacation or give him or her a sizable raise or a new computer, and chances are he or she will soon be as unhappy as before the reward.

Several lines of research lend support to this theory. A study of lottery winners found that they were on the whole no happier a year after their good fortune than they were before. Several studies show that even people with spinal-cord injuries tend to rebound in spirits.[41] Studies of identical twins led one psychologist to conclude that life circumstances like salary, education, or marital status predicted only 2% of the happiness variation within each pair of twins, and that much of the rest was simply determined by the person's genes. In fact, the results of several long-term studies that followed people over many years suggest that the people who are happiest today will also be the happiest 10 years from now.

Like testing employees for any traits, coming up with a set of tests or interview questions to identify happier, high-set-point people requires careful consideration and probably the help of a licensed psychologist. However, the following might provide some insight into the tendency to be relatively happy:

Indicate how strongly (high, medium, low) you agree with the following statements:

- ■ "When good things happen to me, it strongly affects me."
- ■ "I will often do things for no other reason than they might be fun."
- ■ "When I get something I want, I feel excited and energized."
- ■ "When I'm doing well at something, I love to keep at it."

Agreeing with more statements and agreeing with them more strongly *may* correlate with a higher happiness set-point.[42]

Interviews

Both before and after any testing occurs, several interviews are usually in order. The interview is probably the single most widely used selection device.

How to Be a Good Interviewer   The problem is that while almost everyone gets a job interview, most interviews don't produce very reliable information. However, a manager can boost the usefulness of selection interviews by following sound procedures like these:[43]

Plan the interview Begin by reviewing the candidate's application and résumé, and note any areas that are vague or may indicate strengths or weaknesses. Review the job specification and start the interview with a clear picture of the traits of an ideal candidate.

If possible, use a structured form. Interviews based on a structured guide, as in Figure 9.10, usually result in the best interviews.[44] At a minimum, write out your questions prior to the interview. The interview should take place in a private room where telephone calls are not accepted and interruptions can be minimized.

Delay your decision. Interviewers often make snap judgments even before they see the candidate—on the basis of the application form, for instance—or during the first few minutes of the interview. Plan on keeping a record of the interview and review it afterward. Make your decision then.[45]

◄ FIGURE 9.10

Structured Interview Form for College Applicants

CANDIDATE RECORD — **NAP 100 (10/77)**

CANDIDATE NUMBER: I ☐☐☐ U 921 (1–7)
NAME (LAST NAME FIRST): ☐☐☐☐☐☐☐☐☐☐☐☐☐☐☐☐☐☐☐☐ (8–27)
COLLEGE NAME: ____________
COLLEGE CODE: ☐☐☐ (28–30)

INTERVIEWER NUMBER: ☐☐☐☐0☐☐☐☐ (33–40)
INTERVIEWER NAME: ____________

SOURCE (41)		RACE (42)		SEX (43)		DEGREE (53)		AVERAGE	CLASS STANDING (59–59)	
Campus	☐ C	White	☐ W	Male	☐ M	Bachelors	☐ B	(A = 4.0)	Top 10%	☐ 10
Walk-in	☐ W	Black	☐ B	Female	☐ F	Masters	☐ M	Overall ☐☐ (54-55)	Top 25%	☐ 25
Intern	☐ I	Asian	☐ A	Init.		Law	☐ L	Acctg. ☐☐ (56-57)	Top Half	☐ 50
Agency	☐ A	Hispanic	☐ H	Cont. ☐☐☐☐☐☐☐		Majors			Bottom Half	☐ 75
		Native Am.	☐ NA	Date						

CAMPUS INTERVIEW EVALUATIONS

ATTITUDE – MOTIVATION – GOALS

POOR ☐ AVERAGE ☐ GOOD ☐ OUTSTANDING ☐

(POSITIVE, COOPERATIVE, ENERGETIC, MOTIVATED, SUCCESSFUL, GOAL-ORIENTED)

COMMENTS:

COMMUNICATIONS SKILLS – PERSONALITY – SALES ABILITY

POOR ☐ AVERAGE ☐ GOOD ☐ OUTSTANDING ☐

(ARTICULATE, LISTENS, ENTHUSIASTIC, LIKEABLE, POISED, TACTFUL, ACCEPTED, CONVINCING)

COMMENTS:

EXECUTIVE PRESENCE – DEAL WITH TOP PEOPLE

POOR ☐ AVERAGE ☐ GOOD ☐ OUTSTANDING ☐

(IMPRESSIVE, STANDS OUT, A WINNER, REMEMBERED, LEVELHEADED, AT EASE, AWARE)

COMMENTS:

INTELLECTUAL ABILITIES

POOR ☐ AVERAGE ☐ GOOD ☐ OUTSTANDING ☐

(INSIGHTFUL, CREATIVE, CURIOUS, IMAGINATIVE, UNDERSTANDS, REASONS, INTELLIGENT, SCHOLARLY)

COMMENTS:

JUDGMENT – DECISION MAKING ABILITY

POOR ☐ AVERAGE ☐ GOOD ☐ OUTSTANDING ☐

(MATURE, SEASONED, INDEPENDENT, COMMON SENSE, CERTAIN, DETERMINED, LOGICAL)

COMMENTS:

LEADERSHIP

POOR ☐ AVERAGE ☐ GOOD ☐ OUTSTANDING ☐

(SELF-CONFIDENT, TAKES CHARGE, EFFECTIVE, RESPECTED, MANAGEMENT MINDED, GRASPS AUTHORITY)

COMMENTS:

CAMPUS INTERVIEW SUMMARY

INVITE (Circle)	AREA OF INTEREST (Circle)		SEMESTER HRS.	OFFICES PREFERRED:	SUMMARY COMMENTS:
Yes No	AUDIT	TAX	Acct'g. ____	No. 1 ____	
DATE AVAILABLE	MCS	ABC	Audit ____	No. 2 ____	
	OTHER		Tax ____	No. 3 ____	

Establish rapport The main purpose of the interview is to find out about the applicant. To do this, start by putting the person at ease. Greet the candidate and begin the interview by asking a noncontroversial question—perhaps about the weather or the traffic conditions that day. As a rule, all applicants—even unsolicited drop-ins—should receive friendly, courteous treatment, not only on humanitarian grounds, but also because your reputation is on the line.

Understand the applicant's status. If you are interviewing someone who is unemployed, he or she may be exceptionally nervous and you may want to take additional steps to relax the person.[46]

Ask questions Try to follow your structured interview guide or the questions you wrote out ahead of time. A list of questions (such as "What best qualifies you for the available position?") is presented in Figure 9.11.

Some suggestions for asking questions include these:

- Avoid questions that can be answered simply *yes* or *no*.
- Don't put words in the applicant's mouth or telegraph the desired answer (for instance, by nodding or smiling when the right answer is given).
- Don't interrogate the applicant as if the person were a criminal, and don't be patronizing, sarcastic, or inattentive.
- Don't monopolize the interview by rambling, or let the applicant dominate the interview so you can't ask all your questions.
- Listen to the candidate and encourage him or her to express thoughts fully. Draw out the applicant's opinions and feelings by repeating the person's last comment as a question (such as "You didn't like your last job?")

Don't just ask for general statements about a candidate's accomplishments, also ask for specific examples.[47] If the candidate lists specific strengths or weaknesses, follow up with, "What are specific examples that demonstrate each of your strengths?" Ask situational questions: make the person explain how he or she would handle a specific hypothetical situation.

Close the interview Toward the end of the interview, leave time to answer any questions the candidate may have and, if appropriate, to promote your firm to the candidate.

Try to close interviews on a positive note. The applicant should be told whether there is an interest in him or her and, if so, what the next step will be. Rejections should be made diplomatically, with a statement like, "Although your background is impressive, there are other candidates whose experience is closer to our requirements." If the applicant is still being considered but a decision can't be reached at once, say so. If it is your policy to inform candidates of their status in writing, do so within a few days of the interview.

Review the interview After the candidate leaves, review your notes, fill in the structured interview guide (if this was not done during the interview), and review the interview while it's fresh in your mind.

Remember that making snap judgments is an all too common interviewing mistake: Reviewing the interview shortly after the candidate has left can help you minimize this problem.

1. Did you bring a résumé?
2. What salary do you expect to receive?
3. What was your salary in your last job?
4. Why do you want to change jobs or why did you leave your last job?
5. What do you identify as your most significant accomplishment in your last job?
6. How many hours do you normally work per week?
7. What did you like and dislike about your last job?
8. How did you get along with your superiors and subordinates?
9. Can you be demanding of your subordinates?
10. How would you evaluate the company you were with last?
11. What were its competitive strengths and weaknesses?
12. What best qualifies you for the available position?
13. How long will it take you to start making a significant contribution?
14. How do you feel about our company—its size, industry, and competitive position?
15. What interests you most about the available position?
16. How would you structure this job or organize your department?
17. What control or financial data would you want and why?
18. How would you establish your primary inside and outside lines of communication?
19. What would you like to tell me about yourself?
20. Were you a good student?
21. Have you kept up in your field? How?
22. What do you do in your spare time?
23. What are your career goals for the next five years?
24. What are your greatest strengths and weaknesses?
25. What is your job potential?
26. What steps are you taking to help achieve your goals?
27. Do you want to own your own business?
28. How long will you stay with us?
29. What did your father do? Your mother?
30. What do your brothers and sisters do?
31. Have you ever worked on a group project and, if so, what role did you play?
32. Do you participate in civic affairs?
33. What professional associations do you belong to?
34. What is your credit standing?
35. What are your personal likes and dislikes?
36. How do you spend a typical day?
37. Would you describe your family as a close one?
38. How aggressive are you?
39. What motivates you to work?
40. Is money a strong incentive for you?
41. Do you prefer line or staff work?
42. Would you rather work alone or in a team?
43. What do you look for when hiring people?
44. Have you ever fired anyone?
45. Can you get along with union members and their leaders?
46. What do you think of the current economic and political situation?
47. How will government policy affect our industry or your job?
48. Will you sign a noncompete agreement or employment contract?
49. Why should we hire you?
50. Do you want the job?

◀ F I G U R E   9 . 1 1

Interview Questions to Ask Candidates

Source: H. Lee Rust, *Job Search, The Complete Manual for Job Seekers* (New York: AMACOM, 1991), pp. 232–33. Reprinted from *Job Search: The Complete Manual for Job Seekers*, copyright © 1990 H. Lee Rust. Reprinted by permission of AMACOM, a division of American Management Association International, New York, NY. All rights reserved. ⟨www.amanet.org⟩

▲ **W E B N O T E**

Improving your interviewing skills using the Internet: The VirtualResume Web site provides information and help in interviewing, as well as a site for posting resumes.

www.virtualresume.com

Used with permission.

Guidelines for Interviewees Before you get into a position where you have to interview applicants, you will probably have to navigate some interviews yourself. What can you do to excel in your interview?

Here are seven things to do to get that extra edge in the interview:

1. *Be prepared.* Before the interview, learn all you can about the employer, the job, and the people doing the recruiting. Look through business periodicals and Web sites to find out what is happening in the employer's company and industry.

2. *Uncover the interviewer's real needs.* Spend as little time as possible answering your interviewer's first questions and as much time as possible getting him or her to describe his or her needs. Determine what the person is looking for and the type of person he or she feels is needed. Use open-ended questions such as, "Could you tell me more about that?" Sample questions you can ask are presented in Figure 9.12. They include, "Would you mind describing the job for me?" and "Could you tell me about the people who would be reporting to me?"

3. *Relate yourself to the interviewer's needs.* Once you know the type of person your interviewer is looking for and the sorts of problems he or she wants solved, you are in a good position to describe your own accomplishments *in terms of the interviewer's needs.* Start by saying something like, "One of the problem areas you've said is important to you is similar to a problem I once faced." Then state the problem, describe your solution, and reveal the results.

▶ **F I G U R E   9 . 1 2**

Questions to Ask the Interviewer

Source: Reprinted from Job Search: The Complete Manual for Job Seekers, copyright © 1990 H. Lee Rust. Reprinted by permission of AMACOM, a division of American Management Association International, New York, NY. All rights reserved. ⟨www.amanet.org⟩

1. What is the first problem that needs attention of the person you hire?
2. What other problems need attention now?
3. What has been done about any of these to date?
4. How has this job been performed in the past?
5. Why is it now vacant?
6. Do you have a written job description for this position?
7. What are its major responsibilities?
8. What authority would I have? How would you define the job's scope?
9. What are the company's five-year sales and profit projections?
10. What needs to be done to reach these projections?
11. What are the company's major strengths and weaknesses?
12. What are its strengths and weaknesses in production?
13. What are its strengths and weaknesses in its products or its competitive position?
14. Whom do you identify as your major competitors?
15. What are their strengths and weaknesses?
16. How do you view the future for your industry?
17. Do you have any plans for new products or acquisitions?
18. Might this company be sold or acquired?
19. What is the company's current financial strength?
20. What can you tell me about the individual to whom I would report?
21. What can you tell me about other persons in key positions?
22. What can you tell me about the subordinates I would have?
23. How would you define your management philosophy?
24. Are employees afforded an opportunity for continuing education?
25. What are you looking for in the person who will fill this job?

4. *Think before answering.* Answering a question should be a three-step process: pause, think, speak. *Pause* to make sure you understand what the interviewer is driving at, *think* about how to structure your answer, and then *speak.* In your answer, try to emphasize how hiring you will help the interviewer solve his or her problem.

5. *Present a good appearance.* Appropriate clothing, good grooming, a firm handshake, and the appearance of controlled energy are important.

6. *Make a good first impression.* Studies show that, although they should wait, most interviewers make up their minds about the applicant during the early minutes of the interview. A good first impression may turn to a bad one during the interview, but it is unlikely. Bad first impressions are almost impossible to overcome. Remember: You have only one chance to make a good first impression.

7. *Watch your nonverbal behavior.* Remember that your *nonverbal behavior* may broadcast more about you than the verbal content of what you say. Maintaining eye contact is very important. Speak with enthusiasm, nod agreement, and remember to take a moment to frame your answer (pause, think, speak) so that you sound articulate and fluent.[48]

Other Selection Techniques

Various other selection techniques are used to screen applicants.

Background Investigations and Reference Checks   Most employers also try to check the job applicant's background information and references. In fact, some estimate that about 95% of U.S. corporations now do so.[49] The vast majority probably use telephone inquiries. The remainder use sources like commercial credit-checking agencies and reference letters.

Background checks can be quite comprehensive. As *Fortune* magazine recently noted (probably with some exaggeration), if you haven't changed jobs in the past few years, you're in for a rude surprise:

Chances are, your new employer will delve into your driving record, check for criminal charges or convictions, survey your creditworthiness, examine whether you've been sued or have run afoul of the IRS, and sometimes even query co-workers and neighbors about your reputation. Your educational history, past employment, and references listed on your résumé are in for fierce scrutiny.[50]

There are two key reasons for conducting reference and/or background checks: to verify the accuracy of factual information previously provided by the applicant and to discover damaging information such as criminal records and suspended driver's licenses.[51] Lying on one's application is apparently not unusual. For example, BellSouth's security director estimates that between 15% and 20% of applicants conceal a dark secret. As he says, "It's not uncommon to find someone who applies and looks good, and then you do a little digging and you start to see all sorts of criminal history."[52]

The most commonly verified background areas are legal eligibility for employment (to comply with immigration laws), dates of prior employment, military service (including discharge status), education, and identification (including date of birth and address).[53]

Background checks can take many forms. Most companies at least try to verify an applicant's current or previous position and salary with the current employer by telephone. Others call current and previous supervisors to discover more about the person's motivation, technical competence, and ability to work with others. Some employers also get background reports from commercial credit-rating companies; this can provide information about an applicant's credit standing, indebtedness, reputation, character, and lifestyle.

Preemployment Information Services Computer databases have made it easier to check background information about candidates. There was a time when the application form provided the only source of background information on a candidate, and in some cases what the employer could obtain through private investigators. Today so-called preemployment information services use databases to accumulate mounds of information about matters such as workers' compensation histories, credit histories, and conviction records. Employers are increasingly turning to these information services to make the right selection decision. Today you can place a call and obtain data on a person's credit, driving, workers' compensation, and criminal records.

To many people, the ethics of using such information is debatable. For example, Theftnet is a database being tested by several large retailers, including Home Depot and JCPenney. The database contains the names of workers across the country who have been prosecuted for theft or who have signed admissions statements with former employers.[54]

On its face, using a database like Theftnet should be straightforward, focusing as it does on convictions or written admissions. Yet in practice using such a database raises several issues. For example, one attorney says supplying information to the database without "clear proof" of an employee's guilt could make an employer liable for defamation.[55] Similarly, employees who have signed admissions statements may in fact be guilty, but may also have signed for unrelated reasons such as coercion or promises by the employer. Sources like these must therefore be used with considerable caution.

Honesty Testing With so many employees working in jobs in which honesty is important—such as in banks, retail stores, and restaurants—paper-and-pencil "honesty testing" has become a mini-industry.[56] These tests ask questions aimed at assessing a person's tendency to be honest. A test might ask questions such as, "Have you ever made a personal phone call on company time?" Sometimes the test assumes that someone who answers all such questions No may not be entirely honest, although the person may actually be telling the truth.

Health Exams A physical examination and drug screening are often two of the final steps in the selection process. A medical exam is used to confirm that the applicant qualifies for the physical requirements of the position and to discover any medical limitations that should be taken into account. By identifying health problems, a physical exam can also reduce absenteeism and accidents and detect communicable diseases that may be unknown to the applicant.

Unfortunately, drug abuse is a serious work problem. Counselors at the Cocaine National Help Line (800-COCAINE) polled callers. They found that 75% admitted to occasional cocaine use at work, and 25% reported daily drug use at work.[57] As a result, more employers are including drug screening as part of their prehiring programs. In one survey, testing rose from 21% of surveyed firms in 1986 to 48% several years later.[58]

▶ ORIENTATION AND TRAINING

Once employees have been recruited, screened, and selected for the company's open positions, they must be prepared to do their jobs; this is the purpose of orientation and training.

Orienting Employees

Employee **orientation** means providing new employees with basic information on things like work rules and vacation policies. In many companies, employees receive a handbook that contains such information. Orientation aims to: familiarize the new employee with the company and his or her co-workers; provide information about working conditions (coffee breaks, overtime policy, and so on); explain how to get on the payroll, how to obtain identification cards, and what the working hours are; and generally reduce the jitters often associated with starting a new job.

This initial orientation is usually followed by a **training program** aimed at ensuring that the new employee has the basic knowledge and skills required to perform the job. Traditional techniques include on-the-job training, lectures, and, increasingly, other methods—using CD-ROMs and the Internet, for example.[59]

Companies like Starbucks invest a great deal of time and money in training employees (indeed, large U.S. companies alone spent over $62 billion training their employees in one recent year).[60] "Brewing the perfect cup" is one of five classes that all Starbucks "partners" (as employees are called) complete during their first six weeks with the company.[61] What are some of the things they learn? Milk must be steamed at temperatures of at least 150°F; orders are "called out," such as "triple-tall nonfat mocha"; and coffee never sits on the hot plate for more than 20 minutes. Starbucks understands that designing an organization and job descriptions is futile unless the carefully selected employees are also well trained.

Training Techniques

Training techniques have been around for many years, and you've probably experienced some of them yourself. For example, **on-the-job training (OJT)** means having a person learn a job by actually performing it. Virtually every employee, from mailroom clerk to company president, gets some OJT when he or she joins a firm. In many companies, OJT is the only type of training available. It usually involves assigning new employees to experienced workers or supervisors, who then do the actual training.[62]

On the other hand, many training techniques are fairly new, and are based on computers and/or telecommunications. For example, companies are now using *teletraining*, through which a trainer in a central location teaches groups of employees at remote locations via television hookups.[63] AMP Incorporated, which makes electrical and electronic connection devices, uses satellites to train its engineers and technicians at 165 sites in the United States and 27 other countries. To reduce costs for one training program, AMP supplied the program content. PBS affiliate WITF of Harrisburg, Pennsylvania, supplied the equipment and expertise required to broadcast the training program to five AMP facilities in North America.[64] Macy's, the New York–based retailer, recently established the Macy's Satellite Network, in part to provide training to the firm's 59,000 employees around the country.[65]

Training on the Internet is already a reality, and many firms are using the Internet to offer at least some of their programs. For example, Silicon Graphics

orientation
the process of providing new employees with basic information about the employer, such as company policies, working hours, or parking arrangements.

training program
the process of providing new employees with information they need to do their jobs satisfactorily.

on-the-job training (OJT)
training in which a person learns a job while he or she is working at it.

▲ Lexus, the luxury car division of Toyota, uses a computerized simulation called Fact Lab for sales training. Trainees can practice handling a variety of situations.

transferred many of its training materials to CD-ROMs. However, since not every desktop computer had a CD-ROM player, many employees couldn't access the training program. Silicon Graphics is therefore replacing the CD-ROM method with distribution of training materials via its Intranet. "Now employees can access the programs whenever they want. Distribution costs are zero, and if the company wants to make a change to the program, it can do so at a central location."[66]

As a result of such benefits, technology-based learning is booming. Management Recruiters International (MRI) uses the firm's desktop ConferView system to train hundreds of employees—each in their individual offices—simultaneously.[67] Instead of sending new rental sales agents to week-long classroom-based training courses, Value Rent-a-Car now provides them with interactive, multimedia-based training programs utilizing CD-ROMs. These help agents learn the car rental process by walking them through various procedures, such as how to operate the rental computer system.[68]

▶ OTHER TOPICS IN HR MANAGEMENT

Chapters 7 through 9 focus on organizing, and so far in this chapter we've emphasized those HR topics—job analysis, recruitment, selection, and training—that relate directly to filling positions. However, there's obviously more to HR management than just filling positions. We'll therefore look briefly at some other important HR topics in this last section.

Employee Appraisal

appraisal

a manager's evaluation of and feedback on an employee's work performance.

Once employees have been at work for some time, their performance should be appraised, or evaluated. Performance **appraisal** is defined as evaluating an employee's current or past performance relative to his or her performance standards. You've probably already had experience with performance appraisals. For example, some colleges ask students to evaluate their professors using an end-of-term rating scale. The scales usually try to evaluate classroom teaching performance—for instance, in terms of dimensions like "prepared for class," "made concepts clear," and "was available for questions." Ratings range from "Poor" to "Excellent" on a 5-point scale.

Indeed, the most familiar performance appraisal approach involves using a form like the one shown in Figure 9.13. This form (traditionally called a "graphic rating scale") lists several job characteristics (like quality of work) and provides a rating scale (from outstanding to unsatisfactory), along with short definitions of each rating. This particular appraisal form is relatively objective because it calls for specific ratings. However, the form also provides space for more subjective examples of particularly good or particularly bad employee performance.

► FIGURE 9.13

Performance Appraisal Form

Source: Gary Dessler, *Human Resource Management*, 9th ed. (Upper Saddle River, NJ: Prentice Hall, 2000).

Performance Appraisal for:

Employee Name _____ Title _____

Department _____ Employee Payroll Number _____

Reason for Review: ☐ Annual ☐ Promotion ☐ Unsatisfactory Performance
                   ☐ Merit   ☐ End Probation Period ☐ Other _____

Date employee began present position _____ / _____ / _____

Date of last appraisal _____ / _____ / _____   Scheduled appraisal date _____ / _____ / _____

Instructions: Carefully evaluate employee's work performance in relation to current job requirements. Check rating box to indicate the employee's performance. Indicate N/A if not applicable. Assign points for each rating within the scale in the corresponding points box. Points will be totaled and averaged for an overall performance score.

RATING IDENTIFICATION

O – Outstanding – Performance is exceptional in all areas.
V – Very Good – Results clearly exceed most position requirements.
G – Good – Competent and dependable level of performance. Meets performance standards.
I – Improvement Needed – Performance is deficient in certain areas.
U – Unsatisfactory – Results are generally unacceptable and require immediate improvement.
N – Not Rated – Not applicable or too soon to rate.

GENERAL FACTORS	RATING	SCALE	COMMENTS
1. **Quality** – The accuracy, thoroughness, and acceptability of work performed.	O ☐ V ☐ G ☐ I ☐ U ☐	100–90 90–80 80–70 70–60 below 60	Points
2. **Productivity** – The quantity and efficiency of work produced in a specified period of time.	O ☐ V ☐ G ☐ I ☐ U ☐	100–90 90–80 80–70 70–60 below 60	Points
3. **Job Knowledge** – The practical/technical skills and information used on the job.	O ☐ V ☐ G ☐ I ☐ U ☐	100–90 90–80 80–70 70–60 below 60	Points
4. **Reliability** – The extent to which an employee can be relied upon regarding task completion and follow up.	O ☐ V ☐ G ☐ I ☐ U ☐	100–90 90–80 80–70 70–60 below 60	Points
5. **Availability** – The extent to which an employee is punctual, observes prescribed work break/meal periods, and the overall attendance record.	O ☐ V ☐ G ☐ I ☐ U ☐	100–90 90–80 80–70 70–60 below 60	Points

Companies use other appraisal techniques today. For example, with **360-degree feedback** (also called *multisource assessment*), performance information is collected all around an employee—from supervisors, subordinates, peers, and internal or external customers.[69] According to one recent study, 29% of the responding employers already use 360-degree feedback and another 11% had plans to implement it shortly.[70] The feedback is generally used for training and development, rather than to determine pay increases.[71]

Most 360-degree feedback systems contain several common features. Appropriate parties—peers, supervisors, subordinates, and customers, for instance—complete

360-degree feedback

a performance evaluation method that involves collecting performance information on an employee all around that person—for instance, from subordinates, supervisors, peers, and internal and external customers.

survey questionnaires on an individual. The questionnaires can take many forms, but often include supervisory skill items such as "returns phone calls promptly," "listens well," and "my manager keeps me informed."[72] Computerized systems then compile all this feedback into individualized reports that are presented to the person being rated.[73]

Compensation

employee compensation

all forms of pay or rewards that go to employees and arise from their employment.

Employee compensation refers to all work-related pay or rewards that go to employees.[74] It includes direct financial payments in the form of wages, salaries, incentives, commissions, and bonuses, and indirect payments in the form of financial fringe benefits like employer-paid insurance and vacations.

fixed salary

compensation based on an agreed rate for a set period of time.

A **fixed salary** or **an hourly wage** is the centerpiece of most employees' pay. For example, blue-collar workers and clerical workers are often paid hourly or daily wages. Some employees—managerial, professional, and often secretarial—are salaried. They are compensated on the basis of a set period of time (like a week, month, or year), rather than hourly or daily.

hourly wage

compensation based on a set hourly pay rate for work performed.

Financial incentives are increasingly important and today are often referred to as *pay for performance*. A **financial incentive** is any financial reward that is contingent on performance. Salespeople are often paid financial incentives called *commissions*, which are generally proportional to the items or services they actually sell. Production workers are often paid a financial incentive called *piecework*, which is a standard sum for each item the worker produces. Many employees periodically receive merit pay or a merit raise, which is a salary increase awarded to an employee based on individual performance. Merit pay differs from a bonus, which is a one-time financial payment. We discuss incentives further in Chapter 11.

financial incentive

any financial reward that is contingent on a worker's performance, such as commissions or piecework.

employee benefits

supplements to wages or pay that employees get as a result of their working for an organization.

Employee benefits are any supplements to wages or pay based on working for the organization. They typically include health and life insurance, vacation, pension, and education plans. Many of these benefits are legally mandated. For example, under federal and state law, **unemployment insurance** is available to most employees and is paid by state agencies to workers who are terminated through no fault of their own. The funds come from a tax on the employer's payroll. **Workers' compensation**, another legally mandated benefit, is a payment aimed at providing sure, prompt income and medical benefits to victims of work-related accidents or their dependents, regardless of fault. Social Security is another federally mandated benefit paid for by a tax on an employee's salary or wages.

unemployment insurance

legally mandated insurance that is paid by state agencies to workers who are terminated through no fault of their own; the funds come from a tax on the employer's payroll.

workers' compensation

a legally mandated benefit that pays income and medical benefits to work-related accident victims or their dependents, regardless of fault.

Starbucks is a good example of how managers use benefits to help build a loyal workforce. Howard Schultz, CEO of Starbucks, places great emphasis on a benefits package that features fully company-paid physicals, dental coverage, eye care, and company-paid disability and life insurance. Also included are stock options, training programs, career counseling, and product discounts for all employees, full time and part time. Schultz sees benefits as the bond that ties workers to the company and inspires loyalty. Perhaps more important, he thinks employees who are treated right treat customers right. "The future of Starbucks" says Schultz, "lies in increasing shareholder value—and increasing employee value will [do that]."[75]

Grievances and Discipline

grievance

a complaint that an employee lodges against an employer, usually one regarding wages, hours, or some condition of employment, such as unfair supervisory behavior.

A **grievance** is a complaint an employee lodges against an employer, usually regarding wages, hours, or some condition of employment like unfair supervisory behavior. Most union contracts contain a grievance procedure whereby the employer and the union determine whether some clause of the contract has been violated. Steps typically include discussing the problem with a supervisor, and then referring the matter to the department head, the personnel department, and finally the head of the facility. A supervisor may fire an employee for excessive absences. The employee might then file a grievance stating that the supervisor had issued no previous warnings or discipline related to excessive absences as was called for in the union agreement and that the firing was unwarranted. Many nonunionized companies also offer grievance procedures.

Supervisors sometimes have to discipline subordinates, usually because a rule or procedure was violated. A company should have clear rules (such as "No smoking allowed when dealing with customers"), as well as a series of progressive penalties that all employees know will be enforced if the rule is broken. One way to set up a discipline system is to follow the so-called FRACT model: Get the *facts*, obtain the *reason* for the infraction, *audit* the records, pinpoint the *consequences*, and identify the *type* of infraction before taking remedial steps.

A recent innovation in this area is called **discipline without punishment**. Here, for example, an employee first gets an oral reminder for breaking the rule and then a written reminder if the rule is broken again. A paid one-day "decision-making leave" is mandated if another incident occurs in the next few weeks. If the rule is broken again, the employee may be dismissed.

discipline without punishment
a multistage disciplinary technique that uses oral reminders of the violated rule; then written reminders; followed by a paid one-day leave; and finally, if the behavior is not corrected, dismissal.

Human Resource Management's Legal Framework

When it comes to personnel practices, managers can't just do whatever they please. Thousands of federal, state, and local laws prescribe what managers can and can't do when it comes to personnel management practices like employee selection.

Equal Employment Laws and Affirmative Action   Equal employment laws prohibiting employment discrimination are among the most important personnel laws. Title VII of the 1964 Civil Rights Act bars discrimination because of race, color, religion, sex, or national origin (see Table 9.1). Its requirements are enforced by the federal Equal Employment Opportunity Commission (EEOC), a five-member commission appointed by the president with the advice and consent of the Senate. It receives, investigates, and may file charges regarding job discrimination complaints on behalf of aggrieved individuals.

Other important antidiscrimination laws include the Equal Pay Act of 1963, which requires equal pay for men and women performing similar work; the Pregnancy Discrimination Act of 1978, which prohibits discrimination in employment against pregnant women; and the Americans with Disabilities Act of 1990, which requires employers to make reasonable accommodations for disabled employees.

These and other antidiscrimination laws mean employers should adhere to certain procedures. For example, employers should confirm that the selection tests they use do not unfairly screen out minorities, and in interviews they should avoid inquiring about an applicant's ethnic, racial, or marital status.

Whereas equal employment opportunity aims to ensure equal treatment at work, **affirmative action** requires the employer to make an effort to hire and promote those in a protected group (such as women or minorities). Affirmative action thus includes taking specific actions (in recruitment, hiring, promotions, and compensation) designed to eliminate the present effects of past discrimination. An example would be setting a goal of promoting more minorities to middle management jobs.

affirmative action
a legislated requirement that employers make an extra effort to hire and promote those in a protected (women or minority) group.

TABLE 9.1   Summary of Important Equal Employment Opportunity Legislation

Action	What It Does
Title VII of 1964 Civil Rights Act, as amended	Bars discrimination because of race, color, religion, sex, or national origin; instituted EEOC
Executive orders	Prohibit employment discrimination by employers with federal contracts of more than $10,000 (and their subcontractors); establish office of federal compliance; require affirmative action programs
Federal agency guidelines	Used by federal agencies for enforcement of laws barring discrimination based on sex, national origin, and religion, as well as employee selection procedures; for example, they require validation of tests
Supreme court decisions: Griggs v. Duke Power Co., Albemarle v. Moody	Ruled that job requirements must be related to job success; that discrimination need not be overt to be proved; that the burden of proof is on the employer to prove that the qualification is valid
Equal Pay Act of 1963	Requires equal pay for men and women for performing similar work
Age Discrimination in Employment Act of 1967	Prohibits discriminating against a person 40 years or over in any area of employment because of age
State and local laws	Often cover organizations too small to be covered by federal laws
Vocational Rehabilitation Act of 1973	Requires affirmative action to employ and promote qualified disabled persons and prohibits discrimination against disabled persons
Pregnancy Discrimination Act of 1978	Prohibits discrimination in employment against pregnant women or workers with related conditions
Vietnam Era Veterans' Readjustment Assistance Act of 1974	Requires affirmative action in employment for veterans of the Vietnam War era
Wards Cove v. Atonio; Patterson v. McLean Credit Union	These Supreme Court decisions made it more difficult to prove a case of unlawful discrimination against an employer
Morton v. Wilks	This case allowed consent decrees to be attacked and could have had a chilling effect on certain affirmative action programs
Americans with Disabilities Act of 1990	Strengthens the need for most employers to make reasonable accommodations for disabled employees at work; prohibits discrimination
Civil Rights Act of 1991	Reverses Wards Cove, Patterson, and Morton decisions; places burden of proof back on employer and permits compensatory and punitive money damages for discrimination

Source: Gary Dessler, *Human Resource Management*, 7th ed. (Upper Saddle River, NJ: Prentice-Hall, 2000), 52.

Sexual Harassment   Sexual harassment is defined as unwelcome sexual advances, requests for sexual favors, and other verbal or physical conduct of a sexual nature that occurs under conditions including the following: when such conduct is made, either explicitly or implicitly, a term or condition of an individual's employment; when submission to or rejection of such conduct by an individual is used as the basis for employment decisions affecting the individual; or when such conduct has the purpose or effect of unreasonably interfering with an individual's performance or creating an intimidating, hostile, or offensive work environment. In other words, if it makes the other person feel uncomfortable, it may be sexual harassment.

In addition to being unfair and detestable, sexual harassment is also illegal. In one famous case, *Meritor Savings Bank, FSB* v. *Vinson*, the U.S. Supreme Court indicated that employers should establish meaningful complaint procedures and head off charges of sexual harassment before they occur. The things an employer should do include:

1. First, take all complaints seriously. As one manual for managers and supervisors advises, "When confronted with sexual harassment complaints or when sexual conduct is observed in the workplace, the best reaction is to address the complaint or stop the conduct."[76]

2. Issue a strong policy statement condemning such behavior.

3. Inform all employees about the policy prohibiting sexual harassment and of their rights under the policy.

4. Establish a complaint procedure so that employees understand the chain of command in filing and appealing sexual harassment complaints.

5. Establish a management response system that includes an immediate reaction and investigation by senior management when charges of sexual harassment are made.

6. Hold management training sessions with supervisors and increase their own awareness of the issues.

7. Discipline managers and employees involved in sexual harassment.

Occupational Safety and Health   The Occupational Safety and Health Act was passed by Congress "to assure so far as possible every working man and woman in the nation safe and healthful working conditions and to preserve our human resources." It sets safety and health standards that apply to almost all workers in the United States. The standards themselves are contained in five volumes and cover just about any hazard one could think of, including, for instance, what sorts of ladders to use, appropriate fire protection, and ways to guard against accidents when using machines and portable power tools. They are administered by the Occupational Safety and Health Administration (OSHA), a U.S. government agency.

Companies can take a number of steps to improve the safety and health of their workforces. One is to reduce unsafe conditions that can lead to accidents. This is an employer's first line of defense. A brief checklist like that in Figure A9.3 can be useful.

Labor–Management Relations   Under the laws of the United States and many other countries, employees are permitted to organize into unions. In the United States, the Norris–LaGuardia Act guarantees each employee the right to bargain with employers for union benefits. The Wagner Act outlaws unfair labor practices such as employers interfering with, restraining, or coercing employees who are exercising their legally sanctioned rights of organizing themselves into a union. The Taft–Hartley Act prohibits unfair labor practices by unions against employers (like refusing to bargain with the employer). The Landrum-Griffin Act protects union members from unfair practices perpetrated against them by their unions.

Other Employment Law Issues   Other employment-related laws affect virtually every HR-related decision managers make. For example, the Fair Labor Standards Act specifies a minimum wage ($5.15 per hour, as of 2000), as well as child-labor and overtime pay rules. The Employee Polygraph Protection Act of 1988 outlaws almost all uses of the polygraph, or lie-detector machine, for employment purposes.

SUMMARY

1. Human resources management is the management function devoted to acquiring, training, appraising, and compensating employees. As workers become more fully empowered, the HR function has grown in importance.

2. Staffing—filling a firm's open positions—starts with job analysis and personnel planning. Recruiting—including the use of internal sources, advertising, employment agencies, recruiters, referrals, college recruiting, and recruiting a more diverse workforce—is then used to create a pool of applicants.

3. With a pool of applicants, the employer can turn to screening and selecting, using one or more techniques—including application blanks, interviews, tests, and reference checks—to assess and investigate an applicant's aptitudes, interests, and background.

4. Once employees have been recruited, screened, and selected, they must be prepared to do their jobs; this is the role of employee orientation and training. Orientation means providing new employees with basic information about the employer; training ensures that the new employee has the basic knowledge required to perform the job satisfactorily.

5. Once they've been on the job for some time, employees are appraised.

6. Employee compensation refers to all work-related pay or rewards that go to employees. It includes direct financial payments in the form of wages, salaries, incentives, commissions, and bonuses, and indirect payments in the form of financial fringe benefits like employer-paid insurance and vacations.

7. In disciplining employees, managers should be sure they have all the facts, and that the discipline is defensible and fair.

8. The HR function is subject to the constraints of numerous federal, state, and local laws. The equal employment laws prohibiting employment discrimination are among the most important of these personnel laws and include Title VII of the Civil Rights Act, various executive orders, the Equal Pay Act of 1963, and the Americans with Disabilities Act of 1990. The Occupational Safety and Health Act sets safety and health standards that apply to almost all workers in the United States. Other laws govern union–management relations and include the Wagner Act.

TYING IT ALL TOGETHER

After planning what's to be done, managers must create an organization. We covered planning in Chapters 4 through 6, and now in this part of the book (Chapters 7 through 9) we have focused on how to design an organization and an organization chart. Of course, an organization—be it GE, GM, or Duncan Group, Inc.—is more than just a chart of reporting relationships and positions. It's the people who make the organization, so in this chapter we focused on the staffing methods managers use to recruit, select, and train employees to fill the organization's positions. Once the organization is staffed with competent and well-trained individuals, the manager's job is still not complete: Employees must then be inspired, motivated, and led, the topics to which we turn in the next part of this book.

human resources (HR) man-
agement 250
strategic HR management 250
staffing 251
job analysis 251
job description 251
job specification 252
job analysis questionnaire 252
personnel planning 254
personnel replacement chart
254
position replacement card 254

recruiting 254
job posting 255
contingent workers 256
executive recruiter 256
application form 263
management assessment
center 265
orientation 273
training program 273
on-the-job training (OJT) 273
appraisal 274
360-degree feedback 275

employee compensation 276
fixed salary 276
hourly wage 276
financial incentive 276
employee benefits 276
unemployment insurance 276
workers' compensation 276
grievance 276
discipline without punishment 277
affirmative action 277

SKILLS AND STUDY MATERIALS

CRITICAL THINKING EXERCISES

1. The United States is a heterogeneous nation. In states like California there is a rich mixture of natives and immigrants from other states as well as from many ancient and emerging nations. Please read the following final thoughts from Ronald Takaki's book on human diversity and the United States, A Different Mirror (Boston: Little, Brown & Company, 1993, p. 428) from a human resources management context. Then write a brief analysis of what the quote means for managing human resources in the 21st century:

   As Americans, we originally came from many different shores, and our diversity has been the center of the making of America. While our stories contain the memories of different communities, together they inscribe a larger narrative. Filled with what Walt Whitman celebrated as the "varied carols" of America, our history generously gives all of us our "mystic chords of memory." Throughout our past of oppressions and struggles for equality, Americans of different races and ethnicities have been "singing with open mouths their strong melodious songs" in the textile mills of Lowell, the cotton fields of Mississippi, on the Indian reservations of South Dakota, the railroad tracks high in the Sierras of California, in the garment factories of the Lower East Side, the canefields of Hawaii, and a thousand other places across the country. Our denied history "bursts with telling." As we hear America singing, we find ourselves invited to bring our rich cultural diversity on deck, to accept ourselves. "Of every hue and caste am I," sang Whitman. "I resist any thing better than my own diversity."

2. As quoted in John Aram's Presumed Superior, affirmative action has different meanings to different people. One observer comments on the double meaning of affirmative action as a means of institutional change: "If civil rights is defined as quotas, it's a losing hand. If it's defined as protection against discrimination and efforts to promote opportunity, then it will remain a mainstream value in American life." John Aram points out, "The dilemma is that progress on civil rights both restricts and opens opportunity. No single, definitive moral premise exists."[77]

   What do you think Aram is trying to say? What aspects of HR can be related to his comments? What are your thoughts and feelings about civil rights and affirmative action as they affect organizational management and jobs?

3. In 1999 the state of California had a population of 34 million, including 51% White, 30% Hispanic, 11% Asian, 7% African American and 0.6% Native American. In 10 years these figures will shift. Total population will be 39.5 million. The population will then include 45% White, 35% Hispanic, 13% Asian, 6% African American, and 0.6% Native American. By 2019 the population is projected to be 45 million. It is projected that the demographics will have changed to 40% White, 39% Hispanics, 14% Asian, 6%

African Americans, and 0.6% Native American.[78] Please think about HR management in California using these three decades of demographics. What are the implications for California? What are the challenges for HR managers? What are the social, political, and cultural challenges to be faced? Will other parts of the country, such as Florida, Texas, New York, and other states, have similar types of demographics? If so, what are the implications for HR managers around the nation?

EXPERIENTIAL EXERCISES

1. *Fast Company*'s September 1999 issue is all about the future. It is titled "21 Rules for the 21st Century." Among the articles is "2004: A Personal Odyssey." The article begins with the following questions: "What are *your* expectations five years from now? As the 21st Century arrives, are you feeling confident about your career and sure of your future? Or does the prospect of ever-more-powerful technology and never-ending change leave you wishing you could return to the simpler days of the Old Economy?" The *Fast Company* Roper Starch worldwide survey found the answers to these questions and more. First think where you will be in 2004 and where you want to be. Then go to *Fast Company* in the library or on the Internet and look at the survey and read the article. When you get to the questions, answer them yourself prior to looking at the survey results. Then compare your responses with those of others who took the survey. You may wish to discuss these issues in small groups in class or as a class.

2. You are the HR director for Manugistics, Inc., a Maryland-based, highly successful software company employing 600 people. Your HR department has 12 employees, representing all areas of human resources. In less than a decade, your company has made a major domestic acquisition and a global acquisition, added new employees, sold a product line, and seen two of the founders leave. How has it managed to remain competitive?

It has "institutionalized change" through its three "elements of excellence": (1) We treat others as we would like to be treated, (2) partnership with our clients results in superior products, and (3) team success is more important than personal glory.[79]

Your department has developed a wide variety of flexible options for employees; for example, 50% of your staff are women with flexible schedules, and 30 to 40% of your employees telecommute.

In March 1997 the company announced a joint venture with Information Resources Inc. (IRI), based in Chicago. The companies will collaborate on the development of an innovative product that integrates point-of-sale data and supply-chain planning, with 20 IRI employees from offices in Chicago, Atlanta, and Waltham, Massachusetts, joining the Manugistics workforce.

Your task as the HR director is to develop an orientation and training program for this joint venture. Also, go to www.manugistics.com and click on the various pages offered. Then determine where the company has gone, where it may be going, and why HR management is important in its efforts.

myPHLIP COMPANION WEB SITE

We invite you to visit the Dessler companion Web site at **www.prenhall.com/dessler** for this chapter's Internet resources.

MONSTER.COM—CAN A FIRM OUTSOURCE ITS RECRUITING?

Most Americans became familiar with Monster.com when it ran the first of its famous advertisements during the Super Bowl in 1999. Monster.com challenged millions of Super Bowl viewers to take stock of their careers with a "when I grow up" spot. The ad features children musing about what they want to be when they grow up. Each child describes a particularly distasteful aspect of a job: "I want to file all day," or "I want to claw my way up to middle management." The spots have been immensely successful in building a brand identity for Monster.com, the online recruitment leader. MediaMetrix, a company that tracks Internet usage, ranks Monster.com as the most utilized Internet job site, boasting more than 2.6 million unique visitors. Since Monster.com reaches so many potential candidates, why should an employer undertake its own candidate search? Why shouldn't firms just outsource their recruiting efforts to a company like Monster.com?

Behind the successful image campaign at Monster.com is a well-organized corporate entity. The company is a subsidiary of TMP Worldwide, the world's largest yellow pages advertising agency and a highly respected provider of direct marketing services. TMP has more than 6,100 employees in 25 countries. The Monster.com subsidiary, a natural extension of TMP's advertising business, is drawing 2.6 million unique visits per month to its job-search Web site. Independent research has estimated Monster.com's share of the Web job search market at over 40%.

One of the most attractive features for employers is Monster.com's ability to attract high-tech employees. Only candidates with a computer, browser, and access to the Internet are likely to use the forum. There are other benefits as well. The Internet can provide instantaneous information, allowing firms to post last-minute openings. A firm can also provide links to its own Web site, offering a prospective employee far more information than is available in a print ad. Monster.com also offers résumé-screening, routing, and searching services. Currently, Monster.com has over a million résumés from active job seekers in its database.

It is common for companies to outsource areas that are not part of their core competence or in areas where they have difficulty in being competitive. Given that Monster.com already has more than a million résumés in its database and the ability to instantly post jobs, should a company give most of its recruiting to Monster.com?

Discussion Questions

1. What competition does Monster.com have in its industry?

2. What strengths does Monster.com bring to recruiting that a hiring company itself might not have?

3. In what ways is Monster.com similar to a personnel agency? Different?

4. What limitations might Monster.com have that might encourage a firm to use other recruiting sources?

CEO SUCCESSION PLANNING AT AMERICAN EXPRESS

American Express is one of the largest diversified financial and network service companies in the world. Since its founding in 1850, it has been a leader in global markets in charge and credit cards, travel and vacation services, financial planning, investment products, insurance, and international banking. Being one of the largest service firms in the world makes American Express one of the most visible. Changing the top leader in a company like this can be a traumatic event. Investors and senior managers come to rely on the consistency of leadership in dynamic or uncertain markets. That is certainly true for American Express.

Typically, when looking for a replacement CEO, companies take into account the candidate's experience within his or her company, track record—how successful the potential CEO was in managing complex tasks in a dynamic environment—and experience with the industry, among other factors. In choosing a new CEO, firms often emphasize consistency. Firms use several methods to attain consistency: having a replacement management team in place for a number of years prior to the CEO change, allowing the financial community to become familiar with the potential CEO's work, appointing a new CEO prior to the departure or

American Express Board of Directors, 1999

Individual	Title
Daniel F. Akerson	Chairman and Chief Executive Officer, Nextlink Communications, Inc.
Anne L. Armstrong	Regent, Texas A&M University System
Edwin L. Artzt	Chairman of the Executive Committee, The Procter & Gamble Company
William G. Bowen	President, The Andrew W. Mellon Foundation
Kenneth I. Chenault	President and Chief Operating Officer, American Express Company
Robert L. Crandall	Former Chairman and Chief Executive Officer, AMR Corporation and American Airlines
Harvey Golub	Chairman and Chief Executive Officer, American Express Company
Beverly Sills Greenough	Chairman, Lincoln Center for the Performing Arts
F. Ross Johnson	Chairman and Chief Executive Officer, RJM Group
Vernon E. Jordan, Jr.	Senior Executive Partner, Akin, Gump, Strauss, Hauer & Feld, LLP
Jan Leschly	Chief Executive, SmithKline Beecham PLC
Drew Lewis	Former Chairman and Chief Executive Officer, Union Pacific Corporation
Richard A. McGinn	Chairman, Chief Executive Officer and President, Lucent Technologies, Inc.
Frank P. Popoff	Chairman of the Board, The Dow Chemical Company

retirement of a new CEO, or asking the CEO to remain with the company as a chair or vice chair of the board to assure continuity of leadership. Of course, the board of directors is intimately involved in the decision.

In the case of American Express, CEO Harvey Golub announced his retirement in 1999, saying Division President Ken Chenault would accept the position of CEO in 2001. In his letter to employees, Golub asserted: "In a sense, there is no ideal time for retirement. There is always more to do, always more challenges to meet, always opportunities to capitalize on and problems to deal with. Nonetheless, succession planning is a critical part of good corporate governance for any company and its board of directors. Indeed, I believe the most important task for any CEO is to ensure the seamless transition of executive authority. This is a process that we began at American Express several years ago with Ken's appointment as president and chief operating officer. Today's announcement is the next step in this process."

Golub also announced that the company would immediately begin to expand Chenault's range of responsibilities. He noted that customers, employees, investors, and suppliers would know that in dealing with Chenault, they were dealing with the next CEO of the company.

One of the key issues in the American Express decision to go with an inside candidate was to maintain a continuity of strategy. Golub's leadership team envisioned several major strategic tasks, among them to

1. Develop and implement a compelling Internet strategy

2. Accelerate growth at American Express Financial Advisors

3. Recognize that in the future limitations on banks from offering both Visa/MasterCard and American Express were likely to be overturned.

The ultimate decision about who would be the new CEO was placed in the hands of the American Express board of directors. The board consists of 14 individuals—2 from American Express and 12 outside directors from a variety of perspectives and backgrounds.

Discussion Questions

1. Given its critical issues, would American Express be better served by promoting from within, or hiring a CEO from outside the company? Why?

2. To what extent does Amex seem to have adhered to the recruitment and selection process as outlined in this chapter? How was the Amex process similar? Different?

3. Should the board accept Golub's recommendation that Chenault succeed him as CEO?

4. What are the strengths and weaknesses of Golub's succession plan for American Express?

IMPLEMENTING A STAFFING/HR PROGRAM AT KNITMEDIA

If you review KnitMedia's latest organization chart, you'll probably note one department conspicuous by its absence. Like most companies with around 100 or so employees, KnitMedia has no separate HR/personnel department. Historically, companies have about one HR person for each hundred employees, but that ratio has been drifting up as companies have tried to become more efficient. So at KnitMedia, there simply aren't enough employees yet to make having an HR manager economically feasible.

This presents several problems. For one thing, from a practical point of view, keeping track of the personnel needs of about 100 employees isn't easy. Think for instance about the challenge of just keeping track of 100 employees' vacation time, sick leave, pension plans, and salary adjustments. That's a lot of paperwork and recordkeeping.

More important perhaps is the fact that when a lot of people have to be hired, how can you be sure that you are hiring the best ones to do the job? For example, here's how Chuck Brownley, the Knitting Factory of New York Club general manager, puts it: "How do we plan for how many staffers we need? It actually starts from the programming when you speak to Glenn, our programming manager. . . . The different artists that we have booked in different programs or events dictates the manpower. . . . If we need extra sound people, or extra technical people or extra door people or extra bar staff to accommodate the overflow." In other words, staffing tends to be pretty much an informal process at KnitMedia. That could be a problem if some people who shouldn't be hired are hired.

There are also legal factors to consider. For example, with about 100 employees, KnitMedia is certainly covered by the various federal, state, and New York City laws regarding equal employment opportunity. Unless the company carefully adheres to these laws and regulations, it could run into problems in the future.

The company has taken some steps to organize its human resource operations. For example, there is an employee manual that is about six pages long and that covers KnitMedia policies regarding matters such as security, environment, probationary periods, at will employment, and time off. Allan Fried recently finished developing a performance appraisal form that the company will use to evaluate employees and that will become part of the company's performance appraisal process. These steps notwithstanding, though, Michael Dorf and his management team are concerned about whether they're doing enough to formalize their HR process, and they've come to you for advice.

Team Exercises and Questions

Use what you learned in this chapter to answer the following questions from Michael Dorf and his management team:

1. What are the main HR areas we should be addressing at KnitMedia and what, in outline form, do they involve?

2. Do you think we're doing an effective job of selecting employees? If not, how exactly would you suggest we go about selecting employees in the future?

3. How would you propose the HR function should be administered at KnitMedia, and why?

► **F I G U R E   A 9 . 1**

Job Analysis Questionnaire for Developing Job Descriptions

A questionnaire like this can be used to interview job incumbents or may be filled out by them.

JOB QUESTIONNAIRE
OZARK MANUFACTURING COMPANY

YOUR NAME _____   PRESENT JOB TITLE _____
DEPARTMENT _____   EMPLOYEE NUMBER _____
SUPERVISOR'S NAME _____   SUPERVISOR'S TITLE _____

1. SUMMARY OF DUTIES: State briefly, in your own words, your main duties.
   _____
   _____

2. SPECIAL QUALIFICATIONS: List any licenses, permits, certifications, etc. required to perform duties assigned to your position.
   _____
   _____

3. EQUIPMENT: List any equipment, machines, or tools (e.g., computers, motor vehicles, lathes, fork lifts, drill presses, etc.) you normally operate as a part of your position's duties.

   MACHINE   AVERAGE NO. HOURS PER WEEK

   _____
   _____
   _____

4. REGULAR DUTIES: In general terms, describe duties you regularly perform. Please list these duties in descending order of importance and give the percent of time spent on them per month. List as many duties as possible and attach additional sheets, if necessary.
   _____
   _____
   _____

5. CONTACTS: Does your job require any contacts with other department personnel, other departments, outside companies or agencies? If yes, please define the duties requiring contacts and how often.
   _____
   _____

6. SUPERVISION: Does your position have supervisory responsibilities? ( ) Yes ( ) No. If yes, please fill out a *Supplemental Position Description Questionnaire for* Supervisors and attach it to this form. If you have responsibility for the work of others but do not directly supervise them, please explain.
   _____
   _____
   _____

7. DECISION MAKING: Please explain the decisions you make while performing the regular duties of your job.
   _____
   _____
   _____

   (a) What might be a likely result of your making (a) poor judgment(s) or decision(s), or (b) improper actions?
   _____
   _____

NO. _____

◀ F I G U R E   A 9 . 2

Job Posting Form

Source: Bureau of National Affairs, Inc.,
Recruiting and Selection Procedures
(Washington, DC, 1988), p. 35.

POSTED: _____
CLOSING: _____

_____

There is a full-time position available for a _____ in the
_____ Department. This position is/is not open to outside
candidates.

PAY SCALE

	Minimum	Midpoint	Maximum
	$ _____	$ _____	$ _____

or
SALARIED

DUTIES
See attached job description.

REQUIRED SKILLS AND ABILITIES
(Must possess all the following skills and abilities to be considered for this
position.)
1. Demonstrated successful performance at past/present positions including:
   – ability to perform tasks in a complete and accurate manner
   – demonstrated timeliness and follow-through on duties and assignments
   – ability to work well with other people
   – ability to communicate effectively
   – reliability and good attendance
   – good organizational skills
   – problem solving attitude and approach
   – positive work attitude: enthusiastic, confident, outgoing, helpful, committed

2.

DESIRED SKILLS AND ABILITIES
(These skills and abilities will make a candidate more competitive.)

Application procedure FOR   EMPLOYEES is as follows:

1. Apply by phoning _____ , on ext. _____ , by 3:00 p.m.
   _____

2. Ensure that a completed Internal Job Application and up-to-date
   resume/application is delivered to _____ by the same
   date.
Applicants will be pre-screened according to the above qualifications.
Selection will be made by the _____ .
     is an equal opportunity employer.
0255M/1

► FIGURE A9.3

Checklist of Mechanical or Physical Accident-Causing Conditions

Source: Courtesy of the American Insurance Association. From "A Safety Committee Man's Guide," pp. 1–64.

I. GENERAL HOUSEKEEPING

Adequate and wide aisles—no materials protruding into aisles

Parts and tools stored safely after use—not left in hazardous positions that could cause them to fall

Even and solid flooring—no defective floors or ramps that could cause falling or tripping accidents

Waste and trash cans—safely located and not overfilled

Material piled in safe manner—not too high or too close to sprinkler heads

All work areas clean and dry

All exit doors and aisles clean of obstructions

Aisles kept clear and properly marked; no air lines or electric cords across aisles

II. MATERIAL HANDLING EQUIPMENT AND CONVEYANCES

On all conveyances, electric or hand, check to see that the following items are all in sound working conditions:

Brakes—properly adjusted

Not too much play in steering wheel

Warning device—in place and working

Wheels—securely in place; properly inflated

Fuel and oil—enough and right kind

No loose parts

Cables, hooks or chains—not worn or otherwise defective

Suspended chains or hooks conspicuous

Safely loaded

Properly stored

III. LADDERS, SCAFFOLD, BENCHES, STAIRWAYS, ETC.

The following items of major interest to be checked:

Safety feet on straight ladders

Guardrails or handrails

Treads, not slippery

No splintered, cracked, or rickety

Properly stored

Extension ladder ropes in good condition

Toeboards

IV. POWER TOOLS (STATIONARY)

Point of operation guarded

Guards in proper adjustment

Gears, belts, shafting, counterweights guarded

Foot pedals guarded

Brushes provided for cleaning machines

Adequate lighting

Properly grounded

Tool or material rests properly adjusted

Adequate work space around machines

Control switch easily accessible

Safety glasses worn

Gloves worn by persons handling rough or sharp materials

No gloves or loose clothing worn by persons operating machines

V. HAND TOOLS AND MISCELLANEOUS

In good condition—not cracked, worn, or otherwise defective

Properly stored

Correct for job

Goggles, respirators, and other personal protective equipment worn where necessary

VI. ELECTRICITY

No frayed, cracked, or deteriorated cords

All portable, as well as fixed machinery grounded by three-wire connectors

No dangling wires

Ground-fault circuit interrupters used in humid conditions

VII. SPRAY PAINTING

Explosion-proof electrical equipment

Proper storage of paints and thinners in approved metal cabinets

Fire extinguishers adequate and suitable; readily accessible

Minimum storage in work area

VIII. FIRE EXTINGUISHERS

Properly serviced and tagged

Readily accessible

Adequate and suitable for operations involved

Fundamentals of Organizing and Staffing

Although many large business firms in the United States and abroad have downsized in recent years—thus reducing their staffing needs and flattening their organizational structures—it will be a long time before KnitMedia adopts such a strategy. The company is growing profitably, and its managers are managing its increase in size by developing a structure that is becoming more hierarchical, not less. As Ed Greer, Senior Vice President of Club Operations, observes, however, KnitMedia can't afford to stand still while it consolidates its new structure. Its business environment is changing too fast. So KnitMedia grows organically, its structure evolving as it goes along.

There are now four major divisions in the organization: New Media, Festival Operations, Club Operations, and the Label Group. There are also separate organizational units for the JazzE Web site, art and graphics, marketing, production, and finance. New positions like chief content officer and chief operating officer have been created, and some jobs have grown big enough to be performed by two people instead of one. There is an official organization chart. We've seen that instead of being at the center of a loose and rather informal structure, as he was a few years ago, Michael Dorf is now at the top of a more conventional hybrid organization.

This new structure actually allows KnitMedia to grow. One of its chief benefits is that it creates a way for Michael to delegate authority to others, who can keep the organization's operations running smoothly while he continues to seek new ventures, new business partners, and new ways to bring KnitMedia's products to a growing audience. One of the drawbacks is that the layers of hierarchical structure tend to distance Michael from others in the company who had become used to having more frequent and more informal contact with him.

An interesting test of the benefits and drawbacks of KnitMedia's increasingly formal structure occurred during Michael's recent three-month trip to the West Coast. Interviewed for the video on the day of his return from Los Angeles, Michael noted that his absence had been helpful in forcing a certain amount of delegation to take place. It also revealed the difference between those employees who could shoulder their responsibilities and those who couldn't. KnitMedia's organizational culture still provides a great deal of freedom, including the freedom to fail, and it lacks the easy fall-back of a large corporate safety net. Thus it is self-motivated individuals who tend to thrive in its still relatively small and constantly evolving environment.

Staffing an organization like KnitMedia presents some interesting challenges. It is an indication of the firm's coming of age as a major force on the Internet that employees are no longer being hired away by record companies; most of those who leave now go to work for Internet start-ups. Turnover can be high in a fast-paced environment where the stakes and the responsibilities are great. Michael believes "the cream rises to the top," however, and he is committed to retaining those employees who have proven their worth to the firm.

A deep commitment to "noncommercial music" and the chance to be creative in many different ways are two of the major draws that bring people from a variety of fields to work at KnitMedia. Competitive salaries, improved benefits and, for the management team, a stock option plan are some of the rewards that keep them there. In the film you'll hear Ed Greer tell of a receptionist's recruitment and promotion to a more responsible position in the JazzE unit. Mary Noelle Dana, Festival Programming Director and Jazzchool Coordinator, talks about the process by which she was hired and how, later, her job grew big enough to be split in half. Sometimes, when the need arises, managers like Mitch Goldman, Chief Content Officer, will hire freelancers who cost the organization less than staff employees and perform valuable short-term services. Recent college graduates work as interns, "floating" throughout the New York office and club, helping where they are needed and picking up valuable skills. (See KnitMedia chart on page 191.)

Questions

Based on the case, the video, the text chapters you've read so far, and your knowledge from other sources, answer the following:

1. What do you think are some advantages and disadvantages of KnitMedia's increasingly hierarchical structure, in addition to those mentioned in the case? How would you recommend it change the structure, if at all?

2. Michael Dorf sees turnover as a way of eliminating employees who aren't working out and identifying those the organization should work to retain. Do you see any negative aspects to frequent or high turnover rates? How would you suggest the company handle ineffective employee performance?

3. How well do you think authority has been delegated at KnitMedia? Do you think it is pushed down too far, or too centralized, or about right?

4. What changes in the organizational structure do you think are suggested by KnitMedia's future plans?

10 ◄ C H A P T E R

BEING A LEADER

AFTER STUDYING THIS CHAPTER, YOU SHOULD BE ABLE TO

- Size up a situation like a leader

- List the foundations of leadership

- Provide a vision for an organization

- Compare and contrast the various leadership styles

- List the specific actions one can take to be a better leader

WHAT'S AHEAD?

Barbara Hyder learned, and fast, that being CEO of a new .com company was different from being a leader in a big, traditional company like Mary Kay Cosmetics.[1] Hyder had been international regional president at Mary Kay before becoming CEO of gloss.com, an on-line beauty startup. How is a .com company different? For one thing, she's now making decisions with her management team on Internet time. For example, when they saw the airwaves clogged with .com ads in December 1999, they made a split-second decision to cancel their ads and instead launch a full $20 million campaign in February 2000. Her new mantra is "You have to act quickly; speed is of the essence."[2]

Hyder's experience says a lot about what leadership is, and how it's different than it was a few years ago. Leaders have always had to say "Here's where we're going to go," and then motivate, cajole, and influence their people to move in that direction. One of the differences today, as we'll see, is that there's a bigger element of consensus-building and teamwork in what leaders do.

Once your organization is staffed with competent employees, these employees must be inspired, motivated, and led. In this part of the book, we'll therefore turn to leadership.

▶ WHAT DO LEADERS DO?

Planning an ad campaign, organizing a management team, and making decisions on when to launch your site is only part of what successful managers like Barbara Hyder do. After plans are set and the organization is in place, nothing is going to happen unless the leader's teammates and subordinates want to move in the direction that's been set. Making sure that happens is a big part of what leaders do.

Leadership is generally defined as influencing others to work willingly toward achieving objectives. As we'll see in this chapter, leadership therefore means crystallizing a direction for subordinates, and then tapping into all the authority, charisma, and traits the leader can muster to make the subordinates want to follow the leader in achieving the leader's goals. In the last two parts of this book we've covered the management functions of planning and organizing. Now we turn to the concepts and skills involved with actually influencing the organization's employees to implement the company's plans. We turn to leadership.

leadership
one person influencing another to willingly work toward a predetermined objective.

Leaders Fill Many Roles

There's a lot more to being a leader than just the contents of this leadership chapter. That's why all of Part 4 of this book is called "Leading," although it also covers topics like motivation, groups, conflict, and change.[3] Leaders simultaneously fill many roles, interacting with and motivating subordinates, leading groups whose members are interacting and in which conflicts might arise, and being part of a group reporting to the leader's own boss. The knowledge contained in this chapter is therefore only part of what leaders must know. This chapter—Being a Leader—will get you started; to really get on the road to being a leader, you'll need the following Part 4 chapters, too. Here's what they cover:

Chapter 11: Motivating Employees Today. Individual differences (for example, in aptitudes and skills) that help to account for why people do what they do, and several theories that help to explain how leaders motivate employees.

Chapter 12: Communicating in Today's Organizations. The barriers that can undermine effective communications, and what a manager has to know about communicating to be an effective leader.

Chapter 13: Managing Groups and Teams. What leaders can do to create more cohesive teams, and the group dynamics leaders should take into account in supervising their own teams.

Chapter 14: Managing Organizational and Cultural Change. Theories and techniques leaders can use to implement changes required to improve an organizational situation.

Don't be overwhelmed by the number of leadership and behavioral science concepts and skills in this and the next four chapters. Instead, think of each as a tool in your leadership toolbox, each useful in its way and under the right conditions.

Leaders Think Like Leaders

How do leaders like Barbara Hyder go about deciding whether the situation calls for applying motivation, communications, team building, organizational change, or some other type of concept or skills? Often, by using a decision process similar to that in the three-step framework shown in Figure 10.1: step back and look at the leadership situation you're facing, and then (1) identify what's happening, (2) account for what's happening, and (3) decide on the actions you'll take.[4] Let's look at a specific example.

Identify What Is Happening   Gus runs a large engineering company in Tampa. He's a genius at what he does, and as a result his company now has about 200 people working for it, including 80 engineers. They've got a recurrent problem though, one that just repeated itself yet again last week. An engineering team will work on a project, send off a proposal, but if the client doesn't like the design or demands time-consuming changes, the project team will often just shelve the project. In other words, they stick the whole project folder on the shelf, go back to working on some other deal, and avoid mentioning anything about the matter to Gus. As you might imagine, Gus is often seen storming around the office yelling "Why didn't you tell me we didn't get that deal, why didn't you tell me we didn't get that deal?" Obviously, what's happening here is that for some reason, Gus's engineers refuse to give him bad news.

Account for What Is Happening   In management, as in other human endeavors, things are not always as they seem. For years, Gus has simply assumed that his engineers are a little irresponsible and that accounts for their walking away from these jobs without a word to him. However, now he's not so sure. He's been reading up on leadership skills for the past few weeks, and now understands there's a lot more than meets the eye when it comes to explaining what people do. Part of being an effective leader, he knows, is understanding how things like motivation, communications, and teamwork can influence what employees do. And he knows that the main purpose of "accounting for what is happening" is to use behavioral science theories and concepts like these to account for why the situations you identified (like the engineers refusing to divulge bad news) are occurring.

Accounting for what is happening in a situation means asking yourself which theory or theories best explain what you see happening, by linking a leadership or other behavioral concept or theory to the issue. In other words, you identify a cause–effect relationship between what has occurred and why. For example, "The engineers here

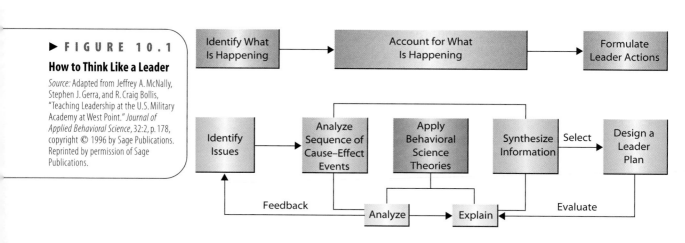

▶ **FIGURE 10.1**

How to Think Like a Leader

Source: Adapted from Jeffrey A. McNally, Stephen J. Gerra, and R. Craig Bollis, "Teaching Leadership at the U.S. Military Academy at West Point." *Journal of Applied Behavioral Science,* 32:2, p. 178, copyright © 1996 by Sage Publications. Reprinted by permission of Sage Publications.

refuse to divulge bad news because they are punished when they do by having Gus yell at them." The *effect* here is the refusal to divulge bad news; the behavioral *cause*—in this case a motivational one—is the fact that they are "punished" when they do.

To account for what is happening you should view the situation as a coherent whole, while at the same time looking for a logical sequence of events. You have to try to identify the root cause of the situation. For example, are the engineers just poorly trained? Are they simply irresponsible? Or are they just reacting to Gus's habit of responding quickly and harshly to any negative news?

In accounting for what is happening, you may find that more than one of the leadership or behavioral science concepts covered in this and the next few chapters applies. In this case, for instance, the engineers may be irresponsible. Or, Gus may have inadvertently created a blame-oriented atmosphere in which his employees know they'll get dumped on when they bring him negative news.

Don't be put off because there may be more than one theory or concept you could use to account for the problem. You may combine several, or choose the one you'll take action on first.

Decide on Leadership Actions   After you have identified and accounted for what is happening, the next step is to decide on the actions that will remedy the situation. Doing so requires applying all the knowledge you gain in this and our other chapters, such as how to motivate employees and how to resolve and manage intergroup conflict.

What actions would you take to help resolve Gus's problem? Gus's assessment of the situation is that he's been too tough and quick to react when people bring him bad news. Good possibilities for action include:

- Getting some counseling.
- Having a meeting with the engineers to explain that things are going to be different.
- Personally working with the engineers to improve a project when the client says it must be redone.

The Building Blocks of Being a Leader

There is no generally accepted theory describing how leaders effectively lead organizations. However, Figure 10.2 provides a useful model for organizing your thoughts. We'll use it to organize this chapter. Leaders with the power and personal traits to be effective in a leadership situation can lead by taking four sets of actions: Think like a leader; provide a vision; use the right leadership style; and apply organizational behavior skills such as motivating. We've discussed thinking like a leader; now let's turn to providing a vision.

How Leaders Provide a Vision

Fortune magazine recently published an issue with a picture of Apple Computer's Steve Jobs on the cover, with the caption "Stevie Wonder!"[5] Why the nickname "Stevie Wonder?" Because in the two or three years he'd been Apple's acting president, the company's financial situation moved from a loss of $600 million to profits of $100 million. Because in the same period the company's stock price jumped from $20 a share to about $100. And because Apple was able to develop and bring to market the brand-new iMac computer, a computer that was so popular and easy to use it was flying off the shelves.

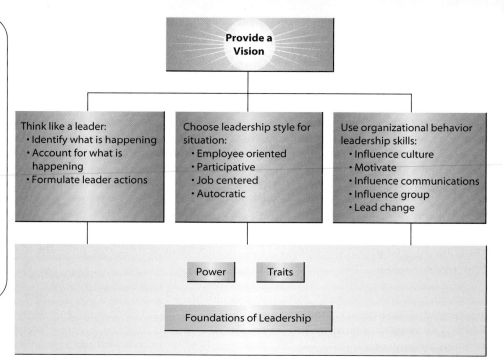

► F I G U R E 1 0 . 2

The Building Blocks of Being a Leader

Note: Leaders with the power and personal traits required to be effective can provide leadership by engaging in four sets of activities: Provide a vision, think like a leader, use the right leadership style, and then use the OB leadership skills explained in the next four chapters.

Source: Adapted from an idea presented in Shelley Kirkpatrick and Edwin A. Luke, "Leadership: Do Traits Matter?" *Academy of Management Executive,* May 1991, pp. 47–60.

Much of Job's success at Apple these last few years has of course resulted from the fact that he's been extraordinarily effective as a manager. He developed the right plans (including introducing the iMac computer). He reorganized the company and hired the right people. And he carefully monitored and maintained control over each of the company's major new products. As the *Fortune* article put it, "No detail was too trivial to escape his scrutiny as he passed final judgment on the look and feel—or what he calls the fit and finish—of a series of ambitious Apple software products and Internet initiatives."[6]

While his management skills undoubtedly had a lot to do with the company's recent success, it was also his visionary leadership that helped make Apple what it is today. He brought to Apple a vision of a company that would produce computers that were extraordinarily easy to use, computers with the most user-friendly interfaces on the market. And with that vision as a guide he was able to motivate Apple's thousands of engineers and employees to work tirelessly to develop the sorts of iMac-type products that would deliver on Job's vision.

As Apple's employees can tell you, there's more to a good, clear vision than a target or plan. The right vision can be so inherently exciting that employees will pursue it with an almost religious fervor. Great leaders like Steve Jobs know that the best kind of motivation is often self-motivation, the kind that drives people to do what they do because they truly believe in doing it. A clear, exciting, and well-communicated vision can help ensure just that kind of self-motivation, by giving employees a target they truly believe in to shoot for.

Today, with the iMac's success guaranteed, Jobs has set Apple off on a new mission: to marry the iMac and the Internet with an easy-to-use new operating system and free Web services for everything from your photos to your homepage. If it works, as *Fortune* says, "Microsoft, AOL, and others will be playing catch-up with a company left for dead two years ago."[7]

The type of direction the leader must set depends on the job that has to be done. Sometimes what's required is a *vision*, a general statement of the organization's intended direction that evokes positive emotional feelings in organization members. Jobs's vision is an example.

Communicating a vision like Jobs's is especially important in today's fast-changing environment, where business conditions are "volatile and carry in them the seeds of rapid and potentially hostile change."[8] Here, "the faster the chief executive officer can conceive a future vision where new products are positioned within emerging product markets the greater is the ability of the firm to control its destiny and affirm a sense of direction."[9] Indeed, CEOs like Barbara Hyder often have to do that at Internet speed.

In turn, the firm's mission statement defines and operationalizes the top manager's vision. A mission statement "broadly outlines the organization's future course and serves to communicate 'who we are, what we do, and where we're headed.'"[10] Mission statements like Apex Elevator's ("Our mission is to provide any customer a means of moving people and things up, down, and sideward over short distances.") are meant to communicate the purpose of the company. If the leader's job is narrower in scale, the task might simply require that he or she provide objectives, which are specific results he or she wants the group to achieve.

MANAGING @ THE SPEED OF THOUGHT

Chris Sinton puts Cisco on the Internet

Leadership—influencing others to move in a desired direction—doesn't necessarily mean being "the person in charge" and supervising hundreds (or even dozens) of subordinates. Sometimes, exerting leadership just means championing a new idea, and having the vision and then the drive and the courage, conviction, and self-confidence to convince others to work with you to implement that vision.

Chris Sinton at Cisco Systems is a case in point. Just a few years ago, Sinton may have been "one of the lowest-tech people at Cisco," but he did know his customers. For example, he knew they hated wasting time phoning and faxing in orders and having to call only when the Cisco salespeople were available to take those orders. And, while he may have been low-tech, he could already see—way back in 1995—that more and more people were using the Internet to place orders for various products from other companies.

At that time, Cisco Systems, although it was the leading firm in providing the various types of electronics that made the Internet work, sold virtually none of its own products via the Internet. But Sinton had a vision, and that was to have Cisco Systems set up Web sites so that customers could, at any time of the day, place orders via the Internet and check the status of those orders, all without ever speaking directly to a salesperson. Sinton first presented his vision to several marketing people two levels above him, and on that basis was given 15 minutes to present his idea at a meeting of senior executives. He urged the company to turn to e-commerce as a way of doing business, and to let customers purchase not only small items like Cisco Systems promotional T-shirts, but also technical support services and even $1.5 million electronic routers.

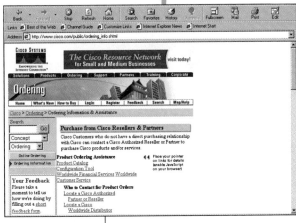

▲ **WEBNOTE**

Today Cisco is using the Internet to communicate directly with vendors, customers, and partners.

www.cisco.com

Used with permission.

Today Cisco, along with pioneers like Dell, "is proving that business to business selling is e-commerce's killer app."[11] By 1999 Cisco was actually selling 80% of its products and services through the Web, thanks to the leadership of people like Sinton.

Where is Sinton today? He is "Managing @ The Speed of Thought" and overseeing the business-to-business e-commerce operation that was his brainchild. As he says, "I just knew the Net could be our business, that it could be a portal to our company."[12] The visionary proposal he wrote to the top executives at Cisco regarding the future of e-commerce is now preserved in the Smithsonian Institution archives.

Sometimes, therefore, you don't have to be leading your own subordinates to be leading other people. In championing a move to e-commerce, Sinton was able to get his bosses and the top executives at Cisco to become excited about his vision. Having done that, he was able to convince them to let him organize the resources that would enable Cisco to become a world leader in business-to-business e-commerce.

▶ THE FOUNDATIONS AND TRAITS OF LEADERSHIP

Whether it is Steve Jobs, Chris Sinton, Barbara Hyder, or the manager at your local dry cleaner, leading is difficult if the leaders don't have "the right stuff." This point has been illustrated clearly by two psychologists, Shelley Kirkpatrick and Edwin Locke. They say that personal traits and power comprise the foundations of leadership—in other words, these are two prerequisites you need before you can lead.[12]

The Leader's Traits

trait theory
in leadership, the theory that leaders have basic identifiable traits or characteristics that contribute to their success as leaders.

Are people like Hyder and Jobs successful as leaders in part because they have the right personality traits for the Job.[13] Identifying what those traits might be is the aim of the **trait theory** of leadership.

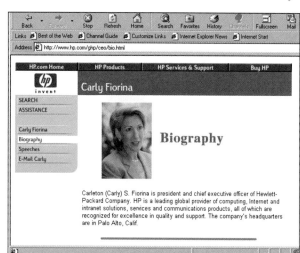

▲ W E B N O T E

Leaders like Carly Fiorina are successful in part because they have the right traits for the job.
www.hp.com
Used with permission.

The Trait Theory The idea that leaders are characterized by certain traits was initially inspired by a "great man" concept of leadership. This concept held that people like Steve Jobs, Microsoft's Bill Gates, and Hewlett-Packard's Carly Fiorina are great leaders because they were born with certain definable personality traits. Early researchers believed that if they studied the personality and intelligence of great leaders, they would sooner or later stumble on the combination of traits that made these people outstanding.

Most of the early research was inconclusive. Some studies asked leaders to describe their leadership traits. Most administered personality inventories to the leaders to assess the traits these people had. In any case, specific traits were related to effectiveness in some situations, but none was found to be consistently related in a variety of different studies and situations. However, recent research "has made it clear that successful leaders are not like other people. The evidence indicates that there are certain core traits which significantly contribute to business leaders' success."[14] Six traits on which leaders differ from nonleaders include drive, the desire to lead, honesty and integrity, self-confidence, cognitive ability, and knowledge of the business. Let's see why each of these matters:

Leaders have drive. They are action-oriented people with a relatively high desire for achievement. They get satisfaction from successfully completing challenging tasks. Leaders are more ambitious than nonleaders. They have high energy because "working long, intense work weeks (and many weekends for many years) requires an individual to have physical, mental, and emotional vitality."[15] Leaders are also tenacious and better at overcoming obstacles than are nonleaders.[16]

Leaders want to lead. Leaders are motivated to influence others. They prefer to be in a leadership rather than a subordinate role, and they willingly shoulder the mantle of authority.

A leader has honesty and integrity. Here's another way to state this: If your followers can't trust you, why should they follow you? Studies have found that leaders are generally rated more trustworthy and reliable in carrying out responsibilities than are followers.[17]

A leader has self-confidence. As two experts summarize, "Self-confidence plays an important role in decision-making and in gaining others' trust. Obviously, if the leader is not sure of what decision to make, or expresses a high degree of doubt, then the followers are less likely to trust the leader and be committed to the vision."[18]

A leader has cognitive ability. By definition, a leader is the one who must pick the right direction and then put into place the mechanisms required to get there. Leaders therefore tend to have more cognitive ability than nonleaders, and a leader's intelligence and subordinates' perception of his or her intelligence are generally highly rated leadership traits.[19]

The leader knows the business. Effective leaders are extremely knowledgeable about the company and the industry; their information helps them make informed decisions and understand the implications of those decisions.[20] There are exceptions: Louis Gertsner, Jr., became IBM chair with no computer experience, and he has excelled at the job. However, these exceptions make the rule: Gerstner has high cognitive ability and quickly immersed himself in absorbing the details of IBM's business. (And he also has a degree in engineering!)

THE **PEOPLE** SIDE OF MANAGING

■ Emotional Intelligence

The idea that great leaders have the right stuff is so seductive that the list of leadership traits is always growing. One of the most interesting lines of trait research focuses on what some experts call "emotional intelligence."[21] According to Daniel Goleman, author of *Working with Emotional Intelligence*, traits like intelligence and technical knowledge matter, but only as "threshold capabilities":

[T]hey are the entry-level requirements for executive positions. But my research, along with other recent studies, clearly shows that emotional intelligence is the *sine qua non* of leadership. Without it, a person can have the best training in the world, an incisive, analytical mind, and an endless supply of smart ideas, but he [or she] still won't make a great leader.[22]

▼ FIGURE 10.3

The Five Components of Emotional Intelligence at Work

Source: Reprinted by permission of the Harvard Business Review. An exhibit from "What Makes a Leader," by Daniel Goleman, November–December 1998. Copyright © 1998 by the President and Fellows of Harvard College. All rights reserved.

	Definition	Hallmarks
Self-Awareness	the ability to recognize and understand your moods, emotions, and drives, as well as their effect on others	self-confidence realistic self-assessment self-deprecating sense of humor
Self-Regulation	the ability to control or redirect disruptive impulses and moods the propensity to suspend judgment—to think before acting	trustworthiness and integrity comfort with ambiguity openness to change
Motivation	a passion to work for reasons that go beyond money or status a propensity to pursue goals with energy and persistence	strong drive to achieve optimism, even in the face of failure organizational commitment
Empathy	the ability to understand the emotional makeup of other people skill in treating people according to their emotional reactions	expertise in building and retaining talent cross-cultural sensitivity service to clients and customers
Social Skill	proficiency in managing relationships and building networks an ability to find common ground and build rapport	effectiveness in leading change persuasiveness expertise in building and leading teams

What is emotional intelligence? Basically, a bundle of people-oriented personality traits which, taken together, reflect a person's emotional maturity, empathy, and social skills. The five component traits of emotional intelligence at work (some of which, like motivation, consistently appear in earlier trait lists as well) are summarized in Figure 10.3. They include self-awareness, self-regulation, motivation, empathy, and social skill. For example, says Goleman, "if there is one trait that virtually all the effective leaders have, it is motivation. They're driven to achieve beyond expectations—their own and everyone else's."[23]

Power

Perhaps you've had the unfortunate experience of being told you are in charge of something, only to find that your subordinates ignore you when you try to assert your authority and give them orders. Such an experience underscores an important fact of leadership: A leader without power is really not a leader at all, since he or she has zero chance of influencing anyone to do anything. Understanding the sources of leadership power is therefore important: It's a second foundation of leadership.

A leader's power and authority derive from several sources. A leader's authority most commonly stems, first, from the *position* to which he or she is appointed. In other words, positions like sales manager or president have formal authority attached to them. As a leader you also have power based on your authority to *reward* employees who do well or coerce or *punish* those who don't do well. As head of, say, the research lab you may also have *expert* power, and be such an authority in your area that your followers do what you ask because of their respect for your expertise. And perhaps you possess *referent* power based on your personal magnetism, so your followers will follow you just because of your charisma.

Notice that whatever your source of power, it must be legitimate if you are to call yourself a leader. A mugger on the street may have a gun and the power to threaten your life, but not qualify as a leader, because leading means influencing people to work *willingly* toward achieving your objectives. That is not to say that a little fear can't be a good thing, at least occasionally. The most famous comment on fear was made in the 16th century by the Italian writer Niccolò Machiavelli, in his book *The Prince*:

> One ought to be both feared and loved, but as it is difficult for the two to go together, it is much safer to be feared than loved . . . for love is held by a chain of obligation which, men being selfish, is broken whenever it serves their purpose; but fear is maintained by a dread of punishment which never fails.

However, while there's more than a germ of truth in what Machiavelli said, there's a danger in relying on fear. A shrewd executive named Chester Barnard wrote in his classic work *The Functions of the Executive* that managers are essentially powerless unless their followers grant them the authority to lead.[24] The reality of leading is that you have to muster all the legitimate power you can get, and that often includes convincing your followers that you have earned the right to lead them.

The issue of power and fear is especially tricky in today's downsized, flattened, and empowered organizations. Increasingly, as we've seen, the tendency is to delegate authority and organize around horizontal, self-managing teams in which the employees themselves have the information and skills they need to control their own activities. Influencing people to get their jobs done by relying too heavily on your own formal authority or even on fear is therefore probably a much less effective tactic today than it would have been even a few years ago.

The idea that the "command and control" approach is increasingly unwieldy is not just theoretical. No less an expert on power than General Peter Schoomaker, commander in chief of the U.S. Special Operations Command (which includes the Army's Delta Force, the Green Berets, the Rangers, and the Navy Seals) argues that the tradi-

▲ Peacekeeping in Bosnia: In a new kind of military operation, U.S. Marines deal with armed guerrillas, discovery of mass graves, and keeping warring ethnic groups apart.

tional military way of issuing orders that are then obeyed unquestioningly is often an outmoded, inaccurate, and dangerous model for leadership today.[25] That's because the armies (and companies) that win today will be those that marshal "creative solutions in ambiguous circumstances"—diffusing ethnic tensions, delivering humanitarian aid, rescuing U.S. civilians trapped in an overseas uprising. And, in such circumstances, Schoomaker says, "everybody's got to know how to be a leader."[26]

Power and the right traits are not enough to make someone a successful leader—they are only a foundation, a precondition. If you have the traits and you have the power, then you have the *potential* to be a leader.[27] As Kirkpatrick and Locke put it, "Traits only endow people with the potential for leadership. To actualize this potential, additional factors are necessary."[28] Specifically, say Kirkpatrick and Locke, the leader must provide a vision (as explained above) and then engage in the behaviors required to get his or her people to implement that vision. Let's therefore turn to leadership style and how leaders behave.

▶ HOW LEADERS ACT LIKE LEADERS

Leadership researchers have formulated several theories to explain how a leader's style or behavior is related to his or her effectiveness. The basic assumption underlying most of these theories is that leaders perform two major functions—accomplishing the task and satisfying the needs of group members. Generally speaking, the functions of a task-oriented leader are to clarify what jobs need to be done and to force people to focus on their jobs. The social or people-oriented role of a leader is to reduce tension, make the job more pleasant, boost morale, and crystallize and defend the values, attitudes, and beliefs of the group. Most experts believe that the task and people dimensions of leader behavior are not mutually exclusive. In other words, most leaders exhibit degrees of both simultaneously.[29]

A number of specific leadership styles are associated with these basic task and people dimensions. In the remainder of this section we'll describe some of the most popular styles.

Structuring and Considerate Styles

Initiating structure and *consideration* have been two of the most frequently used descriptions of leader behavior. They developed out of a research project, originally focused on manufacturing facilities, and launched many years ago at Ohio State University.[30] A survey called the Leader Behavior Description Questionnaire (LBDQ) was developed and was further refined by subsequent researchers.[31] The two leadership factors it measures—consideration and initiating structure—have become synonymous with what experts call The Ohio State Dimensions of Leadership:

Consideration. Leader behavior indicative of mutual trust, friendship, support, respect, and warmth.

Initiating structure. Leader behavior by which the person organizes the work to be done and defines relationships or roles, the channels of communication, and ways of getting jobs done.

The research results unfortunately tend to be somewhat inconclusive. With respect to employee satisfaction, the findings led researcher Gary Yukl to conclude that "in most situations, considerate leaders will have more satisfied subordinates."[32] But the effects of such considerate leadership on employee performance are inconsistent. However, it's obviously foolish to underestimate the importance of being considerate—at least as a rule. Some outstanding leaders, such as Herb Kelleher of Southwest Airlines, take great pains to emphasize the importance of being considerate of one's employees. As he says, "I've tried to create a culture of caring for people in the totality of their lives, not just at work. . . . You have to recognize that people are still most important. How you treat them determines how they treat people on the outside."[33]

Yet leaders also have to remember to avoid what some leadership experts call the "country club" style: all consideration, and no focus on the work.[34] Showing respect for employees, providing support, and generally being considerate of their material and psychological needs are certainly important. But setting goals and getting things done is the name of the game. The leader's support must therefore generally be balanced with an expectation that employees are there to get their jobs done—on initiating structure, in other words.

Yet the effects of initiating structure are inconsistent with respect to performance and satisfaction. In one representative study, structuring activities by the leader and employee grievance rates were directly related: The more structuring the leader was, the more grievances were field. However, where the leader was also very considerate, leader structure and grievances were *not* related.[35] How can we explain such inconclusive findings? Part of the explanation—as we'll see in a moment—is that the style that is right for one situation might be wrong for another. Another part of the explanation, as mentioned above, is that a balance of these two styles generally works best.

Participative and Autocratic Styles

These two styles also stem from the basic "people" and "task" leader dimensions. Faced with the need to make a decision, the autocratic leader solves the problem and makes the decision alone, using the information available at the time.[36] At the other extreme, the participative leader shares the problem with subordinates as a group, and together they generate and evaluate alternatives and attempt to reach consensus on a solution.[37]

We know that encouraging employees to get involved in developing and implementing decisions affecting their jobs can have positive benefits. For example, employees who participate in setting goals tend to set higher goals than the supervisor would normally have assigned.[38] We've also seen that participation brings more points of view to bear and can improve the chances that participants will "buy into" the final decision. On the other hand, there are obviously some situations (like a sinking ship) in which being participative is inappropriate. The tricky part is deciding when to be participative and when not to be.

© 1998 Randy Glasbergen.

GLASBERGEN

"When the boss isn't around to watch us, he loads up this screen saver."

The University of Michigan Studies

At about the same time that researchers at Ohio State were developing their LBDQ, a similar program was beginning at the University of Michigan. Two sets of leadership styles—production-centered and employee-centered, and close and general—emerged from the Michigan studies.

First, Rensis Likert and his associates at Michigan identified two leadership styles. **Employee-oriented leaders** focus on the individuality and personality needs of their employees and emphasize building good interpersonal relationships. **Job-centered leaders** focus on production and the job's technical aspects. Based on his review of the research results, Likert concludes:

> Supervisors with the best record of performance focus their primary attention on the human aspects of their subordinates' problems and on endeavoring to build effective work groups with high performance goals.[39]

Other University of Michigan researchers conducted studies on what they called close and general leadership styles. **Close supervision**, according to these researchers, is at "one end of a continuum that describes the degree to which a supervisor specifies the roles of subordinates and checks up to see that they comply with these specifications."[40] The **laissez-faire leader** who follows a completely hands-off policy with subordinates is at the other extreme, while a **general leader** is somewhere in the middle of the continuum.

The research findings here are much clearer with respect to how close and general leaders affect employee morale than they are with respect to employee performance. Generally speaking, people do not like being closely supervised or having someone constantly checking up on them and telling them what to do. Close supervision is therefore usually associated with lower employee morale.[41] However, no consistent relationship emerged between closeness of supervision and employee performance.

employee-oriented leader
a leader who focuses on the needs of employees and emphasizes building good interpersonal relationships.

job-centered leader
a leader who focuses on production and on a job's technical aspects.

close supervision
a leadership style involving close, hands-on monitoring of subordinates and their work.

laissez-faire leader
a leader who takes a hands-off approach toward supervising subordinates.

general leader
a leader who takes a middle-ground approach between close supervision and laissez-faire leadership.

Transformational Leadership Behavior

A number of years ago James McGregor Burns wrote a book called *Leadership*, which had a major impact on the course of leadership theory.[42] Burns argues that leadership can be viewed as a transactional or a transformational process.[43] Leader behaviors like initiating structure and consideration, he suggests, are essentially based on *quid pro quo* transactions.

Specifically, **transactional behaviors** are "largely oriented toward accomplishing the tasks at hand and at maintaining good relations with those working with the leader [by exchanging promises of rewards for performance]."[44] The key here is that transactional behaviors tend to focus more on accomplishing tasks, and perhaps on doing so by somehow adapting the leader's style and behavior to the follower's expectations.

In today's fast-changing business environment, Burns argues, it's often not transactional behavior, but **transformational leadership** that's needed to manage change: "Transformational leadership refers to the process of influencing major changes in the attitudes and assumptions of organization members and building commitment for the organization's mission, objectives and strategies."[45] Transformational leaders are those who bring about "change, innovation, and entrepreneurship."[46] They are responsible for leading a corporate transformation that "recognizes the need for revitalization, creates a new vision, and institutionalizes change."[47]

What Do Transformational Leaders Do? Transformational leaders do several things. They encourage—and obtain—performance beyond expectations by formulating visions and then inspiring subordinates to pursue them. In so doing, transformational leaders cultivate employee acceptance and commitment to those visions.[48] They "attempt to raise the needs of followers and promote dramatic changes in individuals, groups, and organizations."[49]

Transformational leaders like Steve Jobs do this by articulating a realistic vision of the future that can be shared, by stimulating subordinates intellectually, and by paying attention to the differences among subordinates. Transformational leaders also provide a plan for attaining their vision and engage in **framing**, which means giving subordinates the big picture ("produce a super-easy-to-use iMac computer and user interface") so they can relate their individual activities to the work as a whole.[50]

From the vantage point of their followers, transformational leaders come across as charismatic, inspirational, considerate, and stimulating.[51]

- *Transformational leaders are charismatic.* Employees often idolize and develop strong emotional attachments to them.
- *Transformational leaders are inspirational.* "The leader passionately communicates a future idealistic organization that can be shared. The leader uses visionary explanations to depict what the employee work group can accomplish."[52] Employees are then motivated to achieve these organizational aims.
- *Transformational leaders are considerate.* Transformational leaders treat employees as individuals and stress developing them in a way that encourages the employees to become all they can be.

transactional behaviors
leadership actions that focus on accomplishing the tasks at hand and on maintaining good working relationships by exchanging promises of rewards for performance.

transformational leadership
the leadership process that involves influencing major changes in the attitudes and assumptions of organization members and building commitment for the organization's mission, objectives, and strategies.

framing
in decision making, the idea that the way a problem is presented can influence decisions.

▲ Jeff Bezos, president and founder of Amazon.com, whose vision of selling on the Internet opened up a whole new way of retailing.

- *Transformational leaders use intellectual stimulation.* They "encourage employees to approach old and familiar problems in new ways."[53] This enables employees to question their own beliefs and use creative ways to solve problems by themselves.

Examples of statements used to assess these four characteristics are

1. *Charisma.* "I am ready to trust him or her to overcome any obstacle."
2. *Individualized consideration.* "Treats me as an individual rather than just as a member of the group."
3. *Intellectual stimulation.* "Shows me how to think about problems in new ways."
4. *Inspirational leadership.* "Provides vision of what lies ahead."[54]

Studies of Transformational Leaders Transformational leadership has been studied in many settings.[55] In one study, researchers found that high-performing managers in an express delivery firm used significantly more transformational leader behaviors than did less successful managers in the firm.[56] Another study found that successful champions of technological change used more transformational leader behaviors than did less successful champions.[57]

Other studies suggest that transformational leadership tends to be more closely associated with leader effectiveness and employee satisfaction than are transactional styles of leadership such as general or laissez-faire leadership.[58] It therefore seems clear that a transformational leadership style can be very effective, especially in situations that require managing dramatic change.

Are There Gender Differences in Leadership Styles?

Although the number of women in management jobs has risen to almost 40%, barely 2% of top management jobs are held by women.[59] Women like Carly Fiorina and Barbara Hyder remain the exception. Most women managers are having trouble breaking into the top ranks. Research evidence suggests on the whole that this disparity is caused not by some inherent inability of women to lead, but by institutional biases known as "the glass ceiling" and persistent, if inaccurate, stereotypes. In other words, while there *are* a few differences in the way men and women lead, they do not account for the slow career progress of most women managers. We can summarize some of the more relevant research findings as follows.

▲ Breaking the glass ceiling: Jenny J. Ming, president of Gap Inc.'s Old Navy chain since April 1999, and one of *Business Week*'s Top 25 Managers for 1999.

Persistence of Inaccurate Stereotypes Women's promotions tend to be hampered first by inaccurate stereotypes. Managers tend to identify "masculine" (competitive) characteristics as managerial and "feminine" (cooperative and communicative) characteristics as nonmanagerial.[60] Women tend to be seen as less capable of being effective managers; men are viewed as better leaders. Another stereotype is that women managers tend to fall apart under pressure, respond impulsively, and have difficulty managing their emotions.[61] Such stereotypes usually don't hold up under the scrutiny of the researchers' microscope.

Leader Behaviors Studies suggest few measurable differences in the leader behaviors women and men managers use on the job. Women managers were found to be somewhat more achievement-oriented, and men managers more candid with co-workers.[62] In another study the only gender differences found were that women were more understanding than men.[63] Women and men who score high on the need for power (the need to influence other people) tend to behave more like each other than like people with lower power needs.[64]

Performance   How are women managers rated in terms of performance when compared with men? On the job and in joblike work simulations, women managers perform similarly to men. In actual organizational settings, "women and men in similar positions receive similar ratings."[65] In a special simulation called an assessment center, in which managers must perform realistic leadership tasks (such as leading problem-solving groups and making decisions), men and women managers perform similarly. Only in several off-the-job laboratory studies have men scored higher in performance.[66]

A Gender Advantage   Interestingly, one often-noticed and scientifically supported difference between men and women leaders may actually prove to be a boon to women managers. Women often score higher on measures of patience, relationship development, social sensitivity, and communication. And these may be precisely the skills that managers will need to manage diversity and the empowered members of self-managing teams.[67]

▶ SITUATIONAL THEORIES OF LEADERSHIP

One fact of corporate life is that very often a leader who was eminently qualified and successful in one situation turns out to be much less successful in another. For example, when Steve Jobs returned to Apple, he replaced the former CEO, Gus Amelio. Amelio had spent years as the successful CEO of a high-tech Silicon Valley firm, but lasted less than two years at Apple, where the company's fortunes continued to decline under his administration. Douglas Ivester was the chief operating officer for Coca-Cola Co. for many years, an effective number-two person to the company's CEO, Robert Gouizeta. When Gouizeta passed away the board unanimously chose Ivester to become CEO. Yet he lasted barely nine months before stepping down and being replaced.

It seems that successful leadership in one situation doesn't necessarily guarantee success in another. That fact has driven many experts to try to figure out how to fit the leader and his or her style to the situation. In general, we can say that their research provides some insights into the factors that determine the situational nature of leadership. However, it seems that considerably more research will be required before we have a theory that accurately predicts the conditions under which some leaders succeed while others fail. Let's turn to a synopsis of some of the more widely known approaches to studying the situational aspects of leadership.

Fiedler's Contingency Theory of Leadership

Working at the University of Illinois, psychologist Fred Fiedler originally sought to determine whether a leader who was lenient in evaluating associates was more likely or less likely to have a high-producing group than a leader who was demanding and discriminating.[68] At the core of this research is the least preferred co-worker (LPC) scale. Those who describe their least preferred co-worker favorably (pleasant, smart, and so on) are scored as "high LPC" and considered more people-oriented. "Low LPCs" describe least preferred co-workers unfavorably and are less people-oriented and more task-oriented.

According to Fiedler's theory, three situational factors combine to determine whether the high-LPC or the low-LPC style is appropriate:

1. *Position power*. The degree to which the position itself enables the leader to get group members to comply with and accept his or her decisions and leadership
2. *Task structure*. How routine and predictable the work group's task is
3. *Leader–member relations*. The extent to which the leader gets along with workers and the extent to which they have confidence in and are loyal to him or her

Fiedler initially concluded that the appropriateness of the leadership style "is contingent upon the favorableness of the group-task situation."[69] Basically, he argued that where the situation is either favorable or unfavorable to the leader (where leader–member relationships, task structure, and leader position power all are either very high or very low), a more task-oriented, low-LPC leader is appropriate. In the middle range, where these factors are more mixed and the task is not as clear-cut, a more people-oriented, high-LPC leader is appropriate. Many subsequent research findings cast doubt on the validity of Fiedler's conclusions, and the usefulness of the theory, including its more recent variants, remains in dispute.[70,71]

Path–Goal Leadership Theory

Path–goal leadership theory is based on the expectancy theory of motivation. Expectancy theory states that whether a person will be motivated depends on two things: whether the person believes he or she has the ability to accomplish a task, and his or her desire to do so. Leadership expert Robert J. House developed path–goal leadership theory. He says that in keeping with expectancy motivation theory, leaders should increase the personal rewards subordinates receive for attaining goals, and make the path to these goals easier to follow by reducing roadblocks and pitfalls.

Under this theory, the style a leader uses therefore depends on the situation. For example, if subordinates lack confidence in their ability to do the job, they may need more consideration and support. Or, if it's a situation in which subordinates are unclear about what to do or how to do it, the leader should provide structure (in terms of instructions, for instance) as required.[72] Path–goal leadership theory in general has received little support, in part, perhaps, because of the difficulty of quantifying concepts such as "path."[73]

Leader–Member Exchange Theory

leader–member exchange (LMX) theory

the theory that leaders may use different leadership styles with different members of the same workgroup, based in part on perceived similarities and differences with the leader.

Although a leader may have one prevailing style, you have probably noticed that most leaders don't treat all subordinates the same way. The **leader–member exchange (LMX) theory** says that leaders may use different styles with different members of the same work group.[74,75]

This theory suggests that leaders tend to divide their subordinates into an "in" group and an "out" group (you can imagine who gets the better treatment). What determines whether you're part of a leader's in or out group? The leader's decision is often made with very little real information, although perceived leader–member similarities—gender, age, or attitudes, for instance—are usually important.[76]

A study helps illustrate what makes a follower (or member) fall into a leader's in group or out group.[77] Completed questionnaires were obtained from 84 full-time registered nurses and 12 supervisors in 12 work groups at a large hospital in the southern United States. Of the supervisors (leaders), 83% were women, with an average age of 39 years; the nurses (followers) were mostly women (88.1%), with an average age of 36 years. Various things were measured, including the strength and quality of leader–member relationships or exchanges (friendliness between leader and member, rewards given to members, and so on).

The quality of leader–member exchanges (relationships) was found to be positively related to a leader's perceptions of two things: similarity of leader–follower attitudes and follower extroversion. For example, leaders were asked to assess the similarity between themselves and their followers in terms of attitudes toward six items: family, money, career strategies, goals in life, education, and overall perspective. Perhaps not surprisingly, leaders were more favorably inclined toward followers with whom they felt they shared similar attitudes. Followers were also asked to complete questionnaires that enabled the researchers to label them as introverted or extroverted. The extroverted nurses were more likely to have high-quality leader–member exchanges than were the introverts, presumably because they were more outgoing and sociable in general.

Findings like these suggest at least two practical implications. First, because members of the in group can be expected to perform better than those in the out group, leaders should strive to make the in group more inclusive. For followers, the findings emphasize the obvious importance of being in your leader's in group, and underscore the value of emphasizing similarities rather than differences in attitude—in politics, for instance—between you and your boss.

The Situational Leadership Model

Other behavioral scientists have developed what they call a *situational leadership model* to describe how the leader should adapt his or her style to the task; their model is presented in Figure 10.4.[78] They identify four leadership styles:

- The *delegating* leader lets the members of the group decide what to do themselves.
- The *participating* leader asks the members of the group what to do, but makes the final decisions himself or herself.
- The *selling* leader makes the decision himself or herself, but explains the reasons.
- The *telling* leader makes the decision himself or herself, and tells the group what to do.

According to the situational leadership model, each style is appropriate in a specific situation:

- Delegating works best where followers are willing to do the job and know how to go about doing it.
- Participating works best when followers are able to do the job but are unwilling and so require emotional support.
- Selling works best where followers are neither willing nor able to do the job.
- Telling works best where followers are willing to do the job, but don't know how to do it.

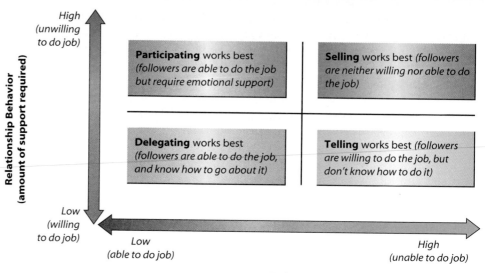

► **FIGURE 10.4**

Situational Leadership Model

Source: Jerald Greenberg. *Managing Behaviour in Organizations: Science in Service* (Upper Saddle River, NJ: Prentice Hall, 1996). Reprinted by permission.

The Vroom-Jago-Yetton Model

Finally, leadership experts Victor Vroom, Arthur Jago, and Philip Yetton have developed a model that lets a leader analyze a situation and decide whether it is right for participation. Being participative, they point out, is usually not an either/or decision, since there are different degrees of participation. These are summarized in Figure 10.5, which presents a continuum of five possible management decision styles. At one extreme is Style I, no participation. Here the leader solves the problem and makes the decision himself or herself. Style V, total participation, is at the other extreme: Here the leader shares the problem with subordinates, and together they reach an agree-

► **FIGURE 10.5**

Five Types of Management Decision Styles

I. You solve the problem or make the decision yourself, using information available to you at that time.

II. You obtain the necessary information from your subordinates, then decide on the solution to the problem yourself. You may or may not tell your subordinates what the problem is when getting the information from them. The role played by your subordinates in making the decision is clearly one of providing the necessary information to you, rather than generating or evaluating alternative solutions.

III. You share the problem with relevant subordinates individually, getting their ideas and suggestions without bringing them together as a group. Then you make the decision, which may or may not reflect your subordinates' influence.

IV. You share the problem with your subordinates as a group, collectively obtaining their ideas and suggestions. Then you make the decision, which may or may not reflect your subordinates' influence.

V. You share a problem with your subordinates as a group. Together you generate and evaluate alternatives and attempt to reach agreement (consensus) on a solution. Your role is much like that of a chairperson. You do not try to influence the group to adopt "your" solution, and you are willing to accept and implement any solution that has the support of the entire group.

ment. You can see that between these two extremes are Style II, minimum participation; Style III, more participation; and Style IV, still more participation.

In their model, the appropriate degree of participation depends on several attributes of the situation that can be quantified by asking a sequence of diagnostic questions. A typical diagnostic question is, "Do I have sufficient information to make a high-quality decision?" Another is, "Is acceptance of the decision by subordinates critical to implementation?" By answering a series of questions like these, a leader, say these experts, can determine whether—and to what extent—to let subordinates participate in making the decision.

▶ BECOMING A LEADER

Being a leader means taking the steps required to boost your effectiveness at filling the leader's role. No formula can guarantee that you can be a leader. However, based on the research presented in this chapter, there are some powerful actions you can take to improve the chances that in a leadership situation you will be a leader. These can be summarized as follows.

Start to Think Like a Leader

It is important to think like a leader, so that you can bring to bear everything you know about leadership and human behavior rather than just react with a knee-jerk response. First, apply the three-step model: Identify what is happening, account for what is happening by bringing to bear all your knowledge of leadership and behavioral theory and concepts, and formulate a response.

Remember that behavioral science knowledge about leading is not limited to just the material contained in this chapter; you need to be able to apply knowledge from the subsequent chapters on motivation, groups, conflict, and change and fit it into your assessment of the situation as you account for what is happening and decide how to influence your followers to deal with the situation. Don't be overwhelmed by the number of theories and concepts that might apply; think of them as tools in your leadership toolbox. There may be—and probably is—more than one way to solve the problem.

Develop Your Judgment

Possessing the traits of leadership gives someone the potential to be a leader. Your ability to be a leader can thus be improved by enhancing your existing leadership traits. Some traits are easier to enhance than others, but all of them can be modified. For example, judgment is important because people will not long follow a leader who makes too many bad decisions. In Chapter 4, we saw that several steps can improve your decision-making ability:

- *Correctly define the problem.* Remember: Don't install new elevators when mirrors will do!
- *Increase your knowledge.* The more you know about the problem and the more facts you can marshall, the more likely it is that your confidence in your decision will not be misplaced.
- *Free your judgment of bias.* A number of cognitive or decision-making biases can distort a manager's judgment. Reducing or eliminating biases like stereotyping from your judgment process is, therefore, a crucial step toward making better decisions.

- *Be creative.* Creativity plays a big role in making better decisions. The ability to develop novel responses—creativity—is essential for decision-making activities like developing new alternatives and correctly defining the problem.
- *Use your intuition.* Many behavioral scientists argue that a preoccupation with analyzing problems rationally and logically can actually backfire by blocking someone from using his or her intuition.
- *Don't overstress the finality of your decision.* Remember that very few decisions are forever; there is more give in more decisions than we realize. Even major, strategic decisions can often be reversed or modified as situations warrant.
- *Make sure the timing is right.* Most people's decisions are affected by their passing moods. Managerial decision makers should therefore take their emotions into account before making important decisions. Sometimes it's best just to sleep on the decisions.

Develop Your Other Leadership Traits

Good judgment is just one of the leadership traits you can enhance. Leaders also exhibit self-confidence. Although developing self-confidence may be a lifelong process, you can enhance it in several ways. One is to focus more on those situations in which you are more self-confident to begin with, such as those in which you are an expert. A stamp collector might exhibit more self-confidence as president of his or her stamp club than in coaching a baseball team, for instance. You can act like a leader by exhibiting self-confidence—by making decisions and sticking with them, and by acting somewhat reserved.

Your knowledge of the business is probably the easiest trait to modify; immerse yourself in the details of your new job and learn as much about the business as you can, as fast as you can. (Figure 10.6 provides a quick test of your leadership readiness).

Start to Build Your Power Base

Remember that a powerless leader is not a leader at all. You can strengthen the foundation of your leadership by enhancing your authority and power. One way to do this is to start acting like a leader. Cracking jokes may get some laughs, but most leaders act at least somewhat reserved to maintain their power base. How much power do you have? Managers with more power generally have:

Reward power if they can:
1. Increase pay levels.
2. Influence getting a raise.
3. Provide specific benefits.
4. Influence getting a promotion.

Coercive power if they can:
5. Give undesirable work assignments.
6. Make work difficult.
7. Make things unpleasant.
8. Influence getting a promotion.

The following self-assessment exercise can give you a feel for your readiness and inclination to assume a leadership role.

INSTRUCTIONS. Indicate the extent to which you agree with each of the following statements, using the following scale: (1) disagree strongly; (2) disagree; (3) neutral; (4) agree; (5) agree strongly.

1. It is enjoyable having people count on me for ideas and suggestions.	1	2	3	4	5
2. It would be accurate to say that I have inspired other people.	1	2	3	4	5
3. It's a good practice to ask people provocative questions about their work.	1	2	3	4	5
4. It's easy for me to compliment others.	1	2	3	4	5
5. I like to cheer people up even when my own spirits are down.	1	2	3	4	5
6. What my team accomplishes is more important than my personal glory.	1	2	3	4	5
7. Many people imitate my ideas.	1	2	3	4	5
8. Building team spirit is important to me.	1	2	3	4	5
9. I would enjoy coaching other members of the team.	1	2	3	4	5
10. It is important to me to recognize others for their accomplishments.	1	2	3	4	5
11. I would enjoy entertaining visitors to my firm even if it interfered with my completing a report.	1	2	3	4	5
12. It would be fun for me to represent my team at gatherings outside our department.	1	2	3	4	5
13. The problems of my teammates are my problems too.	1	2	3	4	5
14. Resolving conflict is an activity I enjoy.	1	2	3	4	5
15. I would cooperate with another unit in the organization even if I disagreed with the position taken by its members.	1	2	3	4	5
16. I am an idea generator on the job.	1	2	3	4	5
17. It's fun for me to bargain whenever I have the opportunity.	1	2	3	4	5
18. Team members listen to me when I speak.	1	2	3	4	5
19. People have asked me to assume the leadership of an activity several times in my life.	1	2	3	4	5
20. I've always been a convincing person.	1	2	3	4	5

Total score: ___

SCORING AND INTERPRETATION. Calculate your total score by adding the numbers circled. A tentative interpretation of the scoring is as follows:

=	90–100	high readiness for the leadership role
=	60–89	moderate readiness for the leadership role
=	40–59	some uneasiness with the leadership role
=	39 or less	low readiness for the leadership role

If you are already a successful leader and you scored low on this questionnaire, ignore your score. If you scored surprisingly low and you are not yet a leader or are currently performing poorly as a leader, study the statements carefully. Consider changing your attitude or your behavior so that you can legitimately answer more of the statements with a 4 or a 5.

▶ **FIGURE 10.6**

Are you Ready to Be a Leader?

Source: Andrew DuBrin, *Leadership: Research Findings, Priorities, and Skills.* Copyright © 1995 by Houghton Mifflin Company. Reprinted with permission.

Legitimate power if they can:

9. Make others feel they have commitments to meet.

10. Make others feel they should satisfy job requirements.

11. Give the feeling that others have responsibilities to fulfill.

12. Make others recognize that they have tasks to accomplish.

Expert power if they can:

13. Give good technical suggestions.

14. Share considerable experience and/or training.

15. Provide sound job-related advice.

16. Provide needed technical knowledge.

Referent power if they can:

17. Make employees feel valued.

18. Make employees feel that I approve of them.

19. Make employees feel personally accepted.

20. Make employees feel important.

Help Others Share Your Vision

Leading means influencing people to work enthusiastically toward an objective. Ensure that your subordinates know and understand the vision, mission, or objective and that you have clarified their assignments. Remember how successful Steve Jobs has been at Apple. As leadership expert John Kotter puts it, "great leaders are all good at getting relevant partners aligned with, buying into, believing in" the direction they have set.

Adapt Your Style and Actions to the Situation

No one leadership style is appropriate for every situation in which you find yourself. Remember that the art of being a leader lies in your being able to identify the leadership-related issues and then being able to determine whether one or more leadership theories and concepts can be applied, and if so, how.

Use Your Other Management Skills to Help You Lead

Research suggests that various management actions can actually function as substitutes for the leadership you may otherwise have to provide.[79] Here are two examples.

Choose the Right Followers If you select and train your followers well, there may be less reason for you to have to exercise leadership on a daily basis. The greater your subordinates' ability, the more their experience, the better their training, and the more professional their behavior, the less direct supervision they will need. Some followers are inherently more effective than others: Choose followers who are cooperative, flexible, and trustworthy and who have initiative and are good at solving problems.[80]

Organize the Task Properly   You may also be able to modify organizational factors to reduce the need for day-to-day leadership. Jobs for which the performance standards are clear, or for which there is plenty of built-in feedback, may require less leadership.[81] Similarly, employees engaged in work that is intrinsically satisfying (work they love to do) require less leadership.[82] Cohesive work groups with positive norms also require less leadership (as do, by definition, self-managing teams).

SUMMARY

1. Leadership means influencing others to work willingly toward achieving objectives. Being a leader requires more than having a command of leadership theories: It also means managing organizational culture; motivating employees; managing groups, teams, and conflict; and facilitating organizational change.

2. Thinking like a leader means reviewing a leadership situation and identifying what is happening, accounting for what is happening (in terms of leadership and other behavioral science theories and concepts), and formulating leader actions.

3. The leader must provide a direction that followers can work toward. This direction may be a statement of vision, mission, or objectives, depending largely on what the leader wants to achieve and the level at which he or she is acting.

4. To be a leader one must also have the potential to be a leader. Having the right stuff (in terms of personality traits) is the second foundation component. Some traits on which leaders differ from nonleaders include drive, the desire to lead, honesty and integrity, self-confidence, cognitive ability, and knowledge of the business.

5. Legitimate power and authority are elements in the foundation of leadership, because a leader without power is not a leader at all. Sources of leader power include position, rewards, coercion, expertise, and referent power or personal magnetism.

6. Leadership style or behaviors include structuring and considerate styles; participative and autocratic styles; employee-centered and production-centered styles; close and general styles; and transformational behavior.

7. Although there are some differences in the way men and women lead, they do not account for the slower career progress of most women managers. Institutional biases such as the glass ceiling and persistent, inaccurate, stereotypes are contributing factors.

8. Situational leadership theories like those of Fiedler and House and the leader–member exchange theory underscore the importance of fitting the style to the situation.

TYING IT ALL TOGETHER

Developing a plan and creating an organization is only part of the task a manager faces. Companies and other organizations are composed of people, and it's the manager's job to inspire, lead, and motivate these people to carry out the company's or the department's mission. In this chapter—the first in Part 4—we looked at what it takes to be a leader, in particular the traits and styles of effective leaders, and how to think like a leader and size up leadership situations. As you know from your own experience, one of the leader's biggest tasks involves actually motivating subordinates. So in Chapter 11 we'll turn to the important topic of motivating employees.

leadership 291
trait theory 296
employee-oriented leader 302
job-centered leader 302

close supervision 302
laissez-faire leader 302
general leader 302
transactional behaviors 303

transformational leadership 303
framing 303
leader–member exchange (LMX) theory 306

SKILLS AND STUDY MATERIALS

CRITICAL THINKING EXERCISES

1. The November 22, 1999, issue of *Fortune* is devoted to the 20th century. In tracing the concept of leadership, *Fortune* divides leadership by decade. In the 1900s it was moguls such as J. P. Morgan. In the 1910s it was the government as regulator, such as breaking up of Standard Oil. By the 1920s celebrities such as Charles Lindbergh attained the sort of media-driven prominence. The union worker led the 1930s. In the 1940s the United States led the rebuilding of Europe. In the 1950s it was the man in the gray flannel suit (think *Father Knows Best*). By the 1960s the conglomerator symbolized the times. Women emerged as leaders in the 1970s. In the 1980s the MBA consultant was the leader. In the decade of the 1990s the e-leaders, cyber chiefs such as Jeff Bezos of Amazon.com, reinvented old business models for a wired world. Think about what leadership will be like in 2000, 2010, 2020, 2030, 2040, and 2050. Base your thinking on what the chapter presents combined with the ideas from *Fortune*.

2. As a group, compare and contrast the perspectives on leadership presented below.[83] What concepts from the chapter would help you in understanding their various perspectives? Which style do you like best and why?

   Leaders can't succeed if they care more about how people feel than how they perform. So focus on output, not attitude. Employees who get results should be taken at face value. Sincerity and competence rarely share a soul. Reward the latter and forget the former.

   Marilyn Moats Kennedy, Managing Partner, Career Strategies, Wilmette, Illinois

   I find it amusing, frustrating, and often, quite appalling, how few business leaders recognize that people should share in the economic value they create. At LifeUSA, our employees have options on 2 million shares of company stock. It seems like common sense to us. So why is it still so uncommon in most companies?

   Sharing the wealth with everyone creates a vested interest for everyone to succeed. It's also a powerful mechanism for accountability. And it encourages people to innovate and provide unbeatable service.

   Nobody wins unless everybody wins.

   Maggie Hughes, COO, LifeUSA Holdings, Inc., Minneapolis, Minnesota

   CEOs are always searching for vision, and I'm no different. But I've come to appreciate the value of bifocals—the kind that let me move from a close up view of Merix to one farther away, and then back again. I try to wear my corporate bifocals regularly, alternating my view so I can get a better look at where we are as an organization and where we are going in the future.

   Sometimes what you see depends on how you look.

   Debi Coleman, Chair and CEO, Merix Corporation, Forest Grove, Oregon

1. Leaders come in all sizes, shapes, genders, and races. Your task is to research five of the following people and then write a brief analysis of what made them leaders. After you have completed that portion of the task, explain what you think an "ideal" leader is and identify someone you think fits that profile best. Write no more than two pages of analysis.

   The leaders are George W. Bush, presidential candidate; Andrew Young, politician; Former first lady Hillary Clinton; Bill Clinton, U.S. president; Mao Zedong, late communist leader of China; Rosa Parks, civil rights leader; Madeline Albright, secretary of state; Bill Gates of Microsoft; Louis Gerstner, CEO of IBM; Helmut Kohl, former chancellor of Germany; and Michael Jordan, former professional basketball star.

2. The November 22, 1999, *Fortune* lists the following men as the four finalists for businessman of the century, in order of time: Henry Ford, founder of Ford Motor Company; Alfred P. Sloan Jr., architect of the modern corporation and CEO of General Motors; Thomas J. Watson Jr., leader of IBM; and Bill Gates, of Microsoft. Which do you think the magazine selected, and why? Do some research on each. Then rank-order the four based on your research. After you have completed the ranking, look at *Fortune* and compare your analysis and theirs.

3. In *The New Global Leaders* (Jossey-Bass, 1999) authors Manfried F. R. Kets de Vries and Elizabeth Florent-Treacy select Richard Branson (United Kingdom) of Virgin Airlines, Percy Barnevik (Sweden) of ASEA Brown Boveri (ABB—engineering), and David Simon (United Kingdom) of British Petroleum as the models for global leadership. Research each of these companies on the Internet or go to the library and find *The New Global Leaders*. Then write a comparative analysis of these individuals' leadership styles and why they are seen as models for the global marketplace.

We invite you to visit the Dessler companion Web site at **www.prenhall.com/dessler** for this chapter's Internet resources.

TURNING AROUND THE U.S.S. BENFOLD

CASE 1

While "leadership" may seem a little theoretical in some situations, that's certainly not the case when it comes to the U.S. Navy. When you're the captain of the ship, the lives of all the people on that ship are in your hands. Leadership style can have a corrosive effect on sailors' morale and on their—and the ship's—performance.

For the past few years, in fact, the U.S. military has been in what one officer calls "deep trouble." Commander Mike Abrashoff says: "People aren't joining. More people are leaving. The attrition rates are going through the roof. In the Navy, 33 percent of those who join never complete their first tour of duty. Combat readiness is declining."[84]

Given those trends, Commander Abrashoff's experience in instituting a new leadership initiative when he took over as captain of the *U.S.S. Benfold* is all the more remarkable. In the two years he was leading the ship, the *Benfold* retention rate went from about 25% to 100% in most of the ship's top job categories. Attrition went from more than 18% to less than 1%, and mission-degrading casualties dropped from 75 to 24. During his final 12 months in command, the ship even ran on 75% of its operating budget, and returned millions of dollars to the Navy. How did he do it?

To a large extent, this turnaround in attitudes was a consequence of a remarkably simple initiative on Abrashoff's part: he brought a new leadership style to the *U.S.S. Benfold* when he took command. Abrashoff says that when he took over, he decided right away that before he could fix the problems on the ship, he had to find out what those problems were. He started his command by interviewing every crew member individually. He'd start each interview with several questions, such as "Where are you from?" "Why did you join the Navy?" "What are your goals in the Navy?" "What are your goals in life?" Then he asked three more questions: "What do you like most about the *Benfold*?" "What do you like least?" "What things would you change if you could?"

As Abrashoff puts it, "The minute I started these interviews, our performance took off like a rocket. Whenever I got an outstanding idea from a sailor—and about 70% of the ideas that I got were, in fact, outstanding—I would implement that idea right on the spot."[85] He used the public address system to tell the rest of the crew what the new idea was, which sailor the idea came from, and that he was implementing it immediately and needed their support in doing so.

Mike Abrashoff says that whenever he needed a reminder about what leadership was all about, he took out an index card he kept in his wallet. On the card were the eight leadership traits he always used as personal guidelines: A leader is trusted. A leader takes the initiative. A leader uses good judgment. A leader speaks with authority. A leader strengthens others. A leader is optimistic and enthusiastic. A leader never compromises his absolutes. A leader leads by example.[86]

Questions

1. How does Commander Abrashoff's leadership style compare with the leadership styles described in this chapter? Do you think his leadership initiative would have been as useful in a company as it was on the *U.S.S. Benfold*? Why or why not?

2. What does Abrashoff's experience on the *U.S.S. Benfold* say to you about how leaders should behave? Why?

3. Abrashoff's index card contains eight leadership traits. How do these eight traits compare with the foundations of leadership covered in this chapter? In what ways are they similar? Different?

4. In addressing the problems on the *U.S.S. Benfold*, did Abrashoff "think like a leader"? In what way?

CAN A MANAGER'S LEADERSHIP STYLE WORK IN MORE THAN ONE SITUATION?

CASE 2

Many analysts would consider leading a manufacturing turnaround the most difficult of all leadership situations. Turnarounds usually require a tough-minded and transformational leader who can make very difficult decisions quickly. Morale can often be difficult in this type of situation as the firm may have been losing money, and radical cost-cutting is often the first move the leader must make. Analysts might prescribe a very different style for the manager of an entrepreneurial start-up or a not-for-profit service provider. Can one leader be successful in this wide range of settings? Consider the case of Vince Naimoli.

Naimoli is currently the managing general partner and CEO of the Tampa Bay Devil Rays baseball organization. It is not his first leadership role. Naimoli has also served in a variety of challenging high-level corporate management situations, including several turnarounds. Will the leadership skills Naimoli developed in industry serve him well in his new career?

As a young man, Naimoli earned a degree in engineering from Notre Dame and an MBA from Fairleigh Dickinson University. He began his career at Continental Group. Over a 12-year period, he progressed through various management positions, eventually becoming a vice president and general manager of Continental Can Company. As general manager of that division, Naimoli had responsibility for over $800 million in sales, the operation of 52 plants, and more than 11,000 employees.

Naimoli then joined Anchor Hocking Corporation as a vice president in the firm's packaging division, which was a money-loser for its parent corporation. Sensing opportunity, in 1983 Naimoli led a group of managers in the purchase of Anchor Glass Container Corporation. The investors named him chairman, president, and CEO. Within a year, the company went from losing over $12 million to making a modest profit. Under his leadership, the company pursued a series of productivity enhancements and acquisitions. Profitability increased and the company grew. By 1986, Naimoli was in a position to take Anchor Glass public again.

By 1987 *Forbes* ranked Anchor Glass as having the third highest return on assets in the nation. In 1989, when Naimoli sold the company, Anchor had revenues in excess of $1 billion and was highly profitable.

After selling Anchor Glass, Naimoli created Anchor Industries International, Inc. (AII), an investment and consulting firm specializing in corporate turnarounds. His new company would acquire companies and appoint Naimoli president and CEO. Through AII and other ventures, Naimoli became CEO of Harding Services, and president and CEO of various portfolio companies, including Electrolux Corporation. Over the next few years, Naimoli successfully orchestrated turnarounds of Doehler-Jarvis, Inc., Ladish Co., Inc., and Harvard Industries. At Harvard Industries, Naimoli became a director one month after the company's bankruptcy reorganization. One year later, the company reported over $7 million in earnings. For his work as chairman, president, and CEO of AII, Naimoli was named 1995 Florida Entrepreneur of the Year in the turnaround category. During his tenure at AII, Naimoli was successful in leading the effort to bring major league baseball to Tampa.

While most leaders would be satisfied with success in one field, Naimoli has triumphed in manufacturing and service environments in many industries. He has also found time to stay active in a leadership role in the community. He has served as chairman of the College of Business, Advisory Board at Notre Dame and chairman of the Board of Trustees of the University of Tampa. He is or has been a director of more than 24 public and private entities and corporations and has received many honors for his corporate, civic, and charitable activity. In 1999 The Northwood University Board of Trustees presented Naimoli with its prestigious Outstanding Business Leader Award.

Discussion Questions

1. Based on what you read in this chapter, list the leadership traits and styles you think Naimoli brings to a leadership situation that make him so successful.

2. To what extent do you feel Naimoli needed to change his leadership style as he moved from turnaround specialist to entrepreneur?

3. To what extent does Naimoli seem to show transformational leadership characteristics? Why?

YOU BE THE CONSULTANT

MICHAEL DORF LEADS KNITMEDIA

If you were to fast forward through KnitMedia's history, you'd find it reflects the leadership of Michael Dorf: Michael manages the band Swamp Thing and starts Flaming Pie Records in Madison, Wisconsin in 1985; the first Knitting Factory opens in 1997; Michael begins recording live Knitting Factory performances and offers them as a "Live at the Knitting Factory" radio series, in part by persuading 30 radio stations to pay $5 a week for the cost of duplication and mailings; Michael begins KnitMedia's Internet operations; and Michael and KnitMedia raise about $5 million and began opening new Knitting Factory clubs abroad.

KnitMedia, in other words has always been driven by Michael Dorf's vision, and to a large extent Dorf still exercises his leadership influence through that vision. As Allan Fried says, "I think Michael leads through his vision; he's got a really powerful instinct and vision for where we need to go, and of what drives our success aesthetically and commercially in terms of achieving our commercial goals as well as our artistic integrity."

However, as in Michael Dorf's case, it's usually not just vision that characterizes successful leaders, but also single-mindedness. Building a business from scratch means overcoming thousands and thousands of obstacles, and an entrepreneur usually can't do that if he or she is weak-willed or does not consistently demand perfection from those who are working for him or her.

This can translate into a sort of austere leadership style. For example, Mark Harabedian, the firm's vice president of finance, says: "What kind of leader is Michael? He's rough. He expects a lot of you, probably more than is possible, and that might create, you know, problems since there's certain things that are physically impossible and that people simply can't do." Michael Dorf himself would probably agree with this assessment. For example, when he left to open the Los Angeles Knitting Factory, he found that while he was gone people had to make decisions on their own and that, as a result, "some of our people completely failed, but [for] those who rose to the occasion, [their ability] was very clear. [My being away], I think, made the cream rise to the top and my being away sort of forced the issue, without having to wait two years to see how well people could do with some initiative."

This all raises several questions for Michael Dorf and his management team, however. For example, as the company grows, how can Dorf's vision continue to penetrate every nook and cranny of the company's worldwide operations so he can continue to provide the sort of leadership he did during the firm's first 10 or 15 years? Second, what sort of consequences do you think Michael's single-mindedness and demanding style of leadership is liable to have—for good or for ill—on the company as it expands?

Team Exercises and Questions

Use what you learned in this chapter to answer the following questions from Michael Dorf and his management team:

1. What exactly can we do to make sure that Michael Dorf's vision does in fact penetrate every nook and cranny of the company as it grows?

2. How would you characterize Michael Dorf as a leader, based on the various styles and approaches management experts use to describe leaders today?

3. What do you see as the pros and cons of this kind of leadership style in terms of the effects it will have on KnitMedia and its employees?

4. Should Michael Dorf modify his leadership style in any way? Why or why not? If so, how would you suggest he go about doing so, and to what end?

MOTIVATING EMPLOYEES TODAY

WHAT'S AHEAD?

General Electric is one of the largest companies in the world. Yet in one recent year its revenues rose 11% to over $100 billion, its earnings rose 13%, and its operating margin (a measure of efficiency) rose a stunning full percentage point, from 15.7% to 16.7%. How can a company so big that makes everything from light bulbs to jet engines to power plants improve its performance so dramatically? The answer can be seen in GE's aircraft engine assembly facility in Durham, North Carolina.[1]

Teams of nine people each are completely responsible for producing entire jet engines, and they operate with just one basic instruction: the day the engine is to be loaded onto a truck.[2] The Durham plant, staffed with highly motivated and self-managing employees, holds the key to motivating employees in a period of global competition and rapid change.

OBJECTIVES

AFTER STUDYING THIS CHAPTER, YOU SHOULD BE ABLE TO

- Compare and contrast three need-based approaches to motivating employees

- Explain the roles of equity, goal setting, and expectations in motivation

- Illustrate the use of the behavior modification approach

- Give examples of how to use 10 methods for influencing behavior and motivating employees

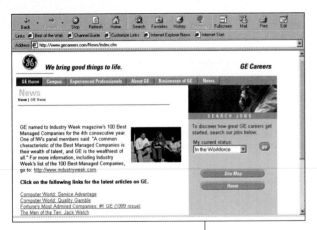

▲ **W E B N O T E**

GE uses the Internet to publicize successful management practices.

www.gecareers.com

Used with permission.

total quality management (TQM)

an organizationwide management system that focuses all functions of the business on maximizing customer satisfaction at continually lower real costs.

Imagine for a moment that you are Jack Fish, the GE Durham plant's founding plant manager. You work for Jack Welch, GE's relentless CEO, a man who's been called "neutron Jack" (for the way he laid off 100,000 workers when he first took over GE), and who still grades each of GE's 85,000 professionals and managers by dividing them into five groups: the top 10%, the next 15%, the middle 50%, the next 15%, and the bottom 10%. You know that while those in the top tier will get bonuses, most of those in the bottom tier will be cut.[3] The company Welch manages strives for continuous progress toward perfection in the products that it makes, continually eliminating defects and wasted effort through a process known as total quality management (TQM).

But your challenge is not just that you work for a demanding boss. You're building a product that simply can't have any defects. Those giant jet engines that your plant builds will drive countless aircraft like the Boeing 777, so you certainly don't want any errors. For example, in measuring the huge 6-foot-wide circular rings that will seal the engine's gases, you know the diameter can be off by no more than half a human hair; that will take a degree of caution and responsibility on the employees' part that can't just be bought with money or assured by supervisors barking orders.

Indeed, your challenge is quite different from that facing the plant manager of the early auto plant shown in Figure 11.1. With relatively little competition and no one's life riding on the results, managers in plants like these could often rely on financial incentives and close supervision to ensure the work got done, and done on time. You can't get away with that today. Somehow, you've got to organize the

▶ **FIGURE 11.1**

An Early Auto Plant

Managers in plants like these could rely on close supervision to be sure the work got done right and on time.

Source: Warner Pflug, The UAW in Pictures (Detroit: Wayne State University Press, 1971), p. 14.

work and motivate the workers so that they're turned on by and committed to their jobs. Somehow, based on your experience and your understanding of human needs and motivation, you've got to organize the work so that the workers, without supervision, will do their jobs as if they own the company.

Today, in other words, at GE's Durham plant, at thousands of new startup .com companies, and at the faraway offices of major companies, intrinsic motivation—motivation that comes from within the individual and which drives the person to do a great job because he or she genuinely wants to do it—is more important than ever. At GE's Durham plant, for instance, employees aren't driving themselves to produce the highest quality engines in the world because they're paid to do so. They're doing it because the job has been organized in such a way and they've been treated in such a way that they're dedicated to doing their jobs in a superior and self-managed manner.

Motivation can be defined as the intensity of a person's desire to engage in some activity. We know that employees can be motivated and that there are few more important leadership tasks than motivating subordinates. In Chapter 10 we discussed leadership, including how to size up and deal with a leadership situation. Knowing how to motivate employees will play a central role in any such analysis. In this chapter, we turn to the studies that help explain what motivates people, and to several specific methods you as a leader can use to motivate subordinates. We'll look first at three approaches that help explain what motivates people: need-based, process-based, and learning/reinforcement-based approaches. Each takes a different perspective in explaining how motivation occurs and how to motivate a person. All are used by managers.

motivation
the intensity of a person's desire to engage in some activity.

▶ **NEED-BASED APPROACHES**

The defense attorney paced back and forth in front of the jury and asked, "Ladies and gentlemen, what possible motive would my client have for committing this crime?" That question is crucial: After all, if there's no motive, then why do it?

Motives and needs also play a central role at work. A **motive** is something that incites the person to action or that sustains and gives direction to action.[4] When we ask why a defendant might have done what he did, or why a football player works to stay in shape all year, or why a sales manager flies all night to meet with a client, we are asking about motives.

A motive can be aroused or unaroused. Everyone carries within him or her **motivational dispositions or needs**—motives that, like seeds in winter, go unaroused until the proper conditions bring them forth. You may have a motivational disposition to enjoy yourself at the movies, but that motive is dormant until Saturday night, when you can put your studies aside. **Aroused motives** are motives that express themselves in behavior.[5] When the conditions are right—when the studies are over, the quiz is done, and the weekend has arrived—the movie-attendance motive is aroused, and you may be off to your favorite flick.

Need-based approaches to motivating employees focus on the role of needs or motivational dispositions in driving people to do what they do. Which needs or motivational dispositions are most important? How and under what conditions do they become aroused and translated into behavior? These are the sorts of questions studied by psychologists like Abraham Maslow, David McClelland, and Frederick Herzberg. (See the chapter appendix for an additional perspective on motives and individual behavior.)

motive
something that incites a person to action or that sustains and gives direction to action.

motivational dispositions or needs
motives that lie dormant until the proper conditions arise to bring them forth or make them active.

aroused motive
a motive that expresses itself in behavior.

Maslow's Needs-Hierarchy Theory

Maslow's needs hierarchy is typical of need-based approaches and is the basis for the other approaches discussed in this section. Maslow argued that people have five increasingly higher-level needs: physiological, security, social, self-esteem, and self-actualization. According to Maslow's *prepotency process principle*, people are first motivated to satisfy the lower-order needs and then, in sequence, each of the higher-order needs.[6] (Psychologist Clay Alderfer, in a variant of this theory, emphasizes that all the needs may be active to some degree at the same time.)

Maslow's hierarchy is widely discussed, and is usually envisioned as a stepladder, as in Figure 11.2. The lower-level needs, once satisfied, supposedly become the foundations that trigger the higher-order needs.[7] In other words, the higher-level needs aren't too important in motivating behavior unless the lower-level needs are pretty well satisfied.

While that's the way the theory is usually presented, its important to remember that there isn't much research supporting the idea that the needs fall into a neat hierarchy or pyramid. In fact, one expert recently said that illustrating the Maslow theory in the form of a pyramid (with the physiological needs on bottom, up to the self-actualization needs on top) "is one of the worst things that has happened to the theory," since it probably wasn't what Maslow himself ever meant.[8] What Maslow's theory does do is emphasize the fact that people have different needs and that, quite possibly, as they go through different stages of their lives, new, "higher level," needs become more important as lower-level needs become more satisfied.[9] The specific needs Maslow describes are as follows.

Physiological Needs   People are born with certain physiological needs. These are the most basic needs, including the needs for food, water, and shelter.

Security Needs   When these physiological needs are reasonably satisfied—when a person is no longer thirsty and has enough to eat, for instance—then security, or safety, needs become aroused. In other words, if you are starving or in the middle of

▼ **FIGURE 11.2**   **Maslow's Hierarchy of Needs**

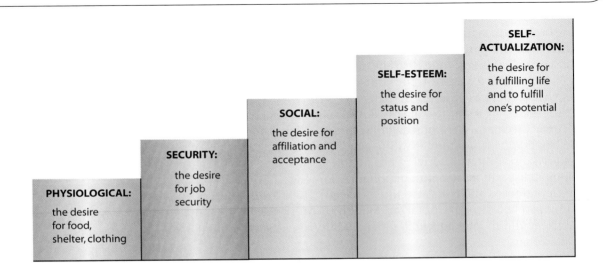

a desert with nothing to drink, the lower-level need for food or water will drive your behavior. You might even risk your life and safety by pursuing that need. But once you have enough to eat or drink, personal safety, security, and protection motivate your behavior.

Social Needs   Once you feel reasonably secure and have had enough to eat and drink, social needs begin to drive your behavior. These are the needs people have for affiliation, for giving and receiving affection, and for friendship.

Self-Esteem Needs   At level four are the self-esteem needs. Psychologist Douglas McGregor says these include the following:

1. Needs that relate to self-esteem—needs for self-confidence, independence, achievement, competence, and knowledge
2. Needs that relate to reputation—needs for status, recognition, appreciation, and the deserved respect of others[10]

Like the social and safety needs, self-esteem needs begin to motivate behavior only when the lower-level needs have been fairly well satisfied.

Some psychologists argue there is a big difference between self-esteem (and the following self-actualization) needs and the lower-level physiological, safety, and social needs: Higher-level needs for things like self-respect and recognition are insatiable—we never get enough of such things. They are also triggered more by factors intrinsic to the job, like challenges and responsibility. Lower-level needs are relatively easily satisfied and tend to be triggered by extrinsic factors like pay and working conditions.

Self-Actualization Needs   Finally, argues Maslow, there is an ultimate need that only begins to dominate behavior once all lower-level needs have been reasonably satisfied. This is the need for self-actualization or fulfillment, the need we all have to become the person we feel we have the potential for becoming. Self-actualization needs motivate us to realize our potential, continue self-development, and be creative.

THE P E O P L E SIDE OF MANAGING

■ The Mother of All Bonuses

When it comes to motivating employees, the bonuses at Kingston Technology must qualify for some sort of record. Kingston is the world's largest supplier of add-on memory boards for personal computers and is run by founders John Tu and David Sun. People have many needs, only some of which are satisfied by money, but the Kingston bonus plan is still something special.

The Kingston bonus plan is fairly simple: Employees receive, overall, 10% of the company's profits. What is a little unusual, though, is that Japanese conglomerate Softbank Corporation bought Kingston for about $1 billion. And, true to their words, Tu and Sun (who will continue managing Kingston) decided to bestow 10% of that—about $100 million—as bonuses to their 523 employees. Some employees got bonuses of up to $300,000, depending on seniority and individual performance.

Carrying through on their "10% of profits" commitment reflects, in part, the owners' understanding that to be useful, an incentive plan like this must be predictable; you can't change the standards every few days. However, at Kingston, the bonus plan is also just one part of a broader effort to make the company feel more like a family. Blurred lines between jobs give employees freedom to do what they think needs to be done, all employees share in free lunches on Friday, and financial seminars help show employees how to invest their windfalls, for example.[11]

Herzberg's Two-Factor Approach

Frederick Herzberg developed a famous motivation theory that divides Maslow's hierarchy into lower-level (physiological, safety, social) and higher-level (ego, self-actualization) sets of needs; he says the best way to motivate someone is to offer to satisfy the higher-level needs.

Hygienes and Motivators Herzberg believes the factors (which he calls *hygienes*) that can satisfy lower-level needs are different from those (which he calls *motivators*) that can satisfy, or partially satisfy, higher-level needs. If hygiene factors (factors outside the job itself, such as working conditions, salary, and supervision) are inadequate, employees will become dissatisfied. But—and this is extremely important—adding more of these hygiene factors (like salary) to the job (providing what Herzberg calls extrinsic motivation) is a very bad way to try to motivate someone because lower-level needs are quickly satisfied. Next week or next month the employee will again be dissatisfied, saying, in effect, "What have you done for me lately? I want another raise."

On the other hand, job content, or motivator, factors that are intrinsic to the work itself (like opportunities for achievement, recognition, responsibility, and more challenge) can motivate employees. They appeal to higher-level needs for achievement and self-actualization, needs that are never completely satisfied and for which most people have an infinite craving. According to Herzberg, the best way to motivate employees is to build challenges and opportunities for achievement into their jobs, to provide intrinsic motivation, in other words. That way even the prospect of doing the job may motivate the employee, much as the thought of doing a favorite hobby may motivate you.

Herzberg's well-known theory didn't stem from an experiment, but from a review he and his colleagues made that focused on employee satisfaction. They concluded from this review that there was a consistent relationship between job satisfaction and certain types of work behaviors, and also between job dissatisfaction and different work behaviors. On this basis, Herzberg's two-factor theory was born.[12] Other studies failed to find such a consistent relationship.[13] On the other hand, a recent study concluded that sustained job performance was directly related to intrinsic feelings that produce positive attitudes, a finding consistent with Herzberg's theory.[14] Herzberg and his colleagues did accomplish two things, however: They popularized the important idea that intrinsic motivation—motivation that comes from within the person—is very important for keeping employees motivated. And they popularized the idea that the nature of the job—such as whether it was sufficiently engaging and challenging—was therefore extremely important too.

Needs for Achievement, Power, and Affiliation

David McClelland and John Atkinson agree with Herzberg that higher-level needs are most important at work. They have studied three needs they believe are especially important—the needs for affiliation, power, and achievement. To understand the nature of these needs, try the following exercise.

Take a quick look (just 10 to 15 seconds) at Figure 11.3. Now allow yourself up to 5 minutes to write a short essay about the picture, touching on the following questions:

1. What is happening? Who are the people?
2. What has led up to this situation? That is, what happened in the past?

◀ **F I G U R E   1 1 . 3**

What's Happening Here?

Source: David A. Kolb, Irwin M. Rubin, and James M. McIntyre, *Organizational Psychology: An Experiential Approach* (Upper Saddle River, NJ: Prentice Hall, 1971), p. 55.

3. What is being thought? What is wanted? By whom?

4. What will happen? What will be done?

Remember that the questions are only guides for your thinking, so don't just answer each one. Instead, make your story continuous and let your imagination roam. No one is going to see your essay except you. Once you have finished writing, resume reading the text.

The picture is from a group of pictures in a test called the Thematic Apperception Test that McClelland and his associates use to identify a person's needs. The picture is intentionally ambiguous, so when you wrote your essay, you were supposedly reading into the picture ideas that reflected your own needs and drives. McClelland has found that this test can be useful for identifying the level of a person's achievement, power, and affiliation needs.[15] This exercise represents only one of several that constitute the Thematic Apperception Test, and it can therefore give you only the most tentative impressions about your needs. It should, however, give you a better understanding of how the needs for achievement, power, and affiliation can manifest themselves.

The Need for Achievement   People who are high in the need to achieve have a predisposition to strive for success. They are highly motivated to obtain the satisfaction that comes from accomplishing a challenging task or goal. They prefer tasks for which there is a reasonable chance for success and avoid those that are either too easy or too difficult. Such people prefer specific, timely criticism and feedback about their performance.

Achievement motivation is present in your essay when any one of the following three things occurs:

1. Someone in the story is concerned about a standard of excellence; for example, he wants to win or do well in a competition, or has self-imposed standards for

a good performance. Standards of excellence can be inferred by the use of words such as *good* or *better* to evaluate performance.

2. Someone in the story is involved in a unique accomplishment, such as an invention or an artistic creation.

3. Someone in the story is involved in a long-term goal, such as having a specific career or being a success in life.

The Need for Power People with a strong need for power want to influence others directly by making suggestions, giving their opinions and evaluations, and trying to talk others into things. They enjoy roles requiring persuasion, such as teaching and public speaking, as well as positions as leaders and members of the clergy. How exactly the need for power manifests itself depends on the person's other needs. A person with a high need for power but a low need for warm, supportive relationships might become dictatorial, while one with high needs for comradeship might become a member of the clergy or a social worker. McClelland believed that "a good manager is motivated by a regimented and regulated concern for influencing others," in other words, that good managers do have a need for power, but one that is under control.[16]

Power motivation is present in your essay when any of the following three things occurs:

1. Someone in the story shows affection or is emotionally concerned about getting or maintaining control of the means of influencing a person. Wanting to win a point, to show dominance, to convince someone, or to gain a position of control—as well as wanting to avoid weakness or humiliation—are obvious examples.[17]

2. Someone is actually doing something to get or keep control of the means of influence, such as arguing, demanding or forcing, giving a command, trying to convince, or punishing.

3. Your story involves an interpersonal relationship that is culturally defined as one in which a superior has control of the means of influencing a subordinate. For example, a boss is giving orders to a subordinate, or a parent is ordering a child to shape up.

The Need for Affiliation People with a strong need for affiliation are highly motivated to maintain strong, warm relationships with friends and relatives. In group meetings they try to establish friendly relationships, often by being agreeable or giving emotional support.[18] Affiliation motivation is present in your essay when one of the following three things occurs:

1. Someone in the story is concerned about establishing, maintaining, or restoring a positive emotional relationship with another person. Friendship is the most basic example, such as when your story emphasizes that the individuals are friends. Other relationships, such as father–son, reflect affiliation motivation only if they have the warm, compassionate quality implied by the need for affiliation.

2. One person likes or wants to be liked by someone else, or someone has some similar feeling about another. Similarly, affiliation motivation is present if someone is expressing sorrow or grief about a broken relationship.

3. Affiliative activities are taking place, such as parties, reunions, visits, or relaxed small talk, as in a bull session. Friendly actions such as consoling or being concerned about the well-being or happiness of another person usually reflect a need for affiliation.

Employee Needs in Practice

As you know from your own experience, what appeals to one person may be inconsequential to another, so you have to use common sense when applying your knowledge of human motives and needs. You see examples of this almost every day. One driver, on the way to work, may find the risks involved with speeding and cutting from lane to lane exciting. Another prefers the security of a more temperate pace and the quiet enjoyment of some music by Brahms. One manager may drive herself relentlessly to obtain a promotion, whereas another, while equally secure, is happier on a slower track if that means spending more time with the spouse.

Here's another example. Different needs also drive our career choices, and we often don't even know it. Thus, psychologist Edgar Schein says that as you learn more about yourself, it becomes apparent that you have a dominant *career anchor*, a concern or need that you will not give up if a choice has to be made. Based on his study of MIT graduates, he identified five career anchors.

Some people had a strong technical/functional career anchor. They made decisions that enabled them to remain in their chosen technical or functional fields. Some had managerial competence as a career anchor. They showed a strong motivation to become managers and (as first mentioned in Chapter 1), they had the analytical, interpersonal, and emotional competence to be successful. Some of the graduates were driven by a need to express their creativity. Many of these went on to be successful entrepreneurs, or to somehow build their personal fortunes by using their creative abilities (for example, by purchasing, restoring, and then renting out homes).

Others made their career decisions because they were driven by the needs for autonomy and independence. These people seemed driven by the need to be on their own, free of the dependence that can arise when a person elects to work in a large organization. Finally, some of the graduates were mostly concerned with long-run career stability and job security; they seemed willing to do what was required to maintain job security, a decent income, and a stable future, including a good retirement program and benefits.[19]

Findings like these illustrate the fact that it's dangerous to generalize when talking about needs. One of your employees may be motivated by a significant raise, while another prefers the security of an employment contract. People even differ in what they need to be recognized for. Some people value dependability and responsibility, and prefer that their supervisors recognize them for things like follow-through, dedication, and loyalty. Others value risk-taking action and the ability to act under pressure, and want to be recognized for responsiveness, cleverness, and ingenuity.[20] Thus, theories like those of Maslow, while useful as approximations, always need to be adjusted to the actual situation you face.

The bottom line is that you have to use common sense and apply your experience when thinking about and motivating employees. For instance, teams are so important at GE Durham that the atmosphere has been described as being like a "tribal community." For example, "there are rules, rituals, and folklore; there is tribal loyalties and tribal accountability."[21] This is obviously not the kind of atmosphere that appeals to everyone: the company therefore takes great pains to select employees whose needs—for affiliation, and for security, for instance—are consistent with the kind of plant this is. Mavericks and loners needn't apply.

▶ PROCESS APPROACHES

Process approaches to motivating employees explain motivation not in terms of specific needs, but in terms of the decision-making process through which motivation takes place. Here we'll focus on the work of psychologists J. S. Adams, Edwin Locke, and Victor Vroom.

Adams's Equity Theory

Adams's equity theory assumes that people have a need for, and therefore value and seek, fairness at work.[22] People are strongly motivated to maintain a balance between what they perceive as their inputs or contributions, and their rewards. Equity theory states that if a person perceives an inequity, a tension or drive will develop in the person's mind, and the person will be motivated to reduce or eliminate the tension and perceived inequity.

Does equity theory work in practice? On the whole, empirical findings regarding underpayment, at least, are consistent with Adams's theory. People paid on a piece-rate basis, per item produced, typically boost quantity and reduce quality when they believe they are underpaid. Those paid a straight hourly rate tend to reduce both quantity and quality when they think they're underpaid. Unfortunately, overpayment inequity does not seem to have the positive effects on either quantity or quality that Adams's theory would predict for it[23] (see Figure 11.4).

Locke's Goal Theory of Motivation

The goal theory of motivation assumes that once someone decides to pursue a goal, the person regulates his or her behavior to try to reach the goal.[24] Locke and his colleagues contend that goals provide the mechanism through which unsatisfied needs are translated into action.[25] In other words, unsatisfied needs prompt the person to seek ways to satisfy those needs; the person then formulates goals that prompt action.[26] For example, a person needs to self-actualize and wants to be an artist: To do so, she must go to college for a fine arts degree, so she sets the goal of graduating from Columbia University's fine arts program. That goal (which is prompted by her need) then motivates her behavior.

Most of the research in this area has been conducted in laboratory settings, with undergraduates as subjects. Many of the studies focus on the results of assigning (or

▶ **F I G U R E   1 1 . 4**

How a Perceived Inequity Can Affect Performance

According to equity theory, how a person reacts to under- or overpayment depends on whether he or she is paid on a piece-rate or salary basis.

	Employee Thinks He or She Is Underpaid	Employee Thinks He or She Is Overpaid
Piece-rate Basis	Quality down Quantity the same or up	Quantity the same or down Quality up
Salary Basis	Quantity or quality should go down	Quantity or quality should go up

getting the subjects to adopt) hard, medium, or easy goals. Although such findings don't necessarily apply to industrial settings, they do tend to support Locke's basic theory. The most consistent finding here is that people who are assigned or who adopt difficult and specific goals rather consistently outperform people who are simply told to "do their best."[27] Such findings have recently been extended to actual workplace settings. Here the evidence also suggests rather strongly that people who are given or who adopt specific and difficult goals tend to outperform people without such performance goals.[28]

Vroom's Expectancy Theory

According to Victor Vroom, a person's motivation to exert some level of effort is a function of three things: The person's **expectancy** (in terms of probability) that his or her effort will lead to performance;[29] **instrumentality**, or the perceived relationship between successful performance and obtaining the reward; and **valence**, which represents the perceived value the person attaches to the reward.[30] In Vroom's theory, motivation is a product of these three things, in other words, Motivation = $E \times I \times V$, where, of course, E represents expectancy, I instrumentality, and V valence.

Vroom actually developed his expectancy theory to try to better understand and explain vocational choice—why people choose the jobs that they do.[31] And (as with equity theory, and goal setting theory, as explained above) expectancy theory views people as "conscious agents" who are continually sizing up the situation in terms of their perceived needs, and then acting in accordance with these perceptions.

What does expectancy theory tell managers about how they can help motivate employees? It says, first, that without an expectancy that effort will lead to performance, no motivation will take place. Managers therefore must be sure their employees have the skills to do the job, and know they can do the job. Confidence building and support are therefore important. The theory also says that subordinates have to see that successful performance will in fact lead to obtaining the reward. That means, for instance, that communicating success stories—employees who did well and were therefore rewarded for it—may help to improve the motivation of other employees. Finally, managers can boost the valence or perceived value their subordinates attach to the rewards. They can do this by better communicating what those rewards are and by making sure that the rewards an employee is offered are actually important to him or her (two extra days off may be more important to one person, while another would rather have two days' extra pay).

While expectancy theory was originally developed to help explain vocational choice, these kinds of real-life applications do come up quite often. One expert recently showed how Vroom's theory could be used to explain why and how fast employees who were injured on the job and then rehabilitated would return. He conducted a study of 32 public sector employees who were off work and receiving compensation for a work-related condition. He concluded that expectancy and valence were both related to the speed with which the employees intended to return to work. Those who saw a clear link between returning to work (and being able to successfully do the job and earn the reward) were more likely to be returned to work more quickly.[32]

Most other research supports Vroom's theory, particularly in studies focusing on job choice. The results suggest that expectancy, instrumentality, and valence combine to influence motivation to choose specific jobs.[33] Studies of the

expectancy
in motivation, the probability that a person's efforts will lead to performance.

instrumentality
the perceived correlation between successful performance and obtaining the reward.

valence
in motivation, the perceived value a person ascribes to the reward for certain efforts.

expectancy approach also provide moderate to strong support for its usefulness in explaining and predicting other types of work motivation.[34] However, one recent study reviewed 77 prior studies of expectancy theory and concluded the results are at best mixed. The researchers questioned the theory's validity, but suggested that many of the prior studies may simply not have tested expectancy theory correctly.[35]

▶ LEARNING/REINFORCEMENT APPROACHES

Learning can be defined as a relatively permanent change in a person that occurs as a result of experience.[36] For example, we learn as children that being courteous is rewarded by our parents, and so we may be motivated to be courteous throughout our lives. There are several theories about how people learn. In this section we'll focus on what may be called learning/reinforcement approaches to motivating employees—how people's behavior is molded by the consequences or results of their actions.

Psychologist B. F. Skinner conducted many of the early studies in this area. Let's apply his theory to a simple example. Suppose you wanted to train your dog to roll over. How would you do it? In all likelihood, you would encourage the dog to roll over (perhaps by gently nudging it down and around), and then would reward it with some treat. Fairly quickly, no doubt, your dog would learn that if it wanted a treat, it would have to roll over. Before you knew it, Fido would be rolling through your house.

In Skinner's theory, the dog's rolling over would be called **operant behavior** because it *operates* on its environment, specifically by causing its owner to give it a treat. (So, who's training whom, you might ask!) In operant conditioning the main question is how to strengthen the association between the **contingent reward** (in this case the treat) and the operant behavior.[37]

Behavior Modification

The principles of operant conditioning are applied at work through behavior modification. **Behavior modification** means changing or modifying behavior through the use of performance-contingent rewards or punishment. It is built on two principles: (1) Behavior that appears to lead to a positive consequence (reward) tends to be repeated, whereas behavior that appears to lead to a negative consequence (punishment) tends not to be repeated. (2) Therefore, by providing the properly scheduled rewards, it is possible to get a person to learn to change his or her behavior.[38] There are two core concepts in behavior modification: The type of reinforcement (reward or punishment) and the schedule of reinforcement.

There are several types of reinforcement. **Positive reinforcement** is a positive consequence, or reward, such as praise or a bonus, that results when the desired behavior occurs. In **extinction**, reinforcement is withheld so that over time the undesired behavior disappears. Extinction is used when someone is inadvertently being rewarded for doing the wrong thing. For example, suppose your subordinate learns that arriving late invariably leads to a scolding by you, which in turn leads to laughter and congratulations from the worker's peers, who think your obvious annoyance is really quite funny. That laughter represents an inadvertent reward to the worker for arriving late. In extinction you would discipline that person in the privacy of your office, thereby removing the attention and the laughter—the reward—the worker gets from his or her friends. **Negative reinforcement** is a bit

---

learning

a relatively permanent change in a person that occurs as a result of experience.

operant behavior

behavior that appears to operate on or have an influence on the subject's environment.

contingent reward

a reward that is contingent or dependent on performance of a particular behavior.

behavior modification

the technique of changing or modifying behavior through the use of contingent rewards or punishments.

positive reinforcement

the act of rewarding desired behavior; or the actual rewards, such as praise or bonuses, given each time the desired behavior occurs.

extinction

the behavioral modification technique of withholding positive reinforcement so that over time the undesired behavior disappears.

negative reinforcement

reinforcing the desirable behavior by removing something undesirable from the situation.

more complicated; it means reinforcing the desirable behavior by removing something undesirable from the situation. Making safety goggles more comfortable is an example.

Punishment, as you know, means adding something undesirable so as to change a person's behavior. For instance, you might reprimand late employees. Punishment is the most controversial method of modifying behavior. Skinner recommends extinction rather than punishment for decreasing the frequency of the undesired behavior.

punishment

a behavioral modification option that applies penalties for the undesired behavior to reduce the possibility that it will recur.

The schedule you use to apply the positive reinforcement is important as well. For example, do you reward someone every time he or she does well, or only periodically? Here behavioral science findings suggest the following:

1. In general, the fastest way to get someone to learn is not to put him or her on a schedule at all. Instead, reinforce the desired behavior continuously, each and every time it occurs. The person learns quickly that doing the job is rewarded. The drawback is that the desired behavior also diminishes very quickly once you stop reinforcing it. This is called continuos reinforcement.

2. *Variable* (also called *partial*) *reinforcement* is the most powerful at sustaining behavior. Here you reinforce the correct behavior not every time the person does the right thing, but every few times he or she does so, around some average number of times. With this type of reinforcement people continue producing the desired behavior for a long time even without reinforcement because they are always expecting to "hit the jackpot" on the next try. This is the theory behind Las Vegas-type slot machines.

Does Behavior Modification Improve Performance?

There seems little doubt that, used appropriately, behavior modification can significantly improve employee performance. One recent study involved a review of 19 prior analyses of the effects of behavior modification.[39] The study's conclusions can be summarized as follows:[40]

1. Organizational behavior modification is effective, regardless of the type of company and reward. Behavior modification generally improved worker performance by 17%.

2. When financial rewards were used with nonfinancial ones (like recognition), there was a 30% performance improvement in service firms, almost twice the effect of each of the individual reinforcers.

3. Performance feedback—telling the employee how he or she is doing and reinforcing performance with praise—helped improve productivity in manufacturing firms by an average of 41%.

4. Paying attention to the employees and providing recognition raised productivity in service firms by 15%.

5. The effect of behavior modification and how it's used seems to depend on the kind of company. Overall, behavior modification had stronger effects in manufacturing than in service organizations. In manufacturing firms, combining financial rewards with nonfinancial reinforcement (such as performance feedback) didn't seem to result in substantially higher performance than using just nonfinancial rewards themselves. On the other hand (as noted in 2, above), combining financial rewards with nonfinancial ones did have much stronger effects in service firms.

As a leader, you'll want to size up the leadership situation and identify what is happening, account for what is happening, and formulate an action or a response. Knowledge about the three approaches to motivating employees (need based, process based, and learning/reinforcement) gives you tools for identifying what is happening and accounting for it. They can also help you formulate an action or a response, using the 10 methods discussed in the next few pages. (Other useful behavioral science topics, including perception and self-concept, are discussed in the chapter appendix).

One reason these motivation methods are widely used is that they have strong foundations in organizational behavior (OB) and motivation theory and research. Table 11.1 presents these foundations. For example, *empowering employees* (column 7) is based in part on what psychologists call self-efficacy—namely, on the idea that people differ in their estimates of how they'll perform on a task. Building up their skills and self-confidence by empowering them should bolster their self-efficacy and thus their motivation.

T A B L E   11.1   The Motivational Underpinnings of 10 Motivation Methods

Foundations of Behavior and Motivation	Pay for Performance	Merit Raises
Self-Concept: People seek to fulfill their potential.		
Self-Efficacy: People differ in their estimates of how they'll perform on a task: self-efficacy influences effort.		
Maslow's Needs Hierarchy: High-level needs are never totally satisfied and aren't aroused until lower-level needs are satisfied.		X
Alderfer: All needs may be active, to some degree, at the same time.		X
McClelland's Ach, Pow, Aff: Needs for achievement, power, and affiliation are especially important in the work setting.		
Herzberg's Dual Factor: Extrinsic factors prevent dissatisfaction; intrinsic factors motivate workers.		
Vroom's Expectancy Approach: Motivation is a function of expectancy that effort leads to performance, performance leads to reward, and reward is valued.	X	X
Locke's Goal Setting: People are motivated to achieve goals they consciously set.		
Adams's Equity Theory: People are motivated to maintain balance between their perceived inputs and outputs.		X
Reinforcement: People will continue behavior that is rewarded and cease behavior that is punished.	X	X

Source: Copyright © 1997 by Gary Dessler, Ph.D.

Using Pay for Performance

pay for performance
any compensation method based on merit or performance rather than across-the-board non-output-based pay.

Pay for performance is probably the first thing that comes to mind when most people think about motivating employees (although, increasingly, challenging jobs and other intrinsic motivators are as or more important). Pay for performance refers to any compensation method that ties pay to the quantity or quality of work the person produces.

Piecework pay plans are probably the most familiar: Earnings are tied directly to what the worker produces in the form of a piece rate for each unit he or she turns out. Thus, if Tom Smith gets 40 cents for each circuit boards he stamps out, he would make $40 for stamping out 100 per day, and $80 for stamping out 200. Sales commissions are another familiar example of pay for performance.

Piecework plans have a firm foundation in motivation theory. Vroom's expectancy approach says motivation depends on employees' seeing the link between performance and rewards, and pay for performance plans should emphasize precisely that. Similarly, behavior modification says people will continue behavior that is rewarded, and pay for performance plans, of course, tie rewards directly to behavior.

variable pay plan
a compensation plan that may reduce or increase some portion of the individual employee's pay, depending on whether the company meets its financial goals.

New pay for performance plans are becoming popular. Variable pay plans, for example, put some portion of the employee's pay at risk, subject to the firm's meeting its financial goals. In one such plan at the DuPont Company, employees could

Motivation Methods								
	Spot Rewards	Skill-Based Pay	Recognition Awards	Job Redesign	Empower Employees	Goal Setting	Positive Reinforcement	Lifelong Learning
		X	X	X	X			X
		X			X			X
	X		X	X	X			X
	X		X	X	X			X
		X	X	X	X			X
				X	X			X
	X		X			X		
					X	X		
	X		X					
	X		X				X	

© 1996 Randy Glasbergen

voluntarily place up to 6% of their base pay at risk.[41] If their departments met their earnings projections, the employees would get that 6% back, plus additional percentages, depending on how much the department exceeded its earnings projections.

Other companies have **gainsharing plans**, incentive plans that engage many or all employees in a common effort to achieve productivity goals.[42] Implementing a gainsharing plan requires several steps. Specific performance measures, such as cost per unit produced, are chosen, as is a funding formula, such as "47% of savings go to employees." The management decides how to divide and distribute cost savings between the employees and the company, and among employees themselves. If employees are then able to achieve cost savings in line with their performance goals, they share in the resulting gains.

Pay for performance plans of all types—including those that let employees share in profits by paying them with shares of company stock—are becoming more popular because they make sense. As Maggie Hughes, President of LifeUSA Holding Inc., of Minneapolis, recently put it:

> I find it amusing, frustrating, and, often quite appalling, how few business leaders recognize that people should share in the economic value they create. At LifeUSA, our employees have options on 2 million shares of company stock. It seems like common sense to us. So why is it still so uncommon in most companies?[43]

Many employers are awarding stock options. For example, when Jim Eckel went to his first interview with Starbucks in 1994, he didn't pay much attention to the stock option plan (affectionately known within the company as Bean Stock). But today, as manager of a Starbucks on Manhattan's Upper West side, Eckel is reportedly a champion of the plan.[44] In fact, as in an increasing number of companies such as IBM, Eckel and about 30,000 other Starbucks partners are part of a new movement in compensation management: Stock options for everyone.

As Bradley Honeycutt, the former vice president of human resources services at Starbucks, put it, "We established Bean Stock in 1991 as a way of investing in our partners and creating ownership across the company . . . it's been a key to retaining good people and building loyalty."[45] By letting all or most employees participate in this way, each employee has a built-in opportunity to see how performance and hard work translate into a rising stock price—and thus more rewards for them.

Not all pay for performance plans succeed. However, the following five suggestions make success more likely, given what we've discussed about motivation:

1. *Ensure that effort and rewards are directly related.* Your incentive plan should reward employees in direct proportion to their increased productivity. Employees must also perceive that they can actually do the tasks required. The standard has to be attainable, and you have to provide the necessary tools, equipment, and training.[46]

2. *Make the plan understandable and easily calculable by the employees.* Employees should easily be able to calculate the rewards they will receive for various levels of effort.

3. *Set effective standards.* The standards should be high but reasonable; there should be about a fifty-fifty chance of success. The goal should also be specific; this is much more effective than telling someone to do your best.

4. *Guarantee your standards.* View the standard as a contract with employees. Once the plan is operational, use great caution before decreasing the size of the incentive in any way.[47]

5. *Guarantee a base rate.* It's often advisable to give employees a safety net by providing them with a base pay rate. They'll know that no matter what happens, they can at least earn a minimum guaranteed base rate.[48]

MANAGING @ THE *SPEED* **OF THOUGHT**

Going On-Line with Incentives

Check out popular Web sites today, and you'll see that many are using on-line incentives to attract crowds to their sites.[49] For example, travel sites like Travelocity offer on-line-only specials, and on-line bookstores like Amazon.com routinely use incentives to attract viewers. They also run contests, like one in which visitors could win thousand-dollar prizes by helping to complete a story, the first paragraph of which was written by the famous author John Updike.

Companies are also using technology to improve the effectiveness of their employee incentive programs. For example, new software charts participants' standings and painlessly tallies the final numbers, and e-mail may be used to send reminders and encouragement like "10 more days to sell, sell, sell!" or "Think Hawaii!"[50] Other companies are using their Intranets to publicize incentive program rules, award details, prize catalogs, and current status to participants. They offer employees exotic prizes like trips to Tahiti. Some companies use their Intranets to provide links to the destination's Internet site.

Software packages help many companies design and manage employee incentive programs. For example, ASPIRE 1.5 (Automated System Promoting Incentives that Reward Excellence) takes incentive planners through the steps required to design a corporate incentive program. The HR department can use the program to indicate how the winners will the judged (such as percentage of sales growth over past performance), and to choose rewards from a menu of incentives options (such as travel, gifts, checks, or paid time off from the office). Another program, Motivation Magic, helps incentive planners custom-design corporate award programs. It comes with a database containing suggestions for all types of incentives, as well as an incentive-design checklist, program timeline, and things like functions for charting results. Another package, Bob Nelson's Reward Wizard, "keeps performance records for all employees in a department or organization, along with their career objectives, personal preferences, hobbies and family circumstances. Space is also provided to enter their accomplishments, award criteria, time allotted to win an award and individual award preferences."[51] Once it's up and running, Reward Wizard can generate prize suggestions adapted to each employee's needs, such as extra Mondays off for Gary and a bigger computer screen for Jeannine.

Using Merit Pay

merit raise

a salary increase—usually permanent—based on individual performance.

Most employees, when they do a good job, expect to be rewarded with at least a merit raise at the end of the year. A **merit raise** is a salary increase—usually permanent—based on individual performance. It is different from a bonus in that it represents a continuing increment, whereas the bonus represents a one-time payment. Gradually, however, traditional merit raises are being replaced by lump-sum merit raises, which are raises awarded in one lump sum that do not become part of the employee's continuing pay.[52]

To the extent that it is actually tied to performance, the prospect of the merit raise may focus the employee's attention on the link between performance and rewards, in line with the expectancy approach to motivation. If it is equitably distributed (which means, among other things, that performance must be evaluated fairly and accurately), a merit raise can enable employees to see the link between their perceived inputs and outputs, in line with Adams's equity approach to motivation.

However, relying too heavily on merit raises is a bit dangerous. A year is a long time to wait for a reward, so the reinforcement benefits of merit pay are somewhat suspect. You may also have personally experienced the questionable nature of some performance appraisal systems, including the fact that some supervisors take the easy way out and rate everyone's performance about the same. Such problems can undermine the motivational basis for the merit plan.[53]

Using Spot Awards

spot award

a financial reward given to an employee as soon as laudable performance is observed.

As its name implies, a **spot award** is a financial award given to an employee literally "on the spot" as soon as the laudable performance is observed. Programs like this have actually been around for some time. For example, Thomas J. Watson Sr., founder of IBM, reportedly wrote checks on the spot to employees doing an outstanding job.[54]

Such cash awards are used increasingly today. FedEx's Bravo-Zulu voucher program is an example. This program was established to let managers provide immediate rewards to employees for outstanding performance. (Bravo-Zulu is a title borrowed from the U.S. Navy's semaphore signal for "well done.") Bravo-Zulu vouchers average about $50 in the form of a check or some other reward, such as dinner gift certificates or theater tickets. More than 150,000 times per year a FedEx's manager presents an employee with one of these awards.[55]

Not surprisingly, spot awards are popular today in the high-tech firms concentrated in northern California. For example, Scitor, a systems engineering consulting firm based in Sunnyvale, California, has an unusual spot awards program called Be Our Guest.[56] This spot awards program is unusual because the small Be Our guest bonuses (which usually range from $100 to $300) are given by employees to their co-workers for doing something beyond the call of duty. The employees give these awards to each other, and supervisors are out of the loop. The question of what qualifies for an award is up to the giver. There are no strict rules regarding what does or does not deserve a bonus, and no manager has to approve. If in the giver's eyes the recipient does something exceptional—stays really late on a project, for instance, or meets an impossible deadline—the giver simply fills out a card indicating the amount of the bonus, and then it's the recipient's to spend as he or she likes. The award comes enclosed in a thank you card that encourages the employee to pamper himself or herself in any way he or she prefers: Most employees reportedly use the award for a fancy dinner, a show, or a day at a spa.

Spot rewards like these have a sound basis in what we know about motivation. To the extent that the rewards are both contingent on good performance and awarded immediately, they are certainly consistent with equity theory and the expectancy approach, with reinforcing desired behavior, and with providing the recognition most people desire.

▲ Ed Matsumoto, a member of Scitor's information systems team, saves up his "Be Our Guest" bonuses. In past years he bought his mother a VCR and his brother-in-law a tool chest. This time, he bought himself a deluxe refrigerator. Says Matsumoto: "Be Our Guest' is not just thank-you, it's a little special."

Using Skill-Based Pay

In most companies pay is determined by the level of job responsibilities. Presidents generally make more than vice presidents, sales managers make more than assistant sales managers, and secretary IVs make more than secretary IIIs, because higher-level jobs are meant to have more responsibility.

Skill-based pay is different in that the employees are paid for the range, depth, and types of skills and knowledge they are capable of using, rather than for the job they currently hold.[57] The difference is important: It is conceivable that in a company with a skill-based pay plan, the secretary III could be paid more per hour than the secretary IV, for instance, if it turns out that the person who was the secretary III had more skills than the person in the secretary IV job.

A skill-based pay plan was implemented at a General Mills manufacturing facility.[58] In this case, General Mills was trying to boost the flexibility of its factory workforce by implementing a pay plan that would encourage all employees to develop a wider range of skills. In turn, that wider range of skills would make it easier for employees to take over whatever job needed to be done in the plant as needs changed.

In this plant, therefore, workers were paid based on attained skill levels. For each of the several types of jobs in the plant, workers could attain three levels of skill: limited ability (ability to perform simple tasks without direction); partial proficiency (ability to apply more advanced principles on the job); and full competence (ability to analyze and solve problems associated with that job). After starting a job, workers were tested periodically to see whether they had earned certification at the next higher skill level. If they had, they received higher pay even though they had the same job.

In other words, higher-skilled workers on the same job received higher pay. Workers could then switch to other jobs in the plant, again starting at the first skill level and working their way up. In this way the workers could earn more pay for having more skills (particularly as they became skilled at a variety of jobs), and the company ended up with a more highly skilled and therefore more flexible workforce.

Skill-based pay plays a big role in performance at the GE Durham engine plant. At Durham, there are no financial incentives for technicians to improve either the productivity or the quality of their work, "[financial incentives] are not part of the culture at GE Aircraft engines" says a former plant manager.[59] Instead, there are three grades of jet-assembly technician—tech 1, tech 2, and tech 3—and one wage rate for each grade. Since each jet engine is built entirely by one dedicated team, most team members are multiskilled, and each team member's pay is based on the skill levels he or she has obtained and been tested for. At Durham, in other words, the emphasis is on making teamwork, challenging jobs, and responsibility and skills the main drivers of motivation, rather than extrinsic factors like financial incentives. The "Entrepreneurs in Action" box shows this works for small firms too.

Skill-based pay makes sense in terms of what we know about motivation. People have a vision—a self-concept—of who they can be, and they seek to fulfill their potential. The individual development that is part and parcel of skill-based pay helps employees do exactly that. Skill-based pay also appeals to an employee's sense of self-efficacy, in that the reward is a formal and concrete recognition that the person can do the more challenging job and do it well.

Using Recognition

If you've ever spent half a day cooking a meal for someone who gobbled it up without saying a word, or two weeks doing a report for a boss who didn't say thanks (let alone good job), you know how important having your work recognized and appreciated can be.

Most people like to feel appreciated. In one study, conducted by the Minnesota Department of Natural Resources, respondents said they highly valued day-to-day recognition from supervisors, peers, and team members; more than two-thirds said it was important to believe that their work was appreciated by others.[60] And recall from our discussion of behavior modification earlier in the chapter that recognition and performance feedback have a significant impact on performance, either alone or in conjunction with financial rewards.

Being recognized—and not necessarily just financially—for a job well done makes a lot of sense in terms of motivation theory. Immediate recognition can be a powerful reinforcer. Recognition also underscores the performance–reward–expectancy link, and it helps appeal to and satisfy the need people have to achieve and be recognized for their achievement.

Many companies therefore formalize the commonsense process of saying thank you for a job well done. Xerox Corporation gives bell-ringer awards: When an employee is recognized, a bell is rung in the corridor while the person is formally recognized by his or her boss.[61] At Busch Gardens in Tampa, Florida, the company reportedly gives a pat-on-the-back award to employees who do an outstanding job, which is a notice of the award in the employee's file.[62] At Metro Motors in Montclair, California, the name of the employee of the month goes up on the electronic billboard over the dealership.[63] Bell Atlantic names cellular telephone sites after top employees.[64]

►Small business owners often face some special challenges when it comes to motivating employees. Many—like Steve Lauer, who runs eight Subway sandwich shops in northern Colorado—have the type of operation that depends heavily on minimum-wage, entry-level workers, many of whom have never worked before.[65] Keeping workers like these motivated while trying to manage all the other functions of a small business can be a challenge.

How do entrepreneurs like Lauer motivate employees? Lauer found that half his turnover occurred in the first 30 days of employment. Remembering his own stress level during his first few days on the job ("standing there in front of a customer, making sandwiches and trying to remember to smile. The first one I did, I forgot to put the meat on"), his first step was to get his new hires' stress levels down. For example, he assigns managers or designated trainers to spend 20 hours periodically with new workers during their first weeks on the job. He also evaluates employees at the end of their first 30 days, rather than waiting until the end of the quarter; this gives him an opportunity to get the new employees the feedback they desire, and gives them a chance to earn more money after their reviews.

Leona Ackerly has a slightly different motivation problem. She runs a residential maid service in Georgia called Mini Maid, Inc. Most of her employees are women in their twenties with little education and few skills, and many have grown up on welfare. Some, says Ackerly, have been abused or otherwise treated badly.

Part of Ackerly's motivation approach is to get her employees to "look at us as their partners in a team effort.

We tell them, 'this is what we give you; this is what you give us.'" Right off the bat, the new employee feels that she is an important part of the company. At this point the employees began to listen.[66] Ackerly says that over the years, she has "watched workers eventually take this philosophy of mutual respect to their homes and apply it in their family lives."

Ackerly's motivation approach is not entirely soft. For one thing, she hires no one with a police record or history of drug use, and if she catches anyone stealing, she presses charges. She insists employees be punctual, clean, and neat. They also earn attendance bonuses each day they come to work on time and in uniform.

Richard Kerley, president and CEO of Fine Host Corporation, runs a food service in Greenwich, Connecticut, that at any time has thousands of people working in convention centers and corporate and college dining facilities, busing tables and cooking and serving food. In this highly competitive business, wages are necessarily very low, but as Kerley says, "Though there may be economic restraints on what we pay them, there are no restraints on the recognition we give them." For example, the company posts workers' names in the company building to recognize good work, gives individual workers quality awards, and makes sure each employee gets a framed certificate for completing training courses. The bottom line is that while running a smaller business may have some special challenges, the intelligent use of respect and recognition can go a long way toward motivating workers who are also entry level and low paid.

These awards seem to be just the tip of the iceberg. According to one survey, 78% of CEOs and 58% of HR vice presidents said their firms were using performance recognition programs.[67] Dallas-based Texas Instruments, for instance, offers a multitude of bonuses as well as nonfinancial recognition, including personalized plaques, parties, movie tickets, golf lessons, and team shirts and jackets. The number of individual Texas Instruments employees recognized in this way jumped by 400% in one recent year, from 21,970 to 84,260.[68]

Using Job Redesign

Highly specialized assembly-line jobs have long had a bad reputation among psychologists. Chris Argyris, for instance, wrote that as people mature into adults, they normally move from a position of dependence and narrow interests to one of independence and broad interests, and that specialized jobs fly in the face of individual development.[69]

The negative impact of monotonous work has been substantiated by studies. In one study of 1,278 blue-collar workers in Israel, the researchers concluded that perceived monotony was moderately related to the objective work conditions; some employees perceived even the same job as more monotonous than did other employees; job satisfaction and psychological distress were related to perceived monotony; and sickness absence was equally related to work conditions and to perceived monotony.[70]

job design

the number and nature of specific tasks or activities in a job.

In the face of problems like these, many employers set up programs aimed at redesigning jobs. **Job design** refers to the number and nature of activities in a job; the basic issue in job design is whether jobs should be more specialized or, at the other extreme, more enriched and nonroutine. It largely grew out of the needs-based motivation theories of Herzberg, who argued that motivation is best accomplished by appealing to workers' higher-order needs.

Job Enlargement and Job Rotation Initial attempts at job redesign centered on job enlargement and job rotation. **Job enlargement** assigns workers additional same-level tasks to increase the number of tasks they have to perform. For example, if the work is assembling chairs, the worker who previously only bolted the seat to the legs might take on the additional tasks of assembling the legs and attaching the back. **Job rotation** systematically moves workers from job to job. A worker on an auto assembly line might spend an hour fitting doors, the next hour installing head lamps, the next hour fitting bumpers, and so on.

job enlargement

an increase in the number of similar tasks assigned to a job.

job rotation

the systematic movement of a worker from job to job to improve job satisfaction and reduce boredom.

Evidence regarding the effects of programs like these is somewhat contradictory. In one study the newly enlarged jobs initially led to improved job satisfaction, reduced boredom, and improved customer satisfaction (because one employee followed the customer's paperwork more or less from beginning to end).[71] However, in a follow-up study two years later, employee satisfaction had leveled off and boredom was on the rise again, suggesting that the motivational value of this technique may be short lived.[72]

Job Enrichment Other psychologists, including Frederick Herzberg, contend that having several boring jobs to do instead of one is not what employees want. Psychologists like Herzberg, Maslow, and Alderfer believe that what employees want from their jobs is a sense of achievement that comes from completing a challenging task successfully and the recognition that comes from using their skills and potential.

job enrichment

the inclusion of opportunities for achievement and other motivators in a job by making the job itself more challenging.

Job enrichment is the method Herzberg recommends for applying his two-factor approach to motivation. **Job enrichment** means building motivators into the job by making it more interesting and challenging. This is often accomplished by *vertically loading* the job, which means giving the worker more autonomy and allowing the person to do much of the planning and inspection normally done by the person's supervisor.

Job enrichment can be accomplished in several ways:[73]

1. *Form natural workgroups.* Change the job in such a way that each person is responsible for, or "owns," an identifiable body of work. Putting a team in charge of building an engine from start to finish is an example.

2. *Combine tasks.* Let one person assemble a product from start to finish, instead of having it go through several separate operations that are performed by different people. This is also a form of job enlargement.

3. *Establish client relationships.* Let the worker have contact as often as possible with the client of that person's work. For example, let an assistant research and respond to customer's requests, instead of automatically referring all problems to his or her boss.

4. *Vertically load the job.* Have the worker plan and control his or her job, rather than let it be controlled by others. For example, let the worker set a schedule, do his or her own troubleshooting, and decide when to start and stop working.

5. *Open feedback channels.* Find more and better ways for the worker to get quick feedback on performance.

Research results show that enrichment programs can be effective, particularly if implemented in association with other changes such as increasing pay along with the increased levels of responsibilities.[74] But it's not necessary to rely on research results to understand that job enrichment really works. For example, enrichment is part of motivation at the GE Durham plant. Remember, for instance, that the facility has more than 170 employees, but just one boss, the plant manager. The nine teams of people who produce each engine get only one marching order—when their engine is to be loaded on the truck—and they make all the other decisions, such as who does what and how to handle teammates who slack off.

▲ Job enrichment at Cin-Made: Boss Bob Frey discusses the company's profit projections with employees.

What they've done in Durham, of course, is to apply many of the job enrichment concepts listed above. They have formed natural work groups so that each team owns an identifiable body of work, in this case an entire engine. They've combined tasks, so that one team is given the responsibility to assemble an engine from start to finish. They vertically loaded the job, since each team makes virtually all its own decisions. (Remember, there are no supervisors in the traditional sense.) In most respects, the Durham plant is proof of the applicability of the job enrichment concept.

Using Empowerment

Empowering employees means giving employees the authority, tools, and information they need to do their jobs with greater autonomy, as well as the self-confidence required to perform the jobs effectively. Empowering is inherently a motivational approach: It boosts feelings of self-efficacy and enables employees to more fully use their potential, thus satisfying higher-level needs for achievement, recognition, and self-actualization. Figure 11.5 lists 10 principles for empowering people, including telling people what their responsibilities are, and giving them authority equal to the responsibilities assigned to them. Today, as at facilities such as GE Durham, work teams are often empowered.

empowering employees
authorizing and enabling employees to do their jobs with greater autonomy.

At Saturn Corporation, for instance, empowered, self-managing work teams are authorized to do a variety of duties. For each team, these duties include resolving its own conflicts, planning its own work schedule, determining its own job assignments, making selection decisions about new members, performing within its own budget, and obtaining its own supplies. Specific examples include these:

▪ *Use consensus decision making.* Decisions are arrived at by consensus. All members of the work unit who reach consensus must be at least 70% comfortable with the decision and 100% committed to its implementation.

► F I G U R E 11.5

Ten Principles for Empowering People

Source: Diane Tracey, *10 Steps to Empowerment* (New York, William Morrow, 1990), 163. Copyright © 1990 by Diane Tracey. By permission of William Morrow & Co., Inc.

1. Tell people what their responsibilities are.
2. Give them authority equal to the responsibilities assigned to them.
3. Set standards of excellence.
4. Provide them with training that will enable them to meet the standards.
5. Give them knowledge and information.
6. Provide them with feedback on their performance.
7. Recognize them for their achievements.
8. Trust them.
9. Give them permission to fail.
10. Treat them with dignity and respect.

- *Make their own job assignments*. A work unit ensures safe, effective, efficient, and equal distribution of the work unit tasks to all its members.

- *Plan their own work*. The work unit assigns timely resources for the accomplishment of its purpose to its customers, while meeting the needs of the people within the work unit.

- *Design their own jobs*. This should provide the optimum balance between people and technology, and include the effective use of human effort, ergonomics, machine utilization, quality, cost, job task analysis, and continuous improvement.

Empowering supports Saturn's enriched jobs. The teams at Saturn also get the training, skills, and tools, such as in consensus decision making, to empower them to do their jobs. Firms like Saturn also make sure managers let their people do their jobs as assigned.

Not all empowerment programs are so comprehensive. At Scandinavian Air Systems (SAS), for instance, empowering the workforce meant letting employees make more decisions themselves. Ticket agents now have the authority to reticket a passenger or even move the passenger up a class, if they feel the situation warrants it. At one Marriott chain subsidiary, each and every hotel employee, from management to maintenance, is empowered to offer guests a free night's stay if, in the employee's opinion, the hotel has been lax in serving the guest. And at engine maker Pratt & Whitney, salespeople can now authorize multimillion-dollar repairs on the spot, instead of having to wait for approvals from up the line.

In virtually all such cases, employees find empowerment exciting, and employers find that it helps workers to self-actualize and exhibit self-efficacy, and thereby boost motivation and employee commitment.[75]

Using Goal-Setting Methods

Have you ever set your sights on some goal—acing a course, graduating from college, or earning enough money for a trip abroad? What effect did setting the goal have on you? If you're like most people, it proved highly motivating: As Locke and his associates have shown time and again, people are strongly motivated to achieve goals they consciously set. Setting specific goals with employees can be one of the simplest yet most powerful ways of motivating them.

The research on how to set goals that motivate employees is voluminous. Indeed, we discussed much of it in Chapter 5, in the context of goal setting for the purpose of planning. Here's a summary:

- *Be clear and specific*. Employees who are given specific goals usually perform better than those who are not.

- *Make goals measurable and verifiable.* Whenever possible, goals should be stated in quantitative terms and should include target dates or deadlines for accomplishment.
- *Make goals challenging but realistic.* Goals should be challenging, but not so difficult that they appear impossible or unrealistic.
- *Set goals participatively.* Participatively set goals usually lead to higher performance, mostly because such goals tend to be more difficult.
- *Make sure the employee has the confidence to do the job.* Research studies show that self-efficacy has an important effect on whether the employee tries to attain the goal. In other words, ability and goal level are important determinants of performance, but having the confidence to do the job is important, too. Therefore, building a person's confidence with honest and supportive comments can help determine whether the goals the two of you set are translated into motivation and performance.[76]

Using Positive Reinforcement

At work, behavior modification programs are often applied by focusing on supplying positive reinforcement to motivate the desired behavior. Positive reinforcement programs (sometimes called organizational behavior management or performance management programs) are widely used.

As summarized in Figure 11.6, modifying behavior with reinforcement is much like balancing a scale. Let's say that wearing a safety helmet is the desired behavior, and not wearing it is the undesired behavior. One way to increase the desired behavior is to add a positive consequence—for instance, by praising the worker each time he or she wears the hat. Another way to do so is to remove the negative

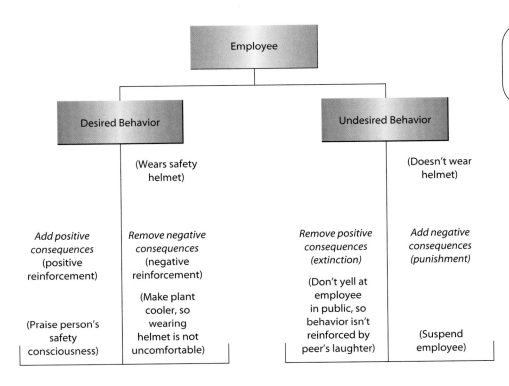

◄ FIGURE 11.6

Options for Modifying Behavior with Reinforcement

consequences of wearing the hat, by lowering the temperature to cool the plant or by making the hat less cumbersome.

Most positive reinforcement/behavior management experts say it's best to focus on improving desirable behaviors rather than on decreasing undesirable ones. If the employee fails to wear a safety hat, stress improving the desired behavior (wearing the hat), rather than reducing the undesirable behavior (not wearing the hat).

Obviously you needn't use just tangible rewards in these types of programs. *Social consequences* include peer approval, praise from the boss, letters of thanks from the company president, and a celebratory lunch. *Intrinsic consequences* include the enjoyment the person gets from engaging in a hobby and the sense of achievement from accomplishing a challenging task. *Tangible consequences* include outcomes like bonuses, incentive pay, and merit raises.

Many employers have implemented positive reinforcement programs, in a multitude of applications. Probably the best-known application in industry was implemented at Emery Air Freight Company.[77] The program grew out of management's discovery that the containers used to consolidate air freight shipments were not being fully utilized. In the air freight business, small shipments intended for the same destination fly at lower rates when shipped together in containers rather than separately. In this case, the workers used containers only about 45% of the time, while they reportedly *thought* they were using them about 90% of the time. Management wanted them to boost the actual usage rate to 90% to 95%.

A behavior management program was implemented. It included an elaborate instruction book for managers that detailed how to use recognition, rewards, feedback, and various other types of social, intrinsic, and tangible consequences. It enumerated no less than 150 kinds of reinforcement, ranging from a smile to detailed praise like "You're running consistently at 98% of standard, and after watching you I can understand why." Intrinsic feedback was used, too; for example, the consultants set up a checklist for a dock worker to mark each time he or she used a container. The results of this program were impressive. In 80% of the offices in which it was implemented, container usage rose from 45% to 95% in a single day.

Using Lifelong Learning

Many employers today face a dilemma. Remaining competitive requires highly committed employees who exercise self-discipline and basically do their jobs as if they owned the company. But competitive pressures have forced many companies to continually downsize; this in turn causes employees to question whether it pays for them to work their hearts out for the company.

Lifelong learning is one method used to build skills and underscore the employer's commitment to employees. **Lifelong learning** provides extensive continuing training, from basic remedial skills to advanced decision-making techniques to college degree programs throughout the employees' careers.

lifelong learning

the organizational program of providing continuing education and training to employees throughout their careers.

For example, although the oil industry is constantly changing, Chevron has survived by dramatically downsizing. But rather than let trained and talented people go, top management used another approach: Reeducate and redeploy Chevron's human resources where the jobs were. At Chevron, lifelong learning was thus used to support the firm's strategy of boosting productivity.

Many of Chevron's bright, qualified employees were in the wrong departments: Some units had too many people, and others had too few. The solution was to give employees the opportunity to be trained to take jobs outside their own specialties or in other Chevron companies. Houston-based Chevron Production Company came up with the idea to mix and match employees from one unit with those of another. In production operations, many employees are petroleum engineers with college degrees. Chevron's refineries traditionally recruit chemical engineers. So with some training and assistance, the petroleum engineers could fill in for the chemical engineers.

To implement this plan, all companies within Chevron were designated either supply (needed to cut employees) or demand (needed staff). Within every operating company, redeployment coordinators were identified to help those who wanted to make the change. There were initial concerns: How far would employees try to stretch in order to jump into an entirely new job? Would surplus employees be low performers whom supply companies just wanted to get rid of?

Overall the plan has worked very well. Of those who entered the redeployment and relearning program, about 80% found work within the companies. The program has saved the company approximately $25 million in severance costs alone and has earned praise from the Department of Labor. Chevron has remotivated an already skilled workforce and changed it into a reskilled, revitalized one, highly motivated by the recognition that it is valued by the firm.[78]

Implemented properly, lifelong learning programs achieve several goals. First, the training and education provide employees with the skills they need to carry out the demanding, team-based jobs that increasingly predominate, even on the factory floor. Second, the opportunity for lifelong learning is inherently motivational: It enables employees to develop and to see an enhanced possibility of fulfilling their potential; it boosts employees' sense of self-efficacy; and it provides an enhanced opportunity for the employee to self-actualize and gain the sense of achievement that psychologists argue is so important. Third, although lifelong learning may not cancel out the potential negative effects of downsizing, it might at least counterbalance them to some degree by giving employees marketable new skills.

Programs like these can be successful. For example, one study concluded that "productivity improvements, greater workforce flexibility, reduced material and capital costs, a better motivated work force, and improved quality of the final product or service are all identified as advantages [of lifelong learning] for commercial enterprises."[79] So, while lifelong learning is not the sort of conventional tool (like incentives or merit pay) that might come to mind when you think about motivating employees, the motivational effect of giving employees the opportunity to develop their skills and self-actualize appears to be considerable.

Putting Motivation Theory into Practice

Can managers really put motivation theories into practice by using techniques like these? The answer is yes. For example, employee theft is a significant problem at work today. It accounts for anywhere between $40 to $250 billion a year in lost merchandise, and it's estimated that $26 billion a year is lost to dishonest employees in the retail industry alone.[80] Here are some examples one expert gives for how various theories of motivation might be used to help prevent employee theft.

With respect to goal-setting theory, for instance, "Set goals for employees, measure the shrinkage levels periodically, and give employees feedback on how they are progressing toward goal attainment."[81] In terms of reinforcement theory, one company instituted a positive reinforcement program to address thefts by truck drivers. Drivers were randomly placed under surveillance, and those who exhibited no incidents of theft were given a small bonus. Expectancy theory can be applied too: Employees need clear communications about the fact that their actions can affect the company's performance. For example, one hospital let employees know that the theft of even one set of surgical room scrubs per employee cost the hospital over $60,000 per year. Even equity theory can be applicable. For instance, employees who view themselves as well-paid and treated fairly may have less motivation to steal.

▶ IN CONCLUSION: HOW DO YOU MOTIVATE TODAY'S EMPLOYEES?

We covered many motivation techniques in this chapter, ranging from pay for performance to spot awards, merit pay, recognition, job redesign, empowerment, goal setting, positive reinforcement, and lifelong learning. All these techniques can be effective; and part of the art of managing is learning when to use—or not use—one or the other.

Yet increasingly, as we've seen, motivating employees seems to require something more. We saw how at GE Durham all operations are run by self-managing teams composed of highly committed employees, none of whom has to be coerced or supervised or in a traditional way motivated to do his or her best. As one observer remarked, "They don't really think that their main job is to make jet engines. They think that their main job is to make jet engines *better*."[82] At another GE facility not too far away, the plant manager describes the difference between GE Durham and his own plant this way: Pointing to the floor upstairs where his own technicians also assembled jet engines, he said: "I think what they've discovered in Durham is the value of the human being. . . . Upstairs, you've got wrench turners. In Durham, you've got people who think."[83]

▲ Mary Garey, manager of the Boca Raton Best Buy store, with some of her 110 employees.

"People who think" is probably as good a way to put it as any. Somehow, at GE and at more and more facilities and offices, companies are finding a way to ignite the kind of self-motivation that drives employees to do their very best. At Durham, employees take such pride in the engines they make that they routinely sweep out the beds of the 18-wheelers that transport those engines just to make sure no damage occurs in transit.[84]

Motivating employees to think and to take responsibility and to do a great job even when you're not around is certainly not something that occurs only in sophisticated manufacturing firms. Mary Garey, general manager of the Boca Raton, Florida, Best Buy store, is a good example. Garey motivates her 110 employees by practicing what she calls "behind the scenes" management. For example, she puts her employees at ease, listens to them, and teaches by example.[85] She interviews all prospective employees and knows each of them by name, and while she might just say a quick hello when she's busy and then go on her way, "she always comes back and says, 'what's happening,' and gives you some time" when she's free again.

Garey's leadership style therefore highlights another important aspect of motivating employees: Understanding employees' needs and the process of motivation are certainly important, as are techniques like incentives and spot awards. However, as Garey's behavior shows, motivation is not just a product of some technique. From your own experience, you know that it's the totality of how you're treated and not simply, say, a merit raise that determines whether you're motivated to get the job done. In Garey's case, as at GE Durham, employees are treated as valued individuals and with respect. The motivation that results therefore comes not just from incentives, spot awards, or even recognition, but from a system that says "We respect you and we believe in you and we know you will do your best."

Managers like Garey know that highly committed and self-motivated employees are their best competitive edge. They therefore work hard to earn commitment—an employee's identification with and agreement to pursue the company's or the unit's mission.[86] That kind of commitment manifests itself in the work behavior at plants like Durham.

SUMMARY

1. Motivation can be defined as the intensity of the person's desire to engage in some activity. Need-based approaches to motivating employees—such as those of Maslow and Herzberg—emphasize the role played by motivational dispositions or needs such as the need for achievement and for self-actualization.

2. An employee's thought process also influences motivation. People want to be treated equitably. Having decided to pursue a goal, they regulate their behavior to try to ensure that a goal is reached. Their expectations—that effort will lead to performance, that performance will lead to reward, and that the reward is valuable enough to pursue in the first place—also influences motivation.

3. Behavior modification means changing or modifying behavior through the use of contingent rewards or punishment. It assumes, for instance, that behavior that appears to lead to a positive consequence or reward tends to be repeated, whereas behavior that leads to a negative consequence or punishment tends not to be repeated.

4. Methods based on motivational approaches like Maslow's theory and behavior modification include pay for performance, spot awards, merit pay, recognition awards, job redesign, empowerment, goal setting, positive reinforcement, and lifelong learning.

TYING IT ALL TOGETHER

In Chapter 10 we saw that a leader has to size up a situation by identifying what is happening, accounting for what is happening, and formulating actions. When it comes to accounting for what is happening and formulating actions, the leader needs a firm understanding of human motivation—what motivates people and how motivation comes about. We therefore emphasized motivation in this chapter, including need-based approaches to motivating employees, process approaches, learning/reinforcement approaches, and methods for influencing behavior.

However, when it comes to motivating employees today, it's also important to take a broader view: Job enrichment and human needs are certainly important, but as our discussions of Best Buy, and the GE Durham and Saturn plants illustrate, the entire management system, including communications and teamwork, determines whether employees are committed and self-motivated to do an exceptional job.

Since effective interpersonal and organizational communications play an important role in this process, we turn to these topics next.

total quality management
(TQM) 320
motivation 321
motive 321
motivational dispositions or
needs 321
aroused motive 321
equity theory 328
expectancy 329
instrumentality 329
valence 329
learning 330
operant behavior 330
contingent reward 330

behavior modification 330
positive reinforcement 330
extinction 330
negative reinforcement 330
punishment 331
pay for performance 333
variable pay plan 333
gainsharing plan 334
merit raise 336
spot award 336
job design 340
job enlargement 340
job rotation 340

job enrichment 340
empowering employees 341
lifelong learning 344
law of individual defferences
353
personality 353
authoritarian personality 355
Machiavellian personality 355
self-concept 356
self-efficacy 357
attributions 359
attitude 359
job satisfaction 359

SKILLS AND STUDY MATERIALS

CRITICAL THINKING EXERCISES

1. It is said the baby boomers (born 1946–1964) "live to work" and that Generation Xers (1965–1981) "work to live." What are the challenges in motivating the two groups? What if they are working on teams together? What job design challenges might you encounter as the team manager?

2. In *Built to Last* (Harper Business, 1994), James Collins and Jerry Porras explore the successful habits of visionary companies. They compare the visionary companies to other companies in the same industry. For example, they com-

pare 3M and Norton, American Express and Wells Fargo, Ford and GM, Disney and Columbia, Merck and Pfizer, Hewlett-Packard and Texas Instruments, and Philip Morris and RJR Reynolds. What do you think makes them visionary? Drawing from the information presented in the chapter, speculate on how you think visionary companies motivate employees. Then go to the Internet to the home pages of these companies. Be prepared to discuss the motivation techniques of each of these firms.

EXPERIENTIAL EXERCISES

1. Interview four or five friends, workmates, or fellow students about what motivates them. Record their responses. Then match the responses with the theories in the chapter and be prepared to discuss in class what you find.

2. Read the business pages of your local newspaper for a week. Also read the sports pages for the same period. Then compare and contrast sports and business examples of motivation. Do you find a difference? How would you describe the differences? Construct a one-page explanation of your findings to share in class.

3. "The Internet lets you distribute your ideas without having to actually put them onto a tape, walk them down the street to your friend's house, and say, 'Can we please listen to this?' Anybody can connect. I've had everything I've written musically online for the past two years."—Joshua McFadden, student and musician, Oberlin College, as quoted (p. 108) in *Business Week*, August 23–30, 1999, "21 Ideas for the 21st Century." What are the implications for motivation in a wired world? How does it and will it increasingly affect values, relationships, loyalty, norms, and the other concepts that inflluence motivation?

We invite you to visit the Dessler companion Web site at **www.prenhall.com/dessler** for this chapter's Internet resources.

DAYTON-HUDSON CORPORATION: LEARNING TO MOTIVATE WOMEN EMPLOYEES

CASE 1

Dayton-Hudson Corporation (DHC) wants to run "the best stores in town." The owner of Dayton's, Hudson's, Mervyn's California, Marshall Fields, and Target, DHC understands that to have the best stores, it needs to attract, retain, and motivate the best employees. Since many retail-shopping dollars are spent by women consumers, DHC also wants to attract and motivate women managers and has developed policies to make the company attractive to prospective women employees.

The stakes are very high in the retail industry. Consider the Target division of DHC. Since opening the first Target store in May 1962, in suburban St. Paul, Minnesota, the company has grown to nearly 900 stores in 44 states. Target provides employment for approximately 189,000 people. The parent company, DHC, is America's fourth largest general merchandise retailer, with more than a quarter of a million team members.

DHC has clearly been successful in its efforts to promote women managers. The company's most recent EEO report noted that in regard to senior management, 26% of DHC managers at the level of vice president or higher are women. Of middle management at the company, 37% are women. Women recently comprised more than 66% of DHC's employee population.

Each of DHC's major divisions has its own program of HR policies and benefits, but they all have several common features:

- Pretax salary set-asides to help pay for dependent care
- Child care resource and referral information
- Employee participation in alternative work arrangements, such as telecommuting, job-sharing, working at home, flextime, and part-time employment
- Time off to care for a sick child or seriously ill family member
- Generous leaves for pregnancy
- 401(k) plan and employee stock option/stock ownership plan that includes a dollar-for-dollar match for the first 5% of salary
- Additional programs in individual divisions, such as expense reimbursement for adoption and prenatal and well-baby care programs

Working Mother magazine has six times named DHC one of the top workplaces for women with children. It has noted a number of key features in the DHC program, including the publication of its overall benefits program. In general, DHC has been recognized for its commitment to enhancing family life.

Discussion Questions

1. In what ways are DHC's policies friendly toward women employees?

2. How might DHC's polices be especially useful for motivating performance among its men and women managers?

3. In your opinion, does DHC have all the programs it needs to motivate managers? Why or why not?

Top management at furniture manufacturer Herman Miller believes that the success of a company is the result of its beliefs. Herman Miller believes that it will be successful only if it defines how it is different from other companies, not just in products but in the way the company gives meaning to its work. In particular, Herman Miller focuses on three key values: good design, participative management, and environmental responsibility. Could a company outperform its competitors because of these values?

Headquartered in Zeeland, Michigan, Herman Miller is a leading multinational provider of office, healthcare, and residential furniture, as well as furniture management services. Herman Miller feels that the source of its vitality has always been its belief systems and its employees. To Herman Miller, a company is a "community of people who firmly believe that doing the right thing and succeeding as a business must be pursued with equal enthusiasm."

The company's executives believe that having a meaningful place to work will unleash creativity and commitment. The company should then be able to deliver better products and services and build longer and stronger relationships with its customers. The company's Web page boasts:

> The mere exchange of goods and services for money is not enough for us. We have a higher aim—to make a meaningful contribution to the people we serve. We must know more about the work environment and potential solutions than anyone else. Knowledge about a customer's needs, problems, and aspirations is a necessary foundation. This knowledge alone, however, is insufficient. We want our products and services to meet customer needs, providing solutions to their problems, enabling them to reach their aspirations. Simply put, the business that understands the diverse needs of its customers and meets those needs best will win. We want to be that company.

To create a more meaningful place to work, the firm tries to create a sense of community. It has a very high level of employee stock ownership. The company began its employee stock ownership plan in 1983. Today, all Herman Miller employees with more than one year of service own stock in the company. The company thinks that owners make better employees because employees and shareholders then have the same interests and goals.

The firm also concentrates on fostering a participative environment. The Herman Miller philosophy has been well articulated in two best-selling books, *Leadership Is an Art* and *Leadership Jazz* by former Herman Miller CEO and the son of its founder, Max DePree. To reinforce its values, the company uses an economic value-added (EVA) accounting system. EVA has been described as a linking measurement of operating and financial performance to incentive compensation for every employee.

Perhaps the most innovative value held by Herman Miller is its concept of environmental stewardship. The company sees itself needing to act with great responsibility in regard to the natural environment. High-level teams work to set environmentally responsible strategies for the present and future operations of the company, while continuous improvement teams attempt to meet and exceed the challenges of being environmentally responsible. Herman Miller executives believe this value has helped the company recruit talented, environmentally responsible employees.

In 1999 Herman Miller was once again selected for the prestigious *Industry Week* magazine list of the 100 best-managed companies in the world. Other recent awards for Herman Miller include the following:

1999—Herman Miller maintains its consistent ranking (since 1986) as *Fortune* magazine's most admired furniture manufacturer in America, with the company's reputation scoring 13th among all American industry, and 3rd among all companies for both innovation and social responsibility.

1999—Herman Miller makes *Forbes* magazine's inaugural platinum list of America's 400 best-managed large companies.

1999—*Fortune* magazine again cites Herman Miller among the 100 best companies to work for in America.

1998—*Industry Week* magazine identifies Herman Miller as one of the world's 100 best-managed manufacturers.

1998—Roney & Co. recognizes Herman Miller among its Michigan Superstar 10 for total financial performance in fiscal year 1998.

1998—Herman Miller receives the Council for Economic Priorities first annual Honor Roll Award for a consistent record of social and environmental leadership.

1998—*Fortune* magazine calls Herman Miller the most admired company in America for social responsibility.

1986 through 1999—*Fortune* magazine consistently lists Herman Miller as the most admired furniture manufacturer in the annual poll of industry executives, board members, and financial analysts.

1998—*Fortune* magazine recognizes Herman Miller among the 100 best companies to work for in America.

1997—Roney & Co. recognizes Herman Miller among its Michigan Superstar 10 for total financial performance in fiscal year 1997.

1997—Business Enterprise Trust recognizes Herman Miller for sound management and social vision.

The company has obviously built an impressive track record for performance.

Discussion Questions

1. How might Herman Miller's values affect the motivation of its employees?

2. Which values do you think would have the greatest impact on performance?

3. Develop a list of specific motivation techniques you would use in a motivation package if you were developing one for this company.

YOU BE THE CONSULTANT

MAINTAINING MOTIVATION AT KNITMEDIA

Developing a package of incentives with which to maintain the motivation of KnitMedia's managers, employees, and artists has become increasingly challenging over the past few years. Michael Dorf and his management team have come to you for advice about what sort of package they should put together.

One problem, particularly recently, has been the explosion of new Internet startups, particularly in "Silicon Alley," the lower Manhattan neighborhood in which many new Internet-related companies are starting up. Many of these startups are offering talented technical people and people with music experience big stakes in their companies in terms of stock options. KnitMedia has recently lost several high-potential employees to these startups since it really can't compete with companies that give people the chance to become multimillionaires in a year or two.

Keeping top-notch artists is a similar but separate problem. KnitMedia recently raised about $5 million, but compared to giants like Warner music and Universal it's still difficult, to say the least, to compete with major record labels' large cash advances at signing. In the past few years, for instance, the company lost four of its rock artists and one jazz

band to major labels. These artists had achieved significant success with the company, and each had contracts expiring with KnitMedia. The artists, including Eric Sanko, who signed with Capital Records for $1 million; Bill Ware, who moved to Warner Music; and the Jazz Passengers, all went on to use their tremendous success to sign with major labels.

This of course could turn out to be a problem: the whole idea of KnitMedia is to attract and showcase new artists at the Knitting Factory clubs and then to develop them into successful recording artists who can be showcased on KnitMedia's record labels and Internet sites and taken out on tours with KnitMedia festivals. That plan will obviously fail unless KnitMedia can retain the artists it identifies as high-potential performers.

As far as attracting and keeping lower-level employees is concerned, the company currently has few incentives. As Chuck Brownley, the New York club's general manager, puts it, to a large extent it's the Knitting Factory itself that's the recruiting magnet, "by virtue of the scene that we create, by virtue of the reputation that we have." As far as the people who actually work as servers at the Knitting Factory, "generally the only incentives that we're utilizing are the potential of tips," a situation that is not at all unusual at clubs like these.

Team Exercises and Questions

Use what you learned in this chapter to answer the following questions from Michael Dorf and his management team:

1. Based on what you know about motivation, how would you describe the motivational needs of recording artists and the other highly creative people who are associated with KnitMedia? What implications does this have for how we should motivate these people?

2. Based on whatever else you know about the music industry and KnitMedia, what exactly do you think we should do to ensure that we could continue to attract and keep high-potential recording artists?

3. What incentive plan do you think would be effective for helping us retain high-potential managers in the face of the sorts of incentives that Internet startups are trying to attract them with?

WHAT MANAGERS SHOULD KNOW ABOUT INDIVIDUAL BEHAVIOR

One of the paradoxes leaders face is that what motivates one person might not motivate another. Any stimulus—an order from the boss, an offer of a raise, or the threat of being fired—has different effects on different people. One person might leap at the chance for a $100 raise, while another might shun it. One might emerge from training with excellent skills, while another might learn nothing. One might jump whenever the boss gives orders, while another might laughingly ignore the boss.

To a large extent, these anomalies occur because of what psychologists call the **law of individual differences**, the fact that people differ in personalities, abilities, values, and needs. As illustrated in Figure 11A.1, these factors act much like filters, adding to, detracting from, and often distorting the effect of any stimulus. It is therefore important for managers to understand the nature of each of these factors.

law of individual differences
a psychological term representing the fact that people differ in their personalities, abilities, values, and needs.

▶ PERSONALITY AND BEHAVIOR

Personality is probably the first thing that comes to mind when most people think about what determines behavior. We tend to classify people as introverted, dominant, mature, or paranoid, for instance, and by and large these labels conjure up visions of particular kinds of behavior.

personality
the characteristic and distinctive traits of an individual, and the way these traits interact to help or hinder the adjustment of the person to other people and situations.

Personality Defined

One way (but by no means the only way) to define **personality** is as "the characteristic and distinctive traits of an individual, and the way the traits interact to help or hinder the adjustment of the person to other people and situations."

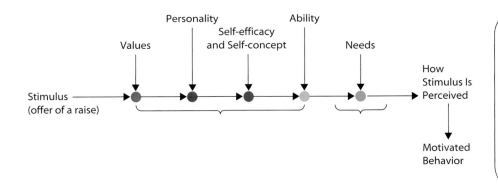

Personality · Ability
Self-efficacy
Values · and Self-concept · Needs

Stimulus
(offer of a raise)

How Stimulus Is Perceived

Motivated Behavior

◀ **FIGURE 11A.1**

Some Individual Determinants of Behavior

A particular stimulus may evoke different behaviors among individuals, because each person's value, personality, self-concept, abilities, and needs influence how he or she reacts.

Psychologist Raymond Cattell used observations and questionnaires to identify 16 primary personality traits, which he then expressed in pairs of words, such as reserved/outgoing, submissive/dominant, and trusting/suspicious.[1] Based on this work, Cattell and his colleagues developed a questionnaire that produced a personality profile for individuals. Figure 11A.2 shows the average personality profiles for people in two sample occupational groups: airline pilots and business executives.

Traits do not just represent characteristics people possess. People do not possess "submissiveness" or "sensitivity"; instead, they act and feel submissive or sensitive. So one way to define personality is in terms of traits, with someone's "personality" being the sum total of his or her traits.

Trait theories hold that someone's traits are a function of both genetic factors and learning, and that, his or her behavior reflects the person's traits—he or she is "extroverted," "agreeable," or "conscientious," for instance. Psychologists like Cattell and Gordon Allport describe an individual's personality in terms of a unique set of personality traits.

More recently, industrial psychologists have emphasized the "big five" personality dimensions as they apply to personnel testing: extroversion, emotional stability, agreeableness, conscientiousness, and openness to experience.[2] In one study of professionals, police officers, managers, sales workers, and unskilled and semi-skilled workers, *conscientiousness* showed a consistent relationship with all job per-

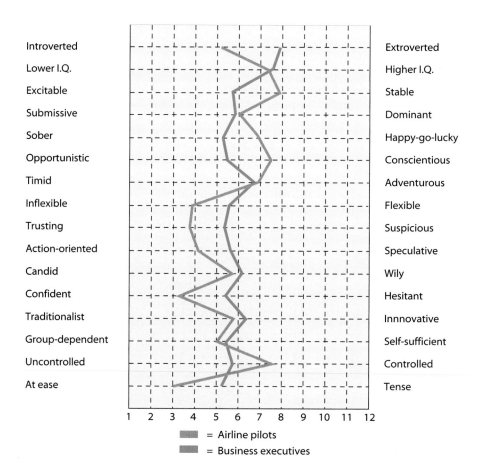

► FIGURE 11A.2

Cattell's 16 Personality Factors

The personalities of various people and even various groups of people are characterized by particular packages of traits, such as introverted, dominant, excitable, and innovative.

Source: Adapted from Gregory Northcraft and Margaret Neale, *Organizational Behavior* (Fort Worth, TX: The Dryden Press, 1994), p. 87.

Introverted		Extroverted
Lower I.Q.		Higher I.Q.
Excitable		Stable
Submissive		Dominant
Sober		Happy-go-lucky
Opportunistic		Conscientious
Timid		Adventurous
Inflexible		Flexible
Trusting		Suspicious
Action-oriented		Speculative
Candid		Wily
Confident		Hesitant
Traditionalist		Innnovative
Group-dependent		Self-sufficient
Uncontrolled		Controlled
At ease		Tense

1 2 3 4 5 6 7 8 9 10 11 12

= Airline pilots
= Business executives

formance criteria for all occupations. *Extroversion* was tied to performance for managers and sales employees, which of course are two occupations involving a lot of social interaction.[3]

Personality Types

At work, you will of course come across many unique personalities, but the following two types are common ones. The **authoritarian personality** has been studied for at least 50 years. Such a person is rigid, is intolerant of ambiguity, tends to stereotype people as good or bad, and conforms to the requirements of authority, perhaps while being dictatorial to subordinates. The **Machiavellian personality** (the name refers to the writings of the 16th-century political advisor Niccoló Machiavelli) tends to be oriented toward manipulation and control, with a low sensitivity to the needs of others.[4]

Measuring Personality

A test and scale known as the Myers-Briggs Type Indicator (MBTI) is one popular tool for measuring personality, particularly in the work setting. The MBTI classifies people as extroverted or introverted (E or I), sensing or intuitive (S or N), thinking or feeling (T or F), and perceiving or judging (P or J). The person's answers to a questionnaire are classified into 16 different personality types (a 4 × 4 matrix); these 16 types are in turn classified into one of four cognitive (thinking or problem-solving) styles:

- Sensation–thinking (ST)
- Intuition–thinking (NT)
- Sensation–feeling (SF)
- Intuition–feeling (NF)

Classifying personality types and cognitive styles in this way has several applications. Some employers have found that they can match the MBTI cognitive styles to particular occupations. This is illustrated in Figure 11A.3. People with the ST approach to problem solving are often well suited to occupations like auditor and safety engineer, for instance.

authoritarian personality
a personality type characterized by rigidity, intolerance of ambiguity, the tendency to stereotype others as being good or bad, and conformity to the requirements of authority.

Machiavellian personality
a personality type oriented toward manipulation and control, with a low sensitivity to the needs of others, the name of which refers to the 16th-century political advisor Niccolò Machiavelli.

	Thinking Style	Feeling Style
Sensation Style	People with this combined thinking/sensation style tend to be *thorough, logical,* and *practical* and to make good *CPAs* or *safety engineers*.	People with this combined sensation/feeling style tend to be *conscientious* and *responsible* and to make *good social workers* and *drug supervisors*.
Intuitive Style	People with this combined intuitive/thinking style tend to be *creative, independent,* and *critical* and to make good *systems analysts*, professors, and *lawyers*.	People with this combined intuitive/feeling style tend to be *people-oriented, sociable,* and often *charismatic* and to make good *human resource managers, public relations directors,* and *politicians*.

◀ **FIGURE 11A.3**

Four Examples of MBTI Styles and Some Corresponding Occupations

► ABILITIES AND BEHAVIOR

Individual differences in abilities also influence how we behave and perform.[5] Even the most highly motivated person will not perform well unless he or she also has the ability to do the job. Conversely, the most able employee will not perform-satisfactorily if not motivated. Some experts summarize this interaction this way:

$$\text{Performance} = \text{Ability} \times \text{Motivation}.$$

There are many types of abilities. Mental, cognitive, or "thinking" abilities include intelligence and its building blocks, such as memory, inductive reasoning, and verbal comprehension. Mechanical ability would be important for mechanical engineers or machinists. Psychomotor abilities include dexterity, manipulative ability, eye–hand coordination, and motor ability: Such abilities might be important for employees who put together delicate computer components or who work as dealers in Las Vegas. People also differ in their visual skills—for example, in their ability to discriminate between colors and between black and white detail.

In addition to these general abilities, people also have specific abilities learned through training, experience, or education. Companies test for these abilities when they are interested in determining a candidate's proficiency on a job such as computer programmer, word processor, or chemical engineer.

► SELF-CONCEPT AND BEHAVIOR

self-concept

the perceptions people have of themselves and their relationships to people and other aspects of life.

Although everyone is different, there is one way in which we are all the same: We all have our own **self-concepts**. Humanist psychologists like Carl Rogers emphasize the role of self-concept in personality. Who we are and how we behave is largely driven, say humanist psychologists, by the perceptions we have of who we are and how we relate to other people and things.

Thus, say humanists, people are motivated by the need for self-actualization—in other words, to strive to achieve their inborn potential and to become the people they believe they can become. Self-concept, in other words, is how we see ourselves, and how we see ourselves has a big influence on how we act and on how we react to the things that happen to us.

It's hard to underestimate the importance of self-concept in shaping the way we behave. Psychologist Saul Gellerman says that we are all driven in a constant quest to be ourselves or the kinds of individuals we think we should be.[6]

The next time you're in class or at work, stop and think about how you feel. Of all the people in the class, or in the company cafeteria, or in the office, around whom, more than anyone, does your world revolve? Who most occupies your thoughts? Would it bother you if your classmates or colleagues ignored you? How would you feel if you came to work every day and your boss or your boss's boss seemed to act as if you didn't exist, although you were knocking yourself out 10 hours per day for the company?

As a manager or future manager, you should keep in mind that every person you meet views himself or herself as being as special as you view yourself to be. The leader who doesn't recognize and act on that fact will be hampered in effectively dealing with people.

Some people have rigid self-concepts and are relatively unable to modify the way they view themselves.[7] Experiences that threaten such a person's self-concept will likely be screened out or distorted. Being turned down for promotion, for example, might be explained away in terms of politics or the supervisor's incompetence.

To some degree, everyone tries to protect his or her self-concept, and doing so is neither unnatural nor unhealthy, at least to a point. However, most psychologists would probably agree that "people with healthy self-concepts can allow new experiences into their lives and can accept or reject them."[8] As these experts put it,

> Such people move in a positive direction. With each new experience, their self-concepts become stronger and more defined, and the goal of self-actualization is brought closer.[9]

In this view, *individual development* plays a major role in helping people fulfill their self-concepts. The person with a healthy (and therefore somewhat flexible) self-concept is on a voyage of discovery, as his or her personality slowly evolves.

▶ SELF-EFFICACY AND BEHAVIOR

As we saw in the chapter, closely related to self-concept is the idea that people differ in their **self-efficacy**, or their belief about their own capacity to perform a task.[10] For a leader, this individual difference is important because self-efficacy has a big effect on how people perform and even on whether they try to accomplish the task.

In a familiar example of self-efficacy, in *My Fair Lady* Professor Higgins convinces Eliza Doolittle that she can do it—and in short order, she's speaking and acting like a proper upper class English person. However, you don't have to rely on movies for proof that self-efficacy works. Research shows that self-efficacy is associated with high work performance in a wide range of settings: life insurance sales, faculty research productivity, career choice, learning and achievement, and adaptability to new technology, to name a few.[11]

self-efficacy

being able to influence important aspects of one's world; the belief that one can accomplish what one sets out to do.

▶ PERCEPTION AND BEHAVIOR

The fact that we all differ in terms of things like personality and self-concept helps to explain why we perceive things differently. We all react to stimuli that reach us via our sense organs, but the way we define or perceive these stimuli depends on what we bring with us from past experiences and on our present needs and personalities.[12] In other words, our behavior is motivated not just by stimuli; it is motivated by our *perceptions* of those stimuli, by the way our personalities and experiences cause us to interpret them.

You are probably familiar with the way perceptual distortion clouds our view of inanimate objects. Consider what happens when we try to match the sizes of near objects with those of far ones. When we look down a row of arches, as in Figure 11A.4, the farthest one usually looks smaller than the closest one, and its perspective size is in fact smaller (because it is farthest away).

Based on experience, however, we know that the arches are actually equal in size, so what we *perceive* is a compromise between the perspective size of the arch and its actual size. In the photo, the nearest arch seems about twice the size of the farthest arch. But if you measure the arches, you will see that it is actually more than four times the size of the farthest arch. Our desire to see objects as we expect them to be causes us to perceive less difference in height than there really is.

Perception and Stereotypes

Just as we read stable, specific characteristics into objects, we also read them into people. This process is called *stereotyping*. For example, some people tend to associate characteristics like industriousness and honesty with certain socioeconomic classes, but not with others. Some managers erroneously assume that women are fit for certain jobs, but not for others. Similarly, we tend to stereotype people according to age, gender, race, or national origin and to attribute the characteristics of this stereotype to everyone we meet who is of that age, gender, race, or national origin. In other words, we all learn to associate certain meanings with certain groups of people.

This process helps us deduce more quickly (but not always accurately) the important characteristics of the people we meet and to avoid having to make fresh guesses every time.[13] Thus, a manager might jump to the conclusion that an older candidate would not be as flexible as a younger one.[14]

Factors That Affect Perception

The way we see or perceive the world is influenced by many things. Some important influences are as follows:

- *Personality and needs.* Our needs affect our perceptions. For example, when shown fuzzy and ambiguous pictures of objects, hungry people tend to see them as food. Tell an insecure employee that you want to see him in your office later in the day, and he might spend the hours worrying about being fired, although you only wanted to discuss vacation schedules.
- *Self-efficacy and abilities.* Someone confident about doing a job might welcome an assignment. Someone who believes he or she will fail might be devastated by the same assignment. Our abilities influence our perceptions of our own success.

- *Values*. Perceptions are also influenced by values, the basic beliefs a person has about what he or she should or shouldn't do. Someone with a strong code of ethics might be horrified at the suggestion of taking a bribe. Someone of lesser character might say, That's not a bad idea.

- *Stress*. People who are under stress tend to perceive things less objectively than those who are not. In one experiment, a group of employment interviewers were put under pressure to hire more employees. They subsequently perceived candidates' qualifications as being much higher than did a group of interviewers who were not under pressure.

- *Experience*. Our perceptions are also influenced by experience. Based on our experiences, for example, we learn to associate certain groups with certain behaviors (in other words, we stereotype them). We then tend to expect everyone from that group to behave in the same fashion.

- *Position*. A person's position in the organization is another important factor. Production managers tend to see problems as production problems, while sales managers see them as sales problems.

- *Attribution*. What people perceive is also strongly influenced by their **attributions**, or the meanings they give to actions. Suppose another car cuts you off as you are driving to work. If you attribute the driver's actions to his temporarily losing control of his car, you may drive on without giving it further thought. If you attribute his actions to his intentionally cutting you off in anger, you may take evasive action to avoid further encounters with someone you now perceive as a hothead.

attributions
the meaning people give to the causes of actions and outcomes.

In summary, our behavior is prompted by our perceptions, not necessarily by reality, and our perceptions, even of the same event, can be different, since our personalities, values, experiences, and needs differ as well.[15]

▶ ATTITUDES AND BEHAVIOR

A person's attitudes can and often will influence performance and behavior at work. An **attitude** is a predisposition to respond to objects, people, or events in either a positive or negative way.[16] When people say things like "I like my job" or "I don't care about my job," they are expressing attitudes, which are important because they can influence the way they behave on the job.

attitude
a predisposition to respond to objects, people, or events in either a positive or negative way.

Because attitudes are important, many companies conduct periodic (and usually anonymous) attitude or opinion surveys of their workforces. IBM, for example, regularly asks employees their opinions about the company, its management, and their work lives. The survey's stated purpose is "to aid management at all levels in identifying and solving problems."[17]

Job satisfaction is probably the most familiar example of attitudes at work. Job satisfaction reflects an employee's attitude about his or her job; in practice, measuring it usually means measuring several specific aspects of the job.

job satisfaction
the measure of an employee's attitude about his or her job.

One popular job satisfaction survey, the Job Descriptive Index, measures the following five aspects of job satisfaction:

1. *Pay*. How much pay is received and is it perceived as equitable?
2. *Job*. Are tasks interesting? Are opportunities provided for learning and for accepting responsibility?

3. *Promotional opportunities.* Are promotions and opportunities to advance available and fair?

4. *Supervisor.* Does the supervisor demonstrate interest in and concern about employees?

5. *Co-workers.* Are co-workers friendly, competent, and supportive?[18]

Good (or bad) attitudes do not necessarily translate into good (or bad) performance.[19] Performance can be affected by many other factors. Engineers may continue to do their best, regardless of how they feel about their employer, because their performance may be governed mostly by professional standards of conduct. Workers on a machine-paced assembly line may have so little discretion over the quantity or quality of what they do that their attitudes might not influence their performance.

COMMUNICATING IN TODAY'S ORGANIZATIONS

WHAT'S AHEAD?

It's 11 A.M. on a recent Wednesday, and 42-year-old Dan Hunt, president of Nortel Network's Caribbean and Latin American operations, is live on the air from the company's South Florida TV studio, answering questions from his far-flung employees.[1] An employee from Mexico wants to know how a new joint venture between Motorola and Cisco will affect Nortel. Another wants to know how Nortel will deal with a new competitive threat by Lucent Technologies. And so goes Hunt's monthly "corporate conversation," an hour-long program that lets him interact live and informally with 2,000 of his employees in 46 countries.[2]

The talk format lets Hunt and Nortel break down the typical one-way, top-down, rigid, corporate way of communicating.

OBJECTIVES

AFTER STUDYING THIS CHAPTER, YOU SHOULD BE ABLE TO

- Define communication

- Improve your interpersonal communication

- List barriers that may undermine organizational communications and ways to avoid them

- Illustrate how improving communications helps companies manage change

- Give examples of how technology improves communications in and among organizations

A man drove up to a gasoline pump to fill his gas tank. The gas station attendant noticed three penguins in the back seat of the car and, curious, asked about them.

"I don't know how they got there," the driver said. "The penguins were there when I took the car out of the garage this morning."

The attendant thought for a moment. "Why don't you take them to the zoo?"

"Good idea," the driver said, and drove away.

The next day, the same man returned to the gas station. In the back seat were the same three penguins, but now they wore sunglasses.

The attendant looked at the car in surprise. "I thought you took them to the zoo!" she exclaimed. "I did," the driver said. "And they had such a good time that today I'm taking them to the beach."

Communications, like patriotism, is something almost everyone agrees is a good thing; the problem is that, like our friend with the penguins, what one person says is not always what the other person hears. As you already know from your own experiences, many things—misunderstandings, semantics, or even fear—can distort the clarity of what you're trying to say. The result, as with the penguins, can range from laughable (if you're lucky) to disastrous.

Just about everything a manager does—setting goals, developing plans, managing teams, or motivating employees, for instance—involves communicating. Indeed, most studies of what managers do conclude that they spend most of their time communicating.[3] One study of supervisors in a DuPont laboratory found they spent 53% of their time in meetings, 15% writing and reading, and 9% on the phone. If we include meetings, interacting with customers and colleagues, and other ways in which managerial communication takes place, managers spend 60% to 80% of their time communicating.[4] In the previous chapter we focused on motivating employees, and on the techniques like job enrichment and recognition. Influencing and motivating employees assumes that you can effectively communicate what you want, and is a good example of why leaders are usually good communicators. In this chapter, we'll turn to the crucial topic of communicating, including communication barriers and how to overcome them.

▶ A COMMUNICATION MODEL

Managers like Daniel Hunt manage based on information—about competitors' tactics, labor and materials, or supplies and assembly line delays. And it's not the events themselves, but the *information* managers receive about them that trigger management action. If that information arrives too late or is wrong or distorted, the company and its managers suffer. **Communication**—the exchange of information and the transmission of meaning—is thus a part of almost everything managers do.[5]

communication

the exchange of information and the transmission of meaning.

As you can see in Figure 12.1,[6] there are five basic aspects to communicating. The sender puts a message in understandable terms and then transmits it via a **communication channel**, a vehicle that carries the message. Face-to-face communication is the most familiar and widely used channel. Memos, reports, policies and procedures manuals, videotape reports, and e-mail are some others.

communication channel

the vehicle that carries the message in the communication process.

But managers like Hunt (and the penguins' chauffeur) know that the information sent isn't always the same as that received. This is because information channels are all subject to noise and distortion. A face-to-face conversation in a restaurant can lead to misunderstandings when the message is overwhelmed by conversations

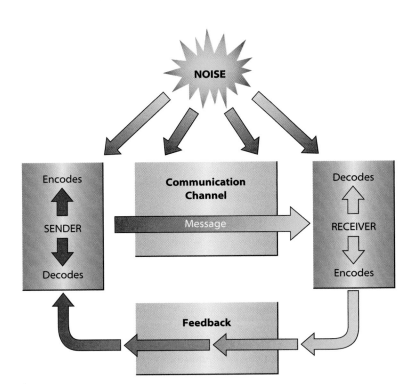

◄ **FIGURE 12.1**

The Communication Process

Source: Carrell/Jennings/Heavrin,
Fundamentals of Organizational Behavior,
© 1997. Reprinted by permission of
Prentice Hall, Inc., Upper Saddle River, NJ.

from surrounding tables. Other noise includes ambiguities in the message and pre-conceptions on the part of the receiver.

The receiver is the person or persons to whom the information is sent. If noise or other barriers like stress or perceptual differences cause the person to decode or hear the message erroneously, feedback can save the situation. **Feedback** is the receiver's response. Air traffic controllers use feedback when they confirm and get reconfirmation of messages they send.

feedback
the receiver's response to the message that was actually received in the communication process.

Interpersonal and organizational communication barriers can lead to problems in any of these five aspects. You might misperceive an event (like a big client lunching with one of your competitors) as a cause for alarm. A communication channel problem (like a subordinate causing a delay in you getting your messages) could cause the message about the event to be delayed for several days. Noise (perhaps distractions) may further delay the message. And then your president, shocked at the long delay in receiving the message, might decode it as if it were accurate, although the lunch was innocent and the client isn't really thinking of switching accounts.

interpersonal communication
communication that occurs between two individuals.

The communication model in Figure 12.1 illustrates both interpersonal and organizational communications. **Interpersonal communication** occurs between two individuals. **Organizational communication** occurs among several individuals or groups. We'll discuss both in this chapter.

organizational communication
communication that occurs among several individuals or groups.

► INTERPERSONAL COMMUNICATION

Managers spend a lot of time communicating face to face, so knowing how to improve interpersonal communication is a basic management skill. Let's look first at barriers to interpersonal communication.

Barriers to Interpersonal Communication

Several interpersonal communication barriers can distort messages and inhibit communication.[7]

Perception   Perceptions are influenced by many things, and it's probably safe to say that no two people perceive a particular message in exactly the same way.

For one thing, people tend to perceive things in a way that reflects what they believe. If you believe that people are good, trustworthy, and honest, then you may tend to perceive people's comments in a supportive way. People also perceive selectively. At the moment, for instance, you are probably concentrating on this book (we hope!) and may, therefore be unaware of the TV blaring in the background. People also tend to screen out messages they don't want which are low-priority or unwelcome.

semantics

the meaning of words.

Semantics   Semantics, the meaning of words, is another barrier, since words mean different things to different people. For example, when the attendant said to take the penguins to the zoo, of course he didn't mean to see the sights. But luckily for the penguins, that's what the driver thought he meant.

Nonverbal Communication   People pick up cues to what you mean not just from your words, but from your manner of speaking, facial expressions, bodily posture, and so on—your nonverbal communication. Thus, coming to work looking perturbed because of traffic may communicate to employees that you're dissatisfied with their work, although that's not the message you planned to send. One expert says, "It has been estimated that in a conversation involving two people, verbal aspects of a message account for less than 5% of the meaning, whereas nonverbal aspects of a message account for 95% of the meaning."[8]

nonverbal communication

the nonspoken aspects of communication, such as a person's manner of speaking, facial expressions, or body posture, that express meaning to others.

You're probably already aware of a lot of the nonverbal distractions that distort what you say, but here's a sampling from one expert's list:

1. Scratching your head indicates confusion or disbelief
2. Biting your lips signals anxiety
3. Rubbing the back of your head or neck suggests frustration, inpatience
4. A lowered chin conveys defensiveness or insecurity
5. Avoiding eye contact conveys insincerity, fear, evasiveness, or (at the very least) lack of interest on what's being discussed
6. A steady stare suggests a need to control, intimidate, and dominate
7. Crossing your arms in front of your chest communicates defiance, defensiveness, resistance, aggressiveness, or a closed mind
8. Hand wringing is a strong sign of anxiety verging on terror
9. At least in North America, getting a limp, dead-fish handshake is almost a disappointment
10. Sighing will be interpreted as a sign of distress or of boredom.[9]

The nonverbal aspects of communication can especially complicate the task of communicating internationally. As one expert recently noted, for instance, if a person travels 10,000 miles to Asia and steps off the plane, the differences in heat, humidity, and culture are immediately apparent, so there's more of a tendency to adapt the message and how it's delivered to the new situation. The problem is that today communications are increasingly sent long distance via e-mail or phone, and this can "increase the potential for misunderstanding by making the need for cultural adjustment less obvious."[10]

For example, a sales manager in Michigan might send a potential customer in Taiwan a brief, uninvited sales pitch via e-mail and be surprised when the message is ignored. Yet to the Taiwanese ignoring such a message is quite understandable. In the United States, Canada, and northern Europe, the verbal content of a message tends to be more important than the setting in which the message is delivered. In such "low-context" cultures, an e-mail is usually accepted as an efficient substitute for an in-person meeting.[11] But in many countries, including many in Asia and the Middle East, context, or setting, with its nonverbal cues, can convey far more meaning than the literal words of a given message.

In cultures like these, in other words, business transactions tend to be ritualized. The style in which they are carried out therefore tends to be more important than the words. There's much more emphasis on face-to-face interaction, and on after-hours socialization. Stripping away the context in a message sent to a "high-context" culture like one in Asia probably helped to torpedo our Michigan sales manager's sales effort: The e-mail message necessarily lacked the nonverbal content and nuances that are so important to doing business in Asia.

This doesn't mean that all global communication needs to be face-to-face, of course. However, it does suggest that it's a good idea to pay attention to the nature of the channel you're going to use. According to what experts call the media richness theory, some communication channels are simply more capable of carrying a rich combination of information than are others.[12] According to the theory, messages should be communicated using channels with sufficient and appropriate media richness capacities. Videoconferencing probably would have made more sense for our Michigan sales manager, since it would have been a closer substitute for an actual face-to-face interaction. Even a telephone call might have been second-best, insofar as it allowed each party to get a better feel for the other person's tone of voice and emphasis.

Ambiguity   Ambiguous messages also tend to get distorted, and here there are three specific problems. Ambiguity of *meaning* occurs when the person receiving the message isn't sure what was meant by the person who said or wrote the message. (For example, does "See me in my office as soon as you can" mean immediately or next week?) Ambiguity of *intent* means that the words may be clear, but the sender's intentions aren't. (You may ask, "Why does she want to see me in her office *now*?") Finally, ambiguity of *effect* represents the receiver's uncertainty about what the consequences of the message might be. (You might understand both your boss's note and her intentions, but still not be able to gauge how noncompliance may affect you.)

Defensiveness   When confronted with information that may clash with their self-concept, many employees react defensively. Defenses, or defense mechanisms, are adjustments people make, often unconsciously, to avoid having to recognize personal qualities that might lower their self-esteem. Defense mechanisms are very important. Everyone has a picture, real or not, of who they are and what they deserve, and most people try hard to screen out experiences that don't fit this self-image. Defenses help people deflect a lot of the things that might otherwise reduce their self-esteem and raise their anxiety.

Effective leaders know that defenses are an important part of interpersonal relations. When someone is accused of poor performance, for instance, his or her first reaction is often denial. By denying fault, the person avoids having to question or analyze his or her own competence. Still others react to criticism with anger and aggression. This helps them let off steam and postpone confronting the problem until they are better able to cope with it. Still others react to criticism by withdrawing.

Improving Interpersonal Communications

Managers have to be effective communicators. Employees who break a rule may have to be disciplined; a new employee may have to be shown how to improve her performance; or a sales manager may want to convince production to get the order out a few days sooner. All these are situations in which interpersonal communications are key. How do you avoid barriers like ambiguity? Some suggestions follow.

Be an Active Listener   Communications pioneer Carl Rogers says that active listeners doesn't just passively hear what the speaker is saying, but also try to understand and respond to the feelings behind the words.[13] The goal is to grasp what the speaker is saying from his or her point of view, and then convey the message that you truly understand. To do this,

- *Listen for total meaning.* For example, if the sales manager says, "We can't sell that much this year," the active listener's response would not be "Sure you can." Instead, the listener would understand the underlying feelings (such as the pressure the sales manager might be under) and let the sales manager know the problem is recognized.

- *Reflect feelings.* Reflecting the speaker's feelings is important because it helps the speaker get them off his or her chest. Reflecting feelings here might mean saying something like, "They're pushing you pretty hard, aren't they?"

- *Note all cues.* Remember that not all communication is verbal. Facial expressions and hand gestures portray feelings, too.

Avoid Triggering Defensiveness   Criticizing, arguing, and even giving advice can trigger defensiveness, as the other person reacts to protect his or her self-image. Trying to influence someone in this way may thus backfire. Similarly, don't try to explain a person to himself or herself by saying things like, "You know the reason you're using that excuse is that you can't bear to be blamed for anything." Instead, focus your comments on the act itself (low sales or poor attendance, for instance). Sometimes it's best to do nothing at all—postpone action. A cooldown period could give both of you a different perspective on the matter.

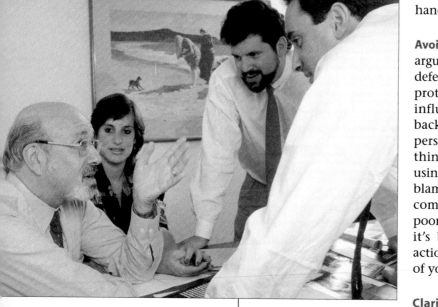

▲   Not all communication is verbal: gestures, posture, facial expression, even distances between people all tell a part of the story.

Clarify Your Ideas Before Communicating
Miscommunication often results from fuzzy thinking or poorly chosen words (consider our friend out on a date with his three penguins, for instance). The way to avoid this problem is to "say what you mean and mean what you say." If you mean "immediately," *say* "immediately,"

rather than "as soon as you can." Also keep in mind the underlying meaning of your message, and make sure your tone, expression, and words all convey a consistent meaning.

Interpersonal Communication in Action

How can you apply guidelines like these to some common business situations? One expert gives the following examples.[14]

Communicating with Your Supervisor   Your boss is a manager, and is therefore responsible for getting results. In general, then, there are some key phrases to avoid when communicating with your boss, since they could be interpreted as a lack of responsibility on your part. These include "I'm only human," "I'm overworked," "It slipped past me," "It's not my fault," "It's not my problem," and "You don't appreciate me."

Similarly, whether you're requesting a raise or a day off next week, or discussing some other matter, body language to avoid includes cringing; looking down; rushing to be seated; slouching in your chair; bringing your hands to your face, mouth, or neck (this suggests anxiety and evasion); and crossing your arms in front of your chest.

Communicating with Colleagues   Getting along with colleagues is important for several reasons: for example, you have to depend on them for help to get your job done, and your career progress and day-to-day peace of mind usually depend to some extent on how well you get along with your peers. In general, therefore, unnecessarily belligerent-sounding words or phrases like "absurd" "bad," "can't," "crazy," "doomed," "unworkable," and "are you out of your mind?" are usually best left unsaid. Body language problems include avoiding eye contact, frowning, shaking your head, and pushing gestures (that is, using the hands as if to push people or things away).

Communicating with Subordinates   Subordinates know that their appraisals and career success are in their supervisors hands. Knowing this makes them more sensitive to any indication of disrespect or unfairness on their managers' part. Words to avoid with subordinates thus include "blame," "catastrophe," "demand," "destroyed," "idiotic," and "misguided." Phrases to avoid include "better shape up," "don't come to me about it," "don't want to hear it," "figure it out for yourself," "you don't understand," and "you'd better." In terms of body language, "it pays to come across as open and receptive."[15] Therefore, maintain eye contact, smile, keep hands away from your face and mouth, use open-handed gestures, and (if you feel you must achieve a touch of a subtle domination) direct your glance to the subordinate's forehead, rather than meeting his or her eyes directly. And, of course, as the cartoon on page 368 illustrates, don't lose your temper.

Negotiating   "Everything," someone once said, "is a negotiation." Whether you're buying a car, requesting a raise, trying to get a better seat on an airplane, or trying to get a cab driver to move faster or an employee to do a better job, negotiations are involved. And negotiations always involve interpersonal communication.

What is the key to being a good negotiator? Negotiating effectively starts with communicating effectively: For example, listen actively so that you understand both the words and the feelings underlying what the other person has just said.

HERMAN® by Jim Unger

"Is that your final answer?"

Don't trigger defensiveness (since that will lead to arguments), and be clear and unambiguous in what you're saying.

Beyond this, there are several tricks of the trade that experienced negotiators recommend. For example, leverage, information, credibility, and judgment are four important negotiating concepts. *Leverage* refers to the factors that either favor or disadvantage a party in a particular bargaining situation.[16] Necessity, desire, competition, and time are four important leveraging factors. For example, it's often the ability to walk away from a deal if acceptable terms can't be hammered out (or to look like you're able to walk away) that wins a negotiator the best terms. The seller who is forced to sell (of necessity) is at an obvious disadvantage. Similarly, who wants the deal more—*desire*—is important. That shiny new car in the showroom may not be a necessity, but if your desire is too obvious, the chances are you won't negotiate as good a deal.

Competition is important, too. In a negotiating situation, a critical factor is whether other potential buyers are vying for the right to make the acquisition; as you know, there is often no more effective ploy then convincing the other party someone else is dying to make the deal. *Time* (and particularly deadlines) can also tilt the tables for or against you. For example, if you've got a deadline the other party knows about but that doesn't particularly affect him or her, chances are you'll be at a relative disadvantage. For example, if the other party knows that your plane leaves tomorrow at 4 P.M. and that if you don't get his deal done you'll have to go back empty-handed, you can probably expect some "take it or leave it" demands as 4 P.M. approaches.

Information, credibility, and *judgment* are the other three basic negotiating concepts. Going into the negotiation armed with information about the other side and about every aspect of the situation can put you at a relative advantage, while a lack thereof (or, even worse, having the other side have the information advantage on you) puts you at a distinct disadvantage. To some extent, all negotiations are a bit like poker, so credibility is also essential. In particular, the other side will always be assessing whether you're bluffing, so convincing them otherwise is an important negotiating skill. Finally, good negotiators always have good judgment: They have "the ability to strike the right balance between gaining advantages and reaching compromises, in the substance as well as in the style of [their] negotiating technique."[17]

So how can you apply some of this, let's say when negotiating with your boss for a raise? First, gather all the information you can. For example, go back over your record and focus on how you meet—and exceed—the demands of your job. Make a list of your accomplishments during the preceding year, and research what others in similar positions and with similar duties and in similar companies get paid.[18] There's nothing quite as effective as making it clear what you're worth and what others in similar situations are being paid for similar jobs. Formulate a target salary level before you begin.

What will you do for leverage? While this tactic is not without risk, having a counteroffer can certainly be effective. It's unfortunate but true that even if your relationship with your boss is great, there's a tendency for the squeaky wheel to get the grease. It often happens in business that what you get is what you ask for, not just what you deserve. Having another job offer and letting your current boss know about it can therefore be effective.

If you've done your homework (and have been doing a good job), then you've already gone a long way toward establishing your credibility. But there is still a lot you can do. Your negotiating tactics and your body language will be important too. For one thing, says one expert, resolve not to "ask" for a raise, since that can seem to put you in a subordinate position. Instead, remember you're *negotiating* for a raise; the leverage you bring to the table means you and your boss are two equal parties trying to work out an equitable deal.

▶ ORGANIZATIONAL COMMUNICATION

Interpersonal communication occurs between two people; organizational communication is the exchange of information and transmission of meaning among several individuals or groups throughout the organization.

Organizational communication can flow downward, laterally, and upward. Downward communications go from superior to subordinate, and consist of messages regarding things like corporate vision, what a job entails, procedures and practices to be followed, and performance appraisals. Lateral, or horizontal, communications go between departments or between people in the same department. Upward communication (from subordinates to superiors) provides management with insights into the company and its employees and competitors.

Managers also distinguish between formal and informal communications. **Formal communication** is messages recognized as official by the organization, including orders (from superiors to subordinates) and various written and unwritten reports. **Informal communication** is not officially sanctioned by the organization; the grapevine (or rumors) is the most familiar example.

formal communication
messages that are recognized as official by the organization, such as orders from superiors to subordinates, sales reports, and status reports.

informal communication
communication not officially sanctioned by the organization, such as rumors heard through the grapevine.

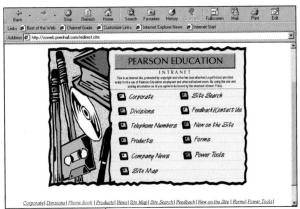

▲ **WEBNOTE**

Pearson uses its intranet to facilitate organizational communications.

©Pearson Education, Inc.

Barriers to Organizational Communication

Several things can diminish the usefulness of a company's organizational communications. For one thing, organizational communication happens between people, so it is susceptible to all the problems discussed above: Noise, defensiveness, criticism, semantics, perception, and filtering can all undermine organizational communication. Organizational communication is also plagued by some special problems because of the number of people involved, and because they often work in different departments and at different organizational levels. These special barriers include the following.

Distortion   Since the message must be relayed from person to person, there are many opportunities for the message to be filtered, embellished, and otherwise distorted. Most people are familiar with the party game in which seven or eight people line up and the first person is given a simple message to relay. Each person whispers the message to the next one in line. The final message usually bears little resemblance to the original one. A similar phenomenon occurs in organizations. Messages transferred from person to person tend to be distorted. The more people involved, the more distortion occurs.

Rumors and the Grapevine   Rumors are a good example of how organizational messages get distorted. Rumors are spread by the grapevine, often at great speed.[19] In one study of 100 employees, the researcher found that when management made an important change in the organization, most employees would hear the news first through the grapevine. Hearing news from a supervisor and official memorandums ran a poor second and third, respectively.[20]

Researcher Keith Davis says there are three main reasons rumors get started: lack of information, insecurity, and conflicts.[21] When employees don't know what's happening, they are likely to speculate about a situation, and a rumor is born. (For example, employees who observe an unscheduled disassembly of a machine may erroneously speculate that machines are being transferred to another plant and that workers will be laid off.) Insecure, anxious employees are especially likely to react in this way.

Conflicts also foster rumors. For example, conflicts between union and management may trigger rumors as each side tries to interpret the situation in a way most favorable to itself. Davis says the best way to refute a rumor is to release the truth as quickly as possible, since the more the rumor is repeated, the more it will be believed and distorted.

Information Overload   Information overload is a familiar problem in today's Internet-based world. For example, you may try to log onto the Internet and find it takes several tries. In this case, the circuits are overloaded and can handle no more users. Similar problems occur within organizations. Managers can juggle only so many problems before they become overloaded and incapable of handling more messages. At that point errors (such as making bad decisions) and omissions (such as ignoring some messages) start to rise.

Narrow Viewpoints   Organizational communication often involves people from different departments, each of whom has his or her own viewpoint and specialty. The problem here, for example, is that sales managers tend to see problems as sales problems, and production managers see them as production problems. Such narrow viewpoints can undermine organizational communication by making it harder for each person to see and understand the other person's point of view.

Status   On the organization chart, it is apparent that the president has more status than the vice president, who in turn has more status than a sales manager, who in turn has more status than a salesperson.

Status differences can translate into communication problems. For example, subordinates may prefer not to relate bad news to a boss, and thus hesitate to be candid about problems. Or, the boss may forget that subordinates need to know what is happening.

Organizational Culture   The organization's culture—its shared values and traditional ways of doing things—can also influence the way messages flow throughout the organization. Dan Hunt of Nortel Networks uses his monthly talk shows to encourage lower-level employees to speak their minds. He encourages all employees to communicate quickly, openly, and with candor. He does this by emphasizing the value of open communication and by instituting organizational changes (including the talk shows) to encourage employees to speak up.

Slowed Communications   The organization chart itself can (and is often meant to) restrict communication to formally sanctioned routes. When Mike Walsh took over as CEO of Union Pacific Railway, he found it sometimes took months for a message about a problem to make its way from one of the railyards to top management.

This example may be extreme, but there's no doubt that much of what is "formal" about formal organizations—sticking to the chain of command, following procedures, filling out the necessary paperwork in order to pass the request up the chain of command, and so on—can slow the flow of communications.

Boundary Differences   You may recall (from Chapter 8, "Designing Organizations to Manage Change") that boundary differences can also inhibit communications. The authority, task, political, and identity boundaries must be pierced if communications are to flow freely. For example, subordinates may tend to be deferential toward their bosses, and may tell them what they want to hear and withhold unwelcome information. Employees also tend to be short-sighted when it comes to interpreting information and understanding organizational problems.

Cultural and Diversity Issues

Finally, whenever many people and groups work together, there's a chance that diversity-driven differences in interpretations will undermine communications. What something means—whether it's a word, tone, hand gesture, or nonverbal behavior—can be dramatically different among different ethnic and cultural groups.

Table 12.1 illustrates the difficulties U.S. and Japanese managers might encounter in that regard. For example, the Japanese tend to be indirect and relationship-oriented, while the U.S. managers (with a more adversarial style) tend to be more direct and task-oriented.

TABLE 12.1 — Some Differences Between Japanese and American Communication Styles

Japanese *Ningensei* Style of Communication	U.S. Adversarial Style of Communication
Indirect verbal and nonverbal communication	More direct verbal and nonverbal communication
Strategically ambiguous communication	Prefers more to-the-point communication
Delayed feedback	More immediate feedback
Patient, longer-term negotiators	Shorter-term negotiators
Uses fewer words	Favors verbosity
Cautious, tentative	More assertive, self-assured
Softer, heartlike logic	Harder, analytic logic preferred
Makes decisions in private venues, away from public eye	Frequent decisions in public at negotiating tables
Decisions via *ringi* and *nemawashi* (complete consensus process)	Decisions by majority rule and public compromise are more commonplace
Uses go-betweens for decision making	More extensive use of direct person-to-person, player-to-player interaction for decisions
Understatement and hesitation in verbal and nonverbal communication	May publicly speak in superlatives, exaggerations, nonverbal projection
Uses qualifiers, tentative, humility as communicator	Favors fewer qualifiers, more ego-centered
Shy, reserved communicators	More publicly self-assertive
Distaste for purely business transactions	Prefers to "get down to business" or the "nitty gritty"
Utilizes *matomari*, or "hints," for achieving group adjustment and saving face in negotiating	More directly verbalizes management's preference at negotiating tables

Source: Adapted from *International Journal of Intercultural Relations*, vol. 18, no. I, A. Goldman, "The Centrality of 'Ningensei' to Japanese Negotiating and Interpersonal Relationships: Implications for U.S.-Japanese Communications," copyright 1994.

▶ IMPROVING ORGANIZATIONAL COMMUNICATION

Communications can flow up, down, and all over organizations, and there are several methods for improving each of these directional flows. We'll look at some techniques here.

Influencing Upward Communication

It's often important to give employees channels through which they can communicate their opinions to their superiors. Doing so can provide superiors with feedback about whether subordinates understand orders and instructions. They contribute to an acceptance of top management's decisions by giving subordinates a chance to express their opinions. And they encourage subordinates to offer ideas to the organization.

Installing and using special upward-communication channels can also provide supervisors with valuable input on which to base decisions,[22] encourage gripes and grievances to surface,[23] and cultivate commitment by giving employees an opportunity to express ideas and suggestions.[24] And, they can help employees "cope with their work problems and strengthen their involvement in their jobs and with the organization.[25] Firms also use upward communication to see how subordinates feel about jobs, superiors, subordinates, and the organization.

While one expert says, "By far the most effective way of tapping the ideas of subordinates is sympathetic listening in the many day-to-day, informal contacts within the department and outside the workplace,"[26] many techniques are used to encourage upward communication. Here are some other popular methods:

1. Social gatherings (including departmental parties, picnics, and recreational events) provide opportunities for informal, casual communication.

2. In unionized organizations union publications can provide useful insights into employee attitudes.

3. Some supervisors schedule formal monthly meetings with their subordinates, in addition to the informal contacts that take place every day.

4. Performance appraisal meetings are good opportunities to seek employees' opinions about their jobs and job attitudes.

5. Grievances provide top management with insights into operational problems.

6. Some companies periodically administer attitude surveys to get answers to questions like, "Are working hours and shift rotations perceived as reasonable?" "Do employees feel the boss has favorites?" and "Do employees consider cafeteria prices fair and the quality of the food good?" Management can then assess the need for change and correct any problems.

7. A formal suggestion system—even a suggestion box—can encourage upward communication.

8. An "open door" policy allows subordinates to transmit concerns through a channel outside the normal chain of command, and can act as a safety valve. Similarly, a formal appeals process (where no formal grievance process is in effect) can show employees that their requests and complaints will be treated fairly.

9. Indirect measures, including absences, turnover rates, and safety records, can be valuable indicators of unstated, uncommunicated problems that exist at the operational level.

Regardless of which mechanisms are used, at least three principles can boost their effectiveness. First, the system should be formalized—through scheduled meetings, suggestion plans, yearly surveys, and so on. Second, there should be a culture of trust in the organization, since subordinates are unlikely to speak (even anonymously) if they mistrust management's motives.[27]

Finally, management has to respond in some way to the opinions and problems expressed in the upward communications. If the problem can't be solved, it should be made clear why; if the problem can be eliminated, it should be. The following are case histories of three effective upward communication programs.

GE's Workout   To make GE a more responsive company, it initiated a series of classroom sessions with executives that became known as the "pit."[28] In these sessions, GE executives were encouraged to put aside decorum and engage the firm's then-CEO Jack Welch in the "rough and tumble debate he relishes."[29] When Welch became concerned that the candor he was experiencing with his executives was not carrying over to lower-level GE employees, the workout was born.

Workout is basically an upward communication channel. It's been described as a forum in which participating employees get a mental workout while engaging in enthusiastic discussions aimed at taking unnecessary work out of their jobs and working out problems together.[30] A group of 40 to 100 employees, "picked by management from all ranks and several functions, goes to a conference center or hotel."[31] The three-day sessions are usually kicked off by a talk by the group's boss, who soon leaves.

An outside consultant/facilitator then divides the group into five or six teams, each of which addresses problems, lists complaints, and debates solutions. When the boss returns, a team-spokesperson makes the team's proposals. The boss is then limited to only three responses: agree on the spot, say no, or ask for more information, "in which case he must charter a team to get it by an agreed upon date."[32]

Sessions like these have been useful for solving problems and for getting employees to express their ideas. As one GE electrician said when told his comments had made his boss really sweat, "When you've been told to shut up for 20 years and someone tells you to speak up—you're going to let them have it."[33]

FedEx's Guaranteed Fair Treatment Procedure The FedEx guaranteed fair treatment procedure is a formal upward communication channel containing three steps. In step 1, *management review*, a complainant submits a written complaint to a member of management. The manager reviews all relevant information, holds a conference with the complainant, and makes a decision to uphold, modify, or overturn the original supervisor's actions.[34] If the person is still not satisfied, then in step 2, *officer review*, the complainant can submit a written complaint to the vice president of his or her division. That person reviews all relevant information, conducts an additional investigation, and makes a decision to uphold, overturn, or modify management's action.

Finally, in step 3, *executive appeals review*, the complainant can submit a written complaint to an appeals board consisting of FedEx's CEO, president, and chief personnel officer, as well as two senior vice presidents. They then review the information and uphold, overturn, or initiate an investigative board of review. (The latter is used when there is a question about the facts in the situation.)

Toyota's Hotline At Toyota Motor Manufacturing, the primary upward communication channel is called the "hotline." Its purpose is to give team members an additional channel for bringing questions or problems to the company's attention. As Toyota tells its employees, "Don't spend time worrying about something . . . Speak up!" Employees are instructed to pick up any phone, dial the hotline extension (the number is posted on the plant bulletin board), and deliver their messages to a recorder, 24 hours a day. All inquiries are guaranteed to be reviewed by the HR manager and to be thoroughly investigated.

The process is basically anonymous. If it's decided that a question would be of interest to other Toyota team members, then the question,

▲ **W E B N O T E**

FedEx uses the Web to maintain open communications between employees and the company.

www.fedex.com

along with the firm's response, is posted on plant bulletin boards. If a personal response is desired, employees must leave their names when they call. However, no other attempt is made to identify hotline callers.[35]

Appraising Your Boss   How would you like to appraise your supervisor, and how (if at all) do you think knowing he or she will be appraised would influence the way the boss acted? A recent study sheds some interesting light on this upward communication channel.

One study examined the effects of such upward feedback by collecting subordinates' ratings for 238 managers in a large corporation at two points in time, six months apart.[36] Subordinates were asked to rate a variety of supervisory behaviors, such as "Regularly challenged me to continuously improve my effectiveness," "Took steps to resolve conflict and disagreement within the team," and "Treated me fairly and with respect."[37]

The study found that the performance of managers whose initial appraisals were high did not improve significantly in six months. However, there *was* a marked improvement among those managers whose initial appraisals were moderate or low. The researchers note that "this is encouraging because these are the managers that most need to improve from the organization's (as well as the subordinates') perspective."[38]

One interesting conclusion of the study was that the managers' performance improved whether or not they received the upward feedback. It's therefore possible, if not likely, that just knowing that their subordinates would appraise them was enough to get the bosses to improve their behavior at work.

Influencing Downward Communication

Downward communication includes many essential types of information: job instructions, rationales for jobs (including how jobs are related to other jobs and positions in the organization), organizational policies and practices, employee performance, and the organization's mission.[39]

Downward communication has probably never been more important than it is today. Developing team-based, boundaryless, and networked organizations depends on having empowered and knowledgeable employees, all of whom are aware of and buy into the company's vision and strategy. Downward communications play a big role in getting this knowledge communicated to employees.

In addition to face-to-face and written messages, firms today use many channels to get data "down to the troops." At Saturn Corporation, assemblers "get information continuously via the internal television network and from financial documents."[40] The firm also has monthly town-hall-like meetings, usually with 500 to 700 attendees. The result is that all employees are familiar with Saturn's activities and performance.

Toyota uses several channels. Employees get the latest plant news at short team meetings at job sites twice each day. A television set at each worksite runs continuously, presenting plantwide information from the in-house Toyota Broadcasting Center. The company

▲   Toyota employees watch in-house programming during a break on the assembly line.

sponsors quarterly roundtable discussions between top management and selected nonsupervisory staff, as well as an in-house newsletter.

Toyota's managers also practice "managing by walking around." The plant's top managers are often on the shop floor, fielding questions, providing performance information, and ensuring that all general managers, managers, and team members are "aware of Toyota's goal and where we are heading."[41]

open-book management
a management style in which a company opens its books to the employees, sharing financial data, explaining numbers, and rewarding workers for improvement.

At other companies, open-book management involves literally opening the books of a company to the employees. Financial data are shared, the numbers are explained, and then workers are rewarded for improvements in the business performance.[42] The basic idea behind open-book management is to foster trust and commitment among employees by treating them, for informational purposes, more like partners than employees.

Open-book programs have been successful in many companies, including Manco, a Cleveland-based manufacturer of industrial products.[43] At Manco, financial information is distributed to employees in three ways. Every month each department gets four books, designated by color, with financial information broken down by company, department, product line, and customer. Monthly meetings are held so employees can see whether they're on track to earn their bonuses and what, if anything, can be and is being done to see that they stay on track. Between meetings, employers can also monitor the firm's financial performance. For example, daily companywide sales totals are posted on the cafeteria walls. Employees are offered classes in finance and accounting to help them understand the numbers.

Influencing Horizontal Communication

Managers also work hard to boost horizontal (interdepartmental) communication. The special channels here usually involve using individuals or committees to bridge departments and to thereby improve the communication flow between them. Examples include:

- *Liaison personnel.* A sales liaison may be employed by the sales department, but be physically located in the factory to advise factory management about the sales department's priorities.

- *Committees and task forces.* Interdepartmental committees, task forces, or teams are usually composed of representatives from several departments; they meet periodically to discuss and solve common problems and to ensure interdepartmental communication and coordination.

- *Independent integrators.* Some companies boost interdepartmental communication by creating special independent integrators. A new-product development department is one example. Its role is to facilitate communication and coordination among the activities of several other departments, such as research and development, sales, engineering, and manufacturing.

The following "Entrepreneurs in Action" box shows that more informal techniques can be effective, too.

Encouraging Informal Communications

One key to improving organizational communication is to make sure that informal communications are encouraged. How can this be done? In a study of innovative companies, Tom Peters and Robert Waterman found that these companies used informal, almost unorthodox, means of communicating to help remain responsive

▶ While formal horizontal communication channels like those above are important, more companies today rely on informal channels too. As the chief financial officer for the electronics firm Adaptec puts it. "We still look at teamwork as interdisciplinary empathy, not just slogans and well-coordinated efforts."[44] In practice, he says, this means that it's not enough for each department manager to view decisions from his or her department's own point of view. Instead, each manager "must understand enough about the company's marketing, sales and operations [and finance]" to understand the impact of each department's activities on the decisions that need to be made.[45]

Adaptec fosters such interdisciplinary empathy in several ways. Interdepartmental brainstorming sessions "let you bounce marketing's great idea off finance and operations, which may change the idea to align more closely with financial and operational realities."[46] Thus, when coordinating major product introductions, "members of the finance, engineering, manufacturing and marketing departments often meet bimonthly to brainstorm problems and solutions. Each participant assesses the situation and can then express an opinion on how, for example, a certain product packaging design could affect manufacturing or engineering processes or how the budget allotted for the project can help define product design or advertising."[47] What emerges from such sessions, says this executive, "is usually an idea or set of ideas that reflects the company's overall competencies better than ideas originating from any one department."

The company also uses more formal interdepartmental communications channels. For example, Adaptec's in-house legal department designed a program to teach other departments about trademarks, and the finance department provided financial training for other departments. "The cross-training sessions make it much easier to achieve understanding and buy-in to corporate strategies."

and manage change.[48] Although some firms subsequently fell off most experts' lists of "excellent" companies, the techniques they used to encourage informal communications provide some useful insights:

> The excellent companies are a vast network of informal, open communications. The patterns and intensity [of informal communication] cultivate the right people getting into contact with each other, regularly, and the chaotic/anarchic properties of a system are kept well under control simply because of the regularity of contact and its nature.[49]

In those outstanding and innovative companies, "the name of the success game" is rich, informal communication:

> The astonishing byproduct is the ability to have your cake and eat it, too; that is, rich informal communication leads to more action, more experiments, more learning, and simultaneously to the ability to stay better in touch and on top of things.[50]

In excellent companies, say Peters and Waterman, the intensity and sheer volume of communications are unmistakable, and usually start with a stress on informality.[51] Specifically, they found that these techniques are used to encourage informal communication:

1. *Informality is emphasized.* At the Walt Disney Company, for instance, everyone from the president down wears a name tag with just his or her first name on it. (These are worn in the parks on a regular basis.) At 3M there are endless meetings, but few are scheduled; most are characterized by the casual getting-together of people from different disciplines who talk about problems in a campuslike, shirt-sleeves atmosphere.

▲ Informal communications: Yahoo! employees.

2. *Communication intensity is maintained at an extraordinary level.* At successful companies, meetings and presentations are held in which "the questions are unabashed; the flow is free; everyone is involved. Nobody hesitates to cut off the chairman, the president or board members."[52] In other words, employees are encouraged to openly confront issues and be blunt and straightforward. Meetings in these companies are not formal and politicized. Instead, they are open, informative discussions in which all points of view can safely be aired.

3. *Communication is given physical support.* Blackboards and open offices facilitate informal interaction. In one high-tech firm, for instance, all employees from the president down work not in offices, but in six-foot-high doorless cubicles that encourage openness and interaction. Corning Glass installed escalators rather than elevators to increase face-to-face contact.[53] Another company eliminated its four-person dining room tables and substituted long rectangular tables that encourage strangers to come in contact, often across departmental lines. Managers are encouraged to get out of their offices, walk around, and strike up conversations with those both in and outside their departments.

Peters and Waterman say all this adds up to "lots of communication." In most of these firms, they say, you can't wander around for long without "seeing lots of people sitting together in a room with blackboards working casually on problems."[54] The "People Side of Managing" feature provides one explanation for the benefits of unrestricted communications in today's fast-changing environment.

THE PEOPLE SIDE OF MANAGING

■ Applying Communications Research in Practice

What happens when organizational communications are restricted to just a few allowable channels, as in more bureaucratic organizations? Psychologist Harold Leavitt addressed this question.[55]

Groups of five persons were arranged in one of the "communication networks" shown in Figure 12.2. Each person was placed in a compartment at a table in such a way that his or her communication was restricted. Each person in the all-channel network could communicate with any other person. People in the wheel network could communicate only with the person in the central position (hub) of the network. This central person could communicate with the four other people in his or her network. (The lines all show two-way linkages.) All each person knew was to whom messages could be sent and from whom messages could be received.

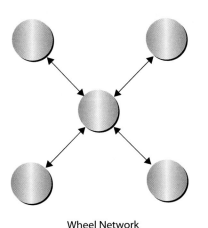

Wheel Network

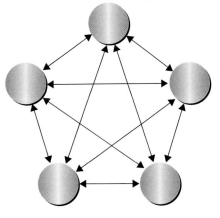

All-Channel Network

◀ **F I G U R E   1 2 . 2**

Two Experimental Communications Networks

In the "centralized" wheel networks, each subject could communicate only with the hub subject; in the all-channel "decentralized" network, each subject could communicate with every other subject, so that ambiguous problems could be solved more quickly.

The researchers found that the best communication network depended on the problem that had to be solved. Where the problem was simple and amenable to a clear-cut yes or no answer (such as "Is this marble blue?"), the wheel network was best. But for complex, ambiguous problems that required lots of give and take, the all-channel network was best. Here, for instance, each person was given marbles that were hard to describe. Two people looking at identical marbles could describe them quite differently; what one might view as "greenish-yellow," another might call "aqua." The person in the center of the wheel network could not himself or herself quickly decide what color was common to all the marbles. Therefore, the all-channel network, where communications could flow freely to and from everyone, arrived at the fastest decision for ambiguous problems.

▶ COMMUNICATING AT THE SPEED OF THOUGHT

It looks like the control room of the USS Enterprise, but it's actually the network-reliability operations center of phone company USWest, in Littleton, Colorado.[56] The center's blinking screens let the 700 USWest people working there instantly see how the firm is performing, in terms of what problems customers in 14 western states may be having with their phones. USWest used to have 100 minicenters sprinkled around various states. However that didn't give employees the comprehensive, 14-state real-time information they needed to react quickly if, for instance, a problem (like a massive storm sweeping across the area) was tying up phone lines.

In USWest's new center, eight large screens show data that are updated every five minutes and alert workers to the nature of specific outages throughout the firm's 14-state region.[57] Every major technical group including engineering and repair is represented in the room; fast, coordinated decisions can thus be made to react to problems. For example, when a team monitoring the screens recently noted a mysterious gridlock in one area, the problem turned out to be the result of "thou-

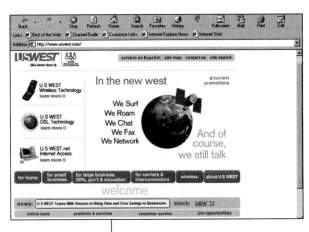

▲   **W E B N O T E**

USWest uses the Web both to communicate with customers and to facilitate internal communications.

www.uswest.com

Used with permission of U.S. West.

▲ Ford designers in Dearborn, Michigan, send design via telecommunications to Turin, where mockups are produced.

sands of people trying to call one merchant that had just received a shipment of beanie babies."[58] The solution was to put controls on the number of calls into that store's region, so the store's neighbors could begin making calls again.

USWest's reliability-operations center puts "crucial, real-time data at everyone's fingertips." It thereby helps teams of dedicated professionals instantly identify problems and formulate coordinated, team-based responses. Telecommunications is helping USWest's departments communicate, quite literally at the speed of thought.

telecommunications

the electronic transmission of data, text, graphics, voice (audio), or image (video) over any distance.

As at USWest, **telecommunications**—the electronic transmission of information—play an important role in managing organizations today. Levi Strauss uses a sophisticated telecommunications system to link its own inventory and manufacturing facilities with point-of-sale processing devices at retail stores. Detailed sales information goes directly to headquarters, where it is analyzed for trends and buying patterns. Management can then make more accurate inventory and production plan decisions. Similarly, retailers like JCPenney use telecommunications to manage in-store inventories. Its buyers get instant access to sales information from the stores and can modify their purchasing decisions accordingly.

As another example, Ford designers at the company's Dearborn, Michigan, headquarters use computers to design new cars like the Lincoln Continental. Digitized designs are then sent electronically and reproduced at Ford's Turin, Italy, design facility, where styrofoam mockups are automatically made to reproduce Dearborn's design.

Telecommunications is also important at work because more and more managerial computer systems applications rely on it. Levi depends on telecommunications in its computerized inventory control systems; radiologists rely on telecommunications for X-rays which can be read from remote locations; your college or university may use telecommunications to allow you to access library information from your office or home; computer-assisted manufacturing systems rely on telecommunications to transmit information from one location in the plant to another; and banks depend on telecommunications to make their remote automatic teller machines operational. Telecommunications also makes possible the use of new group-communication computer systems applications. We'll look at these in the next few pages.

Work Group Support Systems

Work groups and teams play an increasingly important role in managing organizations. The team might be a door-assembly team at Saturn, the sales department at a Levi Strauss subsidiary, or a project team set up in a manufacturing plant to solve a quality-control problem. It might be relatively permanent (as it would be if it were a sales department) or temporary (such as a group formed to solve a one-time quality problem). The team's members might all be at a single site, or they might be dispersed around the city or even around the world. In any case, all the following work group support systems facilitate communication among a team's members.

Electronic Mail   As everyone knows, electronic mail (e-mail) is a computerized information system that lets group members electronically create, edit, and communicate messages to one another, using electronic mail boxes. E-mail's aim is to speed and facilitate intragroup communication and thereby bolster intragroup coordination. An electronic bulletin board is another example. It lets one or more group members file messages on various topics, to be picked up later by other group members.

E-mail systems are not just for messages, though. For example, the e-mail software Eudora Pro helps one company manage its sales operation. The owner set up one computer to check all customers' accounts every 10 minutes so he never misses a rush order. And it lets him sort messages based on key words like *brochure* (so requests for brochures are automatically routed to the person in charge of mailing them).[59]

Videoconferencing   Videoconferencing is a telecommunications-based method that lets group members interact directly with a number of other group members via television links. Firms such as International Open Systems (IOS) of Peabody, Massachusetts, provide videoconferencing via desktop personal computers. It lets users send live video and audio messages, with only a few seconds delay.[60]

Videoconferencing can significantly improve communications and coordination among group members and help a work group achieve its aims more quickly. For example, the team developing the Boeing 777 made extensive use of videoconferencing for meetings with engine suppliers and airlines to discuss the new aircraft's design.[61]

Group Decision-Support Systems   A decision support system (DSS) is an interactive computer-based communications system that facilitates the solution of unstructured problems by a team of decision makers.[62] The general aim of a DSS is to let a team of decision makers get together (often in the same room) and make better and faster decisions and to complete their task more quickly. The DSS (as pictured in Figure 12.3) lets team members interact via their PCs and use several software tools that assist them in decision making and project completion. These software tools include electronic questionnaires, electronic brainstorming tools, idea organizers (to help team members synthesize ideas generated during brainstorming), and tools for voting or setting priorities (so that recommended solutions can be weighted and prioritized).

decision support systems
an interactive computer-based communications system that facilitates the solution of unstructured problems by a team of decision makers.

► FIGURE 12.3

A Decision Support System

The Ventana Corporation demonstrates the features of its GroupSystems for Windows electronic meeting software, which helps people create, share, record, organize, and evaluate ideas in meetings, between offices, or around the world.

collaborative writing systems

a computerized support system that lets group members work simultaneously on a single document from a number of interconnected or network computers.

group scheduling system

a computerized support system that allows each group member to put his or her daily schedule into a shared database so that each can identify the most suitable times to schedule meetings or to attend currently scheduled meetings.

workflow automation system

an e-mail type of system that automates the flow of paperwork from person to person.

telecommuting

the substitution of telecommunications and computers for the commute to a central office.

Using a DSS helps a group avoid a lot of the group decision-making barriers that often occur in face-to-face groups. There's less likelihood that one assertive person will monopolize the meeting, since all the brainstorming and listing of ideas—and the voting—is governed by the computerized programs.

Other Work Group Support Systems   Other work group support systems are also used. **Collaborative writing systems** let a work group's members create long written documents (such as proposals) while working simultaneously at a network of interconnected computers. As team members work on different sections of the proposal, each member has automatic access to the rest of the sections and can modify his or her section to be compatible with the rest.

A **group scheduling system** lets each group member put his or her daily schedule into a shared database, so each can identify the most suitable times for meetings or to attend currently scheduled meetings. A **workflow automation system** uses an e-mail–type system to automate the flow of paperwork.[63] For example, if a proposal requires four signatures, the workflow automation system can send it electronically from mailbox to mailbox for the required signatures.

Telecommuting   Today, millions of people around the world do most of their work at home and commute to their employers electronically. **Telecommuting** has been defined as the substitution of telecommunications and computers for the commute to a central office.[64]

Typical telecommuters fall into one of three categories. Some are not employees at all, but are independent entrepreneurs who work out of their homes—perhaps developing new computer applications for consulting clients. The second (and largest) group of telecommuters includes professionals and highly skilled people who work at jobs that involve a great deal of independent thought and action. These employees—computer programmers, regional salespersons, textbook editors, and research specialists, for instance—typically work at home most of the time, coming to the office only occasionally, perhaps for monthly meetings.[65] The third telecommuter category includes those who carry out relatively routine and easily monitored jobs like data entry or word processing.[66]

Internet-Based Communications

While you are reading this page, millions of people are on the Internet, searching through libraries, talking to friends, and buying and selling products and services. At the same time, countless businesses are using the Internet to help them communicate—at the speed of thought.

The Internet provides enormous communication benefits to organizations. For one thing, since companies can, in a sense, get a "free ride" on the Internet, they can substantially reduce their communications costs. For instance, FedEx clients can track their own packages using FedEx's Web site instead of inquiring by telephone, thus saving the company millions of dollars per year in telephone and customer representative costs.[67] Similarly, the Internet makes it easier and less expensive for companies to coordinate the work of small teams that may be opening new markets in isolated places. The following feature illustrates how.

MANAGING @ THE *SPEED* OF THOUGHT

■ Communicating via the Internet

The Internet-based communications system installed by New York real estate firm Cushman & Wakefield shows how managers use the Internet to communicate today. In addition to being a commercial real estate broker, Cushman & Wakefield manages office buildings, factories, and other commercial properties around the world. With about 2,000 employees, keeping the firm's personnel files up-to-date was an expensive logistical nightmare: Updating each employee's personnel records, benefits, and related legal policies and procedures and keeping track of all the firm's far-flung offices was a problem. For example, each time an employee was out sick, took a vacation, completed a college course, got a raise, or changed his or her job, the person's personnel files had to be changed. Keeping track of all this manually and through traditional telecommunications systems was very expensive.

Since virtually all employees already had Internet access, Cushman & Wakefield decided to use the Internet's low-cost and interactive features to create an Internet-based employee communication network.[68] It then turned out that the firm's policies and procedures and forms were already being stored electronically as Microsoft Word documents, so converting existing documents so they could be displayed on the Web was fairly inexpensive. The new system cost the company less than $10,000 to develop. Then, with all the policies and forms on-line, it was relatively easy for every office to update its files: Managers (or more often the employees themselves) just typed the changes into the Web-based documents using Microsoft Word. The company's new software converted these documents and transferred them through the company's new Internet-based Employee Resource System.[69]

Cushman & Wakefield soon added other communication applications to its Internet system. One uses an internal, Internet-based system to calculate employee commissions, so agents and brokers can get the commission data they want. Another, Site Solutions, is a property tracking system that maintains detailed information on thousands of commercial properties worldwide, including available office space. Today, in other words, more and more of the company's communications, computations, and record-keeping are handled by the Net, making Cushman & Wakefield a good example of managing @ the speed of thought.

Building Internet-Based Virtual Communities

Work group support systems and Cushman & Wakefield's Internet-based communication system provide a glimpse of how companies today use the Internet to build virtual communities—networked, boundaryless, e-based organizations—among their employees.

Companies build virtual communities for many reasons. In one case, a group of managers attended several management development courses; top management wanted to make sure these managers would continue to interact with each other and apply what they learned once they were back on the job. The goals included reinforcing and building on what the managers learned in the courses, and providing ongoing interactive ways for the managers to meet and learn from each other.[70]

The solution was creating a web site. One part, called Management University, contained, for instance, a virtual library that offered a prescreened selection of books, articles, videos, and CD-ROMs on topics that complemented those in the management development course. Another part of the Web site was called the Management Forum. It allowed those who attended the courses to interact and to share problems and examples of how they applied what they had learned.

Some Internet-based virtual communities are much more complex. For example, as prime contractor in a massive effort to obtain a $300 million Navy ship deal, "Lockheed-Martin established a virtual design environment with two major shipbuilders, via a private internet existing entirely outside the firewalls of the three individual companies."[71] Eventually, about 200 suppliers would also be connected to the network via special, secure Internet links. This special Internet-based network "allows secure transfer of design, project management, and even financial data back and forth among the extended design team via simple browser access, with one homepage as its focal point."[72] Its objective was to substantially increase communication among team members and the customer. The result was that the ship would be built in one-third the time and at one-half the cost of previous contracts.

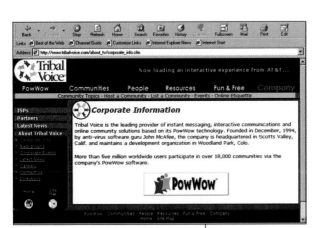

▲ **W E B N O T E**

Tribal Voice lets employees communicate more easily via the Web.

www.tribalvoice.com

Used with permission.

With the need for such virtual communities booming, more companies are introducing Internet-based software applications to help companies establish their own Internet-based virtual communities. Dubbed a "virtual community construction kit," one company has created an application called Tribal Voice. Its features include instant messaging (sending a message that will pop up on the receivers' screens), text to speech (hearing text as it appears in a window), file transfer (exchanging files), a buddy list (keeping track of regular online contacts), a whiteboard (exchanging drawings), and cruising (starting a meeting or conversation with a few people and then directing their Web browsers to the pages of your choosing).[73]

Tribal Voice can help a company let a group of its employees who share a common interest get together via the Internet. For example, says the vice president of marketing for the company that created Tribal Voice, "the sales department could hold forums and share information in an interactive community. A salesperson in a remote location could join this online department and ask for advice on a particular company he wants to call on."[74]

Is There a Company Portal in Your Future?

While most people today are using Web-based portals like Yahoo to surf the Net, more and more employees will soon also be using their employers' company-based business portals.

What is a business portal?[75] For one thing it is, like other Yahoo-type portals, a window to the Internet. But for the companies that are increasingly creating them for their employees, business portals are a great deal more. Through their business portals, categories of employees—secretaries, engineers, salespeople, and so on—are able to access all the corporate applications they need to use, as well as "get the tools you need to analyze data inside and outside your company, and see the customized content you need, like industry news and competitive data."[76] Thus a sales manager could use the portal to access all the information her company has on sales trends, market analyses, and competitors' sales.

Many companies are already rushing into the business of designing business portals for corporate customers. Netscape (which is now a division of America Online) has created business portals for employees at FedEx and Lucent. Another firm, Concur Technologies, just installed business portals for Hearst Corporation's 15,000 employees. So, if communication is indeed "the exchange of information and the transmission of meaning," it looks like a company portal will soon be in most employees' futures, helping them to zero in on just the information they need to do their jobs, and helping them to organize and make sense of all the information that's out there.

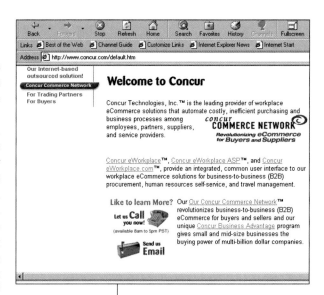

▲ **W E B N O T E**

Concur Technologies develops Internet portals and other Web-based applications that improve organizational communications.

www.concur.com

Used with permission.

SUMMARY

1. There are five elements in the communication process, and errors can occur at any one: sender, communication channel, noise, receiver, and feedback.

2. Several interpersonal communication barriers can distort messages and inhibit communication. These barriers include ambiguity, defensiveness, errors in perception, semantics, and nonverbal communication.

3. You can improve interpersonal communications by being an active listener, avoiding triggering defensiveness, and clarifying your ideas before communicating.

4. Because organizational communication involves people, it is susceptible to all the problems of interpersonal communication and some special problems, including distortion, rumors and the grapevine, information overload, narrow viewpoints, differences in status, organizational culture, structural restrictions, diversity issues, and boundary differences.

5. Upward communication can be encouraged through techniques like social gatherings, union publications, scheduled meetings, and formal suggestion systems. FedEx's Guaranteed Fair

Treatment Procedure, Toyota's hotline, and GE's workout are other examples. Downward communication is encouraged through usual channels (like face-to-face and written messages), as well as techniques like closed-circuit televisions and top managers "walking around."

6. Lateral organizational communication can often be improved through liaison personnel, committees and task forces, and independent integrators.

7. To influence and improve organization-wide communication, a leader can foster informal communication, use networks, encourage boundarylessness, and use electronic networking.

8. Telecommunications and the Internet play an important role in managing organizations today. Companies like Levi Strauss use sophisticated telecommunications systems to link their inventory and manufacturing facilities with point-of-sale processing devices at retail stores. Workgroup support systems allow even geographically dispersed employees to interact in real-time as teams. Internet-based communications systems let companies use the relatively inexpensive Internet to substantially reduce their communications costs. And more and more companies are establishing Internet-based applications to help companies establish their own Internet-based virtual communities.

TYING IT ALL TOGETHER

Motivating and influencing employees—indeed, managing in general—is impossible if the leader can't effectively communicate with his or her employees; therefore, having covered leadership and motivation in the previous two chapters, we turned in this chapter to how communications take place in modern companies today. We saw that communicating today increasingly revolves around telecommunications (including, for instance computer-based decision support systems and videoconferencing). In fact, without the sorts of Internet-based applications discussed in this chapter which make virtual communities possible, it's hard to imagine how most of the twenty-first century management techniques used today (such as networked and boundaryless organizations, and virtual terms) would even be possible. Indeed, today's new telecommunications and Internet-based techniques are to a large extent the foundation on which modern companies are built. Having discussed the telecommunications and Internet bases for group work and virtual teams in this chapter, we'll turn in Chapter 13 to a closer look at how companies use teams today.

KEY TERMS

communication 362
communication channel 362
feedback 363
interpersonal communication 363
organizational communication 363

semantics 364
nonverbal communication 364
formal communication 369
informal communication 369
open-book management 376
telecommunications 380

decision support system 381
collaborative writing system 382
group scheduling system 382
workflow automation system 382
telecommuting 382

CRITICAL THINKING EXERCISES

1. English was the international language for the last half of the 20th century. In the 1980s English was used by at least 750 million people, and barely half of those spoke it as their first language. Today millions of people from every continent and country speak English. Countries such as Taiwan require English as a language as do many other nations. *The Story of English*, by Robert Crum, William Cran, and Robert MacNeil (1986) is a fascinating analysis of the growth and development of the English language. The book opens with the following:

   On 5 September 1977, the American spacecraft Voyager One blasted-off on its historic mission to Jupiter and beyond. On board, scientists, who knew that the Voyager would one day spin through distant star systems, had installed a recorded message greeting from the people of the planet Earth. Preceding a brief message in fifty-five different languages for the people of outer space, the gold-plated disc plays a statement, from the Secretary-General of the United Nations, an Austrian named Kurt Waldheim, speaking on behalf of 147 member states—in English.

   Since then, the world has increasingly embraced English as the language of communications and technology. This is a fine situation for those who use English as a first language, but what happens in an increasingly multi-language world? Americans tend to speak one language—English. In Europe people often speak two or more languages. Obviously, this is true in many other nations that have adapted to English but still have a native tongue. More and more business is done globally, and increasing numbers of organizations are merging across international borders (e.g., DaimlerChrysler). What do you think this all means for the English language as a major language of communication? Should we all be learning other languages as the world globalizes to communicate more effectively? What are the costs and benefits of increasing your language base? Can you effectively negotiate if you do not understand another person's language, nuances and all?

2. Television is a powerful medium of communication, but in general, it is a monologue, not a dialogue. Your challenge as a class is to break up into teams of four to five people. Each team member is then to be assigned one news station to watch all week. For example, you might choose ABC, and another student PBS. At the end of the week, your team is to compare notes as to what news was communicated, how it was presented, who presented the stories, and how balanced they seemed to be. Then be prepared to make a team presentation to the class about your findings and how you see the news shaping our society through the way it is communicated.

EXPERIENTIAL EXERCISES

1. Ours is a world yet to be totally defined in terms of all communication forms. For many, e-mail and the Internet, voice mail, and electronic conferencing are the only ways to conduct business. Others do not own a computer or understand what they would do with an *http://www* address. It is a time perhaps much like the 14th century, when Johann Gutenberg introduced the printing press with movable type and many more people could be reached with new information. This machine helped to lay the foundation for changes such as the Protestant Reformation. In Margaret Wertheim's *The Pearly Gates of Cyberspace: A History of Space from Dante to the Internet* (W. W. Norton & Company, 1999) there is a quote from high-technology entrepreneur Esther Dyson.

   The Net offers us a chance to take charge of our own lives and to redefine our role as citizens of local communities and a global society. It also hands us the *responsibility* to govern ourselves, to educate our children, to do business honestly, and to work with fellow citizens to design rules we want to live by.

   Taking the information provided in the chapter, especially focusing on the section *Communicating at the Speed of Thought*, divide your class into groups of five students. If possible, have a MIS major in each group. Then do research to substantiate and refute the above quote. Choose a side, and then be prepared to debate the issues.

2. Because actions speak louder than words, nonverbal communication can create confusion. Take international gestures. In Britain, secrecy or confidentiality is conveyed by a tap on one's nose, while in Italy it means a friendly warning. A nod in Bulgaria and Greece signifies "no." In most other countries, it means "yes." Placing your fingers in a circle is widely accepted as the U.S. "okay" sign, except in Brazil, where it's considered vulgar or obscene.[77]

Gather 8 to 10 different gestures that mean different things in different nations. Interview classmates, friends, relatives, and co-workers and then come to class ready to discuss what you discovered. Or brainstorm with a group of four to six classmates, generating a list of 8 to 10 U.S. gestures. Then divide the list and seek out what these gestures communicate in other cultures. Report to the class on your findings.

APPROACHING DIVERSITY: BARRIERS OR BREAKTHROUGHS?

CASE 1

You have just been hired by a traditional, paternalistic restaurant chain that has been successfully sued by former employees five times in the last five years for racial and gender discrimination. The company is starting to lose business because of its poor image in the community it serves. Employees are also leaving and others are threatening to sue if conditions do not improve. The workforce is 65 percent women, of which 55 percent are women of color. Twenty-one percent of the male workforce are men of color. Middle management and above are all white males.

The Board of Directors has fired the CEO and replaced her with a young Latina to try to change the company. You are the new Chief Operations Officer. The new CEO has asked you to help her implement a diversity program to reach all aspects of operations. She needs your report by the end of the week.

Questions

1. What communications problems might you expect to unearth in this situation?

2. What means of communication might you use to help the new CEO reach the employees?

3. Given that you are new on the job, how would you collect information to do your analysis in less than a week?

Source: Gillian Flynn, "Do You Have the Right Approach to Diversity?" *Personnel Journal* (October 1995):68–76.

SHOULD WE GO TO THE WEB?

CASE 2

Like most professors who teach the business program's capstone course in strategic management, Cynthia Thomas liked to split her class into groups of five or six students, who then spent the rest of the semester analyzing cases and developing a strategic plan for a company in the vicinity of State University.

From the day they got together to analyze their first case and create their presentation, the five members of one group—Maria, Sid, Len, Hal, and Ruth—seemed to hit it off. During the rest of the semester, their friendship grew. Maria was a specialist in accounting and planned on earning her CPA and then perhaps joining a "big five" accounting firm. Sid was a finance major whose professors described him as "one of the sharpest students ever." Len was a sales and marketing major with a particularly strong interest in small businesses. Hal was majoring in production and operations management and was also a skilled mathematician. Ruth's specialty was human resource management, an area in which her intelligence and understanding of people was especially effective.

Something students generally learn in analyzing strategy management cases is that problems and solutions rarely affect only one department in a company. For example, one case this team of students worked on involved developing a new strategy for Kmart, the big discount firm that was being battered by the increasingly successful Wal-Mart. When group members thought about changing Kmart's computer systems to make the company more competitive, they immediately found that other departments would feel the change. The HR department, for instance, would have to hire new computer people and retrain current employees to use the new systems, and the finance department would have to determine if buying new computers would be cost-effective. So having expertise in several areas was a definite plus in solving problems.

In working together, the group also learned the importance of teamwork. As they analyzed company after company, the confidence of these five young business majors grew. By the end of the semester they'd decided that after graduation, they wanted to set up a consulting firm together. The Business Team, Inc., is the company they formed. The idea was to create a consulting firm in which each person on the team would bring his or her expertise to the analysis of client problems. Clients would thus get complete and comprehensive top-down solutions.

Like many new (as well as large and established) companies, the members of the team are considering whether, and if so how, to use the Web to develop their business. One of the more striking examples of how the Web is making inroads into business-to-business commerce was the announcement in late February 2000 that General Motors, Ford Motor, and DaimlerChrysler had just agreed to join forces to create a single automotive exchange on the Internet. Basically an enormous new Web site, the new exchange was to be an independent company which the major auto companies would use to handle their communications with suppliers and bidding for the $240 billion the three companies spend worldwide each year. "All the world is going to the Net for business-to-business communications" is the way Maria put it.

Discussion Questions

1. How might the partners use the Internet to highlight their multifunction approach to solving business problems?

2. Assuming they decide to "go to the Web" and set up their own site, what communication tasks do you think the new site should accomplish for them?

3. Given your answers to questions 1 and 2 above, design the opening page for The Business Team, Inc.'s new Web site.

4. What concepts and lessons about communications that take place without the use of technology can you apply to Internet-based communications? How might The Business Team, Inc., take advantage of these lessons?

KEEPING THE LINES OF COMMUNICATION OPEN AT KNITMEDIA

As their company grows, Michael and his colleagues have to make sure they take steps to keep the lines of communication open at KnitMedia. One of the main strengths of KnitMedia's large competitors is also potentially one of their greatest weaknesses: size. With a company as big as Warner or Sony, it's sometimes possible for, say, a music manager in London to be unaware that her colleague in New York is working on a project that may be important to her, since communicating across the ocean is still not as easy as just walking down the hall. The major record labels' size can therefore tend to slow their reactions and can lead to late entry into new markets.

Identifying new trends and hopping on to these trends with new artists and new products is therefore at the heart of what music companies like KnitMedia must do. To do that, they have to make sure to institute communication methods that enhance not only organizational communications within KnitMedia, but also communication between KnitMedia and both consumers and artists.

The problem is that, as the company grows, this can actually become more difficult, not easier. For example, consider the way Heather Stamm, the New York Knitting Factory's club production coordinator, describes how e-mail has affected communication at KnitMedia:

> I think it's cut down on face-to-face communication. We don't have time to schedule meetings to sit down and talk every five minutes, but we need to be in constant communication. Although we do have regular weekly meetings for production and weekly meetings for promotion where we talk to each other face-to-face, it's the ability to send instantaneous [e-mails] and to send it to more than one person at a time that's become important. Sometimes [though] I'm e-mailing Glen and he's only three feet away from me, but it's still a useful tool because you can go back and check to see what you said and how they responded. And with artists traveling all over the world all the time, it's a good way to keep in contact with the artists when they're touring.

Particularly as they've become an increasingly global operation, Michael Dorf and his team know that other companies are using many approaches to keep lines of communication open. They have come to you for advice about implementing a new, comprehensive communication package at KnitMedia.

Team Exercises and Questions

Use what you learned in this chapter to answer the following questions from Michael Dorf and his management team:

1. From what you know about our company, do you think interpersonal and organizational communication are currently adequate? Why or why not?

2. Based on what you know about communications from this chapter and based on a review of Internet- and non-Internet-based communications, what methods are other music companies using to maintain open communications both within their organizations, and between their organizations and their artists and consumers?

3. Which communication approaches and techniques do you think KnitMedia should implement, and how would you suggest we do so?

MANAGING GROUPS AND TEAMS

WHAT'S AHEAD?

Anyone who wonders whether organizing employees into teams is a good idea should check out Dayton, Ohio based Monarch Marking Systems, which manufactures labeling, identification, and tracking equipment. In the past few years, Monarch's employee teams have managed to reduce the square footage required for an assembly area by 70%, reduce overdue shipments by 90%, and double productivity, in part by identifying more than 1,400 areas of waste in the company. Which all goes to prove that you can obtain some tremendous benefits by tapping the brainpower and initiative in well-trained employee teams.[1]

OBJECTIVES

AFTER STUDYING THIS CHAPTER, YOU SHOULD BE ABLE TO

- Describe the types of teams

- List the causes and symptoms of unproductive teams

- Explain in detail how to build team performance

- List the problems encountered in making the transition from supervisor to team leader

- Give examples of the values team leaders should have

- Show how to use important team-leader coaching skills

You've probably already had some experience with teams, perhaps as part of a class-room team assigned to make a presentation on some topic (such as using the Internet as a management tool). If so, then you've also already experienced some of the topics addressed in this chapter: the importance of having a clear and agreed-upon goal, hammering out procedures for how work will be done and establishing milestones for getting there; making sure that everyone is pulling his or her own weight; and figuring out how to motivate (or penalize) colleagues who aren't doing their jobs.

From your experience, you also probably know that doing work through teams has both pros and cons. In this chapter we'll discuss the methods leaders use to make their teams more effective. We'll see that to manage teams effectively, you'll have to use many of the people skills we've discussed in the last three chapters, skills like choosing the right style, using recognition to motivate employees, and effectively communicating what you want done. We'll turn first to the topics of employee involvement and group dynamics, and then look more closely at how companies use teams at work, how to build productive teams, and how team leaders lead productive teams.

▶ TEAMS: EMPLOYEE INVOLVEMENT IN ACTION

The use of work teams is now widespread in the United States, so knowing how to organize and manage teams is essential for any manager today.[2] For example, the Center for the Study of Work Teams at the University of North Texas suggests that about 80% of the Fortune 500 companies have half their employees on teams. Another study concluded that 82% of all U.S. firms have organized at least some of their employees into work groups identified as teams. Thirty-five percent of all U.S. organizations also have at least one team classified as self-directed or semi-autonomous (which generally means that the team supervises itself).[3] Yet another study, by the Hay Group, a Philadelphia-based consulting firm, found that 66% of the employers surveyed planned to increase the level of employee participation in teams. Reasons given for organizing more work around teams included improving product quality (chosen by 69% of these respondents), improving pro-ductivity (64%), improving employee morale (17%), and improving staffing flex-ibility (13%).[4]

What Is Employee Involvement?

employee involvement program

any formal program that lets employees participate in formulating important work decisions or in supervising all or part of their own work activities.

Work teams are examples of employee involvement programs. An **employee involvement program** is any formal program that lets employees participate in formulating important work decisions or in supervising all or part of their own work activities.[5]

Managers rate such programs as their biggest productivity boosters. For example, several years ago the editors of *National Productivity Review* mailed a survey to sub-scribers. They found that "increased employee involvement in the generation and implementation of ideas was ranked the highest priority productivity improve-ment action by the respondents." Employee involvement "was similarly ranked number one as the top cause of improvement over the past two years at these firms." (The other eight causes of improvement, in descending order, were quality programs, improved process methods, top management, equipment, technology, training, computers, and automation.)

◄ FIGURE 13.1

Employee Involvement in Your Company: An Informal Checklist

Source: adapted from Jack Osborn, et al., *Self-Directed Work Teams* (Homewood, IL: Business One Irwin, 1990), p. 30.

1. *Information sharing:* Managers make decisions on their own, announce them, and then respond to any questions employees may have.
2. Managers usually make the decisions, but only after seeking the views of employees.
3. Managers often form temporary employee groups to recommend solutions for specified problems.
4. Managers meet with employee groups regularly—once per week or so—to help them identify problems and recommend solutions.
5. *Intergroup problem solving:* Managers establish and participate in cross-functional employee problem-solving teams.
6. Ongoing work groups assume expanded responsibility for a particular issue, like cost reducton.
7. Employees within an area function full time, with minimal direct supervision.
8. *Total self-direction:* Traditional supervisory roles do not exist; almost all employees participate in self-managing teams.

Levels of Employee Involvement

Employee involvement isn't an either–or situation; instead, several levels of involvement can occur. Based on one informal study, for instance (Figure 13.1), the levels range from information sharing (managers make all important operational decisions, inform employees, and then respond to employee questions); to intergroup problem solving (experienced, trained, cross-functional teams meet regularly with a manager to work on problems across several organizational units),[6] to total self-direction (every employee belongs to a self-directed team, starting with a highly interactive executive group).[7]

Level 8 is often seen in the team-based organizations discussed in Chapter 8 (Designing Organizations to Manage Change). In these organizations, management arranges its organizational structure and systems around team-based work assignments. The managers then devote their main efforts to coaching the employees to manage themselves.[8]

▶ GROUP DYNAMICS: THE BUILDING BLOCKS OF GROUPS

How do groups and teams differ, and how—if at all—are they alike?

Groups and Teams

All teams are groups, but not all groups are teams. Whether it's a football team, a commando team, or a self-managing work team, a *team* is always distinguished by the fact that its members are "committed to a common purpose, set of performance goals, and approach for which they hold themselves mutually accountable."[9] A *group* is defined as two or more persons who are interacting in such a manner that each person influences and is influenced by each other person.[10] A work shift or a department's employees may comprise a group, since they work together, but may not share a team's unit of purpose. There's also usually more emphasis in teams on having the members hold one another (rather than an outsider like a supervisor), mutually accountable for achieving goals.[11] However, all teams are also groups, so we'll review some basic group concepts before moving on. Two are especially important: norms and cohesiveness.

Group Norms

Everyone knows that peer pressure is important. To a greater or lesser extent, what we wear, what we drive, and how we behave is geared to make what we do look "right" from the point of view of our peers. It generally takes a strong-willed person to deliberately go against the grain of what the reference group the person admires is doing.

The fact that people act that way is also certainly true at work. A group may not share a team's unity of purpose, but that doesn't mean it can't influence what its members do. For example, in a study titled Monkey See, Monkey Do: The Influence of Workgroups on the Antisocial Behavior of Employees, two researchers studied how individuals' antisocial behavior at work was shaped by the antisocial behavior of their co-workers.[12] They found that ". . . a workgroup was a significant predictor of an individual's antisocial behavior at work." In fact, the more antisocial the group became, the more it was able to pressure its individual members into taking antisocial actions.[13] Neglecting a group's potential influence can therefore be calamitous.

▲ Cohesiveness is essential to the success of work teams as much in traditional business settings as in such high-risk work as capping oil wells.

It's largely through group norms that work groups can have such influence. **Group norms** are "the informal rules that groups adopt to regulate and regularize group members' behavior."[14] They are "rules of behavior, proper ways of acting, which have been accepted as legitimate by members of a group [and that] specify the kind of behaviors that are expected of group members."[15]

By enforcing their norms, workgroups can have an enormous impact on their members' behavior.[16] In fact, studies show that "group norms may have a greater influence on the individual's performance than the knowledge, skills and abilities the individual brings to the work setting."[17] This fact was first revealed by a research project known as the Hawthorne studies. Here researchers described, for instance, how production levels that exceeded the group's norms triggered what the workers called *binging*, in which the producer's hand was slapped by other workers.

group norms

the informal rules that groups adopt to regulate and regularize group members' behavior.

Group Cohesiveness

In turn, the extent to which a group can enforce its norms and influence its members' behavior depends to some extent on the group's attraction for its members—on its **group cohesiveness**.[18]

A group's cohesiveness depends on several things. Proximity and contact are important for group cohesiveness; without them, individuals have little or no opportunity to become attracted to one another. However, proximity doesn't guarantee that people will discover they have something in common; and if the individuals should find they have little in common, bringing them together could actually backfire.[19] Similarly, cohesiveness depends on the interpersonal attraction between the people involved. Individuals tend to be attracted to a group because they find its activities or goals attractive, rewarding, or valuable, or because they

group cohesiveness

the degree of interpersonal attractiveness within a group, dependent on factors like proximity, attraction among the individual group members, group size, intergroup competition, and agreement about goals.

believe that through the group they can accomplish something they couldn't accomplish on their own.

Several other things influence cohesiveness. Intergroup competition can boost cohesiveness (particularly for the winning group), whereas intragroup competition (competition between the group's members) tends to undermine cohesiveness.[20] People join groups in part because they believe the group can help them accomplish their goals; agreement regarding goals therefore boosts cohesiveness, while differences reduce it.[21] Group cohesiveness also tends to decline as group size increases beyond about 20 members.[22]

In summary, proximity, interpersonal attractiveness, homogeneity of interests or goals, intergroup competition, and manageable size tend to boost group cohesiveness. Since all teams are also groups, these factors also influence a team's cohesiveness and therefore its performance. With that in mind, let's return to the subject of teams at work.

▶ HOW COMPANIES USE TEAMS AT WORK

In considering whether and how to rely on teams, management must first decide what sorts of teams to use. There are many choices because teams can be used in various ways. For example, one expert says companies can use four basic categories of teams: suggestion teams, problem-solving teams, semi-autonomous teams, and self-managing teams.[23]

Suggestion teams are usually temporary teams that exist to work on specific tasks such as how to cut costs or increase productivity.

Problem-solving teams "are involved in identifying and researching activities and in developing effective solutions to work-related problems."[24] Most such teams consist of the supervisor and five to eight employees from a common work area; quality circles are an example.

Semi-autonomous teams have a lot of influence and input into the activities in their own work area, but are still managed by a supervisor. Such teams might set their own goals, provide input into solving problems in their work area, and have a lot of input into daily operating decisions such as when to take breaks and which tasks to do first. However, this type of team is still managed by a formal supervisor.

Self-managing teams are also called self-directed work teams. These are like the teams at GE's Durham aircraft engine plant (which we discussed in Chapter 11). Such teams are responsible for managing their work on a daily basis. They do their own scheduling, set their own goals, hire team members, and make operating decisions such as dealing with vendors if parts are defective.[25]

Let's look more closely at several specific subcategories of work teams.

Quality Circles

Companies have long used decision-making committees at the management level for analysis, advice, and recommendations. Often called task forces, project groups, or audit or safety groups, they identify problems or opportunities and recommend courses of action.[26]

Such teams have now become common in the nonmanagerial ranks as well. The quality circle is the most familiar example, and is a special type of problem-solving

suggestion team
a team formed to work in the short term on a given issue such as increasing productivity.

problem-solving team
a team formed to identify and solve work-related problems.

semi-autonomous team
a team that has considerable input into managing the activities in their own work area but are still headed by a supervisor.

self-managing team
a highly trained team of employees, including 6 to 18 people on average, who are fully responsible for turning out a well-defined segment of finished work. Also called a self-directed work team.

team. A **quality circle** is a team of 6 to 12 employees that meets once a week to solve problems affecting its work area.[27] Such teams are first trained in problem analysis techniques (including basic statistics). Then the team is ready to apply the problem analysis process: problem identification, problem selection, problem analysis, solution recommendations, and solution review by top management.[28] One study estimates that "perhaps several hundred thousand U.S. employees belong to QC circles"; most of these are front-line manufacturing employees.[29]

The original wave of employer enthusiasm and support for quality circle programs began to fade several years ago. Many circles failed to produce measurable cost savings. Some circles' bottom line goals were too vague. In other firms, having the employees choose and analyze their own problems proved incompatible with autocratic management styles and cultures.[30]

Today firms are taking steps to make their quality circles more effective. One corporation has replaced about 700 of its original quality circles with 1,000 new work teams. These new teams are generally not voluntary. They include most shop floor employees and, in contrast to the bottom-up approach of quality circles, they work on problems assigned by management.[31]

Project, Development, or Venture Teams

Teamwork is especially important for special, intense ventures or projects like developing new products. The tight coordination and open communications needed here make teams especially useful. Project teams are often composed of professionals like marketing experts or engineers. They work on specific projects like designing new processes (process design teams) or new products (product development teams).

A **venture team** "is a small group of people who operate as a semi-autonomous unit to create and develop a new idea."[32] The classic example is the IBM team organized in Boca Raton, Florida, to develop and introduce IBM's first personal computer. As is usually the case with venture teams, the IBM unit was semi-autonomous: It had its own budget and leader, as well as the freedom to make decisions within broad guidelines.

IBM's venture team experience illustrates both the pros and cons of the venture team approach. Working more or less autonomously outside of IBM's usual network of rules and policies, the team was able to create a new computer system and bring it to market in less than two years. This might have taken IBM years to accomplish under its usual hierarchical, "check with me first" approach to product development. However, many believe the venture team's autonomy eventually backfired. Not bound by IBM's traditional policy of using only IBM parts, the team understandably went outside IBM, to Microsoft (for its DOS, or disk operating system) and to Intel (for the computer processor). This made possible the early introduction of the IBM PC. Unfortunately for IBM, it also let Intel and Microsoft sell the same PC parts to any manufacturer, and led to the proliferation of IBM clones.[33] The bottom line is that team autonomy can be good but should still be tempered by the required controls.

Transnational Teams

What do you do organizationally, as a manager, if you have to complete a project involving activities in several countries at once? Increasingly, managers are solving that problem by creating **transnational teams**, teams composed of multinational members whose activities span many countries.[34]

Transnational teams are used in many ways. For example, Fuji-Xerox sent 15 of its most experienced Tokyo engineers to a Xerox Corporation facility in Webster, New York. They worked there for five years with a group of U.S. engineers to develop a "world copier," a product that proved to be a huge success in the global market-place.[35] Managers and technical specialists from IBM-Latin America formed their own transnational team to market, sell, and distribute personal computers in 11 Latin American countries. A European beverage manufacturer formed a 13-member transnational team called the European Production Task Force, with members from five countries. Its job was to analyze how many factories it should operate in Europe, what size and type they should be, and where they should be located.[36]

Teams like these face special challenges.[37] They typically work on highly complex and important projects. They must coordinate their work over vast distances. And they are subject to what experts have called the special demands of "multicultural dynamics"—in other words, the fact that they are composed of people with different languages, interpersonal styles, and cultures, and are dealing with activities in multiple cultures as well. What can you do to make such teams more effective? Recommendations here include:

■ *Establish the team's driving goal.* With the distances involved being so great, it's especially important that each team member's activities be focused like a laser on the group's common goal. This can ensure a coordinated, unified effort. The team must therefore identify the primary result toward which its time and resources should be applied early in the process.[38]

■ *Provide communications.* The communications system obviously has to enable geographically dispersed team members to communicate with one another, with others in the company, and with outsiders, quickly and in a way that provides for a full understanding of the issues. The preferred information technology therefore typically includes videoconferencing as well as telephone, voice mail, e-mail, and fax. Decision support systems—PC-based groupware that permits, for instance, simultaneous computerized discussions of issues—are used increasingly too.

■ *Build teamwork.* Fostering group cohesiveness is especially important, given the multicultural nature of these groups. "Successful [transnational] teams are characterized by leaders and members who trust each other, are committed to the team's mission, can be counted on to perform their respective tasks, and enjoy working with each other."[39] Team leaders and management therefore have to work hard to provide the training and leadership that foster such characteristics.

Building teamwork in transnational teams can be a tricky problem. On the one hand, one advantage of such teams is the diversity of views they bring to bear, so you want to preserve and encourage different perspectives. On the other hand, you don't want those same differences to lead to unmanageable conflicts, or the team may fall apart. The challenge therefore lies in creating a situation in which different perspectives are encouraged, while the team also works together as a single, goal-oriented unit.

■ *Show mutual respect.* For example, says one expert, rotate the times of conferences so that the same members in a remote time zone don't always have to do business in the wee hours of the morning; hold staff meetings at various geographic locations; link employees at remote sites to the headquarters e-mail system so they feel included; create office space for visiting team members; and learn words expressing respect and gratitude in the languages of other team members.[40]

■ **Virtual Teams**

In some cases today, transnational team members hardly meet face-to-face at all, but instead operate in a virtual environment. Their meetings take place mostly via telecommunications.

Virtual teams are increasingly popular. For one thing, the globalization of trade and of corporate activity practically demands that teams be able to communicate continually regarding their projects and at great distances, but rarely face to face. Furthermore, the increasing emphasis today on strategic partnerships and joint ventures means that employees of various companies must frequently act together as a team, although they work for different companies and may be in different countries or continents. Virtual teams

> are groups of geographically and/or organizationally dispersed co-workers that are assembled using a combination of telecommunications and information technologies to accomplish an organizational task. Virtual teams rarely, if ever, meet in a face-to-face setting. They may be set up as temporary structures, existing only to accomplish a specific task, or may be permanent structures, used to address ongoing issues, such as a strategic planning. Furthermore, membership is often fluid, evolving according to changing task requirements.[41]

Virtual teams depend for their existence on several types of information technology. Desktop videoconferencing systems are often the core systems around which the rest of the virtual team's

▲ Videoconferencing: a virtual team meeting.

technologies are built. Systems like these re-create the face-to-face interactions of conventional groups, so that communication among team members can include the rich body language and nuances of face-to-face communications.[42] (However, some experts contend that the technology most often used by virtual groups is still the jet plane.)

Collaborative software systems (sometimes called group support systems, as noted in chapter 12, or decision support systems) further facilitate decision making in virtual teams. For example, one consulting team used a collaborative software system to research and write a proposal for a major project, letting each member access in real-time the contribution of each other member, while inputting his or her own. Microsoft Corp. offers a NetMeeting conference system. When combined with new products like Framework Technologies Corp.'s ActiveProject 5.0, virtual team members can hold live project reviews and discussions and then store the sessions on the project's Web site.[43]

Finally, companies are creating their own Intranets. With all the virtual teams' required forms and documents available on internal Web sites, these Intranets "allow virtual teams to archive text, visual, audio, and numerical data in a user-friendly format, [and] allow virtual teams to keep other organizational members and outside constituents such as suppliers and customers up-to-date on the team's progress."[44]

Team members in such virtual teams need to keep in mind the cultural differences between team members. One expert therefore suggests removing cultural idioms (like "apples to oranges") from communications, and using multiple channels (such as videoconferencing and e-mail) to build in redundancy to ensure that the message—both verbal and nonverbal—is understood.[45]

Self-Directed Work Teams

As we saw in Chapter 8, self-directed (also called self-managing) teams are the ultimate manifestation of employee involvement programs in many firms. A self-managing self-directed work team is a highly trained group of around eight employees, fully responsible for turning out a well-defined segment of finished work.[46] The "well-defined segment" might be an entire engine or a fully processed insurance claim. In any case, the distinguishing features of self-directed teams are that they are empowered to direct and do virtually all their own work, and that the work itself involves a well-defined item.

In many firms today the whole facility is organized around such self-managing teams. For example, the GE Durham aircraft engine plant is a totally self-managing facility, in which the plant's 170 workers are split into teams, all of whom report to one boss, the factory manager.[47] At Johnsonville Foods, similar self-managing teams recruit, hire, evaluate, and fire (if necessary) on their own. Many of the workers have little or no college background; however, they also "train one another, formulate and track their own budgets, make capital investment proposals as needed, handle quality control and inspection, develop their own quantitative standards, improve every process and product, and create prototypes of possible new products."[48]

Historians like to say that "those who ignore history are doomed to repeat it" and that's also true when it comes to organizing around self-managing teams. While teams like these can be effective, many such efforts (including a major one at Levi Strauss, discussed below) have failed, in part because the companies weren't fully aware of what to expect as they installed self-managing team structures.

What can managers expect when organizing around self-managing teams? Basically, a six-step process involving activities like the following:

1. *Startup*. In this first phase an executive steering committee analyzes the feasibility of a team-based structure, and if it decides to go ahead, takes the preliminary steps required to implement such a program. Measurable goals are identified, the initial sites for the team-based structure chosen, and the actual division of work among teams is assigned. Toward the end of this startup phase, plans for the teams' structure are announced, and the teams and their leaders begin working out their specific roles.

2. *Training*. Experts say "the dominant feature of start up is intensive training for all involved." Team members must learn how to communicate and how to listen, how to use administrative procedures and budgets, and how to develop other skills. Supervisors must learn how to become facilitators and coaches rather than top-down supervisors.[49]

3. *Confusion*. Once the initial enthusiasm wears off, the facility and its teams may enter a period of confusion. Team members may become concerned about whether their new (probably self-imposed) higher work standards may backfire at compensation time; supervisors may become increasingly concerned about their apparently shrinking role in day-to-day operations.

4. *The move to leader-centered teams*. Ideally, the team's confidence will grow as members master their new skills and find better ways to accomplish their work. The chief danger in this stage, according to experts, is that the teams become too reliant on their leaders. Rather than remaining self-directed, some may slip into the habit of letting an elected team member carry out the former supervisor's role. One way to avoid this is "to make sure everyone continues to learn

and eventually exercise leadership skills, . . . [and] allow anyone to exercise leadership functions as needed."[50]

5. *Misplaced loyalty*. Sometimes blinded by their newfound authority and ability to supervise themselves, teams may let loyalty to coworkers hide problems. For example, team members might hide a poorly performing member to protect the person in a misguided fit of loyalty. Management's job here is to reemphasize both the need for intrateam cooperation and the team's responsibility to supervise its own members.

6. *The move to self-directed teams*. Once the new teams rid themselves of the intense team-oriented loyalties that often accompany building self-directed teams, the organization can move to what one researcher calls "the period of true self-direction."[51]

The empowerment of self-directed teams can reportedly be a heady experience for all concerned. As the vice president of one midwestern consumer goods company said about organizing his firm around teams: "People on the floor were talking about world markets, customer needs, competitors' products, making process improvements—all the things managers are supposed to think about."[52]

▶ HOW TO BUILD PRODUCTIVE TEAMS

Requiring several people to work together doesn't make a group a self-directed team, and certainly not a productive one. An underperforming team might simply lack the sort of initiative and sense of urgency that a coach traditionally tries to ignite during halftime breaks. But a lack of initiative is often just one of the problems with which teams must cope.

Does Teamwork Work?

The research regarding the effectiveness and productivity of work teams is unfortunately mixed. Much of the anecdotal evidence is highly favorable. For example, after Kodak's consumer film finishing business division instituted a team-based structure, its division manager reported that unit costs declined by 6% per year over six years, and that productivity increased by over 200% in six years, from 383 units per employee to 836.[53]

One research study recently focused on the impact of work teams on manufacturing performance in a unionized plant operated by a division of a Fortune 500 firm.[54] During a 21-month period, the plant was converted to a team structure. The results of this study indicated that "quality and labor productivity improved over time after the introduction of work teams."[55]

Yet it's clear that team-based structures can also fail. One study surveyed plants of a major U.S. car manufacturer in the early 1980s and found that work teams had a negative impact on plant productivity.[56] In that case the researchers thought the problems might simply be due to startup, and that the team structures would eventually turn out to be effective.

One highly publicized work team program failure occurred in the mid-1990s, in the U.S. factories of Levi Strauss. In an industry famous

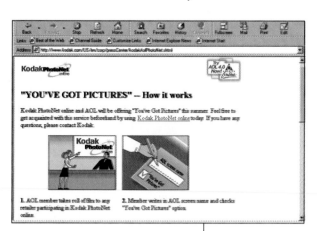

▲ **WEBNOTE**

Kodak relies on its alliance with AOL to boost its film sales.

www.kodak.com

Used with permission.

for low wages and questionable working conditions, Levi Strauss has always right-fully viewed itself as a major exception. However, as competitors with less expensive merchandise manufactured overseas made strong inroads into the Levi's brand the firm sought a way to keep its extensive network of U.S. factories going, but with higher productivity.

The idea it hit on was the Work Team Program. In the early 1990s, most of the Levi Strauss U.S. plants operated on the piecework system. The worker was paid a rate per piece for each specialized task (like attaching a belt loop) that he or she finished.[57] In the new team system, a pair of pants would be constructed entirely by a group of 10 to 35 workers, who would share all the tasks and be paid according to the total number of trousers the group finished each day. The idea was to boost productivity by, among other things, giving employees the flexibility to do several jobs instead of just one.

Unfortunately, it didn't quite work out that way. High-performing faster workers in a group found their wages pulled down by slower-working colleagues (who, conversely, saw their hourly wages rise). Morale began to plummet, arguments ensued, and at some plants, like the Morrilton, Arkansas, factory, a pair of Dockers that previously cost $5 to stitch together now cost $7.50.

The results weren't entirely bleak. Teams that were more homogeneous in terms of work skills did tend to perform better, and their productivity did rise. Furthermore, average turnaround—the time from when an order is received to when the products are shipped to retail stores—improved from nine weeks to seven.

Levi Strauss intends to continue its team program at its remaining U.S. plants, but for 6,000 of its U.S. employees, that is now irrelevant: In the past year or two, Levi's announced it was closing 11 U.S. plants, thus laying off one-third of its U.S. employees. The moral seems to be that the team approach can be effective, but that how it is implemented determines whether it is successful.

The mixed results of the team effort at Levi Strauss also underscores the fact that moving to such a structure is usually merely part of a more comprehensive set of organizational changes. At Levi Strauss, for instance, it wasn't necessarily organizing around teams that created the problem, but the type of incentive plan that was implemented along with it. When teams are introduced, companies also flatten the management hierarchy, cut personnel, restructure tasks, and take other steps, all of which need to be consistent with and make sense in light of the new team-based organization. (In fact, while Levi Strauss was installing its team-based structure, its top management was also busily "taking the company private" by repurchasing its stock from the public shareholders.)

In other words, switching to teams usually also means changing many aspects of the overall management system (how plans are formulated, how employees are selected, and how the company maintains control, for instance). The company could do a good job of organizing its teams but fail to make the required changes in the rest of its management system. This probably helps to explain why some team efforts fail. There are some specifically team-related steps you can take to make teams work better, and we turn to this topic next.

Causes of Unproductive Teams

Let's start by looking at some of the specific things that can cause teams to be unproductive and even to fall apart. For one thing, the purpose of a team is to harness divergent skills and talents for specific objectives. However, *divergent points of view* may lead instead to tension and conflict.[58] *Power struggles*—some subtle, some not—can also undermine a team's effectiveness. Individual members may try to undermine potentially productive ideas with the goal of winning their point, rather than doing what's best for the team. In addition, some team members may be ignored, thus eliminating a potentially valuable resource.[59]

Several recent studies shed further light on why some teams fail. Sometimes an intentionally confusing or *provocative team member* becomes the focus of what turns into a dysfunctional team. We've probably all known someone who seems to spread turmoil wherever he or she goes and the research suggests, to quote the old saying, that one bad apple can actually spoil the bunch.[60] An unequal distribution of *workload* among team members and a lack of institutional/top management support for the team and its members are other factors that have recently been found to undermine the effectiveness of teams.[61]

Irving Janis describes another team problem, one he calls *groupthink*: "the tendency for a highly cohesive group, especially one working on special projects, to develop a sense of detachment and elitism."[62] This sense of detachment, Janis found, can lead the group to press for conformity and to resist examining opposing points of view. Just one powerful point of view prevails, even though cogent arguments against it may exist within the group.

Groupthink may seem academic, but it can have disastrous real-life effects. Just before the explosion of the ill-fated Challenger flight in 1986, one engineer reportedly tried to tell colleagues and managers about his concerns that the low temperatures surrounding the shuttle could cause the engine's sealing rings to leak hot gas. As he put it, "I received cold stares. . . . With looks as if to say, 'go away and don't bother us with the facts.' They just would not respond verbally to . . . me. I felt totally helpless at that moment and that further argument was fruitless, so I, too, stopped pressing my case."[63]

One expert says that some teams fail due to *lack of leadership*, focus, and/or capability, a point summarized in Figure 13.2. For example, in some team situations, the leadership is absent or ineffectual. Where there is (or should be) an elected or appointed team leader, this person is not providing the consistency of direction or vision, or isn't fighting for the required budgets or resources for the team. Where the team itself should be carrying out the leadership role by consensus they're failing to do so, with similar effects. In any case, improving the situation may involve changing the leader, or at least getting the leader to focus on obtaining what the team needs and providing direction in a more consistent manner.

Sometimes it's a *lack of focus* that causes the team to fail. Here, if you spoke with the team's members, it would be apparent that there was a lack of clarity about the team's purpose, roles, strategy, and goals. Comments would be made, such as "why are we organized this way, and what are we supposed to be doing?" Remedial steps include establishing and clarifying the charter or mission for the team, establishing the team's goals, and clarifying members' roles.

Other teams may be motivated, focused, and well led but *lack the capacity* to get their jobs done. Team members may lack critical skills, or not have the knowledge they need to do their jobs. This is one of the reasons why team-based facilities like those at GE's Durham engine plant and Saturn devote enormous resources to training employees. Eliminating this problem involves steps like providing appropriate education and training, and establishing a development plan for the team and its members.

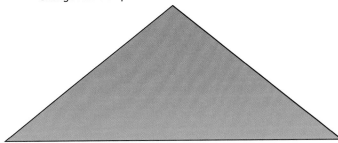

Leadership

Lack of support, consistency of direction, vision, budget, and resources.

Improvement strategy:
- Plan events to ensure demonstrated leadership support
- Increase availability of budget and resources
- Increase communication and contact with leader
- Change leadership

Focus

Lack of clarity about team purpose, roles, strategy, and goals.

Improvement strategy:
- Establish and clarify team charter
- Clarify boundary conditions
- Ensure open channels for communications and information transfer
- Clarify team member roles
- Establish regular team meetings

Capability

Lack of critical skill sets, knowledge, ongoing learning, and development.

Improvement strategy:
- Provide appropriate education and training
- Establish a team development plan
- Establish individual development plans
- Reflect on how group process can be improved
- Regularly assess team effectiveness

◀ **FIGURE 13.2**

Why Teams Fail: The Leadership, Focus, and Capability Pyramid

Each of three factors—leadership, focus, and capability—requires a different improvement strategy to overcome traps that lead to declines in team effectiveness.

Source: Adapted from Steven Rayner, "Team Traps: What They Are, How to Avoid Them." *National Productivity Review,* Summer 1996, p. 107. Reprinted by permission of John Wiley & Sons, Inc.

Symptoms of Unproductive Teams

As at Levi Strauss, various symptoms make it easy to recognize unproductive teams, if you know what to look for. They include[64]:

Non-accomplishment of goals. The team program should be used to accomplish specific goals. If, as at Levi Strauss, these aren't met, the program is not working.

Cautious or guarded communication. When team members fear ridicule or a negative reaction, they may say nothing or be guarded in what they do say. Cautious or guarded communication is thus a symptom of a malfunctioning team.

Lack of disagreement. Lack of disagreement among team members may reflect an unwillingness to share true feelings and ideas. At the extreme, the cause may be group think. Everyone simply feels pressured to "just go along."

Malfunctioning meetings. As in the cartoon on page 404, unproductive teams often have meetings characterized by boredom, lack of enthusiastic participation, failure to reach decisions, or dominance by one or two people.

Conflict within the team. Unproductive teams are often characterized by a suspicious, combative environment and by highly personalized conflict among team members.

"No decision. They're still sleeping on it."

Characteristics of Productive Teams

Of course, you don't want unproductive teams, you want productive ones. How can you make sure a team is more productive? Research findings can be usful here. For example, team members need to recognize the team as a unit and as an attractive work arrangement. In other words, individuals who don't view their team as legitimate or as an attractive way to get the job done are not going to contribute their fair share to the work.[65]

In a study using undergraduate students as subjects, teams in which rewards were distributed based on equity (based on what the person contributed) were more effective than those in which rewards were distributed based on equality (equally, to all the team members).[66] In another study teams composed of agreeable and conscientious employees received higher supervisory ratings and better objective measures of team accuracy and completion than did those with less agreeable and conscientious employees.[67] In other words, many things seem to distinguish productive teams.

Based on an extensive study of work teams, John Katzenbach and Douglas Smith found that productive teams have five characteristics, as follows.

Commitment to a Mission   First, they found that "the essence of a team is a common commitment. Without it, groups perform as individuals; with it, they become a powerful unit of collective performance."[68] Teams therefore need a clear mission, such as Saturn's: "Let's build a world-class quality car."[69] The most productive teams then develop commitment around their own definition of what management wants the teams to do: "The best teams invest a tremendous amount of time and effort exploring, shaping, and agreeing on a purpose that belongs to them both collectively and individually."[70]

Specific Performance Goals Productive teams then translate their common purpose (such as "build world-class quality cars") into specific team goals (such as "reduce new-car defects to no more than four per vehicle"). In fact, "transforming broad directives into specific and measurable performance goals is the surest first step for a team trying to shape a purpose meaningful to its members."[71]

Right Size, Right Mix In their study, Katzenbach and Smith found that the best-performing teams generally have fewer than 25 people, and usually between 7 and 14. (However, while that may be generally true, keep in mind that some firms—such as Microsoft—have been phenomenally successful with development teams of 200 or more.)

Team members also complement each other in terms of skills. Thus, accomplishing the goal usually calls for people with technical expertise as well as those skilled in problem solving, decision making, and interpersonal relationships. Problems arise when the teams are heterogeneous in terms of skill levels (as occurred at Levi Strauss), or when members' skills do not complement each other.

A recent study illustrates the importance of having the right mix. The researchers studied the innovativeness of proposals made by top management teams in 27 hospitals. The question was whether a team's innovativeness reflected the individual innovativeness of team members. Individual innovativeness was measured with items such as "I suggest new working methods to the people I work with" and "I try to introduce improved methods of doing things at work."[72]

In this study team innovation, and specifically the radicalness of the innovations introduced by the teams, apparently depended to a large extent on how individually innovative team members were. The implication is that, at least when it comes to innovation, the team you put together better have a mix that includes at least a few highly innovative people.

THE PEOPLE SIDE OF MANAGING

■ Co-worker Similarity and the Team's Performance

Co-worker diversity can be a tricky issue when it comes to team performances.[73] On the one hand, "a team with a variety of members whose skills and experiences differ and complement each other can take on a wide range of tasks."[74] On the other hand, "be on the alert . . . for teams whose membership is excessively varied, because conflict and communications breakdown can result."[75] (The problems at Levi Strauss, you'll recall, resulted in part from the diversity of skill levels in the teams.) What is a manager to do?

Part of the answer lies in a recent study conducted by three behavioral scientists at the University of Houston.[76] The study examined the impact of various types of similarities (demographic, value, and behavioral style preference) on co-workers' attitudes and behaviors.

Various dimensions of co-worker similarity were measured. Demographic characteristics included age, level of education, country of citizenship, and gender. Information about values included the relative importance that individuals placed, for example, on a world at peace, happiness, freedom, and self-determination. Team members also rated such things as how much they liked each team member and their willingness to work with each of them in the future.

The basic research question was, How did co-workers' similarities influence how well they liked each other and how they felt about working with other team members in the future? Demographic similarity was the strongest predictor of social liking and co-worker preference, but only at the start of the training. Three weeks after the teams had begun work, demographic similarity ceased to be significant in social liking and co-worker preference. Apparently, such differences were overcome by the positive effects that came from working together successfully.

After three weeks of working together, however, similarity in personal values still predicted both liking and preference. Therefore, creating teams whose members share personal values—beliefs about what is good or bad and what one should or should not do—seems to be important for building long-term team cohesiveness. Differences in things like age, education, country of citizenship, and gender seem to fade in significance as the team works together successfully.

A Common Approach   Productive teams also reach agreement on how they will work together to accomplish their mission. For example, team members agree about who does particular jobs; how schedules are set and followed; what skills need to be developed; what members have to do to earn continuing membership in the team; and how decisions are made and modified.

Mutual Accountability   A sense of mutual accountability is the hallmark of productive teams. Members believe "we are all in this together" and "we all have to hold ourselves accountable for doing whatever is needed to help the team achieve its mission." Katzenbach and Smith found that mutual accountability can't be coerced. Instead, it emerges from the commitment and trust that come from working together toward a common goal. The "Entrepreneurs in Action" box on page 408 illustrates how one entrepreneur used teams to help build a newsletter business.

How to Build Team Performance

We've seen that productive teams have certain characteristics (like mutual accountability). How do you foster such characteristics? Guidelines leaders can use to build effective teams include the following:

- *Seek employee input.* The basic reason for organizing around work teams is to tap employees motivation, commitment, and input. Therefore, while a team structure can be installed unilaterally by management, it's probably best to start with a committee of employees. At Levi Strauss, for instance, consultants brought in after the teamwork problems surfaced recommended reorganizing the teams from scratch, using worker input. However by that time, productivity was so low that downsizing was already mandatory.
- *Establish urgent, demanding performance standards.* All team members need to believe the team has urgent and worthwhile goals, and they need to know what their performance standards are.
- *Select members for skill and skill potential.* Choose people both for their existing skills and for their potential to improve existing skills and learn new ones.
- *Pay special attention to first meetings and actions.* Management has to show that it's really committed to the team approach. When potential teams first gather, everyone monitors the signals to confirm, suspend, or dispel concerns. If a senior executive leaves the team kickoff to take a phone call 10 minutes after the session begins and then never returns, people get the message that he or she doesn't care about the team.
- *Set clear rules of behavior.* Good teams develop rules of conduct that help them achieve their goals. The most critical pertain to attendance (for example, "no interruptions to take phone calls"); discussion ("no sacred cows"); confidentiality

("the only things to leave this room are what we agree on"); analytic approach ("facts are friendly"); end-product orientation ("everyone gets assignments and does them"); constructive confrontation ("no finger pointing"); and perhaps the most important, contributions ("everyone does real work").

■ *Move from "boss" to "coach."* Self-directed work teams are, by definition, empowered: They have the confidence, authority, tools, and information to manage themselves. The team leader's job is not to boss, but to see that team members have the support they need.

■ *Set a few immediate performance-oriented tasks and goals.* Effective teams mark their advancement by key accomplishments. This can be facilitated by immediately establishing some short-term goals.

■ *Challenge the group regularly with fresh facts and information.* New information—about performance, or new competitors—causes a team to redefine and enrich its understanding of the challenges it faces. It also helps the team reshape its common purpose and set clearer goals.

■ *Use the power of positive feedback.* There are many ways to recognize and reward team performance besides money. They include having a senior executive speak directly to the team about the urgency of its mission and using praise to recognize contributions.

■ *Shoot for the right team size.*[77] Create teams with the smallest number of employees required to do the work. Large size reduces interaction and involvement and increases the need for extra coordination.

■ *Choose people who like teamwork.* Do what companies like Toyota do: Recruit and select employees who have a history of preferring to work in teams and of being good team members. Increasingly, Internet-based applications are available for helping managers match employees to team needs. For example, one, Kolbe's Warewithal® online (www.warewithal.com), allows potential team members to take an Internet-based test. This identifies and classifies employees based on four Action Mode® basic behaviors—Fact Finder™, Follow-Thru™, Quick Start™, and Implementor™—on the assumption that the best teams require a balance of such skills.[78]

■ *Train, train, train.* Make sure team members have the training they need to do their jobs. Training should cover topics such as the philosophy of doing work through teams, how teams make decisions, interpersonal and communications skills for team members, and the technical skills team members need to perform their jobs.

It's hard to overemphasize the importance of team training. When it opened its new automobile plant in Spartansburg, South Carolina, BMW put its new employees through numerous teamwork-related training sessions. These included sessions on problem solving, communication, and how to deal with conflict within and between teams. Then, during the next 18 months, workers received more than 80 more hours of team skills training each, in areas like problem analysis. As the HR director for BMW Manufacturing put it, training employees about technical matters is straightforward; teaching them how to work well with others is much harder.[79]

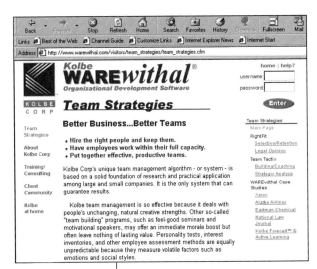

▲ **W E B N O T E**

Kolbe's Warewithal® is an Internet-based software package that helps companies hire, train, and manage effective teams.
www.warewithal.com
Used with permission.

- *Cross-train for flexibility.* Team members should receive cross-training to learn the jobs of other team members. This can help reduce disruptions due to absenteeism and boost flexibility, since all members are always ready to fill in as required.

- *Emphasize the task's importance.* Team members need to know that what they're doing is important for the company, so communicate that message whenever you can. Emphasize the task's importance in terms of customers, other employees, the organization's mission, and the company's overall results.

- *Assign whole tasks.* Try to make the team responsible for a distinct piece of work, such as an entire product, project, or segment of the business. This can boost team members' sense of responsibility and ownership.

- *Encourage social support.* Work teams, like any group, are more effective when members support and help each other. A manager should set a good example by being supportive and taking concrete steps to encourage and reinforce positive interactions and cohesiveness within the team.

- *Provide the necessary material support.* Social support is important, but the results of a recent study showed that material support "may be more important than [just] ensuring group members are cohesive."[80] The researchers found that such material support includes timely information, resources, and rewards that encourage group rather than individual performance. "It also suggests organizations should determine if the necessary support resources are available before creating teams."[81]

Published Image, Inc. Builds Teams

ENTREPRENEURS IN ACTION

▶ Almost from the day he founded Published Image, Inc., and organized the newsletter into self-managed teams, Eric Gershman had in mind the day his own position would become superfluous. His viewpoint was that employees capable of preparing their own work schedules, budgets, and bonuses shouldn't have much use for a boss.

With the growth of mutual funds, Gershman had correctly predicted the need for shareholder newsletters. He spent his entire savings getting Published Image off the ground. Eleven clients and $600,000 in revenue later, things looked bleak: Turnover was high, morale was low, factual errors were common, and a third of the clients were leaving annually. Gershman came up with a 250-page plan of action. "We blew up the whole company and totally changed people's thinking about what their job is," Gershman says. Published Image was divided into four independent teams responsible for client relations, sales, editorial content, and production. Everyone performed a speciality, but everyone shared responsibility for daily deadlines as well. "We work like a unit and pitch in to get out on time whatever has to get done," says Shelley Danse. Her day as an account executive can stretch to cover tasks from research to proofreading to laying out artwork.

Published Image's team approach fostered a sense of ownership of the collective output. It also enhanced appreciation of the work of other employees. Planning was easier, and efficiency improved. Clients were also impressed. "We have one group of people who know all facets of our job, and we can contact any of them during the process," says Peter Herlihy, vice president of mutual funds marketing at Fleet Financial Group.

Gershman soon got his wish of working himself out of a job. After revenues doubled to more than $4 million, his company was bought out by Standard & Poors.

Source: Michael Selz, "Testing Self-Managing Teams, Entrepreneur Hopes to Lose Job," *Wall Street Journal*, 11 January 1994, p. B-1, and Sally Goll Beatty, "Standard & Poors Acquires Published Image, Inc." *Wall Street Journal*, 2 July 1997, p. B7.

▲ Team members at Rodel, Inc., a Delaware manufacturing firm, after completing a rigorous leadership training program aimed at building trust, teamwork, and leadership.

► LEADING PRODUCTIVE TEAMS

You might say that leading productive teams is like leading anything—only more so. In other words, leading a team requires more than just leadership skills; it also requires team-building skills like building mutually supportive relationships, building the team's self-confidence, and learning how to move from boss to coach. In the remainder of this chapter we'll discuss a few uniquely team-related aspects of being a team leader.

How Do Team Leaders Behave?

Leading a team is a lot different from, say, running your average assembly line. We've touched on this elsewhere, but a short review is in order. Team leaders

- coach, they don't boss. They assess members' skills and help members use them to the fullest.
- encourage participation. They solicit input into decisions, share decision-making responsibility, and delegate specifically identified decisions to the team.
- are facilitators.[82] The best team leaders give the other team members the self-confidence, authority, information, and tools they need to get their jobs done. Team leaders don't view themselves as sitting atop an organizational pyramid. Instead, they view the pyramid as upside-down, with their job being to support and facilitate so the team can get the job done.

Typical Transition Problems

Moving from being a traditional in-charge supervisor to being a facilitator/coach team leader isn't easy. As one former executive put it:

> Working . . . under the autocratic system was a lot easier, particularly when you want something done quickly and you are convinced you know the right way to do it. It is a lot easier to say, "OK, . . . we're going to Chicago tomorrow," rather than sit down and say, "All right, first of all, do we want to go out of town? And where do we want to go—east or west?"[83]

Why is it so difficult to make the transition from supervisor to team leader? For at least four reasons.

The Perceived Loss of Power or Status Making the transition from supervisor to team leader often involves a perceived loss of power or status.[84] One day you're the boss, with the authority to give orders and have others obey; the next day the pyramid is upside-down, and you're a facilitator/coach, trying to make sure your team members have what they need to do their jobs—to a large extent, without you. (Self-managing teams often schedule their own work priorities, hire their own co-workers, and decide themselves when to take breaks.)

Unclear Team Leader Roles   Some companies make the mistake of overemphasizing what the former supervisor (now team leader) is *not:* You're not the boss any more; you are not to control or direct any more; you are not to make all the hiring decisions any more. However, telling the new team leaders what they're not, without clarifying what they are, can cause unnecessary problems. It can intensify the new team leader's perceived loss of power or status. And of course it can leave the person with the very real and unnerving question, "What exactly am I supposed to be doing?"

This problem is easily avoided. Team leaders do have important duties to perform—for instance, as coaches, facilitators, and boundary managers. Management's job is to ensure that the team leaders understand what their new duties are, and that they can do their new jobs effectively.

Job Security Concerns   Telling former supervisors/new team leaders they're not in charge anymore understandably undermines their sense of security. After all, it's not unreasonable for someone to ask, "Just how secure is the job of managing a self-managing team?" Some new team leaders will say, "Sure, I know my new duties are to facilitate and coach, but that just doesn't make me feel as irreplaceable as I was when I was in charge." And, there's a lot of truth in that. For example, General Mills claims much of the productivity improvement from its self-directed work teams came from eliminating middle managers. Insecurity is therefore not just a figment of supervisors' imaginations.

Companies handle this problem in several ways. Many—perhaps most—of the resulting teams still need a facilitator/coach, so many of the supervisors can find new jobs as team leaders. What happens when there are too many supervisors? As you know, many companies have been downsized, and supervisors or managers have unfortunately lost their jobs.

Other companies, reluctant to lose the enormous expertise their supervisors have, take steps to retain these valuable human assets. For example, when chemical firm Rohm and Haas's Lousiville, Kentucky, plant changed over to self-directing work teams, the redundant supervisors were turned into training coordinators and made responsible for managing the continuing educational requirements of the plant's new teams.[85]

The Double Standard Problem   Many existing supervisors may feel that the company is treating them as second-class citizens compared with the employees who are being trained to be team members. The smart way to proceed is to create and implement a development and transition plan for the supervisors too—one that clarifies their new duties and identifies the training they'll receive as they make the transition from supervisor to team leader.

What Are Team Leader Values?

Not everyone is cut out to be a leader of a self-managing team. Not every leader is philosophically prepared to surrender the trappings of "being a boss" that leading in such a situation requires.

In particular, being a leader of a self-managing team requires a special set of personal values that derive from the empowered nature of these teams. Important team leader values include the following.

Team Members Come First   Effective team leaders have respect for the individual. At Saturn, for instance, team members carry a card that lists the firm's values, one of which is set forth in these words:

We have nothing of greater value than our people. We believe that demonstrating respect for the uniqueness of every individual builds a team of confident, creative members possessing a high degree of initiative, self-respect, and self-discipline.[86]

You'll find a similar stress on putting people first at Toyota. Here's how one manager puts it:

In all our meetings and in every way, all Toyota top managers continually express their trust in human nature. Mr. Cho [the chief executive of the company] continually reminds us that the team members must come first and that every other action we take and decision we make must be adapted to that basic idea; I must manage around that core idea.[87]

Team Members Can Be Trusted   Some leaders have what Douglas McGregor called Theory X assumptions: They believe that people are lazy, need to be controlled, need to be motivated, and are not very smart.

Assumptions like those obviously won't work when leading self-managing teams. These leaders need what McGregor called Theory Y assumptions about human nature: that people like to work, have self-control, can motivate themselves, and are smart.

In other words, effective team leaders trust team members to do their best. They believe team members can and want to do a good job, and they focus much of their attention on ensuring that team members have what they need to do their jobs.

Teamwork Is Important   It may seem obvious, but team leaders should believe that teamwork is important. They can't just pay lip service to the value of teamwork; they really have to walk the talk.

For one thing, team leaders have to minimize status differences, and may even have to forgo mammoth salary differentials.[88] At Toyota Manufacturing in Lexington, Kentucky, none of the managers—not even the president—have private offices. At Ben & Jerry's Ice Cream, the founders believed that the top manager should earn no more than 7 to 10 times what the lowest-paid employee earned—a far cry from the 100 to 200 times in many other companies.

Support Is Crucial   Team leaders believe in eliminating the barriers to success and are driven by the value of supporting the team's efforts.[89] At Procter & Gamble, for instance, some team leaders refer to themselves as "barrier busters" because "they recognize the primary importance of removing the things that get in the way of the success of their teams."[90]

Probably the biggest difference between team leaders and supervisors is this: Team leaders see themselves as there to support their teams and to eliminate barriers to their team's success. They believe their primary responsibility is to make sure the teams can get their jobs done.

▲ Open plan office at Toyota's Lexington, Kentucky, plant: no one has a private office.

Developing Effective Coaching Skills

We've seen that coaching is a big part of what team leaders do. That's why in his book *Team-Based Organizations*, James Shonk says that leading self-managing teams is a lot like coaching:

> It involves assessing the team's skills and helping them use them to the fullest. Employees tend to contribute more effectively when they are coached to make optimal use of all their strengths and resources.[91]

What is required to be a great coach? Experts list the following guidelines:[92]

- *Know your people*. Assess each employee's skills so you can help team members use them to the fullest.

- *Coach, don't tell*. Remember, a coach's main role is to help people develop their skills. In other words, your job is not to tell people what to do or to sell your own ideas, but to help others define, analyze, and solve problems. Similarly, you should stimulate increased employee initiative and autonomy by raising questions, helping team members identify alternatives, providing general direction, encouraging employees to contribute their own ideas, and supplying feedback.[93]

- *Give emotional support*. Even National Football League coaches know when to back off and be more supportive. Particularly when an employee is new to the task and just developing skills (like how to analyze problems), it's crucial to create a supportive environment.

- *Use Socratic coaching*. Try to refrain from making judgmental statements like, "That won't work." Instead, ask the questions that will lead your team members to find the answers for themselves. For instance, "What is the problem you want to solve?" or "How will you know when you have solved the problem?"[94]

- *Show that you have high expectations*. Empowering employees means giving them not just the authority and tools, but also the self-confidence to get the job done. That's why one expert says, "When I think back on people who have been great coaches in my life, they have always had very high expectations of me."[95]

SUMMARY

1. Work teams are examples of employee involvement programs, which let employees participate in formulating important work decisions or in supervising all or most of their work activities. Managers rank such programs as their biggest productivity boosters.

2. Several aspects of group dynamics are especially important for leaders grappling with how to build more effective teams. Group norms are important because they're the rules groups use to control their members. Group cohesiveness determines the attraction of the group for its members and is influenced by things like proximity, interpersonal attractiveness, homogeneity of interests or goals, and intergroup competition.

3. Leaders can use four general types of teams in organizations: suggestion teams, problem-solving teams, semi-autonomous teams, and self-managing teams. Specific examples of teams include quality circles; project, development, or venture teams; transnational teams; and self-directed work teams.

4. Symptoms of unproductive teams include cautious or guarded communication, lack of disagreement, use of personal criticism, malfunctioning meetings, unclear goals, low commit-

ment, and conflict within the team. Characteristics of productive teams include commitment to a mission, specific performance goals, the right size and mix, a common approach, and mutual accountability.

5. How can a leader go about building a high-performing team? Guidelines include establish demanding performance standards; select members for skill and skill potential; set clear rules of behavior; move from "boss" to "coach"; choose people who like teamwork; train team members, assign whole tasks; and encourage social support. When teams do not succeed, the problem often lies in one of three factors: leadership, focus, or capability.

6. Team leaders have special duties. They coach, encourage participation, are boundary managers, and are facilitators. Moving from boss to team leader can therefore cause transition problems stemming from the perceived loss of power or status, unclear team leader roles, job security concerns, and problems with double standards.

7. Not everyone is cut out to be an effective leader of self-managing teams. A successful team leader must adhere to the right values, including putting team members first, trusting team members to do their best, helping team members to self-actualize, developing team members' capabilities, emphasizing teamwork, delegating, and eliminating barriers to success.

8. Leaders need to develop effective coaching skills. These skills include knowing how to assess employees' skills, developing those skills, giving emotional support, providing specific feedback, using Socratic coaching, and showing high expectations.

TYING IT ALL TOGETHER

Teamwork plays an important role in most companies today. In some companies, the entire structure is organized around teams—as it was, for instance at Published Image, Inc. In other companies, such as GE and Johnsonville Foods, entire facilities are organized around teams; in these organizations self-managing teams of highly trained workers are responsible for discrete, self-contained tasks. In GE's Durham aircraft engine plant, for example, a team builds an entire engine from beginning to end.

Managing teams like these calls on all the leadership skills discussed in the last three chapters. For example, the leadership style that works in one situation may not work in another. Even though coaching and support might be the usual prescriptions for leading a team at work, there are times when some discipline is required. Similarly, motivating a team requires a shrewd balance of material rewards and recognition, and building an effective team requires all the communication skills a leader can muster.

It often happens that teams are created as part of a broader organizational change and development program. Indeed (as companies like Levi Strauss have found to their chagrin), instituting teamwork without considering the broader context of the organization and the other changes that must also take place can lead to problems. In the following chapter we therefore turn to the topic of managing organizational and cultural change.

KEY TERMS

employee involvement program 392
group norms 394
group cohesiveness 394

suggestion team 395
problem-solving team 395
semi-autonomous team 395
self-managing team 395

quality circle 396
venture team 396
transnational team 396

CRITICAL THINKING EXERCISES

1. In many of the exercises throughout this book, you have been working in teams. Compare class and team cohesiveness as the semester or quarter has progressed. What factors have changed and which have remained the same? How do students react to teamwork? Are there demographic or values issues you have noted with the use of teams?

2. One of the keys to effective teams is to assemble what Jennifer James in *Thinking in the Future Tense* (Simon & Schuster, 1996) calls *thinking skills*. She discusses a number of approaches, including evaluating and identifying your thinking (pp. 190–206). Many of her points can be directly applied to teams. Using Edward De Bono's Hat analysis, she gives us an easy way to understand what approach to thinking people take by relating them to imaginary hats they are wearing. This is a condensed version of his guide:

   ■ White hat—The white-hat thinker is mainly concerned with facts and figures.

   ■ Red hat—The red-hat thinker operates from an emotional source.

   ■ Black hat—The black-hat thinker dwells on why something cannot be done.

   ■ Yellow, hat—The yellow-hat thinker is optimistic.

   ■ Green hat—The green-hat thinker is creative and open to new ideas.

   ■ Blue hat—The blue hat thinker is concerned with control.

   Which hat do you wear at school, work, home, or with friends? Does the same hat always apply? If a team had one each of these hat types, how do you think it would solve a problem such as downsizing a company, deciding to merger with another company, or working together on day-to-day projects? What would happen if only green, yellow, and black hats were a team? What about if only white, red, and blue hats were a team? Be prepared to discuss and debate in class.

EXPERIENTIAL EXERCISES

1. Your class has just been appointed by the university administration to form teams to help address racial conflict and hate crimes against minorities. Your goal is to create a plan to promote cultural awareness among the student body and to make positive links with the surrounding ethnically diverse community.

   The administration prefers each team to consist of students from several constituencies. Assume that those represented are to include the African American Honor Society, the Latino Community Outreach Group, the Disabled Students Coalition, the ROTC, the Gay and Lesbian Alliance, Christian Outreach, the Young Republicans, the Asian-Pacific Compact, and the Older Students Awareness Association.

   Break into groups of five and select a team leader for each group. Then try to have each remaining member represent, or role-play that they represent, a group such as those from the list above. Now create the plan requested by the administration.

   When your plan is complete, be prepared to present it to the class, staying in your role. After role playing, discuss the impact the exercise had on you, others, and the team.

2. Some companies have built their management foundation on teams and teamwork rather than a bureaucratic structure. Companies such as Southwest Airlines, Saturn, and Whole Foods Markets decided against a bureaucratic structure and adopted a team approach. Other companies, such as Levi Strauss, have introduced teams with less success. Research each of these companies and, using the chapter, analyze the strengths and limitations of teams, based on these companies' experiences.

We invite you to visit the Dessler companion Web site at **www.prenhall.com/dessler** for this chapter's Internet resources.

MERGING TEAMS AT CANADA'S MOST SUCCESSFUL RAIL COMPANY

CASE 1

Over the past decade, the railway industry has been consolidating. There are fewer and fewer small companies, as large companies acquire more and more firms. There is a clear message in the industry: Unless you are large or have a large partner, you are a likely target for a takeover. Canadian National Railway (CN) understood the market forces clearly. In order to grow in a consolidating industry, it would need to acquire large firms. CN had developed a strong team culture under the leadership of its CEO, Paul Tellier. Would CN be able to absorb another large company and still keep its team-oriented management style? The test came in 1998. First, CN signed a $3 billion merger with the Illinois Central Railroad (IC). Then the newly merged firm formed a marketing alliance with the Kansas City Southern Railroad. Tellier took several steps to make sure the combined firm kept a team-oriented management style.

First, regardless of industry forces, Tellier wanted all the managers to have a shared vision. He understood that Illinois Central provided a perfect complement to CN. The CN–IC merger was a perfect fit (because of complementary assets) at the perfect time (NAFTA was increasing north–south rail traffic). Those facts helped ensure a shared vision of a great railway moving freight north and south.

Second, the management team at CN flooded the employees with communications. Within the first 48 hours of the CN–IC merger, Tellier's team made conference calls to both CN and IC employees. The team also set up a toll-free number to handle employee questions about the merger.

While postacquisition integration can typically take years, it seems apparent from company results that the two formerly separate companies are functioning well as a unit. In 1998, CN announced that it had won the Carrier of the Year 1998 award from Occidental Chemical Corporation for the third consecutive year. CN had been rated first in performance, ranking ahead of eight other Class 1 railroads.

Discussion Questions

1. What concerns might IC managers have about forming teams with their new partner, CN?

2. What steps did Tellier take to build teamwork among his management team?

3. What additional steps would you recommend that Tellier take in the future to build teamwork among managers? Among non-managerial employees?

FROM A UNION TO A COOPERATIVE: TEAM BUILDING AT THE COLORADO SYMPHONY ORCHESTRA

CASE 2

Anyone checking the Web site of the Colorado Symphony Orchestra (CSO) at the turn of the millennium would have been greeted by a friendly message that the weekend concert series was sold out. A first-time visitor to the site would not realize that this orchestra, both artistically and financially successful, was largely the same group of musicians who watched their Denver Symphony Orchestra (DSO) declare bankruptcy in the late 1980s. The group then decided to change its style and create a new team approach to orchestra management and a new orchestra. The CSO was then founded in 1989.

In 1989 the DSO, which had served the community in one form or another for over 55 years, was dissolved. In 1986, the Denver Symphony Association had faced a deficit of close to $750,000. The board told orchestra members they could accept a 20% cut in pay or the organization would file for bankruptcy. With some reluctance, the musicians accepted the cut. In 1987, the musicians agreed to a three-year contract. While the orchestra's future seemed more promising, further difficulties lay ahead. In 1988, the board announced yet another $700,000 shortfall. It asked the musicians to reopen their contract, but they refused.

By 1989, the situation was bleak. The board announced a "comeback season," with a new barebones budget that included a 50% pay cut for the musicians. For 1990, the board was offering musicians a salary of $11,000 for the 21-week season. On August 14, 1989, the musicians unanimously rejected the proposed salary package. Thirty days later, 50 musicians gathered at the Boettcher Hall concert site and voted the CSO into existence.

DSO's traditional orchestra management model was complicated. Ticket sales were never enough to fund the full cost of production, so orchestras relied heavily on contributions from patrons to cover costs. These patrons often had advisory roles, and could exert financial pressure by withholding gifts. An executive director usually managed the business side of an orchestra, while the artistic side was typically managed by a music director. The musicians were usually unionized. At DSO, there was a long history of labor management problems. There were four work stoppages between 1973 and 1980, the longest of which was over 11 weeks.

The newly organized CSO musicians opted for a different model—a partnership, or cooperative team. The basic concept was that all the stakeholders—musicians, staff members, and board—were to share in making decisions that affected the outcomes for the CSO. They planned to share the risks and potential rewards of running the orchestra as a team. According to Erin Lehman, program director of The Arts & Culture Initiative at the Kennedy School of Government, Harvard University, no other orchestra in the country was being managed like the CSO.[97]

One of the key elements that made the agreement unique was the high level of musician involvement in managing the business. The musicians made a substantial financial commitment to the orchestra. They agreed to accept a low salary for the potential to share in surpluses generated at year-end. The goal was to keep musicians' salaries at no more than 50% of the operating budget. Since the musicians were making such a strong financial commitment, they were also given a stronger voice in the operation of the orchestra. They held one-third of the seats on all governing committees, and the majority of seats on the artistic committee (an area usually under the sole control of the artistic director).

The results over the next decade were extraordinary. Ticket sales, a direct measure of customer satisfaction, increased more than 2.5 times from 1991 to 1999. There were also substantial increases in contributions. The organization operated in the black for the entire decade. There was also a big increase in other types of volunteer support.

While the turnaround has not been easy, it has been successful by nearly every measure. However, the CSO isn't standing still. It has hired an experienced professional named Tom Bacchetti, former director of the Atlanta Symphony for over a decade, as executive director. Under Bacchetti's leadership, the Atlanta Symphony performance revenues grew from $1.9 million to $9.4 million. The organization has also invested in developing future audiences with an aggressive youth education program, including two series of free concerts for school groups. Recently, while the orchestra is still not achieving the level of contributions it had hoped for, it is financially stable. The team-based structure at the CSO, such a radical departure from its DSO past, has proved to be a solid base from which to lead the orchestra. One question is, how will the addition of a new, strong executive director change the dynamics of the CSO's team-based structure?

Discussion Questions

1. Based on what you read in this chapter, what team-building values, concepts, and techniques did the CSO musicians use to build their new team approach to managing the orchestra?

2. What managerial role do you see Tom Bacchetti playing in CSO's team-based organization? What skills do you think he'll need? Why?

3. To what extent could CSO's team-based structure work in other orchestras? Why?

TEAMWORK AT KNITMEDIA

One of the biggest challenges KnitMedia faces over the next few years is maintaining the strong sense of team spirit and teamwork that the company had when it was small. Having team spirit when you're only 15 or 20 employees all working together in a small office above the Knitting Factory club in downtown Manhattan is one thing; keeping alive the spirit that "we're all in this together" is quite another when the company is large and when people are scattered all over the world.

Heather Stamm, the New York club's production coordinator, puts it this way: "We do have teamwork, I think, especially in my department with programming and production and the sound stuff—we have pretty good teamwork going on. [However] there's a lot of people and a lot of departments, so you have to try really hard to make sure that everyone stays in communication, because the staff is just so large now and growing . . ."

Keeping the communication open is absolutely critical to the success of a small company like KnitMedia, since the company's size gives it one of its big advantages. Compared to its giant competitors, a small company like KnitMedia should have few of the functional boundaries preventing departments from talking with each other. Emphasizing teamwork more and instituting concrete methods for building more teamwork should therefore be very helpful for a company like KnitMedia. The question is, how to do this as the company grows? Michael Dorf and his team want your advice.

Team Exercises and Questions

Use what you know and what you learned in this chapter to answer the following questions from Michael Dorf and his management team:

1. To what extent and in what manner would you say KnitMedia should be using teams to accomplish its mission? Why?

2. How exactly would you suggest we use teams to more effectively manage our transnational operations, and particularly our expansion into new Knitting Factory clubs abroad?

3. In general, what concrete recommendations would you make regarding how KnitMedia can make more extensive use of teams?

MANAGING ORGANIZATIONAL AND CULTURAL CHANGE

WHAT'S AHEAD?

Just about everyone in the U.S. has a Kodak camera, but by the late 1990s, Kodak's annual operating earnings had fallen by 25%, and sales were stagnant. Faced with what were now insurmountable cost pressures, CEO George Fisher turned to downsizing. He replaced the head of his consumer products division, fired more than 200 high-level executives, and laid plans to eliminate up to 20,000 more jobs. By 1999 profits were on the rise, and Kodak had just introduced, in partnership with AOL, a new Internet-based service called "You've Got Pictures," a process for sharing pictures over the Internet.[1] Slowly but surely, Fisher's transformation of Kodak from a sluggish giant to a lean, mean Internet-oriented fighting machine was taking shape. During 2000, he handed the reins to another CEO.

OBJECTIVES

AFTER STUDYING THIS CHAPTER, YOU SHOULD BE ABLE TO

- List the things managers can change in organizations

- Explain why employees resist change

- Give examples of each of the eight steps for leading organizational change

- Explain how to use five organizational development techniques to change organizations

- Illustrate several techniques for overcoming individual, interpersonal, and intergroup conflicts

Why did Kodak have to change? Because companies that don't adapt to their environments don't survive.[2] For years prior to Fisher's arrival, Kodak was run almost like it had no competition, and it grew slow and unresponsive in the process. For many of these years Kodak in fact had little or no competition, and indeed (particularly in the United States) "Kodak" and "film" were almost synonymous. What the pre-Fisher management didn't recognize, however, was that global competition from firms like Fuji was a growing threat. Unless Kodak changed—unless it began cutting costs and introducing new and innovative products—it could find itself a distant second in the worldwide picture-taking market.

Technological change and intense global competition (as embodied by firms like Fuji film) have made managing organizational change an absolute requirement for millions of companies. We've seen in this book that from small companies like Rosenbluth International to giants like IBM and GE, company after company is downsizing and networking their organizations. And, they are creating self-managing teams, opening up communications (by using techniques like upward appraisals and workout forums), and installing Internet-based decision support systems.

Competition, in a nutshell, means companies have to be leaner and faster. Rapid technological change and intense competition means you either change and adapt, or you die. Here's how the *Harvard Business Review* recently put it, "Companies achieve real agility only when every function, office, strategy, goal, and process— when every person—is able and eager to rise to every challenge. This type and degree of fundamental change, commonly called *revitalization* or *transformation*, is what more and more companies seek but all too rarely achieve."[3]

In the last four chapters we've seen how leaders motivate and influence individuals and teams. Now we'll turn to an explanation of how managers lead and influence organizational and cultural change.

What to Change?

When we say "organizational change," what is it exactly that a manager can change? The answer is the company's strategy, culture, structure, tasks, technologies, and the attitudes and skills of the company's people.

Strategic Change Strategic change refers to a shift in the firm's strategy, mission, and vision. A strategic change may then lead to other organizational changes—for instance, in the firm's technology, structure, or culture.

strategic change
a change in a firm's strategy, mission, or vision.

We've already touched on strategic change examples elsewhere in this book. On becoming Kodak's CEO, for instance, one of Fisher's first strategic changes was to refocus the firm more fully on digital cameras and photography. When Steve Jobs assumed the interim CEO title at Apple Computer several years ago, one of his first strategic moves was to refocus Apple on a much narrower set of products and to emphasize the reemergence of the Macintosh (iMac) computer. Previously focused on PCs, Microsoft's new strategy is to provide the software people need to run their computers "anytime, anywhere"—including, for instance, cell-phone–based Web browsers—to do Internet-based computing. Entrepreneurs must change strategies too, as the *Entrepreneurs in Action* box illustrates.

Strategic changes like those at Apple, Kodak, and Netiva redefine a company's basic direction and are thus among the riskiest (but most important) changes man-

▶ As you can imagine, fast-changing Internet companies also make strategic changes, but at breakneck speed. The experience of Gary Steele, the new CEO of the Internet firm Netiva, is a good example. When he joined Netiva in June 1997, the company seemed a sure bet. It produced and sold an Internet application system that let large companies use the Java programming language to build Web databases.[4]

But after a few months, it became obvious to Steele that something was very wrong. For one thing, technical support was gobbling up Netiva's profits. Netiva had designed its applications for the customer to run and maintain, but Netiva's technical people had to spend days with each customer to get the application up to speed. To make matters worse, the original strategy assumed that customers would develop multiple applications using Netiva's software, and would therefore have to pay multiple license fees. But that wasn't happening: "They were just buying one [license]," said Steele, "so we were doing a lot of work for just $25,000."

By April 1998 Steele knew he was going to have to take drastic measures. Within one week, 40% of the company's employees—including most of the sales and marketing staff—were gone. The next day he met with his executive team to tell them Netiva would no longer be selling Java-based database tools. He spent the rest of the meeting outlining an eight-step plan of action for reformulating the company's strategy over the next six weeks.

Steel and his four executives held 75 fact-finding meetings with executives at-large and midsize companies and swapped notes about what they'd found. One thing they found was that their customers wanted technology, but they wanted that technology without the hassle of installing and endlessly maintaining software. What they wanted, in other words, were "hosted services," where the software vendor runs and maintains complicated applications on its own servers, and the customer's employees access them via the Internet.

Netiva has now changed its name to Portera, and its new product is called ServicePort. Using a Web browser, a customer's employees can use ServicePort to do things like share client reports, schedule group meetings, and get press releases and news. The company has jumped to 70 employees, and a venture capitalist just invested $14 million to help Portera reach the next level.

agers can make. What triggers such changes, and why are they so risky? We can summarize some recent research findings as follows:

1. *Strategic changes are usually triggered by factors outside the company*. External threats or challenges, such as deregulation, intensified global competition, and dramatic technological innovations like the Internet are usually the ones that prompt organizations to embark on companywide, strategic changes.[5]

2. *Strategic changes are often required for survival*. Researchers found that making a strategic change did not guarantee success, but that firms which failed to change generally failed to survive. This was especially true when what they called "discontinuous" environmental change—change of an unexpected nature, such as happened when the Internet made bookselling more competitive—required quick and effective strategic change for the firms to survive.

3. *Strategic changes implemented under crisis conditions are highly risky*. Of all organizational changes, strategic, organizationwide ones initiated under crisis conditions and with short time constraints (like those of Kodak and Apple) were the riskiest. They eventually require changing more aspects of the organization, including its core values.[6] Core values tend to be hard to change, so changing them tends to trigger the most resistance from employees.

Other organizational changes may be required as well, either as a result of the strategic change or for some other reason. For example, it may be impossible to fully implement the strategic change without changing the *culture*—the shared values—

of the firm's employees. When Louis Gerstner took over as CEO of IBM, one of his first tasks was refocusing employees' attention on core values like competitiveness, open communications, and moving fast. Similarly, the new strategy may precipitate a new *structure*: For instance, given Fisher's strategy of emphasizing digital photography, one of his first organizational moves was to group together in one new division all Kodak's digital product teams. Reorganizing is, as we've seen, an increasingly popular approach to change, with companies around the world generally moving to more responsive, team-based, boundaryless type organizations.

In turn, a new organization structure may require a change in tasks, or what experts call *task redesign*. The day-to-day tasks of team members in newly organized teams are generally different than they were when the firm was organized around traditional functions. Many of the preceding changes result from *technological change*, in other words from modifications to the work methods the organization uses to accomplish its tasks, as when a computerized payroll system is installed to replace an antiquated manual system.

Finally, it may be the *employees* themselves who have to change. Perhaps they haven't the skills to do their new jobs, for instance, or morale is so low that steps must be taken to improve attitudes. This is where managers call on training and development techniques like lectures, conferences, and computer-based training to improve employees skills. At other times, the "people" problems stem from misunderstandings or conflicts; in this case organizational development interventions like those discussed below may be used to try to change attitudes and thereby behavior.

MANAGING @ THE *SPEED* OF THOUGHT

Business Process Reengineering

Today, "reorganizing" and task redesign usually doesn't just mean pushing boxes around on an organization chart. Instead, it means reorganizing the company in order to take advantage of some new technology. Business reengineering is one example.

Business reengineering has been defined as "the radical redesign of business processes, combining steps to cut waste and eliminate repetitive, paper-intensive tasks in order to improve cost, quality, and service, and to maximize the benefits of information technology."[7] The approach is to (1) identify a business process to be redesigned (such as approving a mortgage application), (2) measure the performance of the existing processes, (3) identify opportunities to improve these processes, and (4) redesign and implement a new way of doing the work.

A system implemented at Banc One Mortgage provides an example. As illustrated in Figure 14.1, Banc One redesigned its mortgage application process so that it required fewer steps and reduced processing time from 17 days to 2. In the past, a mortgage applicant completed a paper loan application that the bank then entered in its computer system. A series of specialists such as credit analysts and underwriters evaluated the application individually as it moved through eight different departments.

Banc One replaced the sequential operation with a *work cell*, or team, approach. Loan originators in the field now entered the mortgage application directly into laptop computers, where software checked it for completeness. The information was then transmitted electronically to regional production centers, where specialists like credit analysts and loan underwriters convened electronically, working as a team to review the mortgage together—at once. Then after the loan had been formally closed, another team of specialists set up the loan for servicing.

> **business reengineering**
> the radical redesign of business processes to cut waste; to improve cost, quality, and service; and to maximize the benefits of information technology, generally by questioning how and why things are being done as they are.

▼ **FIGURE 14.1**

Redesigning Mortgage Processing at Banc One

By redesigning its mortgage processing system and the mortgage application process, Banc One will be able to handle the increased paperwork as it moves from processing 33,000 loans per year to processing 300,000 loans per year.

Shifting from a traditional approach helped Banc One Mortgage slash processing time from 17 days to 2

BEFORE
Desk-to-desk approach

Paper application

Loan processing in multiple locations by specialists such as credit analysts and underwriters.

Loan servicing by specialists (insurance, escrow, etc.).

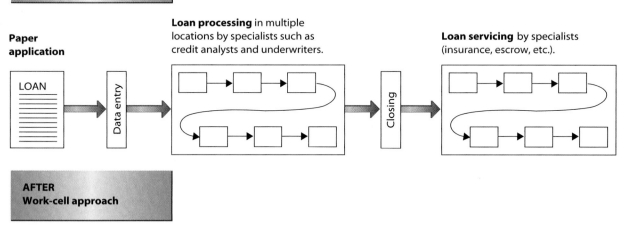

AFTER
Work-cell approach

Application on laptop computer

Regional production center: Teams process open applications.

Servicing: Specialists work together as a team.

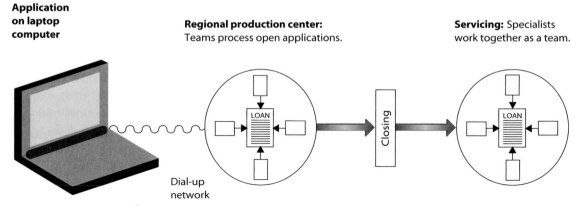

Source: Adapted from Mitch Betts, "Banc One Mortgage Melts Paper Blizzard," *Computerworld*, 14 December 1992. Copyright by Computerworld, Inc., Framingham, MA 01701. Reprinted from *Computerworld* by permission.

Companies' experience with reengineering underscores the importance of the organizational change process. While reengineering with the aid of information technology has had its share of successes, some estimate failure rates to be as high as 70%.[8] When a reengineering effort does fail, it is often due to behavioral factors. Sometimes (as in other change efforts) employees resist the change and deliberately undermine the revised procedures. If business processes are reengineered without considering the new skill requirements, training, and reporting relationships involved, the usual employee resistance problems can be exacerbated. As John Champy, a long-time reengineering proponent, has said, "In short, reducing hierarchy, bureaucracy, and the rest of it is not just a matter of rearranging the furniture to face our customers and markets. It is a matter of rearranging the quality of people's attachments—to their work and to each other. These are *cultural* matters."[9]

Organizational changes differ in their breadth and urgency—changes can range from big to little, in other words. Some changes are *incremental*: They may require reorganizing just one department or establishing work teams in a single plant. At the other extreme, *strategic organizational changes* affect the entire company and usually change not just the company's strategy, but also its structure, culture, people, and processes.[10]

Why Do People Resist Change?

Overcoming resistance is often the hardest part of leading a change. As Niccolò Machiavelli, a shrewd observer of 16th-century Italian politics, once said: "There is nothing so difficult to implement as change, since those in favor of the change will often be small in number while those opposing the change will be numerous and enthusiastic in their resistance to change."[11] Indeed, even the best leaders would agree that implementing large-scale change is enormously challenging. GE's Jack Welch once said that even after 10 years of continual change, he expected that it would take at least 10 more years to rejuvenate GE's culture.[12]

The fact that a change is advisable or even mandatory doesn't mean employees will accept it. In fact, it's often the company's key people—perhaps even some top and middle managers—who are the most resistant; they may just prefer the status quo.

It's easy to see how such resistance might arise. Take a personal example: Suppose you've been attending a college class in management, with the college's best professor, and several weeks into the semester the dean comes in and announces that some students will have to be moved to another professor and class because the fire marshal says the lecture hall is overcrowded. You've been asked to move. How would you react? What would go through your mind? Probably several things: that your grade might be adversely affected; that you don't want to leave the friends you've made in this class and start all over again; that it might be just a tad embarrassing to have to get up and leave (although obviously it's not your fault); and that it's not fair that you should be one of those singled out to leave. You don't want to go!

In his book *Beyond the Wall of Resistance*, author-consultant Rick Maurer says resistance can stem from two sets of things. What he calls Level 1 resistance is based on lack of information or on honest disagreement over the facts. In this case, everything is on the table, and there are no hidden agendas. Level 2 resistance is more personal and emotional. Here, people are afraid—that the change may cost them their jobs, or to lose face, or reduce their control (or in our case, lower their grades). Maurer points out that treating all resistance as if it were Level 1 (and simply caused by an honest disagreement and lack of information) can make a company miss the mark in its change efforts. For example, using "slick visual presentations to explain change with nice neat facts, charts, and time lines, when what people really want to hear is: 'what does this mean to them?'" can be a recipe for disaster.[13]

Years ago, Professor Paul Lawrence said it's usually not the technical aspects of a change that employees resist, but its social consequences, "the changes in their human relationships that generally accompany the technical change."[14] Thus, they may see in the change diminished responsibilities for themselves and therefore lower status in the organization and less job security. Sometimes it's not fear of the obvious consequence, but rather apprehension about the unknown consequences that produces resistance. For example, how much do you know about the professor who'll be teaching that new class you're being moved to, and about the new classmates you'll be joining? Not much, unfortunately.

You've also probably noticed that some people are inherently more resistant to change than others. At the extreme, in fact, some people are simply recalcitrant, which basically means they'll almost always resist change as a knee-jerk reaction. People like these are continually "fighting the system." As you might imagine, they are usually not the sorts of employees who contribute in a positive way to organizational change.

One recent study took place in six organizations—two large European companies, two Australian banks, a large U.S. university, and a Korean manufacturing firm. Its aim was to determine the extent to which managers' responses to organizational change were influenced by various personality traits. Three personality traits—tolerance for ambiguity, having a positive self-concept, and being more tolerant of risk—significantly predicted effectiveness in coping with change.[15] Those with the lowest self-image, least tolerance for ambiguity, and least tolerance for risk appeared, as expected, to be the most resistant.

Overcoming Resistance to Change

unfreezing

a step in psychologist Kurt Lewin's model of change that involves reducing the forces for the status quo, usually by presenting a provocative problem or event to get people to recognize the need for change and to search for new solutions.

What tools are available to overcome resistance? In Table 14.1, John Kotter and Leonard Schlesinger summarize the pros and cons of some methods leaders use to deal with resistance to change. For example, education and communication are appropriate where inaccurate or missing information is contributing to employee resistance. Negotiation and agreement may be appropriate if one group will clearly lose by the change and that group has considerable power to resist. Coercion—forcing the change—can be a fast way of pushing through a change and is widely used, particularly when speed is essential. It can be effective when the manager has the power to force the change, but risky if it leaves influential employees with a residue of ill will.

Psychologist Kurt Lewin proposed a famous model to summarize the basic process for implementing a change with minimal resistance. To Lewin, all behavior in organizations was a product of two kinds of forces: those striving to maintain the status quo, and those pushing for change. Implementing change thus meant either reducing the forces for the status quo or building up the forces for change. Lewin's process consists of three steps: unfreezing, moving, and refreezing.

Unfreezing means reducing the forces that are striving to maintain the status quo, usually by presenting a provocative problem or event to get people to recognize the need for change and to search for new solutions. Without unfreezing, said Lewin, change will not occur. Attitude surveys, interview results, or participatory informational meetings are often used to provide such provocative events. For example, when he took over as CEO of the Dutch electronics firm Philips, Jan Timmer invited the company's top 100 managers to an off-site retreat. Here he gave them a shock: a hypothetical press release that said Philips was bankrupt and that it was up to the 100 managers to bring the company back from the brink.[16] In the fast-changing electronics industry, Timmer then got a shock of his own: Within three years he was replaced by Cor Boostra, who pledged to make the ruthless cost-cutting changes that Timmer—despite his start—failed to implement.[17]

▲ Jan Timmer, former CEO of the Dutch electronics firm Philips.

TABLE 14.1 Six Methods for Dealing with Resistance to Change

Method	Commonly Used in Situations	Advantages	Drawbacks
Education + communication	Where there is a lack of information or inaccurate information and analysis.	Once persuaded, people will often help with the implementation of the change.	Can be very time-consuming if lots of people are involved.
Participation + involvement	Where the initiators do not have all the information they need to design the change, and where others have considerable power to resist.	People who participate will be committed to implementing change, and any relevant information they have will be integrated into the change plan.	Can be very time-consuming if participators design an inappropriate change.
Facilitation + support	Where people are resisting because of fear and anxiety.	No other approach works as well with employee adjustment problems.	Can be time-consuming and expensive, yet still fail.
Negotiation + agreement	Where someone or some group will clearly lose out in a change, and where that group has considerable power to resist.	Sometimes it is a relatively easy way to avoid major resistance.	Can be too expensive in many cases if it prompts others to negotiate.
Manipulation + co-optation	Where other tactics will not work or are too expensive.	It can be a relatively quick and inexpensive solution to resistance problems.	Can lead to future problems if people feel manipulated.
Coercion	Where speed is essential, and the change initiators possess considerable power.	It is speedy and can overcome any kind of resistance.	Can be risky if it leaves people angry at the initiators.

Source: Adapted and reprinted by permission of *Harvard Business Review.* "Six Methods for Dealing with Change," from "Choosing Strategies for Change," by John P. Kotter and Leonard A. Schlesinger, March–April 1979. Copyright © 1979 by the President and Fellows of Harvard College; all rights reserved.

Lewin's second step aims to shift or alter the behavior of the people in the department or organization in which the changes are to take place. **Moving** means developing new behaviors, values, and attitudes, sometimes through structure changes, and sometimes through the sorts of change and development techniques in Table 14.1, and which we'll discuss later in this chapter.

Lewin assumed that organizations tended to revert to their old ways of doing things unless the new ways were continually reinforced. This reinforcement is

moving

a step in psychologist Kurt Lewin's model of change aimed at using techniques and actually altering the behaviors, values, and attitudes of the individuals in an organization.

accomplished by **refreezing** the organization into its new state of equilibrium. Lewin advocated instituting new systems and procedures that would support and maintain the changes that were made. For example, Gerstner installed new pay and incentive plans at IBM to emphasize the superiority of performance over seniority.

▶ AN EIGHT-STEP PROCESS FOR LEADING ORGANIZATIONAL CHANGE

Changes may involve the firm's strategy, culture, structure, tasks, or technologies, or the attitudes and skills of its people. The changes may have to be incremental or strategic. And they may trigger various levels of resistance. In any case, the manager needs a basic process for leading and implementing the organizational change. In this section we focus on an eight-step process: creating a sense of urgency; creating a guiding coalition and mobilizing commitment; developing and then communicating a shared vision; empowering employees; generating short-term wins; consolidating gain; anchoring the new ways of doing things; and monitoring progress and adjusting the vision. In applying this 8-step process, keep in mind that implementing a change is like solving any problem: You have to recognize the problem, diagnose it, and then formulate and implement a solution.

Create a Sense of Urgency

You've become aware of the need for change, what do you do now? Do you simply paper over the problems (see the cartoon), or do you take more positive steps? Most experienced leaders instinctively know they've got to unfreeze the old habits, often by creating a sense of urgency. Timmer knew he had to rouse his top managers out of their status-quo thinking. He did this with his hypothetical bankruptcy press release.

Urgency does more than overcome employees' traditional reasons for resisting change: It can also jar them out of their complacency. In organizations, several things can leave employees feeling complacent.[18] These include the absence of a major and visible crisis, too many visible resources, low overall performance standards, and a lack of sufficient performance feedback from external sources. When

© 1997 Randy Glasbergen.

"Your job will be to walk funny and look really cute, so nobody notices how horrible it is to work here."

complacency sets in (as it did in many companies, including IBM and Kodak in the 1980s), something must be done to create a sense of urgency so that employees will be more open to change. How do you create such a sense of urgency?[19] A partial list includes the following:

- Create a crisis by allowing a financial loss or exposing managers to major weaknesses relative to competitors.

- Eliminate obvious examples of excess such as company-owned country club facilities, numerous aircraft, or gourmet executive dining rooms.

- Set targets for revenue, income, productivity, customer satisfaction, and product development cycle time so high that they can't be reached by conducting business as usual.

- Send more data about customer satisfaction and financial performance to more employees, especially information that demonstrates weaknesses relative to competitors.

Create a Guiding Coalition and Mobilize Commitment

Major transformations—such as Fisher accomplished in 1998 by transforming Kodak into an Internet- and digital-oriented company—are often associated with one highly visible leader. But no leader can accomplish any major change alone. That's why most leaders create a guiding coalition of influential people who can be missionaries and implementers of change. The coalition should include people with enough power to lead the change effort, and it's essential to encourage the group to work together as a team.

In this process, the managers have to choose the right lieutenants. One reason to create the coalition is to gather political support; the leader therefore has to ensure that there are enough key players on board so that those left out can't easily block progress.[20] The coalition's members should also have the expertise, credibility, and leadership skills to explain and implement the change.

Many leaders then create one or more broad, employee-based task forces to diagnose the company's problems. This can produce a shared understanding of what can and must be improved, and thus mobilize the commitment of those who must actually implement the change.

Develop and Communicate a Shared Vision

In Chapter 10 ("Being a Leader") we saw that it's the leader's job to provide direction. Whether that "direction" is a statement of vision, mission, or objectives depends on what the leader wants to achieve and the level at which he or she is acting.

To transform an organization, a new vision is usually required, "a general statement of the organization's intended direction that evokes emotional feelings in organization members." For example, when Barry Gibbons became CEO of a drifting Spec's Music retail chain, its employees, owners, and bankers—all its stakeholders—required a vision of a renewed Spec's around which they could rally. Gibbons's vision of a leaner Spec's offering a diversified blend of concerts and retail music helped to provide the sense of direction they all required.

Change expert Kotter says that "the real power of a vision is unleashed only when most of those involved in an enterprise or activity have a common understanding of its goals and direction."[21] In other words, fostering support for the new vision is impossible unless the vision has been effectively communicated. What are the key steps in effectively communicating a vision? They include the following:

- *Keep it simple.* Here is an example of a good statement of vision: "We are going to become faster than anyone else in our industry at satisfying customer needs."
- *Use multiple forums.* Try to use every channel possible—big meetings and small, memos and newspapers, formal and informal interaction—to spread the word.
- *Use repetition.* Ideas sink in deeply only after they have been heard many times.
- *Lead by example.* "Walk the talk" so that your behaviors and decisions are consistent with the vision you espouse.

Empower Employees to Make the Change

Accomplishing a change that transforms an organization usually requires the assistance of the employees themselves. To get that assistance, change experts advise empowering the employees. As one expert explains:

> Major internal transformation rarely happens unless many people assist. Yet employees generally won't help, or can't help, if they feel relatively powerless. Hence the relevance of empowerment.[22]

The next step, therefore, is to empower employees, to give them the wherewithal to help make the change. This starts with removing the barriers to empowerment. This idea is summarized in Figure 14.2. By now employees understand the vision and want to make it a reality, but they're boxed in: lack of skills means they can't act; formal structures and systems make it difficult to act; or bosses may discourage implementing the new vision. The leader's job is to see that such barriers are removed.

There are many potential barriers, and therefore many ways to remove them. When he took over as CEO of Sony and its loss-making movie studios, Nobuyuki Idei proceeded, in a most un-Japanese way, to fire all the studio executives and install a new team of industry veterans, with a mandate to fix Sony's movie business.[23] At Allied Signal, CEO Lawrence Bossidy put all of his 80,000 people through quality training within two years. He also created area "councils" (for instance, for Asia), so that employees who were undertaking initiatives in those areas could get together, share market intelligence, and compare notes.[24]

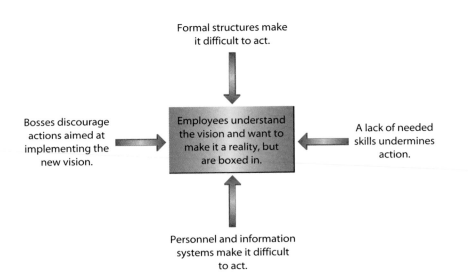

► FIGURE 14.2

Barriers to Empowerment

Source: Reprinted by permission of Harvard Business School Press. From *Leading Change* by John P. Kotter. Boston, MA, 1996, p. 102. Copyright © 1996 by the President and Fellows of Harvard College; all rights reserved.

Formal structures make it difficult to act.

Bosses discourage actions aimed at implementing the new vision.

Employees understand the vision and want to make it a reality, but are boxed in

A lack of needed skills undermines action.

Personnel and information systems make it difficult to act.

Jacques Nasser, Ford Motor Company's newly appointed CEO, took a similar approach. His vision at Ford was aimed at getting employees to think like shareholders and at having the company as a whole respond swiftly to and anticipate customers' needs. Ensuring that Ford's employees had the knowledge and skills they needed to operate at this level was central to Nassers transformation; he therefore implemented an extensive program of what he called "teaching" throughout the giant corporation. As he put it, "the programs we use are many and varied— Capstone, the Business Leadership Initiative, and Executive Partnering, to name just three."[25]

Table 14.2 summarizes four of the most widely used programs in the new curriculum at Ford. The Business Leadership Initiative, for example, is open to all salaried employees. In this program, the employees' managers provide three days of teaching and discussion on such matters as the contrast between the old and new Ford Motor Company.

Chevron uses a change process it calls "direct participation" to help strip away the barriers and give its employees what they need to help with the change. Large-scale conferences—basically two- to three-day

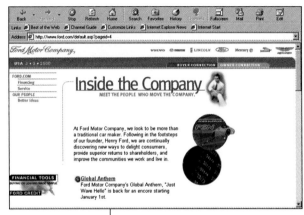

▲ **W E B N O T E**

Ford uses the Web to communicate with customers as well as to interact with vendors and help train its employees.

www.ford.com

Used with permission.

TABLE 14.2 The New Curriculum at Ford

Program	Participants	Teachers	Components
Capstone	24 senior executives at a time	Jacques Nasser and his leadership team	▪ Conducted once a year ▪ About 20 days of teaching and discussion ▪ Teams given six months to solve major strategic challenges ▪ 360-degree feedback ▪ Community service
Business Leadership Initiative	All Ford salaried employees—55,000 to date	The participants' managers	▪ Three days of teaching and discussion ▪ Teams assigned to 100-day projects ▪ Community service ▪ 360-degree feedback ▪ Participants make videos that contrast the old with the new Ford
Executive Partnering	Promising young managers—12 so far	Nasser and his leadership team	▪ Participants spend eight weeks shadowing seven senior executives
Let's Chat About the Business	Everyone who receives e-mail at Ford— about 100,000 employees	Nasser	▪ Weekly e-mails describing Ford's new approach to business

Source: Reprinted by permission of the Harvard Business Review, An exhibit from "Driving Change: An Interview with Ford Motor Company's Jacques Nasser" by Jacques Nasser and Suzy Wetlaufer, March–April 1999 Copyright © 1999 by the President and Fellows of Harvard College; all rights reserved.

▲ Chevron training teams: Y2K contingency planning workshop, where direct participation is a key change process.

events—are at the heart of the direct participation process. During these conferences, large numbers of employees and other participants meet to address a problem or an issue that calls for change, and to produce detailed recommendations that can be implemented fast. In addition to the exhilaration that can result from participating in such an exercise, direct participation conferences like these "bring multiple perspectives to bear on the problem and identify the changes needed to resolve it."[26]

Sometimes empowerment just means letting the employees find their own way, rather than forcing the changes on them. In one successful change, an engineering department spent nearly a year analyzing how to implement the team concept: The engineers conducted surveys, held off-site meetings, and analyzed various alternatives before deciding on a matrix management approach that the department members felt would work for them.[27]

Generate Short-Term Wins

Transforming a company can take time, but most people need reinforcement periodically to see that their efforts are working. Maintaining employees' motivation to stay involved in the change therefore requires planning for and creating short-term wins.

The leader can't just hope that short-term wins will materialize.[28] For example, the guiding coalition in one manufacturing company intentionally set its sights on producing one highly visible and successful new product about 20 months after the start of an organizational renewal effort.[29] The new product was selected in part because the coalition knew that its introduction was doable. And they knew that the introduction would provide the positive feedback required to renew the sense of urgency and motivation.

Consolidate Gains and Produce More Change

As momentum builds and changes are made, the leader has to guard against renewed complacency. That's why it's crucial, while employees are generating short-term wins, to consolidate the gains that have been made and produce even more change. How?

One approach is to use the increased credibility that comes from short-term wins to change all the systems, structures, and policies that don't fit well with the company's new vision. In one company, for example, when a vice president for operations saw the writing on the wall and left the firm, the position was left vacant; the two departments that had reported to him—engineering and manufacturing—now reported to the general manager. This helped to formalize the cross-functional nature of the new team approach at this firm.[30]

Anchor the New Ways of Doing Things in the Company Culture

The organizational change won't survive without a corresponding change in employees' shared values. A "team-based, quality-oriented, adaptable organization" is not going to happen if the company's shared values still emphasize selfishness, mediocrity, and bureaucratic behavior. We'll look more closely at how to mold culture in the following pages.

Monitor Progress and Adjust the Vision as Required

Finally, it's essential that the company have a mechanism for monitoring the effectiveness of the change and for recommending remedial actions. One firm appointed an oversight team composed of managers, a union representative, an engineer, and several others to monitor the functioning of its new self-managing teams. In another firm, regular morale surveys were used to monitor employee attitudes.

Change in Action: Becoming an E-Business

Every business is becoming an e-business today. As *Fortune* recently put it, "e or be eaten": Either link your business to the Web, or say goodbye to your business.

As a result, just about every business today—not just familiar e-businesses like Amazon.com—is getting on the Web. GM, Ford, and the other automakers are marketing cars over the Web, and will soon purchase all or most of their billions of dollars of supplies via Internet links with suppliers. Banc One recently sponsored an "immersion day" in New York City to introduce the press to its new online spin-off—an Internet bank called wingspanbank.com.[31] At Sears, CEO Arthur C. Martinez said he was "a serious skeptic for a long time," but Sears too has jumped on the e-business bandwagon, as have Procter & Gamble, Toys "Я" Us, Southwest Airlines, Lands' End, and even the U.S. Postal Service.

The problem, as one observer put it, is that "blending old business and e business—'clicks and mortar' as some call it—is for the most part a difficult, awkward process."[32] For one thing, the cultures are often widely different. Most Sears headquarters employees are housed in comfortable offices in company headquarters. In their Internet division at Hoffman Estates, Illinois, Sears's e-employees, including its former treasurer, have small cubicles and "boxes lie everywhere."[33]

Major strategic and structural changes may be required when moving into e-business as well. For example, when Charles Schwab first established its Internet-based trading system, the strategy was to run it as a separate business from its conventional office-based trading network. Within two years, however, it became apparent that the two were competing, so Schwab had to take the painful steps required to actually merge two different businesses.

What sorts of organizational changes can you expect when moving from a conventional to an Internet-based business? "Entering the e-commerce realm is like managing at 90 mph. E-business affects finance, human resources, training, supply-chain management, customer-resource management, and just about every other corporate function. This puts the managers of these departments in a new light," says the chief strategist for one e-business.[34]

For example, you have to decide whether to blend the new e-business into the company's existing structure or organize the e-commerce operation as a completely separate entity. If the decision is made to blend the two entities, some argue that rather than assigning one manager the job of coming up with an e-strategy, "it's far better to develop an organizational structure that puts the Web and e business at the central focus of a cross-departmental business group, rather than merely adding Web responsibilities to a preexisting task list."[35] Greg Rogers, who heads up Whirlpool Corporation's e-commerce operation, points out that the company's strategy will have to change, too: "Internet strategy is really business strategy."[36] The company's new business strategy will have to reflect the fact that the company now embraces e-commerce as part of its competitive advantage.

As with any major change, there is resistance.[37] For example, "one of the early organizational barriers (Michael) Dell had to overcome was convincing everybody that the Web wasn't just a science project—that the Web could be used to conduct a real business," says the director of Dell Online. That means, of course, that top executives need to understand and be committed to the Web and then take a leadership role in overcoming resistance.

▶ THE LEADER'S ROLE IN ORGANIZATIONAL AND CULTURAL CHANGE

change advocate

leader who champions organizational change, often by cajoling, inspiring, and negotiating it.

charismatic leadership

guidance from leaders who possess envisioning, energizing, and enabling qualities that mobilize and sustain activity within an organization.

Organizational and cultural changes usually don't take place spontaneously. Instead, they're triggered by problems and opportunities, and then driven by leaders like Gary Steele and Steve Jobs. And the "leader" doesn't necessarily mean just the CEO or top executive. While the person leading the change is often the CEO (like Kodak's Fisher), the leader may also be an office manager, or perhaps a champion who assumes the role of cajoling, inspiring, and negotiating a new product successfully through the firm until it's produced. Such leaders—called **change advocates**, or champions—also play a major role in any organizational change.

We've looked so far at the nature of organizational change and at an 8-step process for leading change. Now we'll look more closely at what change leaders actually do.

▲   Louis Gerstner, former chairman and CEO of IBM, in his office. Gerstner's instrumental leadership skills turned IBM around.

The Leader's Role in Strategic Change

Nowhere is the role of leadership more obvious or more important than in the sorts of organizationwide strategic changes implemented at firms like Kodak, Apple, and Netiva. A careful analysis of leaders in firms like these suggests three crucial change leader functions: charismatic, instrumental, and missionary leadership.[38]

Charismatic Leadership   David Nadler and Michael Tushman say that leading a successful change requires charismatic leaders who possess "a special quality that enables the leader to mobilize and sustain activity within an organization."[39] **Charismatic leadership** consist of three behaviors: envisioning, energizing, and enabling. As summarized in Figure 14.3, the charismatic leader is an envisioning leader who is capable of articulating a compelling vision, setting high expectations, and being a model of behaviors that are consistent with that compelling vision. He or she is also an energizing leader who can demonstrate personal excitement, express personal confidence, and seek, find, and use success among his or her colleagues. Finally, charismatic leaders are enabling leaders who are able to express personal support, empathy, and confidence in people and thereby inspire them to undertake the required changes.

Instrumental Leadership   Charismatic leadership alone doesn't explain the sort of success that executives like Louis Gerstner had in turning IBM around. Effective leaders of change must also "build competent teams, clarify required behavior, build in measurements, and administer rewards and punishments so that individuals perceive

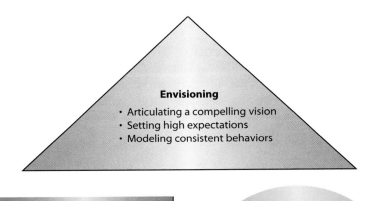

◀ FIGURE 14.3

Charismatic Leadership Behaviors

Charismatic change leadership plays a major role in driving through a change. Its components are envisioning, energizing, and enabling leadership.
Source: Copyright © 1990, by The Regents of the University of California. Reprinted from the *California Management Review*, Vol. 32. No. 2. By permission of The Regents.

that behavior consistent with the change is essential for them in achieving their own goals." Nadler and Tushman call this the change leader's **instrumental leadership** role: it's the managerial aspect of change leadership that puts the instruments in place through which the employees can accomplish their new tasks. For example, leaders must ensure that the necessary structure is in place to carry out the change. They must invest in building teams, creating new organizational structures, setting goals, establishing standards, and defining roles and responsibilities.[40]

instrumental leadership
the managerial role of building and clarifying organizational changes so that employees can accomplish their new tasks.

Missionary Leadership Few leaders can turn an organization around by themselves; instead, as we've seen, they must enlist the aid of others. They must then depend on this new coalition to spread the top manager's vision; this is **missionary leadership**.

In practice, successful leaders communicate their visions to three groups: their own senior teams, senior management, and leadership throughout the organization. They generally look first for opportunities to extend and institutionalize their vision for the firm to the group of individuals who comprise their own senior team. (This, in part, is why CEOs seeking to implement major changes often seek and hire subordinates whose values and visions are consistent with theirs. For example, Gerstner quickly hired several new senior vice presidents for finance, HR management, and several other functions within months of assuming the reins at IBM.) Then, senior managers just below the top executive team are encouraged to buy into the vision and become missionaries for the change.

missionary leadership
a leadership style characterized by influencing an organization to move toward a vision by winning the commitment of others who then aid in the process.

Finally, the vision and details of the change need to be "sold" throughout the organization. This means creating cadres of employees who are capable of helping to lead the change and are eager to do so. Ford does this with its teaching programs, by annually training hundreds of employees—not just managers, but engineers, chemists, and others throughout the firm. In this way, Ford provides employees with the values and skills they will need to make their units consistent with Nasser's vision of a lean, competitive, agile organization.

■ Training Leaders to Lead Change

Can leaders be trained to be better leaders of change? The answer, based on one recent study, is yes.

Much of what change leaders do—being charismatic, exercising instrumental leadership, and being missionaries, for instance—is part of what being a transformational leader is all about. We've seen (in Chapter 10) that transformational leaders can be influential in shaping organizational change. Transformational leaders tend to be charismatic, stimulating, inspirational, and to treat employees as individuals..[41]

But can a person be trained to be more transformational? The results of one study suggest that the answer is a definite yes.[42] The study took place at one of the five largest banks in Canada. The managers of the 20 branches in one region were randomly assigned to receive transformational leadership training or not to receive it. The training group ended up with 5 male and 4 female managers; the no-training group had 6 male and 5 female managers.

The first part of the two-part training program consisted of a one-day training session that familiarized participants with the meaning of transformational leadership and explained and illustrated how it might be implemented in the managers' branches. The second part consisted of several one-on-one "booster" sessions. Here a trainer met individually with each of the managers to go over the latter's leadership style and to develop personal action plans for the manager to become more of a goal-oriented, transformational leader.

The results of this study clearly indicate that managers can be trained to be transformational leaders. For example, the subordinates of the managers who received the training subsequently perceived their managers as higher on intellectual stimulation, charisma, and individual consideration than did subordinates of managers in the no-training group.

Influencing Organizational Culture

Leaders who effectively transform their organizations recognize the important role that organizational culture always plays in such a process. As we saw in Chapter 3, organizational culture is defined as the characteristic traditions, norms, and values that employees share. Values and norms (such as "be honest," "be thrifty," and "don't be bureaucratic") are basic beliefs about what you should or shouldn't do, and what is or is not important.

Norms and values guide and channel all our behavior, and so successfully changing an organization (for instance, changing it from "bureaucratic" and "stick to the chain of command" to "let's be responsive and get the job done") requires a new set of values—a new culture—as well. As reengineering advocate John Champy has said, reducing hierarchy and bureaucracy is not just a matter of rearranging the furniture: these are cultural matters.

You know from your own experience that changing someone's values involves a lot more than just talk. Parents might tell their children repeatedly to eat only healthy foods, but if the children see their parents saying one thing and doing another, chances are the parents' actions—not simply what the parents say—will mold their children's eating habits.

Much the same is true when it comes to creating or changing a company's culture. When he decided to transform Kodak, for instance, Fisher knew he had to do more than talk. Top executives who weren't performing were replaced; new incentive plans were instituted; and new, more results-oriented appraisal systems were introduced. The net effect was to send a strong signal to employees throughout the firm that the values of being efficient, effective, and responsive were a lot more important today then they'd been the week before.

▲ Jacques Nasser, CEO of Ford: Getting employees to respond quickly was central to his transformation plan.

Creating and Sustaining the Right Corporate Culture   There are a lot of things a leader can do to create and sustain the required corporate culture. In many firms, for instance, publishing a formal core values statement is a logical first step in creating a culture. For example (as we saw in Chapter 3) the core values credo of Johnson & Johnson starts with "We believe our first responsibility is to the doctors, nurses, and patients, to mothers and all others who use our products and services. In meeting their needs, everything we do must be of high quality."

Of course the leaders' own words and actions are important, too. For example, the foundations of Wal-Mart's values can be traced to the late Sam Walton's personal values of "hard work, honesty, neighborliness, and thrift." Under Walton's leadership, the firm developed an almost religious zeal for doing things efficiently, and hard work became a requirement for getting promoted.

Your management practices also send a strong signal about what you do and do not think is important. For example, at Toyota, where quality and teamwork are essential, much of the training process focuses on how to work in teams and how to solve quality problems. Similarly, one of the first things Gerstner did when he took over at IBM was to institute a bonus-based approach to paying employees that emphasized performance much more heavily than did the company's old compensation plan.

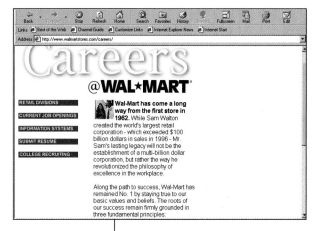

▲ **W E B N O T E**

Wal-Mart uses the Web to underscore core values like respect, service, and excellence.

www.walmart.com

Source: Used with permission.

Signs, symbols, stories, rites, and ceremonies are important, too. In fact many believe that symbolism—what the manager says and does and the signals he or she sends—ultimately does the most to create and sustain the company's culture. At Ben & Jerry's, for instance, signs and symbols are used throughout to create and sustain the company's culture. The joy gang, for example, is a concrete symbol of the firm's values, which emphasize charity, fun, and goodwill toward fellow workers. And at JCPenney, where loyalty and tradition are values, new management employees are inducted at ritualistic conferences into the "Penney partnership," where they commit to the firm's ideology as embodied in its statement of core values of honor, confidence, service, and cooperation.

How to Change a Company's Culture   Imagine you are swept into the CEO's position in a company long known for its culture of backbiting, bureaucratic behavior, and disdain for clients: What steps would you take to change the company's culture? Management expert Edgar Schein has proposed a sort of shorthand list of mechanisms leaders can use to establish, embed, and reinforce organizational culture.[43] Schein advocates five "primary embedding mechanisms":

1. *Make it clear to your employees what you pay attention to, measure, and control.* For example, you can direct the attention of your employees toward controlling costs or serving customers if those are the values you want to emphasize.

2. *React appropriately to critical incidents and organizational crises.* For example, if you want to emphasize the value that "we're all in this together," don't react to declining profits by laying off operating employees and middle managers while leaving your top managers intact.

3. *Deliberately role model, teach, and coach the values you want to emphasize.* For example, Wal-Mart founder Walton truly embodied the values "hard work, honesty, neighborliness, and thrift" that he wanted all Wal-Mart employees to follow. Although he was one of the richest men in the world, he drove a pickup truck, a preference he explained by saying, "If I drove a Rolls Royce, what would I do with my dog?"

4. *Communicate your priorities by the way you allocate rewards and status.* Leaders communicate their priorities by the way they link pay raises and promotions (or the lack thereof) to particular behaviors. For example, when the top management at General Foods decided several years ago to reorient its strategy from cost control to diversification and sales growth, it revised the compensation system to link bonuses to sales volume (rather than just to increased earnings) and to new-product development.

5. *Make your HR procedures and criteria consistent with the values you espouse.* When he became chairperson and CEO of IBM, Gerstner brought in a new top management team whose values were consistent with shaking up IBM's traditionally bureaucratic and politicized culture.

Schein suggests not stopping there. As you can see in Table 14.3, he also recommends using secondary mechanisms—such as redesigning the organizational structure, using new organizational systems, and redesigning physical space—to further reinforce the desired cultural changes. However, Schein believes that these secondary mechanisms are just that—secondary—because they work only if they are consistent with the five primary mechanisms.

TABLE 14.3 — Mechanisms for Embedding and Reinforcing Organizational Culture

Primary Embedding Mechanisms	
1.	What leaders pay attention to, measure, and control
2.	Leader reactions to critical incidents and organizational crises
3.	Deliberate role modeling, teaching, and coaching
4.	Criteria for allocation of rewards and status
5.	Criteria for recruitment, selection, promotion, retirement, and excommunication

Secondary Articulation and Reinforcement Mechanisms	
1.	Organization design and structure
2.	Organizational systems and procedures
3.	Design of physical space, facades, buildings
4.	Stories about important events and people
5.	Formal statements of organizational philosophy, creeds, charters

Source: Reprinted with permission from E. H. Schein, *Organizational Culture and Leadership.* Copyright © 1985 Jossey-Bass, Inc. A subsidiary of John Wiley & Sons, Inc. All rights reserved.

▶ USING ORGANIZATIONAL DEVELOPMENT TO CHANGE AN ORGANIZATION

Whether managing IBM or Netiva, the person contemplating the change must decide what basic process he or she will use. At one extreme, the top executive might ram through most of the changes somewhat autocratically, perhaps because of time constraints or the nature of the changes that have to be made. After a few months on the job, for instance it was apparent to Netiva's Gary Steele that finances were so tight dramatic staff cuts were simply essential, and there wasn't much room for participative decision-making.

At the other extreme, the situation is often such that the best way to make some change is to get the employees themselves to analyze the problem, develop the solution, and implement the change. This can be especially useful when getting the employees' commitment to the change is crucial, for instance, or when the employees are in the best position to understand what the problems are and how to solve them. In these situations the change process of choice is often organizational development, the topic to which we now turn.

What Is Organizational Development?

Organizational development (OD) is a special approach to organizational and cultural change in which the employees themselves formulate and implement the change that's required, often with the assistance of a trained facilitator. As an approach to changing organizations, OD has several distinguishing characteristics:

1. It is usually based on **action research**, which means collecting data about a group, department, or organization, and then feeding that data back to the employees so the group members themselves can analyze them and develop hypotheses about what the problems in the unit might be.

organizational development (OD)

an approach to organizational change in which the employees themselves formulate the change that's required and implement it, usually with the aid of a trained consultant.

action research

the process of collecting data from employees about a system in need of change, and then feeding that data back to the employees so that they can analyze it, identify problems, develop solutions, and take action themselves.

2. It applies behavioral science knowledge for the purpose of improving the organization's effectiveness.

3. It changes the organization in a particular direction—toward improved problem solving, responsiveness, quality of work, and effectiveness.[44]

Types of OD Applications

The number and variety of OD applications (also called *OD interventions* or *techniques*) have increased substantially over the past few years. OD got its start with what were called **human process interventions**. These were aimed at helping employees better understand and modify their own and others' attitudes, values, and beliefs, and thereby improve the company.

Today, as illustrated in Table 14.4, a much wider range of applications is available. Indeed, the once-clear lines between OD and other types of organizational change efforts (such as reorganizing) are starting to blur. This is happening because OD practitioners have become increasingly involved not just in changing participants' attitudes, values, and beliefs, but also in directly altering the firm's structure, practices, strategy, and culture. However, OD's distinguishing characteristic always has been, and is, having the employees themselves analyze the situation and develop the solutions.

There are four types of OD applications: human process, technostructural, HR management, and strategic. All are based on action research—on getting the employees themselves to collect the required data and to create and implement the solutions. The "Entrepreneurs in Action" box (page 440) shows some examples.

Human Process Applications   The human process OD techniques generally aim at improving employees' human relations skills. The goal is to provide employees with the insight and skills required to analyze their own and others' behavior more effectively so they can solve interpersonal and intergroup problems more intelligently. **Sensitivity training**, team building, confrontation meetings, and survey research are in this category. Sensitivity, laboratory, or t-group training (the *t* is for training) was one of the earliest OD techniques. It aims to increase the participant's insight into his or her own behavior and the behavior of others by encouraging an open expression of feelings in the training group. Typically, 10 to 15 people meet, usually away from the job. The focus is on the feelings and emotions and interactions of the members in the group. Participants are encouraged to portray themselves as they are now, in the group, rather than in terms of past experiences.[45] T-group training is obviously very personal in nature, so it's not surprising that it is controversial and that its use has diminished markedly.[46]

OD's characteristic action research emphasis is perhaps most evident in **team building**, which refers to the process of improving the effectiveness of a team. Data concerning the team's performance are collected and then fed back to the members of the group. The participants examine, explain, and analyze the data and develop specific action plans or solutions for solving the team's problems. The typical team-building meeting begins with the consultant interviewing each of the group members and the leader prior to the meeting.[47] They all are asked what their problems are, how they think the group functions, and what obstacles are keeping the group from performing better. The consultant might then categorize the interview data into themes and present the themes to the group at the beginning of the meeting. (Themes like lack of time or lack of cohesion might be culled from such statements as "I don't have enough time to get my job done" or "I can't get any cooperation

---

human process interventions

organizational change techniques aimed at enabling employees to develop a better understanding of their own and others' behaviors for the purpose of improving that behavior such that the organization benefits.

sensitivity training

also called laboratory or t-group training, the basic aim of this organizational development technique is to increase participants' insight into their own behavior and that of others by encouraging an open expression of feelings in a trainer-guided group.

team building

the process of improving the effectiveness of a team through action research or other techniques.

TABLE 14.4 **Examples of OD Interventions and the Organizational Levels They Affect**

Interventions	Primary Organizational Level Affected		
	Individual	Group	Organization
Human Process			
T-groups	X	X	
Process consultation		X	
Third-party intervention	X	X	
Team building		X	
Organizational confrontation meeting		X	X
Intergroup relations		X	X
Technostructural			
Formal structural change			X
Differentiation and integration			X
Cooperative union-management projects	X	X	X
Quality circles	X	X	
Total quality management		X	X
Work design	X	X	
Human Resource Management			
Goal setting	X	X	
Performance appraisal	X	X	
Reward systems	X	X	X
Career planning and development	X		
Managing workforce diversity	X		
Employee wellness	X		
Strategic			
Integrated strategic management			X
Culture change			X
Strategic change			X
Self-designing organizations		X	X

around here.") The group then explores and discusses the issues, examines the underlying causes of the problems, and begins working on some solutions.

Other human process interventions aim to bring about intergroup or organizationwide change. Organizational **confrontation meetings** can help clarify and bring into the open misperceptions and problems so that conflicts can be resolved. The basic approach is that the participants themselves provide the data for the meeting and then, with the help of a facilitator/moderator, confront and thrash out any misperceptions in an effort to reduce tensions.

confrontation meeting
an organizational meeting aimed at clarifying and revealing intergroup misperceptions, tensions, and problems so that they can be resolved.

survey research

the process of collecting data from attitude surveys filled out by employees of an organization, then feeding the data back to workgroups to provide a basis for problem analysis and action planning.

Survey research requires that employees throughout the organization fill out attitude surveys. The data are then used as feedback to workgroups. They use it as a basis for problem analysis and action planning. In general, such surveys are a convenient and widely used method for unfreezing an organization's management and employees by providing a lucid, comparative, graphic illustration of the fact that the organization has problems that should be solved.

Technostructural Applications   OD practitioners are increasingly involved in efforts to change the structures, methods, and job designs of firms. Compared with human process interventions, technostructural interventions (as well as the HR management interventions and strategic interventions described in the following sections) generally focus more directly on productivity improvement and efficiency.

formal structure change program

an intervention technique in which employees collect information on existing formal organizational structures and analyze it for the purpose of redesigning and implementing new organizational structures.

OD practitioners use a variety of technostructural interventions. For example, in a **formal structure change program**, employees collect data on existing structures and analyze them. The purpose is to jointly redesign and implement new organizational structures. OD practitioners also assist in implementing employee-involvement programs, including quality circles and job redesign.

Dream Weavers and Startups

ENTREPRENEURS   IN   ACTION

■ Startup companies are often much different today than they were a few years ago. Entrepreneurs traditionally started their businesses from scratch, and then slowly grew them, brick by brick and customer by customer. Because the process was a relatively slow and continuous one, the entrepreneur was usually able to grow his or her company's vision, and to put all the values and systems in place that were needed to help the employees implement that vision.

Today, many startups like Netiva are technology-based and often emerge, full-blown, out of large parent companies (or with the enormous financial backing of venture capital firms). As a result, a startup firm—say, one born to create a new Internet portal—may begin life with millions of dollars of cash and hundreds of employees, but without the traditions and values that normally go along with growing a business from scratch.

OD consultants today therefore often play the role of what one calls "dream weavers": They are asked to take all the necessary elements for success that are already in place and help pull them together into a smoothly working whole by working with the entrepreneur and his or her employees as a facilitator/transition agent.

How exactly can OD consultants help? Here are some examples:

Establish a new identity. When a giant company spins off a new startup, OD consultants can help the new entity establish an independent identity, for instance by working with the new team to help flesh out value, vision, and mission statements.

Build teams. The new company may be staffed with people who haven't worked together before or who have little or no experience in building effective teams. The OD consultants can use their facilitation skills to create a smoothly functioning team. For example, one startup was having a serious interpersonal communications problem. In this case, the new company's software engineers complained about each other to third parties and did poorly in one-on-one interactions. The OD consultant worked with the people involved during staff meetings to identify and address the counterproductive behavior and facilitate teamwork.[48]

Manage cultural change. Sometimes a new spinoff company's culture may reflect the culture of the parent firm. In one of these startups, for instance, the fear of challenging the system was so ingrained that true creativity was thwarted. In this case the OD consultant was able to work with the team to help instill—through a new core value statement, new leadership and management practices, and new signs and symbols—a more risk-oriented and creative set of values.

HR Management Applications OD practitioners also use action research to help employees analyze and change personnel practices. Targets of change include the performance appraisal system and reward system. Changes might include instituting workforce diversity programs aimed at boosting cooperation among a firm's diverse employees.

Strategic Applications Among the newest OD applications are **strategic interventions**, organizationwide interventions aimed at bringing about a better fit between a firm's strategy, structure, culture, and external environment. **Integrated strategic management** is one example of using OD to create or change a strategy. This intervention consists of four steps:

1. *Analyze current strategy and organizational design.* Senior managers and other employees utilize models such as the SWOT matrix (explained in Chapter 5) to analyze the firm's current strategy and organizational design.

2. *Choose a desired strategy and organizational design.* Based on the analysis, senior management formulates a strategic vision, objectives, and plan, as well as an organizational structure for implementing them.

3. *Design a strategic change plan.* The group designs a strategic change plan, which "is an action plan for moving the organization from its current strategy and organizational design to the desired future strategy and design."[49] The plan explains how the strategic change will be implemented, including specific activities as well as the costs and budgets associated with them.

4. *Implement a strategic change plan.* The final step is to implement a strategic change plan and measure and review the results of the change activities to ensure that they are proceeding as planned.[50]

strategic intervention
an organization development application aimed at effecting a suitable fit among a firm's strategy, structure, culture, and external environment.

integrated strategic management
an organizational development program to create or change a company's strategy by analyzing the current strategy, choosing a desired strategy, designing a strategic change plan, and implementing the new plan.

▶ CONFLICT-MANAGEMENT TECHNIQUES

The need to implement an organizational change doesn't always stem from things external to the organization. Sometimes, for instance, a conflict between departments or managers makes the need for change apparent, as when two departments resist working cooperatively to achieve some goal. Organizational development, as you might imagine, is often the process of choice for handling interpersonal problems like these. But whether it's OD or some other technique, knowing how to manage conflict is a crucial part of knowing how to manage change.

Conflict's Pros and Cons

Conflict, as you probably know, can have dysfunctional effects on an organization and its employees. Opposing parties in conflicts tend to put their own aims above those of the organization, and the organization's effectiveness suffers. Time that could have been used productively is wasted as people hide valuable information and jockey for position. Opponents can become so personally involved in the tensions produced by conflict that they undermine their emotional and physical well-being. Perhaps the most insidious effect of conflict is that it doesn't remain organization bound for long. Its effects are observed by customers and stockholders and are taken home by the opponents, whose families are caught in the fallout.

Despite its adverse effects, conflict is viewed by most experts today as potentially useful because it can, if properly channeled, be an engine of innovation and change. This view explicitly encourages a certain amount of controlled conflict in organizations because lack of active debate can permit the status quo or mediocre ideas to prevail.

This more positive view of conflict is supported by surveys of management practice. In one survey of top and middle managers, for example, managers rated conflict management as of equal or slightly higher importance than topics like planning, communication, motivation, and decision making. The managers spent about 20% of their time on conflicts, yet they did not consider the conflict level in their organization to be excessive. Instead, they rated it as about right—that is, at the midpoint of a scale running from "too low" to "too high."

Individual, Interpersonal, and Intergroup Organizational Conflict

Three types of conflict—individual, interpersonal, and intergroup/organizational—exist in organizations.

role conflict

a situation in which an employee has conflicting orders, such that compliance with one would make it difficult or impossible to comply with the other.

Role conflict is a familiar example of conflict within the individual. It occurs when a person is faced with conflicting orders, such that compliance with one would make it difficult or impossible to comply with the other. Sometimes role conflict arises out of obviously conflicting orders, as when a corporal receives orders from a captain that would force her to disobey an order from her sergeant. Sometimes, however, the role conflict's source is not so obvious: Obeying an order might force a person to violate his or her own cherished values and sense of right and wrong. In any case, role conflict is a serious problem in organizations, and it can be stressful to the people involved and adversely affect morale and performance.[51]

While the term *role conflict* can sound theoretical, its effects in practice are very real. This is illustrated by a study that included, among others, 68 supervisors employed by a large midwestern university.[52] The basic question in this study was whether the stress resulting from supervisors experiencing role conflict would result in a deliberate inflation of performance ratings for the subordinates they were rating.

Surveys were used to measure two things: the extent to which the supervisors experienced role conflict, and the degree to which their subordinates' performance ratings were inflated. An example of an item used to measure a supervisor's self-reported tendency to deliberately inflate performance ratings is "At times I find it necessary to deliberately inflate performance evaluation ratings of my subordinates." An example of an item used to measure the supervisor's role conflict is "I receive incompatible requests from two or more people."[53]

The findings show the sorts of subtle but serious consequences role conflict can have. In this case role conflict and inflated appraisals went hand in hand. The more supervisors saw themselves as receiving conflicting orders and instructions, the more leniently they tended to appraise their own subordinates. Why might that be the case? It's not clear, but perhaps the supervisors with more role conflict felt that their own authority was less clear and secure, so they were less apt to take a chance on being strict with subordinates.

interpersonal conflict

a conflict occurring between individuals or between individuals and groups.

Conflicts in organizations can also be **interpersonal conflicts** and occur between individuals or between individuals and groups. Sometimes, of course, such conflicts arise from legitimate sources, as when real differences in goals or objectives exist between the parties involved. Often, however, they arise not from legitimate differences, but from personalities. Some people are more aggressive and conflict prone than others, and some are so hypersensitive that they view every comment as an insult that provokes a response.

Finally, there are **intergroup organizational conflicts**, such as between line and staff units or between production and sales departments. Effectively managing intergroup conflict is especially crucial today as firms increasingly try to manage change by moving toward boundaryless organizations. We'll therefore focus on the causes and management of intergroup conflict in the remainder of this section.

Causes of Intergroup Conflict

There are many reasons intergroup conflicts occur, but research suggests that four factors create most of the problems: interdependencies and shared resources; differences in goals, values, or perceptions; authority imbalances; and ambiguities.

Groups that don't have to depend on each other or compete for scarce resources will generally not get involved in intergroup conflict. Conversely, groups that work interdependently or that must compete for scarce resources may eventually come into conflict.[54] Conflicts thus tend to be a way of life for members of quality control and production departments, sales and production departments, and other departments that depend on each other.

Similarly, people who agree in terms of their *goals*, values, or perceptions are less likely to find themselves arguing than are those with fundamental differences. Researchers Richard Walton and John Dutton found that the preference of production departments for long, economical runs conflicted with the preference of sales units for quick delivery to good customers and that these differing goals often led to intergroup conflict.[55] Other differences in goals that led to intergroup conflicts include those between flexibility and stability, between short-run and long-run performance, between measurable and intangible results, and between organizational goals and societal needs.[56] In any case, the bottom line is that when the goals of two groups are similar or identical, there is little chance of serious conflict arising; when there is a fundamental difference in goals, conflicts are likely to arise.

Researchers Paul Lawrence and Jay Lorsch found that what they call "organizational differentiation" is a similar source of intergroup conflict.[57] As each department in an organization tries to cope with the unique demands of its own environment, it necessarily develops its own types of procedures, cherished values, and point of view. For example, a research department in a chemical firm might be run very democratically, and its employees might develop a rather long-term time perspective, because most of the things they are working on will not reach fruition for years. The production department might be run more autocratically, and its managers might be expected to put more emphasis on immediate results. Lawrence and Lorsch believe that the greater the differentiation between co-workers' departments, the more potential for conflict there is.

We also know that when a group's actual *authority* is inconsistent with its prestige, intergroup conflicts are more likely to arise. For example, a researcher found that in one company, the production department had to accept instructions from a production engineering department composed of employees with skills no greater than (and in fact quite similar to) those possessed by production employees. As a result, "production managers spent an inordinate amount of time checking for consistency among the various items produced by production engineering,"[58] in order to catch the engineers in a mistake.

Ambiguity—for instance, regarding who does what, or in assigning credit or blame between two departments—also boosts the likelihood of conflict between units. If both the quality control and production departments can claim credit for the cost savings resulting from a change in production procedures, a conflict may well result. Similarly, if it's hard to place the blame for a problem, conflicts may emerge as departments attempt to shed the blame, say, for a cost overrun or machine breakdown.

Techniques for Managing Intergroup Conflict

The many techniques for managing or resolving conflicts generally fall into four categories: superordinate goals, structural approaches, conflict-resolution modes of solving problems, and OD techniques (described above).

Institute Common or Superordinate Goals   One of the most familiar and sensible ways of short-circuiting conflicts is to find some common ground on which the parties can agree. In labor-management negotiations, for example, arbitrators generally begin their work by finding some point on which both sides can agree and then building a solution from that point of agreement.

As another example, national leaders such as Cuba's Fidel Castro often use the ploy of claiming that their countries are about to be attacked in order to bring about unification of the opposing factions in their own countries. Invoking such a superordinate ("it's bigger than both of us") goal can be an effective conflict-management tactic.

Use Structural Approaches   Other conflict-management methods are based on using the organization's structure. For example, the most frequent way of resolving disagreements between departments is to refer them to a common superior. If the vice presidents for sales and finance cannot reach agreement on some point, they would typically refer their disagreement to the president for a binding decision. Another structural approach is to reduce the interdependencies or the need to compete for scarce resources. Sometimes the changes are as simple as separating the units physically, so that the members of one group no longer have to confront members of the other each day.[59] Another change is to increase the available resources so that both groups can get what they want.

Lawrence and Lorsch, in the study mentioned earlier, found that many companies have reduced interdepartmental conflict by setting up special liaisons between warring departments. In the high-technology plastics industry, for example, successful companies set up special "integrator" new-product development departments; their job was to coordinate the work of the research, sales, and manufacturing departments.

Use the Right Conflict-Resolution Styles   There are different ways to settle an argument, and some are usually better than others. For example, having both parties meet to confront the facts and hammer out a solution is usually more effective than simply smoothing over the conflict by pushing problems under a rug. The following are some popular conflict-management styles and statements that illustrate them:

■ *Confrontation.* "In recent meetings we have had a thrashing around about our needs. At first we did not have much agreement, but we kept thrashing around and finally agreed on what was the best we could do."

■ *Smoothing.* "I thought I went to great lengths in our group to confront conflict. I said what I thought in the meeting, but it did not bother anybody. I guess I should have been harsher. I could have said I won't do it unless you do it my way. If I had done this, they couldn't have backed away, but I guess I didn't have the guts to do it. I guess I didn't pound the bushes hard enough."

- *Forcing.* "If I want something very badly and I am confronted by a roadblock, I go to top management to get the decision made. If the research managers are willing to go ahead [my way], there is no problem. If there is a conflict, then I take the decision to somebody higher up."[60]

- *Avoidance.* "I'm not going to discuss that with you."

- *Competitive.* "You don't know what you're doing." "You need to get to work; if you can't get your job done, get out." "This is your doing, not mine."

- *Compromise and collaboration.* "I'm sure we can figure out a way to solve this together." "We're all in the same boat in this matter." "Let's see how we can work this out."

- *Accommodating.* "Calm down so we can work this out." "Please tell me what is wrong."[61]

There are several general rules for which style to use and when. **Avoidance** or **smoothing over** usually won't resolve a conflict and may actually make it worse if bad feelings fester. However, some problems—especially small ones—sometimes do go away by themselves, and avoidance or smoothing over may be the only choices if the other party is highly emotional. **Accommodation** can help calm an opponent who is not uncontrollably irate, but this is another stop-gap measure, since the disagreement itself remains unresolved.

Other approaches are more direct. **Competition** presumes a win–lose situation and sometimes works best when it's all right to resolve the conflict with a clear winner or loser, such as in sports. However, if you need to continue to work with someone, this approach may leave a residue of ill will. **Compromise** means each person gives up something in return for reaching agreement. This approach can work well, but may leave one or both parties feeling that they could have done better if they'd bargained harder.

Collaboration—with both sides on the same side of the table to work out the agreement—is often the best approach, especially when differences are confronted and aired in a civil, problem-solving manner. **Forcing** can be effective as a brute show of power, but it can backfire if the person who is forced has the option of wiggling out of the deal.

A recent study of how supervisors and subordinates actually handled conflicts provides an interesting perspective on which conflict-resolution styles are best. In practice, people usually don't rely on a single conflict-resolution mode. In other words, they don't just confront or smooth over a situation, but rather use these and other approaches together to some degree.[62] The researchers therefore focused on seven possible conflict-resolution styles. These and the researchers' definitions are presented in Table 14.5: forcing, confronting, process controlling, problem solving, compromising, accommodating, and avoiding. The basic idea the researchers wanted to study was whether some combination of these styles was more effective than others. They analyzed videotapes of 116 male police sergeants handling a standardized, scripted conflict with either a subordinate or a superior.

It was clear that to resolve the conflict most effectively, the sergeant had to use several styles at once. For example, problem solving tended to enhance the sergeant's effectiveness, especially if he combined it with forcing. However, process controlling—dominating the conflict-resolution process to one's own advantage, for instance by not letting the conversation stray off track—was even more effective than trying to force the issue by insisting that the adversary do what he or she

---

avoidance

moving away from or refusing to discuss a conflict issue.

smoothing over

in conflict management, diminishing or avoiding a conflict issue.

accommodation

giving in to the opponent in an attempt to end a conflict.

competition

an approach to conflict management and negotiating that presumes a win–lose situation.

compromise

settling a conflict through mutual concessions.

collaboration

a conflict-management style in which both sides work together to achieve agreement.

forcing

a direct, contentious method of resolving conflict that utilizes one negotiator's superior position.

TABLE 14.5 Conflict-Resolution Modes

Component	Definition
Forcing	Contending the adversary do what you say in a direct way
Confronting	Demanding attention to the conflict issue
Process controlling	Dominating the conflict-resolution process to one's own advantage
Problem solving	Reconciling the parties' basic interests
Compromising	Settling through mutual concessions
Accommodating	Giving in to the opponent
Avoiding	Moving away from the conflict issue

Source: Evert Van De Vliert, Martin C. Euwema, and Sipke E. Huismans, "Managing Conflict with a Subordinate or a Superior: Effectiveness of Conglomerated Behavior," *Journal of Applied Psychology*, April 1995, pp. 271–81. Copyright © 1995 by the American Psychological Association. Reprinted by permission.

was told. In this study the sergeants also boosted their conflict-management effectiveness by being somewhat accommodating.

The bottom line seems to be that for these police sergeants, the use of three conflict-resolution styles together—problem solving while being moderately accommodating and still maintaining a strong hand in controlling the conflict-resolution process—was an especially effective combination. Whether this combination would prove equally effective for other types of supervisors would have to be addressed by other studies.

SUMMARY

1. Thinking like a leader involves reviewing a leadership situation and identifying what is happening, accounting for what is happening (in terms of leadership and other behavioral science theories and concepts), and formulating leader actions. Knowledge of organizational change and development can be useful tools.

2. Managers in their leadership roles can focus on various change targets. They can change the strategy, culture, structure, tasks, technologies, or attitudes and skills of the people in the organization.

3. The hardest part of leading a change is overcoming resistance. Resistance stems from several sources: habit, resource limitations, threats to power and influence, fear of the unknown, and altering employees' personal compacts.

4. Methods of dealing with resistance include education and communication, facilitation and support, participation and involvement, negotiation and agreement, manipulation and co-optation, and coercion. Psychologist Kurt Lewin suggests unfreezing the situation, perhaps by using a dramatic event to get people to recognize the need for change.

5. Implementing a change is basically like solving any problem: The manager must recognize that there's a problem, diagnose the problem, and then formulate and implement a solution.

6. An eight-step process for actually leading organizational change includes creating a sense of urgency; creating a guiding coalition and mobilizing commitment to change through joint diagnosis of business problems; developing and then communicating a shared vision; removing barriers to the change and empowering employees; generating short-term wins; consolidating gains and producing more change; anchoring the new ways of doing things in the company's culture; and monitoring progress and adjusting the vision as required.

7. Organizational changes almost never take place spontaneously; instead, they are pushed or driven by leaders. If you are a change leader, important functions to keep in mind include the need for charismatic leadership, instrumental leadership, missionary leadership, and transformational leadership.

8. Organizational development is a special approach to organizational change that basically involves letting the employees themselves formulate and implement the change that's required, often with the assistance of a trained consultant. Types of OD applications include human process applications, technostructural interventions, HR management applications, and strategic applications.

9. Conflict can have dysfunctional effects on an organization and its people, although it can be a positive force as well. At least three types of conflict can be identified in organizations: individual, interpersonal, and intergroup. Intergroup conflicts often stem from interdependencies and shared resources; intergroup differences in goals, values, or perceptions; authority imbalances; or ambiguity. Problems like these can be solved by establishing superordinate goals, eliminating interdependencies, using one or more conflict-resolution modes, or through OD conflict-resolution techniques like confrontation meetings.

TYING IT ALL TOGETHER

Managers plan, organize, lead, and control. Planning (the subject of Chapters 4–6) involves making decisions, laying plans and setting goals, and developing a strategy and mission for the firm. Organizing (Chapters 7–9) means putting an organization in place to implement those plans by creating reporting relationships, delegating authority, writing job descriptions, and hiring and training the employees who will staff those positions and implement the plans. With the employees in place, the manager's leadership role becomes more important. Organizations are not just organization charts and machines, but people, and the manager in his or her leadership role is responsible for influencing and motivating the company's employees to achieve their goals.

Leadership therefore involves the distinctly interpersonal aspects of what managers do. In the last five chapters we have therefore focused on the people side of the manager's job, including leadership style, motivation, communication, groups and teams, and now, in the current chapter, on leading organizational and cultural change.

In the next chapter we'll turn to the fourth, and last, of a manager's main functions. But in fact controlling is, in most respects, inseparable from and largely an extension of the other three functions. Controlling, for instance, traditionally means setting standards, measuring performance, and then taking corrective action as required. Thinking of controlling separately from planning (and setting standards) is therefore somewhat meaningless. Similarly, "controlling someone" is, to a large extent, an extension of the manager's leadership or people-oriented duties.

You know from your own experience that the best way to control someone is to get that person to control himself or herself so that they do the job right because they want to. To that extent controlling, as we'll see, really calls on all the leadership skills you can muster. Indeed, particularly in today's fast-changing, empowered companies, it's best not to think of control as a mechanical process imposed on employees. Keeping track of what's happening in the organization will always be important, of course, but now, more often than not, the key to control is getting employees to want to excel. That is why the following chapter is called not "Control," but "Controlling and Building Commitment."

KEY TERMS

strategic change 419
business reengineering 421
unfreezing 424
moving 425
refreezing 426
change advocate 432
charismatic leadership 432
instrumental leadership 433
missionary leadership 433
organizational development (OD) 437
action research 437

human process interventions 438
sensitivity training 438
team building 438
confrontation meeting 439
survey research 440
formal structure change program 440
strategic intervention 441
integrated strategic management 441
role conflict 442

interpersonal conflict 442
intergroup organizational conflict 443
avoidance 445
smoothing over 445
accommodation 445
competition 445
compromise 445
collaboration 445
forcing 445

SKILLS AND STUDY MATERIALS

CRITICAL THINKING EXERCISES

1. MIT economist Lester Thurow is well known for his views on the economics of change and economic changes. *Rethinking the Future*, edited by Rowan Gibson (Nicholas Breakely, 1998), includes an article by Thurow, "Changing the Nature of Capitalism." Causing the change are what he terms five economic tectonic plates that are driving all the economic changes and fundamentally remaking the economic surface of the earth: the end of Communism; the movement from natural resource–based industries to human-created brainpower industries; the world population's growth, movement, and aging; the new global economy; and the fact that the world does not have one dominant economic, political, or military power. He argues that these changes are shaking the foundations of 21st century capitalism because technology and ideology are moving apart. He says, "We know the forces that are going to determine the future of capitalism. But what we don't know is the exact shape of the future, because that's not

determined by the stars; it's determined by what we do." What do you think of Thurow's analysis? What sorts of organizational changes do you think they'll trigger for companies?

2. One change that many authors have identified is the change from a brawn-based economy to a brain- and knowledge-based economy. In Peter Drucker's *The New Realities* (1989) he noted that only one of the 19th-century business builders had any advanced schooling: That was J. P. Morgan, and he was a college dropout. Since the later part of the 20th century knowledge has become the capital of a developed economy. This has occurred in one generation. What are the implications for leadership in this new world of knowledge capital? How will those trained and educated in the 1980's survive the changes of today? What techniques discussed in this chapter may help leaders create knowledge-friendly companies?

1. You are now a citizen of the 21st century. The rules of the job and career game appear to be changing rapidly as machines such as ATMs replace bank tellers, you can bank and pay bills with your computer, and you can even order products, including groceries, over the Internet. In groups of 5 students, preferably from different majors, explore how you think the profession you are now preparing for will look like in the future, 10 years from now and then 30 years from now. Be prepared to share your discussion with other groups.

2. In *Owning the Future* (Houghton-Mifflin, 1999) Seth Shulman warns that freely shared knowledge is fast becoming a valuable asset. We face imminent threats from new monopolies that concentrate vital information in the hands of a few. Shulman writes of today's battles for control over the intangible new assets—genes, software, databases, and scientific information—that make up the lifeblood of our new economy. What do you think of his warnings? Interview five people who are involved in one of these subjects (genes, software, databases, or scientific information), and be prepared to discuss what you find in class.

We invite you to visit the Dessler companion Web site at **www.prenhall.com/dessler** for this chapter's Internet resources.

JOB SURFING: CATCHING THE NEW WAVE

CASE 1

Switching jobs is no longer viewed as irresponsible behavior. In fact, it makes sense to stay mobile and increase your skills whenever you can.

David Friedensohn is a case in point. Over the last decade he has worked for four different employers, including Citicorp and Viacom. In addition, he has been a self-employed consultant. David has continually learned new skills, increased his responsibilities, and bumped up his income. Currently, he is vice president for new business at Prodigy, running a couple of the online service's startup ventures in New York City and earning a steady six-figure income. His advice: "You have to be disciplined to get the skills to stay in the race. You can't force the ocean to throw a good wave at you either. You have to seize opportunities when they come."

Questions

1. What are the implications of David's philosophy for leading organizational change today?

2. Why do you think David does not resist change but rather embraces it?

3. Could you manage your career as does David?

4. Do you think constant change is the wave of the future for most job seekers? Why or why not?

Source: Justin Martin, "Job Surfing: Move On to Move Up." *Fortune*, 13 January 1997, 50–4.

When he first came to office, Vice President Al Gore proposed a major process redesign of all government agencies. He asked for nothing short of the "reinvention of government." As part of that initial proposal, the administration asked federal agencies to create "reinvention laboratories (RLs)." RLs were empowered to test radical new processes for doing the government's business. If successful, they would share ideas, successes, and lessons with other agencies. Could an idea as simple as process redesign lead to a reinvention of government?

There are approximately 350 national RLs. At the first RL Conference at Hunt Valley, Maryland, an RL was defined as:

> a place that cuts through "red tape," exceeds customer expectations, and unleashes innovations for improvements from its employees.

One of the first groups to test a planned change of processes through organizational redesign was the U.S. Environmental Protection Agency (EPA). After a few minor successes and some failures, the EPA reported that its reinvention efforts had "dramatically increased public access to environmental information and saved businesses and communities more than $2.4 billion a year." All this was accomplished while still ensuring the protection of public health and the environment.

The EPA outlined its successes in an annual report that highlighted the environmental and economic benefits from the agency's partnership programs. The latest data showed that in one year businesses and communities saved $1.6 billion by eliminating 7.6 million tons of solid waste, preventing 79 million metric tons of air pollution, saving nearly 6 million gallons of clean water, and conserving enough energy to light 56 million households for a year. The EPA RLs not only cut costs by directly reducing pollution, but saved another $807 million by cutting unnecessary paperwork. By streamlining regulatory processes and abolishing outdated provisions, the time businesses and communities spend on paperwork has been reduced by 26.9 million hours per year (more than 3,100 years of labor).

At the core of this organizational change effort is employee empowerment. RLs were envisioned as places where managers could fully delegate authority and responsibility, unshackling workers to fully accomplish their mission. Instead of using bureaucratic measures like hours worked, the RLs measured success by customer satisfaction.

In comparing successful RL programs, several benchmarks for successful organizational change became evident. Process champions in an RL need to be recognized and supported at the highest levels. RLs also need to create a win–win environment. Risk taking has to be encouraged and safe harbors for innovation established. RLs need to celebrate and publicize successes. Successful RLs put the spotlight on heroes and let people tell their stories. RLs found that this not only improved motivation, but allowed other organizations to learn from experiences, both successful and unsuccessful. A key rule for successful RLs was to maximize doing and minimize reporting. Strong RLs had also adopted a strategy for long-term change. At their best, RLs became identifiable rallying points for employees, managers, customers, and other stakeholders.

In its evaluation of the RLs, the General Accounting Office (GAO) said,

> the reinvention lab effort has produced hundreds of ideas to reengineer work processes and improve agencies' performance—ideas drawn from employees with hands-on experience in operating government programs. Many of the labs are addressing issues that are at the cutting edge of government management . . . more innovations are possible in these and other areas as agencies review and rethink their existing work process.
>
> (Management Reform: Status of Agency Reinvention Lab Efforts, GAO/GGD-96-69)

Discussion Questions

1. In what ways are the principles and methods for managing change at an RL similar to the recommendations in this chapter?

2. What elements does this chapter recommend that seem to be absent from the RLs?

3. What suggestions would you make for improving the RL process?

HOW CAN WE KEEP THE SPIRIT OF CHANGE ALIVE?

To see how important the spirit of change can be at a company like KnitMedia, consider the following comments from John Swenson, KnitMedia's senior editor at jazze.com:

It's a new Web site we started up Thanksgiving, and it's going to be the most comprehensive jazz and blues Web site. We're going to have over 20,000 titles. We've only been going since Thanksgiving, so we're building as we go. We're about 20 percent completed with a biography section. We donated daily news updates and there will be live music clips and videos available for downloading. Working here is like being in a beehive. Everybody's constantly busy whirling around: If you go out for lunch, when you come back, somebody will be working on your computer because there aren't enough to go around. I mean we probably need about twice as much office space for the amount of activity that's going on here. But surprisingly, everybody's very industrious and polite, contrary to what you might expect under the circumstances. I love editing a jazz Web site on a day-to-day basis.

Of course a lot of that sort of spirit goes back to the culture—the underlying values—that Michael Dorf has cultivated at KnitMedia. In terms of values, for instance, Michael has said, "We always allow, we hope, for caprice, spontaneity and the unexpected . . . The secret is improvisation, and constant improvising."

The potential problem for KnitMedia, of course, is that a creative, improvisational culture becomes increasingly difficult to sustain as companies grow, and as employees become further removed from the visionary leader—in this case, Michael Dorf. The last thing Dorf and his team want is for a "that's not my job, you'll have to do your job alone" type of culture. But that's the risk as more managers and employees are brought in. Needless to say, Dorf and his team want to make sure that doesn't happen, and have come to you for advice.

Team Exercises and Questions

Use what you learned in this chapter to answer the following questions from Michael Dorf and his management team:

1. What is KnitMedia's culture? In answering, please make sure to tell us the underlying values and assumptions, as well as any of the physical or procedural manifestations of that culture.

2. Do you see any need for us to change KnitMedia's culture? Why or why not? If so, what suggestions would you make for changing it?

3. Michael Dorf is both the company's visionary leader and the main person molding its company culture. How would you suggest Dorf ensure that KnitMedia's culture continues to reflect his vision, and continues to provide the guidance for all employees that it has in the past?

4. Do you see any reason to institute a formal organizational change program? If so, how would you suggest we proceed? Please explain your answer.

Leading and Motivating

It would be difficult to imagine how KnitMedia's successful start-up and subsequent growth could have been accomplished without the vision and leadership of Michael Dorf. Michael's love for a particular kind of music, his vision of the Knitting Factory club as an incubator for talent—and eventually as a brand name for the many new ventures that became KnitMedia, Inc.—and his energy and commitment to sharing that vision with others are widely acknowledged as the organization's single guiding force.

It becomes clear from listening to the managers, employees, and artists associated with KnitMedia that all of them share Michael's attraction to jazz music. Music is what draws many people to work at KnitMedia, and it is very often what keeps them there. The chance to bring noncommercial music to the widest possible audience, to participate in Michael's creative vision, is a major motivator, particularly when coupled with the organization's ambitious plans to tap cutting-edge media such as Webcasting and new ventures like e-commerce.

None of this heady appeal should suggest that KnitMedia is all play and no work. A strong degree of self-motivation is needed to survive in the organization's growing and evolving culture. Most of the managers try to hire people with experience and specific technical skills, and hard work and a certain level of intensity and dedication—along with the camaraderie inspired by Michael's shared vision—are the norm.

Michael himself is known as a very demanding leader who admits to being somewhat difficult to work for. He has been criticized, even by those who admire him, for being a workaholic with unrealistic expectations of others. He is also recognized as brilliant, inspiring, and a savvy business thinker. As Ed Greer, Senior Vice President of Club Operations, sees it, the new position of Chief Operating Officer, now held by Allan Fried, was a necessary step in creating a kind of buffer between Michael and the rest of the company. This change has allowed Michael to do what he does best, which is to go out and "challenge the world" on behalf of KnitMedia, while Allan undertakes the day-to-day operation of the firm, making sure, as he puts it, that Michael's "vision gets implemented."

Ed Greer sees himself as another facilitating leader, pointing people in the right direction, checking that they are doing what they need to do, but refraining from micro-managing or telling people in detail what to do. His hope is that he can develop his employees sufficiently so they can see for themselves what needs doing and be able to do it independently.

Dave Brenner, Vice President for New Media, describes himself as the first to come in and the last one to leave, a leader "by example." He relies on his interpersonal skills to help him work with people on a day-to-day basis, letting his staff know what is expected of them and finding out what their concerns are in return.

For Stephanie Oxley, Vice President of KnitMedia Labels, who runs what she terms "a tight ship," leadership means motivating people to feel as if the company were their own. The factors that make that happen, she feels, are being honest and straightforward with her staff, offering encouragement, and making it known that her expectations are very high. Although two of her staff members work in the Amsterdam office, Stephanie feels there is a high degree of closeness and cohesion. Those team members who work in New York often socialize together, for example.

Questions

Based on the case, the video, the text chapters you've read so far, and your knowledge from other sources, answer the following:

1. Evaluate Michael Dorf's leadership style and characteristics. What benefits do you think the organization derives from his strengths? How do you think he might improve his effectiveness as a leader?

2. Contrast the leadership styles of the other KnitMedia managers who have been profiled in the case and the video. What do you think are some of their strengths and weaknesses? Which one do you think you most resemble as a leader?

3. In addition to love of KnitMedia's brand of jazz and financial compensation, what other motivators do you think are operating at this organization? Which ones are appealing to you? As the firm continues to grow and change, what new incentives do you think might motivate employees to join or stay with KnitMedia?

CHAPTER ▸ 15

CONTROLLING AND BUILDING COMMITMENT

WHAT'S AHEAD?

Craig Miller, CEO of MM & A Group, was getting a sinking feeling. Not long ago, the fast-growing software consulting and personnel placement firm in Atlanta was overwhelmed with information—by phone, mail, fax, and e-mail—flooding in from customer orders and invoices, and from financial and legal documents. He knew his firm wouldn't be able to fill software engineering positions for its corporate clients or complete its own consulting projects if he didn't get control of all that data.[1] Craig knew he had to keep track of what was happening in his company, and knew he needed the information in a form that would enable him to take fast corrective action if corrective action was required. He also knew that installing a system to control what was happening at his firm was therefore one of the most important things he could do as a manager.

OBJECTIVES

AFTER STUDYING THIS CHAPTER, YOU SHOULD BE ABLE TO

- Explain each of the three steps in the traditional control process

- Compare and contrast traditional control methods and commitment-based control methods

- Give examples of traditional diagnostic, boundary, and interactive control methods

- List the unintended behavioral consequences of control

- Illustrate how managers can use belief systems and employee commitment to maintain better control

▶ THE ROLE OF CONTROL IN THE MANAGEMENT PROCESS

Craig Miller is only one of millions of managers trying to deal with the question of how to keep his or her business under control. Sometimes being out of control doesn't have especially serious consequences, as when your dry cleaner is "only" an hour late in finding your freshly cleaned blouse. Often, though, the consequences are more severe, as when Barings, the British banking firm, saw its business ruined by multimillion-dollar losses run up unnoticed by one of its traders in Asia. Upon assuming responsibility for a unit, managers decide "where we're going" (Planning, Chapters 4–6), who will do what (Organizing, 7–9), and how to motivate their troops (Leading, 10–14). Now, in Chapter 15, we'll see how to keep things under control.

control

task of ensuring that activities are getting the desired results.

Control is the task of ensuring that activities are providing the desired results. In its most general sense, *controlling* means setting a target, measuring performance, and taking corrective action as required. As control expert Kenneth Merchant says, "The goal [of the control system] is to have no unpleasant surprises in the future."[2]

Why Control Is Required

If managers could be sure that every plan they made and every task they assigned would be perfectly executed, they really wouldn't need to "control." All the results could be expected to be as planned, with no unpleasant surprises. But things rarely go this smoothly. Most plans are executed by people, and people vary widely in abilities, motivation, and even honesty. Furthermore, particularly in today's fast-changing business environment, who can assume that the plans themselves might not suddenly become outdated? (One can only imagine the kind of scrambling booksellers like Barnes & Noble had to do to change their five-year plans when Amazon.com was first introduced, for instance). So even the validity of the plans themselves and the results originally desired must be monitored and controlled.

Making Sure There's a Timely Response

As Kenneth Merchant said, the manager's aim is to have no unpleasant surprises, and so the manager has to be sure he or she can make a timely response. It would surely do Craig Miller no good, for instance, to find out in June that in March a large client had called to ask Craig to fill a position.

steering control

control that predicts results and takes corrective action before the operation or project is completed.

When it comes to being able to take timely action, some controls are more timely than others. For example, experts distinguish between steering controls, yes/no controls, and post-action controls. With **steering controls**, corrective action is taken before the operation or project has been completed.[3] For example, the flight path of a spacecraft aimed at Mars is tracked continuously, since you would not want to find out after the fact that you missed your mark. Its trajectory is modified so that flight path corrections can be made days before the spacecraft is due to reach a target. In the same way, most managers set intermediate milestones so they can check progress long before a project is to be completed. If a problem is found, it can be corrected in time to save the project.

yes/no control

a control system in which work may not proceed to the next step until it passes an intermediate checkpoint step.

A **yes/no control** means work may not proceed until it passes an intermediate control step. For example, most companies have a rule forbidding employees from entering into contracts with suppliers or customers unless the agreements have been approved ahead of time by the firm's legal staff. Yes/no controls help to head off problems before they occur.

Post-action controls are ones in which results are compared to the standard after the project has been finished. Budgets are examples of post-action controls, as are the end of term grades students receive. The problem with post-action controls, as with grades, is that you usually can't do much to remedy the situation once the time period is over and the results are in. Most students therefore prefer finding out how they're doing during the semester. Similarly, with things changing so fast, Craig Miller doesn't want to find out after the fact that his plans were ill-conceived or his employees didn't follow through. Most managers try to build in the timeliness provided by steering controls, such as by monitoring weekly or monthly performance reports. This can help identify problems before they get out of hand.

post-action control

any control tool in which the project or operation being controlled is completed first, and then results are measured and compared to the standard.

MANAGING @ THE *SPEED* OF THOUGHT

■ Controlling on Internet Time

As you can imagine, the Internet has improved managers' abilities to make timely mid-course corrections if they see activities trending out of control. Boeing's use of the Web is a good example. Boeing has an Internet-based network used by 1,000 other companies, including aluminum supplier Alcoa, Inc.[4] To gain access to this network, external users (including most of Boeing's suppliers and customers) receive "digital certificates" from Boeing, with passwords authorizing them to access the network.

The network allows both Boeing and its suppliers to maintain better, more timely control, "by reducing the number of misunderstandings with business partners and customers," according to Boeing's Web program manager. Access to the e-network means suppliers can continually get real-time updates regarding required delivery dates and schedule changes, and can make course corrections if these are required. And, since Boeing's e-commerce system is linked to tracking tools supplied by delivery services such as FedEx, customers can view the status of their orders at anytime over the Web. Delivery surprises are thus kept to a minimum.

Boeing's Internet-based system has improved the timeliness of the company's control system in many other ways. For example, employees can use the system to monitor production lines: "We use the Web to keep track of shortages on airplane production lines so that everyone in the whole organization can know where the hot spots are, not just management."[5]

The system even made it easier to control activities in more specific areas, such as training. For example, as soon as each instructor was required to publish his or her course lists on the Internet-based system, the training department realized different instructors were sometimes teaching the same thing. This allowed the training department to eliminate redundant courses and better control the costs of the courses the company makes available to its employees.

Everything Managers Do Relates to Control

Since managing involves planning, organizing, leading, and controlling, one might easily get the impression that maintaining control is just something managers do after they're finished planning, organizing, and leading, but in fact nothing could be further from the truth. In fact, just about everything managers do that we've touched on in the last 14 chapters relates to control. For example, controlling always requires that some desirable outcomes like targets, standards, or goals be set, so that the word *planning* is almost always used along with the word *control*. Similarly, "how to control" is often an underlying concern when decisions are made regarding how to *organize*. For example, self-contained autonomous divisions (like GM's Saturn division) can, due to their relative freedom, easily overspend and spin out of control unless their profits and other results are carefully monitored. And even the most sophisticated, computerized control system won't prevent unpleasant surprises if the company's *staffing*—hiring people with the right skills and then giving them the training and orientation that they need—is not up to par.

Similarly, much of what managers do when they have their *leadership* hats on involves making sure that employees are doing and will do the things they're supposed to do. As we saw in Chapters 10–14, for instance, close supervision—literally monitoring each and every thing employees do—is certainly one way to accomplish that. However, today the sort of self-motivation that derives from empowering teams and putting them in charge is often the better alternative. Let's look more closely at how managers maintain control.

▶ TWO APPROACHES TO MAINTAINING CONTROL

What is the best way to stay in control? We'll see in this chapter that there are two basic options: **traditional** and **commitment-based control methods**. Let's look at each.

The Traditional Control Process

What's the first thing you think of when someone mentions the word *control*? Chances are, you think of somehow exerting influence to ensure that some person or group is doing what he or she is supposed to do. When most people think of control, in other words, they generally think of some kind of external process that's somehow used to keep a person's behavior in line. Whether you're controlling your neighbor down the block, or the sales team at your company, or the City of New York, control traditionally includes three steps:

1. Establishing a standard, goal, or target so that you know in advance what the results ought to be.

2. Using some type of external monitoring system (such as personal observation or a budget) to compare actual performance to that standard.

3. Taking corrective action, if necessary, to get the actual performance in line with what you planned.[6] Let's look at the three traditional steps in control in more detail.

Step 1: Establish a Standard   Standards can be expressed in terms of money, time, quantity, or quality (or a combination of these). Thus, a salesperson might get a dollar-based quota of $8,000 worth of products per month, or a production supervisor might be told to cut costs by $2,000 per week. Performance standards are also expressed in terms of time—a person might have to meet a certain sales quota in a week or complete a report by May 1.

Some standards are quantity based. For example, production supervisors are usually responsible for producing a specified number of units of product per week. Sometimes standards are qualitative, such as the reject rates in quality control, the grades of products sold (such as "grade A"), or the quality of a student's report.

Whatever the category—quantity, quality, timeliness, dollars—the usual procedure is to choose a specific yardstick and then set a standard, as shown in Figure 15.1. For quantity, yardsticks include units produced per shift and grievances filed per month.[7] Specific quantitative goals then might be set for each.

---

traditional control methods

control procedures that are based on maintaining control generally through external means, by setting standards, comparing the actual results to the standard, and then taking corrective action, and including diagnostic, boundary, and interactive control systems.

commitment-based control methods

a category of control tools that rely on the employees' self-control and commitment to doing things right to make sure things stay in control.

AREA TO CONTROL	POSSIBLE YARDSTICK	STANDARD/GOAL TO ACHIEVE
Quantity	Number of products produced	Produce 14 units per month
Quality	Number of rejects	No more than 10 rejects per day
Timeliness	Percentage of sales reports in on time	Return 90% of sales reports on time
Dollars	Percentage of deviation from budget	Do not exceed budgeted expenses by more than 5% during year

◀ F I G U R E   1 5 . 1

Examples of Control Standards

Step 2: Measure Actual Performance and Compare It to the Standard   The next step is to install a "control system" and then use it to measure actual performance or results.[8] Personal observation is the simplest and most common way of comparing actual performance to standards: You keep monitoring subordinates to make sure things are being done right.

While nothing substitutes for the interactive give-and-take of this sort of personal supervision, it becomes increasingly difficult to monitor everyone personally as the manager assumes more responsibilities. One way to handle this is to add supervisors; for example, a hospital director might hire two assistant directors to observe employees on different floors. But in practice, personal control must at some point be supplemented by formal, more impersonal control systems. Budgetary and financial reports, quality control reports, and inventory control reports are three examples of traditional control systems used to measure and compare actual performance to standards.

Step 3: Take Corrective Action   Taking corrective action is essentially a problem-solving activity. In some instances the deviation—such as sales that are too low—can be easily explained. However, as we saw in Chapter 4 ("Making Decisions"), things are often not what they seem. Perhaps the sales target was too high, or your firm could not supply the products or couldn't supply them on time. The point is that a deviation from the standard merely flags a problem that may or may not require further analysis. You may then have to diagnose and solve the problem.

Commitment-Based Control

As companies expand worldwide and compete in fast-changing markets, the problems of relying on traditional controls like budgets have become increasingly apparent. Sears, Roebuck, and Company, as we saw in Chapter 3, took a $60 million charge against earnings after it admitted that some of its service writers and mechanics recommended unnecessary automobile repairs to customers. Kidder, Peabody & Company lost $350 million when a trader allegedly reported fictitious profits.

Problems like these were not—and probably could not have been—anticipated with traditional controls. Particularly today, when markets change quickly and more employees are empowered, managers need a way to ensure that their employees won't let activities slip out of control, or that, if they do, the managers will discover it before catastrophe strikes. Harvard professor and control expert Robert Simons puts it this way:

> A fundamental problem facing managers [today] is how to exercise adequate control in organizations that demand flexibility, innovation, and creativity. . . . In most organizations operating in dynamic and highly competitive markets, managers cannot spend all their time and effort making sure that everyone is doing what is expected. Nor is it realistic to think that managers can achieve control by simply hiring good people, aligning incentives, and hoping for the best. Instead, today's managers must encourage employees to initiate process improvements and new ways of responding to customers' needs—but in a controlled way.[9]

Companies are therefore increasingly relying on employees' commitment and self-control to keep things under control. One sign of this is the widespread use of self-managing teams, wherein employees are given the self-confidence, tools, training, and information they need to do their jobs as if they owned the firm. The idea here is that the best way to keep things on track is to get the employee to want to do so.

This leaves us with two basic ways to maintain control. While any classification scheme is bound to be somewhat arbitrary, we can conveniently distinguish (see Figure 15.2) between traditional control systems and commitment-based control systems:

- Traditional control systems, as we've seen, are based on setting standards and then monitoring performance. These systems include three categories of controls: diagnostic controls, boundary systems and interactive controls.[10] **Diagnostic control systems** (such as budgets) allow managers to determine whether important targets have been met and, if necessary, to figure out why they haven't been. **Boundary control systems** are policies that identify the boundaries within which employees are to operate. Ethical rules against accepting gifts from suppliers are an example. **Interactive control systems** involve controlling employees interactively, by questioning them face to face.

diagnostic control system
a control method, such as a budget, that ensures that standards are being met and that variances are diagnosed and explained.

boundary control system
policies, such as codes of conduct, that establish rules and identify the actions and pitfalls that employees must avoid.

interactive control system
control methods that involve direct, face-to-face interaction with employees so as to monitor rapidly changing information and respond proactively to changing conditions.

▼ **FIGURE 15.2**   **Two Basic Categories of Control Systems**

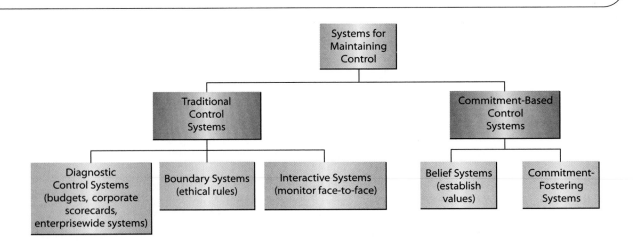

- Commitment-based control systems rely on getting the employees themselves to want to do things right—they emphasize self-control, in other words. For example, companies like Toyota and Saturn work hard to socialize all employees in the companies' belief systems and values, such as the importance of teamwork, quality, and respect for people, to foster self-control. The employees then, they hope, are more inclined to control their own actions. Other companies emphasize systems for building commitment to doing what is best for the company, and doing it right.

Let's look at these two types of systems in more detail.

▶ TRADITIONAL CONTROL SYSTEMS

We can start by exploring the three main types of traditional control systems: diagnostic control systems, boundary control systems, and interactive control systems.

Diagnostic-Control Systems

When most people think of controls, they think of *diagnostic control systems*. These aim to ensure that the firm's targets and goals are being met and that any discrepancies can be diagnosed and explained. Budgets and performance reports are examples. Semi-annual performance reviews are another.

Diagnostic controls reduce the need for managers to constantly monitor everything.[11] Once targets have been set, managers can (at least in theory) leave the employees to pursue the goals, supposedly secure in the knowledge that if the goals aren't met, the deviations will show up as variances that must be explained. This idea is at the heart of what managers call the principle of exception. The **principle of exception** (or management by exception) holds that to conserve managers' time, only significant deviations or exceptions from the standard, "both the especially good and bad exceptions," should be brought to the manager's attention.[12]

The Basic Management Control System There are any number of things that a manager might want to control, ranging from employees' performance to the progress of a report. However, there's no doubt that in virtually every organization it's the financial aspects of how the company is doing that's the bottom line of what needs to be controlled. At the end of the day, it's usually whether the manager achieved his or her sales, expense, and profit targets that largely determines whether or not that person succeeded in the past year or not. The basic management control system is therefore usually financially based.

As a result, the management functions of planning and controlling are inseparable. As explained in Chapters 5 and 6, planning generally begins with formulating a strategic plan for the enterprise, including a strategy or course of action that explains how the enterprise will move from the business it's in now to the business it wants to be in. This provides an overall direction for the enterprise and creates a framework within which the rest of the planning process can take place.

Subsidiary, lower-level plans and a hierarchy of goals are then produced. At the top, the president and his or her staff might set strategic goals (such as to have 50% of sales revenue from customized products by 2001), to which each vice president's goal is then tied. A chain or hierarchy of supporting departmental goals and short-term operational goals can then be formulated. (We covered this

principle of exception sometimes called management by exception, this rule holds that employees should be left to pursue the standards set by management, and only significant deviations from the standard should be brought to a manager's attention.

process in detail in Chapter 5.) At each step in this hierarchical process, the goals and plans are almost always translated into financial targets and embodied in financial reports of various kinds. Financial statements and budgets comprise the heart of the basic management control system. Let's look more closely at these statements and budgets.

budget
formal, financial expression of a manager's plans.

sales budget
shows the number of units to be shipped in each period (usually per month) or in general the sales activity to be achieved and the sales revenue expected from the sales.

operating budget
shows the expected sales and/or expenses for each of the company's departments for the planning period in question.

production and materials budget
shows what the company plans to spend for materials, labor, and administration in order to fulfill the requirements of the sales budget.

income statement
shows expected sales, expected expenses, and expected income or profit for the year.

cash budget
shows, for each month, the amount of cash the company can expect to receive and the amount it can expect to disperse.

balance sheet
is a projected statement of the financial position of the firm.

Budgets are formal financial expressions of a manager's plans. They show targets for things such as sales, cost of materials, production levels, and profit, usually expressed in dollars. These planned targets are the standards against which actual performance is compared and controlled. The first step in budgeting is generally to develop a sales forecast and sales budget. The **sales budget** shows the number of units to be shipped in each period (usually per month) or in general the sales activity to be achieved, and the revenue expected from the sales.

Various operating budgets can then be produced. **Operating budgets** show the expected sales and/or expenses for each of the company's departments for the planning period in question. For example, a **production and materials budget** or plan might show what the company plans to spend for materials, labor, administration, and so forth in order to fulfill the requirements of the sales budget.

For the organization as a whole, the data from all of these budgets or plans are generally compiled into a tentative profit plan for the coming year. This tentative profit plan is usually called the budgeted **income statement** or pro forma income statement. It shows expected sales, expected expenses, and expected income or profit for the year. In practice, cash from sales usually doesn't flow into the firm in such a way as to coincide precisely with cash disbursements. (Some customers may take 35 days to pay their bills, for instance, but employees expect to be paid every week). The **cash budget** or plan shows, for each month, the amount of cash the company can expect to receive and the amount it can expect to disperse. Any expected cash shortage can then be planned for, perhaps with a short-term loan.

There will also probably be a budgeted **balance sheet** for the company. This is a projected statement of the financial position of the firm; it shows assets (such as cash and equipment), liabilities (such as long-term debt), and net worth, (the excess of assets over other liabilities). The budgeted balance sheet shows managers, owners, and creditors what the company's projected financial picture should be at the end of the year.

Budgets are probably the most widely used control device. Each manager, from first-line supervisor to company president, usually has an operating budget to use as a standard of comparison. Remember, however, that creating the budget (as shown in Figure 15.3) is just the standard-setting step in the three-step control process. Actual performance still must be measured and compared to the

▶ FIGURE 15.3
Example of a Budget

BUDGET FOR MACHINERY DEPARTMENT, JUNE 2000

Budgeted Expenses	Budget
Direct Labor	$2,107
Supplies	$3,826
Repairs	$ 402
Overhead (electricity, etc.)	$ 500
TOTAL EXPENSES	$6,835

FIGURE 15.4

Example of a Performance Report

PERFORMANCE REPORT FOR MACHINERY DEPARTMENT, JUNE 2000

	Budget	Actual	Variance	Explanation
Direct Labor	$2,107	$2,480	$373 over	Had to put workers on overtime.
Supplies	$3,826	$4,200	$374 over	Wasted two crates of material.
Repairs	$ 402	$ 150	$252 under	
Overhead (electricity, etc.)	$ 500	$ 500	0	
TOTAL	$6,835	$7,330	$495 over	

budgeted standards and, if necessary, the problem diagnosed and corrective action taken.

The organization's accountants are responsible for collecting data on actual performance. They compile the financial information and feed it back to the appropriate managers. The most common form of feedback is a performance report, such as the one in Figure 15.4. The manager typically receives a report like this for his or her unit at the end of some time period (say, each month).

As in Figure 15.4, the performance report shows budgeted or planned targets. Next to these numbers, it shows the department's actual performance. The report also lists the differences between budgeted and actual amounts; these are usually called **variances**. A space is sometimes provided for the manager to explain any variances. After reviewing the performance report, the manager can take corrective action. The firm's accountants will also conduct an audit of the firm's financial statements and financial results. An **audit** is a systematic process of objectively obtaining and evaluating evidence regarding important aspects of the firm's performance, judging the accuracy and validity of the data, and communicating the results to interested users such as the board of directors and the company's banks.[13] The purpose of the audit is to make sure the firm's financial statements accurately reflect its performance.

Ratio Analysis and Return on Investment   Most managers and accountants maintain control in part by monitoring various **financial ratios**, which compare one financial indicator on a financial statement to another. The rate of return on investment (ROI) is one such ratio: It is a measure of overall company performance and equals net profit divided by total investment. Return on investment measures net profit not as an absolute figure, but rather in relation to the total investment in the business. A $1 million profit, for example, would be more impressive in a business with a $10 million investment than in one with a $100 million investment. Figure 15.5 presents some commonly used financial ratios.

Figure 15.6 shows how financial ratios can be used to analyze a firm's performance. For example, a missed net income target may be due to low sales or high sales costs. Similarly, earnings divided by sales (the profit margin) reflects management's success or failure in maintaining satisfactory cost controls. As another example, a low ROI can be influenced by factors like excessive investment. In turn, excessive investment might reflect inadequate inventory control, accounts receivable, or cash.[14]

Financial Responsibility Centers   Particularly in larger departments, the managers' operating budgets usually reflect the fact that the managers are in charge of financial responsibility centers. **Financial responsibility centers** are

variance
the difference between budgeted and actual amounts.

audit
a systematic process of objectively obtaining and evaluating evidence regarding important aspects of the firm's performance, judging the accuracy and validity of the data, and communicating the results to interested users.

financial ratio
an arithmetic comparison of one financial measure to another, generally used to monitor and control financial performance.

financial responsibility centers
individuals or groups who are assigned the responsibility for a particular set of financial outputs and/or inputs.

NAME OF RATIO	FORMULA	INDUSTRY NORM (AS ILLUSTRATION)

1. Liquidity Ratios (measuring the ability of the firm to meet its short-term obligations)

Current ratio	$\dfrac{\text{Current assets}}{\text{Current liabilities}}$	2.6
Acid-test ratio	$\dfrac{\text{Cash and equivalent}}{\text{Current liability}}$	1.0
Cash velocity	$\dfrac{\text{Sales}}{\text{Cash and equivalent}}$	12 times
Inventory to net working capital	$\dfrac{\text{Inventory}}{\text{Current assets} - \text{Current liabilities}}$	85%

2. Leverage Ratios (measures the contributions of financing by owners compared with financing provided by creditors)

Debt to equity	$\dfrac{\text{Total debt}}{\text{Net worth}}$	56%
Coverage of fixed charges	$\dfrac{\text{Net profit before fixed charges}}{\text{Fixed charges}}$	6 times
Current liability to net worth	$\dfrac{\text{Current liability}}{\text{Net worth}}$	32%
Fixed assets to net worth	$\dfrac{\text{Fixed assets}}{\text{Net worth}}$	60%

3. Activities Ratios (measures the effectiveness of the employment of resources)

Inventory turnover	$\dfrac{\text{Sales}}{\text{Inventory}}$	7 times
Net working capital turnover	$\dfrac{\text{Sales}}{\text{Net working capital}}$	5 times
Fixed-assets turnover	$\dfrac{\text{Sales}}{\text{Fixed assets}}$	6 times
Average collection period	$\dfrac{\text{Receivables}}{\text{Average sales per day}}$	20 days
Equity capital turnover	$\dfrac{\text{Sales}}{\text{Net worth}}$	3 times
Total capital turnover	$\dfrac{\text{Sales}}{\text{Total assets}}$	2 times

4. Profitability Ratios (indicates degree of success in achieving desired profit levels)

Gross operating margin	$\dfrac{\text{Gross operating profit}}{\text{Sales}}$	30%
Net operating margin	$\dfrac{\text{Net operating profit}}{\text{Sales}}$	6.5%
Sales (profit) margin	$\dfrac{\text{Net profit after taxes}}{\text{Sales}}$	3.2%
Productivity of assets	$\dfrac{\text{Gross income less taxes}}{\text{Total assets}}$	10%
Return on investment	$\dfrac{\text{Net profit after taxes}}{\text{Total investment}}$	7.5%
Net profit on working capital	$\dfrac{\text{Net operating profit}}{\text{Net working capital}}$	14.5%

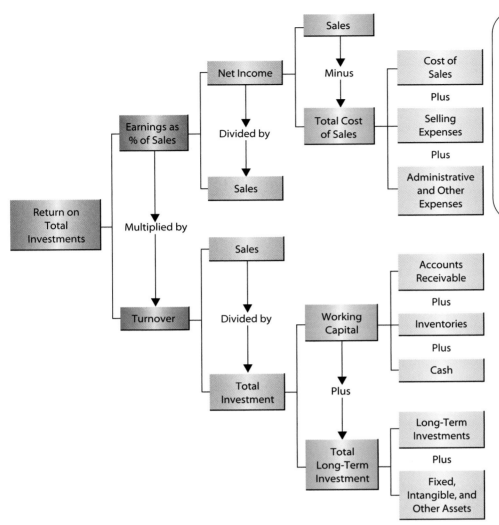

Relationship of Factors Affecting Return on Investment

The firm's overall profitability—its return on total investments—can be better understood by analyzing its components, including earnings as a percentage of sales and turnover.

individuals or units who are responsible for and measured based on a specific set of financial activities. For example, **profit centers** are responsibility centers whose managers are held accountable for profit, which is a measure of the difference between the revenues generated and the cost of generating those revenues.[15] The Saturn division of General Motors is a profit center and the performance of the person managing that division is controlled in large part in terms of whether or not he or she meets the division's profit goals. **Revenue centers** are responsibility centers whose managers are held accountable for generating revenues, which is a financial measure of output. Sales managers are generally measured in terms of the sales produced by their revenue center/departments.

profit centers

responsibility centers whose managers are held accountable for profit.

revenue centers

responsibility centers whose managers are held accountable for generating revenues, which is a financial measure of output.

■ **Using Technology to Stay in Control at UPS**

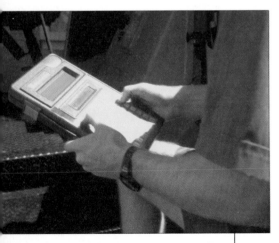

UPS is the world's largest air and ground package distribution company, delivering close to three billion parcels and documents each year in the United States and more than 185 other countries. Critical to its success has been the $1.8 billion UPS invested in the mid 1990s in information technology. Each UPS driver uses a hand-held computer called a Delivery Information Acquisition Device (pictured below) to capture customers' signatures along with pick-up, delivery, and time card information and automatically transmit this information to headquarters via a cellular telephone network.

Through TotalTrack, its automated package-tracking system, UPS can control packages throughout the delivery process. And with its own global communication network called UPSnet, UPS not only tracks its packages, but electronically transmits documentation on each shipment directly to customs officials prior to arrival. Shipments are therefore either cleared for shipment or flagged for inspection when they arrive.

Today, UPS uses the Internet to help it and its customers monitor and control the progress of all those millions and millions of packages. For example, the UPS Internet-based tracking system lets a customer store up to 25 tracking numbers and then monitor the progress of each package. That not only lets the customer (and UPS) keep on top of each package's progress, but it is also a "value added" feature for the customer, which can easily keep its customers informed about the progress of the ultimate customer's package.

▲ **W E B N O T E**

UPS Internet-based tracking system lets customers monitor their package's progress without contacting UPS customer representatives.

www.ups.com
Used with permission.

▲ The UPS portable scanner system allows drivers to relay information about each delivery to headquarters so the firm can monitor the whereabouts of every package it ships.

The Corporate Scorecard Today, more and more companies are experimenting with a diagnostic control tool called a **corporate scorecard**. Its basic purpose is to provide managers with an overall impression of how their companies are doing.[16]

Corporate scorecards are basically computerized models. Like other traditional diagnostic control tools, they measure how the company has been doing and help managers diagnose exactly what (if anything) has gone wrong. However, they differ from their simpler control cousins, such as budgets, in several ways. First, they mathematically trace a multitude of performance measures simultaneously, and show the relationships between these various measures. The manager therefore generally gets several measures of overall performance, rather than just one or two. At Shell Oil, for instance, the Shell Business Model (as Shell's scorecard is called) shows revenue growth, overall company market value, rate of return compared to the cost of borrowing money, and rate of return of the firm as a whole.

Like the dials on your car's dashboard, corporate scorecards help managers better analyze and control what's happening in their companies. For example, before using the Shell Business Model, Shell's managers didn't understand the mathematical link between revenue growth and shareholder value (especially stock price). As a result, they wouldn't try to rush a new oil rig into operation, since fast growth was not so important to them. With the new scorecard model, they could see that faster growth translates into higher shareholder value, so they're more anxious to get those oil rigs on-line fast.

Enterprise Resource Planning Systems   Corporate scorecards are actually components of larger control systems known as **enterprise resource planning systems**. Systems like these are produced by companies like SAP of Germany, Oracle, and PeopleSoft. They are basically companywide integrated computer systems that integrate a firm's individual control systems (such as order processing, production control, and accounting) in order to give managers real-time, instantaneous information regarding the costs and status of every activity and project in the business.[17]

Using one of these products, for example, the check-printing company Deluxe Paper Payment Systems was able to "get a clearer picture of which of its customers were profitable and which were not."[18] When it discovered how much more profitable an order from a bank for checks could be when it came via electronic ordering, the company launched a campaign to increase electronic ordering—particularly by its 18,000 bank and small-business customers. As a result, the number of checks ordered electronically jumped from 48% to 62% in just a few months, dramatically improving profits at Deluxe. The box below shows another example.

With results like that, some glowingly refer to enterprise software as "the stuff that puts the information age to work for corporations.[19] By integrating all the company's various control systems, "managers will now be able to receive daily online reports about the costs of specific business processes, for example, and on the real-time profitability of individual products and customers."[20]

corporate scorecard

a management tool, usually a computerized model, that traces a multitude of performance measures simultaneously and slows their interactions.

enterprise resource planning system

a companywide integrated computer system that gives managers real-time, instantaneous information regarding the costs and status of every activity and project in the business.

Using Enterprise Software to Get in Control

ENTREPRENEURS IN ACTION

While enterprise software systems can be very expensive—one Fortune 500 company reportedly spent $30 million in license fees and $200 million in consulting fees to install one—smaller firms are increasingly using them, too.[21] For example, thanks to its new enterprise software system, "three people at Harman Music Group that once worked nearly full-time planning what products to make at its factory [have been replaced by] two people who do that work part time each week."[22]

According to Harman's director of operations, Matthew Bush, the stacks of reports (including production schedules, orders, and inventory reports) that he used to analyze each day to begin developing his production plans now come right off his personal computer: "I just call it up and, in a matter of seconds, there it is."

Harman hired Hewlett-Packard to install its new software, and Hewlett-Packard assigned a five-person full-time team to the project. The team began by developing a blueprint of how Harman music operates by interviewing employees

and by mapping out exactly how information (such as a new order) went from one activity to another, and analyzing which managers needed what kind of information.

The team made some interesting discoveries along the way. For example, they discovered that three people at Harman spent part of their workday literally "taking out the trash," getting rid of scrap and obsolete inventory. When it became obvious how expensive that basically unproductive activity was, the process was streamlined.

There were other discoveries, and many other benefits. For example, while the company reportedly always knew how many units of a model it planned to build in any given week, and how many were in stock and how many were ordered, "there was a lot of guesswork" in matching all that information. The new enterprise system updates the forecast whenever the company gets an order. It also automatically updates production plans, while providing Harman's managers with a real-time estimate of the profitability of each of its products. Now that's control!

On September 30, 1999, SAP launched a new Web site called mysap.com. Companies can use the site to download SAP software components, as well as to link with other companies using SAP—for instance, to link their sales and inventory systems—and interact more seamlessly with them.[23]

Boundary Control Systems

Boundary control systems are a second traditional category of ways to maintain control. They "establish the rules of the game and identify actions and pitfalls that employees must avoid."[24] In other words, they set the boundaries within which employees should operate. Examples include standards of ethical behavior and the codes of conduct to which employees are told to adhere.

Johnson & Johnson's credo (explained in Chapter 3), illustrates the heart of a boundary control system. It contains fundamental ethical guidelines (such as, "We believe our first responsibility is to the doctors, nurses, and patients . . . who use our products" and "Our suppliers and distributors must have an opportunity to make a fair profit"). These are supposed to provide the boundaries within which Johnson & Johnson employees are to keep. Selling a product that might be harmful, for example, would obviously be out of bounds. This helps explain why when several bottles of poisoned Tylenol were found some years back, Johnson & Johnson decided to recall the entire stock of the product.

Ethical or boundary control systems require more than just drawing up a list of guidelines. In Chapter 3, for instance, we emphasized that fostering ethics at work involves at least five steps.

1. Emphasize top management's commitment.
2. Publish a code.
3. Establish compliance mechanisms.
4. Involve personnel at all levels.
5. Measure results.

Boundary control systems are important for any company, but they're especially important for firms that depend on trust.[25] Large consulting firms like McKinsey & Company and the Boston Consulting Group must be able to assure clients that the highly proprietary strategic data they'll see will never be compromised. They must therefore enforce strict rules "that forbid consultants to reveal information—even the names of clients—to anyone not employed by the firm, including spouses."[26]

The boundaries a firm lays down are not limited to ethical guidelines: "Strategic boundaries focus on ensuring that people steer clear of opportunities that could diminish the business's competitive position."[27] Thus managers at Automatic Data Processing (ADP) use a strategic boundary list that lays out the types of business opportunities ADP managers should avoid. Another company, a large Netherlands-based multinational, has a strategic policy of discouraging its executives from forming joint ventures with firms in the United States because of the greater possibility of litigation in U.S. courts. The basic idea of such rules and policies is to delineate and control the boundaries within which employees should stay.

Interactive Control Systems

The typical small, entrepreneurial company has at least one big control advantage over its huge multinational competitors: Mom and Pop can talk face to face with almost everyone in the firm to find out immediately how everything is going.

Indeed, such face-to-face interaction is at the heart of how most smaller companies traditionally maintain control. It is perhaps the most basic traditional way to stay in control.

Of course, as companies grow, this kind of direct interaction becomes more difficult. However, most firms still use these controls. Interactive strategic control is one example. It is a real-time, usually face-to-face method of monitoring both a strategy's effectiveness and the underlying assumptions on which the strategy is built.[28]

Senior managers at *USA Today* use interactive control.[29] Three weekly reports delivered each Friday give senior managers an overview of how they have done in the previous week and what they may expect in the next few weeks. This "Friday packet" includes information ranging from year-to-date advertising and sales figures to specific information regarding particular advertisers.

▲ The *USA Today* newsroom, where managers can meet and monitor both the news and the newspaper's activities, minute by minute.

Weekly face-to-face meetings among senior managers and key subordinates are part of interactive control at *USA Today*. Regular meeting topics include advertising volume compared to plan, and new business by type of client. Senior managers don't just look for unexpected shortfalls; they also look for unexpected successes that might suggest putting more emphasis on particular areas, such as approaching more software suppliers to advertise. Several strategic innovations have emerged from these meetings. Among them are exclusive advertising inserts dedicated to specific customers and products, and a new market-survey service for automotive clients.

How does information like this help *USA Today*'s senior managers? It helps them to look at the big picture regarding how the paper is doing versus its competitors. And it helps them identify trends, such as decreasing or increasing advertising expenditures by specific advertisers, or changing sales patterns in various states. At *USA Today*, interactive controls give senior managers a formal procedure through which they can monitor strategic information and get a feel for the importance of that information by interacting face to face with key subordinates.

▶ HOW DO PEOPLE REACT TO CONTROL?

Every organization has to ensure that its employees are performing as planned. Every day managers face questions like "How can I make sure that Marie files her sales reports on time?" and "How can I make sure John doesn't close the store before 10:00 P.M.?" To a large extent, the answer to both questions is to impose controls. Unfortunately, relying on controls is not as easy as it may seem.

The Negative Side of Control

If controlling employees' behavior were the only (or the best) way to ensure effective performance, we could disregard much of this book. For example, we wouldn't need to know much about what motivates people, what leadership style is best, or how to win employee commitment. We could just "control" employees' work.

But the fact is that managers can't just rely on controls for keeping employees in line. For one thing, from a practical point of view, it's impossible to have a system of rules and controls so complete that you can track everything employees say or do, even with enterprise software. For another, employees often short-circuit the controls, sometimes with ingenious techniques. Let's look more closely at this second problem.

Some Unintended Behavioral Consequences of Controls

How can employees evade controls? One expert classifies these employee tactics as behavioral displacement, gamesmanship, operating delays, and negative attitudes.[30]

behavioral displacement
a reaction to being controlled in which employees concentrate too narrowly on the company's control standards and thereby miss the company's more important objectives.

Behavioral Displacement Behavioral displacement occurs when the behaviors encouraged by the controls are inconsistent with what the company actually wants to accomplish. "You get what you measure," in other words. Employees focus their efforts where results are measured and disregard the company's more important goals.

The problem stems mostly from limiting the measures to just one or two control standards. For example, Nordstrom, a retailer famed for its extraordinary customer service, found itself involved in a lawsuit related to its policy of measuring employees in terms of sales per hour of performance.[31] Unfortunately, tracking its salespeople's performance by simply monitoring sales per hour backfired. Without other measures, the sales-per-hour system didn't work. Some employees claimed their supervisors were pressuring them to underreport hours on the job to boost reported sales per hour. Nordstrom ended up settling the claims for over $15 million.

gamesmanship
management actions that try to improve the manager's apparent performance in terms of the control system without producing any economic benefits for the company.

Gamesmanship Gamesmanship refers to management actions aimed at improving the manager's performance in terms of the control system, without producing any economic benefits for the firm. For example, one manager depleted his stocks of spare parts and heating oil at year's end, although he knew these stocks would have to be replenished shortly thereafter at higher prices. By reducing his stocks, the manager reduced his expenses for the year and made his end-of-year results look better, although in the long run the company spent more than it had to.[32] In another example, a division overshipped products to distributors at year-end. The aim was to ensure that management could meet its budgeted sales targets, even though the managers knew the products would be returned.[33]

Operating Delays Operating delays are another unintended consequence of control, and they are especially dangerous when quick, responsive decisions are required. When he became CEO of GE, for instance, Jack Welch knew that it sometimes took a year or more for division managers to get approval to introduce new products; the problem was the long list of approvals required by GE's control system. Flattening the organization and streamlining the approval process are two ways to solve this problem.

Negative Attitudes In addition to displacement, gamesmanship, and operating delays, controls can have more insidious effects by undermining employee attitudes. One study that focused on first-line supervisors' reactions to budgets found that the budgets were viewed as pressure devices. Supervisors came to see them as prods by top management and in turn used them to prod their own subordinates. As a result of this pressure, employees formed antimanagement work groups, and the supervisors reacted by increasing their compliance efforts.[34]

"Intelligent" employee ID badges provide a more high-tech example. Italy's Olivetti holds the basic patent on the Active-Badge System and began marketing it commercially in the early 1990s. The Active Badge looks like a clip-on ID card. It's actually a small computer that emits infrared signals to strategically located sensors, which can then track the wearer anywhere within an equipped facility. The system can also keep tabs on visitors. Knowing where people are avoids interruptions, wasted phone calls, and useless trips to empty offices. But questions arise: How much privacy can managers expect employees to surrender in the name of control? How much control is too much? And what effect will these badges have on morale? Proponents say effective safeguards can be implemented. Critics fear that once such a system is in place, there will be no defense against abuse.[35] Let's look more closely at this.

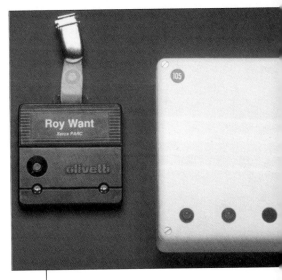

▲   Xerox uses a form of the Active Badge as a management control device: It allows managers to find employees quickly for meetings and phone calls.

■ Electronic Performance Monitoring and Control

When it comes to monitoring employees electronically, computerized badges are the tip of the iceberg. As two researchers recently put it: "As many as 26 million workers in the United States are subject to electronic performance monitoring (EPM)—such as having supervisors monitor through electronic means the amount of computerized data an employee is processing per day—on the job."[36]

Jeffrey Stanton and Janet Barnes-Farrell studied the effects of such monitoring on individuals working on computers in an officelike environment.[37] The 108 participants were recruited from introductory psychology classes. The researchers wanted to study several things: one was whether a worker's feelings of personal control were affected by having the ability to lock out the performance monitoring; another was whether informing the person he or she was being monitored affected performance.

The results show why it's important for employees to believe they have some personal control over their environments. "Participants with the ability to delay or prevent electronic performance monitoring indicated higher feelings of personal control and demonstrated superior task performance."[38] The findings also suggest that if you *are* going to monitor employees' performance electronically, it's probably best not to let them know when they're actually being monitored. Participants who knew exactly when they were being monitored expressed lower feelings of personal control than did those who were not told when they were being monitored.

By the way, don't assume that electronic performance monitoring will apply only to subordinates and not to bosses. For example, the Japanese company that controls 7-Eleven is gradually trying to impose an EPM system on its store managers in Japan and in the United States. Like all 7-Eleven stores, the ones belonging to Michiharu Endo use a point-of-sale computer to let headquarters know each time he makes a sale. In the case of 7-Eleven's new system, headquarters monitors how much time Endo spends using the analytical tools built into the computerized cash register to track product sales, and how effective he is at weaning out poor sellers. Headquarters then ranks stores by how often their operators use the computer as a measure of how efficient they are.

The system has run into particular resistance in the United States. Many 7-Eleven managers, thinking they escaped the bureaucratic ratrace by taking over their own stores, have been surprised at the degree of control this new EPM system has exposed them to.[39]

▶ USING COMMITMENT-BASED CONTROL SYSTEMS

This all presents an interesting dilemma for those managing today's organizations. For one thing, globalized and team-based organizations complicate the task of keeping everything under control: Distance makes monitoring what your employees are doing day-to-day much more difficult, especially since there's a tendency to try to evade the control system. A second problem is that imposing too much control on self-managing teams may well backfire: How can you feel empowered if someone else is controlling everything you do?

How then do today's managers ensure that everyone does what they're supposed to do and that things stay under control? Increasingly, the answer is by supplementing traditional controls with systems that encourage employees to exercise self-control. The idea here is that employees are then driven to do what they're supposed to do not because they have to, but because they want to. As management guru Tom Peters once put it:

> You are out of control when you are "in control." You are in control when you are "out of control." [The executive] who knows everything and who is surrounded by layers of staffers and inundated with thousands of pages of analyses from below may be "in control" in the classic sense but in fact really only has the illusion of control. The manager has tons of after-the-fact reports on everything, but (almost) invariably a control system and organization that's so ponderous that it's virtually impossible to respond fast enough even if a deviation is finally detected. . . . In fact, you really are in control when thousands upon thousands of people, unbeknownst to you, are taking initiatives, going beyond job descriptions and the constraints of their box on the organization chart, to serve the customer better, improve the process, [or] work quickly with a supplier to nullify a defect.[40]

There are at least three approaches managers can use to encourage self-control and employee commitment: motivation techniques, belief systems, and commitment-building systems. Obviously, highly motivated employees are generally more likely to do their jobs right. We discussed motivation techniques at length in Chapter 11. In the remainder of this chapter, we'll look at how managers use *belief systems* and *commitment-building systems* to encourage and foster employee self-control.

Using Belief Systems and Values to Foster Self-Control

We've seen at several points in this book (particularly in Chapter 3, Ethics, and Chapter 14, Managing Change) that a person's behavior tends to be a function of his or her values and beliefs. For example, if one of your values is "always do your best at everything you do, and never do more than you can do well," you'll probably do a better job than someone who takes a more flippant approach to the quality of his or her work. Since values can have a powerful influence on controlling one's behavior, managers often try to instill the right values in their employees.

This helps to explain why companies work hard to create a belief system—a culture—that is consistent with what the company wants to achieve. At the Toyota Manufacturing plant in Lexington, Kentucky, for instance, quality and teamwork are crucial to everything the facility wants to do. Its managers therefore steep their employees in the culture and values of quality and teamwork. They do this by selecting new employees based on the extent to which they evidence such traits, and then by emphasizing quality and teamwork in orientation, training, and appraisal and incentive systems. To a large extent, in other words, the superior quality and high productivity that characterizes Toyota's Lexington facility is a result not of technology (since all auto plants have similar machines), but of the employees' dedication to a handful of core values that drive their behavior.

It's hard to overestimate how important shared values like these can be in managing far-flung global operations. Shared values like Wal-Mart's "hard work, honesty, neighborliness, and thrift" provide it's employees with a common ideology or way of looking at the world. They give Wal-Mart's employees a sort of built-in compass, one that gives them the direction and sense of purpose that's required to do the job right, no matter how far from headquarters they are, and without a rulebook or supervisor to watch their every move.

In a study of successful and long-lived companies, James Collins and Jerry Porras made similar observations. In their book *Built to Last*, they describe how firms like Boeing, Disney, GE, Merck, and Motorola put enormous effort into creating shared values, values that answer questions such as "What are we trying to achieve together?" and "What does this organization stand for?"[41] As they say,

> More than at any time in the past companies will not be able to hold themselves together with the traditional methods of control: hierarchy, systems, budgets, and the like. Even "going into the office" will become less relevant as technology enables people to work from remote sites. The bonding glue will increasingly become *ideological*.[42]

In explaining why shared values are so important for managing today, Collins and Porras emphasize that a strong set of shared values "allows for coordination without control, adaptation without chaos."[43] In other words, employees who buy into the company's values don't need to be coaxed, prodded, or controlled into doing the right thing: They'll do the right thing because they believe it's the right thing to do. They'll control themselves.

This helps to explain why organizational change efforts (discussed in the preceding chapter) often put a premium on achieving cultural change. When Louis Gerstner took over as IBM's CEO, he knew that reorganizing and instituting a new strategy wouldn't be enough to transform his giant company into a highly responsive and efficient competitor. In many parts of the company, more lethargic values had taken root: these emphasized, for instance, seniority rather than performance;

waiting for approvals rather than acting; and sticking to the chain of command. It took several years of Gerstner leading by example, instituting new systems (such as performance-based pay), and evangalizing about the firm's new values before IBM's new culture could emerge.

Today, at IBM as at many other change-oriented companies, the values that tend to be cherished include beliefs in teamwork, openness, candor, trust, and being number one. To the extent that employees share these values, the task of controlling what employees do becomes easier: Again, for example, assemblers at Toyota's Camry plant in Lexington, Kentucky, build quality into their cars not because they're being supervised or told to do so, but because they're driven to do so by their own deep-seated beliefs.

Using Commitment-Building Systems to Foster Self-Control

Fostering the right values is one way to encourage self-control; building employees' commitment is another.

Viacom several years ago reached agreement to sell its Prentice Hall publishing operations to Pearson PLC, for $4.6 billion. In announcing the sale, Prentice Hall's president thanked its employees for their past hard work and dedication, and reminded them that during the transition, "It's more important than ever to focus on our individual responsibilities to ensure that our company performs at the highest levels."[44] His message spotlights a dilemma all managers have today: maintaining employee commitment—an employee's identification with and agreement to pursue the company's or the unit's mission—in the face of downsizings, mergers, and turbulent change.[45] In other words, how do you get your employees to exercise self-control and do their jobs as if they own the company at a time when loyalty seems to be going out of style?

Over the past 30 years or so, we've learned quite a bit about how to earn employee commitment. The evidence suggests that doing so requires a comprehensive, multifaceted management system, one that draws on all the managers' planning, organizing, leading, and controlling skills, and one consisting of an integrated package of concrete managerial actions. These actions would include the following: foster people-first values, guarantee organizational justice, build a sense of community, communicate your vision, use value-based hiring, plus financial rewards, and encourage personal development and self-actualization.

Foster People-First Values   Building employee commitment usually starts by establishing a strong foundation of "people-first values." Firms that hold to these values literally put their people first: They trust their employees, assume their employees are their most important assets, believe strongly in respecting their employees as individuals and treating them fairly, and maintain a relentless commitment to each employee's welfare. As one United Auto Workers (UAW) officer at Saturn Corporation's Spring Hill, Tennessee, plant put it:

> Our philosophy is, we care about people—and it shows. We involve people in decisions that affect them. I came from the Messina, New York, GM foundry, and managers there, like a lot of the other managers you'll come across, take the position that "I'll tell you what to do, and that's what you'll do." In fact, some of those managers from the foundry are here now. But on the whole those who are here now are different, and the basic difference is wrapped up in the question "Do you really believe in people?" Saturn's commitment really comes down to how you feel about people—your attitudes—more than

commitment

the relative strength of an individual's identification with and involvement in an organization.

anything, because all the other Saturn programs—the work teams, the extensive training, the way people are paid—all stem from these people attitudes.[46]

One way firms like Saturn foster such people-first values is by emphasizing them in all their communications to employees. For example, all Saturn employees carry a card that lists the firm's values, one of which is:

> Trust and respect for the individual: We have nothing of greater value than our people. We believe that demonstrating respect for the uniqueness of every individual builds a team of confident, creative members possessing a high degree of initiative, self-respect, and self-discipline.[47]

The UAW officer's comment that "commitment really comes down to how you feel about people" underscores another way in which people-first values are institutionalized throughout these firms: They hire managers who already have people-first values, and then promote them in part based on their people skills. In fact, it's almost impossible for antisocial people to move into management at such firms—or to stay. People-first values permeate everything these managers say and do. The idea that these values should be applied to every one of its decisions was summed up by one officer at JC Penney this way:

▲ Fostering people-first values: Charles Wang, CEO of Computer Associates, in the company's daycare center.

> Our people's high commitment stems from our commitment to them, and that commitment boils down to the fundamental respect for the individual that we all share. That respect goes back to the Penney idea—"To test every act in this wise: Does it square with what is right and just?" As a result, the value of respect for the individual is brought into our management process on a regular basis and is a standard against which we measure each and every decision that we make.[48]

Guarantee Organizational Justice Commitment is built on trust, and trust requires being treated fairly. Managers in firms like Saturn, FedEx, and GE do more than express a willingness to hear and be heard. They also establish programs that guarantee employees will be treated fairly. As explained in Chapter 12 (Communications), these programs include: guaranteed fair treatment programs for filing grievances and complaints; "speak up" programs for voicing concerns and making inquiries; periodic survey programs for expressing opinions; and various top-down programs for keeping employees informed.

Build a Sense of Shared Fate and Community High-commitment firms also work hard to encourage a sense of community and shared fate, a sense that "we're all in this together." They do so by pursuing what Rosabeth Moss Kanter calls commonality, communal work, and regular work contact and ritual.[49]

For one thing, they try to minimize status differences. In many new Internet firms, for instance, all managers and employees share one large space, perhaps (as at Sears) with some movable cubicles. Other employers have eliminated status differences like executive washrooms and executive parking spaces; these too are usually efforts at building a sense of community.

Managers further emphasize this sense of community by encouraging joint effort and communal work. At Saturn new employees are quickly steeped in the terminology and techniques of teamwork: There are no employees in the plant, only team members working together on their communal tasks (like installing all dashboard components). Team training starts with the employee's initial orientation, as new members meet their teams and are trained in the interpersonal techniques that make for good teamwork. The resulting closeness is then enhanced by empowering work teams to recruit and select their own new members. Periodic job rotation reinforces the sense that everyone is sharing all the work.

Kanter found that the feeling of "we're all in this together" is further enhanced by bringing individual employees into regular contact with the group as a whole.[50] Ben & Jerry's hosts monthly staff meetings in the receiving bay of its Waterbury, Vermont, plant. It also has a "joy gang," whose function is to organize regular "joy events," including Cajun parties, ping-pong contests, and manufacturing appreciation day.

Thanks to the Internet, employees don't necessarily have to be at the same location to cultivate the feeling that they're part of a close-knit community. Using Internet-based group communication systems such as Tribal Voice, companies can build virtual communities by letting teams of employees communicate easily and in real-time, even if they are dispersed around the globe.[51] As one expert puts it, "The sales department could hold forums and share information in an interactive community." Said another, "When people interact in a virtual community, there is an exchange of ideas and information, which becomes powerful and generates excitement."[52]

Communicate Your Vision   Committed employees need missions and visions to which to be committed, preferably missions and visions that they can say "are bigger than we are." With such missions to commit to, workers at firms like Saturn and Ben & Jerry's become almost soldiers in a crusade, one that allows them to redefine themselves in terms of the mission. In that way, says Kanter, the employee can "find himself anew in something larger and greater."[53] Employee commitment in high-commitment firms thus derives in part from the power of the firm's mission and from the willingness of the employees to acquiesce, if need be, to the needs of the firm for the good of achieving its mission.

Ben & Jerry's is an example. The company's mission still symbolizes its founders' idea of what a business should be and provides the firm and its employees with an ideology that represents a higher calling to which they can commit themselves. The mission is presented in Figure 15.7. Ben & Jerry's employees don't just make ice cream, in other words: They are out to change the world.

▶ **FIGURE 15.7**

Some Elements of Ben & Jerry's Mission

Ben & Jerry's mission is "charismatic" in that it links employees' actions with the transcendent goal of helping humankind.
Source: Adapted from Ben & Jerry's Homemade, Inc., *Employee Handbook.*

Ben & Jerry's mission consists of three interrelated parts:
   Product Mission: Making, selling, and distributing the best all-natural ice cream and related products in a wide variety of innovative flavors made from Vermont dairy products.
   Social Mission: Operating the company in a way that actively recognizes the central role that business plays in the structure of a society by initiating new ways to improve the quality of life of the broad community, including local, national, and international.
   Economic Mission: Operating the company on a sound financial basis of profitable growth, increasing value for our shareholders and creating career opportunities and financial rewards for our employees.

Use Value-Based Hiring   As we saw in Chapter 9 (Staffing), many firms today also practice **value-based hiring**. Instead of just looking for job-related skills, they try to get a sense of the applicant's personal values. To do this, they look for common experiences and values that may signal the applicant's fit with the firm and give applicants realistic previews of what to expect when they come to work there. At UPS and Delta Airlines, for instance, you must be ready to start at the bottom. At UPS, you may have a new college degree, but chances are you'll start working on a delivery truck. At Delta you may well start cleaning planes. That may seem onerous to some, but it does help sift out people who may not fit with those firms' ways of doing things. The idea is that if you don't fit in, you probably won't become committed to the company.

Use Financial Rewards and Profit Sharing   You may not be able to buy commitment, but most firms don't try to build commitment without good financial rewards. Intrinsic motivators like work involvement, a sense of achievement, and the feeling of oneness are usually not enough. To paraphrase psychologist Abraham Maslow, you can't appeal to someone's need to achieve until you've filled his or her belly and made the person secure. That is why Kanter says "Entrepreneurial incentives that give teams a piece of the action are highly appropriate in collaborative companies."[54] Firms like these generally provide above-average pay and incentives. FedEx, for instance, provides a half-dozen types of incentive awards, including "Bravo-Zulu," that a manager can award on the spot.

Encourage Employee Development and Self-Actualization   Few needs are as strong as the need to fulfill our dreams, to become all we are capable of being. In Chapter 11 (Motivation), we discussed Maslow's theory that "the desire to become more and more what one is, to become everything that one is capable of becoming" is the ultimate need. Self-actualization, to Maslow, means that "what man can be, he *must* be . . . it refers to the desire for self-fulfillment, namely, to this tendency for him to become actualized in what he is potentially.[55]

At work, promotions are important. But the real question is whether employees get the opportunity to develop and use all their skills and become, as Maslow would say, all they can be. Training employees to expand their skills and to solve problems, enriching their jobs, empowering employees to plan and inspect their own work, and helping them to continue their education and to grow are some other ways to accomplish employee self-actualization, as we've seen in earlier chapters.

Having the company explicitly commit to the goal of helping workers to self-actualize is an important part of the process. Here's what one Saturn assembler said:

> I'm committed to Saturn in part for what they did for me; for the 300 hours of training in problem solving and leadership that help me expand my personal horizons; for the firm's Excel program that helps me push myself to the limit; and because I know that at Saturn I can go as far as I can go—this company wants its people to be all that they can be. But I'm also committed to Saturn for what I saw where I came from: the burned out workers, the people who were so pressed down by the system that even if they saw their machines were about to break from poor maintenance, they'd say, "Leave it alone. Let management handle it." This is like a different world.[56]

value-based hiring

the practice of screening and hiring people whose values are consistent with those of the company, rather than looking just at an applicant's job-related skills.

Similarly, one FedEx manager described his firm's commitment to actualizing employees as follows:

> At Federal Express, the best I can be is what I can be here. I have been allowed to grow with Federal Express. For the people at Federal Express, it's not the money that draws us to the firm. The biggest benefit is that Federal Express made me a man. It gave me the confidence and self-esteem to become the person I had the potential to become.[57]

Summary: How Do You Foster Employees' Self-Control?

In today's globalized, quality-conscious, and teamwork-based world, managers can't rely on traditional control systems to ensure that results are up to par. Financial statements, budgets, and profit centers—all those elements of traditional control systems—only go so far. They can't easily monitor what a young trader is buying and selling in Asia (as Barings discovered to its chagrin). And they can't ensure the kind of continuous attention to detail and initiative that producing high-quality Camry cars or a new Windows application requires of the teams that are working on these projects. Today, you have to supplement traditional control systems with employee self-control. You have to make the workers want to do their jobs as if they own the company.

We've looked at several ways to do this. Motivation techniques like those discussed in Chapter 11 can certainly help, since motivated employees can usually be expected to perform better. Fostering the right culture of shared values can be useful too. What people do tends to reflect what they believe, and if employees believe, for instance, in doing high-quality work, then their performance will more likely reflect such values.

Finally, we've seen on the last few pages that fostering commitment is another powerful way to encourage employee self-control. Committed employees, by definition, identify with and agree to pursue the company's or the unit's mission. They exercise self-control because, in a very real sense, their companies' missions are their own, and because they do their jobs as if they own the company. Getting employees to actually think of the company's goals as their own isn't easy. It requires most of your management skills, and the creation of an integrated, commitment-oriented management system. You must:

Foster people-first values

Encourage extensive two-way communications

Build a sense of shared fate and community

Provide a vision

Use value-based hiring

Use financial rewards and profit sharing

Encourage self-actualizing

SUMMARY

1. Control is the task of ensuring that activities are providing the desired results. In its most general sense, controlling therefore means setting a target, measuring performance, and taking corrective action. Experts distinguish between steering controls, yes/no controls, and post-action controls.

2. As companies expand worldwide and compete in fast-changing markets, the problems of relying on a traditional control system (set standards, compare actual to standard, and take corrective action) have become increasingly apparent. Employees have had to become more empowered to be more responsive, and "controlling" can detract from that.

3. While the classification is somewhat arbitrary, there are three types of traditional control methods. Diagnostic control systems like budgets and performance reports are intended to ensure that goals are being achieved and that variances, if any, are explained. Boundary control systems establish the rules of the game and identify actions and pitfalls employees must avoid. Interactive control systems are real-time, usually face-to-face methods of monitoring both a plan's effectiveness and the underlying assumptions on which the plan was built.

4. Budgets and ratio analysis are among the most widely used diagnostic control tools. Budgets are formal financial expressions of a manager's plan and show targets for yardsticks such as revenues, cost of materials, and profits, usually expressed in dollars. Most managers also achieve control by monitoring various financial ratios.

5. A big problem with relying on traditional controls is that they can lead to unintended, undesirable, and often harmful employee reactions, such as behavioral displacement, gamesmanship, operating delays, negative attitudes, and reduced empowerment.

6. Achieving control in an age of empowerment relies on employees' self-control. Motivation techniques and building value systems are two important ways to tap such self-control. Another powerful way is to get employees to think of the company's goals as their own—to earn their commitment.

TYING IT ALL TOGETHER

In this book—and in this and the preceding 14 chapters—we have talked about the management process—namely, planning, organizing, leading, and controlling. Since this is a textbook, we necessarily covered the topics sequentially, one topic at a time. But as you can probably imagine, that's not the way managers really manage day to day. In other words, you generally won't have the luxury to spend Monday planning, Tuesday organizing, Wednesday and Thursday leading, and Friday controlling. Instead, you'll be doing all these tasks simultaneously. For example, as part of your planning function you'll be sitting with your subordinates trying to formulate goals and to motivate them to accept them. You may be monitoring and controlling the progress of a project, only to discover that the people staffing the project are not up to the job, or that the milestones you set when the project was planned are no longer valid. Management is really an integrated, "tying it altogether" process, in other words.

That fact is particularly evident when it comes to controlling and building commitment, the subject of this last chapter. For one thing, planning and controlling are merely two sides of the same coin: what you control and how you're doing depends entirely on where you want to go, so that deciding where planning leaves off and controlling begins is bound to be somewhat arbitrary.

Similarly, effectively controlling your organization will demand all the people skills you can muster. Employees can be enormously creative when it comes to getting around control systems, and getting them to *not* want to get around those systems is therefore a very demanding task. Also, and perhaps more important, controlling someone is usually not the best way to stay in control. You can lower your "control costs"—not to mention your aggravation level—enormously by getting your employees to want to do a great job. Doing this of course is essentially a behavioral, not a technical, process.

When you ask most people how they maintain control, their first reaction might be "we use budgets," "we use timeclocks," or "we watch what our people are doing." But getting employees to want to do a great job is in many respects the best way to keep your firm under control, and doing so, as we have seen, relies on behavioral activities like fostering people-first values and building a sense of shared fate and community. And it's just such an "integrating the people side of managing into all that they do" that top managers do best.

KEY TERMS

control 454
steering control 454
yes/no control 454
post-action control 455
traditional control methods 456
commitment-based control methods 456
diagnostic control system 458
boundary control system 458
interactive control system 458
principle of exception 459

budget 460
sales budget 460
operating budget 460
production and materials budget 460
income statement 460
cash budget 460
balance sheet 460
variance 461
audit 461
financial ratio 461

financial responsibility centers 461
profit centers 463
revenue centers 463
corporate scorecard 465
enterprise resource planning system 465
behavioral displacement 468
gamesmanship 468
commitment 472
value-based hiring 475

SKILLS AND STUDY MATERIALS

CRITICAL THINKING EXERCISES

1. The budget is a traditional means of control, usually established by the top management. Now think about establishing a budget for a company by using committed and empowered employees to develop it. Who would be involved and why? How would your approach differ from traditional budgeting?

2. We are increasingly dependent on technology and the flow of information provided by means such as the Internet. Yet there is ongoing debate about the control and privacy aspects of both the Internet and intranets. What do you think about using electronic monitoring technology as a control device? What about the privacy issues? Should our boss be able to monitor us and our use of computers?

EXPERIENTIAL EXERCISES

1. You are one of the founding engineers in your 6-month-old firm, and you brought to the firm values of environmental awareness, quality, and excellence. These values have united the original members, but you are concerned that they might change with the addition of 50 new people needed by your fast-growing company to meet demand. What type of control system would you develop to ensure your values are adhered to, based on the concepts in this chapter?

2. When you next eat at a fast food restaurant, or go to the gas station to fill up your tank or get service, or go shopping at the grocery store, note the control systems in place. Then be prepared to discuss them in class in terms of what you have read in this chapter.

myPHLIP COMPANION WEB SITE

We invite you to visit the Dessler companion Web site at **www.prenhall.com/dessler** for this chapter's Internet resources.

CONTROLLING QUALITY WITH COMMITTED EMPLOYEES AT RITZ-CARLTON

CASE 1

Many consider business hotels as offering a generic service—a safe, clean, comfortable room in a city away from home. Ritz-Carlton Hotel Company viewed its business differently. Targeting industry executives, meeting and corporate travel planners, and affluent travelers, the Atlanta-based company manages 25 luxury hotels that pursue the goal of being the very best in each market. Ritz-Carlton succeeded with more than just travelers; it was awarded the U.S. government's Malcom Baldrige National Quality Award. Given a mission of true excellence in service, what types of control systems did Ritz-Carlton need to achieve its goals?

In the presentation of the Baldrige award, the committee commended Ritz-Carlton for a management program that included participatory leadership, thorough information gathering, coordinated planning and execution, and a trained workforce empowered "to move heaven and earth" to satisfy customers. Of all the elements in the system, Ritz-Carlton felt the most important control mechanism was committed employees.

All employees are trained in the company's "Gold Standards," which set out Ritz-Carlton's service credo and the basics of premium service. The company has translated key product and service requirements into a credo, and 20 "Ritz-Carlton Basics." Each employee is expected to understand and adhere to these standards, which describe processes for solving any problem guests may have.

The corporate motto is "ladies and gentlemen serving ladies and gentlemen." Like many companies, Ritz-Carlton gives new employees an orientation followed by on-the-job training. Unlike other hotel firms, Ritz-Carlton then "certifies" employees. Corporate values are reinforced continuously by daily "line ups," frequent recognition for extraordinary achievement, and a performance appraisal based on expectations explained during the orientation, training, and certification processes.

All workers are required to act at the first sign of a problem, regardless of the type of problem or customer complaint. Employees are empowered to do whatever it takes to provide "instant pacification." Other employees must assist if a coworker requests aid in responding to a guest's complaint or wish. There is never an excuse for not solving a customer problem.

Responsibility for ensuring high-quality guest services and accommodations rests largely with employees. All employees are surveyed annually to determine their understanding of quality standards and their personal satisfaction as a Ritz-Carlton employee. In one case, 96% of all employees surveyed singled out excellence in guest services as the key priority.

Discussion Questions

1. What steps does Ritz-Carlton take to control the quality of its service?

2. What does Ritz-Carlton do to foster its employees' high level of commitment?

3. How does the company's value system foster employee self-control?

Andy Grove, former CEO of Intel, once called his company the laboratory of contemporary management.[58] The maker of the famous Pentium chip that drives most of today's desktop computers employs more than 64,000 employees in what many consider the most complex industry in which to manage. In this industry it is not uncommon for new competitors to launch previously unheard-of technologies that can unseat market leaders. Grove developed a phrase that described what he considered to be an essential way for managers of high-tech companies to operate. He later turned that phrase into a best-selling book: *Only the Paranoid Survive.* How do you maintain control in a "paranoid" environment? Are Intel's values and norms sufficiently strong to hold managers in a high-powered company in line?

The semiconductor industry is known for its breathtaking pace of change. On-line firms like Monster and Amazon can move from startups to publicly traded market leaders in the space of a year. As a $27 billion-per-year company with a great track record of success, it might be easy for Intel to become complacent—hence Grove's warning. In Grove's vocabulary, industries reach inflection points where the paradigm is about to shift. It would be easy for a manager to miss the new signals consumers are sending, and missing these signals at Intel could mean that the company could be driven from its "number 1" pedestal. In Grove's world, paranoia is healthy. To be sure, he is not describing the irrational fear a true paranoid would have. What he is describing is a need for constant vigilance. To keep managers motivated to stay in constant touch with a changing world, Intel has installed a complex management motivation and control system.

The company has grouped its human resource practices into three areas: benefits and compensation, flexible work options and benefits, and personal development and training. Central to the Intel system is the value of rewarding individual excellence. The merit-based performance system ties compensation increases and career advancement opportunities to personal performance.

Intel uses three basic types of incentive programs: an employee cash bonus program, a general bonus program, and stock incentives. The bonus programs are generally profit-sharing programs with the unique twist of rewarding both company performance and the performance of the small group in which the employee participates. Stock programs include a stock options program and stock participation plan, in both of which Intel subsidizes the purchase of

company stock. The importance of share ownership among managers is well documented; the more shares a manager holds in Intel, the greater the effect of company performance on that employee's compensation.

Intel also offers a variety of performance awards. These awards may or may not involve financial incentives, but they always involve personal recognition. Managers can achieve awards that lead to formal recognition at the corporate level or spontaneous employee-to-employee awards at the department level.

Intel also uses a number of alternative work schedule arrangements (each business group can establish its own work methods, for instance). The range of methods is quite broad and includes compressed workweeks; part-time positions; telecommuting; personal absence days; and family, medical, and personal leaves.

Intel is also deeply concerned about the personal and intellectual renewal of its employees, its core resource. In one of the most innovative programs, Intel offers all its full-time U.S. employees the opportunity to take a sabbatical leave. Every seven years, all regular full-time employees in the United States are entitled to an eight-week sabbatical with pay, in addition to normal vacation and personal time off. Intel also encourages intellectual development in more traditional ways. In 1998 the company spent more than $300 million for ongoing employee education. Under Grove's leadership, Intel had also developed a university that offers more that 3,400 courses worldwide. In addition to Intel University courses, employees may also receive full reimbursement for tuition, books, and fees for university-level courses and programs that have present or future application at the company. Finally, Intel has developed and launched a formal mentoring system.

While there are formal control systems at Intel, there is also a great reliance on individual self-control. By sharing its vision and values, and developing incentives to reinforce those values, the top management team at Intel is expressing its belief that motivated employees will control themselves to the good of the firm. So while Grove speaks of only the paranoid surviving, his company has invoked a full range of traditional and commitment-based control mechanisms to help its employees succeed. Still, the competitive dynamics in Intel's industry make it one of the most demanding environments in the world. Has Intel installed the correct mix of motivational methods to assure its survival and success?

Discussion Questions

1. In what ways do Intel's compensation packages function as a control system?

2. To what extent do you feel a company can rely on financial benefits for the self-control of its employees? Why?

3. Would traditional control systems work in the high-velocity environment in which Intel operates? Why or why not? What elements of commitment-based control systems are evident at Intel?

KEEPING THINGS UNDER CONTROL AT KNITMEDIA

KnitMedia's plans to establish a network of Knitting Factory clubs around the world means that it will need sophisticated new methods for maintaining control. That was one of the reasons Mark Harabedian was asked to join the management team. Harabedian has an accounting degree and about 15 years of strong systems background in various companies ranging from startups to rapidly growing firms. When he came in, the first thing he needed to do was "some cleanup work," as well as choose an auditor to review the company's financial situation.

Mark has already made many control systems changes. For example, he instituted an accounts payable approval process: A manager now needs to approve whenever a bill needs to be paid. He also installed a new budgeting process, "All the managers came back to me with information that we put into financial plans, and we put a budget together. There's a budget of employee spending, capital improvements, and so on. There are also budgets for the Web site activity, the festival activity, and the club activity." These new systems, says Mark, help to show the management team what they're going to spend for things like capital improvements in the future. Now they can make sure that money is available, and also that the budget figures are not exceeded.

That's just the tip of the iceberg when it comes to maintaining control at KnitMedia. As Harabedian points out, the company also has extensive retail sales of things like CDs. And it has to be able to monitor the finances of the Knitting Factory clubs in Los Angeles and Berlin, since the cash coming in—when people pay admission, for example, or buy a soft drink—can "disappear" if the company isn't careful. KnitMedia therefore should have a way for each individual club to report to company headquarters in New York the exact ticket, merchandise, and bar sales on a nightly basis. That way, Michael Dorf and his staff can keep a firm grip on revenues generated by each club. The management team would like you to review its current control efforts and to make some recommendations regarding possible improvements.

Team Exercises and Questions

Use what you learned in this chapter to answer the following questions from Michael Dorf and his management team:

1. How do other companies, including specifically restaurants and nightclubs, maintain control over their national or global locations?

2. Given what you know about the enthusiasm with which managers and employees are drawn to work for KnitMedia, and given what you know about our culture, to what extent do you think we can rely on employee commitment for making sure that things stay under control?

3. What specifically would you suggest we do to foster increased commitment? Which of our company's values do you think would be most influential in keeping things under control here, and why?

4. Finding out two weeks later that an employee may have run off with several days' worth of club receipts is pretty useless, since at that point the money is probably gone. What controls would you suggest we implement to try to make sure that (1) an employee can't hide any significant amount of money that comes into a club, and (2) if someone does manage to hide some cash, we find out about it as quickly as possible?

5. We know that boundary control systems basically lay out the boundaries within which employees must operate, for example in terms of the ethical and other rules of behavior employees are required to follow. What are some of the important ethical and other rules you think we should be enforcing in order to make sure things stay under control?

A MODULE

MANAGING OPERATIONS AND SERVICES

WHAT'S AHEAD?

As a small manufacturer of precision metal parts, Cook Specialty Company knew it had to be quick and efficient to survive. When its customers started trimming the number of suppliers they bought from, Cook decided it needed a new competitive advantage. As we'll see in this module, their approach involved installing a new computerized manufacturing system, one that gave Cook the advantages of small-volume custom manufacturing, combined with the efficiencies of large scale. Like many successful manufacturing and service businesses, Cook was applying modern operations and services management and control techniques to stay ahead of the competition.

OBJECTIVES

AFTER STUDYING THIS MODULE, YOU SHOULD BE ABLE TO

- Give examples of the three main elements in any production system

- List the four production design decisions operations managers must make

- Demonstrate how to use two basic inventory management systems

- Compare and contrast five tools used to improve quality

- Explain each of the five steps in a service management program

To this point in the book, we've focused on the functions all managers perform, specifically planning, organizing, leading, and controlling. All managers—whether they're sales managers, personnel managers, accounting managers, production managers, or some other type—engage in these basic activities as part of their jobs. While it's beyond the scope of this book to describe the inner workings of all these managers' jobs, we'll look more closely here at how one type of manager—the operations manager—does his or her job.

▶ BASICS OF OPERATIONS MANAGEMENT

Operations management is the process of managing the resources required to produce the organization's goods and services.[1] Like all managers, operations managers plan, organize, lead, and control. However, unlike other managers, operations managers focus on the direct production resources of a firm, often called the five P's of operations management: people, plants, parts, processes, and planning and control systems.

The *people* include the direct and indirect workforce, such as assembly workers, inventory clerks, and clerical staff. *Plants* are the factories or service branches where the product or service is produced. *Parts* include the raw materials and other inputs that will be transformed into finished products or services. *Processes* represent the technology, the equipment, and the steps required to accomplish production. The *planning and control* systems are the procedures management uses to operate the system (such as the methods used to schedule the work) and to control quality.[2]

operations management
the process of managing the resources that are needed to produce an organization's goods and services.

The Production System

At the heart of operations management is a production system; whether producing goods or services, this system always has three main components, summarized in Figure A.1. **Inputs** are all the resources required to manufacture the product or service. The main inputs include materials and supplies, personnel, and capital. Other inputs include data on the competition, the product, and the customer. Environmental inputs include data on the legal aspects of doing business, social and economic trends, and technological innovations.

input
a resource required for the manufacture of a product or service.

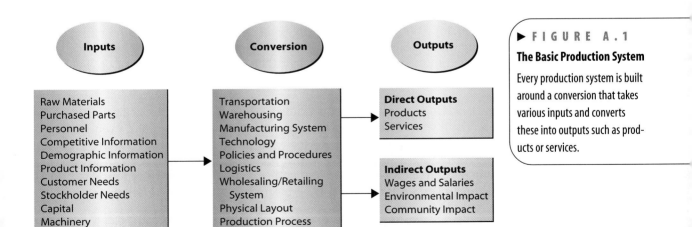

▶ FIGURE A.1

The Basic Production System

Every production system is built around a conversion that takes various inputs and converts these into outputs such as products or services.

Production System	Primary Inputs	Purpose of Conversion Subsystem	Outputs
1. Pet food factory	Grain, water, fish meal, personnel, tools, machines, paper bags, cans, buildings, utilities	Converts raw materials into finished goods	Pet food products
2. Public accounting firm	Supplies, personnel, information, computers, buildings, office furniture, machines, utilities	Attracts customers, compiles data, supplies management information, computes taxes	Management information, tax services, and audited financial statements
3. College or university	Students, books, supplies, personnel, buildings, utilities	Transmits information and develops skills and knowledge	Educated persons

Source: Adapted from Norman Gaither, *Production and Operations Management*, 5th ed. (Fort Worth, TX: The Dryden Press, 1992), pp. 22–23.

conversion system

any production system that converts inputs (material and human resources) into outputs (products or services); sometimes called the production process or technology.

output

a direct outcome (actual product or service) or indirect outcome (tax, wage, salary) of a production system.

Any production system takes inputs and converts them into products or services called outputs. The conversion system (also called the production process or technology) has several components. These include the production machinery and its physical layout, the transport services that bring in the inputs and deliver the final products to customers, and storage services for goods awaiting shipment. The production system's outputs may be divided into direct outputs (the actual products or services) and indirect outputs (such as taxes, wages, and salaries).

The same sequence applies to a service business like a university (see Table A.1).[3] Here inputs include students, books, supplies, professors, and buildings. The conversion system consists of the technology used to transmit information to the students (lectures, exams, computerized instruction, and so forth). The output is educated persons.

Designing Production Systems

Whether you're producing goods or services, designing a production system requires four basic decisions: Where will the facility be located? What type of production process will be used? What will be the layout of the plant or facility? And what will be the layout of the production system itself?

The Facility Location Decision   Deciding where to locate the facility is always crucial. For a service firm like a retail store or fast-food restaurant, even placing the facility on the wrong side of the road can spell disaster if the location is inaccessible. For example, in 1999 the British retailer Marks & Spencer had to close more than 30 of its European Stores because it had chosen poor locations. For a manufacturer, plant location influences crucial factors like transportation costs and labor availability.

Locating a facility requires managers to apply both subjective and objective criteria. On the subjective side are things like the owner's personal preference. If Mr.

Suarez loves to sail and his whole family lives in Miami, then the plant may be located in nearby Hialeah, even if transportation costs there are somewhat higher than they might be elsewhere.

As production becomes more globalized, selecting a site tends to rest on a variety of country-, region-, and site-specific objective criteria.

Typical country-related considerations include, for instance, government rules and attitudes, cultural and economic issues, location of markets, availability of labor and supplies, and exchange rates. Region/community considerations include corporate management's desires, attractiveness in terms of things like taxes, labor availability, utilities, environment regulations, government incentives, and proximity to supplies and customers. Once these decisions are made, management turns to finding a specific site. Considerations here include things like the cost of the site, transportation availability, zoning restrictions, and environmental impact issues.

Managers ignore country, region, and site-specific considerations at their peril, especially if they're looking to expand abroad. For example, today the $64 million Hilton Hanoi Opera Hotel stands nearly empty, as do most of the city's eight other new luxury hotels. What went wrong? In the first half of the 1990s, many believed Vietnam was the next great "Asian tiger" in terms of projected economic growth.[4] Today, reality has set in. Vietnam is still communist, and is reportedly "closer to Cuba than to today's market oriented China."[5] It's also still one of the poorest countries in Asia, with many antibusiness government policies and tariffs. Corruption is reportedly rampant. So, it looks like the Hanoi Hilton may be empty for years to come.

Basic Types of Production Processes   We can distinguish between two broad types of production systems: intermittent production systems and continuous production systems.

In **intermittent production** systems, production is performed on the product on a start-and-stop basis.[6] Automobile repair shops, custom cabinet shops, and construction contractors are examples. They are generally characterized by made-to-order products and relatively low product volumes, as well as frequent schedule changes and the use of general-purpose equipment that can make a variety of models or products.

Mass production is a special type of intermittent production process in which standardized methods and single-use machines produce long runs of standardized items. Most mass production processes use assembly lines, fixed sequences of specialized (single-use) machines. In a typical assembly line, the product moves from station to station, where one or more employees and/or specialized machines perform tasks such as inserting bumpers or screwing on doors. Mass production systems may in fact run more or less continuously and may stop and start very few times over the course of a year.

Continuous production processes run for very long periods. Chemical plants, paper plants, and petroleum refineries are examples. Enormous capital investments are involved in building highly automated continuous process facilities such as these. They are therefore usually designed for high volume and use special-purpose equipment.

As we will see, the traditional dividing line between intermittent and continuous processes is beginning to blur. For example, computer-assisted manufacturing processes at Mead Corporation, which produces and sells paper, merge the flexibility of intermittent production with the efficiency of continuous production.

intermittent production
a system in which production is performed on a start-and-stop basis, such as for the manufacture of made-to-order products.

continuous production
a production process, such as those used by chemical plants or refineries, that runs for very long periods without the start-and-stop behavior associated with intermittent production.

facility layout

the configuration of all the machines, employee work stations, storage areas, internal walls, and so forth that constitute the facility used to create a firm's product or service.

product layout

a production system design in which every item to be produced follows the same sequence of operations from beginning to end, such as an assembly line.

process layout

a production system design in which similar machines or functions are grouped together.

fixed-position layout

a production system arrangement in which the product being built or produced stays at one location and the machines and tools required to build the product are brought to that location as needed, as for the building of ships or other bulky products.

cellular manufacturing

usually a combination of process and product layouts, in which machines and personnel are grouped into cells containing all the tools and operations required to produce a particular product or family of products.

Facility Layout   **Facility layout** refers to the configuration of the total facility—not just the machines, but also the employee workstations, storage areas, internal walls, and so forth. Important objectives here usually include reducing materials-handling costs, providing sufficient capacity, and allowing for safe equipment operation and ease of maintenance.

Facility layout is important for service firms, too. Retailers lay out their stores to improve sales, raise customer satisfaction, and increase convenience. Thus food stores typically put products like meats toward the back, to draw customers past the other aisles to get to them. Similarly, office managers may try to promote communication between departments and to provide adequate privacy with movable partitions.

Production System Layout   Whether in a factory or a service business like a car wash, there are basically four ways to lay out the production (conversion) system itself. In a **product layout**, every item to be produced follows the same sequence from beginning to end, moving from one specialized tool and operation to another. An assembly, or production, line is one example. Product layouts are not restricted to manufacturing. For example, automatic car washes use product layouts, as Figure A.2 illustrates.[7]

In a **process layout**, similar machines or functions are grouped together; for example, all drill presses may be positioned in one area and all lathes in another. As Figure A.3 illustrates,[8] service businesses like universities and hospitals are usually organized around process layouts. Separate locations exist for classrooms, libraries, offices, and computer centers, for instance. In a **fixed-position layout**, the product stays at one location, and the manufacturing machines and tools required to build the product are brought to that location as needed. Bulky or heavy products like ships are built in this way.

In **cellular manufacturing**, machines are grouped into cells, each of which contains all the tools and operations required to produce a particular product or family of products. This is shown in Figure A.4.[9] Cellular manufacturing layouts may combine aspects of both process and product layouts. As in product layouts, each cell is usually dedicated to producing particular parts or products. As in

---

▼ FIGURE A.2   **Product Layout**

A car wash is an example of an assembly-line-type product layout, where each special-purpose machine performs its function as the product moves from station to station.

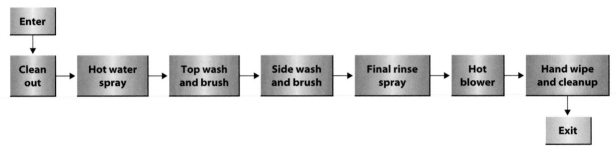

Source: Everett Adam, Jr., and Ronald Ebert, *Production and Operations Management* (Englewood Cliffs, NJ: Prentice Hall, 1992), p. 254.

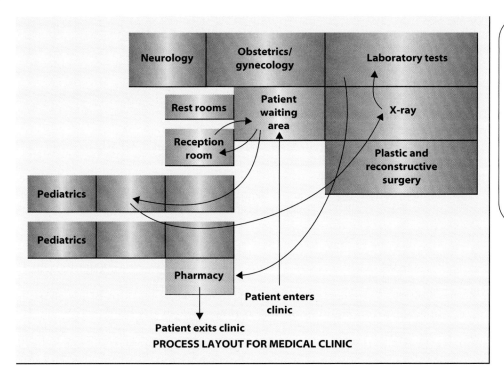

PROCESS LAYOUT FOR MEDICAL CLINIC

◄ FIGURE A.3

Process Layout

In a process layout like this, each process has its own area, and the "product" (in this case the patient) is directed to the processes (such as x-ray and pediatrics) that are appropriate.

Source: Everett Adam, Jr. and Ronald Ebert, *Production and Operations Management* (Englewood Cliffs, NJ: Prentice Hall, 1992), p. 254.

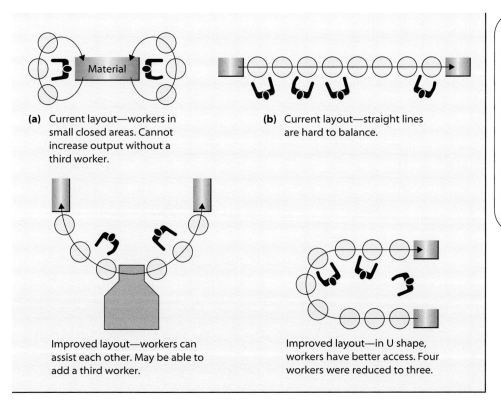

(a) Current layout—workers in small closed areas. Cannot increase output without a third worker.

(b) Current layout—straight lines are hard to balance.

Improved layout—workers can assist each other. May be able to add a third worker.

Improved layout—in U shape, workers have better access. Four workers were reduced to three.

◄ FIGURE A.4

Improving Layouts by Moving to the Work Cell Concept

Note in both **(a)** and **(b)** that U-shaped work cells can reduce material and employee movement. The U shape may also reduce space requirements.

Source: Render/Heizer, *Principles of Operations Management*, 2nd ed., © 1997. Reprinted by permission of Prentice Hall, Inc., Upper Saddle River, NJ.

process layouts, each cell is also sometimes designed to perform a specific set of manufacturing operations (such as all the grinding and buffing needed to produce one of the valves that goes into the company's car engines).

▶ OPERATIONS PLANNING AND CONTROL TECHNIQUES

production planning
the process of deciding what products to produce and where, when, and how to produce them.

production control
the process of ensuring that the specified production plans and schedules are being adhered to.

Gantt chart
a production scheduling chart (named after management pioneer Henry Gantt) that plots time on a horizontal scale and generally shows, for each order, the start and stop times of each operation.

Whether you're producing cars or Broadway shows, a system for planning and controlling production is required. **Operations** or **production planning** is the process of deciding what products to produce and where, when, and how to produce them. **Operations** or **production control** is the process of ensuring that the specified production plans and schedules are being met. We'll look at some important techniques used in this process.

Scheduling and Gantt Charts

Production schedules can be presented on charts that show what operations are to be carried out and when. The **Gantt chart** shown in Figure A.5 is one example.

Henry Gantt, a management pioneer, devised several versions of his chart. In the example shown in Figure A.5, time is presented on the horizontal scale. For each order, the start and stop times for each operation are shown sequentially. In another type of Gantt chart, each operation is listed separately in the left column, one under the other, and time is again shown horizontally. That way, the start and stop times for all operations in a complex project can be scheduled and tracked.

In practice, schedulers work from the required delivery date backward. They determine how long each assembly will take, how long it will take to obtain raw materials, and so forth. Based on the results, schedulers can determine whether the required delivery date can be met and what bottlenecks they must prepare to unclog.

▶ FIGURE A.5

A Gantt Chart

This Gantt chart shows the step and timing of each step for each order.

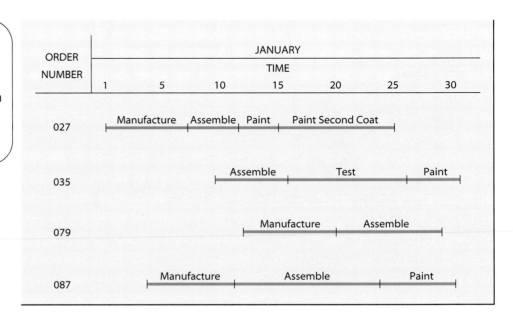

Network Planning and Control Methods

The Gantt chart is adequate for managing relatively simple projects (with not too many subassemblies or activities). More complex projects usually require computerized network charting to show how one activity affects the others.

Network planning and control methods graphically represent the project steps and the timing and linkages among those steps. A project is a series of interrelated activities aimed at producing a major, coordinated product or service. Examples include introducing a new Ford Taurus or planning a wedding reception.

PERT and CPM are the two most popular network planning and control methods. PERT (program evaluation review technique) and CPM (critical path method) were invented at about the same time and are similar, although several details (for instance, CPM shows the cost of each step) set PERT apart from CPM.

Events and activities are the two major components of PERT networks. As Figure A.6 shows, **events**, depicted by circles, represent specific accomplishments such as "foundation laid." **Activities** are the time-consuming aspect of the project (like laying the foundation) and are represented by arrows. By studying the PERT chart, the scheduler can determine the **critical path**, the sequence of critical events that in total requires the most time to complete. Computerized programs (see Figure A.7) are used to create PERT networks for very complex projects.

network planning and control methods
ways of planning and controlling projects by graphically representing the projects' steps and the timing and links between these steps.

events
the specific accomplishments in a project, represented by circles in a PERT chart.

activities
the time-consuming aspects of a project, represented by arrows in a PERT chart.

critical path
the sequence of events in a project that in total requires the most time to complete.

▼ **FIGURE A.6**   **PERT Chart for Building a House**

In a PERT chart like this one, each event is shown in its proper relationship to the other events. The blue circles show the critical—or most time-consuming—path.

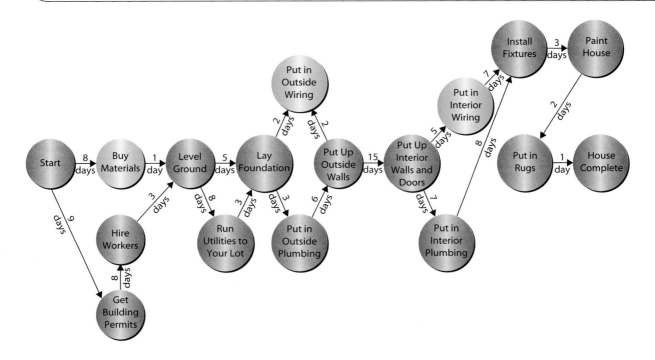

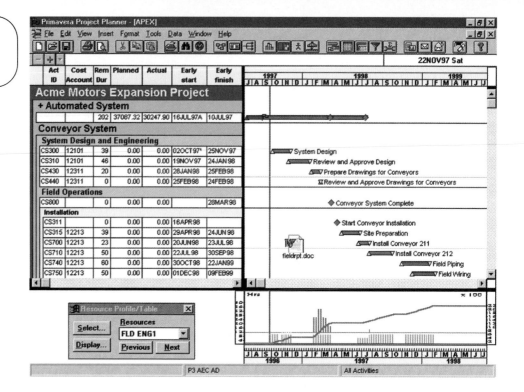

Purchasing

Purchasing departments buy all the materials and parts the firm needs to conduct its business, including the raw materials that go into the firm's products, as well as machinery, tools, purchased components, and even paper clips and computer paper.

Purchasing is a more important function than many managers realize. Some experts estimate that 60% of a manufacturer's sales dollars are paid to suppliers for purchased materials.[10] Furthermore, manufacturers striving to maintain quality levels know that the quality of their finished products can't be any better than the quality of their components. Purchasing departments can affect a firm's cost-effectiveness as well as its reputation. Today, in fact, many firms work closely with suppliers to create better-quality parts. Many firms, such as Ford, send engineers to help suppliers boost their quality-management systems.

Purchasing managers engage in several activities.[11] They maintain a database of available suppliers. They are also responsible for selecting suppliers and negotiating supply contracts with them. Purchasing managers try to minimize the costs of materials and supplies, but it would be an oversimplification to say that this is their only (or even their main) concern. For many firms, high-quality, reliable, on-time deliveries outweigh costs. And, increasingly, firms are automating their purchase decisions by having suppliers bid for their business via the Internet.

► INVENTORY MANAGEMENT TECHNIQUES

Firms keep inventories of five types of items.[12] *Raw materials* and purchased parts are obtained from outside suppliers and used in the production of finished products. *Components* are subassemblies that are awaiting final assembly. *Work in process* refers to all materials or components on the production floor in various stages of production. *Finished goods* are final products waiting to be purchased or about to be sent to customers. Finally, *supplies* are all items the firm needs that are not part of the finished product, such as paper clips, duplicating machine toner, and tools.

The Role of Inventory Management

Inventory management is the process of ensuring that the firm has enough inventories of all parts and supplies needed, within the constraint of minimizing total inventory costs.

In practice, inventory managers must address four specific costs. **Ordering, or setup, costs** are the costs of placing the order or setting up machines for the production run. For purchased items, ordering costs might include order-processing costs and the cost of inspecting goods when they arrive. For items made in-house, setup costs include the labor involved with setting up the machine and the cost of preparing the paper-work for scheduling the production run.

Ordering, or setup, costs are usually fixed, meaning that they are independent of the size of the order. **Acquisition costs**, the total cost of all units bought to fill an order, vary with the size of the order. For example, ordering required parts in larger quantities may reduce each unit's cost thanks to quantity discounts. This in turn will lower the total acquisition costs of the order, whereas ordering smaller quantities may raise the unit cost.

Inventory managers focus on two other inventory costs. **Inventory-holding** (or carrying) **costs** are all the costs associated with carrying parts or materials in inventory. The biggest specific cost here is usually the firm's cost of capital, which in this case is the value of a unit of the inventory times the length of time it is held times the interest rate at which the firm borrows money.[13] **Stockout costs** are the costs associated with running out of raw materials or finished-goods inventory. For example, if a company cannot fill a customer's order, it might lose both the current order and any profits or future sales the customer may have delivered.

Inventory managers want to avoid three basic problems. The first is overinvestment in inventories, which ties up money, crowds available space, and hikes losses when stored products deteriorate or become obsolete. At the other extreme, inventory managers want to avoid underinvestment, which leaves the firm unable to fill production orders and discourages customers. The third problem is unbalanced inventory, which means some items are understocked while others are overstocked.

Basic Inventory Management Systems

Many quantitative and nonquantitative systems are available for managing inventory. The ABC and EOQ systems are two of the most popular.

ABC Inventory Management   Most firms find that a small proportion (25% to 30%) of the parts in their inventory accounts for a large proportion (70% or 80%) of their annual dollar volume of inventory usage. (A part's annual dollar volume is computed by multiplying its cost per part by the number of parts used in a year.)

When using the ABC system, the manager divides the inventory into three dollar-volume categories—A, B, and C—with the A parts being the most active. The manager then concentrates most of his or her checking and surveillance on the A

inventory management
the process of ensuring that the firm has adequate inventories of all parts and supplies needed, within the constraint of minimizing total inventory costs.

ordering, or setup, costs
the costs, usually fixed, of placing an order or setting up machines for a production run.

acquisition costs
the total costs of all units bought to fill an order, usually varying with the size of the order.

inventory-holding (carrying) costs
all the costs associated with carrying parts or materials in inventory.

stockout costs
the costs associated with running out of raw materials, parts, or finished-goods inventory.

parts. For example, the A parts are ordered most often so that their total in inventory is minimized and so that they are not in the inventory bins too long.

At the other extreme, the inventory manager might find that perhaps 50% of the parts in inventory account for, say, 15% of annual dollar volume. Why spend as much time closely monitoring all those parts when in total they account for only 15% of the firm's annual dollar volume of inventory usage? The idea is to focus on the high-annual-dollar-volume A inventory items, and to a lesser extent on the B items and even less on the C items.

The Economic Order Quantity Inventory Management System   The idea behind the **economic order quantity (EOQ)** system or model is to determine the most economic quantity to order—in other words the quantity that will minimize total inventory costs. EOQ is the best-known and probably the oldest inventory system.

Figure A.8 illustrates the relationships involved in EOQ. As shown, the two major costs, inventory carrying costs and ordering costs, vary inversely with each other. For example, ordering in large quantities usually allows the firm to order more economically, but it means higher storage costs (because the firm would have, on average, more inventory in stock).

In its simplest form the economic order quantity is

$$Q = \sqrt{2US/CI}$$

where Q is the economic order quantity (the most economical quantity to order), U is the annual usage of the item, S is the restocking or ordering costs, C is the cost per unit, and I is the annual carrying costs.

This EOQ equation is widely used, but it is based on some simplifications. For example, it assumes that the same number of units are taken from inventory periodically, such as 10 units per day. It also assumes that the supplier does not offer quantity discounts for ordering in large batches. More sophisticated EOQ versions are available for handling these and other complications.[14]

economic order quantity (EOQ)

an inventory management system based on a simple formula that is used to determine the most economic quantity to order so that the total of inventory and set-up costs is minimized.

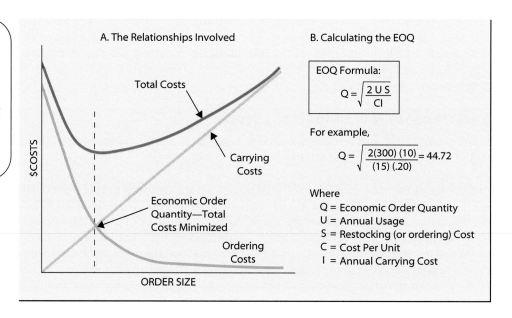

▶ **FIGURE A.8**

The Economic Order Quantity Model

When order size goes up, ordering costs per order go down, but carrying costs go up because more items are left longer in inventory.

▶ CONTROLLING FOR QUALITY AND PRODUCTIVITY

Quality can be defined as the totality of features and characteristics of a product or service that bears on its ability to satisfy given needs. To put this another way, "quality measures how well a product or service meets customer needs."[15]

This definition highlights several important things about quality. First, the customer's needs are the basic standard for measuring quality. An airplane seat in coach can be as "high quality" as one in first class, in terms of the coach passenger's expectations and the competitor's services. Second, high quality does not have to mean high price. Again, the basic consideration should be the extent to which the product or service meets the customer's expectations.

Quality standards today are international. Doing business in Europe often means the firm must show it complies with ISO 9000, the quality standards of the 15-nation European Union (EU).

Total Quality Management Programs

Total quality management (TQM) programs are organizationwide programs that aim to integrate all functions of the business such that all aspects of the business, including design, planning, production, distribution, and field service, are aimed at maximizing customer satisfaction through continuous improvements.[16] In the United States, this approach is also often called *continuous improvement, zero defects*, or *six sigma*; in Japan it is known as *Kaizen*.[17]

W. Edwards Deming, who is credited with bringing quality control to Japan in the 1950s, is generally regarded as the intellectual father of TQM. His concept of total quality is based on the following 14-point system, which he says must be implemented at all organizational levels:

1. Create consistency of purpose toward improvement of product and service and translate that into a plan.

2. Adopt the new philosophy of quality.

3. Cease dependence on inspection to achieve quality, by building quality into the product from the beginning.

4. End the practice of choosing suppliers based solely on price. Move toward a single supplier for any one item and toward a long-term relationship of loyalty and trust.

5. Improve constantly and forever the production and service system in order to improve quality and productivity and thus constantly decrease cost. In other words, aim for continuous improvement.

6. Institute extensive training on the job.

7. Shift your focus from production numbers to quality.

8. Drive out fear, so that everyone may work effectively for the company.

9. Break down barriers between departments. People in research, design, sales, and production must work as a team to foresee problems of production as well as problems that may occur after sale when the product or service is actually used.

10. Eliminate slogans and targets for the workforce for zero defects and new levels of productivity, particularly where new methods for achieving these targets are not put in place.

---

quality
the extent to which a product or service is able to meet customer needs and expectations.

ISO 9000
the quality standards of the European Union.

total quality management (TQM) program
a specific organizationwide program that integrates all the functions and related processes of a business such that they are all aimed at maximizing customer satisfaction through ongoing improvements.

11. Eliminate work standards (quotas) on the factory floor.

12. Remove barriers that rob employees of their right to pride of workmanship. Among other things, this means abolishing the annual merit rating and all forms of management by objectives or management by numbers.

13. Institute a vigorous program of education and self-improvement.

14. Create a structure within top management that will push every day for each of the preceding 13 points. Make sure to put everybody in the company to work to accomplish the transformation.[18]

Malcolm Baldrige Award
a prize created in 1987 by the U.S. Department of Commerce to recognize outstanding achievement in quality control management.

The U.S. Department of Commerce has also created the **Malcolm Baldrige Award**, in part to recognize organizations that adhere to Deming-type quality principles. The award is named after former President Reagan's Secretary of Commerce, who died while in office. Most U.S. manufacturing firms, service firms, and small businesses are eligible to apply for the Baldrige Award. Winners include Motorola, FedEx, Cadillac Motor Car, and Xerox Business Products and Systems.

Quality Control Methods

In addition to building an organizationwide commitment to quality, companies use various tools and techniques to monitor product or service quality. First, most firms have a formal inspection procedure, in which inspectors test and measure the product against quality standards. Sometimes (such as when producing heart pacemakers), a 100% inspection is typical. More common is **acceptance sampling**, in which only a portion of the items are inspected, perhaps 2% or 5%. Have you ever called an airline and been told "The conversation may be recorded for quality or training purposes? That airline is using acceptance sampling to check on its reservations clerks.

acceptance sampling
a method of monitoring product quality that requires the inspection of only a small portion of the produced items.

Firms also use quality control charts like the one in Figure A.9. There are many charts, but the basic idea is always the same. Upper and lower control limits are

► F I G U R E   A . 9

Example of Quality Control Chart

The idea behind any control chart is to track quality trends to ensure that they don't go out of control.

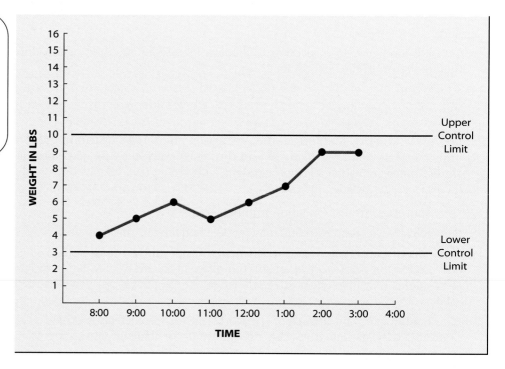

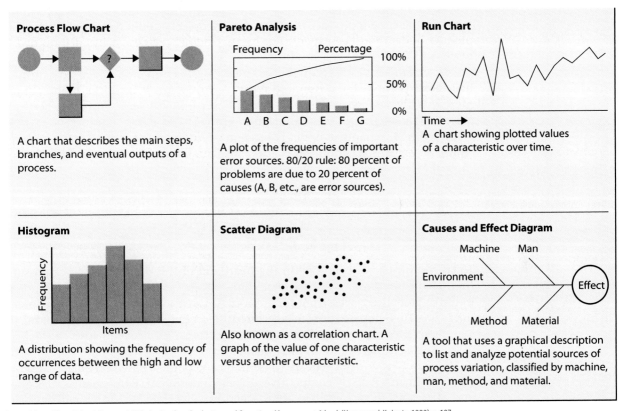

Process Flow Chart

A chart that describes the main steps, branches, and eventual outputs of a process.

Pareto Analysis

A plot of the frequencies of important error sources. 80/20 rule: 80 percent of problems are due to 20 percent of causes (A, B, etc., are error sources).

Run Chart

A chart showing plotted values of a characteristic over time.

Histogram

A distribution showing the frequency of occurrences between the high and low range of data.

Scatter Diagram

Also known as a correlation chart. A graph of the value of one characteristic versus another characteristic.

Causes and Effect Diagram

A tool that uses a graphical description to list and analyze potential sources of process variation, classified by machine, man, method, and material.

Source: Adapted from Richard Chase and Nicholas Aquilero, *Production and Operations Management*, 6th ed. (Homewood, IL: Irwin, 1992), p. 197.

drawn to show the range within which some measurable characteristic is to fall. Then the chosen characteristic (such as length or weight) is inspected and measured. (Kellogg might want to make sure each box of corn flakes contains no more than 20 ounces and no fewer than 19.5 ounces.) If the measures begin to move toward the upper or lower control limits, it's time to see what is causing the variation.

Employees typically use several tools to monitor quality problems. Some of these are summarized in Figure A.10.[19] For example, a scatter diagram shows the magnitude of one trait (such as the number of defects) versus a second trait (such as time). A cause-and-effect (or fishbone) diagram outlines the four main categories of problems—machine, human (personnel), method, and material—and helps employees analyze the problem and devise solutions.

Design for Manufacturability

Designing for manufacturability means designing products with ease of manufacturing in mind. Its aims are to develop a product that can

- Exhibit the desired level of quality and reliability
- Be designed in the least time with the least development cost
- Make the quickest and smoothest transition into production

designing for manufacturability
designing products with ease of manufacturing and quality in mind.

- Be produced and tested with the minimum cost in the minimum amount of time
- Satisfy customers' needs and compete in the marketplace[20]

Designing for manufacturability is increasingly important. As one expert points out, "By the time a product has been designed, only about 8 percent of the total product budget has been spent. But by that point, the design has determined 80 percent of the cost of the product!"[21] For example, Hewlett-Packard's LaserJet III printer had dozens of parts more than the IBM laser printer. Because IBM's printers had fewer points where assembly errors could occur, it could be manufactured more quickly, less expensively, and with fewer initial defects. As one expert said, "The design determines the manufacturability."[22]

Designing for manufacturability often means designing products using multidisciplinary teams. This approach is also called simultaneous design or **concurrent engineering**. It ensures that all departments involved in the product's success contribute to its design.[23]

concurrent engineering

designing products in multidisciplinary teams so that all departments involved in the product's success contribute to its design.

▶ WORLD-CLASS MANUFACTURING AND MANAGING CHANGE

Today, no firm—not even one in the heartland of the United States—can assume that it will be immune from global competitors.[24] Virtually every firm finds its industry globalized, which means it faces not just local competitors, but foreign ones too. This globalization means intensified competition, as firms around the world strive to improve quality, lead time, customer service, and costs in the hope of gaining a stronger hold on their markets.

World-class companies are those that can compete based on quality and productivity in an intensely competitive global environment. Firms such as UPS, Sony, and Microsoft, to name a few, set the performance standards for their industries and are able to respond swiftly and effectively to changing conditions.

World-class manufacturers are world class in part because they use modern production techniques and management systems to boost productivity, quality, and flexibility. These techniques and systems include TQM (already described), just-in-time manufacturing, computer-aided design and manufacturing, automation and robotics, flexible manufacturing systems, and computer-integrated manufacturing.

world-class company

an organization that can compete successfully based on quality and productivity in an intensely competitive global environment.

world-class manufacturer

an organization that uses modern production techniques and management systems to boost manufacturing productivity, quality, and flexibility in an environment of international competition.

just-in-time (JIT)

a production control method used to attain minimum inventory levels by ensuring delivery of materials and assemblies just when they are to be used; also refers to a philosophy of manufacturing that aims to optimize production processes by continuously reducing waste.

The Basic Components of Just-in-Time Systems (JIT)

The concept called **just-in-time (JIT)** has two related definitions. In the narrowest sense, JIT refers to production control methods used to attain minimum inventory levels by ensuring delivery of materials and assemblies "just in time"—in other words, just when they are to be used. JIT also refers to a *philosophy* of manufacturing that aims to optimize production processes by continuously reducing waste. One expert explains JIT's benefits this way:

> JIT streamlines production, based on demand-driven, just-in-time arrival of components at each assembly's stage. JIT strives to simplify manufacturing and reduce material burden by operating with minimum lot sizes, no queues (products waiting in line to be used), and minimum inventory levels. . . . JIT means producing each day only that day's demand so material "flows" through production. [But] JIT also can serve as a focal point for other approaches to world-

1. *Waste of overproduction.* Eliminate by reducing setup times, synchronizing quantities and timing between processes, compacting layout, visibility, and so forth. Make only what is needed now.

2. *Waste of waiting.* Eliminate through synchronizing workflow as much as possible, and balance uneven loads with flexible workers and equipment.

3. *Waste of transportation.* Establish layouts and locations to make transport and handling unnecessary if possible. Then rationalize transport and material handling that cannot be eliminated.

4. *Waste of processing itself.* First question why this part or product should be made at all, and then why each process is necessary. Extend thinking beyond economy of scale or speed.

5. *Waste of stocks.* Reduce by shortening setup times and reducing lead times, by synchronizing workflows and improving work skills, and even by smoothing fluctuations in demand for the product. Reducing all the other wastes reduces the waste of stocks.

6. *Waste of motion.* Study motion for economy and consistency. Economy improves productivity, and consistency improves quality. First improve the motions, then mechanize or automate. Otherwise there is danger of automating waste.

7. *Waste of making defective products.* Develop the production process to prevent defects from being made so as to eliminate inspection. At each process, accept no defects and make no defects. Make processes failsafe to do this. From a quality process comes a quality product—automatically.

◀ **F I G U R E   A . 1 1**

The Seven Wastes JIT Aims to Eliminate

Source: R. Hall, *Attaining Manufacturing Excellence* (Homewood, IL: Dow Jones-Irwin, 1987), p. 26.

class manufacturing. . . . JIT demands zero defects and other total quality management efforts to eliminate waste. It calls for individual responsibility and empowerment. The ideal of continuous improvements—making products ever better, cheaper and faster—is likewise the mission of JIT.[25]

Reducing seven main wastes lies at the heart of the JIT philosophy. As summarized in Figure A.11,[26] these are the wastes of overproduction, waiting, transportation, processing, stock, motion, and making defective products. As you can see, JIT is a thorough management approach. It is also sometimes called **lean manufacturing** or **value-added manufacturing** (meaning that any manufacturing process that does not add value to the product for the customer is wasteful).[27]

In practice, JIT has several basic components. For example, the Japanese business community (where JIT was invented) tends to build small, specialized plants rather than large ones. It is easier to manage small plants, and it is easier to organize the workflow and to staff highly specialized plants. Few Japanese plants have as many as 1,000 employees; most have fewer than 30.[28] And, inside their plants, the Japanese tend to lay out facilities around the cell or group technology we discussed earlier. In JIT firms, cells are formed instead in which *all the processes required to complete a major part of the product are grouped together*. One employee can then perform all the processes. The worker will have to be more highly trained and flexible, but the moving and waiting time between processes is reduced or eliminated.

JIT-based firms also function on the idea that every worker is personally responsible for the quality of the item he or she produces. Thus, quality goes in "at the source," when the product is actually made.

Computer-Aided Design and Manufacturing

Computer-aided design (CAD) is a computerized process for designing new products or modifying existing ones. Designers sketch and modify designs on a computer screen, usually with an electronic pencil. CAD facilitates the actual

lean manufacturing
a management philosophy that assumes that any manufacturing process that does not add value to the product for the customer is wasteful; also called value-added manufacturing.

value-added manufacturing
a management approach that emphasizes the idea that any manufacturing process that does not add value to the product for the customer is wasteful; also called lean manufacturing.

computer-aided design (CAD)
a computerized process for designing new products, modifying existing ones, or simulating conditions that may affect the designs.

design of the item, makes it easier to modify existing products, and lets designers expose their designs to simulated stresses such as wind resistance.

Computer-aided manufacturing (CAM) uses computers to plan and program the production equipment. For example, CAM allows for computerized control of tool movement and cutting speed so that a machine can carry out several sequential operations on a part, all under the guidance of the computer-assisted system.

CAD and CAM are often used together. For example, with the design already in place within the CAD system, the computer "knows" a component's specifications and can thereby "tell" the production equipment how to cut and machine it.

Companies are using the Internet today to expand the potential of such computer-based systems. For example, when Motorola's plant in Mansfield, Massachusetts, got the green light to begin producing new cable modems, the plant manager knew he needed a faster and cheaper way to get the engineering documents to the assemblers on the plant floor.[29] The manager and his staff created an internal plant Intranet, using the power of the Web and the simplicity of the Netscape Navigator browser. Now, with a $500 digital camera to take pictures of each component, digitized images of the parts to be built are simply placed online, along with step-by-step instructions for assembly and testing. This not only eliminates having to produce all those expensive paper engineering drawings, but also helps Motorola update its drawings instantaneously.

Flexible Manufacturing Systems

In many firms today, flexible manufacturing systems are at the heart of managing change. **Automation** can be defined as the automatic operation of a system, process, or machine. A robot is a programmable machine capable of manipulating items and designed to move materials, parts, or specialized devices through programmed motions. A **flexible manufacturing system (FMS)** is "a system in which groups of production machines are connected by automated materials-handling and transfer machines, and integrated into a computer system."[30] Computers route parts and components to the appropriate machines, select and load the proper machine tools, and then direct the machines to perform the required operations. The items are then moved from machine to machine by computerized automated guided vehicles (AGV). These form a computer-guided cart system that picks up and delivers tools and parts from multiple workstations.

Several things combine to provide such a system with its flexibility: Machine setup times are reduced by computerized instructions; each machine can be quickly retooled to produce a variety of parts; reduced setup times cut required manufacturing lead times; automated guided vehicles move parts with relative speed and efficiency; and the firm can respond more quickly to new competing products or changing consumer tastes by using CAD to redesign products and CAM to reprogram its machines.

In fact, says Toshiba President Funio Sato, the aim of flexible manufacturing at his firm "is to push Toshiba's two dozen factories to adapt faster to markets . . . customers wanted choices. They wanted a washing machine or TV set that was precisely right for their needs. We needed variety, not mass production."[31]

Flexible manufacturing lets Toshiba and other firms combine the advantages of customized, one-at-a-time production with mass production's efficiency. At the Toshiba plant in Ome, Japan, for instance, workers efficiently assemble 9 word processor models on one line and 20 laptop computer models on another.[32] Such flexibility helps Toshiba be very responsive to customer requirements.

computer-aided manufacturing (CAM)

a computerized process for planning and programming production processes and equipment.

automation

the automatic operation of a system, process, or machine.

flexible manufacturing system (FMS)

the organization of groups of production machines that are connected by automated materials-handling and transfer machines, and integrated into a computer system for the purpose of combining the benefits of made-to-order flexibility and mass-production efficiency.

The National Bicycle Industrial Company, a subsidiary of electronics giant Matsushita, is another example.[33] With only 20 employees, National Bicycle's factory can produce more than a million variations of 18 bicycle models, each custommade to a customer's unique requirements.

Computer-Integrated Manufacturing   Many firms aim to integrate automation, JIT, flexible manufacturing, and CAD/CAM into one self-regulating production system. **Computer-integrated manufacturing (CIM)**, defined as the total integration of all production-related business activities through the use of computer systems,[34] gives the firm a competitive advantage based on speed, flexibility, quality, and low cost. This process is summarized in Figure A.12.

CIM's advantages usually exceed those of the sum of its component parts. In other words, CIM can yield synergistic results. For example, CAD facilitates CAM by feeding design changes directly to the machinery tools. Automated guided vehicles can facilitate JIT systems by eliminating human variability from the system.[35]

Why is an integrated approach important? As one Japanese executive put it, "In the past, manufacturing was characterized by large (production run) quantities, with few varieties. Today's customers are asking for small quantities in very many varieties. CIM adds flexibility to help make those very short production runs economical."[36] CIM can thus be an essential part of managing change.

computer-integrated manufacturing (CIM)

the total integration of all production-related business activities through the use of computer systems, usually including automation and automatic guided vehicles.

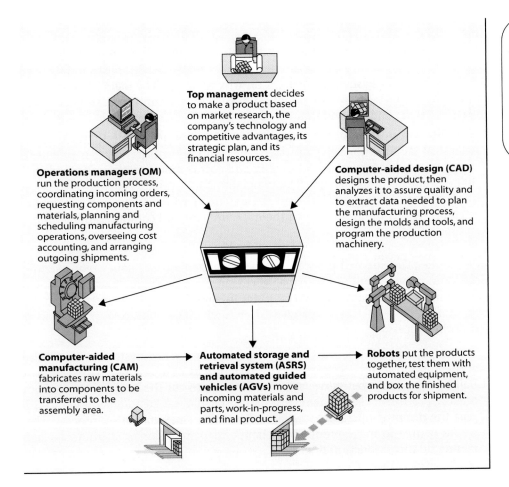

◀ **F I G U R E   A . 1 2**

The Elements of CIM

Source: Render/Heizer, *Principles of Operations Management*, 2nd ed. © 1997. Reprinted by permission of Prentice Hall, Inc., Upper Saddle River, NJ.

Top management decides to make a product based on market research, the company's technology and competitive advantages, its strategic plan, and its financial resources.

Operations managers (OM) run the production process, coordinating incoming orders, requesting components and materials, planning and scheduling manufacturing operations, overseeing cost accounting, and arranging outgoing shipments.

Computer-aided design (CAD) designs the product, then analyzes it to assure quality and to extract data needed to plan the manufacturing process, design the molds and tools, and program the production machinery.

Computer-aided manufacturing (CAM) fabricates raw materials into components to be transferred to the assembly area.

Automated storage and retrieval system (ASRS) and automated guided vehicles (AGVs) move incoming materials and parts, work-in-progress, and final product.

Robots put the products together, test them with automated equipment, and box the finished products for shipment.

Cook Specialty Company, a small manufacturer of precision metal parts, is an example of CIM.[37] As its customers trimmed the number of suppliers from whom they purchased parts, Cook needed a way to stay competitive. Its solution was to switch to being a custom manufacturer, one that not only made products based on customer-supplied blueprints, but that actually helped customers design their products.

A new CIM system enables Cook to do that. By linking its CIM system with customers' CAD systems, Cook and its customers can now swap drawings and send instructions for final designs directly to Cook's computer-automated machines for exact manufacture. The company's robots then handle welding and other repetitive tasks. By integrating its CIM system with customers' CAD systems and linking both with its own computer-controlled machines and robots, Cook now has a highly integrated system that gives it a competitive edge.

As mentioned earlier in the book, today many companies are using the Web to conduct virtually all of their business. For example, Boeing's electronic commerce site basically strips away the barriers that traditionally separated the company from suppliers and customers, so that all can now interact automatically and in real-time over the Web. Boeing sells more than $1 million in parts each day over the Internet, and suppliers like Alcoa use the Web site to coordinate shipments of materials to Boeing. Increasingly, in other words, internal manufacturing systems are not only becoming more integrated within themselves, but are becoming integrated with customers' and suppliers' systems.[38]

Combining Computers and People to Build Flexibility   Unfortunately, many CIM installations fail. Some companies spend millions of dollars installing CIM systems, only to discover that their plants are no more productive or flexible than they were before. A recent study sheds some light on why this is so. The main discovery concerned the important role of people—both managers and operators. Harvard Professor David Upton found that

> The flexibility of the plants depended much more on people than on any technical factor. Although high levels of computer integration can provide critically needed advantages in quality and cost competitiveness, all the data in my study point to one conclusion: operational flexibility is determined primarily by a plant's operators and the extent to which managers cultivate, measure, and communicate with them. Equipment and computer integration are secondary.[39]

An Example   The successful computerization experience of paper manufacturer Mead Corporation's mill in Escanaba, Michigan, is an example.[40] Because some of its machines were already highly computer integrated, Mead managers knew that computerization itself was no panacea. Here's what they did to keep the workers part of the process:

- They replaced their existing computer systems with a new system called Quality and Information for Decisions. "The system was designed from the outset to help workers make better decisions rather than to cut them out of the decision making process."[41] The system (nicknamed QUID) was custom designed to support the machine operators who actually ran the manufacturing process. They would be free to make production changes depending on what they saw happening on the production line.

- From the outset, the plant's managers insisted that operators be involved in the system's design and development.

- The plant managers saw to it that the computer system was designed mostly in-house. In particular, the people at each work function in the plant designed their own computer interface to ensure that operators got the information they felt they needed to do their jobs, and in the format that was easiest for them to understand.

The plant's responsiveness and customer satisfaction increased dramatically, and the plant recently sold the most paper in its history. Escanaba is now the most productive mill in Mead's fine-paper group and has dramatically increased its market share. This plant's experience and results underscore the need to combine computers and people when a plant sets out to computerize in order to build flexibility.

▶ MANAGING SERVICES

It's likely that after college you will go to work for a firm in a service-producing industry like transportation, communications, wholesale or retail trade, finance or insurance, or government, or in the legal, educational, or health sectors. Currently, about 75% of people working are employed in the service-producing sector. Managing services is therefore a "growth industry" itself.

Managing services is especially challenging because it's different from managing the creation of tangible products.[42] First, a service is generally created the instant it's used; it can't be produced and held in stock awaiting demand. Second, most services are provided with little or no supervision. Usually no production supervisor or quality-control clerk is hovering around the arrogant waiter who ruins a customer's meal, for example.

Karl Albrecht, a famous service management expert, defines **service management** as "a total organizational approach that makes quality of service, as perceived by the customer, the number one driving force for the operation of the business."[43]

Service management thus means more than just managing a service firm. Certainly, Jan Carlson was a "service manager" insofar as he was the president of SAS, which is a service firm. But "service management" also means managing an enterprise (whether a service firm like SAS or a manufacturing firm like Honda) in such a way that *quality of service* becomes the basic standard for evaluating everything the company does or should do.

service management
a total organizationwide approach that makes quality of service the business's number one driving force.

Why Service Management Is Important

Service management is important because of the intense global competition all companies face today. That means everyone has to fight harder for customers than ever before. Service management is important today for at least three specific reasons.

Service Is a Competitive Advantage   In Chapter 6 we explained that one way for a company to compete is to differentiate its product or service by creating something that is perceived as unique.[44] Many firms today differentiate themselves, at least in part, on customer service. For example, Mercedes-Benz North America offers its customers a toll-free phone number they can call 24 hours a day, seven days a week if they need road assistance. Crown Cork and Seal custom-builds a manufacturing plant near each of its major customers, thereby providing customized services for each one of them. Microsoft provides a 24-hour telephone help line.

Bad Service Leads to Lost Customers   Good service is also important because companies never hear from most of their dissatisfied customers; they just lose them.

This point is illustrated by a series of studies undertaken by the Technical Assistance Research Program, Inc. (TARP), in Washington, D.C.[45] TARP found that the average business never even hears from 96% of its unhappy customers. In other words, if 4 people complain to a company, there are probably another 96 or so unhappy customers who don't. However, TARP also found that while the company may not hear from these unhappy customers directly, they are out there spreading the word nevertheless. Each of them will tell an average of 9 or 10 people about the problems they had with the firm. So in addition to reducing its competitive edge, bad service will siphon off many current and potential customers.

Customer Defections Drain Profits   Effective service management is also crucial because in most industries the longer a firm keeps a customer, the more profit it stands to make from that customer.[46]

There are three reasons for this. First, long-term customers tend to spend more than new customers. Second, they tend to generate profits in other ways, such as referrals. Third, customers generally become more profitable over time. For example, it usually costs a credit card company about $51 to recruit a new customer. If that customer then stays only about a year and uses the card once or twice before leaving in disgust over an error on a bill, the credit card company might not even earn back the $51 acquisition cost. On the other hand, if the company can keep that customer for several years, her value to the company rises because the customer generates a profit in each of those years through credit card fees.

Karl Albrecht's Service Triangle

The actual techniques of service management focus on three core concepts: the moment of truth, service cycles, and the service triangle.[47]

moment of truth

the instant when the customer comes in contact with any aspect of a business, and based on that contact forms an opinion about the quality of your service or product.

The Moment of Truth   The core concept in service management is the **moment of truth**, which service management expert Karl Albrecht defines as "that precise instant when the customer comes into contact with any aspect of your business and, on the basis of that contact, forms an opinion about the quality of your service and, potentially, the quality of your product."[48]

The moment of truth plays a central role in service management because it is, as Albrecht says, "the basic atom of service, the smallest indivisible unit of value delivered to the customer."[49] When you as a customer call FedEx or go to a movie theater or supermarket, you experience moments of truth—precise instants when you come into contact with any aspect of the business.

On the basis of those accumulated moments of truth you then form an opinion about the quality of the service you have received and, potentially, about the quality of the product as well.

Here are some typical moments of truth in a supermarket shopping experience:

1. You look for a place to park in the supermarket's lot.
2. You walk to the supermarket from your car.
3. You look for a shopping cart.
4. You get your check approved.
5. You ask a clerk how to find a product.
6. You pick up your item.

7. You wait in the checkout line.

8. Your order is added up.

9. Your items are placed in the bag.

10. You take your purchases back to your car.

This is a simplified example, of course, but consider how many opportunities the supermarket's management has to create a good (or bad) service quality impression. In fact, if the supermarket were really interested in improving quality, it would have to manage the service experience in such a way that each of those moments of truth proved to be as positive an experience as possible. How might management do this? By taking actions like reducing waiting time at the checkout lines, expediting the check approval process, and ensuring that stock clerks are ready and eager to answer your questions.

One of the main points service management experts like Albrecht make is that when the moments of truth go unmanaged, the quality of service quickly declines. In other words, if the supermarket manager does not actually sit down and consider what his or her customer's typical moments of truth are and then see to it that they are positive, they will likely be unhappy experiences. And for the supermarket (or almost any other business), the accumulation of negative experiences embodied by the bad moments of truth will undermine the customer's perceptions of the quality of the firm.

In today's highly competitive world, that could be deadly. To take our supermarket example, management may stock the shelves with the finest products and perhaps even offer competitive prices. But if the moments of truth go unmanaged and the customer's experience is sufficiently bad, the market will lose out to its competitors down the road.

The Cycle of Service Albrecht therefore suggests thinking of the customer's moments of truth in terms of a **cycle of service**. Start with the first instance in which a customer comes into contact with any aspect of the organization, and then include, in sequence, every other moment of truth.

cycle of service
includes all the moments of truth experienced by a typical customer, from first to last.

The manager and his or her team will want to map out a cycle of service for three reasons. First, by carefully thinking through each contact from beginning to end, they can identify a complete list of all the moments of truth. Second, once identified, the critical moments can be focused on. Finally, with a list of moments of truth (and particularly the critical ones), management can turn to actually managing the service experience. But such service management also means creating a service strategy and attending to the service people and the service system.

The Service Triangle Albrecht says it's useful to think of a successful service management effort in terms of a service triangle, as presented in Figure A.13. Service management experts know these three factors must work together to achieve service quality. Here's how Albrecht describes each of the three elements:

- *A well-conceived service strategy.* Outstanding organizations have a unifying idea about what they do. This service concept, or service strategy . . . directs the attention of the people in the organization toward the real priorities of the customer. It becomes . . . the nucleus of the message to be transmitted to the customer. For example, McDonald's focuses on "quality, service, cleanliness, and price."

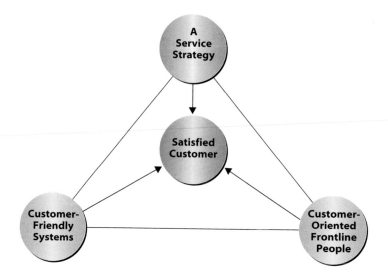

- *Customer-oriented front-line people.* [T]he managers of such organizations have [also] encouraged and helped the people who deliver the service to keep their attention fastened on the needs of the customer. . . . This leads to a level of responsiveness, attentiveness, and willingness to help that marks the service as superior in the customer's mind. . . .

- *Customer-friendly systems.* The delivery system that backs up the service people is truly designed for the convenience of the customer rather than the convenience of the organization. The physical facilities, policies, procedures, methods, and communication processes all say to the customer, "This apparatus is here to meet your needs."[50]

Jan Carlson's and his efforts at SAS Airlines provide an example. On becoming CEO, Carlson decided to build SAS's competitive advantage around customer service. He therefore formulated a strategy aimed at giving business travelers top-notch service for which they were willing to pay top-notch prices—special business-class seats and service, for instance.

But he knew that to implement his strategy, he had to modify both the people and the systems at SAS. For example, the SAS *people* had to be trained and retrained and empowered to cut through red tape to help customers. In terms of the *systems,* Carlson had to eliminate first-class service, expand business-class service, institute new check-in systems for business customers, and install business equipment like fax machines that his customers could use.

Implementing a Service Management Program

What is the overall process involved in creating a service-oriented, customer-driven organization? Service management experts Karl Albrecht and Ron Zemke say it has five steps.[51]

customer report card

lists the service attributes for which customers are looking, as well as the relative weights or priorities of each attribute and how the customers score your company on each of them.

Step I: The Service Audit The first step is to conduct a service audit, often using a **customer report card**. The customer report card lists the service attributes for which your customers are looking, as well as the relative weights or priorities of each attribute and how the customers score your company on each of them.

	Report Card for Downtown Ten-Plex Movie Theater		
TABLE A.2			

Desirable Service Attributes	Customer Priority	Our Score (Based on Audit)
Convenient parking	High	Medium
Safe parking	High	Low
First-run movies	High	High
Clean theater	High	Medium
Unobstructed view	High	High
Comfortable seats	Medium	Medium
Courteous clerks	Low	Low
Short waits for tickets	Medium	Low

If the information can be obtained, it's also useful to add your competitors' scores on each attribute for comparison purposes. One way to obtain the information required to compile the report card is to conduct in-depth interviews with a sample of the company's customers.[52]

An example of a report card for the Downtown Ten-Plex Movie Theater is presented in Table A.2. As you can see, the movie theater's customer research found eight service attributes typical theatergoers look for in the Ten-Plex Theater. These attributes include convenient parking, first-run movies, and a clean theater. In the next column, each of these attributes is given a priority ranking. For example, convenient parking, safe parking, and first-run movies are all high-priority services, while courteous clerks is rated lower. Finally, the customer report card includes a column called "Our Score." Management can use this space to record how customers rated the Downtown Ten-Plex Movie Theater on each of these service attributes.

Step 2: Strategy Development The second step is to formulate a **service strategy**, which has been defined as "a distinctive formula for delivering service; such a strategy is keyed to a well-chosen benefit premise that's valuable to the customer and that establishes an effective competitive position."[53]

In the simplest terms, the service strategy should answer the question "Why should the customer choose us?" It should be clear and brief enough to be easily communicated to and grasped by company employees. McDonald's Corporation's strategic emphasis on "quality, service, cleanliness, and price" and Carlson's SAS strategy emphasizing "high-quality service for business travelers" are examples.

service strategy
the company's plan for achieving superior service.

Step 3: Education The next step in implementing a service program is to spread the gospel of service throughout the organization. At companies like SAS, "wall-to-wall training" is often the method of choice. This means doing short bursts of 100% participation training: Everyone is trained at about the same time during a one- or two-day period.

Step 4: Implementation The next phase is the "implementation of grass-roots improvements in the way the organization produces and delivers its service products."[54]

Several activities take place here. Service quality teams are often created, each of which serves as a source of specific recommendations on how to improve service and also functions as a conduit to get information back to the departments. The application lab is another implementation technique. Here, a trainer (often a member of the firm's human resources department) is invited to meet with a department to discuss the group's service mission and to identify operational aspects the department would like to improve.

Other companies use service quality circles, small groups of employees who meet on a regular basis to identify and solve service problems. Useful tools include the service report card and an analysis of the moments of truth and the cycle of service.

The most important implementation activity is redesigning service systems using what you know about the moments of truth. For example, in one bank the system required that you stand in one line to get a check approved and then stand in a second, longer line to pick up your money. A system like this would undermine the customers' service experience even with the best, most customer-oriented employees.

Redesigning service systems can involve making many changes. Grass-roots improvements might include modifying how the firm is organized, as well as its data systems (to avoid having to respond to customer concerns with "Sorry, the computer can't do that"), customer rules, and serial procedures (the actual sequence of steps used to handle the customer's problem).

Step 5: Maintenance—Making the Change Permanent Making the change permanent requires all a manager's planning, organizing, leading, and controlling skills. For example, making high-quality service the norm requires control—in this case polling customers to ensure that the service attributes (such as speed of delivery) do not have to be revised, and to continually assess each attribute's relative importance.

Employees need to be empowered and given customer-oriented goals. Employee selection and training must be effective so that the emotionally laden customer-contact jobs are properly staffed. Top managers have to "walk their talk" and show by word and deed that they take service seriously. Service standards must be set, performance measured, and rewards distributed to ensure that customer service remains top-notch. Making the change permanent requires, in other words, effective management.

SUMMARY

1. Operations management is the process of managing the resources required to produce an organization's goods and services. The direct production resources of a firm are often called the five P's of operations and production management: people, plants, parts, processes, and planning and control systems.

2. Any production system consists of inputs, a conversion system, and outputs. Inputs are the primary resources used in the direct manufacture of the product or service. The conversion system converts those inputs into useful products or services called outputs.

3. The production system is the heart of the operation. Four production design system decisions include the facility or plant location, the type of production processes that will be used, the layout of the plant or facility, and the layout of the production system itself.

4. Production planning is the process of deciding what products to produce, and where, when, and how to produce them. Production control is the process of ensuring that the specified production plans or schedules are being met.

5. The production schedule is often presented on a chart that shows what operations are to be carried out and when. Network planning and control methods are used to plan and control complex projects. Purchasing departments buy the materials and parts the firm needs to conduct its business.

6. Inventory management ensures that the firm has adequate inventories of all needed parts and supplies, within the constraint of minimizing total inventory costs. Many quantitative and nonquantitative systems are available for managing inventory; ABC and EOQ systems are two of the most popular.

7. Quality reflects how well a product or service meets customer needs. Many firms use a process called designing for manufacturability to improve quality. Quality control in many firms involves a total, companywide effort. A number of quality-control techniques are used to monitor and control product quality, including inspection procedures and acceptance sampling.

8. World-class companies compete based on quality, productivity, and responsiveness in an intensely competitive global environment. World-class manufacturers use modern production techniques and progressive management systems to boost manufacturing productivity, quality, and flexibility. These production techniques and management systems include TQM, JIT manufacturing, CAD and CAM, automation and robotics, FMS, CIM, and mass customization.

9. In today's increasingly competitive business world, service management is important: it provides a competitive advantage, and reduces the costs associated with lost customers. To some experts, effective service management focuses on three core concepts: the moments of truth, service cycles, and the service triangle. The five steps in implementing a service management program are the service audit, strategy development, education, implementation, and maintenance.

KEY TERMS

operations management 483
input 483
conversion system 484
output 484
intermittent production 485
continuous production 485
facility layout 486
product layout 486
process layout 486
fixed-position layout 486
cellular manufacturing 486
production planning 488
production control 488
Gantt chart 488
network planning and control
 methods 489
events 489
activities 489
critical path 489

inventory management 491
ordering, or setup, costs 491
acquisition costs 491
inventory-holding (carrying)
 costs 491
stockout costs 491
economic order quantity
 (EOQ) 492
quality 493
ISO 9000 493
total quality management
 (TQM) program 493
Malcolm Baldrige Award 494
acceptance sampling 494
designing for manufacturability 495
concurrent engineering 496
world-class company 496
world-class manufacturer 496

just-in-time (JIT) 496
lean manufacturing 497
value-added manufacturing
 497
computer-aided design (CAD)
 497
computer-aided manufacturing (CAM) 498
automation 498
flexible manufacturing system (FMS) 498
computer-integrated manu-
 facturing (CIM) 499
service management 501
moment of truth 502
cycle of service 503
customer report card 504
service strategy 505

CUSTOMER SERVICE AT KNITMEDIA

KnitMedia's new six-page brochure for its just-opened Hollywood/Los Angeles Knitting Factory describes the new club in glowing terms. The club is on Hollywood Boulevard, not far from the future home of the Academy Awards and Disney's El Capitan Theater, and the "walk of fame" near Grauman's Chinese Theater. The club's features include separate soundproof performance spaces, a state-of-the-art sound system, state-of-the-art video and audio systems, high-tech Internet fully wired facilities, a large, well-equipped kitchen, and facilities for private parties.

However, while location, great artists, and technology like state-of-the-art sound systems certainly accounts for much of the success of a club like this, Michael Dorf and his management team know that another ingredient is crucial too: the quality of the service customers receive. Like hotels, restaurants, dry cleaners, and thousands of other service businesses, Dorf and his team know that a Knitting Factory club is, when it comes down to it, a hospitality business. If the service isn't good, it will detract from the overall success of the operation. Since the clubs have been very successful, Michael and his team have obviously been doing most things right. But they want to make sure that as they grow, they're making specific provision for building high-quality service into everything the Knitting Factory clubs do.

When it comes to great service, KnitMedia already has a lot it can build on. For one thing, most employees are highly enthusiastic about coming to work at KnitMedia. On the other hand, Dorf and his management team have never had to give a lot of thought to building a service strategy for their company: after all, it was a local operation that they could watch on a day-to-day basis. Now, with new clubs opening out of town, they want to take a more formal approach to building high-quality service. They've therefore approached you for advice.

Team Exercises and Questions

Use what you learned in this chapter to answer the following questions from Michael Dorf and his management team:

1. What are some of the main "moments of truth" we can expect our customers and prospective customers to encounter in dealing with a Knitting Factory club? What cycle of service can our customers expect to encounter?

2. We want to conduct a service audit of our New York club. Please design for us a customer report card, including desirable service attributes, each with a customer priority.

3. We know that the five steps in implementing a service management program include the service audit, strategy development, education, implementation, and maintenance. What will be the components of each of those steps for a service management program that we could implement at the Knitting Factory in New York?

MANAGING WITH INFORMATION TECHNOLOGY

WHAT'S AHEAD?

While most people don't know it, buying a pair of Levi's jeans at a big chain like Macy's makes the consumer a part of the Levi's information system—at least for a moment. As we'll see in this module, Levi's has installed a vast information network to help it manage and control its sales, and that network begins, in a sense, with the point of sale cash register where you pay for those jeans. That sale automatically triggers a series of automated decisions—for instance, telling Levi's computer systems to produce another pair of jeans in that size and model, and to ship them to that store to replace its inventory. We'll see in this module that, as at Levi's, information technology—combining telecommunications systems and computers—is today an integral part of the way that firms do business, and an essential ingredient in managing change.

OBJECTIVES

AFTER STUDYING THIS MODULE, YOU SHOULD BE ABLE TO

■ Give examples of why managers at different organizational levels require different types of information

■ Give examples of information systems used by managers

■ Illustrate telecommunication's role in managing organizations

■ Give examples showing how information technology and the Internet can help managers plan, organize, lead, and control more effectively

Throughout this book (and particularly in the "Managing @ the Speed of Thought" boxes), we've seen how managers are using information technology like computers and the Internet today. In this module we'll take a more comprehensive look at information technology and management, and particularly at what information technology is and how it's used to manage organizations.

▶ MANAGEMENT IN THE INFORMATION AGE

Information technology refers to any processes, practices, or systems that facilitate processing and transporting information. You are no doubt already very familiar with information technology's modern components. For example, you probably use a personal computer and are familiar with management information systems from the work you do. You probably use cellular phones, facsimile machines, and e-mail and voice-mail systems. Information technologies like these have dramatically altered the way people do their jobs and the way companies are managed.

The Nature of Information

Information is data presented in a form that is meaningful to the recipient.[1] "Information," as Peter Drucker said, "is data endowed with relevance and purpose."[2] Knowledge, on the other hand, has been defined as "information . . . distilled via study or research and augmented by judgment and experience."[3]

To put these definitions into managerial terms, consider this example. PepsiCo Inc., wants to determine why consumers are not buying its new Pepsi Light drink. To search for an answer, the company's market researchers conduct a survey containing 25 multiple-choice questions. The answers to the questions are put on computer disks, where by themselves they would appear to the untrained eye as nothing but long streams of unrelated numbers.

When market researchers summarize these *data* for presentation to management, the result is *information*, such as graphs showing average responses by age level and other demographic traits for each question. The marketing department can then apply its *knowledge* to draw meaningful conclusions, such as (in PepsiCo's case), a hypothesis about why older consumers seem less inclined to purchase Pepsi Light than younger ones.

What Is "Information Quality"

Managers are, of course, inundated with information all the time. What they need is high-quality information. High-quality information has several characteristics.[4] As in the PepsiCo example, good information must be *pertinent* and related to the problem at hand. It must also be *timely*. For example, the Pepsi Light survey information would be useless if it came rolling in two years after the product was pulled off the shelf. Good information must also be *accurate*. Finally, good information reduces *uncertainty*, which we can define as the absence of information about a particular area of concern.[5]

In the PepsiCo example, to meet these last criteria, the survey information should help the marketing manager answer the question "Why aren't people buying Pepsi Light the way we thought they would?"

Yet, even good information is relatively useless without the knowledge that comes from analysis, interpretation, and explanation.[6] Managers are, as we said, deluged by information—on competitors' practices, consumers' buying habits, machinery breakdowns, and many other relevant issues. The role of information technology today is thus not just to generate and transfer more (or even better-quality) information. It is to contribute to the manager's knowledge of what is happening, through analysis, interpretation, and explanation. Its ultimate aim is to make the manager's company more competitive.

Data mining is one example.[7] This means using special computer software to analyze vast amounts of customer data stored in a company's data banks to obtain information the firm can use to be more competitive. When it comes to making decisions, managers don't want to be deluged by truckloads of numbers; they want to receive reports that let them see meaningful patterns and relationships. New data-mining software products like Intelligent Miner from IBM let them do just that.

For example, like most phone companies, MCI Worldcom Communications Corp. wants to keep its best customers. To do this, it's helpful to identify early those customers who might be thinking of jumping to another long-distance carrier. But how do you screen telephone data on more than 100 million households to try to find patterns in characteristics like lifestyle and past calling habits that may suggest the customer is a likely candidate for switching phone companies? In this case, MCI Worldcom uses its IBM supercomputer and special data-mining software to analyze a set of 22 detailed and highly secret statistical profiles of customers to monitor the patterns that it believes can help identify customers' intentions.

data mining
using special computer software to analyze vast amounts of customer data stored in a company's data bank to obtain information the firm can use to be more competitive.

Knowledge Management

Knowledge—no matter how high-quality it is—is totally useless if the people who need that knowledge don't know it exists or can't get to it. This fact has given rise to a new area called **knowledge management**, which one expert refers to as "the task of developing and exploiting an organization's tangible and intangible knowledge resources".[8] The company's tangible knowledge assets include things like patents, licenses, and information on customers and competitors. Intangible knowledge assets are the knowledge employees possess, including their experiences and the methods they've discovered for solving problems. The basic purpose of knowledge management "is to leverage and reuse resources that already exist in the organization so that people will seek out best practices rather than reinvent the wheel."[9]

As we noted in earlier chapters, using computerized systems to enable employees to easily access their companies' knowledge bases has proved to be a boon to companies. For example, IBM consultants reportedly cut their proposal-writing time from an average of 200 hours to 30 because they can now share information.[10] Sales and technical support reps at Dell Computer's call centers solve more problems more easily thanks to a central knowledge base that advises them on what questions to ask and what solutions to suggest. As we saw in Chapter 3, Xerox Corp.'s copier repairers have reduced average repair time by 50% thanks to a knowledge base comprised of suggestions and solutions from the company's repair staff.

knowledge management
the task of developing and exploiting an organization's tangible and intangible knowledge resources.

Managers' Requirements for Information

Managers at different levels in the organization require different types of information.[11] First-line managers (like the front-desk manager at a Hilton Hotel) tend to focus on short-term, operational decisions. At this level, information should emphasize activities such as accounts receivables, order entry, inventory control, and cash management.

Middle managers tend to focus more on intermediate-range decisions, like events that might affect the company in the coming year or so. They therefore require information for use in budget analysis, short-term forecasting, and variance analysis. A marketing manager needs consumer data to plan her next ad campaign, for instance.

Top managers (including the firm's CEO and vice presidents) focus more on long-range strategic decisions. They therefore need information that enables them to make, for example, factory location decisions, merger and acquisition decisions, and new-product planning decisions.

Because of these different information requirements, different types of information systems are needed at each level of the organization, as we'll see next.

▶ INFORMATION SYSTEMS FOR MANAGING ORGANIZATIONS

What Is an Information System?

information system

a set of people, data, and procedures that work together to retrieve, process, store, and disseminate information to support decision making and control.

An **information system** is a set of people, data, technology, and organizational procedures that work together to retrieve, process, store, and disseminate information to support decision making and control.[12] We'll focus here on *managerial* information systems, which are systems that support managerial decision making and control.

Information systems are more than computers. The information system also usually includes major parts of the organization, such as the employees who input data into the system and retrieve its output. Managers are (or should be) part of the information system too, since it's their specific needs for information (like an MCI Worldcom managers' need for information about customers' calling patterns) that the information system is designed to serve.

Information Systems = Technology + People   Recent changes at Schneider National, North America's biggest carrier of full truckload cargoes, help show why information systems include technology, people, and organizations.

After deregulation revolutionized the trucking industry, Schneider National knew it had to do something quickly to get itself into more competitive shape.[13] The regulations that had made it difficult for customers to change carriers were gone, so the firm suddenly faced more competition than ever before.

Schneider National managers decided on a two-pronged strategy. First, to prepare the organization for other changes to come, management focused on making sweeping changes in its corporate culture. The main aim was to replace its "regulated-utility" mentality with a sense of urgency to get things done fast.

The company's CEO took several steps to change the culture and values of the company: He encouraged everyone from drivers on up to suggest ways to improve operations, eliminated status symbols like reserved parking spaces, began calling all employees *associates*, and drew attention to the new emphasis on performance by awarding bonus paychecks based solely on performance.

Information technology changes were then built on this new cultural foundation. All trucks were equipped with computers and rotating antennas, so that a satellite could track every rig and make sure it stuck to its schedule. When a customer called to request a pick-up, dispatchers knew exactly which truck to assign to the job. The order was sent directly to that driver's on-board terminal, complete with directions to the destination and instructions about what gate to use.

The new information system has been very successful. However, it's doubtful that it would have been if management hadn't had the wisdom to design the system around the people—by changing the culture, by making sure the drivers who had to use the system were made to feel like involved participants in the process, and by designing a system the drivers wanted to use.

Levels of Information Systems   Because information requirements at each organizational level tend to be unique to that level, there is a corresponding hierarchy of information systems, from strategic-level systems at the top, to operational systems at the bottom.[14]

As in Figure B.1, **executive support systems** provide information for strategic-level decisions on matters such as five-year operating plans. **Management information systems** and *decision support systems* provide middle managers with reports regarding matters such as current versus historical sales levels.

▼ **FIGURE B.1**   **Applications of Information Systems for Each Organizational Level**

Managers at each level of the organization have unique information requirements. Various types of information systems have thus been developed to serve the needs at each management level.

TYPES OF SYSTEMS

STRATEGIC-LEVEL SYSTEMS

	Sales and Marketing	Manufacturing	Finance	Accounting	Human Resources
Executive Support Systems (ESS)	5-year sales trend forecasting	5-year operating plan	5-year budget forecasting	Profit planning	Manpower planning

MANAGEMENT-LEVEL SYSTEMS

	Sales and Marketing	Manufacturing	Finance	Accounting	Human Resources
Management Information Systems (MIS)	Sales management	Inventory control	Annual budgeting	Capital investment analysis	Relocation analysis
Decision-Support Systems (DSS)	Sales region analysis	Production scheduling	Cost analysis	Pricing/ profitability analysis	Contract cost analysis

KNOWLEDGE-LEVEL SYSTEMS

	Sales and Marketing	Finance	Human Resources
Knowledge-Level Work Systems (KWS)	Engineering workstations	Graphics workstations	Managerial workstations
Office Automation Systems (OAS)	Word processing	Document imaging	Electronic calendars

OPERATIONAL-LEVEL SYSTEMS

	Sales and Marketing	Manufacturing	Finance	Accounting	Human Resources
		Machine control	Securities trading	Payroll	Compensation
Transaction Processing Systems (TPS)	Order tracking	Plant scheduling		Accounts payable	Training & development
	Order processing	Material movement control	Cash management	Accounts receivable	Employee record keeping

Source: Adapted from Laudon and Laudon, *Management Information Systems* 6th ed. (Upper Saddle River, NJ; Prentice Hall, 1998), p 39.

management information system

an information system that provides decision support for managers by producing standardized, summarized reports on a regular basis.

transaction processing system

an information system that provides detailed information about short-term, daily activities.

Transaction processing systems provide detailed information about the most short-term, daily activities, such as accounts payables and order status. We'll look more closely at each type of system.

Transaction Processing Systems

A *transaction* is an event that affects the business. Hiring an employee, selling merchandise, paying an employee, and ordering supplies are transactions. In essence, transaction processing systems collect and maintain detailed records regarding the organization's transactions. These records are generally used for making operational-level decisions. For example, a university must know which students have registered, which have paid fees, which members of the faculty are teaching, and what secretaries are employed in order to conduct its business.

The collection and maintenance of such day-to-day transactions were two of the first procedures to be computerized in organizations. As is still the case today, early transaction processing systems automated the collection, maintenance, and processing of mostly repetitive transactions. Examples include computing withholding taxes and net pay, and processing accounts payable checks.

Transaction processing systems (TPSs) can be put to five uses.[15] They may have to classify data based on common characteristics of a group (such as finding all sales employees with five years' service, for instance). They are used to do routine calculations (such as computing net pay after taxes and deductions for each employee) and can be used for sorting (for instance, grouping invoices by zip code). The TPS can also be used for summarization (such as summarizing for each department's manager what his or her average payroll is compared to the other departments). Finally, the TPS can be used for storage (for example, storing payroll information for, say, the past five years).

Management Information Systems

A management information system (MIS) provides decision support for managers by producing standardized, summarized reports on a regular basis.[16] It generally produces management level reports, reports for longer-term purposes than typical transaction processing systems.

In a university, for instance, a TPS is used to print class rolls and grade rolls. An MIS, in contrast, can measure and report class size and enrollment trends by department and by college. The deans (who are midway between the president and other executives, and operating managers such as department heads) can then use the MIS reports to increase or decrease class sizes or to drop some courses from next semester's schedule while adding others. MISs condense, summarize, and manipulate information derived from the organization's TPS. They then present the results in the form of routine summary reports to management, often with exceptions flagged for control purposes.[17]

Decision Support Systems

Decision support systems (DSSs) "assist management decision making by combining data, sophisticated analytical models, and user-friendly software into a single powerful system that can support semi-structured or unstructured decision making."[18] In other words, systems like these can help managers (again, usually midlevel managers but occasionally executives) make decisions that are relatively unstructured when compared to those addressed by the typical MIS.

TABLE B.1	**How Firms Use Their DSS**
American Airlines	Price and route selection
Champlin Petroleum	Corporate planning and forecasting
Equico Capital Corporation	Investment evaluation
Frito-Lay, Inc.	Price, advertising, and promotion selection
General Dynamics	Price evaluation
Juniper Lumber	Production optimization
Kmart	Price evaluation
National Gypsum	Corporate planning and forecasting
Southern Railway	Train dispatching and routing
Texas Oil and Gas Corporation	Evaluation of potential drilling sites
United Airlines	Flight scheduling
U.S. Department of Defense	Defense contract analysis

At the university, for instance, an MIS is used to make course addition and deletion decisions, decisions that are fairly routine. However, suppose the university's faculty threatens to strike. The university could use a decision support system to estimate the impact on university revenues of having to drop various combinations of classes.

An MIS differs from a DSS in several ways.[19] A DSS is more capable of analyzing alternatives. This is because decision support systems let the user (in this case, the vice president for academic affairs) include subprograms showing how various components of the university (such as revenues and enrollments in various courses) are related. Furthermore, a DSS does not rely just on internal information from the TPS the way the MIS typically does. Instead, a DSS is built to absorb new external information into the analysis.

Thus, the university's academic vice president, faced with a strike, may want to include in her or his analysis an estimate of the likelihood that a number of the university's students will move across town to a competing school, given the competing school's ability (or inability) to expand its class offerings.

Table B.1 gives some examples of how companies use DSS systems. For example, American Airlines uses its system for price and route selection, General Dynamics for price evaluation, and Southern Railway for train dispatching and routing.

Executive Support Systems

Executive support systems (ESS) are information systems designed to help top-level executives acquire, manipulate, and use the information they need to maintain the overall strategic effectiveness of the company. Such systems often focus on providing top management with information for making strategic decisions. They help top management match changes in the firm's environment with the firm's existing and potential strengths and weaknesses.[20]

Executive support systems perform several specific tasks. Executives such as Cypress Semiconductor's president use their ESS for keeping informed about and monitoring the pulse of their organizations. For example Cypress monitors the weekly compliance of all its 4,000 employees (for instance, how each worker stands in terms of project progress or sales productivity). Second, executives use ESS to quickly identify and understand evolving competitive situations.

A university president could thus use an ESS to keep tabs on and analyze the following questions:

- Is the average student taking fewer courses?
- Are costs for maintenance labor substantially higher than they have been in the past?
- Is there a significant shift in the zip codes from which most of our students come?

An ESS also makes it easy for executives to browse through the data. One executive describes the capability this way:

I like to take a few minutes to review details about our customers, our manufacturers or our financial activities first hand. Having the details flow across the screen gives me a feel for how things are going. I don't look at each record, but glance at certain elements as they scroll by. If something looks unusual, it will almost jump out at me and I can find out more about it. But if nothing is unusual, I will know that, too.[21]

A top executive can also use an ESS to monitor a situation. Thus, a university president could use an ESS to monitor the new dining facilities management firm running the student cafeteria by reviewing information such as student usage, student complaints, and revenues. Executives also use ESSs to facilitate environmental scanning. For example, a wealth of information is available in commercial computerized data banks, including financial information on tens of thousands of U.S. companies. Executives can use an ESS to tap into such data banks in order to glean competitive data regarding other firms in their industry.

An ESS can also support analytical needs. For example, it may allow the university president to create what-if scenarios that show the probable effects on revenues of increasing faculty salaries or adding new programs. Finally, an ESS may enable the executive to get at data directly. Using terminals and telephone lines, executives can use an executive support system to tap directly into the company's data files in order to get specific information that may be of interest, without waiting for others to assemble it.[22]

Enterprisewide Information Systems and the Company's "Digital Nervous System"

As we saw in Chapter 15 companies today are increasingly implementing enterprisewide information systems. Basically, systems like these—produced by companies like SAP of Germany—are companywide integrated computer systems that integrate a firm's individual systems (such as order processing, production control, and accounting) in order to give managers real-time, instantaneous information regarding the costs and status of every activity and project in the business.

Today, in other words, more and more managers don't rely just on the sorts of executive, management, and transaction information systems that parallel the company's executive, managerial, and operational levels. Instead, enterprisewide systems are being used to integrate these various systems. For example, a point-of-sale device at a Wal-Mart store might signal Levi Strauss to produce 50 more size 34

501 jeans. Levi's enterprisewide system than automatically acknowledges the order, produces a production schedule, monitors the order's progress, and provides top managers with real-time information regarding the profitability of that order as well as total Wal-Mart orders by geographic region for that day.

Microsoft chairman Bill Gates, says that "like a human being, the company has to have an internal communication mechanism, a 'nervous system,' to coordinate its actions."[23] Like world-class athletes, world-class companies need superfast reflexes. And just as it's hard for someone to have great reflexes with a malfunctioning nervous system, companies with inadequate "digital nervous systems" can't respond fast enough to customers' requests or competitors' moves. Enterprisewide information systems like the one at Levi can form the backbone of the company's digital nervous system. It's easier for companies with systems like these to literally "do business at the speed of thought."

Systems like these are already in place and working effectively at many firms. For example, you'll recall that Harmon Music Group uses a type of enterprisewide system to integrate its order processing, production scheduling, and accounting systems and to thereby run its business very efficiently. Similarly, Deluxe Paper Payment systems was able to dramatically improve its profitability by using information from its enterprisewide information systems to get many of its smaller customers to switch to electronic check ordering.

Yet installing one of these highly integrated systems can also be fraught with peril. For example, October 31, 1999 turned out to be a scary Halloween for Hershey Foods, the largest U.S. candymaker. During the summer, "Hershey flipped the switch on a $112 million computer system that was supposed to automate and modernize everything from taking candy orders to putting palettes on trucks."[24] But instead of speeding the flow of orders and information, the system has apparently gummed up the works. Orders, even from huge customers like Wal-Mart, were being delayed, and Hershey sales reps actually had to call customers to find out what products they'd received, because the new information system couldn't tell which orders Hershey had delivered and which it had not. The mix up was a boon to competitors like Mars Inc. and Nestle USA, both of which saw their Halloween chocolate orders jump as customers scrambled to keep their shelves stocked with candies.

Part of the problem, experts now say, may be that Hershey tried to implement its system all at once, putting it online in what computer people call a "big bang" approach. Whatever the cause, it's apparent that while enterprisewide information systems can certainly help managers manage, implementing a project of that magnitude requires the most effective planning, organizing, leading, and controlling (in other words, management) skills the company can muster.

▶ **NETWORKS FOR MANAGING ORGANIZATIONS**

Organizations make extensive use of networks to better manage their operations. A network "is a group of interconnected computers, work stations or computer devices (such as printers and data storage systems)."[25] Local area networks, wide area networks, and distributed networks are three examples of managerial networks.

Local Area Networks

A local area network (LAN) spans a limited distance, such as a building or several adjacent buildings, using the company's own telecommunications links (rather than common-carrier links such as those provided by AT&T's phone lines). In an

network
a group of interconnected computers, workstations, or computer devices.

local area network (LAN)
a communications network that spans a limited distance, such as a building or several adjacent buildings, using the company's own telecommunications links.

office, a LAN may be used to support a workgroup information system such as e-mail, and a factory may use a LAN to link computers with computer-controlled production equipment.

More generally, LANs are used for one or more of the following reasons: to distribute information and messages (including e-mail); to drive computer-controlled manufacturing equipment; to distribute documents (such as engineering drawings from one department to another); to interconnect the LAN's computers with those of a public network such as Prodigy or the Internet; and, given the high cost of certain equipment such as laser printers, to make equipment sharing possible (including not just printers but disk storage file servers, for instance).

Wide Area Networks

Wide area networks (WANs) are networks that serve microcomputers over larger geographic areas, spanning distances that can cover a few miles or circle the globe. Early WANs utilized common carrier networks, such as the telephone links provided by AT&T. However, many firms today operate their own WANs, which are essentially private, computerized telecommunications systems.

The Benetton retail store chain uses its WAN to enable both store managers and headquarters staff to identify local trends and improve inventory and production management. The stores accumulate sales data during the day and keep them on computer disks. At night, another, larger computer at corporate headquarters polls the individual retail stores' computers, accessing data that are then transmitted over telephone lines back to headquarters. Here, the information is processed and a summary of sales trends is forwarded to headquarters and individual store managers.[26]

As at Benetton, WANs are often used to achieve distributed processing. **Distributed processing** generally uses small local computers (such as point-of-sale systems) to collect, store, and process information, with summary reports and information sent to headquarters as needed.[27]

Managing and The Internet

While you're reading this page, millions of people around the world are "on the Internet," searching through libraries, talking to friends, and buying and selling products and services, from firms ranging from Amazon.com to Sony to Deutsche Telecom. The value of the Internet lies in its ability to easily and inexpensively connect so many people from so many places; the miracle of the Internet is that no one owns it and it has no formal management organization. Instead, to become part of the Internet, an existing network simply pays a small registration fee and agrees to comply with certain electronic standards, such as Transmission Control Protocol/Internet Protocol (TCP/IP), originally developed by the U.S. Department of Defense.

As most of us are aware, the boom in e-commerce has turned most business people into Web believers. It's probably harder to find companies that don't use the Web today than those that do. Hundreds of thousands of merchants around the world now sell products or services via the Web. Hershey Foods, for instance, offers a personal address book and a service that reminds users of special dates and anniversaries, thus allowing them to conveniently send Herhsey products to mark special occasions. In July 1999, BarnesandNoble.com launched its music site. Another site, onlineofficesupplies.com, is open 24 hours a day, seven days a week, offering more than 30,000 products at reduced prices.[28] Business sales (if not profits) are thus booming on the Internet.

But all those Internet-based sales sites are only the tip of the iceberg when it comes to managerial uses of the Internet. For one thing, since companies can, in a sense, get a "free ride" on the Internet, they can substantially reduce their communications costs by building their management systems around the Internet.

This book's "Managing @ the Speed of Thought" features and Webnotes present many examples of how managers use the Internet. Remember, for instance, how the New York real estate firm Cushman & Wakefield uses the Internet to let its 2,000 employees around the world communicate with each other and with the headquarters staff. Similarly, Schlumberger Ltd., the New York and Paris oil drilling equipment company, relies on the Internet to communicate with and stay in control of vast projects in 85 countries.

Other companies use the Internet for strategic planning. With so many firms having Web sites today, the Internet has become a useful device for collecting information on competitors, for example. (One company, visiting a competitor's site, reportedly found a preview of an upcoming promotional campaign, and was able to quickly revise its own plans and get the jump on its competitor).[29] Other companies actually build Web pages to help employees gather information about competitors or customers; the Web pages contain, for instance, links to published news accounts, press releases, and government statistics.[30]

The bottom line is that information technology and the Internet are literally helping managers to "manage @ the speed of thought." Many or most of today's virtual corporations and strategic alliances—all of which depend for their existence on rapid, relatively inexpensive multimedia communications—would be impossible without such tools. Similarly, many team-based organizations would be unmanageable without systems such as Lotus Notes groupware, through which geographically dispersed team members can communicate virtually "face-to-face." Indeed, when it comes to leading and influencing employees, information technology and the Internet now almost always play a major role.

When the president of Xerox recently wanted to motivate his troops, he sent them all what Xerox calls a "vmail," a voicemail note that goes automatically to each employee's voicemail box. Dell Computer, the direct sales computer firm, relies heavily on information technology to stay close to its customers and to control the progress of its orders. For example, employees who take customers' calls work on PCs linked by a network to a large central computer that contains the company's customer database. As the calls come in, the telephone representatives input the information to the database, and follow up inquiries by triggering the mailing of customized sales letters to inquiry customers. Customers can then easily track the progress of their orders on Dell's Web site and can do this without tying up a Dell telephone representative's time. Thus, whether it's planning, organizing, leading, or controlling, information technology and the Internet are vital management tools today.

SUMMARY

1. Information technology refers to any processes, practices, or systems that facilitate the processing and transportation of data and information. The increasingly rapid deployment of information technology in organizations has sped the transformation of many businesses today into information-based organizations.

2. Information is data presented in a form that is meaningful to the recipient. Knowledge, on the other hand, has been defined as information distilled via study or research and augmented by judgment and experience. Good-quality information must be pertinent, timely, and accurate and reduce uncertainty. But even good information is relatively useless without knowledge. The role of information technology at work is to contribute to the manager's knowledge of what is happening through analysis, interpretation, and explanation.

3. Managers at different levels in the organization require different types of information. First-line managers tend to focus on short-term, operational decisions and therefore need information that focuses on operational activities. Middle managers tend to concentrate on the intermediate range and so require information for use in such tasks as budget analysis, short-term forecasting, and variance analysis. Top managers make long-range plans and, therefore, require information that will enable them to make better strategic decisions.

4. Information systems are people, data, hardware, and procedures that work together to retrieve, process, store, and disseminate information to support decision making and control. The hierarchy of information systems used in management includes executive support systems, management information and decision support systems, and transaction processing systems.

5. Managers today rely heavily on telecommunication-based networks such as LANs, WANs and the Internet. We've seen in this books *Managing @ the Speed of Thought* features that all management functions—from planning to organizing to leading to control—are often Internet-assisted today.

KEY TERMS

information 510	management information system 513	network 517
data mining 511		local area network (LAN) 517
knowledge management 511	transaction processing system 514	wide area network (WAN) 518
information system 512		distributed processing 518
executive support system 513		

YOU BE THE CONSULTANT

KNITMEDIA

IT'S A HIGH-TECH WORLD AT KNITMEDIA

The growing popularity of the Internet has turned out to be a tremendous shot in the arm for KnitMedia and its management team. Its various online properties and Internet partners (like AOL) have provided an amazing opportunity to get its music and other content directly to its customers, and to that extent the Internet has diminished the competitive advantage of industry giants like Warner music. The company already has a growing list of e-commerce sites, including jazze.com, knittingfactory.com, jazzschool.com, and knitfilms.com.

KnitMedia also uses technology, and in particular telecommunications technology, to link its growing network of Knitting Factory clubs. As KnitMedia's literature points out:

All locations will be connected by high-speed links providing streaming audio and video of performances, and both artist and customer interactions between venues. The Knitting Factory is a pioneer in networks integrating Internet and broadband technology, creating a digital playground for both the consumer and the artist. Each club will have video screens in the bars, allowing patrons thousands of miles apart to toast each other.

KnitMedia management will combine its local support and global reach to form a unique, extended international cyber community of both musicians and fans.

Michael Dorf and his management team have several questions for you regarding the further use of information systems and technology for running KnitMedia.

Team Exercises and Questions

Use what you learned in this chapter to answer the following questions from Michael Dorf and his management team:

1. Do you think that linking the Knitting Factory clubs in this way (so that, say, performances at one club can be shown simultaneously at the others) will be a big competitive advantage? Why or why not?

2. We know that other companies are using the Internet to facilitate communications and control. How would you suggest we use information technology and the Internet to improve the performance of KnitMedia and its various businesses? (We need specific examples, please).

Controlling and Building Commitment

For a growing organization like KnitMedia, the checks and balances of an effective control process become more important all the time. If they performed no other function than to let managers know when it is time to revise or change their plans, controls would still perform a valuable service. However, they also prompt improved performance.

We've seen that a high degree of employee commitment to the brand, the product, or the organizational vision does exist at KnitMedia. Vice President of KnitMedia Label Stephanie Oxley wants her staff members to feel that the company is their own, and that kind of identification with the organization is an equally strong goal among her colleagues. So employee commitment already supplements traditional control in situations involving team effort, particularly in the more creative aspects of the organization.

As new clubs are opened, both in the United States and abroad, a dual set of more traditional controls comes into play. Each club has its own local manager who is responsible for overseeing operations, and these managers report in turn to Ed Greer, Senior Vice President of Club Operations. Ed has written a new operations manual for running the clubs that includes all kinds of housekeeping details, spelling out standards for cleaning and maintenance that are the responsibility of the club managers and night managers. At weekly management meetings for the New York staff, Ed personally reinforces the standards, and he encourages his staff to walk through the club frequently (particularly before the doors open) to make sure that all is in order, from the supply of toilet paper in the rest rooms to the replacement of a broken light bulb. The artists' dressing rooms get the same meticulous attention as the rest of the club.

While "control rests completely in attention to details," as Ed says, it also begins at the top, with the simple question whether the club is clearly visible from 100 yards away. Ed continually works with his staff to ensure that they can see the club's facilities as he sees them—as expectant customers see them—and that they can follow through on their responsibilities for ensuring that every visitor's experience is a pleasant one.

Mark Harabedian, Vice President of Finance, describes the ways in which cash inflows and outflows are controlled in the club's bar. Cash disappears easily, he admits, and it is necessary to have strong control systems to ensure that it all ends up in the safe at the end of the night. New cash registers have arrived that use touch screens; they also boast many inventory features and controls that will simplify the process of accurately measuring nightly cash income. In addition, weekly meetings keep the staff "ahead of the snowball," and monthly reports on bar performance measure average dollars spent, types of drinks sold and in what quantities, and so on.

A check approval process operates to control the outflow of funds, and stricter budgets are now drawn up, particularly for larger projects like building a new Web site or upgrading the organization's office computers or adding to staff. CEO Michael Dorf jokes that the process of budgeting is so new he still has trouble pronouncing the word, and sometimes adhering to the plan as well. But there is no question that this kind of financial control tool is critical to KnitMedia's future success.

Questions

Based on the case, the video, the text chapters you've read so far, and your knowledge from other sources, answer the following:

1. Characterize the types of controls in use at KnitMedia. Do you think the right types are operating in each area?

2. Do you foresee any downside to the increasing use of controls at KnitMedia? What might the organization's managers do to prevent these?

3. Which of the tools described in Modules A and B would you suggest KnitMedia think about using, and why?

CHAPTER 1

1 David Kirkpatrick, "The Second Coming of Apple," *Fortune*, 9 November 1998, pp. 87–104.

2 David Kirkpatrick, "IBM: From Blue Dinosaur to E-Business Animal," *Fortune*, 26 April 1999, pp. 119–125.

3 Joan Magretta, "The Power of Virtual Integration: An Interview with Dell Computer's Michael Dell," *Harvard Business Review*, March–April 1998, pp. 73–84.

4 Henry Mintzberg, "The Manager's Job: Folklore and Fact," *Harvard Business Review*, July–August 1975, pp. 489–561.

5 See, for example, ibid.; and George Copeman, *The Chief Executive* (London: Leviathan House, 1971), p. 271. See also George Weathersby, "Facing Today's Sea Changes," *Management Review*, June 1999, p. 5; and David Kirkpatrick, "The Second Coming of Apple," *Fortune*, 9 November 1998, pp. 86–104; and Jenny McCune, "The Changemakers," Management Review, May 1999, pp. 16–22.

6 Peter Drucker, "The Coming of the New Organization," *Harvard Business Review*, January–February 1988, p. 45. See also Fred Andrews, "The Sage of Value and Service," *New York Times*, 17 November 1999, pp. C-1, C14.

7 Geoffrey Colvin, "How to be a great ECEO," *Fortune*, 24 May 1999, pp. 104–110.

8 G. William Dauphinais and Colin Price, "The CEO as a Psychologist," Management Review, September 1998, pp. 1–15.

9 Claudia H. Deutsch, "A Hands-on-the-Helm Leader," *New York Times*, 13 June 1999, Money and Business Section, p. 2.

10 Noel Tichy and Ram Charan, "The CEO as Coach: An Interview with Allied-Signal's Lawrence A. Bossidy," *Harvard Business Review*, March–April 1995, pp. 69–78.

11 Ibid., p. 70.

12 Ibid., p. 73.

13 Ibid., p. 70.

14 Ibid.

15 Ibid., p. 76.

16 These are based on Henry Mintzberg, "The Manager's Job: Folklore and Fact."

17 Sumatra Ghoshal and Christopher Bartlett, "Changing the Role of Top Management: Beyond Structure to Processes," *Harvard Business Review*, January–February 1995, pp. 86–96.

18 Ibid., p. 89.

19 Ibid., p. 91.

20 Ibid., p. 96.

21 Ibid., p. 94.

22 John Holland, *Making Vocational Choices: A Theory of Careers* (Upper Saddle River, NJ: Prentice-Hall, 1973); see also John Holland, *Assessment Booklet: A Guide to Educational and Career Planning* (Odessa, FL: Psychological Assessment Resources, Inc., 1990).

23 Edgar Schein, *Career Dynamics: Matching Individual and Organizational Needs* (Reading, MA: Addison-Wesley, 1978), pp. 128–129.

24 A. Howard and D. W. Bray, *Managerial Lives in Transition: Advancing Age and Changing Times* (New York: Guilford, 1988); discussed in Dwayne Schultz and Sydney Ellen Schultz, *Psychology and Work Today* (New York: Macmillan Publishing Co., 1994), pp. 103–104.

25 Ibid., Schultz and Schultz, p. 104.

26 Ibid.

27 "Riding the Storm," *Economist*, 6 November 1999.

28 Rebecca Buckman, "Wall Street Is Rocked by Merrill's On-Line Moves," *Wall Street Journal*, 2 June 1999, p. C1.

29 Nina Munk, "How Levi's Trashed a Great American Brand," *Fortune*, 12 April 1999, pp. 83–90.

30 Henry Mintzberg, "The Manager's Job: Folklore and Fact," *Harvard Business Review*, July–August 1975, 489–561. For a discussion of critical management trends, see Sharon Lobel, et al, "The Future of Work and Family: Critical Trends for Policy, Practice, and Research," *Human Resource Management*, Fall 1999, pp. 243–254.

31 See, for example, ibid.; and Copeman, p. 271. See also Weathersby, p. 5.

32 Thomas Stewart, "Welcome to the Revolution," *Fortune*, 13 December 1993, p. 66.

33 Charles W. Hill, *International Business* (Burr Ridge, IL: Irwin, 1994), p. 6.

34 Ibid., p. 9.

35 Amy Barrett, Peter Elstrom, and Catherine Arnst, "Vaulting the Walls with Wireless," *Business Week*, 20 January 1997, pp. 85, 88.

36 Bryan O'Reilly, "Your New Global Workforce," *Fortune*, 14 December 1992, pp. 52–66. See also "Charting the Projections: 1996–2006," *Occupational Outook Quarterly*, Winter 1997–1998, pp. 2–5. See also Floyd Kemske, "HR 2008: A Forecast Based on our Exclusive Study," *Workforce*, January 1998, pp. 46–58.

37 Richard Crawford, *In the Era of Human Capital* (New York: Harper, 1991), p. 10. See also Kemske, pp. 46–58. See also Sharon Lobel, Bradley Googins, and Ellen Bankert, "The Future of Work and Family: Critical Trends for Policy, Practice, and Research," *Human Resource Management*, Fall 1999, pp. 243–254.

38 Ibid.

39 "Charting the Projections: 1996–2006," *Occupational Outlook Quarterly*, Winter 1997–1998, pp. 2–24.

40 James Brian Quinn, *Intelligent Enterprise* (New York: The Free Press, 1992), p. 3.

41 Ibid., p. 26.

42 Thomas Stewart, "Brain Power," *Fortune*, June 3, 1991, p. 44; See also Thomas Stewart, "Brain Power," *Fortune*, 17 March 1997, pp. 105–10.

43 Bill Gates, *Business @ the Speed of Thought* (New York: Warner Books, 1999), p. 289.

44 Francis Fukuyama, "Are We at the End of History?" *Fortune*, 15 January 1990, p. 68.

45 Peter Drucker, "The Coming of the New Organization," *Harvard Business Review*, January–February 1988, p. 45.

46 Joan Magretta, "The Power of a Virtual Integration: An Interview with Dell Computers Michael Dell," *Harvard Business Review*, March–April 1998, pp. 73–84.

47 Ibid., p. 74.

48 Ibid., p. 82.

49 Ibid.

50 Ibid., p. 76.

51 Ibid., p. 75.

52 Tom Peters, *Liberation Management* (New York: Alfred Knopf, 1992), p. 9.

53 Ibid., and www.abb.com, 31 December 1999.

54 Eryn Brown, "Nine Ways to Win on the Web," *Fortune*, 24 May 1999, p. 125.

55 Ibid., p. 125.

56 Bryan Dumaine, "What the Leaders of Tomorrow See," *Fortune*, 3 July 1989, p. 58. See also Weathersby, p. 5. See also, Gary Hamel and Jeff Sampler, "The eCorp.: Building a New Industrial" *Fortune*, 7 December 1998, pp. 80–112.

57 These are based on Walter Kiechel III, "How We Will Work in the Year 2000," *Fortune*, 17 May 1993, p. 79.

58 Karl Albrecht, *At America's Service: How Corporations Can Revolutionize the Way They Treat Their Customers* (Homewood, IL: Dow-Jones Irwin, 1998).

59 Bryan Dumaine, "What the Leaders of Tomorrow See," *Fortune*, 3 July 1989, p. 51.

60 Rosabeth Moss Kanter, "The New Managerial Work," *Harvard Business Review*, November–December 1989, p. 88.

61 Ibid.

62 Drucker, "The Coming of the New Organization," p. 45.

63 Peters, *Liberation Management*.

64 Bryan Dumaine, "The New Non-Managers," Fortune, 22 February 1993, p. 81. See also David Kirkpatrick, "IBM: from Big Blue Dinosaur to e-Business Animal," *Fortune*, 26 April 1999, pp. 116–127. See also McCune, pp. 16–22. See also Brent Schlender, "Larry Ellison: Oracle at Web Speed," *Fortune*, 24 May 1999, pp. 128–137.

65 Thomas Stewart, "How GE Keeps Those Ideas Coming," *Fortune*, 12 August 1991, p. 42. See also Kirkpatrick, "IBM: from Big Blue Dinosaur to e-Business Animal," pp. 116–127; and Kirkpatrick, "The Second Coming of Apple," Fortune, pp. 86–104.

66 Peter Drucker, "The Coming of the New Organization," p. 43.

67 Stratford Sherman, "A Master Class in Radical Change," *Fortune*, 13 December 1993, p. 82. See also McCune, pp. 16–22.

68 Michael Dorf, Knitting Music (New York: Knitting Factory Works, 1992) p. 4.

CHAPTER 1 APPENDIX

1 Alvin Toffler, *Future Shock* (New York: Bantam Books, 1971), p. 43.

2 Adam Smith, *An Inquiry into the Nature and Causes of Wealth of Nations*, ed., Edward Cannan, 4th ed. (London: Methuen, 1925). Published originally in 1776.

3 Alfred Chandler, *Strategy and Structure* (Cambridge, MA: MIT Press); see also Daniel Wren, *The Evolution of Management Thought* (New York: John Wiley, 1979).

4 D. S. Pugh, Organization Theory (Baltimore: Penguin, 1971), pp. 126–127.

5 Claude George, Jr., *The History of Management Thought* (Upper Saddle River, NJ: Prentice-Hall, 1972), pp. 99--101.

6 Richard Hopeman, Production (Columbus, OH: Charles Merrill, 1965), pp. 478–485.

7 Henri Fayol, *General and Industrial Management*, translated by Constance Storrs (London: Sir Isaac Pitman, 1949), pp. 42–43.

8 Based on Richard Hall, "Intra-Organizational Structural Variation: Application of the Bureaucratic Model," *Administrative Science Quarterly*, December 1962, pp. 295–308.

9 William Scott, Organization Theory (Homewood, IL: Richard D. Irwin, 1967).

10 F. L. Roethlisberger and William Dickson, *Management and Worker* (Boston: Harvard University Graduate School of Business, 1947), p. 21.

11 Chandler, *Strategy and Structure*, pp. 19–51.

12 Warren G. Bennis, "Organizational Development and the Fate of Bureaucracy." Address at the Division of Industrial and Business Psychology, American Psychological Association, 5 September 1964. Reprinted in L. L. Cummings and W. E. Scott, Jr., *Organizational Behavior and Human Performance* (Homewood, IL: Richard D. Irwin and Dorsey, 1969), p. 436.

13 Douglas McGregor, "The Human Side of Enterprise," Edward Deci, B. Von Haller Gilmer, and Harry Kairn, *Readings in Industrial and Organizational Psychology* (New York: McGraw-Hill, 1972), p. 123.

14 R. Likert, *New Patterns of Management* (New York: McGraw-Hill, 1961), p. 6.

15 Ibid., p. 103.

16 Chris Argyris, *Integrating the Individual and the Organization* (New York: John Wiley, 1964).

17 Likert, New Patterns of Management, p. 91.

18 Ibid., p. 100.

19 Ibid.

20 Ibid.

21 Chester Barnard, *The Functions of the Executive* (Cambridge: Harvard University Press, 1968), p. 84.

22 Ibid., p. 167.

23 Ibid., p. 143.

24 Herbert A. Simon, *Administrative Behavior* (New York: Free Press, 1976), p. 11.

25 C. West Churchman, Russell Ackoff, and E. Leonard Arnoff, *Introduction to Operations Research* (New York: John Wiley, 1957), p. 18.

26 Daniel Wren, *The Evolution of Management Thought* (New York: John Wiley, 1979), p. 512.

27 C. West Churchman, *The Systems Approach* (New York: Delta, 1968).

28 Joan Woodward, *Industrial Organizations: Theory and Practice* (London: Oxford University Press, 1965), pp. 64–65.

CHAPTER 2

1 Jeremey Kahn, "Wal-Mart Goes Shopping in Europe," *Fortune*, 7 June 1999, pp. 105–12.

2 Wiliam Echikson, "Michael the NBA, and the Slam-Dunking of Paris," *Business Week*, 3 November 1997, p. 82.

3 Neel Chowdhury, "Dell Cracks China," *Fortune*, 21 June 1999, pp. 120–24.

4 Ted Rakstis, "Going Global," *Kiwanis Magazine*, October 1981, pp. 39–43.

5 Thomas Clasen, "An Exporter's Guide to Selecting Foreign Sales Agents and Distributors," *The Journal of European Business*, November–December 1991, pp. 28–32.

6 Albert G. Holzinger, "Paving the Way for Small Exporters," *Nation's Business*, June 1992, pp. 42–43.

7 Charles Hill, *International Business* (Bun Ridge, IL: Irwin, 1994), p. 402.

8 Art Garcia, "It's in the Mail," *World Trade*, April 1992, pp. 56–62.

9 See, for example, John Daniels and Lee Radebaugh, *International Business* (Reading, MA: Addison-Wesley, 1994), p. 544.

10 Michael Czinkota, Pietra Rivoli, and Ilka Ronkinen, *International Business* (Fort Worth: The Dryden Press, 1992), p. 278.

11 Hill, p. 411.

12 Daniels and Radebaugh, p. G-19.

13 Kenichi Ohmae, "The Global Logic of Strategic Alliances," *Harvard Business Review*, March–April 1989, pp. 143–154.

14 Katherine Rudie Harrigan, "Joint Ventures and Global Strategies," *Columbia Journal of World Business*, (Summer 1984, pp. 7–16; Czinkota et al., *International Business*, p. 320.

15 Jube Shiver Jr., "AOL Jumps into Race to Deliver Net on TV," *Los Angeles Times*, 12 May 1999, p. C1.

16 "Ace Signs Second Joint Venture Agreement," *Do-It-Yourself Retailing*, April 1999, p. 95.

17 Barry James, "Air France and Delta Pave the Way for the Third Alliance," *International Herald Tribune*, 23 June 1999, p. 1.

18 Ohmae, p. 143.

19 Wilfred Vanhonacker, "Entering China: An Unconventional Approach," *Harvard Business Review*, March–April 1997, pp. 130–140.

20 Robert Neff, "Guess Who's Selling Barbies in Japan Now?" *Business Week*, December 1991, pp. 72, 74, 76; See also Jeffrey Garten, "Troubles Ahead in Emerging Markets," *Harvard Business Review*, May–June 1997, pp. 38–50 and Yagang Pan and Peter Chi, "Financial Performance and Survival of Multinational Corporations in China," *Strategic Management Journal*, April 1999, p. 359.

21 Hill, p. 4; Dawn Anfuso, "Colgate's Global HR United Under One Strategy," *Personnel Journal*, October 1995, p. 44ff; See also Marlene Piturro, "What Are You Doing About the New Global Realities?" *Management Review*, March 1999, pp. 16–22; and Maureen Minehan, "Changing Conditions in Emerging Markets," *HR Magazine*, January 1998, p. 160.

22 For a discussion see, for example, Arvind Phatak, *International Dimensions of Management* (Boston: PWS-Kent, 1989), p. 2.

23 Paul Doremus, William Keller, Louis Pauly, and Simon Reich, *The Myth of the Global Corporation* (Princeton: Princeton University Press, 1998).

24 Theodore Levitt, "The Globalization of Markets," *Harvard Business Review*, May–June 1983, pp. 92–102; For an example see Thomas Stewart, "See Jack. See Jack Run Europe," *Fortune*, 27 September 1999, pp. 124–127.

25 Note that there are few, if any, "pure" market economies or command economies anymore. For example, much of the French banking system is still under government control. And it was only several years ago that the government of England privatized (sold to private investors) British Airways.

26 Jeffrey Garten, "Troubles Ahead in Emerging Markets," *Harvard Business Review*, May–June 1997, pp. 38–48.

27 "Countries with Highest Gross Domestic Product and Per-Capita GDP," *The World Almanac and Book of Facts, 1998* (Mahwah, NJ: K-III Reference Corporation, 1997), p. 112.

28 David Kemme, "The World Economic Outlook for 1999," *Business Perspectives*, January 1999, pp. 6–9.

29 For a discussion see, for example, Czinkota et al., Chapter 2, James Flanigan, "Asian Crisis Could Bring New Threat: Protectionism," *Los Angeles Times*, 3 February 1999, p. N1.

30 Ibid., p. 116.

31 Daniels and Radebaugh, p. 409.

32 Molly O'Meara, "Riding the Dragon," *World Watch*, March/April 1997, pp. 8–18.

33 See, for example, Susan Lee, "Are We Building New Berlin Walls?" *Forbes*, January 1991, pp. 86–89; Tom Reilly, "The Harmonization of Standards in the European Union and the Impact on U.S. Business," *Business Horizons*, March–April 1995.

34 Bryan Moskal, "The World Trade Topography: How Level Is It?" *Industry Week*, 18, May 1992, pp. 24–36.

35 Daniels and Radebaugh, p. 138.

36 Czinkota et al., p. 640.

37 Benjamin Weiner, "What Executives Should Know About Political Risk," *Management Review*, January 1992, pp. 19–22; see also Maria Kielnas, "Political Risks Emerged as Global Landscape Changes: Managing Risks of Doing Business Internationally Requires Knowledge of Culture and Infrastructure," *Business Insurance*, 14 June 1999, p. G2.

38 Laura Pincus and James Belohlav, "Legal Issues in Multinational Business Strategy: To Play the Game, You Have to Know the Rules," *Academy of Management Executive*, (November 1996), pp. 52–61.

39 Ibid., pp. 53–54.

40 Ibid., p. 53.

41 Philip Harris and Robert Moran, *Managing Cultural Differences*, pp. 227–228. See also Jack N. Behrman, "Cross-Cultural Impacts on International Competitiveness," *Business and the Contemporary World*, 1995, pp. 93–113 and Lorna Wrighte, "Building Cultural Competence," *Canadian Business Review*, Spring 1996, p. 29ff.

42 Catherine Tinsley, "Models of Conflict Resolution in Japanese, German, and American Cultures," *Journal of Applied Psychology*, Month 1998, pp. 316–322.

43 Ibid., p. 321.

44 Geert Hofstede, "Cultural Dimensions in People Management," in Vladimir Pucik, Noel Tichy, and Carole Barnett, eds., *Globalizing Management*, (New York: John Wiley & Sons, Inc., 1992), 139–158.

45 Ibid., p. 143.

46 Ibid.

47 Ibid., p. 147.

48 "Hard Labor," *Economist*, 27 February 1999, p. 62.

49 "Sweatshop Wars," *Economist*, 27 February 1999, p. 62.

50 Czinkota et al., 205.

51 United Nations, Draft International Code of Conduct on the Transfer of Technology (New York: United Nations, 1981), p. 3; quoted in Michael Czinkota et al., *International Business*, p. 313.

52 Czinkota et al., p. 314.

53 Jeremy Main, "How to Go Global—and Why," *Fortune*, 28 August 1989, p. 70, See also Kasra Ferdows, "Making the Most of Foreign Markets," *Harvard Business Review*, March–April 1997, pp. 73–88 and Liane Ladarba, "A.M. Report: Olivetti Reshapes Global Landscape," *Telephony*, 31 May 1999.

54 *www.wal-mart.com/newsroom/firstquarter99.html.*

55 Hill, pp. 5–6.

56 Ibid., p. 6; and Michael McGrath and Richard Hoole, "Manufacturing's New Economies of Scale," *Harvard Business Review*, May–June 1992, p. 94; See also Thomas Kochan and Russell Lansbury, "Lean Production and Changing Employment Relations in the International Auto Industry," *Economic and Industrial Democracy*, November 1997, pp. 597–620 and John Sheridan, "Bridging the Enterprise," *Industry Week*, 5 April 1999, p. 17.

57 Based on McGrath and Hoole, pp. 94–102.

58 Kasra Ferdows, "Making the Most of Foreign Factories," *Harvard Business Review*, March–April 1997, pp. 80–81.

59 Kenneth Laudon and Jane Laudon, *Management Information Systems* (Upper Saddle River, NJ: Prentice Hall 1998), p. 348.

60 Ibid., p. 348.

61 Based on Brian O'Reilly, "Your New Global Workforce," *Fortune*, December 1992, pp. 52–66, See also Charlene Solomon, "Don't Get Burned by Hot New Markets," *Global Workforce*, a supplement to *Workforce*, January 1998, p. 12.

62 Ibid., p. 64. See also Shirley R. Fishman, "Developing a Global Workforce," *Canadian Business Review*, Spring 1996, pp. 18–21.

63 See Mariah E. DeForest, "Thinking of a Plant in Mexico?" *Academy of Management Executive*, February 1994, pp. 33–40.

64 Ibid., p. 34.

65 Ibid., p. 37.

66 Ibid., p. 38. See also Randall S. Schuler, Susan E. Jackson, Ellen Jackofsky, and John W. Slocum, "Managing Human Resources in Mexico: A Cultural Understanding," *Business Horizons*, May 1996, pp. 55–61.

67 Robert Reich, "Who Is Them?" *Harvard Business Review*, March–April 1991, pp. 77–88.

68 Philip Harris and Robert Moran, *Managing Cultural Differences* (Houston: Gulf Publishing Company, 1979), p. 1.

69 "On a Wing and a Hotel Room," *Economist*, 9 January 1999, p. 64.

70 Ibid., p. 64.

71 Gail Dutton, "Building a Global Brain," *Management Review*, May 1999, pp. 34–38.

72 Ibid., p. 35.

73 Ibid., p. 36.

74 Ibid., p. 37.

75 Ibid., p. 35.

76 Ibid., p. 35.

77 Ibid., p. 35.

78 Gretchen Spreitzer, Morgan McCall, Jr., and Joan Mahoney, "Early Identification of International Executive Potential," *Journal of Applied Psychology*, February 1997, pp. 6–29.

79 Phatak, pp. 46–49.

80 John Rossant, "After the Scandals," *Business Week*, 22 November 1993, pp. 56–57; William Duggan, "Global Dangers: Political Risks," *Risk Management*, September 1999, p. 13.

81 Anant Negandhi, *International Management* (Newton, MA: Allyn & Bacon, Inc., 1987), 61. See also Keith W. Glaister and Peter J. Buckley, "Strategic Motives for International Alliance Formation," *Journal of Management Studies*, May 1996, pp. 301–322.

82 Richard D. Robinson, *Internationalization of Business: An Introduction* (Hillsdale, IL: The Dryden Press, 1984), pp. 227–28; See also "Organizing for Europe," *International Journal of Retail and Distribution Management*, Winter 1993, pp. 15–16.

83 PR Newswire, 27 March 1997, "Reynolds Metal Announces Organizational and Management Changes."

84 See, for example, S. M. Davis, "Managing and Organizing Multinational Corporations," in C. A. Bartlett and S. Ghoshal, eds. *Transnational Management* (Homewood, IL: Richard D. Irwin, 1992). See also Oliver Gassnann and Maximilian von Zedtwitz, "New Concepts and Trends in International are & the Organization," *Research Policy*, March 1999, pp. 231–232.

85 Paul Blocklyn, "Developing the International Executive," *Personnel*, March 1989, p. 44. Overseas assignments can also be risky for the managers who are sent abroad, with one recent study concluding that these managers' employers don't reward their international experience. See Linda Grant, "That Overseas Job Could Derail Your Career," *Fortune*, 14 April 1997, p. 167; see also Martha I. Finney, "Global Success Rides on Keeping Top Talent," *HRMagazine*, April 1996, pp. 69–72; and Reyer A. Swaak, "Expatriate Failures: Too Many, Too Much Cost, Too Little Planning," *Compensation and Benefits Review*, November 1995, pp. 47–55.

86 Jackqueline Heidelberg, "When Sexual Harassment Is a Foreign Affair," *Personnel Journal*, April 1996.

87 Madelyn Callahan, "Preparing the New Global Manager," *Training and Development Journal*, March 1989, p. 30. See also Charlene Marmer Solomon, "Big Mac's McGlobal HR Secrets," *Personnel Journal*, April 1996, p. 46ff; and Lorna Wrighte, "Building Cultural Competence," *Canadian Business Review*,Spring 1996, p. 29ff.

88 Joseph Fucini and Suzy Fucini, *Working for the Japanese* (New York: The Free Press, 1990), pp. 122–123. See also Richard Kustin and Robert Jones, "The Influence of Corporate Headquarters on Leadership Styles in Japanese and US Subsidiary Companies," *Leadership Organizational Development Journal*, 1995, pp. 11–15.

89 Ken Siegmann, "Workforce," *Profit*, November 1999, p. 47.

CHAPTER 3

1 "A Global War Against Bribery," *Economist*, 16 January 1999, pp. 22–24.

2 Manuel Velasquez, *Business Ethics: Concepts and Cases* (Upper Saddle River, NJ: Prentice-Hall, 1992), p. 9; Kate Walter, "Ethics Hot Lines Tap into More Than Wrongdoing," *HRMagazine*, September 1995, pp. 79–85. See also Skip Kaltenheuser, "Bribery Is Being Outlawed Virtually Worldwide," *Business Ethics*, May 1998, p. 11.

3 The following, except as noted, is based on Manuel Velasquez, *Business Ethics*, pp. 9–12.

4 Ibid., p. 9.

5 This is based on ibid., pp. 12–14.

6 Ibid., p. 12. For further discussion see Kurt Baier, *Moral Points of View*, abbr. ed. (New York: Random House, 1965), p. 88. See also Milton Bordwin, "The 3 R's of Ethics," *Management Review*, June 1998, pp. 59–61.

7 For further discussion of ethics and morality see Tom Beauchamp and Norman Bowie, *Ethical Theory and Business* (Upper Saddle River, NJ: Prentice Hall, 1993), pp. 1–19.

8 See Michael McCarthy, "James Bond Hits the Supermarket: Stores Snoop on Shoppers' Habits to Boost Sales," *Wall Street Journal*, 25 August 1993, p. B12. See also Rene Bos, "Business Ethics and Human Ethics," *Organization Studies*, vol. 18, no. 6, 1997, pp. 997–1014.

9 Sara Morris et al., "A Test of Environmental, Situational, and Personal Influences on the Ethical Intentions of CEOs," *Business and Society*, August 1995, pp. 119–147.

10 Justin Longnecker, Joseph McKinney, and Carlos Moore, "The Generation Gap in Business Ethics," *Business Horizons*, September–October 1989, pp. 9–14.

11 Ibid., 10. For a discussion of the development of a scale for measuring individual beliefs about organizational ethics, see Kristina Froelich and Janet Kottke, "Measuring Individual Beliefs About Organizational Ethics," *Educational and Psychological Measurement*, vol. 51, 1991, pp. 377–383.

12 Thomas Tyson, "Does Believing that Everyone Else is Less Ethical Have an Impact on Work Behavior?" *Journal of Business Ethics*, vol. 11, 1992, pp. 707–717. See also Basil Orsini and Diane McDougall, "Fraud Busting Ethics," *CMA 1973*, June 1999, pp. 18–21.

13 Lynn Sharp Paine, "Managing for Organizational Integrity," *Harvard Business Review*, March–April 1994, p. 106. See also Susan Gaines, "Continuing to Make Sears a Compelling Place to Work, Shop, and Invest," *Business Ethics*, November 1997, p. 10.

14 Ibid., pp. 107–117.

15 Ibid., p. 108.

16 Ibid., p. 108. For a recent analysis of the financial consequences of illegal corporate activities, see Melissa Baucus and David Baucus, "Paying the Piper: An Empirical Examination of Longer-term Financial Consequences of Illegal Corporate Behavior," *Academy of Management Journal*, February 1997, pp. 129–51; Dale Kurschner, "Five Ways Ethical Business Creates Fatter Profits," *Business Ethics*, March 1996, p. 20ff. James Hunter, "Good Ethics Means Good Business," *Canadian Business Review*, Spring 1996, pp. 14–17.

17 This is from Saul Gellerman, "Why Good Managers Make Bad Ethical Choices," *Harvard Business Review*, July–August 1986, p. 86. Some experts argue that a mature organization sometimes needs a crisis to shake itself out of its ethical lethargy. See, for example, Christopher Boult, Stephen Drew, Alan Pearson, Guy Saint-Pierre, James C. Rush, and Brenda Zimmerman, "Crisis and Renewal: Ethics Anarchy in Mature Organizations," *Business Quarterly*, Spring 1996, pp. 24–32.

18 Gellerman, ibid.

19 Ibid.

20 Baucus and Baucus, p. 149.

21 For a discussion, see Steen Brenner and Earl Molander, "Is the Ethics of Business Changing?" *Harvard Business Review*, January–February 1977, pp. 57–71; Robert Jackyll, "Moral Mazes: Bureaucracy and Managerial Work," *Harvard Business Review*, September–October 1983, pp. 118–30. See also Ishmael P. Akaah, "The Influence of Organizational Rank and Role of Marketing Professionals' Ethical Judgments," *Journal of Business Ethics*, June 1996, pp. 605–614.

22 From Guy Brumback, "Managing Above the Bottom Line of Ethics," *Supervisory Management*, December 1993, p. 12.

23 Deon Nel, Leyland Pitt, and Richard Watson, "Business Ethics: Defining the Twilight Zone," *Journal of Business Ethics*, vol. 8, 1989, p. 781; Brenner and Molander, "Is the Ethics of Business Changing?" See also Daniel Glasner, "Past Mistakes Present Future Challenges," *Workforce*, May 1998, p.117.

24 Robert Sweeney and Howard Siers, "Survey: Ethics in Corporate America," *Management Accounting*, June 1990, pp. 34–40.

25 Ibid., p. 34.

26 Ibid., p. 35.

27 Rochelle Kelin, "Ethnic versus Organizational Cultures: The Bureaucratic Alternatives," *International Journal of Public Administration*, March 1996, pp. 323–344.

28 Paine, "Managing for Organizational Integrity," p. 110.

29 Discussed in Samuel Greengard, "Cheating and Stealing," *Workforce*, October 1997, pp. 45–53.

30 *Corporate Ethics: A Prime Business Asset* (New York: The Business Round Table, February 1988), p. 81.

31 Ibid., p. 78.

32 Ibid., p. 79.

33 Ibid.

34 For a discussion see, for example, Alan Rowe et al., *Strategic Management: A Methodological Approach* (Reading, MA: Addison-Wesley Publishing Co., 1994), p. 101.

35 Ibid., 6.

36 Kate Walter, "Ethics Hot Lines Tap into More Than Wrongdoing," *HRMagazine*, September 1995, pp. 79–85.

37 Rowe et al., *Strategic Management*, p. 7; see also John J. Quinn, "The Role of 'Good Conversation' in Strategic Control," *Journal of Management Studies*, May 1996, pp. 381–395.

38 Ibid., p. 9.

39 Sandra Gray, "Audit Your Ethics," *Association Management*, September 1996, p. 188.

40 James G. Hunt, *Leadership* (Newbury Park, CA: Sage Publications, 1991), pp. 220–224. One somewhat tongue-in-cheek writer describes culture as a sort of "organizational DNA," since "it's the stuff, mostly intangible, that determines the basic character of a business." See James Moore, "How Companies Have Sex," *Fast Company*, October–November 1997, pp. 66–68.

41 Hunt, p. 221. For a recent discussion of types of cultures see, for example, "A Quadrant of Corporate Cultures," *Management Decision*, September 1996, pp. 37–40.

42 *Blueprints for Service Quality: The Federal Express Approach* (New York: AMA Membership Publications, 1991), p. 13.

43 Richard Osborne, "Core Value Statements: The Corporate Compass," *Business Horizons*, September–October 1991, p. 29.

44 Ibid., p. 29.

45 Gary Dessler, *Winning Commitment: How to Build and Keep a Competitive Work Force* (New York: McGraw-Hill, 1993), p. 85.

46 Ibid., p. 85.

47 Daniel Denison, *Corporate Culture and Organizational Effectiveness* (New York: John Wiley and Sons, 1990), p. 12. For a recent discussion see also Daniel Denison, "What Is the Difference between Organizational Culture and Organizational Climate? A Native's Point of View on a Decade of Paradigm Wars," *Academy of Management Review*, July 1996, pp. 619–654.

48 Example is based on Daniel Denison, *Corporate Culture and Organizational Effectiveness*, pp. 147–174.

49 Ibid., p. 148.

50 Ibid.

51 Ibid., p. 151.

52 Ibid.

53 Ibid.

54 Ibid., p. 154.

55 Ibid., p. 155.

56 "Sweatshop Wars," *Economist*, 27 February 1999, pp. 62–63.

57 Ben & Jerry's Homemade, Inc., *Employee Handbook*.

58 Ben & Jerry's *Public Relations Release*, 5 October 1990.

59 Milton Friedman, *Capitalism and Freedom* (Chicago: University of Chicago Press, 1962), p. 133. See also Charles Handy, "A Better Capitalism," *Across the Board*, April 1998, pp. 16–22. See also Robert Reich, "The New Meaning of Corporate Social Responsibility," *California Management Review*, Winter 1998, pp. 8–17. Reich also believes that because of pressure from investors, nonowner stakeholders are being neglected, and that the government should step in to protect them.

60 Tom Beauchamp and Norman Bowie, *Ethical Theory and Business*, pp. 49–52. See also Marjorie Kelly, "Do Stockholders "Own" Corporations?" *Business Ethics*, June 1999, pp. 4–5.

61 Ibid., p. 79.

62 Ibid., p. 60.

63 Ibid., p. 54.

64 William Evan and R. Edward Freeman, "A Stakeholder Theory of the Modern Corporation: Kantian Capitalism," *Ethical Theory of Business*, p. 82. See also Kenneth Goodpaster, "Business Ethics and Stakeholder Analysis," *Business Ethics Quarterly*, January 1991, pp. 53–73. See also Courtney Pratt, "Business Accountability: To Whom?" *CMA*, January 1998, p. 8.

65 John Simon, Charles Powers, and John Gunnermann, "The Responsibilities of Corporations and Their Owners," *The Ethical Investor: Universities and Corporate Responsibility* (New Haven, CT: Yale University Press, 1972); reprinted in Beauchamp and Bowie, pp. 60–65. See also Roger Kaufman et al., "The Changing Corporate Mind: Organizations, Vision, Missions, Purposes, and Indicators on the Move Toward Societal Payoffs," *Performance Improvement Quarterly*, vol. 11, no. 3, 1998, pp. 32–44.

66 Jo-Ann Johnston, "Social Auditors: The New Breed of Expert," *Business Ethics*, March 1996, p. 27.

67 Karen Paul and Steven Ludenberg, "Applications of Corporate Social Monitoring Systems: Types, Dimensions and Goals," *Journal of Business Ethics*, vol. 11, 1992, pp. 1–10.

68 Karen Paul, "Corporate Social Monitoring in South Africa: A Decade of Achievement, An Uncertain Future," *Journal of Business Ethics*, vol. 8, 1989, p. 464. See also Bernadette Ruf et al. "The Development of a Systematic, Aggregate Measure of Corporate Social Performance," *Journal of Management*, vol. 24, no. 1, 1998, pp. 119–133.

69 Ibid. See also John S. North, "Living Under a Social Code of Ethics: Eli Lilly in South Africa Operating Under the Sullivan Principles," *Business and the Contemporary World*, vol. 8, no. 1, 1996, pp. 168–80; and S. Prakash Sethi, "Working With International Codes of Conduct: Experience of U.S. Companies Operating in South Africa Under the Sullivan Principles," *Business and the Contemporary World*, vol. 8, no. 1, 1996, pp. 129–50. Standards similar to the international quality standards that have been used for some time have been put in place for social accountability areas such as child labor and health and safety. See Ruth Thaler-Carter, "Social Accountability 8000: A Social Guide for Companies or Another Layer of Bureaucracy?" *HRMagazine*, June 1999, pp. 106–108.

70 Janet Near, "Whistle-Blowing: Encourage It!" *Business Horizons*, January-February, 1989, p. 5. See also Robert J. Paul and James B. Townsend, "Don't Kill the Messenger! Whistle-Blowing in America: A Review with Recommendations," *Employee Responsibilities and Rights*, June 1996, pp. 149–61. Nick Perry, "Indecent Exposures: Theorizing Whistle Blowing," *Organization Studies*, vol. 19, no. 2, 1998, pp. 235–257.

71 Near, p. 5. See also Fraser Younson, "Spilling the Beans," *People Management*, 11 June 1998, pp. 25–26.

72 Ibid., p. 6. See also David Lewis, "Whistle Blowing at Work: Ingredients for an Effective Procedure," *Human Resource Management Journal*, vol. 7, no. 4, 1997, pp. 5–11.

73 See, for example, Taylor Cox Jr., *Cultural Diversity in Organizations* (San Francisco, CA: Berrett-Koehler Publishers, Inc., 1993), p. 3. See also Geert Hofstede, "Identifying Organizational Subcultures and the Rebel Approach," *Journal of Management Studies*, January 1998, pp.1–12.

74 Ibid. See also T. Horowitz and C. Forman, "Clashing Cultures," *Wall Street Journal*, 14 August 1990, p. A1. See also Emannuel Ogbonna and Lloyd Harris, "Organizational Culture: It's Not What You Think," *Journal of General Management*, Spring 1998, pp. 35–48. See also Gillian Flynn, "White Males See Diversity's Other Side," *Workforce*, February 1999, pp. 52–54.

75 Cox, pp. 3–4.

76 Francis Milliken and Luis Martins, "Searching for Common Threads: Understanding the Multiple Effects of Diversity in Organizational Groups," *Academy of Management Review*, vol. 21, no. 2, 1996, p. 415; see also Patricia Nemetz and Sandra Christensen, "The Challenge of Cultural Diversity: Harnessing a Diversity of Views to Understand Multiculturalism," *Academy of Management Review*, July 21, 1996, pp. 434–462.

77 Cox, p. 11.

78 Michael Carrell, Daniel Jennings, and Christina Heavrin, *Fundamentals of Organizational Behavior* (Upper Saddle River, NJ: Prentice-Hall, 1997), pp. 282–83.

79 George Kronenberger, "Out of the Closet," *Personnel Journal*, June 1991, pp. 40–44.

80 Cox, p. 88.

81 Cox, p. 89.

82 J. H. Greenhaus and S. Parasuraman, "Job Performance Attributions and Career Advancement Prospects: An Examination of Gender and Race Affects," *Organizational Behavior and Human Decision Processes*, 55, July 1993, pp. 273–98.

83 Adapted from Cox, p. 64.

84 Ibid., pp. 179–180.

85 Madeleine Heilmann and Lewis Saruwatari, "When Beauty is Beastly: The Effects of Appearance and Sex on Evaluation of Job Applicants for Managerial and Nonmanagerial Jobs," *Organizational Behavior and Human Performance*, June 1979, pp. 360–72; see also Tracy McDonald and Milton Hakel, "Effects of Applicant Race, Sex, Suitability, and Answers on Interviewer's Questioning Strategy and Ratings," *Personnel Psychology*, Summer 1985, pp. 321–334.

86 Patricia Digh, "Coming to Terms with Diversity," *HRMagazine*, November 1998, p. 119.

87 Cox, p. 236.

88 Digh, p. 119.

89 K. Kram, *Mentoring at Work* (Glenview, IL: Scott Foresman, 1985); Cox, p. 198. See also Ian Cunningham and Linda Honold, "Everyone Can Be a Coach," *HRMagazine*, June 1998, pp. 63–66.

90 See, for example, G. F. Dreher and R. A. Ash, "A Comparative Study of Mentoring among Men and Women in Managerial, Professional, and Technical Positions," *Journal of Applied Psychology*, vol. 75, no. 5, 1990, pp. 1–8.

91 "A Report Card on Diversity," *Harvard Business Review*, January–February 1999, p. 43.

92 "The Impact of Diversity on Education," *Harvard Business Review*, January–February 1999, p. 143.

93 Benjamin Hoff, *The Tao of Pooh* (New York: Dutton, 1992), pp. 109–110.

94 Ibid.

CHAPTER 4

1 Nina Munk, "Title Fight," *Fortune*, 21 June 1999, pp. 84–86.

2 Max Bazerman, *Judgment in Managerial Decision Making* (New York: John Wiley & Sons, Inc., 1994), p. 3.

3 Chris Isadore, "The Fed Ex Making a Heavier Push into Freight; Terrier Coming Out with a More Aggressive Pricing This Week," *Journal of Commerce and Commercial*, 16 March 1999, pp. 7–9.

4 Edward Wyatt, "The Big Board Will Delay Its Decisions on Late Hours," *New York Times*, June 4, 1999, p. C4.

5 See, for example, Herbert Simon, *The New Science of Management Decision* (Upper Saddle River, NJ: Prentice Hall, 1971), pp. 45–47.

6 Larry Long and Nancy Long, *Computers*, (Upper Saddle River, NJ: Prentice-Hall, 1996), pp. M-7.

7 Mairead Browne, *Organizational Decision Making and Information* (Norwood, NJ: Ablex Publishing Corporation, 1993), p. 6.

8 Bazerman, p. 5.

9 For a discussion see, for example, Bazerman, pp. 4–5.

10 Ibid., p. 4.

11 Heath Row, "Chumbo Rewrites the Software Code," *Fast Company*, September 1999, pp. 70–72.

12 Bazerman, p. 4.

13 James G. Miller, "Adjusting to Overloads of Information," in Joseph A. Litterer, *Organizations: Structure and Behavior* (New York: John Wiley, 1969), pp. 313–322. See also Jennifer Laabs, "Overload," *Workforce*, January 1999, pages 30–37.

14 Dewitt Dearborn and Herbert A. Simon, "Selective Perception: A Note on the Departmental Identification of Executives," *Sociometry*, vol. 21, 1958, pp. 140–144. For a recent study of this phenomenon, see Mary Waller, George Huber, and William Glick, "Functional Background as a Determinant of Executives' Selective Perception," *Academy of Management Journal*, August 1995, pp. 943–994. While not completely supporting the Dearborn findings, these researchers did also conclude that managers' functional backgrounds affected how they perceived organizational changes. See also Paul Gamble and Duncan Gibson, "Executive Values and Decision Making: The Relationship of Culture and Information Flows," *Journal of Management Studies*, March 1999, pp. 217–240.

15 See also Janice Beyer, et al, "The Selective Perception of Managers Revisited," *Academy of Management Journal*, June 1997, pp. 716–737.

16 Kenneth Laudon and Jane Price Laudon, *Management Information Systems* (Upper Saddle River, NJ: Prentice Hall, 1996), p. 125. See also Bob F. Holder, "Intuitive Decision Making," *CMA*, October 1995, p. 6.

17 Joan Johnson et al, "Vigilant and Hypervigilant Decision Making," *Journal of Applied Psychology*, vol. 82, no. 4, pp. 614–622.

18 Studies indicate that you can adjust your style and that decision styles are more preferences than set in stone. See Dorothy Leonard and Susan Straus, "Putting Your Company's Whole Brain to Work," *Harvard Business Review*, July–August 1997, pp. 111–121.

19 Bazerman, pp. 6–8.

20 John Hammond, Ralph Keeney, and Howard Raiffa, *Smart Choices* (Boston: Harvard Business School Press, 1999), p. 16.

21 Lester Lefton and Laura Valvatne, *Mastering Psychology* (Boston: Allyn and Bacon, 1992), pp. 248–249. See also Daphne Main and Joyce Lambert, "Improving Your Decision Making," *Business and Economic Review*, April 1998, pp. 9–12.

22 *Bureau of National Affairs Bulletin to Management*, 11 September 1997, p. 293.

23 See, for example, Bazerman, p. 5.

24 James March and Herbert Simon, *Organizations* (New York: John Wiley, 1958), pp. 140–41.

25 Cathy Olofson, "So Many Decisions, So Little Time," *Fast Company*, October 1999, p. 62.

26 Ibid., p. 62.

27 Ibid.

28 Bazerman, p. 93.

29 Quoted from ibid., pp. 105–106.

30 Ibid., p, 108.

31 Prased Padmanabhan, "Decision Specific Experience in Foreign Ownership and Establishment Strategies: Evidence from Japanese Firms," *Journal of International Studies*, Spring 1999, pp. 25–27.

32 Michael Hickins, "Xerox Shares Its Knowledge," *Management Review*, September 1999, p. 42.

33 Ibid., p. 42.

34 Ibid.

35 Quoted in Robert L. Heilbroner, "How to Make an Intelligent Decision," *Think*, December 1990, pp. 2–4.

36 Ibid. See also, Theodore Rubin, *Overcoming Indecisiveness: The Eight Stages of Effective Decision Making* (New York: Avon Books, 1985). See also John Hammond, Ralph Keeney, and Howard Raiffa, Smart Choices, Boston: *Harvard Business School Press*, 1999.

37 See, for example, William Taggart and Enzo Valenzi, "Assessing Rational and Intuitive Styles: A Human Information Processing Metaphor," *Journal of Management Studies*, March 1990, pp. 150–71; Christopher W. Allinson and John Hayes, "The Cognitive Style Index: A Measure of Intuition—Anaylsis for Organizational Research," *Journal of Management Studies*, January 1996, pp. 119–135.

38 This and the following guideline are from Heilbroner.

39 Helga Drummond, "Analysis and Intuition in Technological Choice: Lessons of Taurus," *International Journal of Technology Management*, April 1999, pp. 459–467.

40 James Bowditsch and Anthony Buono, *A Primer on Organizational Behavior* (New York: John Wiley & Sons Inc., 1994), pp. 171–72.

41 Michael Carrell, Daniel Jennings, and Christine Heavrin, *Fundamentals of Organizational Behavior* (Upper Saddle River, NJ: Prentice Hall, 1997), p. 346.

42 For a discussion of these and the following points see, for example, ibid.

43 Irving Janis, Groupthink: *Psychological Studies of Policy Decisions and Fiascos, 2d edition* (Boston: Houghton Mifflin, 1982. See also James Esser, "Alive and Well After 25 Years: A Review of Group Think Research," *Organizational Behavior & Human Decision Processes*, February–March 1998, pp. 116–142.

44 For an additional perspective on many of these see Randy Hirokawa and Marshall Scott Poole, *Communication and Group Decision Making* (Thousand Oaks, CA: Sage Publications, Inc., 1996), pp. 354–364. See also John O. Whitney and E. Kirby Warren, "Action Forums: How General Electric and Other Firms Have Learned to Make Better Decisions," *Columbia Journal of World Business*, Winter 1995, pp. 18–27; Steven G. Rogelberg and Steven M. Rumery, "Gender Diversity, Team Decision Quality, Time on Task, and Interpersonal Cohesion," *Small Group Research*, February 1996, pp. 79–90; Beatrice Shultz, Sandra M. Ketrow, and Daphne M. Urban, "Improving Decision Quality in the Small Group: The Role of the Reminder," *Small Group Research*, November 1995, pp. 521–541.

45 See, for example, Lefton and Valvatne, p. 249.

46 Greenberg and Baron, p. 393.

47 See Ron Zemke, "In Search of Good Ideas," *Training*, January 1993, pp. 46–52; R. Brent Gallupe, Lana Bastianutti, and William Cooper, "Unblocking Brainstorms," *Journal of Applied Psychology*, January 1991, pp. 137–142. Vincent Brown et al., "Modeling Cognitive Interactions During Group Brainstorming," *Small Group Research*, August 1998, pp. 495–526.

48 R. B. Gallupe, A. R. Dennis, W. H. Cooper, J. S. Valacich, J. S. Bastianutti, and J. F. Nunamaker, "Electronic Brainstorming and Group Size," *Academy of Management Journal*, vol. 35, 1992, pp. 350–69.

49 See, for example, Greenberg and Baron, pp. 399–400.

50 See S. G. Rogelberg, J. L. Barnes-Farrell, and C. A. Lowe, "The Stepladder Technique: An Alternative Group Structure Facilitating Effective Group Decision Making," *Journal of Applied Psychology*, vol. 57, 1992, pp. 730–737.

51 Norman R. F. Maier and E. P. McRay, "Increasing Innovation in Change Situations Through Leadership Skills," *Psychological Reports*, vol. 31, 1972, pp. 30–43. See also Jean Phillips, "Antecedents of Leader Utilization of Staff Input in Decision-Making Teams," *Organizational Behavior & Human Decision Processes*, March 1999, pp. 215–217.

CHAPTER 4 APPENDIX

1 The breakeven point is also sometimes defined more technically as the quantity of output or sales that will result in a zero level of earnings before interest or taxes. See for example J. William Petty et al., *Basic Financial Management* (Upper Saddle River, NJ: Prentice Hall 1993), p. 932.

2 Jay Heizer and Barry Render, *Production and Operations Management* (Upper Saddle River, NJ: Prentice Hall, 1996), pp. 240–250.

CHAPTER 5

1 Kenneth Laudon and Jane Laudon, *Management Information Systems* (Upper Saddle River, NJ: Prentice Hall), p. 598; "Wal-Mart to Triple the Size of Data Warehouse," TechWeb <*http://192.21.17.45/newsflash/nf617/0210—st6.htm*> 10 February 1999.

2 George L. Morrisey, *A Guide to Tactical Planning* (San Francisco: Jossey-Bass, 1996), p. 61.

3 Leonard Goodstein, Timothy Nolan, and Jay William Pfeiffer, *Applied Strategic Planning* (New York: McGraw-Hill, Inc., 1993), p. 3.

4 R. R. Donnelley and Sons Company Web site, 10 November 1999. <*wwwrrdonnelley.com*>

5 Ronald Henkoff, "How to Plan for 1995," *Fortune*, 31 December 1990, p. 74.

6 Peter Drucker, "Long Range Planning," *Management Science 5*, (1959), pp. 238–49. See also in Bristol Voss, "Cover to Cover Drucker," *Journal of Business Strategy*, May–June 1999, fall 1991, pp. 1–9.

7 Harvey Kahalas, "A Look at Planning and Its Components," *Managerial Planning*, January-February 1982, pp. 13–16; reprinted in Phillip DuBose, *Readings in Management* (Upper Saddle River, NJ: Prentice Hall, Inc., 1988), pp. 49–50. See also Mary M. Crossan, Henry W. Lane, Roderick E. White, and Leo Klus, "The Improvising Organization: Where Planning Meets Opportunity," *Organization Dynamics*, Spring 1996, pp. 20–35.

8 This is from George Morrisey, *A Guide to Long-Range Planning* (San Francisco: Jossey-Bass, 1996), pp. 72–73.

9 For a discussion, see Peter Wright, Mark Kroll, and John Parnell, *Strategic Management Concepts* (Upper Saddle River, NJ: Prentice-Hall, 1996), pp. 224–225.

10 Ibid.

11 Ibid., p. 225.

12 Goodstein, Nolan, and Pfeiffer, p. 170.

13 Leslie Brokow, "One-Page Company Game Plan," *Inc.*, June 1993, 111–113.

14 Peter F. Drucker, *The Effective Executive* (New York: Harper & Row, 1966); quoted in Keith Curtis, *From Management Goal Setting to Organizational Results* (Westport, CT: Quorum Books, 1994), p. 101.

15 Peter F. Drucker, *The Practice of Management* (New York: Harper & Row, 1954), pp. 65–83, 100.

16 Morrisey, p. 25.

17 Gary Latham and J. James Baldes, "The Practical Significance of Locke's Theory of Goal Setting," *Journal of Applied Psychology*, February 1975. See also Gary Latham, "The Effects of Proximal and Distal Goals on Performance on a Moderately Complex Task," *Journal of Organizational Behavior*, July 1999, pp. 421–430.

18 See, for example, Gary Latham and Gary Yukl, "A Review of Research on the Application of Goal Setting in Organizations," *Academy of Management Journal*, vol. 18, no. 4, 1964, p. 824; Gary Latham and Terrance A. Mitchell, "Importance of Participative Goal Setting and Anticipated Rewards on Goal Difficulty and Job Performance," *Journal of Applied Psychology*, vol. 63, 1978, pp. 163–171; and Sondra Hart, William Moncrief, and A. Parasuraman, "An Empirical Investigation of Sales People's Performance, Effort, and Selling Method During a Sales Contest," *Journal of the Academy of Marketing Science*, Winter 1989, pp. 29–39. See also, Theresa Libby, "The Influence of Voice and Explanation on Performance in a Participative Budget Setting," *Accounting, Organizations, and Society*, February 1999, p. 125.

19 The rest of this section, except as noted, is based on Gary Yukl, *Skills for Managers and Leaders* (Upper Saddle River, NJ: Prentice Hall, 1991), pp. 132–33. See also Gary Latham, "Cognitive and Motivational Effects of Participation: A Mediator Study," *Journal of Organizational Behavior*, January 1994, pp. 49–64.

20 Ibid., p. 133; and Miriam Erez, Daniel Gopher, and Nira Arzi, "Effects of Goal Difficulty, Self-Set Goals, and Monetary Rewards on Dual Task Performance," *Organizational Behavior & Human Decision Processes*, December 1990, pp. 247–269. See also Thomas Lee, "Explaining the Assigned Gold—Incentive Interaction: The Role of Self-Efficacy and Personal Goals," *Journal of Management*, July–August 1997, pp. 541–550.

21 See, for example, Stephan Schiffman and Michele Reisner, "New Sales Resolutions," *Sales & Marketing*, January 1992, pp. 15–16; and Steve Rosenstock, "Your Agent's Success," *Manager's Magazine*, September 1991, pp. 21–23.

22 Yukl, p. 133.

23 Gary Latham and Lise Saari, "The Effects of Holding Goal Difficulty Constant on Assigned and Participatively Set Goals," *Academy of Management Journal*, vol. 22, 1979, pp. 163–68; and Mark Tubbs and Steven Ekeberg, "The Role of Intentions in Work Motivation: Implications for Goal Setting Theory and Research," *Academy of Management Review*, January 1991, pp. 180–99. See also Cathy Durham, "Effects of Leader Role, Team Set Goal Difficulty, Efficacy, and Tactics on Keying Effectiveness," *Organizational Behavior & Human Decision Processes*, November 1997, pp. 203–232.

24 See Latham and Saari, pp. 163–168.

25 Gary Latham, Terence Mitchell, and Denise Dorsett, "Importance of Participative Goal Setting and Anticipated Rewards on Goal Difficulty and Job Performance," *Journal of Applied Psychology*, vol. 63, 1978, p. 170. See also John Wagner III, "Cognitive and Motivational Frameworks in U.S. Research on Participation: A Meta Analysis of Primary Effects," *Journal of Organizational Behavior*, January 1997, pp. 49–66.

26 See, for example, Anthony Mento, Norman Cartledge, and Edwin Locke, "Maryland Versus Michigan Versus Minnesota: Another Look at the Relationship of Expectancy and Goal Difficulty to Task Performance," *Organizational Behavior and Human Performance*, June 1980, pp. 419–440. See also Robert Renn, "Further Examination of the Measurement Properties of Leifer & McGannons 1986 Goal Acceptance and Gold Commitment Scales," *Journal of Occupational and Organizational Psychology*, March 1999, pp. 107–114.

27 William Werther, "Workshops Aid in Goal Setting," *Personnel Journal*, November 1989, pp. 32–38; See also Kenneth

Thompson, et al, "Stretch Targets: What Makes Them Effective?" *Academy of Management Review*, vol. 11, no. 3, 1997, pp. 48–60. See also, Theresa Libby, "The Influence of Voice and Explanation on Performance in a Participative Budget Setting," *Accounting, Organizations, and Society*, February 1999, p. 125.

28 Steven Carroll and Henry Tosi, *Management by Objectives* (New York: Macmillan, 1973).

29 Mark McConkie, "A Clarification of the Goal Setting and Appraisal Processes in MBO," *Academy of Management Review*, December 1991, pp. 29–40. See also Dawn Winters, "The Effects of Learning vs. Outcome Goals on a Simple vs. a Complex Task," *Group and Organization Management*, June 1996, pp. 236–251.

30 *Webster's Collegiate Dictionary of American English* (New York: Simon & Schuster, Inc., 1988).

31 Murray R. Spiegel, *Statistics* (New York: Schaum Publishing, 1961), p. 283.

32 See, for example, Moore, p. 5.

33 George Kress, *Practical Techniques of Business Forecasting* (Westport, CT: Quorum Books, 1985), p. 13. See also Diane Painter, "The Business Economist at Work: Mobil Corp.," *Business Economics*, April 1999, pp. 52–55.

34 Kenneth Laudon and Jane Laudon, *Management Information Systems* (Upper Saddle River, NJ: Prentice Hall), p. 598; and "Wal-Mart to Triple Size of a Warehouse," TechWeb <*http://192.215.17.45/newsflash/nf617/0210—st6.htm.*> 10 February 1999.

35 A. Chairncross, quoted in Thomas Milne, *Business Forecasting*, p. 42.

36 John Chambers, Santinder Mullick, and Donald Smith, "How to Choose the Right Forecasting Technique," *Harvard Business Review*, July–August 1971, pp. 45–74; and Moore, Handbook of Business Forecasting, pp. 265–290. See also John Mentzer, et al. "Benchmarking Sales Forecasting Management," *Business Horizons*, May–June 1999, pp. 48–57. This study of 20 leading U.S. firms found widespread dissatisfaction regarding their current sales forecasting techniques.

37 Philip Kotler, *Marketing Management* (Upper Saddle River, NJ: Prentice Hall, 1997), p. 113.

38 E. Jerome McCarthy and William Perreault, Jr., *Basic Marketing* (Homewood, IL: Irwin, 1990), pp. 131–132.

39 Stan Crock et al., "They Snoop to Conquer," *Business Week*, 28 October 1996, p. 172.

40 Douglas Frantz, "Journalists, or Detectives? Depends on Who Is Asking," *New York Times*, 28 July 1999, p. A1.

41 Arthur Little, *Global Strategic Planning* (New York: Business International Corporation, 1991), p. 3.

42 Melanie Warner, "Nightmare on Net Street," *Fortune*, 6 September 1999, pp. 285–286.

43 Ibid.

44 General Electric Corporation, *Annual Report*, 1998.

45 Andrew Campbell, "Tailored, Not Benchmarked: A Fresh Look at Corporate Planning," *Harvard Business Review*, March–April 1999, pp. 41–50.

46 Ibid., p. 42.

47 Ibid.

48 Ibid., p. 43.

49 Teri Tammers, "The One-Page Strategy Guide," *Inc.*, September 1992, pp. 135–138.

50 Eric Matson, "Now That We Have Your Complete Attention," *Fast Company*, February–March 1997.

CHAPTER 6

1 Peter Drucker, *Management: Tasks, Responsibilities, Practices* (New York: Harper & Row, 1974), p. 611. For an interesting point of view on strategic management, see Daniel W. Greening and Richard A. Johnson, "Do Managers and Strategies Matter? A Study in Crisis," *Journal of Management Studies*, January 1996, pp. 25–52.

2 Andrew Campbell and Marcus Alexander, "What's Wrong with Strategy?" *Harvard Business Review*, November–December 1997, p. 42.

3 Ibid., p. 48.

4 See for example, Allan J. Rowe, Richard O. Mason, Carl E. Dickel, Richard B. Mann, and Robert J. Mockler, *Strategic Management* (Reading, MA: Addison-Wesley Publishing Co., 1989), p. 2; James Higgins and Julian Vincze, *Strategic Management* (Fort Worth, TX: The Dryden Press, 1993), p. 5; Peter Wright, Mark Kroll, and John Parnell, *Strategic Management Concepts* (Upper Saddle River, NJ: Prentice Hall, 1996), pp. 1–15.

5 Arthur Thompson and A. J. Strickland, *Strategic Management* (Homewood, IL: Irwin, 1992), 4; Fred R. David, Concepts of Strategic Management (Upper Saddle River, NJ: Prentice Hall, 1997) 1–27. See also Bob Dust, "Making Mission Statements Meaningful," *Training & Development Journal*, June 1996, p. 53.

6 Higgins and Vincze, p. 5.

7 Warren Bennis and Bert Manus, *Leaders: The Strategies for Taking Charge* (New York: Harper & Row, 1985); quoted in Andrew Campbell and Sally Yeung, "Mission, Vision and Strategic Intent," *Long-Range Planning*, vol. 24, no. 4, p. 145. See also James M. Lucas, "Anatomy of a Vision Statement," *Management Review*, February 1998, pp. 22–26.

8 Melanie Warner, "The Young and the Loaded," *Fortune*, 27 September 1999, pp. 78–118.

9 Thompson and Strickland, p. 4. See also George Morrisey, *A Guide to Strategic Planning* (San Francisco: Jossey-Bass, 1996), p. 7.

10 Ibid., p. 8.

11 This is quoted from, and this section is based on, Allan J. Rowe, et al., pp. 114–116; and Stephen George and Arnold Weimerskirch, *Total Quality Management* (New York: Wiley, 1994), pp. 207–221. See also Jeffrey Sampler and James Short, "Strategy in Dynamic Information—Intensive Environments," *Journal of Management Studies*, July 1998, pp. 429–436.

12 This is based on Higgins and Vincze, pp. 200–204.

13 Rowe et al., pp. 246–247.

14 Thompson and Strickland, p. 169. See also Michael Lubatkin and Sayan Chatterjee, "Extending Portfolio Theory into the Domain of Corporate Diversification: Does It Apply?" *Academy of Management Journal*, February 1994, pp. 109–36.

15 Higgins and Vincze, p. 304.

16 John Byrne, Richard Brandt, and Otis Port, "The Virtual Corporation," *Business Week*, 8 February 1993, p. 99. See also Keith Hammonds, "This Virtual Agency Has Big Ideas," *Fast Company*, November 1999, pp. 70–74.

17 See also J. Carlos Jarillo, "On Strategic Networks," *Strategic Management Journal*," vol. 9, 1988, pp. 31–41; and William Davidow and Michael Malone, "The Virtual Corporation," California Business Review, 12 November 1992, 34–42. See also Hammonds, ibid.

18 Byrne et al., p. 99.

19 Ibid., p. 100.

20 Virtual corporations should not be confused with the Japanese Keiretsus strategy. Keiretsus are tightly knit groups of firms governed by a supra-board of directors concerned with establishing the long-term survivability of the Keiretsus organization. Interlocking boards of directors and shared ownership help distinguish Keiretsus from other forms of strategic alliances, including virtual corporations. See, for example,

Byrne et al., p. 101; Thompson and Strickland, p. 216; and Kenichi Ohmae, "The Global Logic of Strategic Alliances," *Harvard Business Review*, March–April 1989, pp. 143–154. See also Richard Oliver, "Killer Keiretsu," *Management Review*, September 1999, pp. 10–11.

21 Katherine Mieszkowski, "The E.-Lance Economy," November 1999, *Fast Company*, pp. 66–68.

22 Ibid., p. 68.

23 Unless otherwise noted, the following is based on Michael E. Porter, *Competitive Strategy: Techniques for Analyzing Industries and Competitions* (New York: The Free Press, 1980); and Michael E. Porter, *Competitive Advantage* (New York: The Free Press, 1985).

24 Porter, *Competitive Advantage*, p. 14.

25 Porter.

26 Porter, *Competitive Strategy*, p. 17.

27 Based on Tomima Edmark, "Power Play," *Entrepreneur*, March 1997, pp. 104–107.

28 Clayton Christensen, Making Strategy: Learning by Doing," *Harvard Business Review*, November–December 1997, pp. 141–156.

29 Gary Hamel, "Killer Strategies That Make Shareholders Rich," *Fortune*, 23 June 1997, p. 83.

30 Ibid., p. 83.

31 Ibid., p. 83.

32 Philip Evans and Thomas Wurster, "Strategy and the New Economics of Information," *Harvard Business Review*, September–October 1997, p. 72.

33 Ibid., p. 31.

34 Ibid., p. 69.

35 This is quoted from, and this section is based on, Rowe et al.

36 This is based on ibid, p. 116; and George and Weimerskirch, pp. 207–221.

37 Herman Kahn and Anthony Weiner, *The Year 2000: A Framework for Speculation on the Next Thirty-Three Years* (New York: Macmillan, 1967), p. 6; quoted in George A. Steiner, *Strategic Planning: What Every Manager Must Know* (New York: The Free Press, 1979), p. 237; and Nicholas Georgantzas and William Acar, *Scenario-Driven Planning* (Westport, CT: Quorum Books, 1995). See also Diann Painter, "The Business Economist at Work: Mobil Corporation," *Business Economics*, April 1999, pp. 52–55.

38 Adam Kahane, "Scenarios for Energy: Sustainable World vs. Global Mercantilism," *Long-Range Planning*, vol. 25, no. 4, 1992, pp. 38–46.

39 Kerry Tucker, "Scenario Planning: Visualizing a Broader World of Possibilities Can Help Associations Anticipate and Prepare for Change," *Association Management*, April 1999, pp. 70–77.

40 Ibid.

41 Ibid.

42 Gil Ringland, *Scenario Planning: Managing the Future* (New York: Wiley, 1998).

43 Michael E. Porter, "What Is Strategy?" *Harvard Business Review*, November–December 1996, pp. 61–80.

44 This example is based on ibid., pp. 70–75.

45 Ibid., p. 64.

46 For a discussion of core competencies see, for example, C. K. Prahalad and Gary Hamell, "The Core Competence of a Corporation," *Harvard Business Review*, May–June 1990, pp. 80–82. See also Gary Hamel, "Strategy As Revolution," *Harvard Business Review*, July–August 1996, pp. 69–82.

47 Hamel and Prahalad, "Strategy as Stretch and Leverage," *Harvard Business Review*, March–April 1993, pp. 75–84.

48 Ibid., p. 77.

49 Ibid, p. 78.

50 C. K. Prahalad and Gary Hamel, "The Core Competence of a Corporation," p. 82.

51 Ibid., p. 82.
52 Watson Wyatt, Work USA 1997, in BNA *Bulletin to Management*, 4 September 1997, p. 281.
53 Amar Bhide, "How Entrepreneurs Craft Strategies That Work," *Harvard Business Review*, March–April 1994, pp. 150–160. One study suggests that about two-thirds of entrepreneurs—at least owners of family businesses—do not have written strategic plans. See "Planning Lessons from Family Business Owners," *Infoseek/Reuters*, 26 March 1997.

CHAPTER 7

1 <www.starbucks.com/company/timeline.asp211hqv=1a>.
2 David Yoffie, "Building a Company on Internet Time: Lessons from Netscape," *California Management Review*, Spring 1999, p. 8.
3 Ibid., p. 8.
4 "How Can Big Companies Keep the Entrepreneurial Spirit Alive?" *Harvard Business Review*, November–December 1995, pp. 188–189. See also Mary Jo Hatch, "Exploring the Empty Spaces of Organizing: How Improvisational Jazz Helps Redescribe Organizational Structure," *Organization Studies*, vol. 20, no. 1, 1999, pp. 75–100.
5 Ernest Dale, *Organization* (New York: AMA, 1967), p. 109. See also Ed Clark, "The Adoption of the Multidivisional Form in Large Czech Enterprises: The Role of Economics, Institutional and Strategic Choice Factors," *Journal of Management Studies*, July 1999, pp. 535–537; and Tom Peters, "Destruction Is Cool . . . ," *Forbes*, 23 February 1998, p. 128.
6 Rekha Bach, "Heinz's Johnson to Divest Operations, Scrap Management of Firm by Region," *Wall Street Journal*, 8 December 1997, pp. B10, B12.
7 Jana Parker-Pope and Joann Lublin, "P&G Will Make Jager CEO Ahead of Schedule," *Wall Street Journal*, 10 September 1998, pp. B1, B8.
8 Kenneth Laudon and Jane Laudon, *Management Information Systems, 5th edition* (Upper Saddle River, NJ: Prentice Hall, 1998), p. 323.
9 See, for example, Lawton Burns and Douglas Wholey, "Adoption and Abandonment of Matrix Management Programs: Effects of Organizational Characteristics and Interorganizational Networks," *Academy of Management Journal*, February 1993, pp. 106–138.
10 *Organizing for International Competitiveness* (New York: Business International Corp., 1985) p. 117.
11 Burns and Wholey, p. 106.
12 For a discussion of this type of organization and its problems, see Stanley Davis and Paul Lawrence, *Matrix* (Reading, MA: Addison-Wesley, 1967); and Davis and Lawrence, "Problems of Matrix Organizations," *Harvard Business Review*, May–June 1978, pp. 131–142. See also Wilma Bernasco, "Balanced Matrix Structure and New Product Development Process at Texas Instruments Materials and Controls Division," *R&D Management*, April 1999, p. 121.
13 John Hunt, "Is Matrix Management a Recipe for Chaos?" *Financial Times*, January 1998, p. 14.
14 Wilma Bernasco, "Balanced Matrix Structure and New Product Development Process at Texas Instruments Materials and Controls Division," *R&D Management*, April 1999, p. 121.
15 Ibid.
16 Ibid.
17 Rob Walker, "Down on the Farm," *Fast Company*, February–March 1997, pp. 112–122.
18 Jay Galbraith, "Organizational Design: An Information Processing View," *Interfaces*, vol. 4, no. 3, 1974, pp. 28–36; and *Organizational Design* (Reading, MA: Addison-Wesley, 1977). See also Ranjay Gulati, "The Architecture of Cooperation:

Managing Coordination Costs and Appropriation Concerns in Strategic Alliances," *Administrative Science Quarterly*, December 1998, pp. 781–784.
19 Henry Mintzberg, *Structure in Fives: Designing Effective Organizations* (Upper Saddle River, NJ: Prentice-Hall, 1983), pp. 4–9. Cliff McGoon, "Cutting-Edge Companies Use Integrated Marketing Communication," *Communication World*, December 1998, pp. 15–20.
20 Mintzberg, p. 4.
21 Paul Lawrence and Jay Lorsch, *Organization and Environment* (Cambridge, MA: Harvard University Press, 1967). See also Frank Mueller and Romano Dyerson, "Expert Humans or Expert Organizations?" *Organization Studies*, vol. 20, no. 2, 1999, pp. 225–256. Some companies today practice concurrent engineering to improve production coordination, which basically means having all the departments—design, production, and marketing, for instance—work together to develop the product so that its production and marketing is more easily coordinated once the item goes into production. See Hassan Abdalla, "Concurrent Engineering for Global Manufacturing," *International Journal of Production Economics*, April 20, 1999, p. 251.
22 Ibid., p. 6.
23 Christopher A. Bartlett and Sumantra Ghoshal, "Matrix Management: Not a Structure, a Frame of Mind," *Harvard Business Review*, July–August 1990, pp. 138–145. See also K. Simon-Elorz, "Information Technology for Organizational Systems: Some Evidence with Case Studies," *International Journal of Information Management*, February 1999, p. 75; and Alexander Gerybadz, "Globalization of R&D: Recent Changes in the Management of Innovation in Transnational Corporations," *Research Policy*, March 1999, pp. 251–253.
24 Ibid., pp. 143–144.
25 Delia Craven, "Click and Mortar," *Red Herring*, November 1999, p. 208.
26 See for example Scott Chase, "Centralized or Decentralized? A Merger Forces a Company to Decide," *Business Credit*, June 1998, pp. 16–19.
27 Jonathan Day and James Wendler, "The New Economics of Organization," *McKinsey Quarterly*, Winter 1998, pp. 4–18.
28 Joseph Foegen, "Are Managers Losing Control?" *Business Horizons*, March–April 1998, pp. 2–6.
29 Malcolm Warner and Morgan Wetzel, "The Virtual General Manager," *Journal of General Management*, Summer 1999, pp. 71–73.
30 Kenneth MacKenzie, *Organizational Structure* (Arlington Heights, OH: AHM 1978), pp. 198–230.
31 Ibid., p. 201.
32 The foundation study for this conclusion is Alfred Chandler, *Strategy and Structure* (Cambridge: MIT Press, 1962); for a recent literature review and test of the strategy-structure link see Terry Amburgey and Tina Dacin, "As the Left Foot Follows the Right? The Dynamics of Strategic and Structural Change," *Academy of Management Journal*, vol. 37, no. 6, 1994, 1427–1452.
33 Amburgey and Dacin.
34 Chandler, p. 14.
35 Ibid., p. 366.
36 Judith H. Dobrzynski, "Jack Welch: How Good a Manager?" *Business Week*, 14 December 1987, p. 94. See also Thomas Stewart, "Brain Power," *Fortune*, 17 March 1997, pp. 105–10.
37 See, for example, Brian Dumaine, "The Bureaucracy Busters," *Fortune*, 17 June 1991, pp. 36–40; and Todd Vogel, "Where 1990s Style Management Is Already Hard at Work," *Business Week*, 23, October 1989, pp. 92–97.
38 For findings that cast some doubt on the generalizability of this conclusion, see Lyman Porter and Edward Lawler III,

"The Effects of Tall Versus Flat Organization Structures on Managerial Job Satisfaction," *Personnel Psychology*, vol. 17, 1964, pp. 135–148.

39 See, for example, Henri Fayol, *General and Industrial Management*, trans. Constance Storrs (London: Sir Isaac Putnam, 1949).

40 For a discussion of the contingencies affecting span of control (task uncertainty, professionalism, and interdependence), see, for example, Daniel Robey, *Designing Organizations*, 3rd edition (Homewood, IL: Irwin, 1991), pp. 258–259.

CHAPTER 8

1 Tom Peters, *Liberation Management* (New York: Alfred Knopf, 1992), p. 310; see also, Peter Dujardin, "Motivational Speaker Jump-Starts Norfolk Virginia Audience," *Knight-Ridder/Tribune Business News*, 30 September 1999, p. 6.

2 Tom Burns and G. M. Stalker, *The Management of Innovation* (London: Tavistock, 1961), p. 1.

3 Emery and Trist, two other British researchers, referred to this innovative environment as a "turbulent field" environment because changes often come not from a firm's traditional competitors, but from out of the blue. Often, in fact, the changes seem to "arise from the field itself," in that they result from interaction between parts of the environment. The very "texture" of a firm's environment changes because previously unrelated or (from the point of view of the firm) irrelevant elements in its environment become interconnected. F. E. Emery and E. C. Trist, "The Causal Texture of Organizational Environments," *Human Relations*, August 1965, pp. 20–26. As another example, after 1970 (when digital watches were introduced), calculator firms like Texas Instruments suddenly and unexpectedly became competitors in the watch industry.

4 Peter Blau, Cecilia Falbe, William McKinley, and Phelps Tracy, "Technology and Organization in Manufacturing," *Administrative Science Quarterly*, March 1976.

5 However, Allen found that "characteristics, beliefs, and strategies of top management groups were found to be fully as important as contextual factors in predicting organizational choices." Stephen A. Allen, "Understanding Reorganizations and Divisionalized Companies," *Academy of Management Journal*, December 1979, pp. 641–671.

6 How can we explain the fact that an organization's environment and technology influence its structure? One plausible explanation is that some environments and technologies require managers to handle more unforeseen problems and decisions than do others. And, since each person's capacity for juggling problems and making decisions is limited, an overabundance of problems forces managers to respond—often by reorganizing. Thus, when a manager finds himself or herself becoming overloaded with problems, one reasonable response is to give subordinates more autonomy, to decentralize (thus letting employees handle more problems among themselves), and to reorganize around self-contained divisions. By reorganizing in these ways, the manager may surrender some direct control, but at least the organization avoids becoming unresponsive, as might otherwise have been the case.

7 Except as noted, this section is based on Tom Peters, *Thriving on Chaos* (New York: Harper & Row, 1987), pp. 425–438; and Peters, Liberation Management, pp. 90–95.

8 Peters, *Liberation Management*, p. 88.

9 Ibid., p. 90.

10 Jerry Ross, "Review of Rogue Trader: How I Brought Down Barings Bank and Shook the Financial World, by Nicholas Leeson," *Academy of Management Review*, October 1997, p. 10.

11 "Union Pacific's Rail Troubles Take Toll on Texas Business," *New York Times*, 28 November 1997, p. A12.

12 "How Can Big Companies Keep the Entrepreneurial Spirit Alive?" *Harvard Business Review*, (November–December 1996), pp. 188–189.

13 Walker, pp. 112–122.

14 Peters, *Liberation Management*, 49–50.

15 Stephen Baker, "The Perils of Redeployment, or Starting from Scratch," *Computer World*, November 14, 1998, p. S9.

16 Except as noted, the remainder of this section is based on James Shonk, *Team-Based Organizations* (Chicago: Irwin, 1997).

17 Peters, *Thriving on Chaos*, p. 256.

18 Charles Fishman, "Engines of Democracy," *Fast Company*, October 1999, pp. 174–202.

19 Peters, *Liberation Management*, p. 238.

20 William H. Miller, "Chesebrough-Ponds at a Glance," *Industry Week*, 19 October 1992, pp. 14–15.

21 Shonk, pp. 35–38.

22 *Webster's New World Dictionary, 3rd College edition.* (New York: Simon and Schuster, Inc., 1988), p. 911. For a discussion of networked organizations, see James Brian Quinn, Intelligent Enterprise (New York: Free Press, 1992), pp. 213–40.

23 Ram Charan, "How Networks Reshape Organizations—For Results," *Harvard Business Review*, September–October 1991, pp. 104–115.

24 Ibid., pp. 106–107.

25 Ibid., 106; see also Marlene Piturro, "What Are You Doing about the New Global Realities?" *Management Review*, March 1999, p. 16.

26 Ibid., p.108.

27 Christopher Bartlett and Sumantra Ghoshal, "What Is a Global Manager?" *Harvard Business Review*, September–October 1992, pp. 62–74.

28 Cyrus Freidheim, Jr., "The Battle of the Alliances," *Management Review*, September 1999, pp. 46–51.

29 Tom Lester, "The Rise of the Network," *International Management*, June 1992, p. 72.

30 Paul Evans, Yves Doz, and Andre Laurent, *Human Resource Management in International Firms* (London: Macmillan, 1989), p. 123.

31 David Kilpatrick, "Groupware Goes Boom," *Fortune*, 27 December 1993, pp. 99–101.

32 Kenneth Laudon and Jane Laudon, *Essentials of Management Information Systems* (Upper Saddle River, NJ: Prentice Hall, 1997), pp. 413–416.

33 Bob Underwood, "Transforming with Collaborative Computing," *AS/400 Systems Management*, March 1999, p. 59.

34 "Product Development Tool Gets Revamped with Java; Ip Team Integrates Suppliers and Contractors," *Computer World*, 24 May 1999, p. 16.

35 Douglas Johnson, "Discuss Changing Models in Real Time," *Design News*, 3 May 1999, p. 96.

36 Richard Dennis, "Online R&D Management: The Way Forward," *R&D Management*, January 1998, pp. 27–36.

37 Phillip Evans and Thomas Wurster, "Strategy and the New Economics of Information," *Harvard Business Review*, September–October 1997, p. 75.

38 Bill Gates, *Business @ the Speed of Thought* (New York: Warner Books, 1999), pp. 239.

39 Mary Anne Devanna and Noel Tichy, "Creating the Competitive Organization of the 21st Century: The Boundaryless Corporation," *Human Resource Management*, Winter 1990, pp. 455–471.

40 Larry Hirschhorn and Thomas Gilmore, "The New Boundaries of the 'Boundaryless' Company," *Harvard Business Review*, May–June 1992, 104. See also Daniel Denison, Stuart

Hart, and Joel Kahn, "From Chimneys to Cross-Functional Teams: Developing and Validating a Diagnostic Model," *Academy of Management Journal*, August 1996, pp. 1005–1023.

41 This is based on Hirschhorn and Gilmore, pp. 104–108.

42 Except as noted, the remainder of this section is based on Hirschhorn and Gilmore, "The New Boundaries," pp. 107–108.

43 Hirschhorn and Gilmore, p. 107.

44 Ibid., p. 108.

45 Ibid., p. 109.

46 Luc Hatlestad, "New Shades of Blue," *Red Herring*, November 1999, p. 126.

47 Except as noted, this section is based on John A. Byrne, "The Horizontal Corporation," *Business Week*, 20 December 1993, pp. 76–81.

48 Michael Hammer and James Champy, *Reengineering the Corporation* (New York: Harper Business, 1994), p. 35.

49 Ann Majchrzak and Quinwei Wang, "Breaking the Functional Mind-Set of Process Organizations," *Harvard Business Review*, September–October 1996, pp. 93–99.

50 Ibid., 96–99.

51 Ibid.

52 See for example *Webster's New Collegiate Dictionary* (Springfield, MA: G&C Miriam Company), 1973, p. 420.

53 John Byrne, Richard Brandt, and Otis Port, "The Virtual Corporation," *Business Week*, 8 February 1993, p. 99.

54 Marie-Claude Boudreau et al, "Going Global: Using Information Technology to Advance the Competitiveness of the Virtual Transnational Organization," *Academy of Management Executive*, 1998, pp. 121–122.

55 Ibid., p. 122.

56 See for example Gail Dutton, "The New Consortiums," *Management Review*, January 1999, pp. 46–50.

57 Raymond Miles, et al, "Organizing in the Knowledge Age: Anticipating the Cellular Form," *Academy of Management Executive*, 1997, pp. 7–24.

58 Ibid., p. 13.

59 Ibid., p. 13.

60 John Case, "The Open-Book Management Revolution," *Inc.*, June 1995, pp. 26–43.

61 KnitMedia prospectus, pp. 31–32.

CHAPTER 9

1 Cisco Web site <www.cisco.com.>

2 Catherine Truss and Lynda Gratton, "Strategic Human Resource Management: A Conceptual Approach," *International Journal of Human Resource Management*, September 1994, p. 663.

3 See also James Clifford, "Manage Work Better to Better Manage Human Resources: A Comparative Study of Two Approaches to Job Analysis," *Public Personnel Management*, Spring 1996, pp. 89–103.

4 Donald Harris, "A Matter of Privacy: Managing Personnel Data in Company Computers," *Personnel*, February 1987, p. 37.

5 Shari Caudron, "Low Unemployment Is Causing a Staffing Draught," *Personnel Journal*, November 1996, pp. 59–67.

6 "Tight Labor Markets Bring New Paradigm," *BNA Bulletin to Management*, 23 October 1997, p. 344.

7 "High-Stakes Recruiting in High-Tech," *BNA Bulletin to Management*, 12 February 1998, p. 48.

8 Arthur R. Pell, *Recruiting and Selecting Personnel* (New York: Regents, 1969), pp. 10–12; see also Katherine Tyler, "Employees Can Help Recruiting New Talent," *HRMagazine*, September 1996, pp. 57–61.

9 Ibid., p. 11.

10 Allison Thomson, "The Contingent Work Force," *Occupational Outlook Quarterly*, Spring 1995, p. 45.

11 Amy Kover, "Manufacturing's Hidden Asset: Temp Workers," *Fortune*, 10 November 1997, pp. 28–29.

12 One Bureau of Labor Statistics study suggests that temporary employees produce the equivalent of two or more hours of work per day more than their permanent counterparts. For a discussion, see Shari Caudron, "Contingent Workforce Spurs HR Planning," *Personnel Journal*, July 1994, p. 54; See also Brenda Sunoo, "Temp Firms Turn Up the Heat on Hiring," *Workforce*, April 1999, pp. 50–52.

13 "Search and Destroy," *The Economist*, 27 June 1998, p. 63.

14 Ibid.

15 Ibid.

16 The study on employment referrals was published by Bernard Hodes Advertising, Dept. 100, 555 Madison Avenue, NY, NY 10022. See also Allan Halcrow, "Employees Are Your Best Recruiters," *Personnel Journal*, November 1988, pp. 41–49. See also Andy Hargerstock and Hand Engel, "Six Ways to Boost Employee Referral Programs," *HRMagazine*, December 1994, pp.72ff; See also Katherine Tyler, "Employees Can Help Recruiting New Talent," *HRMagazine*, September 1996, pp. 57–61.

17 "High-Stakes Recruiting in High-Tech," *BNA Bulletin to Management*, 12 February 1998, p. 48.

18 Sara Rynes, Marc Orlitzky, and Robert Bretz, Jr., "Experienced Hiring versus College Recruiting: Practices and Emerging Trends," *Peronnel Psychology*, vol. 50 (1997), pp. 309–339.

19 See, for example, Richard Becker, "Ten Common Mistakes in College Recruiting—or How to Try Without Really Succeeding," *Personnel*, March–April 1975, pp. 19–28. See also Sara Rynes and John Boudreau, "College Recruiting in Large Organizations: Practice, Evaluation, and Research Implications," *Personnel Psychology*, Winter 1986, pp. 729–757.

20 Nancy Austin, "First Aide," *Inc.*, September 1999, pp. 68–71.

21 Ibid., p. 78.

22 Ibid., p. 72.

23 "Internships Provide Workplace Snapshot," *BNA Bulletin to Management*, 22 May 1997, p. 168.

24 "Internet Recruitment Survey," *BNA Bulletin to Management*, 22 May 1997, pp. 164–165.

25 Elaine Appleton, "Recruiting on the Internet," *Datamation*, August 1995, p. 39.

26 Julia King, "Job Networking," *Enterprise Networking*, 26 January 1995; see also David Schulz, "Internet Emerging as a Major Vehicle for Mid-Level Retail Recruiting." *Stores*, June 1999, pp. 70–73.

27 Brenda Paik Sunoo, "Thumbs Up for Staffing Websites," *Workforce*, October 1997, pp. 67–73; See also Katherine Hildebrand, "Recruiting on the Internet," *Colorado Business Magazine*, July 1998, pp. 46–48.

28 Gillian Flynn, "Cisco Turns the Internet Inside (and) Out," *Personnel Journal*, October 1996, pp. 28–34.

29 "Retirees Increasingly Reentering the Workforce," *BNA Bulletin to Management*, 16 January 1997, p. 17.

30 Samuel Greengard, "At Peoplesoft, Client/Server Drives the HR Office of the Future," *Personnel Journal*, May 1996, p. 92; see also Bill Gates, *Business @ the Speed of Thought (New York) Warner Books, 1999), pp. 41–42.

31 Jennifer Koch, *"Finding Qualified Hispanic Candidates,"* *Recruitment Today*, Spring 1990, p. 35; see also Shelley Coolidge, "Minority Grads Sought for Jobs," *Christian Science Monitor*, 5 December 1997, p. 8.

32 This compares with 21.5% for black job seekers and 23.9% for white job seekers. Michelle Harrison Ports, "Trends in Job Search Methods, 1990–92," *Monthly Labor Review*, October 1993, p. 64.

33 Bill Leonard, "Welfare Reform: A New Deal for HR," *HRMagazine*, March 1997, pp. 78–86; Jennifer Laabs, "Welfare Law: HR's Role in Employment," *Workforce*, January 1998, pp. 30–39.

34 Herbert Greenberg, "A Hidden Source of Talent," *HRMagazine*, March 1997, pp. 88–91.

35 "Welfare-to-Work: No Easy Chore," *BNA Bulletin to Management*, 13 February 1997, p. 56.

36 "Workplace Testing and Monitoring," *Management Review*, October 1998, pp. 31–42.

37 Ibid.

38 Mel Kleiman, "Employee Testing Essential to Hiring Effectively in the '90s," *Houston Business Journal*, 8 February 1993, p. 31; and Gerald L. Borofsky, "Pre-Employment Psychological Screening," *Risk Management*, January 1993, p. 47; See also Christina Ron Quist, "Pre-Employment Testing: Making It Work for You," *Occupational Hazards*, December 1997, pp. 38–40.

39 Louis Olivas, "Using Assessment Centers for Individual and Organizational Development," *Personnel*, May–June 1980, p. 63–67; Tim Payne, Neil Anderson, and Tom Smith, "Assessment Centers, Selection Systems and Cost-Effectiveness: An Evaluative Case Study," *Personnel Review*, Fall 1992, p. 48; and Roger Mottram, "Assessment Centers Are Not Only for Selection: The Assessment Center as a Development Workshop," *Journal of Managerial Psychology*, January 1992, p. A1; Charles Woodruffe, "Going Back a Generation," *People Management*, 20 February 1997, pp. 32–35.

40 This is based on Daniel Goleman, "Forget Money; Nothing Can Buy Happiness, Some Researchers Say," *Wall Street Journal*, 16 August 1996, pp. B5, B9. See also Shari Caudron, "Hire for Attitude," *Staffing: A Workforce Supplement*, August 1997, pp. 20–26.

41 Golemon, p. B9.

42 Source for questions: Goleman, "Forget Money"; and Dr. Richard Davidson, University of Wisconsin.

43 For a full discussion of this, see Gary Dessler, *Human Resource Management, 8th ed.* (Upper Saddle River, NJ: Prentice-Hall, 2000), chapter 6.

44 R. E. Carlson, "Selection Interview Decisions: The Effects of Interviewer Experience, Relative Quota Situation, and Applicant Sample on Interview Decisions," *Personnel Psychology*, vol. 20, 1967, pp. 259–280; See also Linda Thornburgh, "Computer-Assisted Interviewing Shortens Hiring Cycle," *HRMagazine*, February 1998, pp. 73–76.

45 William Tullar, Terry Mullins, and Sharon Caldwell, "Effects of Interview Length and Applicant Quality on Interview Decision Time," *Journal of Applied Psychology*, December 1979, pp. 669–74; See also Jennifer Burnett, et. al. "Interview Notes and Validity," *Personnel Psychology*, Summer 1998, pp. 375–396.

46 Edwin Walley, "Successful Interviewing Techniques," *The CPA Journal*, September 1992, p. 29.

47 Pamela Paul, "Interviewing is Your Business," *Association Management*, November 1992, p. 29.

48 Gary Dessler, *Human Resource Management, 7th ed.* (Upper Saddle River, NJ: Prentice-Hall, 1997), pp. 242–243.

49 See, for example, George Burgnoli, James Campion, and Jeffrey Bisen, "Racial Bias in the Use of Work Samples for Personnel Selection," *Journal of Applied Psychology*, April 1979, pp. 119–123.

50 Siegel and Lane, *Personnel and Organizational Psychology*, pp. 182–183.

51 Annette Spychalski, Miguel Quinones, Barbara Gaugler, and Katja Pohley, "A Survey of Assessment Center Practices in Organizations in the United States," *Personnel Psychology*, Spring, 1997, pp. 71–90.

52 Steven Norton, "The Empirical and Content Validity of Assessment Centers versus Traditional Methods of Predicting Management Success," *Academy of Management Review*, vol. 20, July 1997, pp. 442–453. Interestingly, a recent review concludes that assessment centers do predict managerial success, but after an extensive review, "we also assert that we do not know why they work." Richard Klimoski and Mary Brickner, "Why Do Assessment Centers Work? The Puzzle of Assessment Center Validity," *Personnel Psychology*, Summer 1987, pp. 243–260.

53 Wayne F. Cascio and Val Silbey, "Utility of the Assessment Center as a Selection Device," *Journal of Applied Psychology*, April 1979, pp. 107–118. See also Paul R. Sackett, "Assessment Centers and Content Validity: Some Neglected Issues," *Personnel Psychology*, vol. 40, Spring 1981, pp. 55–64.

54 "Database Helps Employers Screen Applicants for Theft," *BNA Bulletin to Management*, 12 June 1997, p. 186.

55 Ibid., p. 191.

56 John Jones and William Terris, "Post-Polygraph Selection Techniques," *Recruitment Today*, May–June 1989, pp. 25–31.

57 Ian Miners, Nick Nykodym, and Diane Samerdyke-Traband, "Put Drug Detection to the Test," *Personnel Journal*, August 1987, pp. 191–197; See also Gillian Flynn, "How to Prescribe Drug Testing," *Workforce*, January 1999, p. 107.

58 Eric Rolf Greenberg, "Workplace Testing: Who's Testing Whom," *Personnel*, May 1989, pp. 39–45.

59 See for example Ann Fields, "Class Act," *Inc. Technology*, 1997, pp. 55–57.

60 "Industry Report 1999," *Training*, October 1999, pp. 37–60.

61 Jennifer Reese, "Starbuck," *Fortune*, 9 December 1996, 190–200.

62 Kenneth Wexley and Gary Latham, *Developing and Training Human Resources in Organizations* (Glenview, IL: Scott, Foresman, 1981), p. 107.

63 Mary Boone and Susan Schulman, "Teletraining: A High-Tech Alternative," Personnel, May 1985, pp. 4–9. See also Ron Zemke, "The Rediscovery of Video Teleconferencing," *Training*, September 1986, pp. 28–36; and Carol Haig, "Clinics Fill Training Niche," *Personnel Journal*, September 1987, pp. 134–140.

64 Joseph Giusti, David Baker, and Peter Braybash, "Satellites Dish Out Global Training," *Personnel Journal*, June 1991, pp. 80–84.

65 Macy's Goes 'On Air' to Inform Employees," *BNA Bulletin to Management*, May 15, 1997, p. 160.

66 Larry Stevens, "The Internet: Your Newest Training Tool?, *Personnel Journal*, July 1996, pp. 27–31; see also Samuel Greengard, "Web-Based Training Yields Maximum Returns," *Workforce*, February 1999, pp. 95–96.

67 Shari Caudron, "Your Learning Technology Primer," *Personnel Journal*, June 1996, pp. 120–136.

68 Ibid., p. 130.

69 Kenneth Nowack, "360-Degree Feedback: The Whole Story," *Training and Development*, January 1993, p. 69. For a description of some of the problems involved in implementing 360-degree feedback, see Matthew Budman, "The Rating Game," *Across the Board*, February 1994, pp. 35–38.

70 "360-Degree Feedback on the Rise, Survey Finds," *BNA Bulletin to Management*, 23 January 1997, p. 31; see also Kenneth Nowack et al., "How to Evaluate Your 360-Degree Feedback Efforts," *Training and Development Journal*, April 1999, pp. 48–53.

71 Katherine Romano, "Fear of Feedback," *Management Review*, December 1993, p. 39.

72 Ibid.

73 See, for instance, Gerry Rich, "Group Reviews—Are You Up to It?" *CMA Magazine*, March 1993, p. 5.

74 This is based on Dessler, *Human Resource Management, 8th ed.,* pp. 321–323.

75 Matt Rothman, "Into the Black," *Inc.*, January 1993, pp. 59–65. For a good discussion of what other employers are doing to improve benefits, see, for example, Kimberly Seals McDonald, "Your Benefits," *Fortune*, 3 March 1997, pp. 199–201.

76 This section is based on Gary Dessler, *Human Resource Management, 8th ed.*), pp. 43–44; see also Commerce Clearing House, Sexual Harassment Manual, p. 8.

77 John Aram, *Presumed Superior* (Upper Saddle River, NJ: Prentice Hall).

78 *Sacrmento Bee*, 21 February 1999, Special Report.

79 Gillian Flynn, "It Takes Value to Capitalize on Change," *Workforce,* April 1997, pp. 27–34.

CHAPTER 10

1 Melanie Warner, "Getting up to Internet Speed," *Fortune*, 10 January 2000, pp. 185–186.

2 Ibid., p. 186.

3 Jeffrey McNally, Stephen Gerras, and R. Craig Bullis, "Teaching Leadership at the U.S. Military Academy at West Point," *Journal of Applied Behavioral Science*, June 1996, p. 181.

4 McNally, et al., p. 178.

5 "Steve Job's Apple Gets Way Cooler," *Fortune*, 24 January 2000, pp. 66–76.

6 Ibid., 67.

7 Ibid., 67.

8 M. S. El-Namiki, "Creating a Corporate Vision," *Long-Range Planning*, vol. 25, no. 6, December 1992, p. 25.

9 Ibid.

10 Arthur Thompson and A. J. Strickland, *Strategic Management* (Homewood, IL: Irwin, 1992), p. 7.

11 Shawn Tully, "How Cisco Mastered the Net," *Fortune*, 17 August 1998, pp. 207–210.

12 Tully, p. 210.

13 Shelley Kirkpatrick and Edwin A. Locke, "Leadership: Do Traits Matter?" *Academy of Management Executive*, May 1991, p. 49, and Edwin A. Locke, et al., *The Essence of Leadership: The Four Keys to Leading Successfully* (New York: Lexington/Macmillan, 1991). See also Ruth Tait, "The Attributes of Leadership," *Leadership and Organization Development Journal*, vol. 17, no. 1 (1996), pp. 27–31; David L. Cawthon, "Leadership: The Great Man Theory Revisited," *Business Horizons*, May 1996, pp. 1–4; Robert Baum, "A Longitudinal Study of the Relation of Vision and Vision Communication to Venture Growth in Entrepreneurial Firms," *Journal of Applied Psychology*, February 1998, pp. 43–55.

14 Kirkpatrick and Locke, p. 49.

15 Ibid., p. 50.

16 Except as noted, this section is based on ibid., pp. 48–60; See also Ross Laver, "Building a Better Boss: Studies Show That the Personality of a Chief Executive Can Have a Major Impact on Profits and Productivity," *Maclean's*, 30 September 1996, p. 41.

17 Ibid., p. 53.

18 Ibid., p. 54.

19 Ibid., p. 55.

20 Ibid., pp. 5–6.

21 Daniel Goleman, "What Makes a Leader?" *Harvard Business Review*, November–December 1998, pp. 93–99.

22 Goleman, p. 94.

23 Goleman, p. 99.

24 Chester Barnard, *The Functions of the Executive* (Cambridge, MA: Harvard University Press, 1938). See also Roger Dawson, *Secrets of Power Persuasion* (Upper Saddle River, NJ: Prentice-Hall, 1992); Sydney Finkelstein, "Power in Top Management Teams: Dimensions, Measurement, and Validation," *Academy of Management Journal*, August 1992; and Jeffrey Pfeffer, *Managing with Power: Politics and Influence in Organizations* (Boston: Harvard Business School Press, 1992).

25 Eli Cohen and Noel Tichy, "Operation: Leadership," *Fast Company*, September 1999, p. 280.

26 Cohen and Tichy, p. 280.

27 See, for example, Kirkpatrick and Locke, p. 49.

28 Ibid., p. 56.

29 For a discussion of this issue, see Peter Wissenberg and Michael Kavanagh, "The Independence of Initiating Structure and Consideration: A Review of Evidence," *Personnel Psychology*, vol. 25 (1972) pp. 119–130. See also Gary A. Yukl, *Leadership in Organizations, 3rd ed.* (Upper Saddle River, NJ: Prentice-Hall, 1994). For an interesting example of what can go wrong when the leader uses the wrong leadership style, see Thomas Ricks, "Army at Odds: West Point Posting Becomes a Minefield for 'Warrior' Officer," *Wall Street Journal*, 13 March 1997, pp. A1, A9.

30 Ralph Stogdill and A. E. Koonz, "Leader Behavior: Its Description and Measurement" (Columbus: Bureau of Business Research, Ohio State University, 1957). See also Bernard M. Bass, *Bass & Stogdill's Handbook of Leadership: Theory, Research, & Managerial Applications, 3rd ed.* (New York: The Free Press, 1990).

31 Ralph Stogdill, *Managers, Employees, Organizations* (Columbus: Bureau of Business Research, Ohio State University, 1965).

32 Gary Yukl, "Towards a Behavioral Theory of Leadership," *Organizational Behavior and Human Performance*, July 1971, pp. 414–440. See also Gary A. Yukl, *Leadership in Organizations, 3rd ed.* (Upper Saddle River, NJ: Prentice-Hall, 1994).

33 Hal Lancaster, "Herb Kelleher Has One Main Strategy: Treat Employees Well," *Wall Street Journal*, 31 August 1999, p. B1.

34 Blake and Mouton, *The Managerial Grid*.

35 Chester Schriesheim, Robert J. House, and Steven Kerr, "Leader Initiating Structure: A Reconciliation of Discrepant Research Results and Some Empirical Tests," *Organizational Behavior and Human Performance*, April 1976. See also Bernard M. Bass, *Bass & Stogdill's Handbook of Leadership: Theory, Research, & Managerial Applications, 3rd ed.* (New York: The Free Press, 1990).

36 Victor Vroom and Arthur Jago, "On the Validity of the Vroom-Yetton Model," *Journal of Applied Psychology*, vol. 63, no. 2 (1978), pp. 151–162; Madeleine Heilman et al, "Reactions to Prescribed Leader Behavior as a Function of Role Perspective: The Case of Vroom-Yetton Model," *Journal of Applied Psychology*, February 1984, pp. 50–60. See also Donna Brown, "Why Participative Management Won't Work Here" *Management Review*, June 1992.

37 Vroom and Jago, pp. 151–162.

38 See, for example, Mark Tubbs and Steven Akeberg, "The Role of Intentions in Work Motivation: Implications for Goal Setting Theory and Research," *Academy of Management Review*, January 1991, pp. 180–199.

39 Rensis Likert, *New Patterns of Management* (New York: McGraw-Hill, 1961).

40 Robert Day and Robert Hamblin, "Some Effects of Close and Punitive Styles of Leadership," *American Journal of Psychology*, vol. 69, (1964), pp. 499–510.

41 See for example, Nancy Morse, *Satisfaction in the White Collar Job* (Ann Arbor, MI: Survey Research Center, University of Michigan, 1953).

42 J. M. Burns, *Leadership* (New York: Harper, 1978).

43 For a discussion, see Ronald Deluga, "Relationship of Transformational and Transactional Leadership with Employee Influencing Strategies," *Group and Organizational Studies*, December 1988, pp. 457–458. See also Philip M. Podsakoff,

Scott B. MacKenzie, and William H. Bommer, "Transformational Leader Behaviors as Determinants of Employee Satisfaction, Commitment, Trust, and Organizational Citizenship Behaviors," *Journal of Management*, vol. 22, no. 2 (1996), pp. 259–298.

44 Joseph Seltzer and Bernard Bass, "Transformational Leadership: Beyond Initiation and Consideration," *Journal of Management*, vol. 4, (1990), p. 694. See also Bernard M. Bass, "Theory of Transformational Leadership Redux," *Leadership Quarterly*, Winter 1995, pp. 463–478.

45 Gary Yukl, "Managerial Leadership," p. 269.

46 N. M. Tichy and M. A. Devanna, *The Transformational Leader* (New York: Wiley 1986).

47 Seltzer and Bass, p. 694.

48 Deluga, p. 457.

49 Frances Yamarino and Bernard Bass, "Transformational Leadership and Multiple Levels of Analysis," Human Relations, vol. 43, no. 10 (1990), p. 976; See also David Walman, "CEO Charismatic Leadership: Levels of Management and Levels of Analysis Effects," *Academy of Management Review*, April 1999, pp. 266–268.

50 J. A. Conger, "Inspiring Others: The Language of Leadership," *Academy of Management Executive* vol. 5, (1991), pp. 31–45; See also Linda Hill, "Charismatic Leadership in Organizations," *Personnel Psychology*, October 1999, pp. 767–768.

51 Bernard Bass, *Leadership and Performance Beyond Expectations* (New York: The Free Press, 1985); and Deluga, pp. 457–458; See also Boas Shamir, "Correlates of Charismatic Leader Behavior in Military Units: Subordinates Attitudes, Unit of Characteristics, and Superiors Appraisals of Leader Performance," *Academy of Management Journal*, August 1998, pp. 387–410.

52 Deluga, p. 457.

53 Ibid.

54 Yamarino and Bass, p. 981.

55 For a review, see Robert Keller, "Transformational Leadership and the Performance of Research and Development Project Groups," *Journal of Management*, vol. 18, no. 3 (1992), pp. 489–501.

56 J. J. Hater and Bernard Bass, "Superiors' Evaluations and Subordinates' Perceptions of Transformational and Transactional Leadership," *Journal of Applied Psychology*, vol. 73 (1988), pp. 695–702.

57 J. M. Howell and C. A. Higgins, "Champions of Technological Innovation," *Administrative Science Quarterly*, vol. 35 (1990), pp. 317–341.

58 Yamarino and Bass, p. 981.

59 C. M. Solomon, "Careers Under Glass," *Personnel Journal*, vol. 69, no. 4 (1990), pp. 96–105.

60 See, for example, James Bowditch and Anthony Buono, *A Primer on Organizational Behavior* (New York: John Wiley, 1994), p. 238.

61 Russell Kent and Sherry Moss, "Effects of Sex and Gender Role on Leader Emergence," *Academy of Management Journal*, vol. 37, no. 5 (1994), pp. 1335–46; Jane Baack, Norma Carr-Ruffino, and Monica Pelletier, "Making It to the Top: Specific Leadership Skills," *Women in Management Review*, vol. 8, no. 2 (1993), pp. 17–23.

62 S. M. Donnel and J. Hall, "Men and Women as Managers: A Significant Case of No Significant Difference," *Organizational Dynamics*, vol. 8, (1980), pp. 60–77. See also Jennifer L. Berdahl, "Gender and Leadership in Work Groups: Six Alternative Models," *Leadership Quarterly*, Spring 1996, pp. 21–40.

63 M. A. Hatcher, "The Corporate Woman of the 1990s: Maverick or Innovator?" *Psychology of Women Quarterly*, vol. 5, (1991), pp. 251–259.

64 D. G. Winter, *The Power Motive* (New York: The Free Press, 1975).

65 L. McFarland Shore and G. C. Thornton, "Effects of Gender on Self and Supervisory Ratings," *Academy of Management Journal*, vol. 29, no. 1 (1986), pp. 115–129; quoted in Bowditch and Buono, p. 238.

66 G. H. Dobbins and S. J. Paltz, "Sex Differences in Leadership: How Real Are They?" *Academy of Management Review*, vol. 11 (1986), pp. 118–127; R. Drazin and E. R. Auster, "Wage Differences Between Men and Women: Performance Appraisal Ratings versus Salary Allocation as the Locus of Bias," *Human Resource Management*, vol. 26 (1987):157–168. See also Nancy DiTomaso and Robert Hooijberg, "Diversity and the Demands of Leadership," *Leadership Quarterly*, Summer 1996, pp. 163–187 and Chao C. Chen and Ellen Van Velsor, "New Directions for Research and Practice in Diversity Leadership," *Leadership Quarterly*, Summer 1996, pp. 285–302.

67 M. Jelinek and N. J. Alder, "Women: World-Class Managers for Global Competition," *Academy of Management Executive*, vol. 2, no. 1 (1988), pp. 11–19; J. Grant, "Women as Managers: What Can They Offer to Organizations?" *Organizational Dynamics*, vol. 16, no. 3 (1988), pp. 56–63. On the other hand, one author suggests that women should be more Machiavellian: "War favors the dangerous woman. Women may love peace and seek stability, but these conditions seldom serve them." Harriet Rubin, *The Princessa: Machiavelli for Women* (New York: Doubleday/Currenly, 1997), quoted in Anne Fisher, "What Women Can Learn from Machiavelli," *Fortune*, April 1997, p. 162.

68 Frederick E. Fiedler, *A Theory of Leadership Effectiveness* (New York: McGraw-Hill, 1967), p. 147; See also David Stauffer, "Once a Leader, Always a Leader?," *Across the Board*, April 1999, pp. 14–19.

69 Ibid.

70 See, for example, Robert J. House and J. V. Singh, "Organizational Behavior: Some New Directions for I/O Psychology," *Annual Review of Psychology*, vol. 38, (1987), pp. 669–718; L. H. Peters, D. D. Hartke, and J. T. Pohlmann, "Fiedler's Contingency Theory of Leadership: An Application of the Meta-Analytic Procedures of Schmidt and Hunter," *Psychological Bulletin*, vol. 97, (1985), pp. 274–285.

71 Fred Fiedler and J. E. Garcia, *New Approaches to Effective Leadership: Cognitive Resources and Organizational Performance* (New York: John Wiley and Sons, 1987); and Robert T. Vecchio, "Theoretical and Empirical Examination of Cognitive Resource Theory," *Journal of Applied Psychology*, April 1990, pp. 141–147. See also Robert Vecchio, "Cognitive Resource Theory: Issues for Specifying a Test of the Theory" *Journal of Applied Psychology*, June 1992.

72 Robert J. House and Terrence Mitchell, "Path-Goal Theory of Leadership," *Contemporary Business*, vol. 3 (1974), pp. 81–98; and Abraham Sagie and Meni Koslowsky, "Organizational Attitudes and Behaviors as a Function of Participation in Strategic and Tactical Change Decisions: An Application of Path-Goal Theory," *Journal of Organizational Behavior*, January 1994, pp. 37–48.

73 J. Fulk and E. R. Wendler, "Dimensionality of Leader-Subordinate Interactions: A Path-Goal Investigation," Organizational Behavior and Human Performance vol. 30 (1982), pp. 241–264.

74 G. B. Graen and T. A. Scandura, "Toward a Psychology of Daidic Organizing." L. L. Cummings and B. M. Staw (eds.) *Research in Organizational Behavior*, vol. 9 (Greenwich, CT: J.A.I. Press, 1987), p. 208; See also David Schneider and Charles Goldwasser, "Be a Model Leader of Change," *Management Review*, March 1998, pp. 41–48.

75 Antoinette Phillips and Arthur Bedeian, "Leader-Follower Exchange Quality: The Role of Personal and Interpersonal Attributes," *Academy of Management Journal*, vol. 37, no. 4 (1994), pp. 990–1001; see also Nancy Boyd and Robert Taylor, "A Developmental Approach to the Examination of Friendship in Leader and Follower Relationships," *Leadership Quarterly*, vol. 9, no. 1, 1998, pp. 1–25; Jaesub Lee, "Leader Member Exchange: The "Pelz Effect" and Cooperative Communication Between Group Members," *Management Communications Quarterly*, November 1997, pp. 266–287; and Christopher Avery, "All Power to You: Collaborative Leadership Works," *Journal for Quality and Participation*, March–April 1999, pp. 36–41.

76 Jerald Greenberg, *Managing Behavior in Organizations* (Upper Saddle River, NJ: Prentice-Hall, 1996), p. 215.

77 Phillips and Bedeian, "Leader-Follower Exchange Quality."

78 See Robert P. Vecchio, "Situational Leadership Theory: An Examination of a Prescriptive Theory," *Journal of Applied Psychology*, August 1987, pp. 444–451; and Jerald Greenberg, *Managing Behavior in Organizations* (Upper Saddle River, NJ: Prentice-Hall, 1996), p. 226.

79 Steve Kerr and J. M. Jermier, "Substitutes for Leadership: Their Meaning and Measurement," *Organizational Behavior and Human Performance*, vol. 22 (1978), pp. 375–403. See also Philip M. Podsakoff and Scott B. MacKenzie, "An Examination of Substitutes for Leadership Within a Levels-of-Analysis Framework," *Leadership Quarterly*, Fall 1995, pp. 289–328.

80 David Alcorn, "Dynamic Followership: Empowerment at Work," *Management Quarterly*, Spring 1992, pp. 11–13.

81 Jon Howell, David Bowen, Peter Dorfman, Steven Kerr, and Philip Podsakoff, "Substitutes for Leadership: Effective Alternatives to Ineffective Leadership," *Organizational Dynamics*, Summer 1990, p. 23.

82 Ibid.

83 "What It Means to Lead," *Fast Company*, February–March 1997.

84 Adrian Tomine, "Fast Pack 2000," *Fast Company*, March 2000, pp. 246–247.

85 Ibid., p. 268.

86 Ibid.

CHAPTER 11

1 Charles Fishmen, "Engines of Democracy," *Fast Company*, October 1999, pp. 174–202.

2 Fishmen, p. 20.

3 "The Powerhouse That Jack Built," *Economist*, 18 September 1999, p. 26.

4 Ernest R. Hilgard, *Introduction to Psychology* (New York: Harcourt Brace and World, 1962), pp. 124–125.

5 Ibid., p. 124.

6 See, for instance, Kanfer, "Motivation Theory," in *Handbook of Industrial and Organizational Psychology*, 1990. See also Robert Hersey, "A Practitioner's View of Motivation," *Journal of Managerial Psychology*, May 1993, pp. 110–115, and Kenneth Kovatch, "Employee Motivation: Addressing a Crucial Factor in Your Organization's Performance," *Employment Relations Today*, Summer 1995, pp. 93–107.

7 See Douglas M. McGregor, "The Human Side of Enterprise," in *Management Classics*, Michael Matteson and John M. Ivancevich (Eds.), (Santa Monica, CA: Goodyear, 1977), pp. 43–49; See also Ewart Woolridge, "Time to Stand Maslow's Hierarchy on Its Head?" *People Management*, 21 December 1995, p. 17.

8 John Rowan, "Maslow Amended," *Journal of Humanistic Psychology*, Winter 1998, pp. 81–83; see also Clay Alderfer, "Theories Reflecting My Personal Experience and Life Develop-

ment," *Journal of Applied Behavioral Science*, November 1989, pp. 351–366.

9 See for example Clay Alderfer, "Theories Reflecting My Personal Experience and Life Development," *Journal of Applied Behavioral Science*, November 1989, pp. 351–366.

10 McGregor, p. 45.

11 Carey Goldberg, "Windfall Sets Off a Blizzard of Bonuses for a Company," *New York Times*, 25 December 1996, p. A16.

12 Frederick Herzberg, et al., *Job Attitudes: Review of Research and Opinion* (Pittsburgh, PA: Pittsburgh Psychological Services, 1957).

13 R. B. Ewen, "Some Determinants of Job Satisfaction: A Study of the Generality of Herzberg's Theory," *Journal of Applied Psychology*, 1964, vol. 48, pp. 161–163.

14 Mark Tietjen and Robert Myers, "Motivation and Job Satisfaction," *Management Decision*, May–June 1998, pp. 226–232.

15 This is based on David Kolb, Irwin Rubin, and James McIntyre, *Organizational Psychology: An Experiential Approach* (Upper Saddle River, NJ: Prentice Hall, 1971), pp. 65–69.

16 David McClelland and David Burnham, "Power Is the Great Motivator," *Harvard Business Review*, January–February 1995, pp. 126–136.

17 These are all from Kolb et al.

18 George Litwin and Robert Stringer, Jr., *Motivation and Organizational Climate* (Boston: Harvard University, 1968), pp. 20–24.

19 Edgar Schein, *Career Dynamics: Matching Individual and Organizational Needs* (Reading, MA: Addison-Wesley, 1978); and Thomas Barth, "Career Anchor Theory," *Review of Public Personnel Administration*, vol. 13, no. 4, 1993, pp. 27–42; see also Jeffrey Colvin, "Looking to Hire the Very Best? Ask the Right Questions, Lots of Them," *Fortune*, 21 June 1999, pp. 19–21.

20 Bob Nelson, et al, "Motivate Employees According to Temperament," *HRMagazine*, March 1997, pp. 51–56; See also Donna McNeese-Smith, "The Relationship Between Managerial Motivation, Leadership, Nurse Outcomes and Patient Satisfaction," *Journal Organizational Behavior*, March 1999, p. 243.

21 *Fast Company*, October 1999, p. 186.

22 Kanfer, 102. See also Robert Bretz and Steven Thomas, "Perceived Equity, Motivation, and Final-Offer Arbitration in Major League Baseball," *Journal of Applied Psychology*, June 1992, pp. 280–9; see also Chao Chan, "Deciding on Equity or Parity: A Test of Situational, Cultural, and Individual Factors," *Journal of Organizational Behavior*, March 1998, pp. 115–130.

23 See, for example, J. Greenberg, "A Taxonomy of Organizational Justice Theories," *Academy of Management Review*, vol. 12, 1987, pp. 9–22; See also Armin Falk, "Intrinsic Motivation and Extrinsic Incentives in a Repeated Game with Incomplete Contracts," *Journal of Economic Psychology*, June 1999, pp. 251–254.

24 For a discussion, see Kanfer, 124.

25 Edwin A. Locke and D. Henne, "Work Motivation Theories," in C. L. Cooper and I. Robertson (Eds.), *International Review of Industrial and Organizational Psychology* (Chichester, England: Wiley, 1986), pp. 1–35; see also Maureen Ambrose, "Old Friends, New Faces: Motivation Research in the 1990s," *Journal of Management*, May–June 1999, pp. 231–237.

26 Kanfer, p. 125.

27 A. J. Mento, R. P. Steel, and R. J. Karren, "A Meta-Analytic Study of the Effects of Goal Setting on Task Performance: 1966–1984," *Organizational Behavior and Human Decision Processes*, vol. 39, 1987, pp. 52–83.

28 Gary Latham and T. W. Lee, "Goal Setting," in Edwin A. Locke (Ed.), *Generalizing from Laboratory to Field Settings* (Lexington, MA: Lexington Books, 1986), pp. 101–119.

29 Kanfer, p. 113.

30 For a discussion, see John P. Campbell and Robert Pritchard, "Motivation Theory in Industrial and Organizational Psychology," in Marvin Dunnette, (Ed.), *Industrial and Organizational Psychology*, 1976, pp. 74–75; and Kanfer, pp. 115–116.

31 Peter Foreman, "Work Values and Expectancies in Occupational Rehabilitation: The Role of Cognitive Values in the Return to Work Process," *Journal of Rehabilitation*, July–September 1996, pp. 44–49.

32 Foreman, pp. 44–49.

33 See, for example, Terrence Mitchell, "Expectancy-Value Models in Organizational Psychology," in N. P. Feather (Ed.), *Expectations and Actions: Expectancy-Value Models in Psychology* (Hillsdale, NJ: Erlbaum, 1982), pp. 293–312; see also Mark Tubbs et al., "Expectancy, Valence, and Motivational Force Functions in Goal Setting Research: An Empirical Test," *Journal of Applied Psychology*, June 1993, pp. 36–49; see also Peter Foreman, "Work Values and Expectancies in Occupational Rehabilitation: The Role of Cognitive Values in the Return to Work Process," *Journal of Rehabilitation*, July–September 1996, pp. 44–49.

34 Mark Tubbs, Donna Boehne, and James Dahl, "Expectancy, Valence, and Motivational Force Functions in Goal Setting Research: An Empirical Test," *Journal of Applied Psychology*, June 1993, pp. 361–373; Wendelien Van Eerde and Hank Thierry, "Vroom's Expectancy Model and Work-Related Criteria: A Meta-Analysis," *Journal of Applied Psychology*, October 1996, pp. 575–86; see also Robert Fudge and John Schlacter, "Motivating Employees to Act Ethically: An Expectancies Theory Approach," *Journal of Business Ethics*, February 1999, p. 295; see also Barbara Caska, "The Search for Employment: Motivation to Engage in a Coping Behavior," *Journal of Applied Social Psychology*, 1 February 1998, pp. 206–225.

35 Van Eerde and Thierry, pp. 576–586; see also Jason Colquitt, "Conscientiousness, Goal Orientation, and Motivation to Learn During the Learning Process: A Longitudinal Study," *Journal of Applied Psychology*, August 1998, pp. 654–666.

36 For a definition of learning, see Lefton and Valvatne, p. 161.

37 For a recent review of operant conditioning, see Fred Luthans and R. Kreitner, *Organizational Behavior Modification and Beyond: An Operant and Social Learning Approach* (Glenview, IL: Scott, Foresman, 1985); See also Nancy Chase, "You Get What You Reward," *Quality*, June 1999, p. 104.

38 W. Clay Hamner, "Reinforcement Theory in Management and Organizational Settings," in Henry Tosi and W. Clay Hamner (Eds.), *Organizational Behavior and Management: A Contingency Approach* (Chicago: Saint Claire, 1974), pp. 86–112. See also Donald J. Campbell, "The Effects of Goal-Contingent Payment on the Performance of a Complex Task," *Personnel Psychology*, Spring 1984, pp. 23–40; See also Robert Taylor, "Preventing Employee Theft: A Behavioral Approach," *Business Perspectives*, June 1998, pp. 9–14.

39 Alexander Stajkovic and Fred Luthans, "A Meta-Analysis of the Effects of Organizational Behavior Modifications on Task Performance, 1975–1976," *Academy of Management Journal*, 1997, vol. 40, no. 5, pp. 1122–1149; See also Robert Taylor, "Preventing Employee Theft: A Behavioral Approach," *Business Perspectives*, June 1998, pp. 9–14.

40 Cheryl Comeau-Kirschner, "Improving Productivity Doesn't Cost a Dime," *Management Review*, January 1999, p. 7.

41 Robert McNutt "Sharing Across the Board: DuPont's Achievement Sharing Program," *Compensation & Benefits Review*, July–August 1990, pp. 17–24.

42 Barry Thomas and Madeline Hess Olson, "Gainsharing: The Design Guarantees Success," *Personnel Journal*, May 1988, pp. 73–9. One of the most well known and well-established plans of this type is in place at the Lincoln Electric Company. See, for example, Kenneth Chilton, "Lincoln Electric's Incentive

System: A Reservoir of Trust," *Compensation and Benefits Review*, November 1994, pp. 29–34.

43 "The Fast Company Unit of One Anniversary Handbook," *Fast Company*, February–March 1997, p. 99.

44 James Lardner, "Okay Here Are Your Options," *U.S. News and World Report*, 1 March 1999 p. 44.

45 Naomi Weiss, "How Starbucks Impassions Workers to Drive Growth," *Workforce*, August, 1998, pp. 61–63.

46 See, for example, James Gutherie and Edward Cunningham, "Pay for Performance: The Quaker Oats Alternative," *Compensation & Benefits Review*, March–April 1992, pp. 18–23.

47 See, for example, Graham O'Neill, "Linking Pay to Performance: Conflicting Views and Conflicting Evidence," *Asia Pacific Journal of HRM*, Winter 1995, pp. 20–35.

48 See, for example, Kent Romanoff, "The Ten Commandments of Performance Management," *Personnel*, January 1989, pp. 24–8.

49 Sarah Braley, "Getting Technical: The Incentive Business Gets Wired Slowly," *Meetings and Conventions*, October 1997, pp. 13–16.

50 Braley, p. 13.

51 Braley, p. 43.

52 For a discussion see, for example, Gary Dessler, *Human Resource Management, 8th ed.* (Upper Saddle River, NJ: Prentice Hall, 2000), p. 452.

53 James Brinks, "Is There Merit in Merit Increases?" *Personnel Administrator*, May 1980, p. 60. See also Atul Migra et al., "The Case of the Invisible Merit Raise: How People See Their Pay Raises," *Compensation & Benefits Review*, May 1995, pp. 71–76.

54 Bob Nelson, *1001 Ways to Reward Employees* (New York: Workmen Publishing, 1994), p. 47.

55 Federal Express Corporation, *Blueprints for Service Quality*, pp. 34–35.

56 Cora Daniels, "Thank You Is Nice, But This Is Better," *Fortune*, 22 November 1999, p. 370.

57 Gerald Ledford, Jr., "Three Case Studies on Skill-Based Pay: An Overview," *Compensation & Benefits Review*, March–April 1991, pp. 11–23.

58 Gerald Ledford, Jr., and Gary Bergel, "Skill-Based Pay Case No. 1: General Mills," *Compensation & Benefits Review*, vol. 23, March–April 1991, pp. 24–38.

59 *Fast Company*, October 1999, p. 194.

60 Nelson, *1001 Ways to Reward Employees*, p. 19.

61 Nelson, *1001 Ways to Reward Employees*, p. 6. See also Bob Nelson, "Dump the Cash, Load on the Praise," *Personnel Journal*, July 1996, p. 65ff.

62 Ibid., p. 5.

63 Ibid., p. 5.

64 Ibid., p. 6.

65 Roberta Maynard, "How to Motivate Low-Wage Workers," *Nation's Business*, May 1997, pp. 35–38.

66 Ibid.

67 Scot Hays, "Pros and Cons of Pay for Performance," *Workforce*, February 1999, p. 69–74.

68 Hays, p. 70.

69 Chris Argyris, *Integrating the Individual and the Organization* (New York: John Wiley, 1964).

70 Samuel Melamed, Irit Ben-Avi, Jair Luz, and Manfred Green, "Objective and Subjective Work Monotony: Effects on Job Satisfaction, Psychological Distress, and Absenteeism in Blue Collar Workers," *Journal of Applied Psychology*, February 1995, pp. 29–42.

71 M. A. Campion and C. L. McClelland, "Interdisciplinary Examination of the Costs and Benefits of Enlarged Jobs: A Job Design Quasi-experiment," *Journal of Applied Psychology*, vol. 76, 1991, pp. 186–198.

72 M. A. Campion and C. L. McClelland, "Follow-up and Extension of the Interdisciplinary Costs and Benefits of Enlarged Jobs," *Journal of Applied Psychology*, vol. 78, 1993, pp. 339–351.

73 See, for example, J. Richard Hackman et al., "A New Strategy for Job Enrichment," *California Management Review*, pp. 57–71.

74 See, for example, J. Richard Hackman and Greg Oldham, "Motivation Through the Design of Work: Test of a Theory," *Organizational Behavior and Human Performance*, August 1976, pp. 250–279; and J. R. Hackman and G. Oldham, *Work Redesign* (Reading, MA: Addison-Wesley, 1980).

75 See, for example, Kenneth Thomas and Betty Velthouse, "Cognitive Elements of Empowerment: An Interpretive Model of Intrinsic Task Motivation," *Academy of Management Review*, vol. 15, no. 4, 1990, pp. 666–681. See also Allan J. H. Thorlackson and Robert P. Murray, "An Empirical Study of Empowerment in the Workplace," *Group and Organization Management*, March 1996, pp. 670–683.

76 Gene Phillips and Stanley Gully, "Role of Goal Orientation, Ability, Need for Achievement, and Locus of Control in the Self-Efficacy and Goal Setting Process," *Journal of Applied Psychology*, vol. 82, no. 5, 1997, pp. 790–782.

77 This is based on W. Clay Hamner and Ellen Hamner, "Behavior Modification on the Bottom Line," *Organizational Dynamics* (Spring 1976). For recent applications, see Greg LaBar, "Safety Incentives: Q & A Reveals Best Practices," *Occupational Hazards*, November 1996, pp. 51–56.

78 Gillian Flynn, "New Skills Equals New Opportunities," *Personnel Journal*, June 1996, pp. 77–79.

79 "The Benefits of Lifelong Learning," *Journal of European Industrial Training*, February–March 1997, p. 3.

80 Robert Taylor, "Preventing Employee Theft: A Behavioral Approach," *Business Perspectives*, June 1998, pp. 9–14.

81 Ibid.

82 *Fast Company*, October 1999, p. 202.

83 Ibid., p. 22.

84 Ibid., p. 188.

85 Gary Dessler, "How to Earn Your Employees Commitment," *Academy of Management Executive*, vol. 13, no. 2, 1999, pp. 58–67.

86 Dessler, op cit.

CHAPTER 11 APPENDIX

1 R. Cattel, *The Scientific Analysis of Personality* (Baltimore, Penguin Books, 1965). See also G. Northcraft and M. Neale, *Organizational Behavior* (Hinsdale, IL: Dryden Press, 1994), pp. 64–240.

2 See for example, Jesus Delgado, "The Five Factor Model of Personality and Job Performance in the European Community," *Journal of Applied Psychology*, vol. 82, no. 1, 1997, pp. 30–43.

3 Murray Barrick and Michael Mount, "The Big Five Personality Dimension and Job Performance: A Meta-Analysis," *Personal Psychology*, Spring 1991, pp. 1–26.

4 James Bowditch and Anthony Buono, *A Primer on Organizational Behavior* (New York: John Wiley, 1994), p. 115.

5 Based on Ernest J. McCormick and Joseph Tiffin, *Industrial Psychology* (Upper Saddle River, NJ: Prentice-Hall, 1974), pp. 136–174. See also Marilyn Gist and Terence Mitchell, "Self-Efficacy: A Theoretical Analysis of its Determinants and Malleability," *Academy of Management Review*, April 1992, pp. 183–202.

6 Saul Gellerman, *Motivation and Productivity* (New York: AMACOM).

7 Lefton and Valvatne, p. 412.

8 Ibid.

9 Ibid.

10 Gist and Mitchell, p. 183.

11 For a review and listing of these studies, see Gist and Mitchell, pp. 183–211.

12 Ernest R. Hilgard, *Introduction to Psychology* (New York: Harcourt Brace and World, 1962), p. 86.

13 Timothy Costello and Sheldon Zalkind, *Psychology in Administration* (Upper Saddle River, NJ: Prentice-Hall, 1963), pp. 315–316.

14 Benson Rosen and Thomas Jerdee, "The Influence of Age Stereotypes on Managerial Decisions," *Journal of Applied Psychology*, August 1976, pp. 428–432.

15 Hilgard, p. 476; see also R. Heneman et al., "Attributions and Exchanges: The Effects of Interpersonal Factors on the Diagnosis of Employee Performance," *Academy of Management Journal*, June 1989, pp. 466–478; and Mary Ann Glynow, "Effects of Work Task Cues and Play Task Cues on Information Processing, Judgment and Motivation," *Journal of Applied Psychology*, February 1994, pp. 34–46.

16 Martin Fishbein and Icek Ajzen, *Attitude, Intention and Behavior: An Introduction to Theory and Research* (Reading, MA: Addison-Wesley, 1975).

17 All About Your Company, *IBM Employee Handbook*, p. 184.

18 The Job Descriptive Index is copyrighted by Bowling Green State University, and can be obtained from Dr. Patricia C. Smith, Department of Psychology, Bowling Green State University, Bowling Green, Ohio, 43403.

19 See, for example, M. T. Iaffaldano and M. P. Muchinsky, "Job Satisfaction and Job Performance: A Meta-Analysis," *Psychological Bulletin*, March 1985, pp. 251–273.

CHAPTER 12

1 Paul Roberts, "Live! From Your Office!" *Fast Company*, October 1999, p. 152.

2 Ibid.

3 George Miller, *Language and Communication* (New York: McGraw-Hill, 1951), p. 10, discussed in Gary Hunt, *Communication Skills in the Organization, 2nd ed.* (Upper Saddle River, NJ: Prentice-Hall, 1989), p. 29.

4 This is discussed in and based on Fred Luthans and Janet Larsen, "How Managers Really Communicate," *Human Relations*, 1986, p. 162.

5 Daniel Katz and Robert Kahn, *The Social Psychology of Organizations* (New York: Wiley, 1966).

6 This model is based on the classic and best-known communication model by Claude E. Shannon and Warren Weaver and is adapted by using several improvements suggested by Sanford, Hunt, and Bracey. Both models are presented in Hunt, *Communication Skills*, pp. 34–36.

7 This section on dealing with communication barriers is based on R. Wayne Pace and Don Faules, Organizational Communication, (Upper Saddle River, NJ: Prentice Hall, 1989), pp. 150–162, unless otherwise noted. See also Tom Geddie, "Leap Over Communications Barriers," *Communication World*, April 1994, pp. 12–17.

8 Pace and Faules, p. 153.

9 Jack Griffin, *How to Say It at Work* (Paramus, NJ: Prentice Hall Press, 1998), pp. 26–28.

10 Ernest Gundling, "How to Communicate Globally," *Training and Development*, June 1999, pp. 28–32.

11 Ibid., p. 29.

12 Robert Zmud, "Channel Expansion Theory and the Experiential Nature of Media Richness Perceptions," *Academy of Management Journal*, April 1999, p. 153.

13 For instance, see Jay Knippn and Thad Green, "How the Manager Can Use Active Listening," *Public Personnel Management*, Summer 1994, pp. 357–359. See also Sally Planalp, "Commu-

nicating Emotion: Not Just for Interpersonal Scholars Anymore," *Communication Theory*, May 1999, p. 216.

14 Griffin, pp. 86–220.

15 Ibid., p. 178.

16 James C. Freund, *Smart Negotiating* (New York: Simon & Schuster, 1992), pp. 42–46.

17 Ibid., p. 33.

18 Griffin, pp. 107–109.

19 Bob Smith, "Care and Feeding of the Office Grapevine," *Management Review*, February 1996, p. 6.

20 Eugene Walton, "How Efficient Is the Grapevine?" *Personnel*, March/April 1961, pp. 45–49, reprinted in Davis, *Organizational Behavior, A Book of Readings*.

21 Keith Davis, "Cut Those Rumors Down to Size," *Supervisory Management*, June 1975, p. 206.

22 Jitendra Sharma, "Organizational Communications: A Linking Process," *The Personnel Administrator,* July 1979, pp. 35–43. See also Victor Callan, "Subordinate-Manager Communication in Different Sex Dyads: Consequences for Job Satisfaction," *Journal of Occupational and Organizational Psychology*, March 1993, pp. 13–28.

23 William Convoy, Working Together . . . Communication in a Healthy Organization (Columbus, OH: Charles Merrill, 1976). See also David Johnson et al. "Differences Between Formal and Informal Communication Channels," *Journal of Business Communication*, April 1994, pp. 111–124.

24 Gary Dessler, *Winning Commitment: How to Build and Keep a Competitive Workforce* (New York: McGraw-Hill, 1993).

25 Pace and Faules, pp. 105–106. See also Joanne Yates and Wanda Orlinkowski, "Genres of Organizational Communication: A Structurational Approach to Studying Communication and Media," *Academy of Management Review*, April 1992, pp. 299–327.

26 Earl Plenty and William Machaner, "Stimulating Upward Communication," in Jerry Gray and Frederick Starke (Eds.), *Readings in Organizational Behavior* (Columbus: Merrill, 1977), pp. 229–240. See also Pace and Faules, pp. 153–160.

27 For a discussion of this see Karlene Roberts and Charles O'Reilly III. "Failures in Upward Communication in Organizations: Three Possible Culprits," *Academy of Management Journal*, vol. 17, no. 2, June 1974, pp. 205–215.

28 Based on Stewart, "How GE Keeps Those Ideas Coming."

29 Ibid., p. 42.

30 Ibid.

31 Ibid.

32 Ibid., p. 43.

33 Ibid.

34 *Federal Express Employee Handbook*, p. 89.

35 Toyota Motor Manufacturing, USA, *Team-Member Handbook*, February 1988, pp. 52–53.

36 For a recent review and a discussion see James Smithers et al., "An Examination of the Effects of an Upward Feedback Program Over Time," *Personnel Psychology*, vol. 48, 1995, pp. 1–34.

37 Ibid., pp. 10–11.

38 Ibid., p. 27.

39 Pace and Faules, pp. 99–100.

40 Personal interview, March 1992.

41 Personal interview, March 1992.

42 "Employers Profit from Opening the Books," *Bureau of National Affairs Bulletin to Management*, 5 September 1999, p. 288.

43 Ibid.

44 Paul Hansen, Getting Your Team on the Same Side," *Financial Executive*, March–April 1994, pp. 43–48.

45 Ibid., p. 43.

46 Ibid., p. 44.

47 Ibid., p. 45.

48 This is based on Tom Peters and Robert Waterman, *In Search of Excellence* (New York: Harper & Row), pp. 119–218. On the other hand, creating too much an emphasis on "free speech" can make firms vulnerable to lawsuits and other problems if employees are too quick to speak their minds, according to one expert. See Scott Hayes, "Censored! Free speech at work," *Workforce*, Sept. 1999, pp. 34–38.

49 Ibid., p. 122.

50 Ibid., p. 124.

51 Ibid., pp. 218–220, 122–123.

52 Ibid., p. 219.

53 Ibid., p. 22.

54 Ibid., pp. 122–123.

55 Harold Leavitt, "Some Effects of Certain Communication Patterns on Group Performance," *Journal of Abnormal and Social Psychology*, vol. 46, 1972, pp. 38–50.

56 Ron Lieber, "Information Is Everything," *Fast Company*, November 1999, pp. 246–254.

57 Ibid., p. 253.

58 Ibid.

59 Sarah Schafer, "E-mail Grows Up," *Inc. Technology*, vol. 1, 1997, pp. 87–88.

60 Stephen Loudermilk, "Desktop Video Conferencing Getting Prime Time," *PC Week*, 19 October 1992, p. 81.

61 Paul Saffo, "The Future of Travel," *Fortune*, Autumn 1993, p. 119.

62 Kenneth Laudon and Jane Laudon, *Essentials of Management Information Systems* (Upper Saddle River, NJ: Prentice-Hall, 1997), p. 413.

63 David Kroenke and Richard Hatch, *Management Information Systems* (New York: McGraw-Hill, 1994), p. 359.

64 Robert Ford and Michael Butts, "Is Your Organization Ready for Telecommuting?" *SAM Advanced Management Journal*, Autumn 1991, p. 19; and Laudon and Laudon, *Essentials*, pp. 413–416.

65 Ibid.

66 See Sandra Atchison, "The Care and Feeding of Loan Eagles," *Business Week*, 15 November 1993, p. 58.

67 David Kirkpatrick, "Hot New PC Services," *Fortune*, November 1992, p. 108. See also Amy Cortese, "Here Comes the Intranet," *Business Week*, February 1996.

68 Kenneth Laudon and Jane Laudon, *Management Information Systems* (Upper Saddle River, NJ: Prentice Hall, 1998), p. 128.

69 Ibid., 128.

70 Amy Newman, "How to Create a Virtual Learning Community," *Training & Development*, July 1999, p. 44.

71 Tim Stevens, "Internet-Aided Design," *Industry Week*, 23 June 1997, pp. 50–55.

72 Ibid.

73 Joann Davy, "Online at the Office: Virtual Communities Go to Work," *Managing Office Technology*, July–August 1998, pp. 9–11.

74 Ibid.

75 David Kirkpatrick, "The Portal of the Future? Your Boss Will Run It," *Fortune*, 2 August 1999, pp. 222–227.

76 Ibid.

77 Roger E. Axtell (Ed.), *Do's and Taboos Around the World* (New York: Wiley, 1985), pp. 37–38.

CHAPTER 13

1 Carla Johnson, "Teams at Work," *HRMagazine*, May 1999, pp. 29–36.

2 Ibid., 30.

3 Jack Gordon, "Work Teams: How Far Have They Come?" *Training*, October 1992, pp. 60–65. See also Cheryl Dahle, "Extreme Teams," *Fast Company*, November 1999, pp. 311–326.

4 "Outlook on Teams," *National Affairs Bulletin to Management*, 20 March 1997, pp. 92–93.

5 For employee involvement survey data, see Lee Towe, "Survey Finds Employee Involvement a Priority for Necessary Innovation, " *National Productivity Review*, Winter 1989–90, pp. 3–15. See also Bradley Kirkman and Benson Rosen, "Beyond Self-Management: Antecedents and Consequences of Team Empowerment," *Academy of Management Journal*, February 1999, pp. 58–74.

6 Jack Osburn, Linda Moran, Ed Musselwhite, John Zenger, and Craig Perrin, *Self-Directed Work Teams: The New American Challenge* (Homewood, IL: Business One Irwin, 1990), p. 33. See also Bradley Kirkman, "Beyond Self-Management: Antecedents and Consequences of Team Empowerment," *Academy of Management Journal*, February 1999, pp. 58–74.

7 Ibid.

8 Ibid., p. 34. See also Charles Manz, "Self-Leading Work Teams: Moving Beyond Self-Management Myths," *Human Relations*, vol. 45, no. 11, 1992, pp. 1119–1141.

9 See, for example, John Katzenbach and Douglas Smith, "The Discipline of Teams," *Harvard Business Review*, March–April 1993, pp. 112–113. Note that many researchers do not, however, distinguish between groups and teams. See, for example, Gary Coleman and Eileen M. VanAken, "Applying Small-Group Behavior Dynamics to Improve Action-Team Performance," *Employment Relations Today*, Autumn 1991, pp. 343–353.

10 These definitions are from Marvin E. Shaw, *Group Dynamics: The Psychology of Small Group Behavior* (New York: McGraw-Hill, 1976), p. 11.

11 Jon Katzenbach and Jason Santamaria, "Firing Up the Front-Line," *Harvard Business Review*, May–June 1999, p. 114.

12 Sandra Robinson and Ann O'Leary-Kelly," Monkey See, Monkey Do: The Influence of Workgroups on the Antisocial Behavior of Employees," *Academy of Management Journal* 41, no. 6, 1988, 658–672.

13 Ibid., 667.

14 Daniel Feldman, "The Development and Enforcement of Group Norms," *Academy of Management Review*, vol. 9, no. 1, 1984, 47–53.

15 A. P. Hare, *Handbook of Small Group Research* (New York: The Free Press, 1962), 24. See also S. Barr and E. Conlon, "Effects of Distribution of Feedback in Work Groups," *Academy of Management Journal*, June 1994, pp. 641–656.

16 See Stephen Worchel, Wendy Wood, and Jeffrey Simpson, *Group Process and Productivity* (Newbury Park, CA: Sage Publications, 1992), pp. 45–50.

17 Ibid., p. 245.

18 For a discussion of the difficulty of measuring and defining cohesiveness, see Peter Mudrack, "Group Cohesiveness and Productivity: A Closer Look," *Human Relations*, vol. 42, no. 9, 1989, pp. 771–785. See also R. Saavedra et al., "Complex Interdependence in Task-Performing Groups," *Journal of Applied Psychology*, February 1993, pp. 61–73.

19 See Marvin Shaw, *Group Dynamics* (New York: McGraw-Hill, 1976), Chapter 4.

20 Robert Blake and Jane Mouton, "Reactions to Inter-Group Competition under Win-Lose Conditions," *Management Science*, vol. 7, 1961, p. 432.

21 John R. P. French, Jr., "The Disruption and Cohesion of Groups," *Journal of Abnormal and Social Psychology*, vol. 36, 1941, pp. 361–77.

22 Stanley C. Seashore, *Group Cohesiveness in the Industry Work Group* (Ann Arbor, MI: Survey Research Center, University of Michigan, 1954), pp. 90–5; Joseph Litterer, *The Analysis of Organizations* (New York: Wiley, 1965), pp. 91–101; and J. Haleblian and S. Finkelstein, "Top Management Team Size, CEO Dominance, and Firm Performance: The Moderating Roles of Environmental Turbulence and Discretion," *Academy of Management Journal*, August 1993, pp. 844–864.

23 This material is based on James H. Shonk, *Team-Based Organizations* (Chicago: Irwin, 1997), pp. 27–33.

24 Ibid., p. 28.

25 Ibid., p. 29.

26 Katzenbach and Smith, pp. 116–118.

27 Everett Adams, Jr., "Quality Circle Performance," *Journal of Management*, vol. 17, no. 1, 1991, pp. 25–39.

28 Ibid.

29 Eric Sundstrom, Kenneth DeMeuse, and David Futrell, "Workteams: Applications and Effectiveness," *American Psychologist*, February 1990, p. 120. See also Ruth Wagman, "Task Design, Outcome Interdependence, and Individual Differences: Their Joint Effects on Effort in Task Performing Teams," *Group Dynamics*, June 1999, pp. 132–137.

30 See, for example, Adams, "Quality Circle Performance"; and Gilbert Fuchsberg, "Quality Programs Show Shoddy Results," *Wall Street Journal*, 14 May 1992, pp. B-1, B-4.

31 Gopal Pati, Robert Salitore, and Saundra Brady, "What Went Wrong with Quality Circles?" *Personnel Journal*, December 1987, pp. 83–89.

32 Philip Olson, "Choices for Innovation Minded Corporations," *Journal of Business Strategy*, January–February 1990, pp. 86–90.

33 In many firms, the concept of a venture team is taken to what may be its natural conclusion in that new-venture units and new-venture divisions are established. These are separate divisions devoted to new-product development. See, for example, Christopher Bart, "New Venture Units: Use Them Wisely to Manage Innovation," *Sloan Management Review*, Summer 1988, pp. 35–43; and Robert Burgelman, "Managing the New Venture Division: Research Findings and Implications for Strategic Management," *Strategic Management Journal*, vol. 6, 1985, pp. 39–54.

34 Charles Snow, Scott Snell, Sue Canney Davison, and Donald Hambrick, "Use Transnational Teams to Globalize Your Company," *Organizational Dynamics*, Spring 1996, pp. 50–67.

35 Ibid., p. 50.

36 Ibid.

37 Ibid., pp. 53–57.

38 Lynda McDermott, Bill Waite, and Nolan Brawley, "Putting Together a World-Class Team," *Training and Development*, January 1999, p. 48.

39 Charles Snow et al., p. 61.

40 Based on suggestions by David Armstrong, "Making Dispersed Teams Work," *Bureau of National Affairs Bulletin to Management*, 23 May 1996, p. 168.

41 Anthony Townsend, Samuel DiMarie, and Anthony Hendrickson, "Virtual Teams: Technology and the Workplace of the Future," *Academy of Management Executive*, vol. 12, no. 3, 1998, pp. 17–29.

42 Ibid., 20.

43 Christa Degnan, "ActiveProject Aids Teamwork," *PC Week*, 31 May 1999, p. 35.

44 Ibid., pp. 21–22.

45 Rochelle Garner, "Round-the-World Teamwork," *Computerworld*, 24 May 1999, p. 46.

46 Jack Orsburn et al., p. 8.

47 Charles Fishman, "Engines of Democracy," *Fast Company*, Oct. 1999, pp. 173–202.

48 Tom Peters, *Liberation Management* (New York: Alfred Knopf, 1992), pp. 238–239.

49 Orsburn et al., pp. 20–27.

50 Ibid., p. 21.

51 Ibid., p. 22.

52 Ibid., pp. 22–23.

53 "Kodak's Team Structure is Picture Perfect," *Bureau of National Affairs Bulletin to Management*, 15 August 1996, p. 264.

54 Rojiv Banker, Roger Schroeder, and Kingshuk Sinha, "Impact of Work Teams on Manufacturing Performance: A Longitudinal Field Study," *Academy of Management Journal*, vol. 39, no. 4, 1996, pp. 867–888.

55 Ibid., p. 887–888.

56 Ibid., p. 870.

57 Ralph King, Jr., "Levi's Factory Workers are Assigned to Teams, and Morale has Taken a Hit," *Wall Street Journal*, 20 May 1998, pp. A-1, A-6.

58 Based on Erin Neurick, "Facilitating Effective Work Teams," *SAM Advanced Management Journal*, Winter 1993, pp. 22–26. See also Margarita Alegria, "Building Effective Research Teams When Conducting Drug Prevention Research with Minority Populations," *Drugs & Society*, 1999, vol. 14, no. 1–2, pp. 227—245. George Neuman and Julie Wright, "Team Effectiveness: Beyond Skills and Cognitive Ability," *Journal of Applied Psychology*, June 1999, pp. 376–389.

59 Ibid., p. 23.

60 Joann Keyton, "Analyzing Interaction Patterns in Dysfunctional Teams," *Small Group Research*, August 1999, pp. 491–518.

61 Suchitra Mouly and Jayaram Sankaran, "Barriers to the Cohesiveness and Effectiveness of Indian R&D Project Groups: Insights from Four Federal R&D Organizations," in John Wagner, et al., *Advances in Qualitative Organization Research, vol. 2* (Stanford, CT: A.I. Press, 1999), pp. 221–243.

62 Ibid.

63 Discussed in Paul Mulvey, John Veiga, and Priscilla Elsass, "When Teammates Raise the White Flag," *Academy of Management Executive*, vol. 10, no. 1, 1996, p. 40. See also Richard Hackman, "Why Teams Don't Work," in R. Tindale, et al., *Theory and Research on Small Groups: Social Psychological Applications in Social Issues, vol. 4* (Plenum Press, New York, 1998), pp. 245–267.

64 The following, excerpt as noted, is based on Glenn H. Varney, *Building Productive Teams: An Action Guide and Resource Book* (San Francisco: Jossey-Bass Publishers, 1989), pp. 11–18. See also P. Bernthal and C. Insko, "Cohesiveness without Group Think: The Interactive Effects of Social and Task Cohesion," *Group and Organization Management*, March 1993, pp. 66–88; and Vanessa Druskat, "The Antecedents of Team Competence: Toward a Fine-Grained Model of Self-Managing Team Effectiveness," *Research on Managing Groups and Teams: Groups in Context, vol. 2*, (Stamford, CT: Jai Press, 1999), 1999, pp. 201–231.

65 Svan Lembke and Maria Wilson, "Putting the Team into Teamwork: Alternative Theoretical Contributions for Contemporary Management Practice," *Human Relations*, July 1998, pp. 927–944.

66 Xial-Ping Chen, "Workteam Cooperation: The Effects of Structural and Motivational Changes," in Margaret Foddy, et al., *Resolving Social Dilemmas: Dynamic, Structural, and Intergroup Aspects* (Philadelphia, PA: Psychology Press/Taylor & Francis, 1999), pp. 181–192.

67 George Neuman and Julie Wright, "Team Effectiveness: Beyond Skills and Cognitive Ability," *Journal of Applied Psychology*, June 1999, pp. 376–389.

68 Katzenbach and Smith, p. 112. See also C. Meyer, "How the Right Measures Help Teams Excel," *Harvard Business Review*, May–June 1994, p. 112.

69 See G. T. Shea and R. A. Guzzo, "Groups as Human Resources," K. M. Roland and G. R. Ferris, (Eds.), *Research in Personnel and Human Resources Management*, vol. 5 (Greenwich, CT: JAI Press, 1987), pp. 323–356. See also Sundstrom, DeMeuse, and Futrell, p. 123.

70 Katzenbach and Smith, p. 113.

71 Ibid. The evaluation process is important as well. See R. Saavedra and S. Kwun, "Peer Evaluation in Self-Managing Work Groups," *Journal of Applied Psychology*, June 1993, pp. 450–463.

72 Michael West and Neil Anderson, "Innovation in Top Management Teams," *Journal of Applied Psychology*, December 1996, pp. 680–693.

73 See Campion and Higgs, pp. 102–103. See also Michael Campion, Ellen Papper, and Gina Medsker, "Relations Between Work Team Characteristics and Effectiveness: A Replication and Extension," *Personnel Psychology*, Summer 1996, pp. 429–452.

74 Ibid., p. 102.

75 Ibid., p. 103–104.

76 Joan Glaman, Allan Jones, and Richard Rozelle, "The Effects of Co-Worker Similarity on the Emergence of Affect in Work Teams," *Group & Organization Management*, June 1996, pp. 192–215.

77 The remaining items in this section, except as noted, are quoted from or based on Michael A. Campion and A. Catherine Higgs, "Design Work Teams to Increase Productivity and Satisfaction," *HR Magazine*, October 1995, pp. 101–7. See also Steven G. Rogelberg and Steven M. Rumery, "Gender Diversity, Team Decision Quality, Time on Task, and Interpersonal Cohesion," *Small Group Research*, February 1996, pp. 79–90; Steven E. Gross and Jeffrey Blair, "Reinforcing Team Effectiveness Through Pay," *Compensation & Benefits Review*, September 1995, pp. 34–38; and Joan M. Glaman, Allan P. Jones, and Richard M. Rozelle, "The Effects of Co-Worker Similarity on the Emergence of Affect in Work Teams," *Group and Organization Management*, June 1996, pp. 192–215.

78 John Day, "Warewithal Online: Assemble Teams Based on Employee Instincts," *HRMagazine*, August 1999, pp. 124–130. See also Michael Stevens and Michael Campion, "Staffing Work Teams: Development and Validation of a Selection Test for Teamwork Settings," *Journal of Management*, 1999, vol. 25, no. 2, pp. 207–228.

79 "Getting the Most from Employee Teams," *Bureau of National Affairs Bulletin to Management*, 20 March 1997, p. 96.

80 David Hyatt and Thomas Ruddy, "An Examination of the Relationship Between Workgroup Characteristics and Performance: Once More into the Breach," *Personnel Psychology*, 1997, p. 577.

81 Ibid., p. 578.

82 Kimball Fisher, pp. 151–153.

83 Ibid., p. 44.

84 These are based on Fisher, pp. 48–56.

85 Ibid., p. 53.

86 Gary Dessler, *Winning Commitment* (New York: McGraw-Hill, 1992), p. 28.

87 Ibid., p. 30.

88 For a discussion see Fisher, p. 106.

89 Ibid., pp. 110–111.

90 Ibid., p. 110.

91 Shonk, p. 133.

92 See Shonk, pp. 133–138; Andrew DuBrin, *Leadership: Research Findings, Practice and Skills* (Boston: Houghton-Mifflin, 1995), pp. 224–227.

93 Shonk, p. 133.

94 Fisher, p. 143

95 Ibid., p. 143.

96 "Back in Harmony," The Rocky Mountain News, 6 May 1990, p. 67.

97 Erin V. Lehman, "Is the Glass Half Empty or Half Full? Organizational Change at the Colorado Symphony Orchestra, 1990–1991 to 1998–1999," in *Lessons Learned: Case Studies* (Washington, DC: National Endowment for the Arts).

CHAPTER 14

1 Linda Grant, "Menaced Moments," *Fortune*, 27 October 1997, p. 188; and Linda Grant, "Kodak Still Is in a Fix," *Fortune*, 11 May 1998, pp. 179–181.

2 See for example, Martha Peak, "An Era of Wrenching Corporate Change," *Management Review*, July 1996, pp. 45–49. See also Elias Carayannis, "Organizational Transformation and Strategic Learning in High Risk, High Complexity Environment," *Technovation*, February 1999, pp. 87–94.

3 Melanie Warner, "Nightmare on Net Street," *Fortune*, 6 September 1999, pp. 285–288.

4 Ibid., p. 286.

5 Based on David Nadler and Michael Tushman, "Beyond the Charismatic Leader: Leadership and Organizational Change," *California Management Review*, Winter 1990, p. 80; and Alfred Marcus, "Responses to Externally Induced Innovation: To their Effects on Organizational Performance," *Strategic Management Journal*, vol. 9, (1988), pp. 194–202. See also Steve Crom, "Change Leadership: the Virtues of Obedience," *Leadership & Organization Development Journal*, March–June 1999, pp. 162–168.

6 Nadler and Tushman, p. 80.

7 Gary Dessler, *Winning Commitment: How to Build and Keep a Competitive Work Force* (New York: McGraw-Hill, 1993), p. 85.

8 Ibid., p. 85. See also Varun Grover, "From Business Reengineering to Business Process Change Management: A Longitudinal Study of Trends and Practices," *IEEE Transactions on Engineering Management*, February 1999, p. 36.

9 Denison, Corporate Culture, p. 12. For a recent discussion see also Daniel Denison, "What Is the Difference between Organizational Culture and Organizational Climate? A Native's Point of View on a Decade of Paradigm Wars," *Academy of Management Review*, July 1996, pp. 619–654.

10 Nadler and Tushman, 79.

11 Niccolo Machiavelli (trans. W. K. Marriott), *The Prince*, (London: J. M. Dent & Sons, Ltd., 1958).

12 Richard Osborne, "Core Values Statements: The Corporate Compass," *Business Horizons*, September–October 1991, pp. 28–34.

13 John Mariotti, "The Challenge of Change," *Industry Week*, 6 April 1998, p. 140.

14 Paul Lawrence, "How to Deal with Resistance to Change," *Harvard Business Review*, May–June, 1954. See also Andrew W. Schwartz, "Eight Guidelines for Managing Change," *Supervisory Management*, July 1994, pp. 3–5; Thomas J. Werner and Robert F. Lynch, "Challenges of a Change Agent" *Journal for Quality and Participation*, June 1994, pp. 50–54; Larry Reynolds, "Understand Employees' Resistance to Change," *HR Focus*, June 1994, pp. 17–18; Kenneth E. Hultman, "Scaling the Wall of Resistance," *Training & Development Journal*, October 1995, pp. 15–18; and Eric Dent, "Challenging Resistance to Change," *Journal of Applied Behavioral Science*, March 1999, p. 25.

15 Timothy Judge et al., "Managerial Coping with Organizational Change: A Dispositional Perspective," *Journal of Applied Psychology*, vol. 84, no. 1, 1999, pp. 107–122.

16 Kurt Lewin, "Group Decision and Social Change," in T. Newcomb and E. Hartley, (Eds.), *Readings in Social Psychology* (New York: Holt Rinehart & Winston, 1947). See also Thomas Cummings and Christopher Worley, *Organization Development and Change* (Minneapolis: West Publishing Company, 1993), p. 53. See also Terry Neese, "Convincing Your Employees to Accept Change," *LI Business News*, 7 March 1999, p. 41.

17 Charles Philips, "Can He Fix Philips?" *Fortune*, 31 May 1997, pp. 98–100.

18 John P. Kotter, *Leading Change* (Boston: Harvard Business School Press, 1996), pp. 40–41.

19 Ibid., p. 44.

20 Ibid., p. 57.

21 Ibid., pp. 90–91.

22 Ibid., pp. 101–102.

23 Kathryn Harris, "Mr. Sony Confronts Hollywood," *Fortune*, 23 December 1996, p. 36.

24 Noel Tichy and Ram Charan, "The CEO as Coach: An Interview with Allied Signal's Lawrence A. Bossidy," *Harvard Business Review*, March–April 1995, p. 77.

25 Suzy Wetlaufer, "Driving Change: An Interview with Ford Motor Co.'s Jacques Nasser," *Harvard Business Review*, March–April 1999, pp. 77–88.

26 Christian Ellis and E. Michael Norman, "Real Change in Real-Time," *Management Review*, February 1999, pp. 33–38.

27 Beer, Eisenstat, and Spector, 163.

28 This is based on Kotter, "Leading Change: Why Transformation Efforts Fail," pp. 61–66.

29 Ibid., p. 65.

30 Beer, Eisenstat, and Spector, p. 164.

31 Erin Brown, "Big Business Meets the E World," *Fortune*, 8 November 1999, p. 88.

32 Ibid., p. 91.

33 Ibid.

34 David Baum, "Running the Rapids," *Profit Magazine*, November 1999, p. 54.

35 Ibid.

36 Stewart Alsop, "E or Be Eaten," *Fortune*, 8 November 1999, pp. 94–95.

37 Laurie Windham, "Exec Help Wanted," *Profit Magazine*, November 1999, pp. 13–15.

38 The following is based on Nadler and Tushman, pp. 77–97.

39 Ibid., p. 82.

40 Ibid., p. 85.

41 For a discussion see Julian Barling, Tom Weber, and E. Kevin Kelloway, "Effects of Transformational Leadership Training on Attitudinal and Financial Outcomes: A Field Experiment," *Journal of Applied Psychology*, December 1996, pp. 827–832.

42 Ibid.

43 See, for example, John Rizzo, Robert J. House, and Sydney I. Lirtzinan, "Role Conflict and Ambiguity in Complex Organizations," *Administrative Science Quarterly*, 15 June 1970, pp. 150–63. For additional views on sources of conflict, see Patricia A. Gwartney-Gibbs and Denise H. Lach, "Gender Differences in Clerical Workers' Disputes Over Tasks," *Human Relations*, June 1994, pp. 611–40; and Kevin J. Williams and George Alliger, "Role Stressors, Mood Spillover, and Perceptions of Work-Family Conflict in Employed Parents," *Academy of Management Journal*, August 1994, pp. 837–869.

44 Cummings and Worley, p. 3.

45 Based on J. T. Campbell and M. D. Dunnette, "Effectiveness of T-Group Experiences in Managerial Training and Development" *Psychological Bulletin*, 7, 1968, pp. 73–104, reprinted in W. E. Scott and L. L. Cummings, *Readings in Organizational Behavior and Human Performance* (Homewood, IL: Irwin, 1973), p. 571.

46 Robert J. House, *Management Development* (Ann Arbor, MI: Bureau of Industrial Relations, University of Michigan, 1967), p. 71; and Louis White and Kevin Wooten, "Ethical Dilemmas in Various Stages of Organizational Development," *Academy of Management Review*, vol. 8, no. 4 (1983) pp. 690–697.

47 Wendell French and Cecil Bell, Jr., *Organization Development* (Upper Saddle River, NJ: Prentice-Hall, 1995), pp. 171–193.

48 Chuck McVinney, "Dream Weaver: An OD Consultant Can Get Together All of the Essential Elements for a Successful Startup," *Training and Development*, April 1999, pp. 38–43.

49 Cummings and Worley, p. 501.

50 For a description of how to make OD a part of organizational strategy, see Aubrey Mendelow and S. Jay Liebowitz, "Diffi-

culties in Making OD a Part of Organizational Strategy," *Human Resource Planning*, vol. 12, no. 4 (1995) pp. 317–329.

51 See, for example, John Rizzo, Robert J. House, and Sydney I. Lirtzinan, "Role Conflict and Ambiguity in Complex Organizations," *Administrative Science Quarterly*, June 1970, pp. 150–63; For additional views on sources of conflict, see Patricia A. Gwartney-Gibbs and Denise H. Lach, "Gender Differences in Clerical Workers' Disputes Over Tasks," Human Relations , June 1994, pp. 611–640; and Kevin J. Williams and George Alliger, "Role Stressors, Mood Spillover, and Perceptions of Work-Family Conflict in Employed Parents," *Academy of Management Journal*, August 1994, pp. 837–869. See also Howard Guttman, "Conflict at the Top," *Management Review*, November 1999, p. 49.

52 Yitzhak Fried and Robert B. Tiegs, "Supervisors' Role Conflict and Role Ambiguity: Differential Relations with Performance Ratings of Subordinates and the Moderating Effect of Screening Ability," *Journal of Applied Psychology*, April 1995, pp. 282–291.

53 Ibid., p. 291.

54 See, for example, Richard Walton and John Dutton, "The Management of Interdepartment Conflict: A Model and Review," *Administrative Science Quarterly*, March 1969, pp. 73–84.

55 John Dutton and Richard Walton, "Interdepartmental Conflict and Cooperation: Two Contrasting Studies," *Human Organization*, vol. 25, 1966, pp. 207–220.

56 H. A. Lansberger, "The Horizontal Dimensions in a Bureaucracy," *Administrative Science Quarterly*, vol. 6, 1961, pp. 298–333.

57 Paul Lawrence and Jay Lorsch, *Organization and Environment* (Boston: Harvard University, Graduate School of Business Administration, Division of Research, 1967).

58 John A. Seiler, "Diagnosing Interdepartmental Conflict," *Harvard Business Review*, September–October 1963, pp. 121–132.

59 Eric Neilson, "Understanding and Managing Intergroup Conflict," in Paul Lawrence and Jay Lorsch, *Organizational Behavior and Administration* (Homewood, IL: Irwin, 1976), p. 294. See also Robin L. Pinkley and Gregory B. Northcraft, "Conflict Frames of Reference: Implications for Dispute Processes and Outcomes," *Academy of Management Journal*, February 1994, pp. 193–206.

60 Lawrence and Lorsch, *Organization and Environment*, pp. 74–75.

61 Kenneth Thomas, "Conflict and Conflict Management," in Marvin Dunnette, *Handbook of Industrial and Organizational Psychology* (Chicago: Rand McNally, 1976), pp. 900–902; and Michael Carrell, Daniel Jennings, and Christina Heavrin, *Fundamentals of Organizational Behavior* (Upper Saddle River, NJ: Prentice-Hall, 1997), pp. 505–509.

62 This section is based on Evert Van De Vliert, Martin Euwema, and Sipke Huismans, "Managing Conflict with a Subordinate or a Superior: Effectiveness of Conglomerated Behavior," *Journal of Applied Psychology*, April 1995, pp. 271–281.

CHAPTER 15

1 Tim McCullom, "Getting Control of All That Paper," *Nation's Business*, 1 November 1998, p. 30.

2 Kenneth Merchant, "The Control Function of Management," *Sloan Management Review*, Summer 1982, p. 44.

3 This section is based on William Newman, *Constructive Control* (Upper Saddle River, NJ: Prentice Hall, 1995), pp. 6–9.

4 Kristina Sullivan, "Boeing Achieves Internet Liftoff," *PC Week*, 10 May 1999, p. 67.

5 Ibid.

6 Glenn A. Welsch, *Budgeting: Profit Planning and Control* (Upper Saddle River, NJ: Prentice Hall, 1988), p. 16.

7 Thomas Connellan, *How to Improve Human Performance: Behaviorism in Business and Industry* (New York: Harper & Row, 1978), pp. 68–73.

8 For a discussion, see Joan Woodward, *Industrial Organization: Behavior and Control* (London: Oxford, 1970), pp. 37–56.

9 Robert Simons, *Levers of Control: How Managers Use Innovative Control Systems to Drive Strategic Renewal* (Boston: Harvard Business School Press, 1995), p. 80.

10 This classification is based on Simons, p. 81.

11 For example, see Simons, p. 82.

12 Daniel Wren, *The Evolution of Management Thought* (John Wiley & Sons, 1994), p. 115.

13 Based on Kenneth Merchant, *Modern Management Control Systems* (Upper Saddle River, NJ: Prentice Hall, 1998), p. 642.

14 For a discussion, see Kenneth Merchant, *Modern Management Control Systems* (Upper Saddle River, NJ: Prentice Hall, 1998), pp. 542–545.

15 Ibid., p. 304.

16 Joel Kurtzman, "Is Your Company off Course? Now You Can Find Out Why," *Fortune*, 17 February 1997, pp. 128–130.

17 See for example Matt Hicks, "Tuning to the Big Picture for a Better Business," *PC Week*, 15 July 1999, p. 69.

18 Hicks, p. 69.

19 "The Software War," *Fortune*, 7 December 1998, p. 102.

20 Robin Cooper and Tobert Kaplan, "The Promise and Peril of Integrated Costs Systems," *Harvard Business Review*, July–August 1998, p. 109.

21 "The Software War," *Fortune*, 7 December 1998, p. 102.

22 Guy Bolton, "Enterprise Resource Planning Software Creates Supply Business Revolution," *Knight Ridder/Tribune Business News*, 9 November 1998.

23 Stephen Baker and Steve Hamm, "A Belated Rush to the Net," *Business Week*, 25 October 1999, pp. 152–158.

24 Simons, p. 81.

25 Ibid., p. 84.

26 Ibid., pp. 84–95.

27 Ibid., p. 86.

28 These characteristics are based on Simons, p. 87.

29 This discussion is based on Simons, pp. 87–88.

30 The following, except as noted, is based on Kenneth Merchant, *Control in Business Organizations* (Boston: Pitman, 1985), pp. 71–120. See also Robert Kaplan, "New Systems for Measurement and Control," *The Engineering Economist*, Spring 1991, pp. 201–218.

31 This is based on Simons, pp. 81–82.

32 Merchant, p. 98.

33 "Did Warner-Lambert Make a $468 Million Mistake?" *Business Week*, 21 November 1983, p. 123; quoted in Merchant, pp. 98–99.

34 Chris Argyris, "Human Problems with Budgets," *Harvard Business Review*, January–February 1953, pp. 97–110.

35 Peter Coy, "Big Brother, Pinned to Your Chest," *Business Week*, 17 August 1992, p. 38.

36 Jeffrey Stanton and Janet Barnes-Farrell, "Effects of Electronic Performance Monitoring on Personal Control, Task Satisfaction, and Task Performance," *Journal of Applied Psychology*, December 1996, p. 738; and Paul Greenlaw, "The Impact of Federal Legislation to Limit Electronic Monitoring," *Public Personnel Management*, Summer 1997, pp. 227–245.

37 Stanton and Barnes-Farrell, pp. 738–745.

38 Ibid., p. 738.

39 Norihiko Shirouzu and Jon Bigness, "'7-Eleven' Operators Resist System to Monitor Managers," *Wall Street Journal*, 16 June 1997, pp. B-1–6.

40 Tom Peters, *Liberation Management* (New York: Alfred A. Knopf, 1992), pp. 465–466.

41 Tom Burns and G. M. Stalker, *The Management of Innovation* (London: Tavistock, 1961), p. 119.

42 This quote is based on William Taylor, "Control in an Age of Chaos," *Harvard Business Review*, (November–December 1994), pp. 70–71. James Collins and Jerry Porras, *Built to Last: Successful Habits of Visionary Companies* (New York: Harper and Row, 1994).

43 Ibid., p. 71

44 J. Newcomb, 1998 letter to employees, 17 May 1999.

45 Gary Dessler, "How to Earn Your Employees Commitment," *Academy of Management Executive*, vol. 13, no. 2, 1999, pp. 58–67.

46 Personal interview. See Gary Dessler, Winning Commitment: How to Build and Keep a Competitive Work Force (New York: McGraw-Hill, 1993), pp. 27–28.

47 Ibid., p. 28.

48 Ibid., p. 30.

49 Rosabeth Moss Kanter, *Commitment and Community* (Cambridge, MA: Harvard University Press, 1972), pp. 24–25.

50 See Dessler, p. 64.

51 JoAnn Davy, "Online at the Office: Virtual Communities Go to Work," *Managing Office Technology*, July–August 1998, pp. 9–11.

52 Ibid.

53 Dessler, p. 69.

54 Kanter, p. 91.

55 Abraham Maslow, *Motivation and Personality* (New York: Harper & Row, 1954), p. 336.

56 Interview with assembler Dan Dise, March 1992.

57 Personal interview, March 1992.

58 Address to the Academy of Management, 9 August 1996.

MODULE A

1 Richard Chase and Nicholas Aquilero, *Production & Operations Management* (Homewood, IL: Irwin, 1992), p. 5.

2 Ibid., p. 5.

3 Norman Gaither, *Production and Operations Management* (Fort Worth, TX: The Dryden Press, 1992), p. 22.

4 "Goodnight, Vietnam," *Economist*, 8 January 2000, p. 65.

5 Ibid., p. 65.

6 Gaither, pp. 132–133.

7 Everett Adam, Jr., and Ronald Ebert, *Production & Operations Management* (Upper Saddle River, NJ: Prentice Hall, 1992), p. 254.

8 Ibid., p. 254.

9 Gaither, 135. See also Nancy Hyer, "The Discipline of Real Cells," *Journal of Operations Management*, Aug. 1999, pp. 557–559.

10 Barry Render and Jay Heizer, *Principles of Operations Management* (Upper Saddle River, NJ: Prentice-Hall, 1997), p. 551.

11 Ibid., pp. 551–553.

12 James Evans et al. *Applied Production and Operations Management* (St. Paul, MN: West Publishing Co., 1984), pp. 500–501.

13 Ibid., p. 511.

14 See, for example, Steven Replogle, "The Strategic Use of Smaller Lot Sizes through a New EOQ Model," *Production and Inventory Management Journal* (Third Quarter 1988), pp. 41–44; T. C. E. Cheng, "An EOQ Model with Learning Effect on Set-Ups," *Production and Inventory Management Journal*, First Quarter 1991, pp. 83–84.

15 Evans et al., p. 39.

16 Based in part on Joel E. Ross, *Total Quality Management: Text, Cases and Readings* (Delray Beach, FL: St. Lucie Press, 1993), p. 1. See also James Gaskin, "Bonner Bets on Total Quality Management," *Internet Week*, 6 September 1999, p. 43.

17 Render and Heizer, p. 96.

18 Ross, pp. 2–3, 35–36.

19 Chase and Aquilero, p. 197.

20 These traits are quoted from David Anderson, *Design for Manufacturability* (Lafayette, CA: CI Press, 1990), p. 9.

21 Ibid., p. 16.

22 Anderson, p. 15. See also F. Robert Jacobs and Vincent Mabert, *Production Planning, Scheduling, and Inventory Control* (Norcross, GA: Industrial Engineering and Management Press, 1986), pp. 96–100; and Otis Port, Zachary Shiller, Gregory Miles, and Amy Schulman, "Smart Factories, America's Turn," *Business Week*, 8 May 1989, pp. 142–148.

23 See, for example, Joseph Martinich, *Production and Operations Management* (New York: Wiley, 1997), pp. 215–216.

24 Valerie Reitman, "Global Money Trends Rattle Shop Windows in Heartland America," *Wall Street Journal*, 26 November 1993, p. A–1.

25 David Mandel, "JIT: Strategic Weapon for Aerospace and Defense?" *Industrial Engineering* (February 1993): p. 48. Just-in-time can also be used to improve performance of service organizations. See, for example, W. Calvin Waco, Robert Stonehocker, and Larry Feldman, "Success with JIT and MRP II in a Service Organization," *Production & Inventory Management Journal*, Fourth Quarter 1991, pp. 15–22. See Also Simon Hurley, "Comparing J. I. T. Approaches in a Manufacturing Cell," *Production & Inventory Management Journal*, Spring 1999, pp. 32–38.

26 Adam and Ebert, p. 568.

27 These elements are based on Kenneth Wantuck, *The Japanese Approach to Productivity* (Southfield, MI: Bendix Corporation, 1983); and Chase and Aquilero, pp. 261–72. See Also Mike Kaye, "Continuous Improvement: Ten Essential Criteria," *International Journal of Quality & Reliability Management*, April–May 1999, pp. 485–487.

28 Chase and Aquilero, p. 261.

29 Mary Cronin, "Intranets Reach the Factory Floor," *Fortune*, 18 August 1997, p. 208.

30 Adapted from Gaither, pp. 6–8. See also David Woodruff, "A Dozen Motor Factories—Under One Roof," *Business Week*, 20 November 1989, pp. 93–4. See also Mike Brezonick, "New Vickers Plant Focuses on Flexibility," *Diesel Progress*, North American Edition, January 1999, pp. 32–35.

31 Thomas Stewart, "Brace for Japan's Hot New Strategy," *Fortune*, 21 September 1992, p. 64. See also Bobby Ray Inman, "Are You Implementing a Pull System by Putting the Cart before the Horse?," *Production & Inventory Management Journal*, Spring 1999, pp. 67–72.

32 Ibid., p. 64.

33 Susan Moffat, "Japan's New Personalized Production," *Fortune*, 22 October 1990, pp. 132–135.

34 Mark Vonderem and Gregory White, *Operations Management* (St. Paul, MN: West Publishing, 1988), pp. 44–45. For more information on computer-integrated manufacturing, see Michael Baudin, *Manufacturing Systems Analysis* (Upper Saddle River, NJ: Prentice-Hall, 1990), pp. 2–5. See also Patricia Smith, "CAD/CAM for the Cutting Edge," *Machine Design*, 8 July 1999, pp. 25–29.

35 For additional information, see, for example, Alan Luber, "Living in the Real World of Computer Interfaced Manufacturing" *Production & Inventory Management*, September 1991, pp. 10–11; and Jeremy Main, "Computers of the World, Unite!" *Fortune*, 24 September 1990, pp. 115–22. See also John Teresko, "Japan's New Idea," *Industry Week*, 3 September 1990, pp. 62–66; and David Bak, "Shared Intelligence Guides Control System," *Design News*, 18 October 1999, p. 97.

36 John Teresko, "Manufacturing in Japan," *Industry Week*, 4 September 1989, pp. 35–79. See also Richard Jensen, "How to Be Nimble, How to Be Quick," *CMA Management*, October 1999, p. 34–38.

37 Brian McWilliams, "Re-Engineering of the Small Factory," *Inc. Technology*, 19 March 1996, pp. 4–47, reprinted in Roberta Russell and Bernard Taylor, *Operations Management* (Upper Saddle River, NJ: Prentice Hall), p. 260.

38 Kristina Sullivan, "Boeing Achieves Liftoff," *PC Week*, 10 May 1999, p. 67.

39 David Upton, "What Really Makes Factories Flexible?" *Harvard Business Review* (July–August 1995), p. 75.

40 Ibid., pp. 80–81.

41 Ibid., p. 80.

42 Karl Albrecht, *At America's Service: How Corporations Can Revolutionize the Way They Treat Their Customers* (Homewood, IL: Dow Jones-Irwin, 1988), p. 20. For an analysis of how to organize and manage service businesses, see also James Brian Quinn, *Intelligent Enterprise* (New York: The Free Press, 1992).

43 Michael E. Porter, *Competitive Strategy: Techniques for Analyzing Industries and Competitors* (New York: The Free Press, 1980), p. 37.

44 Based on a discussion in Karl Albrecht and Ron Zemke, *Service America!: Doing Business in the New Economy* (Homewood, IL: Dow Jones-Irwin, 1985), p. 6.

45 Based on Frederick F. Reichheld and W. Earl Sasser, Jr., "Zero Defections: Quality Comes to Service," *Harvard Business Review*, September–October 1990, pp. 105–111.

46 Based on Philip Sadler, Managerial Leadership in the Post-Industrial Society (Gower), as summarized in "When the Product is Service," *Economist*, 7 January 1989, p. 60.

47 Based on Albrecht and Zemke, *Service America!*, pp. 31–47. Albrecht, *At America's Service*, pp. 20–42; and Karl Albrecht and Lawrence J. Bradford, *The Service Advantage: How to Identify and Fulfill Customer Needs* (Homewood, IL: Dow Jones-Irwin, 1990), pp. 24–49.

48 Albrecht and Bradford, p. 30.

49 Albrecht, *At America's Service*, p. 26.

50 Ibid., p. 32.

51 Based on Albrecht and Zemke, *Service America!*, pp. 69–79; and Albrecht, *At America's Service*, pp. 157–223.

52 Albrecht, *At America's Service*, pp. 162–3; Albrecht and Bradford, *The Service Advantage*, pp. 88–91.

53 Albrecht and Zemke, *Service America!*, p. 174.

54 Albrecht, *At America's Service*, p. 198.

MODULE B

1 James Senn, *Information Systems in Management* (Belmont, CA: Wadsworth Publishing Co., 1990), p. 58.

2 Peter F. Drucker, "The Coming of the New Organization," *Harvard Business Review* (January–February 1988), p. 45.

3 Carroll Frenzel, *Management of Information Technology* (Boston: Boyd & Fraser, 1992), p. 10.

4 See, for example, David Kroenke and Richard Hatch, *Management Information Systems* (New York: McGraw-Hill, 1994), p. 20.

5 Senn, p. 58.

6 Kenneth Laudon and Jane Price Laudon, *Management Information Systems, 5th edition* (Upper Saddle River, NJ: Prentice Hall, 1998), p. 5.

7 The following is based on Kenneth Laudon and Jane Price Laudon, *Management Information Systems, 4th edition* (Upper Saddle River, NJ: Prentice Hall, 1996), pp. 11, 41–46. See also John Verity, "Coaxing Meaning out of Raw Data," *Business Week*, 3 February 1997, pp. 134, 138.

8 Jenny McCune, "Thirst for Knowledge," *Management Review*, April 1999, p. 10.

9 Louisa Wah, "Behind the Buzz," *Management Review*, April 1999, p. 17.

10 McCune, p. 11.

11 Frenzel, p. 11.

12 Based on Senn, 8; and Laudon and Laudon, *Management Information Systems, 5th Edition*, p. 5.

13 Kenneth Laudon and Jane Laudon, *Essentials of Management Information Systems, 4th edition* (Upper Saddle River, NJ: Prentice-Hall, 1997), p. 73.

14 Laudon and Laudon, *Management Information Systems, 4th edition*, p. 7.

15 Senn, pp. 14–15.

16 See, for example, Kroenke and Hatch, p. 51.

17 Laudon and Laudon, *Management Information Systems, 4th edition*, p. 24.

18 Laudon and Laudon, *Essentials of Management Information Systems*, p. 405.

19 See, for example, Laudon and Laudon, *Management Information Systems*, p. 24.

20 Larry Long and Nancy Long, *Computers* (Upper Saddle River, NJ: Prentice-Hall, 1996), p. 18.

21 Senn, p. 576.

22 This discussion is based on Senn, pp. 576–577.

23 Bill Gates, *Business @ the Speed of Thought* (New York: Warner Books, 1999), p. 22.

24 Emily Nelson and Evan Ramstad, "Hershey's Biggest Dud Has Turned Out to Be New Computer System," *Wall Street Journal*, 29 October 1999, p. A1.

25 Senn, p. 415.

26 See, for example, Senn, p. 418.

27 Ibid., p. 427.

28 Microsoft Corp., special informational advertising, *Fortune*, 8 November 1999.

29 Kenneth Laudon and Jane Laudon, *Management Information Systems, 5th Edition* (Upper Saddle River, NJ: Prentice Hall, 1998), p. 608.

30 Ibid., p. 608.

A

acceptance sampling a method of monitoring product quality that requires the inspection of only a small portion of the produced items.

accommodation giving in to the opponent in an attempt to end a conflict.

acquisition costs the total costs of all units bought to fill an order, usually varying with the size of the order.

action research the process of collecting data from employees about a system in need of change, and then feeding that data back to the employees so that they can analyze it, identify problems, develop solutions, and take action themselves.

active threats security threats to a company's computer system consisting of attempts to alter, destroy, or divert data or to illegally act as an authorized network terminal point.

activities the time-consuming aspects of a project, represented by arrows in a PERT chart.

affirmative action a legislated requirement that employers make an extra effort to hire and promote those in a protected (women or minority) group.

aggregate output planning a production plan that shows the aggregate (overall) volume of products or services that need to be produced to achieve the sales forecast for each product or service.

anchoring unconsciously giving disproportionate weight to the first information you hear.

application a form that requests information such as education, work history, and hobbies from a job candidate as a means of quickly collecting verifiable historical data.

appraisal a manager's evaluation of and feedback on an employee's work performance.

aroused motive a motive that expresses itself in behavior.

artificial intelligence (AI) a computer's ability to accomplish tasks in a manner that is considered intelligent, and is characterized by learning and making decisions.

attitude a predisposition to respond to objects, people, or events in either a positive or negative way.

attribution the meaning people give to the causes of actions and outcomes.

audioing unconsciously giving disproportionate weight to the first information one hears.

authoritarian personality a personality type characterized by rigidity, intolerance of ambiguity, the tendency to stereotype others as being good or bad, and conformity to the requirements of authority.

authority the right to take action, to make decisions, and to direct the work of others.

authority boundary the boundary represented by differences in organizational level or status across which communications may be distorted or constrained due to the status difference.

automation the automatic operation of a system, process, or machine.

availability heuristic basing a decision on the aspects of the situation that are most readily available in memory.

avoidance moving away from or refusing to discuss a conflict issue.

B

benchmarking a process through which a company learns how to become the best in one or more areas by analyzing and comparing the practices of other companies that excel in those areas.

behavior modification the technique of changing or modifying behavior through the use of contingent rewards or punishments.

behavioral displacement a reaction to being controlled in which employees concentrate too narrowly on the company's control standards and thereby miss the company's more important objectives.

bill of material a computerized record listing the required parts and materials for each manufactured product and where they can be purchased or made.

boundary control system policies, such as codes of conduct, that establish rules and identify the actions and pitfalls that employees must avoid.

boundaryless organization an organization in which the widespread use of teams, networks, and similar structural mechanisms means that the boundaries separating organizational functions and hierarchical levels are reduced and more permeable.

bounded rationality the boundaries on rational decision making imposed by one's values, abilities, and limited capacity for processing information.

brainstorming a creativity-stimulating technique in which prior judgments and criticisms are specifically forbidden from being expressed and thus inhibiting the free flow of ideas which are encouraged.

breakeven analysis a financial analysis decision-making aid that enables a manager to determine whether a particular volume of sales will result in losses or profits.

budget a financial plan showing financial expectations for a specific period.

bureaucracy To Max Weber, the ideal way to organize and manage an organization; generally viewed today as a term reflecting an unnecessarily rigid and mechanical way of getting things done.

business reengineering the radical redesign of business processes to cut waste, to improve cost, quality, and service; and to maximize the benefits of information technology, generally by questioning how and why things are being done as they are.

C

career anchor a dominant concern or value that directs an individual's career choices and that the person will not give up if a choice must be made.

cash cow a business with a high relative market share in a low-growth industry such that minimal investments can and need be made to continue to withdraw relatively high quantities of cash.

causal forecasting estimating a company factor (such as sales) based on other influencing factors (such as advertising expenditures or unemployment levels).

causal methods forecasting techniques that develop projections based on the mathematical relationship between a certain factor and the variables believed to influence or explain that factor.

cellular manufacturing usually a combination of process and product layouts, in which machines and personnel are grouped into cells containing all the tools and operations required to produce a particular product or family of products.

cellular organization an organization composed of small, individual, more-or-less autonomous and self-reliant firms.

certainty the condition of knowing in advance the outcome of a decision.

chain of command the path a directive and/or answer or request should take through each level of an organization; also called a scalar chain or the line of authority.

change advocate a leader who champions organizational change, often by cajoling, inspiring, and negotiating it.

charismatic leadership guidance from leaders who possess envisioning, energizing, and enabling qualities that mobilize and sustain activity within an organization.

close supervision a leadership style involving close, hands-on monitoring of subordinates and their work.

coercive power power based on the real or imagined expectation that one will be punished for failing to conform to the powerful person's attempts at influence.

cognitive biases standard errors in judgment that influence how people make decisions.

cohesiveness the attraction of the group for its individual members.

collaboration a conflict-management style in which both sides work together to achieve agreement.

collaborative writing system a computerized support system that lets group members work simultaneously on a single document from a number of interconnected or network computers.

commitment the relative strength of an individual's identification with and involvement in an organization.

commitment-based control methods a category of control tools that rely on the employees' self-control and commitment to doing things right to make sure things stay in control.

common market a system in which no barriers to trade exist among member countries and a common external trade policy is in force that governs trade with nonmembers; factors of production, such as labor, capital, and technology, move freely among members.

communication the exchange of information and the transmission of meaning.

communication channel the vehicle that carries the message in the communication process.

competition an approach to conflict management and negotiating that presumes a win–lose situation.

competitive advantage the basis for superiority over competitors and thus for hoping to claim certain customers.

competitive intelligence systematic techniques used to obtain and analyze public information about competitors.

competitive strategy a strategy that identifies how to build and strengthen the business's long-term competitive position in the marketplace.

competitor in negotiations or conflict management, a person whose primary motive is to win or to outdo others.

compromise settling a conflict through mutual concessions.

computer-aided design (CAD) a computerized process for designing new products, modifying existing ones, or simulating conditions that may affect the designs.

computer-aided manufacturing (CAM) a computerized process for planning and programming production processes and equipment.

computer-integrated manufacturing (CIM) the total integration of all production-related business activities through the use of computer systems, usually including automation and automatic guided vehicles.

concurrent engineering designing products in multidisciplinary teams so that all departments involved in the product's success contribute to its design.

confrontation meeting an organizational meeting aimed at clarifying and revealing intergroup misperceptions, tensions, and problems so that they can be resolved.

conglomerate diversification diversifying into other products or markets that are not related to a firm's present businesses.

consideration leader behavior indicative of mutual trust, friendship, support, respect, and warmth.

contingent reward a reward that is contingent or dependent on performance of a particular behavior.

contingent worker a temporary worker hired by an employer to fill short-term needs; not a permanent, full-time, or part-time employee.

continuous production a production process, such as those used by chemical plants or refineries, that runs for a very long period without the start-and-stop behavior associated with intermittent production.

control task of ensuring that activities are getting the desired results.

conversion system any production system that converts inputs (material and human resources) into outputs (products or services); sometimes called the production process or technology.

cooperator a person whose primary concern in negotiating or managing conflicts is to maximize outcomes for himself or herself and others.

coordination the process of achieving unity of action among interdependent activities.

core competencies the collective learning in an organization, especially the knowledge of how to coordinate diverse design and production skills and integrate multiple streams of technologies.

corporate-level strategy a plan that identifies the portfolio of businesses that comprise a corporation and how they relate to each other.

corporate scorecard a management tool, usually a computerized model, that traces a multitude of performance measures simultaneously and shows their interaction.

corporate social audit a rating system used to evaluate a corporation's performance with regard to meeting its social obligations.

corporate stakeholder any person or group that is important to the survival and success of the corporation.

cost leadership a competitive strategy by which a company aims to be the low-cost leader in its industry.

critical leadership thinking skills the ability to identify what is happening in a leadership situation, account for what is happening, and decide on the actions to be taken.

critical path the sequence of events in a project that in total requires the most time to complete.

cultural artifacts the obvious signs and symbols of corporate culture, such as organizational structure, policies, and dress codes.

customs union a situation in which trade barriers among members are removed and a common trade policy exists with respect to nonmembers.

customer departmentalization similar to divisional organization except that generally self-contained departments are organized to serve the needs of specific groups of customers.

customer report card lists the service attributes for which customers are looking, as well as the relative weights of priorities of each attribute and how the customers score your company on each of them.

cycle of service includes all the moments of truth experienced by a typical customer, from first to last.

D

data warehouse a computerized repository of information.

decentralized organization an organization in which department heads have authority for most decisions in their divisions, while the company's headquarters office focuses on controlling essential companywide matters.

decision a choice made between available alternatives.

decision making the process of developing and analyzing alternatives and choosing from among them.

decision support system an information system that assists management in semistructured or unstructured decision making by combining data, analytical models, and user-friendly software.

decision tree a technique for facilitating how decisions under conditions of risk are made, whereby an expected value and gain or loss can be applied to each alternative.

decoder/receiver generally, the person or persons to whom the information is sent in the communication process, although this may also refer to any device that converts a message into a usable form.

delegation the act of passing down authority from supervisor to subordinate.

departmentalization the process through which an organization's activities are grouped together and assigned to managers; the organizationwide division of work.

descriptive plan a plan that states in words what is to be achieved and how.

designing for manufacturability designing products with ease of manufacturing and quality in mind.

diagnostic control system a control method, such as a budget, which ensures that standards are being met and that variances are diagnosed and explained.

differentiation strategy a competitive strategy aimed at distinguishing a company from its competitors by focusing on the attributes of its products or services that consumers perceive as important.

discipline without punishment a multistage displinary technique that uses oral reminders of the violated rule; then written reminders; followed by mandatory one-day leaves; and finally, if the behavior is not corrected, dismissal.

discrimination a behavioral bias toward or against a person based on the group to which the person belongs.

dismissal the involuntary termination of an employee's employment with a firm.

distributed processing computerized networks that use small local computers to collect, store, and process information that is sent periodically to headquarters for analysis and review.

diverse describes a workforce comprised of two or more groups, each of which can be identified by demographic or other characteristics.

diversification a corporate strategy whereby managers try to better utilize their organizational resources by developing new products and new markets.

divestment selling or liquidating the individual businesses of a larger company.

divisionalization (product departmentalization) a form of organization in which the firm's major departments are organized so that each can manage all or most of the activities needed to develop, manufacture, and sell a particular product or product line.

dog a business in a low-growth, unattractive industry that also has low relative market share and thus should usually be divested.

downsizing dramatically reducing the size of a company's workforce.

E

economic integration the result of two or more nations minimizing trade restrictions to obtain the advantages of free trade.

economic order quantity (EOQ) an inventory management system based on a simple formula that is used to determine the most economic quantity to order so that the total of inventory and set-up costs is minimized.

electronic bulletin board an example of **e-mail–based communications** that allow one or more group members to file messages on various topics to be picked up by other group members via telecommunications links.

employee benefits supplements to wages or pay that employees get as a result of their working for an organization.

employee compensation all forms of pay or rewards that go to employees and arise from their employment.

employee involvement program any formal program that lets employees participate in formulating important work decisions or in supervising all or part of their own work activities.

employee-oriented leader a leader who focuses on the needs of employees and emphasizes building good interpersonal relationships.

empowering employees authorizing and enabling employees to do their jobs with greater autonomy.

empowerment the act of giving employees the authority, tools, and information they need to do their jobs with greater autonomy and confidence.

encoder/sender the element or person in the communication process that puts a message in a form suitable for transmission.

enterprise resource planning system a companywide integrated computer system that gives managers real-time instantaneous information regarding the costs and status of every activity and project in the business.

environmental monitoring a strategic control method of tracking previously identified events, trends, and premises to see if any of the plan's basic assumptions have changed or require modification.

environmental scanning a strategic control method aimed at identifying previously unidentified or undetected critical events that could influence the company's strategy.

equalizer a person whose primary concern in negotiating or managing conflicts is to equalize outcomes for everyone involved in a situation.

equity theory J. S. Adams's theory that people have a need for, and therefore value and seek, fairness in employer–employee relationships.

ethics the study of standards of conduct and moral judgment; also, the standards of right conduct.

ethnocentric a management philosophy that leads to the creating of home-market–oriented firms.

ethnocentrism a tendency to view members of one's own group as the center of the universe and to view other social groups less favorably than one's own.

events the specific accomplishments in a project, represented by circles in a PERT chart.

exchange rate the rate at which one country's currency can be exchanged for another country's currency.

executive a manager at the top management level of an organization.

executive recruiter an agency retained by employers to seek out top management talent.

executive support system an information system designed to help top-level executives acquire, manipulate, and use the information they need to maintain the company's overall effectiveness.

expectancy in motivation, the probability that a person's efforts will lead to performance.

expected value a calculated value that equals the probability of the outcome multiplied by the benefit or cost of that outcome.

expediting the process of monitoring and adjusting the movement of products and materials from operation to operation.

expert power power that is derived from a person's perceived expertise in some area and the dependence of others on the expert's advice and counsel.

expert system an information system in which computer programs store facts and rules (often called a knowledge base) and which can replicate the abilities and decisions of true human experts.

exporting selling abroad, either directly to target customers or indirectly by retaining foreign sales agents and distributors.

external environment the set of forces with which an organization interacts.

extinction the behavioral modification technique of withholding positive reinforcement so that over time the undesired behavior disappears.

F

facility layout the configuration of all the machines, employee work stations, storage areas, internal walls, and so forth that constitute the facility used to create a firm's product or service.

federal organization an organization in which power is distributed between a central unit and a number of constituent units, but the central unit's authority is intentionally limited.

feedback the receiver's response to the message that was actually received in the communication process.

financial incentive any financial reward that is contingent on a worker's performance, such as commissions or piecework.

financial ratio an arithmetic comparison of one financial measure to another, generally used to monitor and control financial performance.

first-line manager a manager at the bottom management level of an organization, also called a supervisor, who has nonsupervisors as subordinates.

fixed-position layout a production system arrangement in which the product being built or produced stays at one location and the machines and tools required to build the product are brought to that location as needed, as for the building of ships or other bulky products.

fixed salary compensation based on an agreed rate for a set period of time.

flexible manufacturing system (FMS) the organization of groups of production machines that are connected by automated materials-handling and transfer machines, and integrated into a computer system for the purpose of combining the benefits of made-to-order flexibility and mass-production efficiency.

focus strategy a strategy in which a business selects a narrow market segment and builds its strategy on serving those in its target market better or more cheaply than its generalist competitors.

forcing a direct, contentious method of resolving conflict that utilizes one negotiator's superior position.

forecast to estimate or calculate in advance or to predict.

foreign direct investment operations in one country controlled by entities in a foreign country.

formal communication messages that are recognized as official by the organization, such as orders from superiors to subordinates, sales reports, and status reports.

formal organizational network a formally assigned, permanent group of managers or other employees drawn from across a company's functions, geographic areas, and hierarchical levels to take the initiative in finding and solving problems.

formal structure change program an intervention technique in which employees collect information on existing formal organizational structures and analyze it for the purpose of redesigning and implementing new organizational structures.

framing in decision making, the idea that the way a problem is presented can influence decisions.

franchising the granting of a right by a parent company to another firm to do business in a prescribed manner.

free trade the unrestricted exchange of goods among participating countries.

free trade area a type of economic integration in which all barriers to trade among members are removed.

functional authority narrowly limited power to issue orders down the chain of command in a specific functional area such as personnel testing.

functional departmentalization a form of organization that groups a company's activities around essential functions such as manufacturing, sales, or finance.

functional fixedness in decision making, the inability to see other possibilities for an object or idea beyond an object's or idea's stated or usual functions.

functional plan a tactical short-term plan showing how each department of a business will contribute to top management's plans.

functional strategy the overall course or courses of action and basic policies that each department is to follow in helping the business accomplish its strategic goals.

G

gainsharing plan an incentive plan that engages many or all employees in a common effort to achieve a company's productivity objectives and in which they share in the gains.

gamesmanship management actions that try to improve the manager's apparent performance in terms of the control system without producing any economic benefits for the company.

Gantt chart a production scheduling chart (named after management pioneer Henry Gantt) that plots time on a horizontal scale and generally shows, for each order, the start and stop times of each operation.

gender-role stereotype usually, the association of women with certain behaviors and possibly (often lower-level) jobs.

general leader a leader who takes a middle-ground approach between close supervision and laissez-faire leadership.

geocentric *see* regiocentric

geographic expansion a strategic growth alternative of aggressively expanding into new domestic and/or overseas markets.

global corporation a corporation that sells essentially a standardized product throughout the world, components of which may be made or designed in different countries.

globalization the extension of a firm's sales or manufacturing to new markets abroad.

global mercantilism in planning, a scenario in which geopolitical change and international economic tensions lead to more government intervention in managing international trade.

goal a specific result to be achieved; the end result of a plan.

goal commitment the strength of one's determination to reach a goal.

goal-setting studies organizational behavior research that provides useful insights into how to set effective goals.

graphic plan a plans that shows graphically or in charts what is to be achieved and how.

grievance a complaint that an employee lodges against an employer, usually one regarding wages, hours, or some condition of employment, such as unfair supervisory behavior.

group two or more persons interacting in such a manner that each person influences and is influenced by each other person, and who may or may not have unanimity of purpose.

group cohesiveness the degree of interpersonal attractiveness within a group, dependent on factors like proximity, attraction among the individual group members, group size, intergroup competition, and agreement about goals.

group norms the informal rules that groups adopt to regulate and regularize group members' behavior.

group scheduling system a computerized support system that allows each group member to put his or her daily schedule into a shared database so that each can identify the most suitable times to schedule meetings or to attend currently scheduled meetings.

groupthink the mode of thinking in a cohesive group in which the desire to achieve group consensus overrides potentially valuable individual points of view of its members.

H

heuristic a rule of thumb or an approximation applied as a shortcut to decision making.

hierarchy of plans a set of plans that includes the enterprisewide plan and the derivative plans of subsidiary units required to help achieve the enterprisewide plan.

horizontal corporation a structure that is organized around customer-oriented processes performed by multidisciplinary cross-functional teams rather than formal functional departments.

horizontal integration acquiring ownership or control of competitors who are competing in the same or similar markets with the same or similar products.

hot group an energetic, high-achieving workgroup, usually small, whose members are excited by or obsessed with completing a challenging task.

hourly wage compensation based on a set hourly pay rate for work performed.

human process interventions organizational change techniques aimed at enabling employees to develop a better understanding of their own and others' behaviors for the purpose of improving that behavior such that the organization benefits.

human resources (HR) management the management function devoted to acquiring, training, appraising, and compensating employees.

humanistic theories personality theories which assume that people are motivated by the desire to fulfill the potential they see themselves as having.

hyperarchy an organization structure based on electronic networks using the Internet, intranets, and similar links.

I

identity boundary the boundary caused by identifying with those groups with which one has shared experiences and with which one believes one shares fundamental values.

independent integrator an individual or a group that coordinates the activities of several interdependent departments, but is independent of them.

individualist in negotiations or conflict management, a person whose primary motive is to gain as much as possible for himself or herself.

informal communication communication not officially sanctioned by the organization, such as rumors heard through the grapevine.

informal organization the informal contacts, communications, and habitual ways of doing things that employees develop.

informal organizational network cooperating individuals who are interconnected only informally to share information and help solve each other's problems.

information data presented in a form that is meaningful to the recipient.

information superhighway a high-speed digital communications network that may combine telephone lines, cable lines, microwave transmissions, and fiber optics to let anyone anywhere use interactive television, telephones, PCs, or other devices to interact with databases around the world.

information system a set of people, data, and procedures that work together to retrieve, process, store, and disseminate information to support decision making and control.

information technology any processes, practices, or systems that facilitate the processing and transportation of data or information.

initiating structure the leadership factor of being able to organize the work to be done and to define relationships or roles, the channels of communication, and the ways of getting jobs done.

input a resource required for the manufacture of a product or service.

input device a device that receives instructions and data, converts them into electrical impulses, and then transfers the impulses to the computer's storage unit.

instrumental leadership the managerial role of building and clarifying organizational changes so that employees can accomplish their new tasks.

instrumentality the perceived correlation between successful performance and obtaining the reward.

integrated strategic management an organizational development program to create or change a company's strategy by analyzing the current strategy, choosing a desired strategy, designing a strategic change plan, and implementing the new plan.

interactive control system control methods that involve direct, face-to-face interaction with employees so as to monitor rapidly changing information and respond proactively to changing conditions.

intergroup behavior the interactive personal dynamics between groups or departments within an organization.

intergroup organizational conflict a disagreement between organizational units such as production and sales departments or between line and staff units.

intermittent production a system in which production is performed on a start-and-stop basis, such as for the manufacture of made-to-order products.

international business a firm that engages in international trade or investment; also refers to business activities that involve the movement of resources, goods, services, and skills across national boundaries.

international investment the investment of resources in business activities outside a firm's home country.

international management the performance of the management process across national boundaries.

international trade the export or import of goods or services to consumers in another country.

interpersonal behavior how individuals in an organization relate to each other.

interpersonal communication communication that occurs between two individuals.

interpersonal conflict a conflict occurring between individuals or between individuals and groups.

inventory-holding costs all the costs associated with carrying parts or materials in inventory.

inventory management the process of ensuring that the firm has adequate inventories of all parts and supplies needed, within the constraint of minimizing total inventory costs.

ISO 9000 the quality standards of the European Union.

J

job analysis the procedure used to determine the duties of particular jobs and the kinds of people (in terms of skills and experience) who should be hired for them.

job analysis questionnaire a form used by managers to determine the duties and functions of a job through a series of questions that employees answer.

job-centered leader a leader who focuses on production and on a job's technical aspects.

job description a document that identifies a particular job, provides a brief job summary, and lists specific responsibilities and duties of the job.

job design the number and nature of specific tasks or activities in a job.

job enlargement an increase in the number of similar tasks assigned to a job.

job enrichment the inclusion of opportunities for achievement and other motivators in a job by making the job itself more challenging.

job posting publicizing an open job to employees (often by literally posting it on bulletin boards) and listing its attributes, like qualifications, supervisor, working schedule, and pay rate.

job rotation the systematic movement of a worker from job to job to improve job satisfaction and reduce boredom.

job satisfaction the measure of an employee's attitude about his or her job.

job specification the human qualifications in terms of traits, skills, and experiences required to accomplish a job.

joint venture the participation of two or more companies in an enterprise such that each party contributes assets, owns the entity to some degree, and shares risk.

jury of executive opinion a qualitative forecasting technique in which a panel of executives are given pertinent data and asked to make independent sales forecasts, which are then reconciled in an executive meeting or by the company president.

just-in-time (JIT) a production control method used to attain minimum inventory levels by ensuring delivery of materials and assemblies just when they are to be used; also refers to a philosophy of manufacturing that aims to optimize production processes by continuously reducing waste.

K

kanban from the Japanese word for "card," a production control system that operates on the theory that whenever an item is used, it pulls the need for another item (as evidenced by a card containing the part number), which in turn pulls the need for another, and so on.

knowledge management the task of developing and exploiting an organization's tangible and intangible resources.

L

laissez-faire leader a leader who takes a hands-off approach toward supervising subordinates.

law of individual differences a psychological term representing the fact that people differ in their personalities, abilities, values, and needs.

leader–member exchange (LMX) theory the theory that leaders may use different leadership styles with different members of the same workgroup, based in part on perceived similarities and differences with the leader.

leadership one person influencing another to willingly work toward a predetermined objective.

leading getting others to get the job done, maintaining morale, and motivating subordinates.

lean manufacturing a management philosophy that assumes that any manufacturing process that does not add value to the product for the customer is wasteful; also called value-added manufacturing.

learning a relatively permanent change in a person that occurs as a result of experience.

legitimate power authority that is based on a general acceptance of someone's right to influence others, who in turn feel an obligation to accept this influence; the actual source of legitimate power might be tradition or the higher position of the one in power.

leverage to gain a competitive edge by concentrating a company's resources on key strategic goals or competencies

licensing an arrangement whereby a firm (the licensor) grants a foreign firm the right to use intangible property such as patents, copyrights, manufacturing processes, or trade names for a specified period of time, usually in return for a percentage of the earnings, or royalties.

lifelong learning the organizational program of providing continuing education and training to employees throughout their careers.

line adapter a device that modifies the signal from the terminal and computer to match the characteristics of the telecommunications line; a modem is one example.

linear programming a mathematical method used to solve resource allocation problems.

line manager a manager authorized to issue orders to subordinates down the chain of command.

line–staff conflict disagreements between a line manager and the staff manager who is giving him or her advice.

load schedule a plan that compares the labor and machine hours needed to carry out the master production schedule with the labor and machine hours actually available each week.

loading and sequencing assigning individual jobs to machines and work centers.

local area network (LAN) a communications network that spans a limited distance, such as a building or several adjacent buildings, using the company's own telecommunications links.

locus of control the degree of control that individuals believe they have over their lives.

M

Machiavellian personality a personality type oriented toward manipulation and control, with a low sensitivity to the needs of others, the name of which refers to the 16th-century political advisor Nicoló Machiavelli.

Malcolm Baldrige Award a prize created in 1987 by the U.S. Department of Commerce to recognize outstanding achievement in quality control management.

management the managers of an organization; or the study of what managers do.

management assessment center a development and/or selection device wherein management candidates spend two or three days performing realistic management tasks under the observation of appraisers.

management by objectives (MBO) a technique in which supervisor and subordinate jointly set goals for the latter and periodically assess progress toward those goals.

management information system an information system that provides decision support for managers by producing standardized, summarized reports on a regular basis.

management process the manager's four basic functions: planning, organizing, leading, and controlling.

manager a person who plans, organizes, leads, and controls the work of others so that the organization achieves its goals.

managerial competence the motivation and skills required to gain a management position, including intellectual, emotional, and interpersonal skills.

managing diversity planning and implementing organizational systems and practices to manage people in a way that maximizes the potential advantages of diversity while minimizing its potential disadvantages.

market penetration a growth strategy to boost sales of present products by more aggressively permeating the organization's current markets.

marketing channel the means through which a manufacturer distributes its products to its ultimate customers.

marketing-channel departmentalization an arrangement in which departments of an organization focus on particular marketing channels, such as drugstores or grocery stores.

marketing research the procedures used to develop and analyze current customer-related information to help managers make decisions.

mass customization designing, producing, and delivering customized products for or near the cost and convenience of mass-produced items.

mass production type of intermittent production process usually involving an assembly line in which standardized methods and specialized machines produce long runs of standardized items.

master production scheduling (MPS) planning the amounts of all products to be produced for the coming period, and the dates for which they are to be produced.

material requirements planning (MRP) a computer-based system that reviews the master production schedule and specifies the required raw materials, parts, subassemblies, and assemblies needed each week to meet the master production schedule.

matrix organization an organization in which one or more forms of departmentalization are imposed on top of an existing one.

mechanistic organization an organizational structure characterized by close adherence to the established chain of command, highly specialized jobs, and vertical communications.

mentoring a relationship between two people in which the more experienced mentor provides support, guidance, and counseling to enhance the protégé's success at work in other areas of life.

merit raise a salary increase—usually permanent—based on individual performance.

mission statement broadly outlines the enterprise's purpose and serves to communicate who the organization is, what it does, and where it's headed.

missionary leadership A leadership style characterized by influencing an organization to move toward a vision by winning the commitment of others who then aid in the process.

mixed economy an economy in which some sectors are left to private ownership and free market mechanisms, while others are largely owned and managed by the government.

modem the most familiar means of converting telecommunications signals from one type of signal to a more compatible one for the device.

moment of truth the instant when the customer comes in contact with any aspect of a business, and based on that contact forms an opinion about the quality of your service or product.

moral minimum the view that corporations should be free to strive for profits so long as they commit no harm.

morality a society's accepted norms of behavior.

motivation the intensity of a person's desire to engage in some activity.

motivational dispositions or needs motives that lie dormant until the proper conditions arise to bring them forth or make them active.

motive something that incites a person to action or that sustains and gives direction to action.

moving a step in psychologist Kurt Lewin's model of change aimed at using techniques and actually altering the behaviors, values, and attitudes of the individuals in an organization.

multinational corporation (MNC) an internationally integrated company over which equity-based control is exercised by a parent corporation that is owned and managed essentially by the nationals of the country in which it is domiciled.

mutual adjustment achieving coordination through personal interactions and communicated responses to a situation.

N

network a group of interconnected computers, workstations, or computer devices such as printers and data storage systems.

network planning and control methods ways of planning and controlling projects by graphically representing the projects' steps and the timing and links between these steps.

nonprogrammed decision a decision that is unique and novel.

nonverbal communication the nonspoken aspects of communication, such as a person's manner of speaking, facial expressions, or body posture, that express meaning to others.

normative control a characteristic of control processes in responsive organizations in which members are guided in their

behavior by a strong set of shared values, beliefs, and traditions rather than by rules, procedures, and close supervision.

normative judgment a comparative evaluation stating or implying that something is good or bad, right or wrong, or better or worse.

norms the informal rules that groups adopt to regulate and regularize the behavior of group members.

O

objectives specific results toward which effort is directed.

open-book management a management style in which a company opens its books to the employees, sharing financial data, explaining numbers and rewarding workers for improvement.

on-the-job training (OJT) training in which a person learns a job while he or she is working at it.

operant behavior behavior that appears to operate on or have an influence on the subject's environment.

operational plan a short-term plan that shows the detailed daily steps of business operations.

operations management the process of managing the resources that are needed to produce an organization's goods and services.

ordering, or setup, costs the costs, usually fixed, of placing an order or setting up machines for a production run.

organic organization an organizational structure characterized by flexible lines of authority, less specialized jobs, and decentralized decisions.

organization a group of people with formally assigned roles who work together to achieve the stated goals of the group.

organization chart a chart that illustrates the organizationwide division of work by charting who is accountable to whom and who is in charge of what department.

organizational behavior (OB) the study and application of how people behave, individually and as a group, within organizations.

organizational communication communication that occurs among several individuals or groups.

organizational culture the characteristic set of values and ways of behaving that employees in an organization share.

organizational development (OD) an approach to organizational change in which the employees themselves formulate the change that's required and implement it, usually with the aid of a trained consultant.

organizational development interventions in-depth human process interventions such as sensitivity training aimed at changing employees' attitudes, values, and behavior.

organizational network a system of interconnected or cooperating individuals.

organizing arranging the activities of the enterprise in such a way that they systematically contribute to the enterprise's goals.

orientation the process of providing new employees with basic information about the employer, such as company policies, working hours, or parking arrangements.

output a direct outcome (actual product or service) or indirect outcome (tax, wage, salary) of a production system.

P

passive threat a security threat to a computer system that comes from an unauthorized individual or organization monitoring the firm's data transmissions in order to obtain unauthorized information.

path–goal leadership theory a theory that explains a leaders effectiveness in terms of the persons ability to clarify the path to the goal and to make it easier to achieve the goal.

patterns of behavior in organizational behavior, the ceremonial events, written and spoken comments, and actual behaviors of an organization's members that contribute to creating the organizational culture.

pay for performance any compensation method based on merit or performance rather than across-the-board non-output-based pay.

perception the unique way each person defines stimuli, depending on the influence of past experiences and the person's present needs and personality.

personality the characteristic and distinctive traits of an individual, and the way these traits interact to help or hinder the adjustment of the person to other people and situations.

personality trait any readily identifiable and measurable characteristic of an individual.

personnel planning the process of determining the organization's future personnel needs, as well as the methods to be used to fill those needs.

personnel replacement chart company records showing present performance and promotability of inside candidates for the most important positions.

position replacement card a card prepared for each position in a company to show possible replacement candidates and their qualifications.

planning the process of setting goals and courses of action, developing rules and procedures, and forecasting future outcomes.

plan a method for doing or making something and consisting of a goal and a course of action.

policy a standing plan that sets broad guidelines for the enterprise.

political boundary the special interests or agendas within an organization that may oppose each other.

politics the acquisition and use of power.

polycentric a management philosophy oriented toward pursuing a limited number of individual foreign markets.

positive reinforcement the act of rewarding desired behavior; or the actual rewards, such as praise or bonuses, given each time the desired behavior occurs.

postaction control any control tool in which the project or operation being controlled is completed first, and then results are measured and compared to the standard.

power the ability of one person to influence another to do something the latter would not otherwise do.

prejudice a bias that results from prejudging someone on the basis of the latter's particular trait or traits.

premise an assumption made about the future.

primary data information specifically collected to address a current problem.

principle of exception sometimes called management by exception, this rule holds that employees should be left to pursue the standards set by management, and only significant deviations from the standard should be brought to a manager's attention.

problem a discrepancy between a desirable and an actual situation.

problem-solving team team formed to identify and solve work-related problems.

procedure a plan that specifies how to proceed in specific situations that routinely arise.

process analysis solving problems by thinking through the process involved from beginning to end, imagining, at each step, what actually would happen.

process layout a production system design in which similar machines or functions are grouped together.

product development the strategy of improving products for current markets to maintain or boost growth.

product layout a production system design in which every item to be produced

follows the same sequence of operations from beginning to end, such as an assembly line.

production control the process of ensuring that the specified production plans and schedules are being adhered to.

production planning the process of deciding what products to produce and where, when, and how to produce them.

program a plan that lays out all the steps in proper sequence to a single-use, often one-time business project.

programmed decision a decision that is repetitive and routine and can be made by using a definite, systematic procedure.

promotion a reward of an employee's efforts that generally involves moving that person to a job with increased authority and responsibility.

psychoanalytic theory a personality theory developed by Sigmund Freud, that emphasizes the role of past experiences, sexual frustrations, and the unconscious in the determination of personality.

psychological set the tendency to rely on a rigid strategy or approach when solving a problem.

punishment a behavioral modification option that applies penalties for the undesired behavior to reduce the possibility that it will recur.

Q

qualitative forecasting predictive techniques that emphasize logical, unbiased human judgment and may include both technological and judgmental methods.

quality the extent to which a product or service is able to meet customer needs and expectations.

quality circle a team of 6 to 12 employees that meets about once per week on company time to solve problems affecting its work area.

quantitative forecasting a type of forecasting in which statistical methods are used to examine data and find underlying patterns and relationships; includes time-series methods and causal models.

question mark in strategic planning, a business in a high-growth industry, but with low relative market share.

quota a legal restriction on the import of particular goods.

R

recruiting attracting a pool of viable job applicants.

referent power power that stems from one person's identification with or attraction toward another.

refreezing a step in psychologist Kurt Lewin's model of change aimed at preventing a return to old ways of doing things by instituting new systems and procedures that reinforce the new organizational changes.

regiocentric a management philosophy oriented toward larger areas, including the global marketplace; also called geocentric.

related diversification a strategy of expanding into other industries or markets related to a company's current business lines.

retrenchment the reduction of activities or operations to reduce investment.

reward power power based on the ability to raise positive rewards or reduce negative rewards.

risk the chance that a particular outcome will or will not occur.

rites and ceremonies traditional culture-building events or activities that symbolize the firm's values and help convert employees to these values.

role ambiguity a lack of clarity about what or how a person is to do a job.

role conflict a situation in which an employee has conflicting orders, such that compliance with one would make it difficult or impossible to comply with the other.

rule a highly specific guide to action.

S

sales force estimation a forecasting technique that gathers and combines the opinions of the sales people on what they predict sales will be in the forthcoming period.

satisfice to stop the decision-making process when satisfactory alternatives are found, rather than reviewing solutions until an optimal alternative is discovered.

scenario a hypothetical sequence of events constructed for the purpose of focusing attention on causal processes and decision points.

secondary data information for analyzing a situation that has already been collected or published.

self-concept the perceptions people have of themselves and their relationships to people and other aspects of life.

self-efficacy being able to influence important aspects of one's world; the belief that one can accomplish what one sets out to do.

self-managing team a highly trained team of employees including 6 to 18 people on average, who are fully responsible for turning out a well-defined segment of finished work. Also called a self-directed work team.

semantics the meaning of words.

semi-autonomous team a team that has considerable input into managing the activities in their own work area but are still headed by a supervisor.

sensitivity training also called laboratory or t-group training, the basic aim of this organizational development technique is to increase participants' insight into their own behavior and that of others by encouraging an open expression of feelings in a trainer-guided group.

service management a total organizationwide approach that makes quality of service the business's number one driving force.

service strategy the company's plan for achieving superior service.

shop floor control (SFC) the process of overseeing the weekly and daily production schedules to most effectively implement the master production schedules on a week-by-week basis.

signs and symbols practices and actions that create and sustain a company's culture.

similarity heuristic the tendency to base a decision on the aspects of a person or situation that are most familiar or similar to one's own past experience.

simple smoothing average a forecast for the next period that is based on the average sales of the past specified number of periods.

smoothing methods methods used to average the date from a time series so as to remove seasonal and random variations.

smoothing over in conflict management, diminishing or avoiding a conflict issue.

social responsibility the extent to which companies should or do channel resources toward improving the quality of life of one or more segments of society other than the firm's own stockholders.

socializing transforming new employees into committed organizational members by steeping them in the organization's values and traditions.

span of control the number of subordinates reporting directly to a supervisor.

spot award a financial reward given to an employee as soon as landable performance is observed.

staff manager a manager without the authority to give orders down the chain of command (except in his or her own department); generally can only assist and advise line managers in specialized areas such as human resources management.

staffing actually filling a firm's open positions; also, the personnel process that includes six steps: job analysis, personnel planning; recruiting, interviewing, testing and selection, and training and development.

standing plan a plan established to be used repeatedly, as the need arises.

star in strategic planning, a business in a high-growth industry that also enjoys a high relative market share.

statistical decision theory techniques techniques used to solve problems for which information is incomplete or uncertain.

steering control control that predicts results and takes corrective action before the operation or project is completed.

stereotyping attributing specific behavioral traits to individuals on the basis of their apparent membership in a group.

stockout costs the costs associated with running out of raw materials, parts, or finished-goods inventory.

stories the repeated tales and anecdotes that contribute to a company's culture by illustrating and reinforcing important company values.

strategic alliance an agreement between potential or actual competitors to achieve common objectives.

strategic business unit an organizational entity that contains several related businesses.

strategic change a change in a firm's strategy, mission, or vision.

strategic control the process of assessing the firm's progress toward its strategic objectives and taking corrective action as needed to ensure optimal implementation.

strategic HR management the linking of the human resource function with the company's strategies to accomplish that strategy.

strategic intervention an organization development application aimed at effecting a suitable fit among a firm's strategy, structure, culture, and external environment.

strategic management the process of identifying and pursuing the organization's strategic plan by aligning internal capabilities with the external demands of its environment, and then ensuring that the plan is being executed properly.

strategic plan a plan that outlines the course of action a firm plans to pursue in becoming the sort of enterprise it wants to be, given the firm's external opportunities and threats and its internal strengths and weaknesses.

strategic planning identifying the current business of a firm and the business it wants for the future, and the course of action or strategy it will pursue.

strategy a course of action that explains how an enterprise will move from the business it is in now to the business it wants to be in.

subsidy a direct payment a country makes to support a domestic producer.

subsidiary A sub-unit—generally relatively autonomous but wholly owned—of a larger organization. Subsidiaries are often established by foreign firms to manage operations abroad.

suggestion team a team formed to work in the short term on a given issue such as increasing productivity.

survey research the process of collecting data from attitude surveys filled out by employees of an organization, then feeding the data back to workgroups to provide a basis for problem analysis and action planning.

sustainable world a scenario in which economic frictions are resolved and economic trade flows freely, but concern about the environment leads to tightened emissions regulation and higher quality standards for energy products.

SWOT analysis a strategic planning tool for analyzing a company's strengths, weaknesses, opportunities, and threats.

T

360-degree feedback a performance evaluation method that involves collecting performance information on an employee all around that person—for instance, from subordinates, supervisors, peers, and internal and external customers.

tactical plan a plan that shows how top management's plans are to be carried out at the departmental, short-term level.

tariffs government taxes on imports.

task boundary the perceived limited actions of a specific organizational position.

team a group of people committed to a common purpose, set of performance goals, and approach for which they hold themselves mutually accountable.

team building the process of improving the effectiveness of a team through action research or other techniques.

technology transfer the transfer, often to another country, of systematic knowledge for the manufacturing of a product, for the application of a process, or for the rendering of a service; it does not extend to the mere sales or lease of goods.

telecommunications the electronic transmission of data, text, graphics, voice (audio), or image (video) over any distance.

telecommunications lines (links) the medium through which signals are transmitted in a telecommunications system; for example, copper wires, optical fibers, or microwave transmissions.

telecommunications software the computer program that controls input and output activities and other communications network functions.

telecommunications system a set of compatible telecommunications devices that link separate information processing devices for the purpose of exchanging data.

telecommuting the substitution of telecommunications and computers for the commute to a central office.

teletraining providing training to remote employees via telecommunications, such as by video conference.

terminals input/output devices that send or receive data.

time series a set of observations taken at specific times, usually at equal intervals, to identify fundamental patterns.

tokenism symbolically appointing a small number of minority-group members to high-profile positions instead of more aggressively achieving full representation for that group.

total quality management (TQM) an organizationwide management system that focuses all functions of the business on maximizing customer satisfaction at continually lower real costs.

total quality management (TQM) program a specific organizationwide program that integrates all the functions and related processes of a business such that they are all aimed at maximizing customer satisfaction through ongoing improvements.

trade barrier a governmental influence that is usually aimed at reducing the competitiveness of imported products or services.

traditional control methods control procedures that are based on maintaining control generally through external means, by setting standards, comparing the actual results to the standard, and then taking corrective action, and including diagnostic, boundary, and interactive control systems.

training program the process of providing new employees with information they need to do their jobs satisfactorily.

trait theory in leadership, the theory that leaders have basic identifiable traits or characteristics that contribute to their success as leaders.

transaction processing system an information system that provides detailed information about short-term, daily activities.

transactional behaviors leadership actions that focus on accomplishing the tasks at hand and on maintaining good working relationships by exchanging promises of rewards for performance.

transformational leadership the leadership process that involves influencing major changes in the attitudes and assumptions of organization members and building commitment for the organization's mission, objectives, and strategies.

transnational team a work team composed of multinational members whose activities span many countries.

21st-century managing a management approach to the rapidly changing business world that emphasizes responsiveness and effective leadership.

U

uncertainty the absence of information about a particular area of concern.

unemployment insurance legally mandated insurance that is paid by state agencies to workers who are terminated through no fault of their own; the funds come from a tax on the employer's payroll.

unfreezing a step in psychologist Kurt Lewin's model of change that involves reducing the forces for the status quo, usually by presenting a provocative problem or event to get people to recognize the need for change and to search for new solutions.

uniform plant loading establishing monthly production plans and strictly adhering to them so that wide swings in production levels are minimized.

V

valence in motivation, the perceived value a person ascribes to the reward for certain efforts.

value-added manufacturing a management approach that emphasizes the idea that any manufacturing process that does not add value to the product for the customer is wasteful; also called lean manufacturing.

value-based hiring the practice of screening and hiring people whose values are consistent with those of the company, rather than looking just at an applicant's job-related skills.

values basic beliefs about what is important and unimportant, and what one should and should not do.

values and beliefs the guiding standards of an organization, such as "the customer is always right" or "don't be bureaucratic," that affirm what should be practiced, as distinct from what is practiced.

variable pay plan a compensation plan that may reduce or increase some portion of the individual employee's pay, depending on whether the company meets its financial goals.

variance the difference between budgeted and actual amounts.

venture team a small team of people who operate as a semi-autonomous unit to create and develop a new idea.

vertical integration a growth strategy in which a company owns or controls its own suppliers and/or distribution channels.

virtual corporation a temporary network of independent companies linked by information technology.

vision a general statement of an organization's intended direction that evokes emotional feelings in its members.

W

waiting-line/queuing techniques mathematical techniques used to solve waiting-line problems such that the optimal balance of employees available to waiting customers is attained.

whistle-blowing the activities of employees who try to report organizational wrongdoing.

wholly owned subsidiary see subsidiary

wide area network (WAN) a network that serves microcomputers over large geographic areas, spanning distances from a few miles to around the globe, and that may use common carrier networks or private telecommunications systems.

workflow automation system an e-mail type of system that automates the flow of paperwork from person to person.

workers' compensation a legally mandated benefit that pays income and medical benefits to work-related accident victims or their dependents, regardless of fault.

world-class company an organization that can compete successfully based on quality and productivity in an intensely competitive global environment.

world-class manufacturer an organization that uses modern production techniques and management systems to boost manufacturing productivity, quality, and flexibility in an environment of international competition.

Y

yes/no control a control system in which work may not proceed to the next step until it passes an intermediate checkpoint step.

Z

zero-based budgeting a control technique that requires all of a company's budgeted programs to be reviewed every year based on the ratio of their benefits and costs.

CHAPTER 1 Page 3: Stan Godlewski/Liaison Agency, Inc. Page 8: Marty Lederhandler/AP/Wide World Photos. Page 14: Najlah Feanny/SABA Press Photos, Inc. Page 16: Michael Newman/PhotoEdit.

CHAPTER 2 Page 42: Greg Girard/Contact Press Images Inc. Page 52: Spaca Dakic/SIPA Press.

CHAPTER 3 Page 73: Churchill & Klehr Photography. Page 79: George Nikitin/AP/Wide World Photos. Page 86: Alan Levenson.

CHAPTER 4 Page 114: Spencer Grant/FPG International LLC.

CHAPTER 5 Page 138: Roger Mastroianni. Page 141: Copyright © 1999 Saturn Corp. All Rights Reserved. General Motors Media Archives. Page 146: Spencer Grant/PhotoEdit. Page 151: Jim Leynse/SABA Press Photos, Inc.

CHAPTER 6 Page 170: Jeff Greenberg/Photo Researchers, Inc.

CHAPTER 7 Page 201: Koji Sasahara/AP/Wide World Photos. Page 203: White Pine Software, Inc. Page 206: Leif Skoogfors/Rosenbluth International. Copyright Rosenbluth International. Page 213: SABA Press Photos, Inc. Page 214: John Abbott Photography.

CHAPTER 8 Page 224: Mark Richards. Page 224: John Abbott Photography. Page 226: AP/Wide World Photos.

CHAPTER 9 Page 251: Summer Productions. Page 257: Erica Freudenstein. Page 262: Michael Newman/PhotoEdit. Page 274: Internal & External Communication, Inc. Lexus Labs was developed for the luxury division of Toyota Motors Sales, U.S.A. Inc. by Internal & External Communication, Inc. an interactive multimedia training firm based in Marina del Rey, CA. Page 265: The Psychological Corporation.

CHAPTER 10 Page 299: Reuters Newmedia Inc./Corbis. © Reuters Newmedia Inc/CORBIS. Page 303: Paul A. Souders. Page 304: William Mercer McLeod.

CHAPTER 11 Page 320: Wayne State University Archives of Labor and Urban Affairs. Walter P. Reuther Library, Wayne State University. Page 337: Jay Blakesberg. Page 341: Jim Callaway Photography. Page 346: Brian Smith.

CHAPTER 12 Page 366: Byron/Monkmeyer Press. Page 375: Toyota Motor Manufacturing, Kentucky, Inc. Page 378: Mark Richards/PhotoEdit. Page 380: Louis Psihoyos/Matrix International, Inc. Page 380: Louis Psihoyos/Matrix International, Inc. Page 382: Photo courtesy of Ventana Corporation. GroupSystems is a registered trademark of Ventana Corp.

CHAPTER 13 Page 394: Steve Lehman/SABA Press Photos, Inc. Page 398: Jon Riley/Tony Stone Images. Page 409: James Wasserman/James Wasserman Photography. Page 411: Motor Manufacturing, Kentucky, Inc.

CHAPTER 14 Page 424: Leimdorfer/REA/SABA Press Photos, Inc. Page 430: Chevron Corporation. Page 432: James Schnepf/Liaison Agency, Inc. Page 435: Porter Gifford/ Liaison Agency, Inc.

CHAPTER 15 Page 464: Tony Freeman/PhotoEdit. Page 467: John Neubauer/PhotoEdit. Page 469: Brian Tramontana/Xerox Palo Alto Research Center. Page 473: John Abbott Photography.

Conglomerate diversification, defined, 164
Considerate leadership, 300–301, 303
Consultants, for decision making, 112
Contingency theory of leadership, 305–6
Contingent reward, defined, 330
Contingent workers, defined, 256
Continuous change, case example, 246–47
Continuous improvement, 493
   tools for, 495
Continuous production, defined, 485
Control and controlling, 3, 10, 99, 453
   basic management control system,
     459–61
   belief systems and, 471–72, 480
   boundary, 458, 466
   case example, 481, 522
   commitment-based systems, 456,
     457–59, 470–76, 479
   defined, 454
   diagnostic, 458, 459–66
   electronic performance monitoring and,
     469–70
   interactive control systems, 458, 466–67
   Internet-based financial control
     systems, 19–20
   managers and, 455–56
   need for, 454
   negative side of control, 467–68
   network methods for, 489
   post action controls, 455
   production control, 488
   for quality and production, 493–96
   reactions to, 467–69
   role of, 454–56
   steering, 454
   strategic, 162
   timely, 454–55
   traditional methods of, 456–57, 459–67
   unintended behavior consequences of,
     468–69
   yes/no control and, 454
Conversion system, defined, 484
Coordinating, 206–10
   direct supervision for, 208
   divisionalization for, 208
   independent integrators for, 208
   liaisons for, 208
   mutual adjustment for, 207
   rules or procedures for, 207–8
   staff assistants for, 208
   standardization of targets, skills, and
     shared values for, 209
   teams and committees for, 208
Coordination, 206–10
   defined, 206
Core competencies, 180–81
   defined, 180
Core values credo, of Johnson & Johnson,
   435
Corporate culture. See also Organizational
   culture
   creating and sustaining, 435–36
   at Procter & Gamble, 81
Corporate-level strategies, 163–65
   concentration, 163–64
   defined, 162–63
   diversification, 164
   investment reduction strategies, 164

joint ventures, 165
   status quo strategies, 164
   strategic alliances, 165
   vertical integration, 164
   virtual corporation and, 165
Corporate scorecard, 464–65
   defined, 464
Corporate social audit, defined, 85
Corporate stakeholder, defined, 84
Corporation. See also International
   business
   global, 46–47
   horizontal, 237–39
Corrective action, as control method, 457
Cost leadership, defined, 166
Coworkers, team performance and, 405–6
CPM (critical path method), 489
Crawford Small Parts Dexterity Test, 265
Creativity, in decision making, 109–11
Credibility, in negotiating, 368
Critical path, defined, 489
Cross-cultural issues, 53–55
Cross-training, for teams, 408
Cuba, Bay of Pigs and, 116
Cultural artifacts, defined, 79
Cultural change, 418
   control and, 471–72
   startups and, 440
Cultural differences, sensitivity to, 60
Culture. See also Organizational culture
   communication and, 371
   defined, 79
   in global environment, 71
   sociocultural environment of
     international business and, 53–55
CU-SeeMe, 201
Customer departmentalization, defined,
   198
Customer report card, 504–5
   defined, 504
Customer service. See also Service
   management
   case example, 508
Customs, and international business, 55
Customs union, 48–49
   defined, 48
Cycle of service, defined, 503

D

Dairy Council of California, 178
Data. See also Forecast
   primary, 145
   secondary, 145
Databases. See also Computer(s)
   for preemployment information, 272
Data mining, defined, 511
Decentralization, 35
Decentralized organizations, 212–13
   defined, 212
Decision, defined, 98
Decision making, 35
   anchoring and, 107
   breakeven analysis and, 125–26
   case example, 123–24
   creativity and, 109–11
   defined, 98
   empowered, 22

finality of, 114
   group, 115–19
   individual differences and, 105–6
   intuition and, 113–14
   knowledge and, 111–13
   linear programming and, 126–27
   nonprogrammed decisions, 101
   organizational barriers to, 108
   planning and, 130, 133
   problem framing, 107
   process of managerial, 105–9
   programmed decisions, 98–100
   psychological set and, 108
   quantitative aids to, 125–28
   rational, 101–5, 108–9
   shortcuts (heuristics), 106
   statistical decision theory techniques,
     127–28
   strategic decisions, 114
   timing of, 114–15
   waiting line-queuing techniques, 127
Decision support systems (DSSs), 381–82,
   398, 513, 514–15
   defined, 381
Decision tree, defined, 128
Defensiveness, in communication, 365–66
Delegating leader, 307
Delegation
   decentralization and, 213
   defined, 211
   process of, 211–12
Delphi Technique, in group decision
   making, 117
Denmark, 49
Department(s), 29
Departmentalization, 192–206
   customer, 198
   defined, 193
   functional, 193–95
   geographic, 200–201
   hybrid organization and, 204, 205–6
   marketing-channel, 199–200
   matrix, 201–4
   product (divisionalization), 195–98
Deregulation, 15
Descriptive plan, defined, 132
Designing for manufacturability, defined,
   495
Development, employee, 475
Development teams, 396
Devil-advocate approach, to group
   decision making, 117
Diagnostic control systems, 459–66
   defined, 458
Differentiation strategy, defined, 166
Digital nervous system, 516–17
Direct investment, foreign, 44–45
Director, use of term, 4
Direct participation, organizational
   change and, 429
Direct supervision, for coordinating, 208
Disabilities, diversity and, 87
Discipline, employee, 276–77
Discipline without punishment, defined,
   277
Discrimination
   defined, 88
   prohibitions against, 277

Internet. *See also* Telecommunications;
specific companies and products;
specific issues
.com companies and, 295
communication via, 379
company strategy for, 170–71
computer-based manufacturing systems
and, 498
computer preemployment information
services and, 272
controlling on, 455
E-based companies and, 23
electronic networks and, 233–34
employer job postings on, 260
employment services on, 260
financial control systems and, 19–20
global communication and, 201
global production management and, 57
information technology and, 13–14
job-placement and recruiting sources,
260–61
knowledge work and, 16
as management tool, 57
managing and, 517–18
Microsoft and, 173–74
Netscape and, 196
on-line competition and, 12–13
on-line incentives and, 334–35
recruiting on, 260
selling through, 44, 169
strategy for, 170–71
virtual communities and, 384
Web portal strategy and, 420
Internet-based communications, 383
Internet-based job description service, 252
Internet control system, 455
Internships, for college students, 260
Interpersonal communication, 363–69
barriers to, 364–66
in business settings, 367–69
defined, 363
improving, 366–67
Interpersonal conflict, defined, 442
Intervention. *See* specific types
Interviews (staffing), 266–71
guidelines for, 270–71
questioning in, 268, 269, 270
steps in, 266–69
Intranets, 233
Intrinsic consequences, of tangible
rewards, 344
Intuitive decision making, 113–14
vs. systematic decision making, 106
Inventory-holding costs, defined, 491
Inventory management, 490–92
defined, 491
Inventory management systems
ABC inventory management, 491–92
economic order quantity (EOQ) system,
492
Investment, foreign direct, 44–45
Investment reduction strategies, 164
divestment, 164
retrenchment, 164
IPO. *See* Initial public offering (IPO)
IQ tests. *See* Intelligence (IQ) tests
Ireland, 49
ISO 9000, defined, 493

ISO 14001, 94
Issues
controlling in international business, 64
in leading international business, 63–64
organizing, in international
management, 62–63
Italy, 48, 49, 86

J

Japan, 48, 50, 54, 55, 86
communication style in, 372
Java programming language, 148
Jeep (brand name), 185
JIT. *See* Just-in-time (JIT)
Job analysis, defined, 251
Job analysis questionnaire, defined, 252
Job-centered leader, defined, 302
Job description, 251–52
defined, 251
Internet-based service for, 252
sample, 253
Job design, defined, 340
Job enlargement, defined, 340
Job enrichment, 340–41
defined, 340
Job posting
defined, 255
on Internet, 260
Job redesign, 339–41
Job rotation, defined, 340
Job satisfaction
behavior and, 359–60
defined, 359
Job security, team leaders and, 410
Job specification, defined, 252
Job surfing, 449
Joint ventures, 45–46, 165
defined, 45
Judgment, 98
of leaders, 310
in negotiating, 368
Jury of executive opinion, 145
Just-in-time (JIT), 496–97
defined, 496

K

Kaizen, 493
Knowledge
in decision making, 111–12
information and, 510
Knowledge-based organizations, 22
Knowledge management, 112–13
defined, 511
example, 234
Knowledge work, 16–17
Kroll's business intelligence, 147

L

Labor. *See also* Global workforce
global staffing and, 58
Labor-management relations, 279
Laissez-faire leader, defined, 302
Landrum-Griffin Act, 279
Language, and international business, 55
LANs. *See* Local area networks (LANs)

Lateral communication. *See* Horizontal
communication
Latin America, 55, 63
Lattice organization, 247
Law, ethics and, 73
Law of individual differences, defined, 353
Layout
facility, 486
fixed-position, 486
improving, 487
process, 486, 487
product, 486
Leader, roles of, 291
Leader Behavior Description
Questionnaire (LBDQ), 300
Leader-member exchange (LMX) theory,
306–7
defined, 306
Leader role, of managers, 8
Leadership, 3, 23, 99, 290. *See also*
Motivation
actions of, 293
adapting to situation, 313
autocratic style, 301
building blocks of, 293
case example, 452
charismatic, 303, 432, 433
at Cisco Systems, 295
close supervision style, 302
coaching as, 412
considerate style of, 300–301, 303
contingency theory of, 305–6
control and, 456
defined, 291
developing qualities of, 309–13
diversity management and, 88–89
emotional intelligence and, 297–98
employee-oriented style, 302
gender and, 304–5
general leader style, 302
"great man" concept of, 296
of group decision-making discussion,
118–19
inspirational, 303
instrumental, 433
intellectually stimulating, 303
job-centered style, 302
judgment for, 310
laissez-faire style, 302
Leader Behavior Description
Questionnaire and, 300
leader-member exchange (LMX) theory,
306–7
management skills for, 33
in military, 316
missionary, 433
in organizational change, 432–36
organizational culture and, 434–36
participative style, 301
path-goal theory of, 306
power and, 299–300
power base for, 312
as role of managers, 10
self-assessment scale, 311
sharing vision of, 312–13
situational theories of, 305–9
structuring style of, 300–301
styles of, 300–305, 317, 318

Morality, defined, 72
Moral minimum, defined, 85
Mortgage processing, redesigning, 422
Motion study, 31
   Gilbreths and, 31–32
Motivation, 319, 320–21
   bonuses as, 323
   case example, 351–52, 452
   company values and, 350–51
   defined, 320
   empowerment and, 341–42
   foundations of, 332–33
   goal-setting methods and, 342–43
   job redesign and, 339–41
   learning/reinforcement approaches to,
      330–31
   lifelong learning and, 344–45
   merit pay and, 336
   methods of, 332–46
   need-based approaches to, 321–28
   pay for performance and, 334–35
   perceived inequity and, 328
   positive reinforcement and, 343–44
   in practice, 345–46
   process approaches to, 328–30
   recognition as, 338–39
   skill-based pay and, 337–38
   spot award as, 336–37
   successful, 346–47
   of women employees, 349
Motivational dispositions (needs), defined,
   321
Motivational objectives, 140–41
Motivators, in Herzberg's theory, 324
Motive, defined, 321
Moving, defined, 425
Multi-ethnic workforce, 86
Multinational corporation (MNC),
   defined, 46
Multinational organization, organizing
   issues for, 62
Multinational teams. See Transnational
   teams
Multi-national workforce, 86
Mutual adjustment, defined, 207

N

NAFTA (North American Free Trade
   Agreement), 50, 51
Narrow viewpoints, communication and,
   370–71
Nationality, workforce diversity and, 86
National Productivity Review, 392
National Security Council, 116
Need-based approaches to motivation,
   321–28
   achievement, power, and affiliation
      needs, 324–27
   Herzberg's two-factor approach, 324
   Maslow's needs-hierarchy theory,
      322–23
Needs
   of employees, 327–28
   motivational dispositions and, 321
   perception and, 358
Needs-hierarchy theory, of Maslow,
   322–23

Negative attitudes, toward control, 468–69
Negative reinforcement, defined, 330–31
Negotiating, 367–69
Negotiator role, of managers, 9
Net. *See* Internet; Web
Netherlands, 49, 86
NetMeeting conference system, 398
Netscape Navigator, 498
Network(s)
   communications, 379
   local area networks (LANs), 517–18
   for managing organizations, 517–19
   wide area networks (WANs), 518
Network-based organizations. *See*
   Organizational network
Network planning and control methods,
   defined, 489
New-product development, strategy and,
   214
New Realities, The (Drucker), 448
Nominal group technique, in group
   decision making, 117–18
Nonprofits, 2
Nonprogrammed decisions, 98, 100
   defined, 101
Nontariff barriers, 52
Nonverbal communication, 364–65
   defined, 364
Normative judgment, defined, 72
Norms
   defined, 115
   group, 394
Norris-LaGuardia Act, 279
North America, NAFTA and, 50

O

Objectives (goals). *See also* Management by
   objectives (MBO)
   action plan and, 135, 136
   career, 133
   case example, 155–56
   defined, 130
   executive assignment action plan for,
      135, 136
   expressing, 141–42
   hierarchy of, 137–38
   for Internet startup company, 148
   measurable, 140
   motivational, 140–41
   setting of, 138–43
   strategic, 161
   strategic planning and, 188
   types of, 139–40
Occupational safety and health, 279
Occupational Safety and Health
   Administration (OSHA), 279
OD. *See* Organizational development (OD)
Ohio State University, leadership study at,
   300
OJT. *See* On-the-job training (OJT)
Older workers, recruiting for, 262
Olympics (2002), 70, 72
On-line competition, 12–13
On-the-job training (OJT), 273–74
   defined, 273
Open-book management, 181
   defined, 376

Operant behavior, defined, 330
Operating budget, defined, 460
Operating delays, 468
Operational plan, defined, 133
Operations management, 483–88
   defined, 483
Operations planning and control, 488–90
   Gantt charts and, 488
Operations research, quantitative school
   as, 38
Orchestra management, teams in, 415–16
Ordering (setup) costs, defined, 491
Organic management system, 40
Organic organization, 225
   defined, 224
Organization(s). *See also*
   Departmentalization
   boundaryless, 235–39
   cellular, 241–43
   decentralized, 212–13
   defined, 2–3
   delegating authority in, 210–14
   ethical practices shaped by, 74–75
   federal-type, 240–43
   fitting to task, 222–24
   flat vs. tall, 214–15
   informal, 192
   information system objectives by
      organizational level, 513
   line and staff, 211
   mechanistic, 223–24
   modern, 17–20
   moving beyond organic, 222
   network-based, 230–34
   organic, 224
   span of control in, 215
   strategy and structure of, 213–14
   team-based, 227–30
   virtual, 241
Organizational behavior, 36–37
Organizational boundaries, 235–37
   authority boundary, 235–36
   identity boundary, 237
   political boundary, 236–37
   task boundary, 236
Organizational change, 418, 419. *See also*
   Organizational development (OD)
   case example, 451
   to e-business, 431–32
   eight-step process for leading, 426–32
   in governmental agencies, 450
   incremental, 423
   job surfing and, 449
   leadership and, 432–36
   resistance to, 423–26
   strategic change and, 419–23
Organizational communication, 369–71
   barriers to, 370–71
   defined, 363
   improving, 372–78
Organizational culture
   changing, 436
   communication and, 371
   defined, 79
   diversity management and, 90
   ethical behavior and, 78–81
   ethics and, 75
   leadership and, 434

Principles of management, of Fayol, 32–33
Problem
  defined, 98
  framing of, 107
Problem solving, 98. *See also* Decision making
  breakeven analysis and, 125–26
  creativity and, 109–11
  individual differences and, 105–6
  planning and, 130
  team, defined, 395
  tools for, 495
Procedures
  for coordinating, 207–8
  defined, 133
Process analysis, defined, 110
Process approaches to motivation, 328–30
  Adams's equity theory, 328
  Locke's goal theory, 328–29
  Vroom's expectancy theory, 329–30
Process flow chart, 495
Process layout, 487
  defined, 486
Product(s), substitute, 168
Product departmentalization (divisionalization), 195–98
Product development, defined, 163
Production
  control for, 493–96
  globalization of, 56–57
  processes of, 485
Production and materials budget, defined, 460
Production control, defined, 488
Production manager, business decisions of, 99
Production planning, defined, 488
Production system, 483–84
  components of, 484
  designing, 484–88
Productive teams
  building, 400–408
  characteristics of, 404–6
Product layout, defined, 486
Profit, customer service and, 501
Profitability ratios, 462
Profit center, defined, 463
Profit sharing, commitment and, 475
Program, defined, 133
Programmed decisions, 98
  defined, 100
Programming, linear, 126–27
Progress, of organizational change, 431
Project teams, 396
Psychological needs, 322
Psychological set, defined, 107–8
Psychological testing, for employment, 263
Punishment, defined, 331
Purchasing, 490

Q

Qualitative forecasting, 145
  defined, 143
Quality
  control for, 493–96
  defined, 493

Quality circles, 395–96
  defined, 396
Quality control, methods of, 494–95
Quality control chart, 494
Quantitative forecasting, defined, 143
Quantitative school of management, 38–39
Questioning, in staffing interviews, 268, 269, 270, 286–87
Question mark, strategic planning and, 176
Queuing techniques, defined, 127
Quota, defined, 52
QUPID system, 500

R

Race, workforce diversity and, 86, 87
Rating systems, corporate social monitoring and, 85
Ratio, financial, 461, 462
Rational decision making, 101–5
  bounded rationality and, 108
  process of, 103–5
  satisficing and, 108
Raw materials, 490
Recognition, 338–39
  respect and, 339
Recruiting, 254–62. *See also* Personnel planning
  advertising and, 256
  at colleges, 257–60
  contingent workers and, 256
  defined, 254
  for diverse workforce, 260–61
  employment agencies for, 256
  example, 258
  executive recruiters and, 256–57
  on Internet, 260
  job posting and, 255
  outsourcing of, 283
  questions for, 258
  referrals and, 257
  walk-ins and, 257
Reengineering. *See* Business reengineering
Reference checks, for staffing, 271–72
Referrals, 257
Refreezing, defined, 425
Regiocentric, defined, 59
Reinforcement
  negative, 330–31
  positive, 330, 343–44
  punishment as, 331
  variable (partial), 331
Reinvention laboratories (RLs), 450
Related diversification, defined, 164
Renewal process, 9
Research. *See also* Forecast
  action, 437
  communications, 378–79
  for decision making, 111–12
  diversity management and, 89
  marketing, 145
  survey, 440
Resistance to change, 423–26
  methods for dealing with, 425
  overcoming, 424–26
Respect, recognition and, 339

Responsibility, authority and, 211–12
Rethinking the Future (Gibson), 448
Retrenchment strategy, defined, 164
Return on investment, factors affecting, 463
Revenue center, defined, 464
Rewards. *See* Financial incentive; Financial rewards
Risk
  defined, 128
  political, 52
Rites and ceremonies
  corporate culture and, 435
  defined, 81
Rivalry, among competitors, 167
Role(s), of managers, 8–9
Role conflict, defined, 442
Rule(s)
  for coordinating, 207–8
  defined, 133
Rumors, 370
Run chart, 495
Russia, 47–48

S

SABRE system, 169
Safari notebook computer, 165, 241
Safety
  checklist of mechanical or physical accident-causing conditions, 288
  occupational, 279
Salary. *See also* Motivation
  fixed, 276
Sales budget, defined, 460
Sales expansion, globalization and, 42–43
Sales force estimation, defined, 145
Sales forecasting. *See* Forecast
Sales manager, business decisions of, 99
Satellite-based warehousing, 169
Satisfice, defined, 108
Saudi Arabia, 53–54, 55
SBU. *See* Strategic business unit (SBU)
Scalar chain, 190
Scatter diagram, 495
Scenarios, 177–78
  defined, 177
Schedules, of reinforcement, 331
Scheduling, 489
Scientific management, 30–33
  operations research/management science and, 38
Search firms, 256–57
Secondary data, defined, 145
Security needs, 322–23
Self-actualization, employee, 475
Self-actualization needs, 323
Self-concept
  behavior and, 356–57
  defined, 356
Self-control
  belief systems and, 471–72
  commitment-based control systems and, 472–76
Self-directed teams. *See* Self-managing teams
Self-efficacy
  defined, 357
  perception and, 358